May 6, 2002

For Prof. Joseph Schwartzberg

I admire your work on peace and Governance! I hope my book makes a contribution to your efforts.

Sincerely,

INNOVATION IN INTERNATIONAL LAW

General Editor
Richard Falk

Editorial Advisory Board
**Georges Abi-Saab
Antonio Cassese
Samuel S. Kim
Yasuaki Onuma
Edith Brown Weiss
Burns H. Weston**

ACHIEVING INCLUSIONARY GOVERNANCE:
Advancing Peace and Development in First and Third World Nations

Terrence Edward Paupp

Minneapolis, MN 55454

Transnational Publishers, Inc.
Ardsley, New York

Library of Congress Cataloging-in-Publication Data

Paupp, Terrence Edward.
    Achieving inclusionary governance : advancing peace and development in first and third world nations / by Terrence Edward Paupp.
      p. cm. — (Innovation in international law)
    Includes bibliographical references and index.
    ISBN 1-57105-136-8
    1. Democracy. 2. Political participation. I. Title. II. Series.

JC423 .P29 2000
321.8—dc21   00-037811

Copyright © 2000 by Transnational Publishers, Inc.

All rights reserved. This book may not be reproduced, in whole or in part, in any form (beyond that copying permitted by U.S. Copyright Law in Section 107, "fair use" in teaching and research, Section 108, certain library copying, and except in published media by reviewers in limited excerpts), without written permission from the publisher.

Manufactured in the United States of America

For Terry Wayne Sterling

and in memory of

*John Fitzgerald Kennedy
and
Robert Francis Kennedy*

TABLE OF CONTENTS

Acknowledgments .... *xiii*
Foreword by Professor Richard Falk .... *xv*

*Introduction: Inclusion, Exclusion, and the
           Reconstitution of Power*................... *xix*

Part I: Obstacles and Opportunities

Chapter 1. **Preface to Inclusionary Governance:
              The Deepening of Democracy as an
              Aspect of a Peaceful World** 3
  - A. Introduction 4
  - B. To Seek a Newer World. 7
  - C. The Construction of a New
       Sociopolitical Matrix:
       Inclusionary Governance Versus
       Exclusionary Globalization 10
  - D. The Emerging Politics and Law of
       Inclusionary Governance Through
       Democratic Norms 21
  - E. Covenant for a New Democratic Order.... 34
  - F. Building the Institutional and Legal
       Framework for a New Democratic
       Institutional Order................... 35
  - G. Conclusion 41

Chapter 2. **Obstacles and Opportunities: Nuclear
              Disarmament and the Abolition of the
              Globalization of Militarization** 51
  - A. Introduction 52

	B. Building Exclusionary Monopolies: Global Interdependence and Power Under Emergent Nuclearism	57
	C. Beyond Realism: Building "Security Communities" for a Sustainable Peace	62
	D. The Convergence of War, Politics, and International Law in the Post-1945 World	64
	E. The Legality of Nuclear Weapons: International Law and the World Court at the Crossroads of an Historic Encounter	66
	F. Inclusionary Measures for Advancing Peace	78
	G. Sustaining Norms of Nuclear Restraint	84
Chapter 3.	**The Globalization of Media and the Media of Globalization**	113
	A. Introduction	114
	B. Rich Media, Poor Democracy	127
	C. The Rise of Network Society	130
	D. The Electronic Republic and the Manufacture of Consent	136

Part II: Paths to and from Inclusion

Chapter 4.	**Moving Toward Inclusion: Overcoming the Dynamics of Democratic Exclusion**	151
	A. Introduction	151
	B. The Dynamics of Democratic Exclusion	159
	C. The Separation Between the Ideal and Practice of Democracy in First and Third World Settings	179
	D. The State/Society Relationship Revisited	189
Chapter 5.	**Back to the Future: Hobbes's Vision of Sovereignty, Commonwealth, and Anarchy**	209
	A. Introduction	210

	B.	The Role of Nationalism, War, and International Legal Culture.........	214
	C.	Democracy in Conflict With Globalization Under Capitalism...................	222
	D.	Revisting the Hobbesian Dilemma......	223
	E.	The "Rule of Law" Versus "Rule by Law"...	232
	F.	The Founding of the Hobbesian State....	240
	G.	To Create a Global Commonwealth and Culture of Peace.................	256
	H.	The Task of Civil Society in the Commonwealth....................	265

Part III: The Broken and Unbroken Promise of Inclusion

Chapter 6.	**The Promise of Inclusion: Inclusionary Versus Exclusionary Governance............**		287
	A.	Introduction.......................	288
	B.	Identifying the Obstacles to Inclusionary Governance.............	294
	C.	Solutions for Achieving Inclusionary Governance.......................	310
Chapter 7.	**Between Poverty and Polyarchy: The Praxis of Democracy in Third World States........**		349
	A.	Introduction.......................	350
	B.	The Socialization of Poverty and the Fate of Democracy...................	358
	C.	Toward an Illiberal Democracy in Exclusionary States...................	362
	D.	Inclusionary States Measure Developmental Success..............	367
	E.	Democracy in Theory and Practice......	387
	F.	State Power in the Third World and the Extremely Poor.....................	396
	G.	Statism, Presidentialism, Political Parties, and the Dilemmas of Development......	400
	H.	Building the Praxis of the Future by Political Inclusion...................	405

Part IV: Conclusion

Chapter 8. **Establishing Perspectives on Inclusionary Governance, Inclusionary Development, and International Law**................... 419
- A. The Challenge of Inclusion and the Right to Development................ 420
- B. Emerging Preferences and Probabilities for the Realization of Inclusionary Governance 423
- C. The Emerging Inclusionary Principle of Entitlement According to Need 426
- D. The Linkage of Socioeconomic Rights With Political/Civil Rights Is the Task of an Inclusionary Democratic Project 440
- E. Moving Toward Inclusion 462

Index 475

ACKNOWLEDGMENTS

Since the late 1970s I have thought occassionally of developing what I have have called "inclusionary governance." I first chose the term "inclusion" because it conveyed a moral and political imperative to emphasize the dignity and rights of the person. The realities of oppression and exclusion were the shaping realities of my formative experience as one who came to maturity in an age of political assassinations and the crucible of the Vietnam War. At the same time, the civil rights leadership of Martin Luther King Jr., President John F. Kennedy, and Senator Robert Kennedy, inspired a deep sense of dedication, commitment, and tenacity to fight against the evils and injustices of a bitter age.

In my last year at the Lutheran School of Theology at Chicago, I completed a thesis on liberation theology in Latin America. The economic poverty of the continent and the flagrant human rights abuses of exclusionary regimes were then, and remain to this day, a persistent reminder to me of the need to confront and to eliminate these injustices and inspire others to do so. In that task, my professional life has been blessed by my association with Larry Birns, Director of the Council On Hemispheric Affairs, Washington, D.C. His tireless and courageous efforts over many decades has served to enlighten the public at large and the United States Congress in particular with respect to the need to advance human rights concerns above other competing interests.

Inspiration for this book also came from my days at the University of San Diego School of Law, where I had the distinct honor to study labor law under President Kennedy and Johnson's Secretary of Labor, Willard Wirtz. His role in the history of a critical period of American life demonstrated to me the ways in which a commitment to civil rights, labor's rights, and human rights converged in a principled way, not only in the United States, but throughout the world.

Further inspiration and insight for this book came through my work and association with the dean of the University of San Diego School of Law, Sheldon Krantz, who asked me to be his research assistant in updating his book on the law of corrections and prisoners' rights. The abuse of prisoner's and the growth of a "prison-industrial complex" since the 1980s have borne out the veracity of his concerns and warnings regarding the injustices of a system which inherits the excluded, poor, and dispossessed of society without humane purpose but is more than prepared to reap financial profits from growing incarceration rates.

Throughout the years I have been deeply inspired, intellectually and politically, by the work of Professor Richard Falk. For over four decades, his unflagging zeal to promote innovations in the arenas of social action and international law has charted a course on which I have embarked, along with many others. We are all beneficiaries of Professor Falk's commitment to humane governance in its multi-dimensional forms and incarnations, both as practice and as promise.

Also, this book's focus on inclusion has received empirical backing from the work of Professor Arend Lijphart, who has done so much to advance the study and understanding of democratic theory and practice. His emphasis upon more consensual forms of democracy as being more inclusionary than its majoritarian variants was an indispensable contribution to my thought and the claims which I am able to make throughout the course of this book.

I am grateful to the president of Transnational Publishers, Heike Fenton, and her dedicated staff, for their support for this project. For their faith in me and this project, I will be forever indebted. Finally, this book was made possible by the dedication of some true friends who, over many years, made this journey a worthwhile and meaningful one. To name a few, they are: Bill Sims, Rick Schafer, Terry Sterling, Jim Sullivan, Curt Hatch, and Jeremy Kidder. To all of them, I am eternally grateful.

Terrence Edward Paupp

FOREWORD

Innovation in International Law is a series of books that seeks to explore the distinctive challenges of world order that are emerging in the early period of the 21st century. Its focus has been particularly upon the normative dimensions of challenge associated with fairness and equity, as well as with the upsurge of interest in the implementation of human rights and the practice of humanitarian intervention. It is less concerned with the functional dimensions of challenge that involve adaptations to the growing complexity of international life, and a range of uncertainties involving environmental and economic sustainability.

At the most fundamental level of inquiry, the normative challenge centers on the value-generating capabilities of sovereign states, given a variety of transnational pressures evident in the global setting. The state during the Westphalian era of international law has been treated as the only significant actor from the perspective of upholding human well being. The essential normative idea was that of sovereignty exercised within fixed territorial boundaries, enabling governments to provide order internally and security for their citizenry in relation to external threats posed by other states. The state, by defensive capabilities and alliance arrangements, was primarily dedicated to the protection and expansion of its domain, and was not expected until recently to be responsible for addressing internal socio-economic problems of poverty, unemployment, and inequality faced by their population.

These expectations started to change in the 19th century in response to the rise of industrial capitalism in Europe. As tensions mounted along class lines, and a labor movement began to take shape, the role of the state was altered. To offset the danger of revolution, a social contract was informally negotiated, which tempered the workings of the market in the dominant states of Europe, and contributed to a stable social peace within states. The adequacy of this contract was the target of attack by the Communist movement, assuming seriousness in the aftermath of both world wars in the prior century as culminating respectively in the triumph of the Russian Revolution and the outcome of the Chinese Civil War.

International law did not adapt itself very easily to these domestic tensions in state/society relations that gave rise to extremist ideologies in the form of fascism and communism, leading first to World War II and later to the cold war. In a state-centric world order, the role of international law was generally confined to the external relations of states, with the internal domain off-limits, at least among those states that enjoyed full sovereign rights. True, the liberal states mounted interventionary challenges to reverse the Bolshevik takeover of power in Moscow and the Maoist victory in China, but both moves failed completely. The response to Hitler's Germany was accommodating in its essence, even adopting a diplomacy of appeasement in response to German expansionism, and turning a blind eye to the lurid evidence of Nazi racism. Patterns of oppressive behavior, provided it was done internally, as in Germany and the Soviet Union, was castigated by moralists and ideologues, but were not treated as matters of appropriate concern for international law, with the very limited exception of protecting the rights of foreign nationals, especially their property rights.

The colonial order co-existed with statism, creating a hierarchy of domination that put the leading European states in control of most of the non-Western world. Here again, the normative indifference of the international legal order was striking. The role of international law was focused on adjusting relations among the colonial powers for their mutual benefit, and on inventing doctrines that upheld the legality of colonial arrangements, often taking the form of unequal treaties. True, as nationalist energies gained strength, especially in Latin America where the imperial role of the United States was not formalized, it became clear that international law could serve also as a shield against domination, as well as a sword by which to work out the implications of a status of subordination. Relying on the primacy of territoriality and the promise of the equality among states, Latin American jurists began to challenge the economic prerogatives of foreign corporate and financial interests, exposing the incoherence of international law: that is, international law was limited to external relations, but it also was trying to uphold the special claims of Europe and United States to protect the property rights and personal status of their citizens operating in colonized space.

It is against such a background that we best consider the development of international human rights, and its unanticipated impact on international politics. From the perspective of international law this development was potentially subversive from its inception, and only took hold in the atmosphere of the late 1940s because of two convergent political realities: the guilt of the victorious powers in World War II due to their remaining on the sidelines while much of the early dirty work of the Holocaust was being carried out in Germany and the belief that the articulation of international human rights norms was basically a public relations exercise, which would not encroach upon sovereign rights, due to the absence of any intention to press for enforcement. Such an impression is strengthened by the manner in which the Universal Declaration of Human Rights was drafted and then adopted by the United Nations General Assembly in 1948. It is notable that the norms of the Declaration were expressed in a very general and often vague language, and that the essential document was "declaratory" rather than "obligatory." Underlying this kind of symbolic move was the persisting conviction at the time that the world of states would still provide the defining framework of world order, that the state was not seriously challenged by either the establishment of the United Nations or by the articulation of norms that purported to apply internally to state/society relations.

In most respects, this state-centric idea of world order persisted unchallenged during the cold war decades. There was, to be sure, a momentum built from the grassroots to elaborate a more precise and binding framework for international human rights, but still with no serious effort at enforcement. What effort to achieve implementation did arise reflected the rise of transnational human rights organizations that were voluntary associations of citizens. As the cold war came to its abrupt end in the early 1990s, however, the insulation of the sovereign state was eroded from divergent angles in important respects. Above all the rise of global market forces, the mobility of capital, and the character of financial markets, contributed to a perception of "globalization." Additionally, civil society movements in Eastern Europe, as encouraged by the West, appeared to provide an effective kind of implementation for international human rights standards, at least as against these Communist regimes that formed the Soviet bloc. The fall of the Berlin Wall and the collapse of the Soviet Union represented the completion of this process, whose character was further highlighted by the contributions of the international anti-apartheid campaign to the dempocratizing transformation of South Africa in the early 1990s. Such negative developments as the rise of transnational crime and pollution, drug flows, illicit arms trade, ozone depletion, and global warming created a strong impression of a declining capability of states to manage the problems of world order.

A parallel set of developments is associated with the growth of regionalism, especially in Europe. The dynamics of economic coordination in Europe had a cumulative impact upon the role of the territorial state. The gradually increasing relevance of the European Parliament and the European Court of Human Rights was also relevant to the idea that it was no longer helpful to conceive of world order as adequately portrayed by reliance upon the Westphalian framework of territorial sovereignty. Non-state actors came into the picture in ways that could no longer be treated as mere exceptions, and even more significantly, the inside/outside distinction so central to international law could no longer be consistently and usefully maintained.

It is within this context of fundamental change and challenge that it seems most appropriate to locate *Achieving Inclusionary Governance* by Terrence Edward Paupp, the latest, most welcome addition to the Innovation series. Paupp builds on the work of various jurists and political theorists to produce a major contribution to this effort at reformulating the role of international law so as to meet the normative challenges of the present period. He invokes the long tradition of philosophical thought that derives from Immanuel Kant's 1795 *Perpetual Peace* to the effect that world peace depends on the formalized cooperation of democratically organized states. Such an outlook has become very influential as a result of the collapse of the Soviet bloc, the consensus around human rights, and the global trend toward degrees of democratization in various parts of the world. Paupp is also responsive to Thomas Franck's seminal article acknowledging an emergent right to democratic governance, in effect, setting standards as to permissible state/society relations on the basis of systems of governance that are periodically validated by the consent of the citizenry. And Paupp takes due account of the work of David Held and others who seek to promote a conception of democracy that is sufficiently comprehensive to encompass both the internal and external relations of the state, and moves toward a new reality called "cosmopolitan democracy."

What most lends significance to *Achieving Inclusionary Governance* is its comprehensive reinterpretation of the role of the state in relation to the normative agenda of the contemporary world. Paupp draws a basic distinction between inclusionary and exclusionary democracies, and states, with respect to the degree to which priority is accorded human well being. From this perspective, Paupp mounts a powerful critique of neoliberal ideas that have shaped the response of most governments to the growing interdependence of the world economy. By focusing on market efficiencies, neoliberal policies tend toward the social disempowerment of the state with respect to ensuring the economic and social well being of the citizenry. Paupp regards such a narrowing of the role of the state to be a characteristic of "the exclusionary state," which disavows a responsibility for upholding the economic and social rights of persons under its jurisdiction, and undertakes only to protect civil and political rights.

Following Held, Paupp also extends the idea of the inclusionary state to cover regional global arenas of authority and decision that have emerged as so signficant in this era of globalization. It is no longer normatively persuasive to limit either the concerns of the state or the scope of democracy to the territorial domain of sovereignty. In this regard, the encompassing notion of "inclusionary governance" provides students of international law and relations with an elegant and insightful framework for depicting the normative requirements of the present age, with due sensitivity to both the centrality of democracy and human rights.

With an admirable sensitivity to the concerns of Third World disadvantaged countries, Paupp overcomes the First World and Eurocentric biases that distort so much of the literature on international law, especially the work that emanates from North America and Europe. In that regard, Paupp gives belated recognition to the Algiers Declaration on the Rights of Peoples (1976) that represented an early effort by representatives of global civil society to mount a critique of exclusionary governance that extended its concerns to the predatory features of global capitalism as the main embodied form of transnational market operations. Jurisprudentially, the Algiers Declaration, as the Universal Declaration of Human Rights, was born as an aspirational document without obligatory character, but has evolved through practice and later legal initiatives (for instance, the Declaration on the Right of Development) into a perspective that is now embodied in customary international law.

Terrence Edward Paupp has written a stimulating and important book. The Innovation series is proud to add *Achieving Inclusionary Governance* to its list.

Richard Falk
General Editor
April 10, 2000

INTRODUCTION

INCLUSION, EXCLUSION, AND THE RECONSTITUTION OF POWER

Even in nations that call themselves democratic, many groups, classes, and discrete and insular minorities have been and continue to be deprived of a right to have a say in how they are governed. This reality is the reality of political exclusion. And political exclusion, by virtue of the fact that it precludes effective participatory government based on the rule of law, also contributes to peoples' reliance on violence as a means of settling differences. Therefore, political exclusion is antithetical to the task of building a culture of peace.

In the alternative, political inclusion provides the normative and constitutional channels through which people are empowered to have a voice in how they are governed. Further, political inclusion is a universal principle of governance that has the capacity to transcend the limitations which are inherent in traditional political categories and labels, such as democratic, authoritarian, totalitarian. Every political regime is subject to evaluation by the criteria of inclusion and the degree to which a regime does or does not practice inclusionary policies, provides for inclusionary avenues for popular participation, or fails to do so. In this manner, political inclusion provides both a normative and objective basis on which to evaluate current institutional arrangements in politics, economics, and social life. It is also a concept which provides a means of articulating new institutions for governance and ways to express normative concerns and assert rights-claims. This means that we can begin to close the gap between the protection of civil and political rights on the one hand, and unite them with socioeconomic rights on the other. Because it is a concept that is dynamic, not static, political inclusion is a new way to conceptualize the procedure of building a culture of peace.

Throughout this book, I refer to the concept of political inclusion by invoking the term *"inclusionary governance."* The purpose of this term is to present a perspective on governance that transcends the historical perspective offered by democracy. It is also meant to be a term that transcends the dangers of democratic exclusion. Insofar as democracies as well as dictatorships have the capacity to govern by exclusion, I have found it is essential to demarcate the boundaries between inclusionary governance and democracy. Inclusionary governance means that democracy is a subset of political inclusion. The current literature of political science takes cognizance of the problems that arise when democracy fails to embody the claims set forth in its ideal by reference to: "the democratic deficit," "low-intensity democracy," "weak democracy" versus "strong democracy," "semi-democracy," and "polyarchy" (elite rule that is legitimated through formal elections).

Inclusionary governance implies that there are available political institutions and legal regimes that are capable of effectuating its claims. I refer to these institutions as the *"inclusionary state"* (IS). The governing characteristics of the IS are set forth in Chapter 6. The five governing characteristics are designed to promote sociopolitical stability while, at the same time, promoting an inclusionary posture for the state. These five characteristics are: *consensus, consistency, congruence, cohesiveness,* and *coherence*. I maintain that these five characteristics of inclusionary governance enable a nation to embark upon a more equitable approach to economic development and growth, promote effective political institutionalization, serve to create a fair and just legal environment, provide the basis for inclusive constitutional adjudication and procedural due process, and allow for the evolution of mediating institutions at the national level.

The IS is a state that operates under the rubric of constitutionally inclusive principles that promote power-sharing in divided societies. Previously excluded groups and classes are to be afforded formal channels through which they may voice their expectations and demands. Too often, in both First and Third World settings, the national welfare becomes subordinated to elite interests. Over time, divisions emerge between the state and civil society, as well as between classes. As the gap between the rich and poor widens, so too does the degree of political, economic and social exclusion. Economic, political and social inequality works to exacerbate trends which result in the rise of the *"exclusionary state"* (ES).

The ES is not separate from the processes associated with globalization. Rather, the ES represents a state and form of governance which has made concessions to transnational capital, multinational corporate rule, and international organizations such as the WTO. By collusion, reciprocal agreements, and mutually arrived at understandings, as undemocratic as the WTO may be, the fact remains that it is the creation of governments, and most of the powerful players are democracies. Acknowledging this fact serves to demonstrate an important theme of this book: *even though democratic in name, many so-called democratic states do not practice inclusionary democracy*. This finding accounts for the realization that the triumph of corporate trade priorities at the WTO simply reflects the political power that corporations have in those governments. It also underscores the irony of a global situation in which the inability of critics of globalization to transcend a merely defensive criticism of globalization has, at least for the present, foreclosed upon the discovery and promotion of alternative models for a more democratic global economy.

It is one of the major tasks of this book to propose such an alternative model—inclusionary governance/democracy. For, in the absence of inclusionary political activity throughout the global village vis-a-vis a global civilsociety, the disparate and divided claims and concerns of labor movements, environmentalists, and citizen groups will continue to be both marginalized

Introduction

and virtually ineffectual in the task of bringing about major structural transformations at the national, regional, and global levels of governance. This is the challenge that confronts First and Third World peoples alike.

Under these conditions, the question becomes: "How can Third World states accelerate their developmental paths while simultaneously creating more just and equitable societies?" Seeking out the dimensions of this question and provisional answers to it consume the inquiry of this book. The outline of this book is organized so as to examine the following propositions.

First, IS is dedicated to the national welfare and the incorporation of all classes and groups into the life of the nation. Its governmental structure and decision making process accommodates and responds to the grievances of marginalized groups. In short, it is not an apologist for a dominant class or exclusionary alliances, coalitions, and pacts. The principle of constitutional codetermination governs its processes and is linked with a substantive Bill of Rights coupled with international human rights protections that can be incorporated into domestic municipal law.

Second, the IS, as a model of governance, transcends the exclusionary tendencies that are inherent in both authoritarian and democratic forms of governance. Authoritarian governments rely on repression as a means to advance narrow agendas that fail to reflect a more inclusive developmental path with a long-term investment horizon and complementary strategies and policies. Democracies that rely on the mere formalities of electoral procedures, while neglecting the substantive core of socioeconomic rights in conjunction with sociopolitical rights, may create political outcomes which result in sacrificing the principles of social justice, fairness, inclusion, and equitable distribution.

Third, the preconditions for inclusionary and equitable development include the protection and expansion of an autonomous civil society. The civil society is, in its ideal practice, a realm of inclusion, participation and mutual cooperation. Civil society is able to embody these qualities when it is guided by shared norms, values, and aspirations. While the civil society is theoretically autonomous and independent of the state, it still must maintain its links with it. These linkages constitute lines of communication which create vital avenues for dialogue, negotiation, arbitration, and mediation between the two realms. As the bonds between state and society are strengthened, the state becomes better positioned to exert its continued influence in the task of creating new "rules of the game." Whether the rules result in a higher degree of inclusionary outcomes for more classes, groups and interests is of primary concern. It is with this in mind that I turn to to sources of international law as an arena of primary importance in delineating the "rules of the game" for a new millenium of global governance.

INTERNATIONAL LAW AS THE SOURCE GLOBAL GOVERNANCE

International law, like the pursuit of democratic security, must proceed in stages. The pursuit of democratic security involves inventing scenarios that respond to the vagaries and limited priorities of time and place. In this task,

Professor Richard Falk reminds us that "Foucault's imperative *'react to the intolerable!'* cannot be understood as one unified directive" (Falk, 1988, p. 147). There are many intolerable situations in the world, often exacerbated by structural violence and the often unchecked power of nation-states. These situations of "man's inhumanity to man" run the gamut from famines and genocides in Africa to communal violence in India and Kosovo. The ideology, practice and investment in nuclearism in the North finds its deadly counterpart in the national security states and dictatorial regimes of the South. In both First and Third Worlds, nation-states and regional edifices of power commingle to engage in various forms of ecological plunder and the degradation of the enviroment, thereby making sustainable development an increasingly difficult prospect. Recognizing these situations as national, regional, and global tragedies alerts us to the reality that international law's historic fidelity to a state-centric conception of sovereignty, as the cornerstone of international law and practice, is no longer tolerable.

In beginning our discussion of the role and significance of international law as it relates to the concept and practice of inclusionary governance, we must recognize that "the move from describing the world to prescribing for it forms the core of international law" (Ratner, 1998, p. 65). On this matter, I am deeply grateful to Professor Ratner for making the conceptual and practical distinction between "description" and "prescription" as the most important feature which resides within the very core of what we call international law. From this distinction we can better appreciate what constitutes the mission of international law, as described in 1950 by Hersch Lauterpact, which is to lead "to enhancing the stability of international peace, to the protection of the rights of man, and to reducing the evils and abuses of national power" (*Id.*, pp. 65–66).

The protection of the rights of man from the abuses of national power has been the normative and objective challenge to political theorists and international law experts since the civil wars between the Tudors and Stuarts in the 17th century England of Thomas Hobbes. The fear and dread of uncontrolled and uncontrollable anarchy within and between states has served as a continual reminder that the containment of conflict was going to be, in large measure, dependent upon the rules of and for governance. The political realm and the legal realm would have to be united, at least in theory, at that point where ethics and international affairs were conjoined. In this critical respect, rights, responsibilities, obligations, duties, consensus, norms, and customs, have all been historical components of the working vocabulary and conceptual universe of an emerging system of international law.

The 18th century saw the first important steps in the direction of "inclusionary governance" and "inclusionary democracy," embodied in the recognition of Immanuel Kant's view that international law and domestic justice are fundamentally connected (Tesón, 1998, p. 1; Kant, 1795, trans., 1983: Kant, 1794, trans., 1983; Kant, 1793, trans., 1983). Despite the prominence of the international law of human rights in the mid- to late-20th century, the dominant discourse has failed to recognize the important normative status of the individual. The contours of traditional international legal theory outline the concerns associated with the rights and duties of states and seems to reject the contention that the rights of states are merely derivative of the rights and interests of the individuals that reside within them. It is for this reason that the cosmopolitan tradition of world order, which finds its origins in the Stoics and emerges in the modern world by stages through Hugo Grotius, Immaneul Kant, and Woodrow Wilson, can now be understood as that tradition of international law which serves as the conceptual and legal underpinnings for inclusionary governance/democracy.

Inclusionary governance/democracy needs to be differentiated from the idea that international legitimacy and sovereignty are merely a function of whether or not a government effectively *controls* its population. Rather, inclusionary governance/democracy asks whether a government justly *represents* its people. The distinction is crucial. Returning to Ratner's observation that "the move from describing the world to prescribing for it forms the core of international law" exposes the fact that the issues of a government's *"control"* over its population (which is largely an expression of the notion of juridical sovereignty) versus a government's *"representation"* of its people presents us with the *description* of un-democratic forms of control, on the one hand, versus the *prescription* for consensual democratic forms of representation and participation, on the other.

Control implies subjugation, repression, authoritarianism, and anti-democratic norms and practices. Control also obviates normative concerns with human rights and justice by emphasizing order and stability as the primary ordering principles or values of national and international life. In short, control connotes exclusion and the impulse to engage in exclusionary forms of governance. Alternatively, representation implies the primacy of participation in decision making, for all individuals, groups, and classes affected by governing processes and/or economic policies. The difference between control and representation is a difference between forms of inclusionary or exclusionary governance. In other words, the idea, force, and meaning of inclusionary governance (as an innovative concept in international law and political science) points to the fundamental need to unite the descriptive with the prescriptive if there is to be genuine coherence in the theory and practice of international law and its application to the plight of the poor, excluded and marginalized of the planet.

The emphasis upon control and the power to control are inherently antithetical to a normatively democratic framework of thought and action which values and protects the individual. The emphasis upon the value and practice of representation (as well as participation in decision making) serves to remove the duality in international law between justice and legitimacy as conceptually separate. When the duality between justice and legitimacy is removed, the core value of inclusionary governance is exposed as the legitimate expression of an interpretation of international law which holds that "the end of states and governments is to benefit, serve, and protect human being, and not its components, states, and governments" (Tesón, 1998, p. 1; see also Popper, 1966, p. 288). Understood in this way, "respect for states is merely derivative of respect for persons." Therefore, sovereignty itself is redefined because the sovereignty of the state is "dependent upon the state's domestic legitimacy" and, therefore, "the principles of international justice must be congruent with the principles of internal justice" (*Id.*, p. 1).

Richard Falk has invoked a similar orientation in his criticism of global economic policy as increasingly shaped by neoliberal criteria that emphasizes the primacy of capital efficiency (i.e., privatization and liberalization) at the expense of the individual as social and economic functions shift from the public to private the sector. Domestically, he argues, "the *intranational result* is the partial social disempowerment of the state. The *international result* is the decline of direct development assistance by the World Bank and International Monetary Fund. In effect these institutions mount pressure to assure that a governmental recipient of funds does not use public resources for poverty alleviation and social distress, but rather to build a high-growth economy" (Falk, 1998, p. 430; italics are mine).

The emphasis upon building a high-growth economy sacrifices the union of justice and legitimacy. Such an emphasis places the individual outside the mainstream of legal and political protections and social and economic rights. In short, such an emphasis creates an exclusionary state (ES) and produces more and more excluded, poor, dispossessed, and marginalized persons. It is a permanent state of injustice. It is an anti-democratic state for it fails to include large segments of its population in the decision making processes that affect their lives.

The traditional foundations of international law protect and serve this order because these traditional foundations are illiberal and authoritarian in their exaltation of state power as an end in itself. The exercise of power attains moral legitimacy only when it is the result of political consent and respects the basic rights of the individuals subject to that power. In sum, then, it follows that if international law is to be morally legitimate, "it must mandate that states respect human rights as a precondition for joining the international community" (Tesón, 1998, p. 2). Kant was the first to promote this thesis, as exemplified in his essay *Perpetual Peace*. In Kant's view, a morally legitimate international law is founded upon *"an alliance of separate free nations, united by their moral commitment to individual freedom, by their allegiance to the international rule of law, and by the mutual advantages derived from peaceful intercourse"* (Tesón, 1998, p. 2).

In the centuries since Kant, international human rights law has been state-centric. What this means is that governments have agreed on standards, their degree of bindingness, and on issues concerning enforcement. According to Falk, "such a feature of human rights law reflects a wider pattern of international law-making which tends to view state consent as a precondition to the formation of valid rules of law" (Falk, 1981, pp. 190–191); each government has veto power over the formation of rules or standards which violate its own policy perogatives. However, in the post-1945 era, a shift began in which higher degrees of *consensus* began to be a precondition to consent (or at least to complement consent as a source of international norm creation).

As a consequence of this shift, it has been argued that the law-making stature of UN General Assembly Resolutions has created milestones "in what is properly perceived as the progressive development of international law" (*Id.*, p. 191). As examples of the progressive development of international law, the following have been cited: the Universal Declaration of Human Rights, the resolution affirming the Nuremberg Principles, the Resolution on Permanent Sovereignty over Natural Resources, and the Declaration on the Granting of Independence to Colonial Countries and Peoples. The net result of these trends, however, is that the role of consent as a community-based source of law remains controversial and indefinite (*Id.*, p. 191). This is especially the case in the post-1980s, where trade regimes and international finance have increasingly worked through treaties, often negotiated above and beyond the reach of ordinary citizens. Not being subjected to democratic controls, scrutiny or the influence of democratic forms of representation, these treaties have often sought to control shifts in wealth and power without having to seek democratic consensus in the process.

In response to multinational power and initiatives, many Third World governments and their peoples, in the midst the US intervention in Vietnam, sought to press the core capitalist countries by either seeking to join the nonaligned nations movement (in a bipolar Cold War context), or, in the alternative, by beginning to build an international legal regime that would hold these great powers accountable for their interventionism, imperial undertakings, and violations of both self-determination and national sovereignty. In this task, Third World peoples began to revive Immanuel Kant's view of a morally legitimate international law. That undertaking found its most profound expression in the Algiers Declaration (adopted July 4, 1976).

By the 1970s, it had become clear that consensus had its limits. After all, consensus can only function when most states are in agreement. A problem arises when international society is divided, or if a large number of individual governments are guilty of objectionable policies. At that point in historical time, it was impossible to mobilize a meaningful consensus. By the mid-1970s, an atmosphere of crisis contaminated the international community of nations, largely derived from the structural features and logic of capital accumulation by market-oriented systems, not to mention superpower intervention in Vietnam and other Third World states. Given this state of affairs, liberal declarations on human rights, written by those representing the centers of capitalism's power, now increasingly rang hollow by virtue of their failure to acknowledge their own complicity in practices and policies which deepened repression and exploitation around the globe. In other words, it had become abundantly clear that the failure to admit complicity in this version of world order revealed the fact that "imperial centers of power are unable to pursue human rights without dismantling their economic and political structures of domination" (Falk, 1981, p. 191). The Algiers Declaration of the Rights of People responded to this situation.

The preamble of the Algiers Declaration made clear its preoccupation with the sources of global human misery, including "as basic explanation of the general failure to realize those minimal rights associated with the basic needs of the peoples of the world" (*Id.*, p. 192). In short, the Algiers Declaration stands as an indictment of exclusionary governance at the national and international levels. While issued as a nongovernmental document, with no accountability to governing powers within the UN, it was free of political constrictions in outlining its criticisms of the international system. Its greatest virtue and greatest strength is found in the fact that it is itself "an assertion of popular sovereignty, asserting that it is the peoples of the world that are the fundamental sources of authority with respect to the governing process" (*Id.*, p. 192).

With this declaration, the first major global impulses of the demand for inclusionary governance were felt. Its reverberations still resound, "drawing inspiration from the Magna Carta tradition," for it "is a framework of rights asserted by and for the peoples of the world over and against the claims and activities of governments, multinational corporations, and international institutions" (*Id.*, p. 192). The preamble of the Universal Declaration on the Rights of Peoples states: "that the effective respect for human rights necessarily implies respect for the rights of peoples, we have adopted the UNIVERSAL DECLARATION OF THE RIGHTS OF PEOPLE."

It sets forth the following seven sections "for those who, throughout the world . . . find in this Declaration the assurance for the legitimacy of their struggle": right to existence; right to political self-determination; economic rights of peoples; right to culture; right to environment and common resources; rights of minorities; guarantees and sanctions. There could be no more eloquent starting point in international law or politics than the Algiers Declaration for the articulation of the claims of inclusionary governance and its claims for the realization inclusionary democracy in the global village.

A FRAMEWORK OF RIGHTS ASSERTED BY AND FOR THE PEOPLE

Kant is usually regarded as the pioneering advocate of an international organization that would be capable of securing a lasting peace. While his views are credited with foreshadowing the creation of modern conceptions of international law associated with the United Nations, the true scope and vitality of his vision transcends such a narrow institutional context. Beyond his originality in advocating and predicting the rise of a global political organization, his major contribution has been to show the strong linkages which exist between international peace and personal freedom, as well as between the exercise of arbitrary government at home and aggressive behavior abroad. In recognition of these linkages, Kant's first principle of international ethics, found in *Perpetual Peace*, stresses the idea that "the constitution of every nation should be republican" (Kant, 1795, p. 112). The corollary to this assertion is found in his second article "The law of nations shall be based upon a union of republican states" (Kant, 1795, p. 115). Taken together, these principles seek to promote a constitutional regime in every republican state that subscribes to three central principles: (1) the liberal principle of respect of individual autonomy and the government's (relative) neutrality of ends; (2) the independence of the constitutional system, meaning that all legal acts (or dependence of all subjects) must derive from a single common legislation; (3) the principle of the equality of all citizens, that is, equality before the law (Tesón, 1998, pp. 3–6). Viewed in combination, these principles exemplify the heart of the Kantian thesis, which is that "observance of human rights is a primary requirement to join the community of nations under international law" (*Id.*, p. 7).

The observance of human rights, understood in light of the Kantian thesis, has direct implications for traditional thinking about democracy. Insofar as "traditional thinking about democracy has been severely limited by national blinders that in practice encourage us to ignore the rights of people outside our own nation" (Johansen, 1993, p. 41), Kant's emphasis upon the "community of nations" draws us into a larger framework of thinking about democracy and governance—inclusionary governance/democracy. What this suggests is that "principled governing authority must be developed not only 'vertically' within domestic societies from the local to the national level, but also 'horizontally' across national borders and 'vertically' to encompass world society at the global level" (*Id.*, p. 41). The implications of this vertical/horizontal accountability for local, national, and global governance reverberates in the writings of Richard Falk ("humane governance"), David Held ("cosmopolitan democracy"), and Terrence Paupp ("inclusionary governance/democracy").

The lasting importance of the Algiers Declaration may be seen in the matrix of this "vertical/horizontal" nexus. There are three reasons for this assessment. First, on an ideological level, the declaration condemns the denial of human rights and associates this denial with capitalism in its international aspect. The emasculation of the rights of people is antithetical to the Kantian thesis on republican government and constitutionalism, the claims of democracy, and the covenants and charters of the international community which have embraced human rights as the *sine qua non* of the post-1945 international legal order. Second, with respect to legitimacy, as a political necessity and as a legal norm of governance, the declaration calls into question the legitimacy of practices which systematically deny human rights that occur outside of the authoritative and legitimating functions of various international arenas. In this respect, the "Algiers Declaration serves notice on governments, multinational corporations, and international institutions . . . that their activities are subject to scrutiny from a vantage point that is higher than that of national governments" (Falk, 1981, p. 193). Third, and finally, the declaration asserts the rights of all peoples to question the state system because the "peoples of the world possess the ultimate law-making authority, and that the validity of governmental law-making capacity rests on a prior delegation of competence by the people" (*Id.*, 1981, p. 199).

Further, by virtue of having vested ultimate law-making authority in the people, neither "sovereignty" nor "globalization" are immune from accountability to the people. While the phenomenon of globalization finds its way into the literature of international relations (IR) theory in the form of claims about a loss of "state capacity," the reality is that globalization "cannot be construed as a force set apart from the practice of sovereignty, reshaping it from the outside" when, in reality, "sovereignty and globalization actively refashion each other, and should not be thought of as each other's negations" (Clark, 1999, p. 170). In other words, changes in state power or state capacity do not reveal a "diminution" of that power, but rather a "reconstitution" of power around the consolidation of domestic and international linkages

(*Id.*, p. 171). Extrapolating from this interpretation, the question then becomes: "How does this reconstitution of power work to effect exclusionary or inclusionary tendencies in national and international arenas?"

We do know that the reconstitution of power, its linkages and alignments on a global scale, have caused tremendous exclusionary forces to be let loose (or at least exacerbated), inducing higher levels of poverty and social and political exclusion, along with anti-democratic practices which devalue citizenship and the rights attached to it. As the rights of citizenship diminish, so too do democratic protections and procedures at the national and international levels. In this respect, the reconstitution of power, on a global scale, has reflected an inclination to become increasingly "predatory." The dimensions of this globalized reconstitution of power have resulted in exclusionary trends of governance. And yet, in spite of inclusionary pressures, "democratizing social forces have been increasingly, if unevenly, effective in their capacity to erode statist forms of oppressive rule" (Falk, 1999(b), p. 21).

In large measure, the advance of these exclusionary practices and reconstituted forms of power present subversive challenges to the core Westphalian notion of territorial supremacy and, at the same time, have enlisted states themselves in endorsing and adopting exclusionary and predatory policies which dramatically affect the poor, marginalized, excluded, and dispossessed within their own sovereign borders (Report of the Independent Commission on International Development Issues, 1980; The Report of the Commission on Global Governance, 1995; Papers written for the Commission on Global Governance, 1995; Brandt, 1986; George, 1977; Chossudovsky, 1997 and 1998; Falk, 1975, 1998, 1999; Petras and Polychroniou, 1998, pp. 187–208).

In combination, the literature on international law, international institutions, globalization, regionalization, and inequality (on national and international levels), points toward the view that "'globalization' can be defined as the growth, or more precisely the accelerated growth, of economic activity that spans politically defined national and regional boundaries" (Oman, 1999, p. 37). The nature of the expansion of these changes has resulted in the reconstitution of power arrangements, as well as newly fashioned legal, political, and economic linkages. The net result of this global reconstitution of power is a new dynamic for the fueling of disparities of wealth, power, and resources within and between exclusionary states (ES). These disparities and inequalities are the direct result of anti-democratic and inherently exclusionary policies that fail to meet the needs and democratic demands of citizens. At the same time, these exclusionary policies and structures effectively deny international human rights protections which should be afforded refugees and migrants (Klingemann and Fuchs, 1995, pp. 1–23).

These exclusionary trends and impulses, at the international level, to the extent that they mirror the exclusionary predicament of nation-states, serve to demonstrate that even so-called democratic states have their limitations in effectuating justice, democracy, and inclusion within their own borders. By exposing these limitations, it has been argued that "democratic states are not exogenous social actors that can *reconstitute* an externalized international order along non-authoritarian lines; nor, for that matter, can they build a liberal peace. If a liberal peace exists, they are already a part of it,

Introduction　　　　　　　　　　　　　　　　　　　　　　　　　　　xxix

just as the order is a part of them. And if globalization is unsettling democracy, it does not do so from the outside but is instead a manifestation of the changing form of the democratic state itself" (Clark, 1999, p. 158; italics are mine).

A major manifestation of this phenomenon was launched in 1995, with the creation of the World Trade Organization (WTO). The WTO is the zealous handmaiden of corporate globalization. In the name of promoting free trade, the WTO works to codify the rules of the global economic game. Compared to the General Agreement on Tariffs and Trade (GATT) that preceded it, the WTO has more power. The manifestation of its power is displayed through its dispute panels. When decisions of its dispute panels are binding (and a consensus of all 134 member governments is needed to block them), the WTO usually wins. In fact, so far, no democratically achieved environmental, health, food safety, or environmental law challenged at the WTO has been upheld. As of 1999, all of these challenges have been declared "barriers to trade" (Wallach and Sforza, 1999).

The manifestation of exclusionary forms and norms of exclusionary governance arise in a dialectical matrix of national and international factors. To the extent that exclusionary forms of governance are on the rise, these forms are largely a manifestation of a growing congruence between anti-democratic norms and practices within nations, as well as between nations, in relation to transnational non-governmental actors (such as banks, multinational corporations, and other international institutions linked to the processes of capital accumulation such as the WTO, GATT, and NAFTA).

With the reconstitution of power arrangements (as discussed above), at the regional level we find the juxtaposition of a worst-case assessment and a best-case scenario. A worst-case assessment would suggest that "regionalism is serving as a cover for the re-entrenchment of relations of privilege and domination that were challenged during the revolt against colonialism" (Falk, 1999(b), p. 79). Alternatively, a best-case scenario would "attribute inequality in benefits and burdens to the short run, with a more equitable, sustainable, and democratic global economic order emerging in response to grass-roots and other challenges mounted against negative globalism" (*Id.*, p. 79).

These alternative scenarios, associated with the reconstitution of power, are not limited to a Third World setting, although they are a graphic and intimate part of it. A perfect case-study for these phenomena may be found, in a First World setting, with the struggle over European integration, inaugurated by the Single European Act (1986) and continued in the Maastrict Treaty (1993). These treaties exemplify the fact that European integration, from the early 1980s through the late 1990s, has been a polity-creating as well as a market-deepening process (Hooghe and Marks, 1999, p. 70). As a dual process—polity-creating and market-deepening—the struggle over European integration allows for the examination of intertwined dynamics that point toward new directions for governance, international law, and international institutions. It is with reference to this struggle that we must now turn. But before undertaking a case-study the European Union (EU), a more comprehensive background review of international law and international institutions is in order.

THE RECONSTITUTION OF GOVERNANCE, INTERNATIONAL LAW, AND INTERNATIONAL INSTITUTIONS

To analyze world politics in the 1990s is to discuss international institutions. International institutions are leading actors in world politics because the rules that govern world politics also govern organizations that serve to implement those rules. Questions involving the expansion of NATO, the ability of the UN Security Council to assure UN inspectors access to sites where Iraq might be conducting banned weapons activity, the conditions under which China should or should not be admitted to the World Trade Organization (WTO), the function of the International Monetary Fund (IMF) as a "lender of last resort," the future of UN peacekeeping practices and their effectiveness—all are examples of the growing importance of international institutions for maintaining world order (Keohane, 1998, p. 82). Still, the question of the role of international institutions cannot be limited to these aspects of interdependence.

Equally important are considerations of the nature and scope of international institutions as they operate at the regional and domestic levels of the individual nation-states through an emerging regime of international law and its normative context. Municipal law and international law are co-equally responsible for the scope and quality of governance within and between nations. For within the context of regional institutions (which must adhere to some guidance and democratic demands from nation-states), such as the emerging European Union (EU), there are still two processes at work that are deeply intertwined with one another. First, the Single European Act (1986) and the Maastrict Treaty (1993) are part of a process of market integration in which a great variety of nontariff barriers have been effectively reduced or entirely eliminated. Second, these institutional reforms have led to the creation of a single, though diverse, polity. The polity itself is reflective of of a system of multilevel governance which encompasses a variety of authoritative institutions. These authoritative institutions exist at the supra-national, national, and subnational levels of decision making. Within and between these various levels have emerged issues associated with democratic governance and international law that bear directly on whether or not the inauguration of 21st century legal norms and values will usher in an age of inclusionary or exclusionary governance on the European stage. The implications for other parts of the First and Third Worlds are tremendous.

As already noted, Steven Ratner, in his article, "International Law: The Trials of Global Norms," states that "the move from describing the world to prescribing for it forms the core of international law" (Ratner, 1998, p. 65). This is especially the case for the emerging European Union. Historically, international lawyers have faced the dual task of coming to terms with the two cardinal challenges: (1) how to make international law precepts legitimate in a diverse community of nations; and (2) how to make them stick in the absence of any one sovereign authority or supranational enforcement mechanism (*Id.*, p. 65). These formerly distinct concerns and sets of issues are now converging in the context of the Europe of the late 1990s and on into the new milennium as the European Union matures.

Introduction xxxi

At risk and in question is nothing less than political concerns and legal issues that were formerly regarded as "purely domestic." A bold new paradigm is needed and must be constructed in order to realize a more comprehensive legal, social, economic, and political order. Such a new paradigm for governance must be capable of blending the *descriptive* elements of law and governance with the *prescriptive* elements of law and governance. While the suffusion of norms into decision making is a long-term process, it is integral to building the European Union.

The European political economy has witnessed the collapse of national Keynesianism in a context of poor economic performance and declining international competitiveness. This has forced a reconstitution of power which, in turn, has meant that the two most fundamental issues of political life had to be dealt with: (1) the scope and structure of political authority, and (2) the scope of authoritative decision making in the economy. While the European Union "continues to serve as a means for achieving narrow collective goods . . . these larger questions are never far from view" (Hooghe and Marks, 1999, p. 96). Hence, the normative aspects of democratic governance, international law, economic policy, and the force of treaties all converge at this point. Recognizing this reality is to realize that *description* has merged into *prescription* in the formation and formulation of international law. Before proceeding with the European Union as a case study in global governance, the international legal norms and institutions affecting its evolution need to be demarcated within the larger global context. It is to this new global context of international law that we now turn.

THE EMERGING GLOBAL CONTEXT OF INTERNATIONAL LAW

International law has entered a new global context. New realities demand new ideas as well as new approaches. The new global context of international law has led to three fundamental shifts: (1) new forms and new players around the globe have led to treaties effectively displacing much customary law; (2) the legitimacy problems associated with a history of Western dominance of law, politics, and economics have been challenged; and (3) new linkages between trade, the environment, human rights, issues of social justice, and the unequal distribution of wealth have transformed the nature and scope of international regulations that were once purely within the scope of domestic/municipal law and jurisdiction. We shall briefly examine each of these shifts in turn.

First, with respect to new forms and new players, we find most rules of international law have traditionally been found in one of two places: treaties—binding written agreements between states; or customary law— uncodified but equally binding rules based on long-standing behavior that states accept as customary. Historically, treaties have increasingly displaced much customary law insofar as international rules have become increasingly codified. The figures are staggering. The total number of bilateral and multilateral treaties registered with the UN since 1945 is approximately 50,000. Of these, the total number of registered treaties to which the United States is a party is approximately 10,000. The major multilateral treaties to which the United States is not a party are the following: (a) Convention on Rights of the Child (1989)—191 parties, all but the United States and Somalia; (b) Convention on Biological Diversity (1992)—172 parties; (c) Convention on the Elimination of All Forms of Discrimination Against Women (1979)—161 parties; (d) Comprehensive Nuclear Test Ban Treaty (1996)—149 signatories (not yet in force, and defeated by the United States Senate in October 1999); (e) International Covenant on Economic, Social, and Cultural Rights (1966)—137 parties; (f) UN Convention on the Law of the Sea (1982, amended, 1994)—123 parties; (g) Convention on the Prohibition of the Use, Stockpiling, Production and Transfer of Anti-personnel Mines and on Their Destruction (1997)—122 signatories (not yet in force).

As international law and the international community of nation-states have progressively moved forward in significant areas of inclusionary governance, on a national and global basis, the United States, despite its claim to being a democratic state, has continually failed to embark upon an inclusionary path that would lead to the endorsement and enforcement of a treaty regime which would have principled force and inclusionary normative capacity at the international level. Given the disparity between its announced adherence to democratic principles and norms, and its practices, the United States has refused to live up to its claims vis-a-vis this treaty regime. Insofar as the new global context of international law is reliant upon treaties as the principal means for advancing inclusionary governance—*both descriptively and prescriptively*—the glaring absence of the support of the world's leading, dominant, and sole superpower is disturbing at the very least.

The ominous absence of the imprimatur of US approval for these treaties, as well as the global initiatives which they represent, raises the question of whether the US has embarked upon the path of being a benevolent hegemony or upon a path of neo-isolationism. In either case, the US has followed a path of global governance which has precluded popular participation in sustainable development and, even worse, created a mandate for exclusionary states and impulses to, once more, form a multipolar world where competition and increasing rivalry could lead to war (Kupchan, 1999, p. 26).

In Professor Falk's analysis, US behavior can best be evaluated from the perspective of a distinction between "globalization-from-above" versus "globalization-from-below." Under the rubric of "globalization-from-above," the reconstitution of power involves the restructuring of the world economy on a regional and global scale "through the agency of the transnational corporation and financial markets." Under the rubric of "globalization-from-below," the restructuring of the world economy involves the rise of transnational social forces "concerned with environmental protection, human rights, peace, and human security," which has led to the emergence of a "global civil society" (Falk, 1998, p. 167).

The US opposes "globalization-from-below," as demonstrated in its statist backlash, designed to cut off various inclusionary arenas of participation by transnational political forces. The result of this policy is not only evident in a deliberate reaction against the claims of cosmopolitan democracy, but it is seen as "also mixed with ideological perceptions that globalization-from-below seeks to moderate market forces and takes issue with the laissez-faire tenets of neo-liberalism" (*Id.*, p. 168).

Throughout this book, I identify this statist backlash as the *"exclusionary impulse"* which undergirds US support for exclusionary states (ES) that are more dedicated to following the prescriptions of neoliberal economic and political principles than in meeting the needs of their own people, as mandated by international law charters, treaties, and practices. For if the model of inclusionary governance is pursued in place of the neoliberal model of development, then inclusionary/democratic norms are placed on a collision course with reconstituted capital power and its logic of accumulation at all costs. The dangers for law and democracy come into sharper focus when it is recognized that, by adopting the ideology of "globalization-from-above," both the WTO and the European Union, acting as exclusionary states (ES), are more "inclined to support supernationalizing transfers of sovereignty over economic policy-making" (Falk, 1998, p. 168). Such a consequence results in the automatic transfer of democratic accountability from the people to realms of power and decision making beyond the reach, participation, or deliberative power of the people.

The antagonistic posture of the the United States to implementing the claims of global civil society (as demonstrated by its continued refusal to sign the above-referenced treaties), exposes the power-centers' attempt to legitimate the rule of capital on a global basis, thereby inviting the dangers of "democratic fatigue" at the nation-state level. In the US, third-party "reform parties" and movements, the rise of right-wing militias, the growth in the rates of various hate crimes, all give testimony to the fact that new avenues for authoritarian politics are emerging, as occured in Germany's first failed democracy, the Weimar Republic.

In combination with this historical possibility, there is also a growing recognition that the so-called "Washington Consensus" is either dying or dead. Between the early 1980s and late 1990s this elite consensus swept the globe, alleging that unfettered markets provided the formula to make rich countries out of poor ones. In policy circles, this formula came to be known as the "Washington Consensus." At the dawn of a new century, however, spreading cracks in the consensus are more visible as its hegemonic *legitimacy* has come into question. The cracks in the consensus have emerged in the face of an effective citizens' backlash in North and South, in response to the exclusionary tendencies and impulses embodied in the consensus.

In an emerging global village, "what is being suggested is the need for a jurisprudence of international law that encompasses globalization in both its main expressions: from above and from below" (Falk, 1998, p. 170). Yet the very articulation of this need is resisted by the old order, which seeks retrenchment behind walls of elite governance, which is to say exclusionary governance. Law, economics, politics, and even religion have been enlisted in an attempt to legitimate the illegitimate. It dates back to 1980.

Supported by the capitalist triumvirate of Thatcher, Reagan, and Kohl, it championed free trade, free investment, deregulation, and privatization as the holy grails of economic growth. The only problem is that it was and is an edifice of power built upon exclusionary governance and policies. Consequently, it never gained *legitimacy* outside of a technocratic elite. The national and international order that supported it is in the midst of decline. By 1999, the combined wealth of the world's 475 billionaires exceeded the income of the poorest half of the world's people (Broad and Cavanagh, 1999, pp. 81 and 88).

This regime of exclusionary governance has had the effect of delegitimating governments, economic policies, and those elements of national and international law which have advanced its incorporation into the world's economy and furthered a paradigm of imperial rule. It is primarily for this reason that globalization seems to spiral out of control. Yet "the more it does so, the more it evokes counter-tendencies that express themselves at the state level, in the absence of effective sites for doing so" (Clark, 1999, p. 174). In almost Hegelian terms, the thesis of "globalization-from-above" collides with "globalization-from-below," exposing the claims of inclusionary governance and the outlines of a legitimacy problem underlying the current order. A new synthesis is in the making, which is what makes the outcome of this particular historical period very open-ended. It is to this *legitimacy problem* that we now turn in order to examine the second aspect of the new global context for international law.

Second, the new global context for international law reveals the outlines of a legitimacy problem. While legal scholars debate over how to shape better enforcement mechanisms, another expanding debate is emerging about the legitimacy of such measures. At the heart of the matter is the question of whether Western dominance of the Organization for Security and Cooperation in Europe, the UN, the WTO, and other international institutions, is not merely a case of raw power asserting its might through multilateral bodies, all to the ultimate detriment of a genuine rule of law (Ratner, 1998, p. 73). The restoration of a genuine rule of law is potentially emerging as a "right to democratic governance" (Franck, 1992, pp. 46ff.; Falk, 1998, pp. 165–171). I have devoted Chapter 1 to this topic and its ramifications. Suffice it to say, by way of introduction, that both the prescriptive and descriptive legal history and normative structure of such an emerging right to democratic governance is well-grounded in international law. It is, obviously, a view which is at odds with the Washington Consensus.

In this regard, an analogy can be drawn between the closing months of the Second World War and the close of the 1990s, with the neoliberal paradigm largely discredited. The analogy is this: at the end of 1945, "a small group made up primarily of men from the richer countries sketched the architecture of the postwar global economy. The institutions they created are no longer serving the needs of the majority of people on earth. In the closing months of the twentieth century, there is at last the opportunity for a larger, more representative group to create new global rules and institutions for the twenty-first century. Indeed, since the Washington Consensus swept the globe two decades ago, the possibility of reading its obituary has never been greater" (Broad and Cavanagh, 1999, p. 87). Inherent in the promise of neoliberalism's obituary is the ascendant promise of what I have called inclusionary governance—a global commonwealth whose prescriptive norms and descriptive political, legal, and economic structures rest on the foundation of inclusionary principles and practices. The promise and potential of the emerging democratic entitlement also points to new linkages at the national, regional, and global levels.

Third, the new global order is in the process of establishing new linkages. The merger of globalization "from above" and "from below" point to a new kind of democracy—a cosmopolitan model (Held, 1995; Kant, 1795). This vision enables us to imagine the outlines of a new global context for the exercise of international law insofar as the establishment of new linkages lays to rest "the notion of hermetically sealed areas of international law—each a nice chapter in a treatise" (Ratner, 1998, p. 74). Such a view is increasingly anachronistic, for it fails to take into account the fact that trade law and environmental law are no longer distinct arenas of legal concern. The existence of NAFTA and GATT, as part of an emergent treaty regime in international law, all exemplify the overlap between not only trade and the environment, but labor law standards, human and civil rights concerns, issues of inequality, and the distribution of wealth on a global scale.

Beyond artificially-induced debates about the clash of cultures and/or civilizations (in many respects more reflective of the thinking embodied in the Washington Consensus and neoliberal paradigm), the core reality of the new global context is that "the proliferation of new norms has direct effects on the debates over globalization—the 'Jihad versus McWorld' controversy" (Ratner, 1998, p. 75). What this means is that a global treaty on environmental concerns will be able to accommodate different perspectives on the priority of environmental protection versus development. The conclusion to be drawn from this shift is, almost by definition, one where "the decision by states to subject a once strictly domestic concern to international regulation means that cultural, value-based, or 'sovereignty' arguments no longer enjoy the upper hand" (Ratner, 1998, p. 75). When this trend is viewed within the matrix of regional arrangements, the European Union comes to mind. The example of the EU provides us with a perspective of structural reform. As such, the birthplace of the modern state system of sovereign states is now the birthplace for innovations in modeling a new form of political community "in which state boundaries are of greatly reduced significance and regional operating space becomes the dominant economic and political motif" (Falk, 1993, p. 30).

In the event that the EU experiment enjoys success in the task of improving Europe's position in the world market, it will be heralded as a worthy precedent for experiments elsewhere. Alternatively, if it fails to deal with what its critics refer to as its "democratic deficit" (Martin and Ross, 1999, pp. 171–175)—a failure to incorporate and include the marginalized, dispossessed, jobless, poor, unemployed and under-employed—then it could be a warning sign that old modes of exclusionary/neoliberal governance have merely undergone a mutation under the rubric of regionalization—again asserting the primacy of capital accumulation over and against the needs and aspirations of its entire citizenry. Should the EU create a new organization of democratic disempowerment, then its promise to be a zone of peace with rising levels of democratic governance and human rights, will be severely compromised. It will, at that point, stand as warning sign, rather than as a sign post to a new promised land.

THE EUROPEAN UNION AS A CASE STUDY IN NATIONAL/REGIONAL GOVERNANCE: THE DYNAMICS OF INCLUSION VERSUS EXCLUSION

The treaties of the three European Communities (the ECSC, the EC, and EURATOM) as amended, and the Maastrict Treaty on European Union, are the "primary" sources of EU law. The EU treaties have had a common set of institutions since 1967. These institutions are as follows: the Council of Ministers, the Commission, the Parliament, and the Court of Justice (to which the Court of First Instance was attached in 1989). These institutions, supplemented by national legislatures, courts and tribunals, have been actively engaged in generating a complex body of "secondary" European Union law. While some of this law is adopted directly at the EU level, a great deal more of it is enacted by national governments under the "direction" of the Union.

Beyond this, the power to legislate resides in the founding treaties. While some of the secondary case law of the EU is created by decision of the European Court of Justice or Court of First Instance, much more of the developing Union law occurs in the national courts, acting in many instances with "advisory rulings" from the Court of Justice. European Union secondary law includes international obligations, often undertaken through "mixed" EU and national negotiations and ratifications.

What is being created under the auspices of the EU is a polity. It also represents a market-deepening process. While a wide variety of nontariff barriers have been reduced or eliminated, these institutional reforms have led to a more fundamental restructuring of power—a system of multileveled governance that encompasses a variety of authoritative institutions, intersecting at the supranational, national, and subnational levels of decision making.

From the early 1980s though the 1990s, two decades of economic developments—internationalization of markets for goods and capital, the decline of traditional industry and industrial employment, growing pressures toward flexible specialized production, the decentralization of industrial relations, the decline of economic competitiveness, and high levels of long-term unemployment—have inaugurated fundamental shifts in the organization of political authority in western Europe. These trends combine to expose the main underlying fact that the so-called "social quality" of Europe is what is ultimately at risk. Further, these trends expose the fact that "the concerns of social policy, traditionally the prerogative of sovereign states, have become supranational and global in scope" (Deacon, 1999, p. 211).

These converging trends have forced to the surface the underlying fact that the management of economic activity impinges directly upon concerns with social justice. Therefore, the management of economic activity is increasingly called upon to serve the purposes of social justice, making social justice concerns high on the agenda for global actors such as the G-7, the World Bank, and the World Trade Organization (WTO). Whether these global actors take social justice concerns as seriously as the affected states do is another question. The point is that these global actors, at the very least, are being forced to address these concerns whether they wish to or not.

Introduction

While the implications for national, supranational, and transnational social policy has been both "under-theorized" and "under-researched" within the topic of "social policy," it is one of the main tasks of this book to advance understanding in this critical domain. At the heart of the matter, as far as the EU is concerned, is the fact that "the deepening of the market did not determine how the market was to be governed. That was—and is—subject to an intense and highly politicized struggle among national government leaders, Commissioners and high-level European Commission administrators, judges in the European Court of Justice, party representatives in national parliaments and the European Parliament, alongside a variety of social movements and interest groups" (Hooghe and Marks, 1999, p. 71). To reach this conclusion is to acknowledge that *European integration is an irreducibly political process* and not just an economic one. Still, politics impacts upon economic decision making and vice versa. Both economics and politics are legally accountable to the rule of law and legal standards as they have evolved and as they are currently evolving. In a more tempered vein of analysis, Vobruba has asserted that "the development of European social policy is neither economically determined nor can [it] be freely built according to political aims. Thus, the problem is the balance between economic realism and political requirements" (Vobruba, 1997, p. 105). Still, between these two interconnected extremes lies the question of the "social quality" of Europe.

A good definition of the "social quality" (or "social question") revolves around such concepts as optimal social participation, integration, solidarity, a sense of belonging and a sense of purpose to one's existence. Fundamental to these concepts are employment, security of income, adequate housing, and good health. These are also the material "fundamentals" (or basic human needs), which constitute some central goals associated with inclusionary governance and inclusionary democracy in both First and Third World settings. In the European Union today, over 20 million citizens are unemployed and 55 million citizens are living in relative poverty (Beck, van der Maesen, and Walker, 1997, p. 274). Given these numbers, it has become increasingly clear that Europe "not only needs a new social order, it requires a common moral order to sustain new forms of societal networks, based on the modern conception of citizenship. The social rights of citizenship will sustain social freedom in order to defend and to develop forms of social cohesion" (*Id.*, p. 275).

The needs and requirements for new forms of governance, capable of sustaining this new enterprise, were foreshadowed as early as 1990. The European Community (EC) strategy for completing a single, integrated market by 1992 reflected the interests of big European capital. In the early 1990s, it had become apparent that abolishing all frontier, social, industrial, technological, and other barriers to a single market would facilitate progress toward another wave of industrial restructuring. So conceived, it was assumed that big European capital would enjoy an era of growth and expansion for a new breed of European multinationals, capable of confronting American and Asian multinationals in an all-out struggle for world markets in the 1990s. Given the dynamics of this strategy, Palmer noted that "to this end, big European capital wants remaining working class, trade union and social welfare 'obstacles' to increased competitiveness swept away" (Palmer, 1990, p. 60). The potential victims of this move would be workers in industrial sectors, left unable to meet the new targets of global productivity and competitiveness. The economic and social threats associated with this trend would spread to communities which depended on such industries and to the more vulnerable regions and unprotected social groups (including migrant and immigrant workers).

As these trends accelerated, they reached a point of critical mass in which "social exclusion" became a new development and a pressing concern. It was no longer just a question of "poverty," for a conceptual shift had occurred in the late 1980s making "social exclusion" a distinct category of social assessment. The EC was instrumental in the definitional and conceptual shift, stating that: "(Recognizing) that social exclusion is not simply a matter of inadequate [resources], and that combating exclusion also involves access by individuals and families to decent living conditions by means of measures for social integration and integration into the labour market; accordingly request the Member States to implement or promote measures to enable everyone to have access to education, by acquiring proficiency in basic skills, training, employment, housing, community services, medical care" (as quoted in Abrahamson, 1997, p. 129, from, Council resolution of 29 September 1989).

Yet "social exclusion" is also transnational. It can be identified in the devaluation of unskilled jobs and the displacement of jobs. It can be found even in restrictions placed on public budgets, for these restrictions are often the consequence of phenomena originating at the international level as much, if not more, than at the national and local level. For example, when the IMF or the Maastrict treaty requirements dictate how much, and sometimes where, the social budget should be cut or reduced, even national policies against social exclusion may be constrained or negotiated at the international level (Saraceno, 1997, p. 163). The implications for the legitimacy of democratic national governments are tremendous.

The problem-solving capacity, and hence the democratic legitimacy of national governments, is being weakened by the dual processes of legal and economic integration in Europe. The loss is not fully compensated by the development of effective and legitimate problem-solving capabilities at the European level. There are unresolved contradictory trends at work. On one level, there is the structural assymmetry between the effectiveness of the legal instruments of "negative integration," which prevents governments from interfering with the free movements of goods, services, capital, and persons. On another level, there are the political constraints which act to impede positive action at the European level. This is especially the case for policies pertaining to the welfare state. The challenge, then, has become one where new strategies are required at the national level which could potentially succeed in maintaining welfare state goals—even under the brutal conditions of international economic competition.

In this regard, European income maintenance policy could have a salutory effect in mitigating the harmful affects of globalization and play a protective and enabling role with respect to these national solutions. Should a more inclusionary policy and politics emerge, then multi-level governance

Introduction xxxix

in Europe would not only regain its effectiveness and legitimacy, but also deepen the roots of cosmopolitan democracy by actualizing its humane and inclusionary goals and values. In the context of the EU there are three central challenges to realizing the promise and potential of inclusionary democracy: (1) capitalist democracy itself, as a threat to legitimacy and the establishment of conflict-minimizing policies; (2) global intervention in national policy by international institutions such as the IMF and the domestic sphere of income maintenance policy; (3) an outdated and antiquated notion of "sovereignty" which fails to comprehend the true nature of sovereignty in its encounter with globalization. Each of these issues is related to both governance and international law. Each will of these issues will be addressed in turn.

First, the EU finds itself having to confront the legal, political, and economic dimensions of establishing legitimacy in an age of globalization and a declining welfare-state. The problem to be resolved is rooted in capitalist democracy itself. Insofar as the "democratic state and the capitalist economy coexist in symbiotic interdependence," this symbiotic relationship is characterized by fundamental tensions: "The sovereignty of the state is territorially limited, while the capitalist economy tends toward global interaction" (Scharpf, 1999, p. 30). The social and environmental costs of the logic of capital accumulation compel enterprises to exploit all factors of production. But along with generating material abundance for consumers, jobs for workers, and tax revenues for governments, there is the downside of highly unequal income distributions and regional and sectoral winners and losers, accompanied by cyclical and structural crises "which may result in mass unemployment and mass poverty" (*Id.*, p. 30).

By contrast, the democratic state "derives its claim to legitimacy from a commitment to the public interest and to distributive justice." Insofar as democratic governments are constrained by the mechanisms of electoral accountability, they are obliged to orient their policies toward the interests of the broad majority of their voters. The tasks of democratic governance, therefore, are to be directed to the protection of groups within the electorate who are subject to losses due to structural change. Part of structural change involves mass unemployment. Therefore, democratic governance must be engaged in regulating labor markets and production processes in order to protect the interests of the affected workers and, at the same time, to achieve a normatively defensible distribution of incomes.

Second, intervention in national policy by international institutions underscores the web of interconnectedness which the reality of globalization has unleashed. This is especially difficult in the context of the EU's emerging regional polity and the internal dynamics associated with its legitimation and accountability to democratic norms and welfare issues involving the "social quality" of Europe. The reality of global intervention in national policy serves to capture the web of interconnectedness that, for example, would loom large in the aspirations of an East European country seeking to join the EU. It finds itself tangled in a sphere of income maintenance policy. What this reveals are the contending influences of the IMF (concerned with balancing the state budget) on the one hand, and the

International Labor Organization (ILO) (concerned with the adoption of decent social security conventions) on the other. The tension between the budget-balancing requirements of the IMF and, for example, the expenditure requirements of the Social Charter of the Council of Europe exposes a great range of contending influences on income maintenance policy in the European region.

Global intervention in the context of Europe's national policy was accelerated by the collapse of communism and the end of the Cold War. Further both the threat of global migration and the transnationalism of the environment has served to unleash a global discourse about the best way to regulate global capitalism, both in terms of the defense of Northern welfare states and the export of welfare capitalism to the South. At its core, this global discourse must address the most effective way to engage in a transnational redistribution of wealth and, at the same time, afford adequate income maintenance and provision for the poor, excluded, unemployed, underemployed, and marginalized sectors of the national, regional, and international polity. In this context, foreign policy and diplomatic concerns are shifting from military and security matters, through the auspicies of trade and economic concerns, to a greater concentration upon social and environmental matters (Deacon, 1999, p. 214).

Within the context of the EU itself, these pressures can be outlined by reviewing three contending influences on national income maintenance policy in the European region. First, all countries must negotiate with agencies such as the IMF and World Bank. The various types of influence exerted range from public expenditure limitations (as loan conditions affect the income maintenance budget) to advice on constructing a social "safety net" policy and structure of social security expenditures. Quite often, these loans are given on the condition of social reform. Correspondingly, the International Labor Organization attempts to influence income maintenance policy through various conventions on social security systems and offer advice on tripartite forms of government. Second, the Council of Europe is legally mandated to recognize and enforce in its member states those legal requirements which arise out of the following influences: (a) obligatory Charter of Human Rights; (b) the Strasbourg Court of Human Rights; (c) independent expert judgments; and (d) optional conventions on social security. Third, and finally, countries within the EU are subject to EU influences emanating from: (a) the obligatory Social Charter (except for the UK); (b) the Luxembourg Court of Justice; (c) the requirement of participation in the Social Exclusion Project; and (d) the determination of net winner/loser calculations in the redistribution of structural funds (*Id.*, p. 216).

Third, the final major challenge to realizing the promise and potential of inclusionary democracy is in the encounter between the traditional concept of sovereignty and its encounter with globalization. The EU has brought to the forefront of international law the idea that sovereignty, as an attribute of statehood, is not an innate condition but is deemed to be a social, rather than a natural creature. This is largely because sovereignty now inhabits the world of intersubjective meaning rather than the dense primordial forests of the state of nature. Understanding this new situation in international rela-

Introduction

tions and law leads to the conclusion that supranational bodies, such as the EU or intergovernmental regimes, could be accorded sovereignty in particular functional areas. In other words, "some such approach seems essential to comprehending the encounter between sovereignty and globalization, if the superficialities of 'the end of sovereignty' and 'the demise of the state' are to be avoided" (Clark, 1999, p. 72).

The implications for inclusionary governance, which stem from the aforementioned issue areas, are tremendous in terms of the emergence of supranational citizenship in the sphere of human and social rights. There are already global and regional agencies in place (UN, World Bank, IMF, OECD, WTO, EU, NAFTA, ILO) that are engaged in aspects of supranational policies and have the instruments with which they either: (a) facilitate redistribution, or (b) seek to regulate activity. These supranational and global agencies already shape national policy and the terms of economic competition by laying down social policy conditions on governments. As will be discussed in Chapter 1, this form of intervention vitiates the conventional/traditional notions of sovereignty. This is because of the fact that when global agencies lay down such conditions, as conditions on governments for the receipt of financial assistance, they are engaged in both redistributing resources *between* governments and/or establishing conventions, offering technical advice so as to affect legal and social regulation *within* governments.

In the international law environment there are three central institutions which have authority in the EU. They are as follows: (1) the European Court (Luxembourg), with competencies in both the social rights sphere and in the human rights sphere; under its protective rubric are EU member state governments and citizens of EU member states; (2) the Court of Human Rights (Strasbourg), with competencies in the human rights sphere; under its protective rubric fall the Council of Europe member state governments and citizens of Council of Europe member states; (3) the International Court of Justice (The Hague), with competencies in the human rights sphere; under its protective rubric are UN member state governments and countries of the UN member states.

What the EU legal environment embodies is a new set of possibilities and opportunities for the realization of inclusionary democracy. This is, in large measure, "because individual citizens are empowered to appeal to an authority above the state, a world within which universal human and social rights are recognized and reinforced as a principle already possible" (Deacon, 1999, p. 219).

Such a possibility in the realm of international law and regional protections is especially relevant with respect to the "social quality"of Europe and all issues associated with building an income maintenance policy in the European region. While global conventions are silent on the right to social assistance, the right to work is acknowledged. On the level of the EU, a critical issue remains as to whether any practical meaning, backed up by judicial force, could be given to the idea of the right to social assistance. It has been suggested that "it is not fanciful to suggest that in some decades' time the right to social assistance or to a minimum income could be enshrined as one of the global citizenship entitlements that the reformed UN system would expect its member states to uphold" (*Id.*, p. 245). This idea is already a past of the more visionary picture painted by David Held in his vision for a future cosmopolitan democracy (discussed in Chapter 1).

From an international law perspective, Held has called for the creation of a new International Human Rights Court (Held, 1995), reflective (on a global level) of the work already undertaken on the European continent by the Council of Europe's Strasbourg Court of Human Rights. Held would seek to advance the realization of a global cosmopolitan democracy by inaugurating the creation of a global parliament, with revenue-raising capacity and sharing in global governance with an International Court which empowers global citizens to take their "local" national governments to court if they are denied basic citizenship rights. Among these rights would be the inclusion of a guaranteed basic income for all adults (Held, 1995, p. 249).

The rights of citizenship are in the process of being reconfigured within the parameters of a new paradigm in the European Union. In particular, the membership status of immigrants and refugees is directly affected by the development of citizenship rights in the EU. This is because the concept of citizenship is not static. Rather, it constitutes a forever changing concept with flexible limits, both in the formal and substantive senses. Historically, the concept has evolved in the direction of a more egalitarian and inclusive paradigm of belonging (Sorensen, 1996, p. 3). However, in the EU, contemporary debates are simultaneously debates about nationhood in an increasingly international and migrant world (*Id.*, pp. 56–57).

The harmonization of immigration controls within the EU, which began in the mid-1980s, coincided with an increased flow of refugees from central and eastern Europe as well as from Africa, the Indian subcontinent, and Southeast Asia. Given the predominance of the logic of exclusion, the harmonization process has been affected not only by policies limiting the admission and settlement of refugees but, throughout Western Europe, the logic of exclusion has also reawakened racism and xenophobia (Thranhardt and Miles, 1995, pp. 3–4). These developments have brought into question the relationship between migration and the democratic context of European political institutions.

From the perspective of international law, the territorial principle of *jus soli* has only recently become the principle of bounding the demos in several large-scale democracies. In the past, political theorists have assumed that the boundary of the demos coincided with the geographical boundaries of the democratic state (Koslowski, 1997, p. 83). That is no longer the case. In fact, the old principle of *jus sanguinis* is rapidly deteriorating under the impact of an EU that eclipses previous notions and concepts of boundaries and citizenship and raises questions of whether democracy and *jus sanguinis* are compatible (*Id.*, p. 82). The burden on welfare states, as a consequence of this departure from past norms, such as the notion of closed membership (in which citizens are entitled to universal health care, extensive child care benefits, liberal unemployment benefits, and state financed higher education), have crumbled insofar as the welfare state's own legitimizing principles are undermined. They are undermined because effective and legitimate welfare states may have been possi-

Introduction

ble in the context of increasing population growth within established membership, but increasing proportions of resident aliens (characteristic of postwar European demography) have made these forms of the welfare state almost unsustainable (*Id.*, p. 87).

In terms of the concerns of this book, the issues associated with migration, in a democratic context, reveal the fact that inclusion and exclusion, within the different dimensions of civil, social, and political rights, are interrelated. For example, the increasing costs involved in the extension of social rights serves to prompt political pressure for a more restrictive redefinition of nationality laws. In turn, this pressure limits the extension of political rights to resident aliens as well as their children. Hence, the practical and normative question of whether to extend full citizenship rights has increasingly come to depend on the question of social rights. A balancing act reappears as policy makers have to decide between being attentive to fiscal constraints on the one hand, and the social rights of citizens and the political rights of resident aliens on the other. A serious compromise of either set of rights may very well constitute a violation of liberal principles.

By the mid-1980s, for the first time, the EU and member states found it useful to exchange information on their immigration policies. By 1991, the member states found it was useful to agree to harmonize them. Until the entry into force of the Treaty on European Union—the Maastrict Treaty (November 1, 1993)—immigration policy matters were discussed in the context of purely intergovernmental cooperation. Now, under the terms of the treaty, immigration concerns are addressed in its Title VI on cooperation in the fields of justice and home affairs. There now exists a non-binding information and consultation procedure with respect to the European Parliament. Now, member states may include immigration provisions in conventions, thus rendering the European Court of Justice competent to deal with their interpretation (de Jong, 1997, pp. 325–326). Still, immigration policies remain primarily within the context of national policy making. Looking to Europe's responses in the 21st century, it has been suggested that the appropriate European response to the challenges of immigration would have to be multidimensional—an approach capable of strengthening cooperation within an enlarged EU with an extensive dialogue with the major countries of origin (*Id.*, p. 328).

While advocates of European integration generally view increasing cooperation among member states in a positive light, human rights advocates argue that greater cooperation among EU member states might well result in human rights violations if cooperation means increasingly restrictive policies. Such policies, if they bar the entry of legitimate asylum-seekers, may exhibit racist overtones, especially if enforcement is directed at migrants from non-European countries and governed by ascriptive physical characteristics (Koslowski, 1998, p. 180). Given the scope of this problem, it has been suggested that Europe needs to develop a comprehensive system for managing migration that also protects the basic human rights of those forced to move. The suggestion takes concrete embodiment in the proposal that "the formulation of such a system is possible if the various European countries coordinate their policies to promote human approaches" and that these countries should accept the use of international institutions and non-governmental organizations (NGOs) in order to facilitate the humane management of migration (Helton and Birchenough, 1996, p. 89).

This proposal makes sense on five levels and has implications for new uses of international law and international institutions. With nearly 50 million refugees and displaced persons around the globe, the stakes are very high. In the context of Europe alone, the search for solutions to the crisis will involve addressing a combination of critical issues, including repatriation, local integration, and resettlement. Therefore, the issues associated with what I have termed the *"inclusion/exclusion dilemma"* need to be addressed in the context of international law by the international community for the following reasons:

First, many West European leaders have invoked the imagery of an "asylum crisis" (based upon escalating arrivals) to justify various nonentry strategies (such as readmission agreements). Such agreements serve merely to impose refugee status determination responsibilities on less capable governmental structures in Central and Eastern Europe.

Second, there is a body of classical refugee protection law in international law. As early as 1951, the United Nations Convention relating to the Status of Refugees was intended to address the needs of those uprooted during the Second World War. As the problem of refugee movements proved to be permanent and universal, a basic remedy which emerged was the right (protected under international law) not be returned to a place where he/she might face persecution. This is the principle of *nonrefoulement*. The problem is that subsequent convention and protocol has led to a situation where the meanings of "persecution," "fear," and "well-founded" vary dramatically from country to country. Given this result, the quality of reception and protection extended to refugees is not consistent throughout Europe. Hence, convention and protocol have not significantly evolved or adapted to meet the exigencies of those persons persecuted in the post-Cold War World. The result is that the growing view of asylum as an expensive loophole in immigration control regimes has severely eroded the ability of those persecuted to receive protection in Western Europe.

Third, the failure to move toward an effective international law regime in this area has left a legal gap between the practice of "asylum" versus "temporary protection." Recent practice in Europe has resulted in the creation of "temporary protection" regimes, along with a variety of special "humanitarian," "exceptional" or "tolerated" statuses for approximately a quarter of the more than eighty percent of asylum seekers who are refused refugee status.

Fourth, while the Organization for Security and Cooperation in Europe (OSCE) is one of many security-related entities that are beginning to address post-Cold War issues, including migration, and has been working with the United Nations High Commissioner for Refugees (UNHCR), as well as the International Organization for Migration (IOM), the fact remains that organizations faced with issues of international migration (especially forced migration), remain relatively weak and need to be strengthened. This is especially critical at a time when armed conflicts have combined with ethnic overtones to produce human tragedies in Armenia, Azerbaijan, Chechnya, Georgia, Tajikistan, East Timor, and Bosnia-Herzegovina.

Fifth, a beginning has been made to undertake efforts at enhancing international cooperation through nongovernmental consultations and refugee advocacy groups. Regional organizations are emerging under the rubric of the European Council on Refugees and Exiles. Voluntary agencies, NGOs, and European asylum lawyers have contributed toward the formulation and implementation of a comprehensive European asylum and refugee policy. While the development of these elements of civil society are crucial in the task of protecting those who have been forcibily displaced, more needs to be accomplished at the international level.

Finally, the need for more work at the international level in establishing a more comprehensive transnational legal regime to deal with the global refugee crisis can be best understood by recognizing that "the absence of comprehensive regional and subregional arrangements to ensure that states and their local populations do not become overburdened by migration or refugee emergencies only exacerbates the very same political and economic pressures (such as high unemployment or ethnic tension) in the receiving country that often cause persons to flee their countries of origin in the first place" (Helton and Birchenough, 1996, p. 98). Further, insofar as member state cooperation on migration to the EU has largely remained outside of the Community framework, it may be asserted that "the secrecy and lack of parliamentary oversight that such cooperation entails increases the democratic deficit" (Koslowski, 1998, p. 180). This possibility also opens up questions for the traditional welfare state and the new paradigm of governance (largely exclusionary) that has threatened the democratic vestiges of a social contract forged over many generations. Therefore, the conclusion that can easily be asserted, with transnational legal ramifications, is that "only through the elaboration of policies that promote effective migration management, while ensuring respect for the basic human rights of noncitizens, will this dilemma be addressed" (Helton and Birchenough, 1996, p. 98). This proposed direction is another central aspect of inclusionary governance and inclusionary democracy that transcends the borders of the nation-state and enters into the realm of international law.

The question as to whether the new paradigm constitutes new inroads for inclusion or, in the alternative, a fundamental reversal of the historical role of the welfare state, is now coming into sharper focus. Within the context of the EU, as the foregoing discussion demonstrates, the historical role and purpose of the welfare state, under siege since the 1980s, has now reached crisis proportions. Needs have increased with lasting unemployment. Further, the social consequences of the neoliberal project, with its emphasis upon privatization and technocratic decisionmaking, is disturbing for everybody concerned with the quality of society one lives in. After all, the welfare state has been the end product of a social contract forged through generations. Most of the components of the European welfare state "grew organically, prompted by, proposed to, perhaps forced on, but eventually legitimated by, the electorate" (Ferge, 1997, p. 174). Given this history, proposals for further integration will have to be evaluated in terms of their systemic implications as well as their policy effects.

Take, for example, the difference between the decision-making styles which are "technocratic" versus those that are "politicized." In "technocratic" decision making, we find: (1) basic policy goals are shared among key actors; (2) the means for achieving policy goals involve scientific-rational methods; and (3) issues are dealt with in compartmentalized policy areas. In contrast, "politicized" decision making is characterized by the following: (1) basic policy goals are contested among key actors; (2) the means for achieving policy goals involve basic political choices; (3) issues are dealt with in interconnected policy arenas (Hooghe and Marks, 1999, p. 73). There are corresponding distinctions to be noted with respect to "actor involvement," i.e., elitist or participatory. With respect to elitists, the following characteristics exist: (1) only a small number of social groups are politically mobilized; (2) the boundary rules for participation are elite-determined; (3) decision makers are insulated from group pressures. Alternatively, with respect to the "participatory" model, the following characteristics exist: (1) a large number of social groups are politically mobilized; (2) the boundary rules for participation are contested; (3) decision makers are vulnerable to group pressures (*Id.*, p. 73).

What these distinctions embody is that the development of a Europolity (the EU) has gone hand in hand with fundamental shifts in decision making. First, decision making has become increasingly politicized. Second, the scope of political participation in the EU has widened. As a result, the fundamental finding is that EU decision making has become less technocratic and more contentious (*Id.*, pp. 72–74). As fewer decisions are resolved by rational-scientific methods, there is increasing "politicized" pressure to have decisions relinquished to arenas of political contention concerning the fundamental goals of European integration. Some have argued that this politicization was triggered by the internal market program which accompanied institutional reforms (*Id.*, p. 74). Hence, elites have become more vulnerable to generalized public pressure. More critically, however, what is exposed is the fact that while societies have been "thought of in terms of split spheres in which the economic and social dimensions seem to work against each other," this can no longer continue to be the case insofar as issues of efficiency can no longer be artificially divorced from issues of equity. The historical trade-off has meant that "in the name of efficiency, states must reduce the public sector and restore market mechanisms. In the name of equity, they must combat social injustice, poverty and social exclusion" (Bouget, 1997, p. 41).

In this new arena of contention, it may be argued that "the strongest asset of the union is, in fact, its civil society." Europe's civil society was not only deeply involved in the creation and construction of the welfare state, but has also been actively resistant to onslaughts upon welfare arrangements throughout the 1990s. Even in the absence of mass protests and mobilizations, civil society has the capacity to support trade unions in the shaping of new systems. But, in the search for avenues to secure inclusionary socioeconomic rights and inclusionary democracy, civil society may find allies in supranational agencies that have begun to take a strong stance on behalf of the excluded, thereby birthing into existence the foundations of *inclusionary*

Introduction   xlvii

governance and *inclusionary democracy*. In this regard, "the Council of Europe in its most recent revision of the European Social Charter (open for signature since the 3rd May 1996) aims at strengthening safeguards of fundamental economic and social rights. The United Nations declared 1996 the International year for the Eradication of Poverty and the next decade 1997–2006 the International Decade for the Eradication of Poverty. The European Commission set up a *'Comité des Sages'* in 1995. This *Comité* has emphasized the importance of a social dimension of an integrated Europe" (Ferge, 1997, p. 174).

These advances toward inclusionary governance are well-articulated in the view of the Chair of the *Comité*, who stated that, "'civic rights and social rights are becoming interdependent'. In the European tradition they are inseparable. 'Freedom and the conditions of freedom' are the mirror image of 'democracy and development'" (European Commission, 1996, p. 5). The *Comité* also expressed its feeling that "Europe was in greater danger than it realized and that the 'social deficit' was fraught with menace. Europe cannot be built on unemployment and social exclusion, nor on an inadequate sense of citizenship. Europe will be a Europe for all, or it will be nothing at all" (*Id*., p. 13).

The sentiments and principles stated by the *Comité* represent the primary and central elements of what constitutes what I am describing by the term *inclusionary governance*: a dedication in legal, political, economic, and social life to (1) remove all vestiges of a "social deficit"; (2) erradicate poverty; (3) build, protect, and maintain the full rights of citizenship within a democratic framework (consensual, not majoritarian in emphasis); (4) rely on fidelity to consitutional procedures to guarantee social justice. The project of inclusionary governance is diametrically opposed to the neoliberal project, which "attempts to insulate markets from political interference by combining European-wide market integration with minimal European regulation. The neoliberal project rejects democratic institutions at the European level capable of regulating the market, but seeks instead to generate competition among national governments in providing regulatory climates that mobile factors of production find attractive" (Hooghe and Marks, 1999, p. 75). Insofar as a polity is an arena for contention about the authoritative allocation of values, it follows that "institutional architecture is intimately connected with policy outcomes. The contention that underlies European integration concerns nothing less than the question of how Europe should be organized politically" (*Id*., p. 82). In other words, it is a question of pursuing inclusionary or exclusionary governance. On this point, there is no grey area. It is an either/or question.

THE WIDENING SCOPE OF EXCLUSIONARY GOVERNANCE AND THE EMERGING MANDATE FOR GLOBAL INCLUSIONARY GOVERNANCE

At the close of the 1990s, widening circles of exclusion can be discerned at every level of global life: local, national, regional, international. This introduction has already covered many of them. To this list, the following should be itemized: unrepresentative institutions, non-pariticipatory forms of governance (public and private); the failure of the international community to place meaningful controls on the international arms trade; exclusionary decision making at elite centers of power; the failure to amend international charters of institutions, such as the IMF, to make their agendas and policies more inclusionary; the failure to adopt an effective nuclear test ban and legal prohibitions to halt nuclear proliferation. All of these issues expose the existence of unaccountable centers of power and the dire consequences which stem from their lack of accountability to international legal standards, the mandates of democratically elected governments, and the aspirations of an emerging global civil society.

Given the widening scope of global exclusion, in all of its forms, there is an objective need for a corresponding expansion of inclusionary governance and inclusionary democracy at all levels of global life: local, national, regional, and international. Recently, the linkage between development, democracy, human rights, and peace has served to inaugurate a more widely recognized and articulated consciousness of a collective aspiration to approximate and eventually realize the goals associated with a sustainable peace. The synthesis of these elements of global governance is useful in altering the old North-South development-versus-security debate. They have converged into one major element: *the need for a fairer process*, a process capable of reducing major grievances before they grow into problems. In this regard, some have suggested that what is needed to create the opportunity for both development and peace is "good governance," which would allow people to determine their own priorities (Peck, 1998, p. 17).

Similarly, on the subject of *fairness in international law and institutions*, Thomas Franck has advocated new ways to shape the global discourse by acknowledging that "fairness discourse is necessary for the implementation of international human rights, self-determination, collective security, and free trade." Additionally, he asserts that "it is a necessary part of decision making in the International Court of Justice, the UN Security Council, and the Office of the Secretary-General, as also in GATT, ICSID, and FTA arbitrations" (Franck, 1996, p. 478). Fairness is "embedded in the decision making processes of numerous treaty-based organizations and non-governmental institutions" (*Id.*, p. 478). Given, as previously mentioned, the descriptive and prescriptive core of international law, it logically follows that identifying the principle of fairness as central to the discursive enterprise of international law and international institutions is no accident. Rather, it is the recognition that fairness constitutes the basis for lasting and sustainable forms of security, justice, and democratic decision making (in its participatory, consensual, and representational aspects), and is intimately linked to what is mandated by the core values, principles and goals of inclusionary governance and inclusionary democracy.

Franck has argued that "since fairness discourse is central to the concept of fairness, attention must be paid to how the discourse is organized: who has a voice and how decisions are reached. While the institutions of international governance are gradually changing shape as their importance increases, two characteristics have remained dominant. Firstly, the discourse tends to give each state an equal voice. Secondly, it tends to give voice only to representa-

Introduction

tives of governments" (*Id.*, pp. 478–479). As to the first characteristic, equal voice, Franck acknowledges that, apart from the Security Council or the Bretton Woods Institutions, most international discourse operates on the principle of one state, one vote (or voice). As to the second characteristic, the fact that voice and vote are reserved exclusively for governments "is both manifestly unfair and, ultimately, destructive discourse" (*Id.*, p. 480). As has already been noted, and will be throughout the course of this book, the larger and wealthier states are able "to staff the forums of discourse in ways which give them an advantage over the understaffed, smaller, poorer participants" (*Id.*, p. 481). The goal of David Held's conception of "cosmopolitan democracy" (as discussed in Chapter 1) is a means of overcoming this historical disadvantage.

Franck argues that there are ways in international law and institutions to ameliorate the problem of formal state equality. He suggests that "a forum in which the participants represented persons rather than governments would establish some correlation between population and representation" (*Id.*, p. 482). In this way, representation and participation could, theoretically, reach a point of critical mass so as to affect decision making processes in a meaningful way. Yet, beyond this hopeful aspiration, he argues that "perhaps of equal importance is the opportunity which such a systemic reform wold provide for institutionalizing the democratic entitlement and certifying the authenticity of the link between people and their representatives in the fairness discourse" (*Id.*, p. 482). On this matter, Franck's thesis that there is an "emerging right to democratic governance" will be addressed in Chapter 1 (in relationship to Held's conception of "cosmopolitan democracy"). Suffice it to say, for the purposes of this introduction, that it is increasingly acknowledged that essential international institutions are facing an imminent breakdown. In large measure, this breakdown coincides with widespread dissatisfaction over what governments do and how they do it (*Id.*, p. 483).

The dissatisfaction with governments, to which Franck and others refer, raises questions concerning "fairness about fairness" in the shaping of global discourse. On this subject, some have also suggested that the 1990s "were a unique moment when real global reform for sustainable development, based upon global cooperation and international institution-building, could have been achieved under Atlantic leadership. But that opportunity has been utterly squandered as so often in earlier moments of victory" (Gowan, 1999, p. 138). Instead, reliance on the current catchphrase of "The Third Way" is seen as an easy way to abandon social liberal or social democratic values "for the sake of overcoming . . . cognitive dissonance with an Americanised Europe." By taking the path of "The Third Way," many European intellectuals have begun to "abandon the struggle for egalitarian and cosmopolitan solutions" (*Id.*, p. 138). In the alternative, "inclusionary governance" and "inclusionary democracy" represent the antithesis of a watered-down "Third Way" and denounce the tenets, ideology, and practices of the neoliberal project and creed.

Inclusionary governance embraces cosmopolitan law and democracy because, in the words of Jurgen Habermas, "cosmopolitan law is a logical consequence of the idea of the constitutive rule of law. It establishes for the first time a symmetry between the jurisdiction of social and political relations both within and beyond the states' borders" (Habermas, 1998, p. 199). It is also an extension and revision of Kant's idea of Perpetual Peace. It is empowered to do this for three reasons. In spite of the stratification of world society, a consensus emerges in three areas: (1) a shared historical consciousness which is dependent on peaceful coexistence; (2) normative agreement concerning human rights (inspite of momentary dispute between the West on the one hand and Africans and Asians on the other); and (3) a shared conception of a desirable state of peace (*Id.*, p. 185).

When viewed in combination, these areas have the capacity to transform the shape of international discourse because "discourse theory invests the democratic process with normative connotations stronger than those of the liberal model" and, at the same time, "it conceives the basic principles of the constitutional state as a consistent answer to the question of how the demanding communicative presuppositions of a democratic opinion-and will-formation can be institutionalized" (*Id.*, p. 248). This unfolding of the democratic entitlement (Franck and Held) is effectuated through how discourse theory works in the context of "institutionalized deliberations in parliamentary bodies, on the one hand, and in the informal networks of the public sphere, on the other" (*Id.*, p. 248).

The central goal of what I call the "discourse of inclusion" shares with Franck's "right to democratic governance," Held's "cosmopolitan democracy," Falk's "humane governance," and Habermas's "discourse theory" an emphasis upon the capacity of international law, international institutions, and the validity of claims to democratic governance to meet a normative demand for inclusionary governance that cannot be denied, suppressed or revoked. It can only be realized as innovations in international law and politics force the processes associated with the reconstitution of power, on a global basis, to address and answer the claims set forth by the poor, excluded, marginalized, and dispossessed of the globe. As this process proceeds in the first decades of the 21st century, the normative implications are obvious. The integrative force of solidarity will be developed through widely autonomous public spheres of action throughout an emerging global civil society. As the various forms of this solidarity take on institutional expression, it will be accomplished vis-a-vis legally institutionalized procedures of democratic deliberation and decision making. In this manner, it will be able to hold its own against two other major social forces—money and administrative power (Habermas, 1998, p. 249). In this regard, as already suggested by Richard Falk, Thomas Franck, and David Held, "the point of cosmopolitan law is . . . that it bypasses the collective subjects of international law and directly establishes the legal status of the individual subjects by granting them unmediated membership in the association of free and equal world citizens" (*Id.*, p. 181). It is to this project that Chapter 1 is dedicated and serves as prologue to the chapters that follow.

THE STRUCTURE OF THE BOOK

The political legitimacy of the state is placed at risk when the regime of the state allows for the practice of exclusionary governance and builds an

Introduction

exclusionary state (ES). Throughout the Third World, most lesser developed countries (LDCs) have political systems that do not have very deep roots. Most of these political states are not deeply embedded in their respective societies. Consequently, that state-society linkages remain weak. Even in supposedly democratic systems, shifting majorities and coalitions may use elections and manipulate their outcomes so as to load the ranks of the bureaucracy with their own cadres. Within the new guard of bureaucrats, we often find the reinforcement of preexisting patterns and practices of serving particular clients, classes, and groups at the expense of others. This atmosphere of exclusionary politics serves to perpetuate exclusivity. It also serves to undermine equitable economic growth and development. For development, broadly conceived, is more than just a matter of economic calculation, it is also a measure of human welfare and the ability and capacity of states and their respective civil societies to address basic human needs.

In order to address the full scope of this challenge, the book is divided into five parts. This *Introduction* frames the international law context in which the political, social, and economic aspects of inclusionary governance need to be considered. Each chapter is designed to elucidate particular problems and to provide specific proposals and provisional remedies for overcoming the dynamics of exclusion.

Part I, beginning with Chapter 1, outlines the arguments of how the deepening of democracy is an aspect of a peaceful world. The starting point of analysis is the recognition that the deepening of democracy on a national and transnational scale must deal with the fact that exclusionary states, incomplete legal practices and norms, and state and non-state actors continue to dominate the international environment. These obstacles constitute barriers to the deepening of democracy. Insofar as a world government capable of controlling nation-states has never evolved, the neoliberal perspective presents the argument that markets and globalized capitalism are sufficient for organizing efforts to open the door to democratic development and consolidation. In contrast to this view, I present the following counter-arguments: (1) there is no democracy without a national constitutional state; (2) while the market may be necessary for civil society, its sustaining role must be buttressed by the constitutional state; (3) the market requires the legal support and sociopolitical mediations of the state to function properly; (4) most democratic states have been based on a "welfare compromise," which reconciles the reproduction of capital with the reproduction of popular consent. The nature of popular consent, as conceived under the rubric of inclusionary governance, mandates the need for national and international accountability so that the legal, political, economic, and social contexts of power can move toward a functional system of inclusionary governance. The central thesis of this chapter is that the broadening and deepening of democracy (in its consensual forms) is dependent on the degree to which inclusionary governance can be incorporated into both the nation-state system and the international system.

To make the deepening of democracy contingent upon inclusionary governance is to speak of new relations between state and society. Also, it is contingent upon the recognition of the need to construct a new sociopolitical matrix which exposes the differences between inclusionary governance on the one hand and exclusionary globalization on the other. In so doing, there is a proposed outline for a new security agenda which transcends old power logics. In place of these failed logics, the chapter details alternatives, such as Richard Falk's conception of humane governance, David Held's model of cosmopolitan democracy, and the conception of inclusionary governance as a radical demand insofar as it departs from the logic of classical security thinking. It postulates that the achievement of peace, on a national and international scale, is ultimately predicated upon building a transnational network of laws, institutions, and political practices that advocate the practices associated with "sustainable development" and security. The path to this goal is outlined in an analysis of the emerging politics and law of inclusionary governance through the deepending of democratic norms. Compliance with the emerging right to democratic governance is linked to a right of representation in international organizations, as well as international fiscal trade and development benefits.

Specific attention is given to the creation of an international democratic polity. The UN Rights Conventions and UN Charter are the historical grounding for this undertaking. The UN General Assembly and World Court are also included in this regard. From this point, there is an emphasis upon the need to delineate traditional notions of sovereignty from the legal principle of self-determination. In so doing, the reform, containment, or amendment, of the G-7, GATT, the EU, NAFTA, the IMF and World Bank are considered. The rationale for this analysis arises out of the recognition that part of the global "democratic deficit" is due to the unaccountability of these international institutions and the international legal environment, as currently constituted, which allows them to operate in defiance of democratic norms, human rights, UN conventions, and the UN Charter, as well as other recognized instruments of international law. The ensuing growth of islands of poverty within and between nations, in both First and Third World contexts, is testimony to this democratic deficit. Therefore, current regional experiments with reconstituting democracy, as in the European Union context, are discussed in relationship to the possibilities for framing a global social charter for the 21st century which would have the capacity to unleash the dynamics inherent in the concept of cosmopolitan democracy.

The international asymmetries of power find expression through violations of Westphalian sovereignty, thereby bringing into question the durability, applicability, and current relevance of that particular model of international governance. The chapter concludes with a proposed "covenant for a new democratic order." It addresses the task of building the institutional and legal framework for a new democratic institutional order at the nation-state and international levels.

In Chapter 2, the obstacles and opportunities for inclusionary governance will be analyzed by reference to struggles over the control of nuclear weapons and the historic opinion of the World Court that they are illegal. In Chapter 3, the role of media globalization as a threat to the deepening of democracy will be analyzed with respect to its capacity for disinformation as well as enlightenment. Both nuclear weapons and the media are discussed in terms of their monopolizing tendencies.

Nuclear weapons possess a monopoly on terror. Nuclear weapons also distort culture, nationally, regionally, and internationally, by virtue of creating an armaments culture. The dimensions of the armaments culture leaves no area of civil society or government unaffected. Hence, the armaments culture distorts democracy as it leads to secrecy, the distortion of budgetary priorities, and the squandering of wealth so as to exacerbate conditions of inequality, poverty, and a growing incapacitation for self-determination around the globe.

The effects of media globalization demonstrate a monopoly on information. The media, while seeming to display an apparent variety of views and competition for audiences, actually compete more in terms of variations on a few standardized themes than of clashing issues. The resulting harmonization of themes reveals a strong corporate bias which distorts information, perceptions, and analysis. The monopoly of information becomes a monopolization of thought and dialogue, thereby rendering any form of democracy weak because the potential for democratic dialogue and argument has been so seriously compromised.

When viewed in combination, there are obstacles and opportunities attendant upon each of these arenas of human endeavor. For the maintenance of a monopoly in terror or information is not a foregone conclusion if new forms of accountability are mandated by a national and international order which promotes inclusionary governance in place of exclusionary governance, in the halls of decision making as well as the market. In fact, in the marketplace of ideas, neither monopoly can survive once subject to scrutiny and accountability, mandated by the rule of law and a deepening of democratic norms. Hence, the identification of the obstacles presented by these monopolies is, simultaneously, an identification of those arenas for opportunities to dismantle their exclusionary tendencies and powers.

Part II, beginning with Chapter 4, examines the dynamics of democratic exclusion in both First and Third World settings. The United States, Brazil, and South Africa are examined for comparative purposes. Building a culture of peace and inclusion depends on many interrelated factors. Primary among these factors is the fundamental right of people to have a say in how they are governed. The implications of this right revive the Hobbesian notion of a vibrant commonwealth and the Lockean notion of a social contract. The articulation of this right demands that people are included in the political, economic, and social decisions that affect their lives.

In Chapter 5, I review Hobbes' vision of state sovereignty, the responsibilities of leadership, the nature of the social compact, and the promise of a stable and peaceful commonwealth versus the dangers of anarchy and civil war. Hobbes's concerns are as relevant at the close of the 20th century as when he produced his classic Leviathan 350 years ago. This chapter allows for the development of an historical perspective on the issues of sovereignty, nationalism, war, and the nature of the international legal culture of the 20th century. The entire set of relationships that have been established by First and Third World states are prefigured in Hobbes' vision. Therefore, attention to the Hobbesian dilemma is an important consideration in advancing peace and development in First and Third World nations.

Part III, beginning with Chapter 6, outlines the promise of peaceful development inherent in building inclusionary states and identifying the obstacles to their institutionalization. Having identified the obstacles, the chapter concludes with solutions for achieving inclusionary governance by reference to the criteria of what I call its "Five C's": *consensus, consistency, congruence, cohesiveness, and coherence*. These criteria are examined in relation to the scholarly literature which has identified the underlying causes of internal conflict. This examination of the dynamics of conflict and strategies for its prevention allows me to frame the dimensions of the "inclusion/exclusion dilemma"—how organizational fragmentation in society and in the state has created crucial impediments to redistributive reform, equitable growth and development, and more humane forms of governance. This problem is given greater attention in Chapter 7.

Chapter 7 examines the praxis of democracy in Third World states. Latin America and Africa are given special attention. By examining the predominant trends of Third World states, trapped between polyarchy and poverty, the chapter explains how many exclusionary states (ES) have justified their exercise of power by reliance on the strength of the economic records of economic growth without making reference to how that growth is distributed and how problems of poverty and conflict remain unaddressed as a result. The ES and its predominance in the Third World demonstrates that the state is no longer playing the role of the Hobbesian protector of the commonwealth and, instead, works to advance the accumulation of private wealth. At both the national and international levels the expansion of the practices of the ES have resulted in the socialization of poverty and weakened effective democratic forms of governance that collapse under exclusionary pressures and practices. In response, the chapter discusses the requirements associated with accommodating new demands and social classes. It contrasts the state's primary function in class-formation under the ES —what Tilly calls "durable inequality"—with the policies, practices and goals of the IS.

The failure to identify the role of the state as central to development, the alleviation of poverty and the institutionalization of inclusionary practices, entails a corresponding failure to identify the characteristics of successful states. By emphasizing formal distinctions, as between democratic and authoritarian states, the substantive characteristics of styles of governance (exclusionary versus inclusionary) have been left largely unexamined. This omission has created the crisis of exclusion in the praxis of Third World nations. I argue that it is time to correct this grievous omission.

In Part IV, the conclusion summarizes the major sources of international law and particular transnational institutions that may be used to consolidate the foundations for global forms of inclusionary governance. The role of international law in the prevention and resolution of ethnic conflict is discussed in determining in which ways international law might limit the use of force, tighten prohibitions on genocide, strengthen protection for refugees, and reevaluate standards of citizenship and ethnic identity. These concerns are interrelated and, because they share a common arena of concern in the context of global governance, they also constitute the matrix in which global governance and inclusionary governance have the capacity to evolve on a national, regional, and international scale. Further, these concerns also are salient in terms of building a sustainable peace. Because intrastate conflict does not always remain within international boundaries, conflict in one country can have repercussions in another, due to cross-border movement by rebels and refugees, the mobilization of ethnic kin in adjacent states, or the subsequent reciprocal repression of minorities in neighboring states. Given these national, regional, and international dynamics, it is vital that the international community come to realize the need to address grievances about discrimination before they escalate into conflict. The concept and practice of inclusionary democracy provides such an avenue, with precise proposals and analysis for addressing these concerns across regions.

There are significant differences across regions in the form and magnitude of communal conflict. While nonviolent protest has been the most common form of communal action in western democracies, Latin America, Eastern Europe, and the former Soviet Union, violent protest has become more common in Eastern Europe and the Middle East. Further, rebellions have occurred with greater frequency and intensity in Asia, the Middle East, and Africa. Yet, despite these differentiations between regions, there is something much more fundamental that they all share in common—the impulse to exclude, to segregate, to repress large segments of their respective populations. The forms of exclusion, of segregation, and repression are found in massive islands of poverty, which some have referred to as a "Fourth World." Additionally, the scourge of poverty is reinforced by a crisis in international justice, as economic exploitation ravages the dispossessed and marginalized of every nation.

The conclusion suggests that, in following the lead of the Brundtland Commission, which worked to blend environmental responsibility and development into a more dynamic and cohesive concept of "sustainable development," inclusionary governance will be capable of producing a transnational society which respects human rights and international justice, not only in covenants and charters, but in the affairs of state and with respect to the practice of global/humane governance at all levels. This will mean adherence to the following: (1) an expanded scope of representation and participation for the agenda of previously excluded and marginalized individuals and groups which provides them with an effective voice in the processes of decision making; (2) the construction of an international order which posits the "right to development," the "principle of entitlement according to need," a reconstituted norm of "self-determination" which protects, extends, and widens the writ of human rights, and the union of political and civil rights with socioeconomic rights; (3) a debt-forgiveness regime which removes the stranglehold which international banks and multinational corporations have on the great majority of Third World people; and (4) a UN-supervised process of charter amendments which will effectively amend the charters of the IMF and World Bank so as to make them accountable to the entire international community, especially those most severely hurt and damaged by their interventionary structural adjustment policies, in violation of the Westphalian model, the purposes of the UN Charter, and the promises inherent in humane governance, cosmopolitan democracy, and inclusionary governance.

In the alternative, should these directions not be taken in the 21st century, it has been suggested that "as global laissez faire breaks up, a deepening international anarchy is the likely human prospect" (Gray, 1998, p. 218). Insofar as the global free market throughout the 1980s and 1990s has been increasingly emancipated from social control and political governance, it has come to resemble other 20th century experiments in utopian social engineering. The common thread that is woven into the fabric of all of these grand designs is that "each was convinced that human progress must have a single civilization as its goal. Each denied that a modern economy can come in many varieties. Each was ready to exact a large price in suffering from humanity in order to impose its single vision on the world. Each has run aground on vital human needs" (*Id.*, p. 235). Inclusionary governance presents a corrective to the failures of law, of economics, of governments and governance, to meet vital human needs. It is with the recognition that an inter-civilizational dialogue is required if international law is to be effective, if different forms of democracy are to be deepened across cultures, if the chains of poverty and exclusion are to be undone, that the approach and path of inclusionary governance is presented for consideration.

BIBLIOGRAPHY

Peter Abrahamson, "Combating Poverty and Social Exclusion in Europe," *The Social Quality of Europe*, edited by Wolfgang Beck, Laurent van der Maesen, and Alan Walker, Kluwer Law International, 1997.

Michael Banton, *International Action Against Racial Discrimination*, Clarendon Press, Oxford, 1996.

Wolfgang Beck, Laurent van der Maesen, and Alan Walker, "Social Quality: From Issue To Concept," *The Social Quality of Europe*, edited by Wolfgang Beck, Laurent van der Maesen, and Alan Walker, Kluwer Law International, 1997.

Denis Bouget, "The Maastrict Treaty and Social Quality: A Divorce?," *The Social Quality of Europe*, edited by Wolfgang Beck, Laurent van der Maesen, and Alan Walker, Kluwer Law International, 1997.

Willy Brandt, *North-South—A Program for Survival: The Report of the Independent Commission on International Development Issues under the Chairmanship of Willy Brandt*, The MIT Press, 1980.

Willy Brandt, *Arms and Hunger*, Pantheon Books, 1986.

Robin Broad and John Cavanagh, "The Death of the Washington Consensus?," *World Policy Journal*, Volume XVI, No. 3, Fall 1999.

Michel Chossudovsky, *The Globalisation of Poverty: Impacts of IMF and World Bank Reforms*, Zed Books Ltd., 1997.

Michel Chossudovsky, "Global Poverty in the Late 20th Century," *Journal of International Affairs*, Volume 52, No. 1, Fall 1998.

Ian Clark, *Globalization and International Relations Theory*, Oxford University Press, 1999.

Commission on Global Governance, *Our Global Neighborhood: The Report of the Commission on Global Governance*, Oxford University Press, 1995.

Commission on Global Governance, *Issues in Global Governance: Papers Written for the Commission on Global Governance*, Kluwer Law International, 1995.

Robert Cox, "Structural Issues of Global Governance: Implications for Europe," *A New Europe in the Changing Global System*, edited by Richard Falk and Tamas Szentes, United Nations University Press, 1997.

Peter Cumpter and Steven Wheatley, *Minority Rights in the "New" Europe*, Martinus Nijhoff Publishers, 1999.

Bob Deacon, "Social Policy in a Global Context," *Inequality, Globalization, and World Politics*, Oxford University Press, 1999.

Corneilus D. de Jong, "European Immigration Policies in the Twenty-First Century?," *Immigration into Western Societies: Problems and Policies*, edited by Emek M. Uncarter and Donald J. Puchala, Pinter Publishers, 1997.

Michael W. Doyle, *Ways of War and Peace: Realism, Liberalism, and Socialism*, W.W. Norton & Company, 1997.

European Commission, "For a Europe of Civil and Social Rights," *Report by the Comité des Sages chaired by Maria de Lourdes Pintasilgo*, Brussels,

Directorate-General for Employment, Industrial Relations and Social Affairs, 1996.

Richard A. Falk, *A Study of Future Worlds*, The Free Press, 1975.

Richard A. Falk, *Human Rights and State Sovereignty*, Holmes & Meier Publishers, Inc., 1981.

Richard A. Falk, "Document: Openings for Peace and Justice in a World of Danger and Struggle," *Alternatives: Social Transformation and Humane Governance*, Volume XIII, 1988.

Richard A. Falk, "The Pathways of Global Constitutionalism," *The Constitutional Foundations of World Peace*, edited by Richard A. Falk, Robert C. Johansen, and Samuel S. Kim, State University of New York Press, 1993.

Richard A. Falk, "Failure in Europe: Regional Security after the Cold War," *A New Europe in the Changing Global System*, edited by Richard Falk and Tamas Szentes, United Nations University Press, 1997.

Richard A. Falk, *Law In An Emerging Global Village: A Post-Westphalian Perspective*, Transnational Publishers, Inc., 1998.

Richard A. Falk, "The Pursuit of International Justice: Present Dilemmas and an Imagined Future," *Journal of International Affairs*, Volume 52, No. 2, Spring 1999(a).

Richard A. Falk, *Predatory Globalization: A Critique*, Polity Press, 1999(b).

Zsuzsa Ferge, "A Central European Perspective on the Social Quality of Europe," *The Social Quality of Europe*, edited by Wolfgang Beck, Laurent van der Maesen, and Alan Walker, Kluwer Law International, 1997.

Ralph H. Folsom, *European Union Law in a Nutshell*, Second Edition, West Publishing Co., 1995.

Thomas M. Franck, *Fairness in International Law and Institutions*, Oxford, 1995.

Dieter Fuchs and Hans-Dieter Klingemann, "Citizens and the State: A Changing Relationship?," *Citizens and the State*, edited by Hans-Dieter Klingemann and Dieter Fuchs, Oxford University Press, 1995.

Johan Galtung, "Global Governance for and by Global Democracy," *Issues in Global Governance: Papers written for the Commission on Global Governance*, Kluwer Law International, 1995.

Susan George, *How the Other Half Dies: The Real Reasons for World Hunger*, Allanheld, Osmun & Co. Publishers, 1977.

Peter Gowan, *The Global Gamble: Washington's Faustian Bid for World Dominance*, Verso, 1999.

John Gray, *False Dawn: The Delusions of Global Capitalism*, The New Press, 1998.

Jurgen Habermas, *The Inclusion of the Other: Studies in Political Theory*, edited by Ciaran Cronin and Pablo De Greiff, The MIT Press, 1998.

David Held, *Democracy and the Global Order: From the Modern State to Cosmopolitan Governance*, Stanford University Press, 1995.

Arthur C. Helton and Pamela Birchenough, "Forced Migration in Europe," The Fletcher Forum Of World Affairs, Volume 20, No. 2, Summer/Fall 1996.

Liesbet Hooghe and Gary Marks, "The Making of a Polity: The Struggle Over

European Integration," *Continuity and Change in Contemporary Capitalism*, edited by Herbert Kitschelt, Peter Lange, Gary Marks, and John D. Stephens, Cambridge University Press, 1999.

Robert C. Johansen, "Toward a New Code of International Conduct: War, Peacekeeping, and Global Constitutionalism," *The Constitutional Foundations of World Peace*, edited by Richard A. Falk, Robert C. Johansen, and Samuel S. Kim, State University of New York Press, 1993.

Immanel Kant, "Idea for a Universal History with a Cosmopolitan Intent" (1794), in *Perpetual Peace and Other Essays*, translated by Ted Humphrey, 1983.

Immanuel Kant, "To Perpetual Peace: A Philosophical Sketch" (1795), in *Perpetual Peace and Other Essays*, translated by Ted Humphrey, 1983.

Robert O. Keohane, "International Institutions: Can Interdependence Work?," *Foreign Policy*, No. 110, Spring 1998.

Rey Koslowski, "Migration and the Democratic Context of European Political Institutions," *Immigration Into Western Societies: Problems and Policies*, edited by Emek M. Ucarer and Donald J. Puchala, Pinter Publishers, 1997.

Rey Koslowski, "European Union Migration Regimes, Established and Emergent," *Challenge to the Nation-State: Immigration in Western Europe and the United States*, edited by Christian Joppke, Oxford University Press, 1998.

Charles A. Kupchan, "Life After Pax Americana," *World Policy Journal*, Volume XVI, No. 3, Fall 1999.

Pual G. Lauren, *Power and Prejudice: The Politics and Diplomacy of Racial Discrimination*, Westview Press, 1988.

G. F. Mancini, "The Making of a Constitution for Europe," *The New European Community: Decisionmaking and Institutional Change*, edited by Robert O. Keohane and Stanley Hoffmann, Westview Press, 1991.

Robert Miles and Dietrich Thranhardt, editors, *Migration and European Integration: The Dynamics of Inclusion and Exclusion*, Pinter Publishers, London, 1995.

Myres S. McDougal, Harold D. Lasswell, and Lung-chu Chen, *Human Rights and World Public Order: The Basic Policies of an International Law of Human Dignity*, Yale University Press, 1980.

Myres S. McDougal and W. Michale Reisman, *International Law Essays: A Supplement to International Law in Contemporary Perspective*, The Foundation Press, Inc., 1981.

Myres S. McDougal and W. Michael Reisman, "The Prescribing Function in the World Constitutive Process: How International Law Is Made," *International Law Essays: A Supplement to International Law in Contemporary Perspectives*, The Foundation Press, Inc., 1981.

Pippa Norris, "Introduction: The Growth of Critical Citizens?," *Critical Citizens: Global Support for Democratic Government*, edited by Pippa Norris, Oxford University Press, 1999.

Charles Oman, "Globalization, Regionalization, and Inequality," *Inequality, Globalization, and World Politics*, edited by Andrew Hurrell and Ngaire Woods, Oxford University Press, 1999.

John Palmer, "Europe 1992: A Socialist Perspective," *New Politics*, Volume II, No. 4, Winter 1990.
Connie Peck, Sustainable Peace: *The Role of the UN and Regional Organizations in Preventing Conflict, Carnegie Commission on Preveting Deadly Conflict*, Rowman & Littlefield Publishers, Inc., 1998.
James Petras and Chronis Polychroniou, "Rethinking Globalization: From the Future to the Past," *Socialism and Democracy*, Volume 12, Nos. 1–2, 1998.
Steven R. Ratner, "International Law: The Trials of Global Norms," *Foreign Policy*, No. 110, Spring 1998.
Anee Sa'adah, *Germany's Second Chance: Trust, Justice, and Democratization*, Harvard University Press, 1998.
Fritz Scharpf, *Governing in Europe: Effective and Democratic?*, Oxford University Press, 1999.
Jems M. Sorensen, *The Exclusive European Citizenship: The Case for Refugees and Immigrants in the European Union*, Avebury, 1996.
Fernando R. Tesón, *A Philosophy of International Law*, Westview Press, 1998.
Dietrich Thranhardt and Robert Miles, "Introduction: European Integration, Migration and Processes of Inclusion and Exclusion," *Migration and European Integration: The Dynamics of Inclusion and Exclusion*, edited by Robert Miles and Dietrich Thranhardt, Pinter Publishers, 1995.
Amado S. Tolentino, "Good Governance Through Popular Participation in Sustainable Development," *Sustainable Development and Good Governance*, edited by Konrad Ginther, Erik Denters, and Paul de Wart, Martinus Nijhoff Publishers, 1995.
Emek M. Ucarer and Donald J. Puchala, editors, *Immigration Into Western Societies: Problems and Policies*, Pinter Publishers, London, 1997.
Georg Vobruba, "Social Policy for Europe," *The Social Quality of Europe*, edited by Wolfgang Beck, Laurent van der Maesen, and Alan Walker, Kluwer Law International, 1997.
Lori Wallach and Michelle Sforza, *Whose Trade Organization?: Corporate Globalization and the Erosion of Democracy—An Assessment of the World Trade Organization*, Public Citizen, 1999.

Part I

OBSTACLES AND OPPORTUNITIES

CHAPTER 1

PREFACE TO INCLUSIONARY GOVERNANCE: THE DEEPENING OF DEMOCRACY AS AN ASPECT OF A PEACEFUL WORLD

The lights begin to twinkle from the rocks:
The long day wanes: the slow moon climbs: the deep
Moans round with many voices. Come, my friends,
'Tis not too late to seek a newer world.
Push off, and sitting well in order smite
The sounding furrows; for my purpose holds
To sail beyond the sunset, and the baths
Of all the western stars, until I die.
Alfred Lord Tennyson

There is a tide in the affairs of men
Which, taken at the flood, leads on to fortune;
Omitted, all the voyage of their life
Is bound in shallows and in miseries.
On such a full sea we are now afloat;
And we we must take the current when it serves
Or lose our ventures.
Julius Caesar, Act IV, Scene III

We are entering what might be called the Age of Ambiguity, where out postmodern, postindustrial, postinternational viewpoints lead to the conclusion that our social relations today and into the future will be characterized by a discomforting—yet full of potential—ambiguity.
Kurt Mills, *Human Rights in the Emerging Global Order*, 1998, p. 53

> Globalization causes polarization and seems to spiral out of control. The more it does so, the more it evokes counter-tendencies that express themselves at the state level, in the absence of effective alternative sites for doing so. The outcome at any one historical period is, to this extent, open-ended.
>
> Ian Clark, *Globalization and International Relations Theory*, 1999, p. 174

A. INTRODUCTION

World order is being shaped by a variety of social forces, resulting in a transition from a world of sovereign, territorial states to an emergent global village. A global media, in combination with global market forces, in the form of multinational corporations and banks, have reached escape velocity from the mitigating features of state regulation (Falk, 1999(a), p. 33). These phenomena are currently placed under the generalized rubric of "globalization."

Yet globalization does not automatically equate with other values that exist beyond the calculus of market logic. For example, the supposed triumph of market logic encompasses the efficient movement of capital without the hindrance of governmental regulation (Falk, 1999(c), p. 422). The problem is that market logic excludes all of the values and functions associated with international justice, as well as the role of states and international law in effectuating the promotion of justice, human rights, democracy, and policies and practices (local, national, regional, international) that are inclusionary. The resulting disparity between the "magic of the market" and the disempowered state has created an ever-expanding gulf between the haves and the have-nots, the included versus the excluded. The various forms within which international disparities take shape range from the non-realization of the democratic promise of participation to core issues concerning the failure of states and the international system itself to effectively deal the dynamics of economic growth and the distribution of wealth in relation to meeting basic human needs and rights.

The concept and meaning of *"inclusionary governance"* are dedicated to explicating the nature of these disparities and finding solutions to overcoming them. The matrix for the resolution of these disparities is found in the intersection of law, politics, economics, and culture (national and global). The culmination of the decade of the 1990s and the dawning of the 21st century exposes the fact that geopolitical governance under the domination of market capitalism and its logic have extended and deepened global poverty. It is a poverty of not only economics, but a poverty of politics and a poverty of the human spirit. The promise of democracy as "deep," "strong," "consolidated," has yet to be realized. In fact, the promise of these forms of democracy is threatened because its promise is at odds with market logic, rationality, and dynamism as ends in themselves. The Kantian imperative governing means and ends has removed human rights and human dignity from the equation of development due to the weight and force of the logic of "turbo capitalism" in the service of profit for the sake of profit. These forces impel and empower what I call the *"exclusionary impulse"* and *"exclusionary governance."* Exclusionary governance is a way of shaping and maintaining political, social, and economic relationships that remain beyond the regulation, intervention, and influence of democratic accountability and norms. As a consequence, the rise of the *"exclusionary state"* (ES) has created a world order that is more inclined to spawn conflict, civil wars and genocide, than to pursue human rights, meet basic human needs or to accommodate democratic values and norms that are inherently inclusionary in theory and in practice.

The deepening of democracy, on a national and transnational scale, demands full recognition of the fact that exclusionary states, incomplete legal practices and norms, and state as well as non-state actors (i.e., multinational corporations and banks) continue to dominate the international environment. These obstacles constitute barriers to the deepening of democracy and include, but are not limited to, the absence of consent, compromise, and participation in natonal and international forums, and the subordination of the constitutional state to the logic of the capitalist market. According to David Held, "the problem, for defenders and critics alike of modern democratic systems, is that regional and global interconnectedness contests the traditional national resolutions of the key questions of democratic theory and practice. The very process of governance can escape the reach of the nation-state. National communities by no means exclusively make and determine decisions and policies for themselves, and governments by no means determine what is exclusively for their own citizens" (Held, 1995, pp. 16–17).

The implications for a state-centric view of international law and politics are enormous. For if national communities no longer are the sole or even primary actors in effectuating the forms and norms of governance, then democracy itself is placed at risk. Yet this crisis of democracy is not of recent vintage insofar as "for most of the nineteenth and twentieth centuries democracy *in* nation-states has not been accompanied by democratic relations *among* states" (Held, 1993, p. 27). Hierarchy and unevenness have been the dominant characteristics of the international system since its inception.

A world government capable of controlling nation-states has never evolved. Nonetheless, considerable governance underlies the current order among states. Because the ordering of human affairs transcends the institutionalism of power in a single political form or structure, I use the term "inclusionary governance" in order to explicate the fact that the ordering of human relations, on both a national and international scale, is comprised of more than a bureaucratic structure termed "government." The task of governing and governance is to weigh, balance and choose between competing normative and institutional frameworks that reach into almost every aspect of human interaction. Employing the terminology of "governance" rather than "government" is important in this context. While various reasons may be cited, the primary rationale in doing this is to emphasize the fact that the term "governance" is attributable to the mutiplication of international actors on the global scene. Further, the fact that many of these international forces and actors are not regulated (or well-regulated) points to the reality that they transcend the control of and increasingly infringed-upon power of the nation-state. In short, the use of the term "governance" serves to focus attention on various forms of institutional and collective efforts to organize human affairs on a global scale. Governance, therefore, spans a vast spectrum of global institutions from the UN system to local grassroots initiatives. In between these arenas of power and influence are multinational corporations, banks, and various non-governmental organizations (NGOs) (Falk, 1999(c), p. 420).

Still, use of the term governance should not be automatically equated with the principles of democracy. The historical reality of the modern interstate system, and of international relations more generally, has exhibited little relation to any democratic principle of organization (Held, 1993, pp. 27–28). This reality points to the fact that nation-states and the international system have exhibited exclusionary tendencies that are, in a word, anti-democratic. The anti-democratic history of this system constitutes a defense of hierarchy, asymmetrical relationships, and the protection and defense of privilege in a world capitalist economy.

For centuries, the non-European world has been placed at the bottom rungs of a hierarchy of power which has and continues to be part of the structure of economic globalization and subordination to the centers of capitalist power. In this respect, "the other side of hierarchy is unevenness" (Held, 1993, p. 31). Because of this unevenness of power, most contemporary discussions do not incorporate the *political economy* component of sovereignty. This blind spot in political and legal analysis constitutes a serious omission in understanding the true nature of international power relationships. Among these interpretative gaps are the following realities: (1) the motives of the colonizing European states were fundamentally linked to the dynamic of expanding the power and reach of capitalism, as well as capitalist requirements for resources and larger markets; (2) the colonizers worked to transform their colonies into regions of specialized production which would also create, on a global scale, an expanding division of labor centered around European states' competitive needs; and (3) Third World states were required to relinquish their sovereignty by effectively grafting it on to a productive structure that was and is historically constructed to deprive their economies of autonomy, diversity, and true independence (Inayatullah, 1996, p. 53).

The exclusion of these three ideas in many political and legal discussions about the nature of the international order makes the unwarranted presumption that Third World states have now finally overcome their historical status as agents of international processes of capitalist accumulation within a global division of labor. Too often there is also the presumption that Third World states can compete as equals within a global market while meeting their own needs with their own efforts and resources (*Id.*, p. 53). These presumptions, taken together, represent the neoliberal perspective.

The neoliberal perspective presents the argument that markets and capitalism constitute a nearly sufficient key to opening the door to democratic development and democratic consolidation. However, it may be argued that the neoliberal perspective is a project that all too easily overlooks the role of the national constitutional state. The national constitutional state plays an especially preeminent role in the newly emerging democracies of the "Third Wave," commonly found in the post-communist world and in Latin America. Based on this alternate view to the neoliberal consensus, the following points can be made:

1. There is no democracy without a national constitutional state, because the constitutional state is the essential agent in the development and operation of a democratic civil society.
2. The market may be necessary for civil society, but it is not sufficient, and it is not, at any rate, a direct agent. Its sustaining role must be buttressed and possibly corrected by the constitutional state.
3. The market is not in a position to operate in a socially and contractually congenial environment without the legal buttressing and the sociopolitical mediation of the state. Therefore, the antinomy between state and market (less state, more market) is similarly misplaced, precisely from the perspective of the market.
4. The most successful democratic states, both politically and economically, have been based on a "welfare compromise," reconciling the reproduction of capital with the reproduction of popular consent (Di Palma, 1997, p. 290; Almond, 1991; Lijphart, 1999).

The above-referenced critique of the neoliberal project is beneficial in bringing to the forefront of discussion the necessary components of what constitutes a deepening and consolidation of democracy: consent, compromise, constitutionalism, consolidation of a democratic culture and a constitutional state, and civil society. If these components of democratic accountability are placed in appropriate legal, political, and international contexts of power and practice, then both nation-states and the international system can move toward a functional system of *inclusionary governance*. In the alternative, if these components for the deepening of democracy are not brought to the forefront, then exclusionary impulses from the world capitalist market and the hierarchical features of the dominant Western system of geopolitical governance will triumph. For, in the absence of inclusionary governance, exclusionary trends have and will continue to dominate the centers of power and decision making at both the national and international levels of global governance (Pereira and Nakano, 1998, pp. 21–41; Waisman, 1999, pp. 43–59; Garreton, 1999, pp. 61–78). The consequence of this trend toward exclusion will be to exacerbate disparities in wealth and power, thereby creating islands of poverty and deprivation throughout the international system.

B. TO SEEK A NEWER WORLD

In the contemporary world, the largest markets tend to be concentrated in small areas where the bulk of skilled labor also lives (i.e., North America, Western Europe, Japan). The logic of power and capital requires the leading capitalist state (the United States) to strengthen its dominance in these restricted areas of the global economy. But what does this capitalist map of the world mean for the majority of humanity? In answer, it may be argued that "as for the great mass of the earth's territory outside these areas, it is of little significance and the people who live there can be of no more than auxiliary interest, or even of no interest at all, except insofar as one has to contain disturbances and a slide into forms of barbarism that may have international spillovers" (Gowan, 1999, p. 67).

Such a result is antithetical to the deepening of democracy on a global basis. Given the decline of the Westphalian notion of territorial supremacy and sovereign prerogative, the implication is that political independence often provides only a brief respite from the process of marginalization in the world economy (Held, 1993, p. 32). The very structure of the international system leaves individual nation-states trapped in patterns of behavior seeking the means to engage in the competitive pursuit of their own security and interests "without systematic means to pursue the accountability and regulation of some of the most powerful forces ordering national and international affairs" (*Id.*, p. 32). In the final analysis, "it is the political and economic might which ultimately determines the effective deployment of rules and resources within and across borders in the Westphalian world" (*Id.*, p. 32).

In the absence of an alternative discourse, it has often been assumed that social and political segmentation is necessary and that it will be permanent. However, assuming that there could be a global transformation of state capacity and civil society so as to affect economic practices and institutional arrangements (as currently vested), it may be possible for a deepening of democracy to effectuate a new kind of global order that is increasingly inclusionary. If an alternative discourse to the logic of market capitalism can gain momentum, it could potentially affect the international division of labor, transform economic performance, and begin to determine the extent to which civil society and autonomous democratic participation may broaden, thicken, and deepen (Waisman, 1999, p. 58).

In the post-Cold War era, the cycle now opening is that of mass liberal democracy and its politics will be increasingly governed by the dynamics of association and autonomy. The good news for inclusionary governance is that, "unlike the previous cycles, this one is not grounded in inherently self-limiting institutions (economic in the first case and political in the second) but allows for the institutionalization of very different kinds of polities" (*Id.*, p. 58). Different polities are more consensual and more inclusionary. For example, in a study of thirty-six countries, Lijphart has noted that "the conventional wisdom" erroneously argues that "majoritarian democracy is better at governing, but admits that consensus democracy is better at representing—in particular, representing minority groups and minority interests, representing everyone more accurately, and representing people and their interests more *inclusively*" (Lijphart, 1999, p. 275, italics mine).

My central thesis is that the broadening and deepening of democracy (in its consensual forms) is dependent on the degree to which inclusionary governance can be incorporated into both the nation-state system and the international system. This is because what has made governability and reform in places such as Latin America so difficult is the absence of a social contract that is inclusive, consensual, equitable, and committed to a developmental path that will permanently reduce inequalities. In this regard, in Latin American societies, given their heterogeneity and deep inequality, civil society is poorly structured. In fact, "there is no broad political agreement on the prevailing economic regime, particularly on the pattern of income distribution. The long-term solution for this would be economic reforms that permanently reduce inequalities" (Pereira and Nakano, 1998, p. 22).

The primary obstacles to this goal are local elites who oppose distributional policies and seek to place their energies into promoting development-oriented political pacts between the middle-class and workers. This path leaves the poor, marginalized, dispossessed and excluded individuals and classes in a permanent state of structural exclusion from national life and the world capitalist market economy. The success of this compromise continues, as in the past, to depend on the resumption of this particular developmental process which is centered on market-oriented reforms—macroeconomic adjustment price stabilization and trade liberalization. The problem with this path is that such reforms are contingent on a stronger state that is able to implement social policies and promote economic growth. If the state fails in this task, governability will not be achieved (*Id.*, p. 22). Governability has usually not been achieved. It has often not been achieved, for example, because stabilization policies fail to meet their announced goals. But they also fail because they "involve unnecessary transition costs that eventually make the stablization program unviable in political terms" (*Id.*, p. 32). In other words, exclusionary states (ES) suffer from a missing social contract. It is missing because there is an objective failure to include the poor and marginalized.

In this task, the World Bank has been of little help. The World Bank's pro-poor polices of the 1970s, which were intended to be permanent, and implied an effective redistribution of income, were never implemented on a large scale, because of the resistance of privileged groups in each of the countries—i.e., exclusionary states (ES). The problem was compounded by the debt crisis, making the 1970s Latin America's "lost decade." When pro-poor policies reappeared in the late 1980s, in the form of targeted social expenditures, these policies employed very limited resources and merely sought to bring temporary political support for limited reforms (*Id.*, p. 34). These policies were not intended to inaugurate an era of inclusionary governance. For inclusionary governance would seek to not only promote economic and political reforms, assure a more efficient allocation of resources, and build an adequate institutional framework for the future, but also guarantee a permanent reduction in income inequalities. The usual suspects constituted the opposition to this "expensive alternative"—the rich and middle class, not to mention the authors of the "Washington consensus."

To speak of the "Washington Consensus" is to identify the rational role of the advanced capitalist state. Whether or not it claims to be "democratic," the state is not simply its elected politicians. After all, politicians come and go but the state must remain and "it is the primary task of the top civil servants to present their political masters with the facts: the systemic facts of the state's situation and interests within a much longer time horizon than the electoral cycle" (Gowan, 1999, p. 65). When viewed from this perspective, "the state must ensure the best possible conditions for its capitalists to want to invest and improve productivity and expand output—the material basis of the state's own resource strength" (*Id.*, p. 65). It is this consensus that stands in the way of new relations between state and society in the Third World and, increasingly, within First World nations as well. Yet, inclusionary governance and deepening democracy demands the formation of new relations between state and society at the national and international level. It is to this challenge that we now turn.

1. New Relations Between State and Society

Insofar as governance has been associated with the nation-state system since 1648 (the Peace of Westphalia), individual states within the international system have claimed to hold exclusive jurisdiction over their territories and citizens, in light of their status as sovereign entities. This mode of governance has effectuated what has been referred to as statism. The Westphalian view of international society, as constituted by territorial sovereign states, consigns democratic norms and constitutional practice to the margins of governance and power.

The marginalization of democratic norms and constitutional practice has detrimental consequences for the international system by making exclusionary trends and impulses even more exclusionary of democratic norms, values, and practices. If democracy is primarily defined as rule where rulers have the consent of the ruled, then many states within the international system, as well as the international system itself, must be defined as un-democratic and even anti-democratic. Further, the lack of consent is testimony to the lack of inclusion and the presence of exclusion in the social, political, and economic dimensions of national and international life. A visionary picture of inclusionary governance, from the standpoint of *"cosmopolitan democracy"* is portrayed throughout the work of David Held. In his view, a future cosmopolitan democracy would develop a global parliament, with revenue-raising capacity, share global governance with an International Court that empowers global citizens to take the "local" national governments to court if they deny them their basic citizenship rights, which would include a "guaranteed basic income for all adults" (Held, 1995, p. 279). Similarly, Garreton maintains that "the crucial issue today is the reconstruction of a political system that allows for the simultaneous strengthening of the state and the autonomous capacity of collective actors to define the type of modernity they want. Such a system requires the construction of a new sociopolitical matrix" (Garreton, 1999, p. 77).

C. THE CONSTRUCTION OF A NEW SOCIOPOLITICAL MATRIX: INCLUSIONARY GOVERNANCE VERSUS EXCLUSIONARY GLOBALIZATION

Why does democracy matter? Because human beings matter. The dignity, worth, and human rights of the person constitute the most persuasive case for the embodiment of democratic norms and values into political life

Preface to Inclusionary Governance 11

and in the formal and informal aspects of law at both the national and international level. It is at the level of consent that democracy as a set of norms obtains value for the person, for consent demands and requires dialogue as a means and method to iron out difficulties and differences. The very quality and scope of governance is shaped by this dialogue.

Rousseau made reference to the "General Will" as an expression of the consent that was to be generated by dialogue. Kant founded the search for perpetual peace upon a complex system of law that vested legitimacy within the institutions of government by virtue of the fact that law's primary purpose was to effectuate peace through the municipal law of states. The premise of his argument was that unless people were associated together in subjection to the law and constitutional order maintained in the states, then the condition of mutual society would remain that of the natural state of war (Covell, 1998, p. 168).

Not unlike Hobbes, Kant saw the war of all against all lurking within and between states. The absence of law and consent to the law was vital not only for political legitimacy but also for the sake of peace itself. The absence of consent points toward the absence of democratic norms of inclusion that are capable of forging and formulating the foundations of consent. The exclusionary impulses that arise out of this matrix of exclusionary practices create anarchic features at the national and international levels. In a paper written for the Commission on Global Governance, Johan Galtung noted: "The world as a political system combines anarchic features of non-rule with hierarchical features of non-democratic rule, and the world as an economic system is based on hidden rule. As a consequence, development- environment policies tend to hurt lower-class people in lower class countries badly, and security-peace policies tend to be in the interests of upper-class countries, launching, for instance, international crimes tribunals against marginalized people in marginalized countries. The world is not a democracy, meaning that everybody cannot be given a voice; there is little or no dialogue toward consensus, and the majority will of humans or even states plays a minor role" (Galtung, 1995, p. 197).

The effects of globalization have exacerbated the damage to the practice of democracy, already largely accomplished under the auspices of capitalist expansion in both First and Third World states. Globalization has unleashed the full brutality of the Hobbesian war of all against all, through the vicissitudes of the market, as well as new and old forms of state violence—dedicated, as always, to the maintenance of privileged and elite access to wealth and power (Kaldor, 1999; Robinson, 1996; Petras and Polychronious, 1998; Arrighi and Sliver, 1999; Vasquez, 1993; Rosenau, 1990). This dynamic is what I call the *"exclusionary impulse."*

The dynamics of the *exclusionary impulse* are historically conditioned. Therefore, it changes over time and in relationship to successive and distinct stages in the evolution of capitalist expansion. On this point, it has been observed that "while system-wide financial expansions come and go, the transformations in systemic organization that accompany them do not. They constitute successive and distinct stages in the process of formation, widening and deepening of a world market and a world capitalist system" (Arrighi and Silver, 1999, p. 279). There is growing agreement on this point among scholars. This emerging consensus of interpretation has come as a consequence of identifying the pitfalls of the *"globalization thesis."*

Increasingly, it has been observed that "the *globalization thesis* ignores the fact that the movement toward the international integration of national economies is as old as the history of capitalism itself" (Petras and Polychroniou, 1998, p. 189). The historical antecedent for the current phase of globalization began in the late 15th century with the rise of capitalism and its overseas expansion. The exploitation and conquest of large segments of the Third World—Asia, Africa, Latin America—as well as settlements in Australia and the United States, are all instances of "globalization." Given this view, globalization is not a new phenomenon. Rather, it consitutes a new name, "a subcode for international capitalism, that subsumes diverse sociopolitical and economic processes" (*Id.*, p. 189).

In this context, the dynamics of the *"exclusionary impulse"* have been accelerated by the complex set of linkages which exist between the characteristics of informational capitalism on the one hand, and the rise of inequality, social polarization, poverty, and misery in most of the world on the other. In this regard, Manuel Castells notes: "globalization proceeds selectively, including and excluding segments of economies and societies in and out of networks of information, wealth, and power, that characterize the new dominant system" (Castells, Vol. III, 1998, p. 162).

The trend toward including some segments of economies while excluding others serves, in part, to explain the crisis of the nation-state and of the institutions of civil society constructed around it. The reason for this result is that technological advances lead to the greater individualization of work. Each person is left to bargain away their fate vis-a-vis constantly changing market forces. The collective consequence of this trend allows markets to undermine the institutional capacity of the nation-state, as well as the institutions of civil society, to correct the social imbalances which are the consequence of unrestricted market logic (*Id.*, p. 162).

Looking to the future of global politics, Cox cautions: "It is of the first importance to consider the sources of conflict that may be exacerbated by the globalization trend" (Cox, 1992, p. 145). Conflicts may arise from a variety of sources, including ecological issues, migration, social polarization in response to the development of new structures of production, and the dynamics of economic competition, as well as from ethnic and group differentiations. Whatever the source of these differentiations, the point to be made is that they are capable of being "manipulated in the interest of economic and social cleavages" (*Id.*, p. 145). In turn, these conflicts can have consequences that are not confined to communities within states, but may transcend borders and can become extended into the interstate system "through the differential responses of particular states and the transnational linkages of social groups" (*Id.*, p. 145).

Of equal importance is the necessity to identify probable sources of opposition to globalization, such as the relatively disadvantaged. These people, classes, and groups are the victims of what I have called the "exclusionary impulse." Their very status as excluded, marginalized, and dispossessed persons serves as the global space where new sources of opposition may arise, including social movements (Johnston and Klandermas,

1995, pp. 3–24; Jenkins and Klandermas, 1995, pp. 3–13; Kriesi, Koopmans, Duyvendak, and Giugni, 1995; Tarrow, 1994). Such movements may include labor movements that have proven themselves capable of transcending national boundaries, as well as what Gramsci called the economic-corporate level of consciousness (Mark Robinson, 1998, pp. 150–186). Additionally, democratization movements may also arise and become more assertive in their struggles to enhance popular control over those aspects of social organization that directly affect people's lives actively work to exclude people from exercising their right to democratic control, the practice of giving their consent (or withholding it), their right to participate.

In this new era of globalization, political transitions brought about by the collapse of authoritarian rule, democratization, or political reforms also contribute to making nation-states more prone to violence. In his examination of the causes and regional dimensions of internal conflict, Michael Brown has noted that "the emergence and rise of exclusionary national ideologies, such as ethnic nationalism and religious fundamentalism" can act as destabilizing forces (Brown, 1996, p. 577). Further, "the emergence of dehumanizing ideologies" is especially dangerous "because it is often the precursor to genocidal slaughter." Also, the rise of new groups or changes in the inter-group balance of power "can intensify inter-group competition and anxieties, making political systems more volatile" (*Id.*, p. 577). Additionally, the emergence of power struggles between and among elites "can be particularly problematic" in light of the fact that desperate and opportunistic politicians are especially prone to employing divisive ethnic and national appeals (*Id.*, pp. 577–78).

The onset of globalization "has disclosed political elites far more disposed than their citizens to transfer sovereignty over economic activities to international institutions, as in relation to the establishing of the World Trade Organization or such regional initiatives as North American Free Trade Association" (Falk, 1998, p. 223). As the Western hemisphere is forced to embrace the treaty terms of NAFTA, so too, much of Europe is forced to embrace the emergent European Union (EU), as prescribed in the Maastrict treaty process. In both First and Third World settings, the threats to democracy increase along with an exponential proclivity to employ violence and engage in conflict, as a means of opposing the perceived tyranny of globalization, exclusionary trends and impulses that impact on the lives of millions of people who have little or no recourse. From these observations of international trends, there is a growing appreciation of the linkage between inequality on the one hand and the generation of insecurity and violence on the other.

1. Developing a New Security Agenda

Globalization, mass communications, and the liberalism of economic exchanges have all converged to make a new security agenda rather problematic. In large measure, this is because the convergence of these trends have served to facilitate illicit flows of drugs, weapons, or mass migration

(Hurrell, 1999, p. 263). There is, in short, an expanding range of connections between inequality and security. Three major connections may be readily identified.

First, despite the official pronouncement that the Cold War is ended, "old power logics remain firmly established within several important and volatile regions" (*Id.*, p. 265). So, while the major power centers of the international system have experienced a lessening of tensions, it does not follow that other power centers and unequal power asymmetries would be less prone to conflict and violence. In fact, just the opposite has occured, as in the cases of East Timor, Bosnia, Rwanda, and Haiti.

Second, the importance of issues associated with inequality, as well as social, economic, and political exclusion, have taken on new significance in relationship to maturing notions of what a new security system should look like and take into account. In this respect, "classic understandings of security have been supplemented by a new security agenda in which inequality plays a central role" (*Id.*, p. 265). The challenge of developing a new security agenda constitutes one of the major tasks associated with deepening democracy. The importance of what I have termed *"inclusionary governance,"* Falk has termed *"humane goverance,"* and Held has termed *"cosmopolitan democracy,"* reflects a common concern with the establishment of democratic norms that are capable of effectively creating a security environment that transcends reliance on military solutions and/or financial domination. All three models address the connection between inequality and security and the need to find and implement new policies, values, and institutions that promote democratic norms, inclusionary practices, and humane values.

Third, by expanding the range of connections between inequality and global security, it is becoming even more evident that "inequalities of power determine why certain issues come to be treated as security issues and whose security needs are to be protected" (*Id.*, p. 265). In this regard, the history of classical and 20th century notions of security have been severely circumscribed by their failure to take into account the normative ambitions of international society in relation to security.

In terms of security, as with many other issues in this new phase (era) of globalization, "our understandings of what is legitimate, indeed perhaps necessary, to expect from the international political system have grown enormously. These expectations lead inevitably away from a pluralist security order built around minimalist norms of co-existence . . . and towards a security order that both seeks much tighter control over the use of force in states' relations with each other and reaches deep into the ways in which domestic societies are organized" (*Id.*, p. 269). This insight has tremendous implications for the deepening of democracy on both the national and international levels, as well as for the way in which we assess the "logic" and the "triumph" of capitalism's market economy.

Throughout the Third World, it is clear that capitalism does not strengthen democracy. According to Denitch, "political and economic elites who insist on carrying out the cruel Social Darwinian mandates of the international financial community, regardless of the social and political price,

Preface to Inclusionary Governance 15

make democracy very unlikely" (Denitch, 1996, p. 28). Similarly, Falk maintains that "the current phase of capitalism is especially polarizing with respect to both class relations and center/periphery patterns. That is, capitalism is in the midst of an especially cruel phase" (Falk, 1995, p. 48). This is due, in part, to an ideology of triumph, wherein "capitalism is essentially uncontested ideologically, and capitalist dominance is accepted globally as a fact of life, with socialist, and even strong welfare alternatives, being discredited, at least temporarily" (*Id.*, p. 48).

With the expanding range of connections between inequality and security becoming more firmly established in the consciousness of people around the globe, however, it may well be that submerged alternatives and discourses may be ascendent. Take, for example, the fact that, at the close of 1999, the normative ambitions of international society have come to include demands for more effective control over the development and proliferation of weapons of mass destruction. Additionally, normative ambitions, on a global level, have pulled for progressively tighter limits on legitimate justifications for the use of force by states. Also, there has been an increase in concern for the security of an expanded range of social groups against an expanded range of threats (Hurrell, 1999, p. 269). In short, at the dawn of the 21st century, there is a widening "inclusionary impulse" which seeks to encompass an entire range of previously neglected issues and persons. This global trend of articulated normative ambitions constitutes what I call the "inclusionary impulse," pursuant to growing global aspirations for peace and the rubric of international law which places new demands upon the international agenda for the realization of inclusionary governance.

2. Inclusionary Governance as a Radical Demand

The demand for inclusionary governance is a radical demand because it is a radical departure from the intellectual framework of classical security thinking. By identifying ever widening parameters of what is truly inclusive of human security, more forms of deadly conflict and violence may be avoided. A more peaceful world, premised upon international justice, is in the making. In part, the demand for inclusionary governance and the deepening of democratic norms arises from the recognition that many contemporary security problems, especially the problems of civil violence, migration, and environmental degradation, are not readily susceptible to military responses. Rather, the causes of these problems are largely the consequence of *inhumane governance*. As such, inhumane governance stands under a triple indictment (Falk, 1995, pp. 47–78).

The first indictment is *global apartheid*. The matrix of international power relations, first inaugurated by the Westphalian conception of international society (with its reliance on sovereign norms), and further entrenched by the statist hierarchies, reflective of the inequalities of international life, collapsed in the aftermath of the superpower bipolarity of the Cold War years

(1945–1989). The view of conventional geopolitics, by focusing primarily upon the top of the pyramid of power, neglected those at the bottom. Hence, the South Commission, in its report *The Challenge to the South*, served to exemplify this basic concern with the dynamics of inequality and its relationship to conventional notions of security:

> Were all humanity a single nation-state, the present North/South divide would make it an unviable, semi-feudal entity, split by internal conflicts. Its small part is advanced, prosperous, powerful; its much bigger part is underdeveloped, poor, powerless. A nation so divided within itself would be recognized as inherently unstable. (The South Commission, 1990, p. 2).

In light of this objective reality of modern history, the term "global apartheid" has been invoked in order to evoke a recognition of the fact that what is unacceptable at the national level is also unacceptable at the international level. Further, the term has the purpose of mobilizing transnational forces dedicated to fostering "the transition to geogovernance in the form of humane governance" (Falk, 1995, p. 52). Because global apartheid is inherently exclusionary, it supports and sustains inequality within and between nations and "indicates the hidden racist and classist structure of geopolitics" (*Id.*, p. 52). In order to rescue geopolitics from the grip of global apartheid, it is necessary to adopt a reformist obligation. *The Human Development Index* and *The Human Development Report* are two such reformist attempts to depict where the locus of suffering exists and to identify the necessary steps toward its mitigation. In this sense, these UN reports constitute part of the work of the international community to construct not only "humane governance," but also to create a new developmental agenda that stresses "inclusionary governance" for those who have been victimized by global apartheid.

The Human Development Report has been commissioned by the United Nations Development Program (UNDP) since 1990 as an independent report on the state of human development. It has been instrumental in explicating the concept of human development. It has also advanced the international debate on issues such as the measure of development, the environmental aspects of development, gender equality and development, as well as the links between economic growth and development and the concept of human poverty. In its 1997 report, the report's authors found that nearly one-third of the people in the least developed countries, most of them in sub-Saharan Africa, could not expect to live beyond the age of 40 (UNDP, 1997, p. 5).

Coupled with this finding was the discovery that poverty was linked to adult illiteracy. This means that the poor are not only severely restricted in their access to knowledge, information, and the press, but also in their ability to exercise connected rights such as political participation (Speth, 1998, p. 282). The democratic deficit emerges from the realm of poverty as an obstacle to the deepening of democracy. Although the political aspects of poverty eradication have often been neglected in debates on poverty, there is increasing evidence that the pendulum is starting to swing the other way so that the "non-economic aspects of the eradication of poverty are perceived as essential to empower the poor and to open the political space for the success of poverty eradication strategies" (*Id.*, p. 291).

The second indictment of inhumane governance involves the concept of *"avoidable harm."* In this respect, "the first indictment implicates structure, the second indictment relates to policy failure in relation to matters of normative concern" (Falk, 1995, p. 55). Insofar as the historical and current dynamics of world order have and continue to generate many varieties of avoidable harm, "the commitment to humane governance implies intolerance toward all forms of avoidable harm" (*Id.*, p. 55). In this regard, the second indictment begins with both the existence and spread of poverty. The elimination of poverty is within fiscal reach. Had an additional $50 billion dollars a year been committed to this goal throughout the 1990s, the basic needs of every person on the planet (adequate food, water, health care, education) would have been met. Instead, poverty has worsened, widened its scope, and deepened into a global crisis. Not only have the poor and excluded been deprived of their basic needs, they have been disempowered as well. Hence, inhumane governance has exacerbated the problem of exclusionary governance. In this sense, the problem of povery has also created a crisis for global politics and the search for peace, conflict prevention, and conflict resolution. For the disempowerment of the poor and the resulting inequality associated with it have also formed and forged the conditions for social conflict, ethnic strife, and war around the globe.

The non-economic aspects of empowering the poor, excluded, dispossessed, and marginalized has implications for the process of building a global culture of peace. Peace, after all, is not something caused by inanimate forces, but something that is consciously made by human beings. In this regard, Vasquez observes that "how well it is made determines how long it will last, for it is the success or failure of a peace in creating a global political system that will determine the frequency of war in the presence of intractable issues" (Vasquez, 1993, p. 266). The structure of global peace during the 1990s was not well made. Among its numerous failures is the role and extent of global oppression. While there are many varieties of oppression "that arise from intolerance and the abuse of power and authority," it is also true that "oppressive violence can emanate from the state or its enemies in civil society, or from prejudiced elements embedded in civil society" (Falk, 1995, p. 63). The 1999 involvement of NATO in the affairs of Kosovo is graphic testimony to this reality.

The third indictment of inhumane governance involves the concept of *"Eco-Imperialism."* The third indictment "involves the political consequence of two interactive processes: the worsening of environmental conditions and the persistence of dominant growth-oriented economic priorities" (Falk, 1995, p. 75). These processes have largely been advanced and worsened by two major Western international financial lending institutions, the IMF and the World Bank. The damage they have inflicted is well-documented (Hancock, 1999; Caufield, 1996; Rich, 1994).

Alternatives to these institutions and their approaches to development have emerged over the decade of the 1990s. The terms "sustainable development" and "sustainability" have come to dominate the field of environmental policy and politics. The widespread recognition of the so-called "Brundtland Report" (the report of the United Nations Commission on Environment and Development), published in 1987, inaugurated the use of these terms. As a result, *"sustainable development"* rapidly became the key principle underpinning official environmental policy at both national and international levels. Evidence of its impact became clear during the 1992 "Earth Summit" in Rio de Janeiro (the UN Conference on Environment and Development). The conference not only generated formal endorsement for the concept from over 150 governments, but also generated a wide range of policy initiatives under the sustainable development heading.

The central ideas which emanate from the discourse of sustainable development find expression in six "core ideas" represented by the term. These are:

1. Environment-economy integration: ensuring that economic development and environmental protection are integrated in planning and implementation.
2. Futurity: an explicit concern about the impact of current activity on future generations.
3. Environmental protection: a commitment to reducing pollution and environmental degradation and to the more efficient use of resources.
4. Equity: a commitment to meeting at least the basic needs of the poor of the present generation (as well as equity between generations).
5. Quality of life: a recognition that human well being is constituted by more than just income growth.
6. Participation: the recognition that sustainable development requires the political involvement of all groups or "stakeholders" in society (Jacobs, 1999, pp. 26–27).

In conclusion, Falk's triple indictment of inhumane governance is nothing less than the recognition of the fact that, to become a reality, "humane governance will have to address the economic and environmental agenda by adopting appropriate procedures and establishing institutions of a magnitude capable of overcoming global apartheid" (Falk, 1995, p. 78; Held, 1993, p. 40). In this task, the goals of humane governance converge with the goals of inclusionary governance and cosmopolitan democracy. At their core, they represent a call for principled participation by the poor and excluded to remake and reshape the global arena of humankind. At issue is whether or not a peaceful planet is within humanity's grasp. Bringing about such a result will require a pattern or mode of governance that is conducive to peace and adopts an institutional framework (economic, legal, political, social), that is capable of objectively sustaining a normative framework based on these principles. In sum, "sustainable development is a crucial idea in relation to reconciling policy responses to environment and poverty in a world of very uneven economic and social circumstances" (Falk, 1999(b), p. 178). It is to these alternative patterns of governance that we now turn.

3. Achieving Peace Through Sustainable Development and Security

The making of peace is largely determined by the mode or pattern of governance that is chosen and eventually adopted as the objective and normative framework for state and international relations. Table 1.1 provides a schematic description of the relationship between patterns of governance and forms of security, as well as how this relationship would vary according to competing visions.

With respect to the cited possibilities for patterns of governance and the various forms of security which have the potential to be established on their respective foundations, it may legitimately be argued that the idea of "perpetual peace," as formulated by Immanuel Kant, demonstrates that the globalization of civility, the development of cosmopolitan forms of governance, the deepening of democracy, and the evolution of "inclusionary governance" are real possibilities.

Still, an expansion of debate on the non-economic aspects of poverty does not mitigate the fact of how far the world is from the benefits we might expect from democratization. According to the UNDP Human Development

TABLE 1.1 Patterns of Governance

Patterns of Governance	Political Institutions	Source of Legitimacy	Mode of Security
States system	Nation-states	Nation-building, patriotism	External defense, internal pacification
Cold War	Nation-states, blocs, transnational institutions	Ideology—freedom/socialism	Deterrence, bloc cohesion
Clash of civilizations	Nation-states, civilizational blocs	Cultural identity	Civilizational defense at home and abroad
Coming anarchy	Pockets of authority	Non-existent	Fortified islands of civility amidst pervasive violence
Cosmopolitan governance	Transnational institutions	Humanism	End of modern war, cosmopolitan law-enforcement

SOURCE: Mary Kaldor, *New & Old Wars: Organized Violence in a Global Era*, Stanford University Press, 1999, p. 150.

Report 1992, "the richest 20 percent of the world's people get at least 150 times more than the poorest 20 percent." But if the comparison is based on the richest and poorest countries only, disregarding the maldistribution within countries, "in 1960, the richest 20 percent of the world's population had incomes 30 times greater than the poorest 20 percent. By 1990, the richest 20 percent were getting 60 times more." In other words, "a scandalous situation is getting even worse. A more democratic world would not have tolerated this" (Galtung, 1995, p. 199). Therefore, the possibilities and prospects for deepening democracy have implications for civil society, the distribution and redistribution of national and international wealth, as well as the eradication of poverty and hunger.

Moving toward the actual development of a more democratic world is increasingly seen as an "emerging right to democratic governance" (Franck, 1992, pp. 46–91). Franck has underscored the power of democratic legitimacy as a new global consensus emerges to declare democratic governance as a right. He cites the fact that more than two centuries have elapsed since the signatories of the US Declaration of Independence manifested two radical propositions. The first is that governments are instituted to secure the "inalienable rights" of their citizens. The second is that a nation earns "separate and equal station" in the community of states by demonstrating "a decent respect to the opinions of mankind." Given these propositions, Franck insists that "democracy . . . is on the way to becoming a global entitlement, one that increasingly will be promoted and protected by collective international processes" (Franck, 1992, p. 46). While the transformation of the democratic entitlement from moral prescription to legal obligation has evolved gradually, it has evolved to a new status. Like Galtung, Franck holds that "consent benefits the governing as much as the governed: that sociological truism is at last becoming a political axiom" (*Id.*, p. 48).

Similarly, Falk has argued that "implicitly at least . . . many of the elements of a democratic public order system were affirmed as morally and legally mandatory for states from the time that the Universal Declaration of Human Rights was adopted in 1948" (Falk, 1998(a), p. 314). Still, there have been limitations to this mandate. The mandate is neither binding nor fully articulated. While it is true that the Universal Declaration and the two covenants of 1966 affirm social, economic, cultural, civil, and political rights, they also "refrain from any direct attempt to prescribe the constituent elements of a legitimate public order system of a state or to insist that the implementation of human rights depends on the establishment of democracy in the form of a non-authoritarian political order" (*Id.*, p. 314).

Nevertheless, Falk asserts that a question persists as to whether the realization of human rights "is not virtually synonymous with a wider move in international political life towards the affirmation of democracy as the only legitimate system of governance in the contemporary world" (*Id.*, p. 314). While the equation of democracy with human rights is tenable, the capacity of those at the bottom of the international system to adjust to multinational corporate power is less so. For while the affirmation of democracy and human rights has the capacity to guide international political life, the separate sphere of "market logic" remains largely immune from accountability to these principles. As Robinson cautions, the "way in which the overwhelming majority of humanity's resources is used is decided not on the basis of humanity's needs but on the basis of the drive for profit by transnational corporations. The burning challenge of our time is how to wrest such enormous power away from transnational capital and its agent, the transnational elite. This challenge amounts to no more or less than how to democratize global society" (Robinson, 1996, p. 385). It is to the challenge of how to democratize global society that we now turn.

D. THE EMERGING POLITICS AND LAW OF INCLUSIONARY GOVERNANCE THROUGH DEMOCRATIC NORMS

International law is more than a set of rules or mandates. It is also comprised of the interplay between politics, values, and functions. This is because international law is comprised of evolving standards and practices. Henkin has observed two major elements that make up the totality of international law: first, that law is politics and, second, that law is the normative expression of a political system (Henkin, 1989). While there has been an attempt to draw a dividing line between law and politics, this line constitutes an artificial distinction. While law is normative and involves legal obligations which invite legal remedies, it cannot be divorced from the practice of politics which encompasses freedom of choice, diplomacy, bargaining, and negotiation. The fact remains that law is made by political actors. As such, international law has evolved from the interplay of political forces that have developed political procedures for political ends. The history of the post-World War II process of decolonization provides an excellent example of this evolutionary process (Nardin, 1983; Arend, 1999; Beitz, 1979; Hasenclever, Mayer, and Rittberger, 1997; George, 1994; Franck, 1995; Franck, 1992).

At the time of decolonization (the post-1945 world), political decisions were taken which instituted the negative sovereignty regime as the sole successor to colonialism. The implications this has had for the international legal order have been enormous insofar as "this ruled out alternative institutional arrangements which might have been better suited to the different circumstances and needs of particular colonial populations" (Jackson, 1990, p. 198). As far as global governance is concerned, the political choice of negative sovereignty created an international legal order in which "legal uniformity triumphed despite the fact that the emerging world of states was anything but uniform and was indeed highly pluralistic in almost every respect" (*Id.*, p. 198).

Similarly, in the post-Cold War era (1990–present), the same observation can be made with respect to the highly pluralistic nature of international society. The close of the 20th century is not all that dissimilar to the mid-20th century insofar as the highly stratified system of international relations that developed under the auspices of the Cold War are currently becoming more stratified under the auspices of "globalization" (in its new and revised phase of capitalist expansion) (Booth, 1998). The crisis of the nation-state and of the institutions of civil society are constituent elements of the current crisis of democracy. The social, political, and economic imbalances which are derived from the practice of unrestricted market logic have created a situation in some Latin American or African states where the state, "emptied of representativeness, becomes a predator on its own people. New information technologies tool this global whirlwind of accumulation of wealth and diffusion of poverty" (Castells, Vol. III, 1998, p. 162).

The challenge to articulating democratic norms and deepening democratic practices in the global environment is vividly exposed in those situations where the state itself is emptied of its capacity to practice representativeness. At that point, the state becomes an exclusionary state (ES). If democracy is to triumph in the longer term, "compliance with the democratic entitlement should also be linked to a right of representation in international organs, to international fiscal, trade and development benefits, and to the protection of UN and regional collective security measures" (Franck, 1992, p. 91). In addition to linking the deepening of democracy to a right of representation, it is essential to emphasize democratic accountability at the state, regional, and international levels of global governance. Fundamentally this means that, in the contemporary world, "democracy can only be fully sustained by ensuring the accountability of all related and interconnected power systems, from economics to politics" (Held, 1995, p. 267).

Given this perspective, "if the history and practice of democracy has until now been centered on the idea of locality (the city-state, the community, the nation), it is likely that in the future it will be centered on the international or global domain" (Held, 1993, p. 45). With the undeniable reality of globalization and the interconnectedness it implies, there are still no straightforward solutions to the problems it poses for inclusionary governance, humane governance, or the deepening of democracy. It is, as already acknowledged, an uneven process with uneven impacts. However, the capacity to envision and work toward a different international order constitutes not merely an aspiration but an obligation for all those who seek what some have described as "a newer world" (Kennedy, 1967).

1. The First Steps Toward the Creation of an International Democratic Polity

According to David Held, "a first step in the direction of an international democratic polity . . . lies within the grasp of the UN system, but would involve the latter actually living up to its charter" (Held, 1995, p. 269). This task would entail "pursuing measures to implement key elements of the UN Rights Conventions, enforcing the prohibition of the discretionary use of force, and activating the collective security system envisaged in the Charter itself" (*Id.*, p. 269). The extension of the Charter model would also encompass the following elements: (1) adding the requirement of compulsory jurisdiction in the case of disputes falling under the UN rubric; (2) providing the means of redress in the case of human rights violations through a new international human rights court; (3) making a (near) consensus vote in the General Assembly a legitimate source of international law (and recognized as such by the World Court); and (4) modifying the veto arrangement in the Security Council and reassessing representation on it to allow for adequate regional accountability (*Id.*, p. 269). In all of these endeavors, the Charter model provides a basis for deepening democracy at the global level, thereby extending the democratic entitlement through what has been identified as "the emerging right to democratic governance" (Franck, 1992, pp. 46–91). In so doing, the UN Charter system has the capacity to generate political resources of its own and to act as a politically independent decision-making center (Held, 1995, p. 269).

The implications for the search for international justice and peace are enormous. To begin with, maintaining the "rule of law" and its impartial administration in international affairs constitutes a move away from the accusation of "double-standards" and toward the steps necessary for enhancing the prospects of a global peace. This is an especially vital undertaking when, in the wake of globalization, transformations in the international arena are placing increasing strain on both the Westphalian and Charter concepts of international governance (Held, 1995, p. 270). The maintenance of the "rule of law" serves to bring global governance into conformity with the claims of democratic norms and the capacity of those norms to effectuate the pursuit of peace in the long run. Fidelity to democratic norms enhances the global prospects for peace because "peace is an historically determined process, a social construction of a political system—complete with rules of the game, allocation mechanisms, and decision games. Each historical period (and its global culture) has its own form of war and its own form of peace, and the nature of its peace will determine whether war can be avoided for a long or short period of time" (Vasquez, 1993, p. 266).

The historically dominant modes of geo-governance, the model of Westphalia and the UN Charter model, both constitute a model of governance based on taking the political world as one finds it and then accommodating the international legal structure to it. In the case of the Westphalian system, there was always a gulf between the recognition of states (equal in status before the law), and the actual asymmetries of power (which pervaded the states system) (Held, 1995, p. 79). Similarly, in the case of the UN Charter model, the architecture of the UN "was drawn up to accommodate the international power structure as it was understood in 1945" (Held, 1995, p. 87).

An examination of the shift in the structure of international regulation from the Westphalian to the UN Charter model serves to raise fundamental questions about the nature and form of international law. At bottom, these questions point toward "a significant disjuncture between the law of national states—of the states system—and of the wider international commmunity. At the heart of this shift lies a conflict between the claims made on behalf of individual states and those made on behalf of an alternative organizing principle of world affairs: ultimately, a democratic community of states, with equal voting rights in the General Assembly of nation-states, openly and collectively regulating international life while constrained to observe the UN Charter and a battery of human rights conventions" (Held, 1995, p. 85). Such a democratic community of states would work collectively to maintain what has been termed "cosmopolitan democratic law" (*Id.*, pp. 270–272).

The cosmopolitan model of democracy would be upheld and guarded by its participants. But its participants would be constrained by the institutional components of the cosmopolitan model of democracy. In other words, "participants act in institutional mileux and the nature of these is, of course, of the utmost significance in the determination of political processes and outcomes." In this context, "the cosmopolitan model of democracy would seek the entrenchment of cosmopolitan democratic law in order to provide shape and limits to political decision-making" (*Id.*, p. 272).

The entrenchment of cosmopolitan democratic law would be effectuated as it is enshrined within the constitutions of parliaments and assemblies at the national and international level. Further, international courts would enjoy an extension of their influence so that previously excluded groups and individuals would have an effective avenue to sue political authorities for the enactment and enforcement of key rights and obligations, both within and beyond formal political associations. Hence, what is mandated by the cosmopolitan model of democracy translates into the operational and institutional foundation of what I have termed *"inclusionary governance."* For, once the legal, political, and economic rules of the game are set, there remains the task of articulating the normative and substantive components of the realm of democratic entitlements. Such entitlements must transcend the exclusionary nature and character of traditional liberal democracy and the institutions and laws reflective of their exclusionary purposes. Therefore, inclusionary governance, as an innovative model for the expansion of consent and participation by and for the previously excluded persons, classes, and groups of humankind, becomes an evolving set of principles, goals, and institutions, through which the practice of cosmopolitan democracy may be assessed and assisted.

2. First Principles: Self-Determination and Its Struggle With Sovereignty

At the close of the 20th century, the process of decolonization is nearly complete. Nevertheless, the principle of self-determination retains much of its original energy. It can be observed in having contributed to the withdrawal of the Soviet Union from Eastern Europe and the Baltic states in 1989 and throughout the 1990s. The pull of self-determination has also been felt in South Africa's decision to give independence to Namibia. In 1991, the civil war in Angola was ended on the basis of an agreement to hold free and internationally observed elections, thereby giving Angola the legitimate regime it had failed to acquire at the moment of its independence.

In short, the ascendency of the principle and practice of self-determination has evolved into a "building block in the creation of a democratic entitlement" (Franck, 1992, p. 55). As such, the principle of self-determination now emerges, at the dawn of the 21st century, as a legal and political basis on which to enact historic transformations. Additionally, the "deeply embedded roots of self-determination also anchor the legitmacy claims of other, more recent components of the democratic entitlement" (*Id.*, p. 56).

Preface to Inclusionary Governance

Self-determination constitutes a central attribute not only of the notion of democratic entitlement, but also of the claims inherent in the practice of inclusionary governance. Self-determination, democratic entitlement, inclusionary governance, and the model of cosmopolitan democracy all constitute what I call the "inclusionary impulse," especially when juxtaposed with the current system of exclusionary states (ES) and exclusionary policies.

The so-called "New World Order" inaugurated by the G-7, GATT, the IMF, and the World Bank, all under the auspices of the "Washington-concensus," has sought to legitimize exclusionary practices and policies within and between nations (Bello, 1994). The rationale is largely premised on the pursuit of elite profit and the protection of vested wealth (Gowan, 1999). In this process of social restructuring there is more than growing inequality and poverty. There is also the actual exclusion of people and territories which, "from the perspective of dominant interests in global informational capitalism, shift to a position of structural irrelevance" (Castells, 1998, Vol. III, p. 162).

This widespread, multiform process of social exclusion leads to what Manuel Castells has metaphorically referred to as "the black holes of informational capitalism." He defines these black holes as "regions of society from which, statistically speaking, there is no escape from the pain and destruction inflicted on the human condition for those who, in one way or another, enter these social landscapes" (*Id.*, p. 162). Castells postulates that this will remain a global reality, unless there is a change in the laws that govern the universe of informational capitalism. For the fact remains that only "purposive human action can change the rules of social structure, including those inducing social exclusion" (*Id.*, p. 162).

It is indeed more than unlikely that such an historic shift will emerge in the absence of purposive human action in the service of the cosmopolitan model of democracy and the ideals, values, and substantive policy and structural changes which are both mandated and articulated within the framework of inclusionary governance. With respect to the cosmopolitan model, it posits that people can enjoy membership in diverse communities which significantly affect them and, accordingly, gain access to a variety of forms of political participation. In this context, citizenship would be extended, in principle, to membership in all cross-cutting political communities, from the local to the global (Held, 1995, p. 272). With respect to inclusionary governance, the agenda of individual states and international organizations would extend the scope, breadth and reach of their policies to encompass the needs and claims of all previously excluded individuals, classes, groups, nationalities into their respective deliberations. In the absence of the principles of cosmopolitan forms of democracy and inclusionary governance, the situation of the excluded and marginalized throughout Latin America, Asia, and Africa can only worsen.

Take, for example, Latin America. Through the 1980s poverty increased by 60 million, reaching 196 million Latin Americans (Vilas, 1996, p. 298). The region produced poor people at double the rate of total population growth: 44 percent as against 22 percent growth, respectively, throughout the decade. Although the proportion of the population living below the poverty line is greater in rural areas (two-thirds) than in the cities (one-third), the urban poor (115.5 million) outnumber the rural poor (80.4 million).

Given these percentages, it is clear that the urbanization of poverty accelerated during the Reagan-Thatcher era of neoliberalism. For Latin Americans, this era signaled a new reality: 80 percent of the decade's growth took place in the cities, with approximately 48 million new urban poor becoming its casualties.

The main finding to be drawn is that the growth of urban poverty is mainly a response to the economic crisis and to policies implemented by governments. These governments constitute what I call the "exclusionary state": a state that not only tolerates, but actively promotes poverty as an unfortunate consequence of adopting a neoliberal agenda in combination with the protection and maintenance of vested elite interests and enclaves of privilege and indifference. Insofar as poverty implies exclusion and inequality, it is antithetical to democracy, understood as a system of inclusion. The very fact that the magnitude of a population living in expanding islands of poverty is allowed to exist threatens the consolidation of democratic regimes. As the consolidation of democratic regimes is threatened, so too is the emerging right to democratic governance, understood as both inclusionary and cosmopolitan. In fact, some scholars argue that "the third wave seems to be losing the tremendous momentum of democratic expansion that it had gathered over two decades. In all likelihood, the number of electoral democracies will not increase significantly in the next few years and could even diminish sharply" (Diamond, 1999, p. 64).

There are many conceptual approaches to democratic consolidation in the literature on democracy. Therefore, in order to escape the dangers of tautology, the study of the processes of democratic consolidation must rest on more than the dominant hypothesis for democratic consolidation: the stability and persistence of democracy (*Id.*, p. 65). If democratic consolidation is construed as the process of achieving deep and broad legitimation, capable of affecting political actors at both elite and mass levels, it becomes the most principal principle. Norms and beliefs must, in this process, be linked to political behavior. Elites (leaders of opinion, culture, business and social organizations) must believe in the legitimacy of democracy. The mass public, in turn, must consistently believe that democracy is preferable to any other form of government. In practice, this translates into elite behaviors where leaders of government, state institutions, and political parties and interest groups respect each other's rights to compete peacefully for power. Similarly, at the mass public level, there must be no antidemocratic movement, party, or organization that benefits from a mass following. Further, violence, fraud, and other unconstitutional methods are not accepted as means to advance political preferences or to pursue political interests (*Id.*, p. 69). In short, "democratic consolidation can . . . only be fully understood as encompassing a shift in *political culture*" (*Id.*, p. 65). Such a shift in political culture has both political and legal ramifications.

I would argue that, in relation to political culture, both political and legal concerns center largely upon the legal principle and right of self-determination. Since the principle and right of self-determination is contingent upon democratic autonomy, there is the practical question of how it is practiced and protected as both an inherent legal right as well as a political obligation between persons, civil society, the state, and the international community. The principle of autonomy, as formulated by David Held, states, "persons should enjoy equal rights (and accordingly equal obligations) in the framework which generates and limits the opportunities available to them; that is, they should be free and equal in their determination of the conditions of their own lives, so long as they do not deploy this framework to negate the rights of others" (Held, 1991, p. 228).

3. From the European Social Charter to a Global Social Charter

The practical and normative question that arises from the principle of autonomy in relationship to the legal principles of self-determination and sovereignty is: How can states consider themselves sovereign when the IMF imposes conditionality requirements on loans that have the direct consequence of altering their domestic social, economic, and political agendas? In response, consider the observation in the most recent (ninth) edition of Oppenheim on International Law: "Sovereignty is supreme authority, which on the international plane means . . . legal authority which is not in law dependent on any other earthly authority" (Oppenheim, 9th ed., p. 122, as quoted in Franck, 1995, p. 4). In spite of the legal definition of sovereignty and the norms associated with it, international financial institutions (IFIs) are a new organizational form that was initiated with the creation of the International Bank for Reconstruction and Development, commonly known as the World Bank, and the International Monetary Fund (IMF) at the close of the Second World War. They were followed by the so-called Bretton Wood twins—the Inter-American Development Bank, the Asian Development Bank, and the European Bank for Reconstruction and Development. All of these institutions engage in sovereign lending.

In the post-World War II period, the agreements between these IFIs and sovereign borrowers have taken the form of contracts (rather than coercion or imposition), Nevertheless, these contracts have "routinely contained invitations that violate the Westphalian model. The terms included in contractual arrangements between borrowing countries and IFIs have often involved detailed specifications of domestic economic behavior" (Krasner, 1999, p. 143). In so doing, these IFIs effectively compromise the domestic autonomy of borrowing states. By these means, the IMF creates new forms of dependence that allow for an erosion of political independence.

In altering the domestic agenda by the contractual obligations subsumed under the rubric of conditionality, these IFIs impose added burdens on the poor by restricting wage levels, cutting government subsidies on food and energy, and reduce credit available to those with low income (Falk, 1995, p. 61). While Third World debtors would have preferred contractual arrangements that would have allowed them access to IMF resources without the need to make such painful political choices, they were forced to compromise their domestic autonomy as a condition of receiving needed international finance. The ultimate reason for this structure was the consequence of American rulers wanting the World Bank and IMF to have financial leverage so that these institutions "could support a specific vision of how domestic polities and economies should be organized" (Krasner, 1999, pp. 145–146). When this strategy failed, as in the case of Chile under the democratically elected leadership of Salvador Allende, IMF and World Bank support was withdrawn and a CIA supported coup by the generals brought General Pinochet to power.

From an international law perspective, given the history of IFIs in the 20th century, the question arises: How can the function and purpose of IFIs be transformed into international actors that promote international justice concerns, in compliance with international law norms and the governing charter of the United Nations? First, it has been suggested that IFIs will require a considerable change in their organizational culture. Second, and more realistically, the only real, practical changes that will help to produce inclusionary governance, humane governance, and deepened forms of democracy will be changes in the mandates and charters of IFIs that will serve to bring them into greater compliance with the norms of sovereignty, human rights, self-determination, and international justice concerns. Such changes may also have marked effects a the ability of IFIs to engage in a conflict prevention and management strategy (Chayes and Chayes, 1998, p. 192).

The World Bank has traditionally focused its attention on the developmental needs of less developed countries. The Bank has traditionally insisted that under Article IV of its charter it could only consider the economic soundness of the projects it funds and cannot be diverted by social or political considerations. In practice, however, the Bank took the position that it could not respond to UN General Assembly resolutions calling for an embargo on economic relations with South Africa and Portugal because of their racial policies (*Id.*, p. 192). Supposedly, this purist perspective has begun to change. But whether it does or not, the fact remains that until that future point in time when the IFIs become legally accountable for their violations of the Westphalian model, human rights covenants and charters, the principles of international law, and UN General Assembly resolutions, these international actors will continue to operate "above the law."

In sum, since the 1950s sovereign lending to developing countries has been governed by an international regime that violates the Westphalian model. This has led to a situation in which poorer countries were effectively forced to sacrifice their domestic autonomy and capacity for democratic decision making on matters internal to their respective states. The forced agreement to compromise their domestic autonomy is the consequence of IMF and World Bank "conditionality" lending which reflected the values and preferences of the more powerful market-oriented industrialized economies. This political and economic reality has encroached on international legal norms and mandates that could have, had they been observed and respected, halted the deepening poverty of millions of people in Third World states. The exclusionary impulse embodied in various IMF agreements, in particular, has often strengthened exclusionary states and practices by virtue of the fact that these loan agreements transgressed the lines protecting sovereign autonomy and democratic accountability. With the effective decline if not outright removal of their legal rights and protections, the relative bargaining power of the individual states was not merely diminished but effectively nullified. In this critical regard, "different preferences over outcomes and power asymmetries have resulted in violations of Westphalian sovereignty through both intervention and invitation" (Krasner, 1999, p. 151).

In light of this history, it can easily be argued that "the increasing levels of global poverty resulting from economic restructuring are casually denied by the G7 governments and international institutions (including the World Bank and IMF); social realities are concealed, official statistics are manipulated, economic concepts are turned upside down" (Chossudovsky, 1998, p. 297). The purpose of engaging in these efforts is to vindicate the free market system. In 1990, Peru was the victim of IMF-sponsored "Fujishock" while the prevailing situation in Sub-Saharan Africa and South Asia was so serious that a majority of the population suffered from chronic undernourishment. The poverty indicators of the World Bank misrepresented country-level situations in order to underplay the seriousness of the dimensions of global poverty. The poor are 20 percent of world population (1.3 billion people). In order to protect the "Washington Consensus," the free market is presented as "the most effective means of achieving poverty alleviation, while the negative impact of macroeconomic reform is denied" (*Id.*, p. 302). In a world of greater global integration, there is also local disintegration insofar as "expansion and profitability for the world's largest corporations is predicated on a global contraction of purchasing power and the impoverishment of large sectors of the world population" (*Id.*, p. 307).

The exclusionary impulse has taken as its credo: survival of the fittest (i.e., enterprises with the most advanced technologies or command over the lowest wages survive). While this trend has historically been contrived for use in the Third World, a parallel process can be observed in Western Europe under the auspices of the Maastricht Treaty. The treaty process has resulted in a political restructuring under the auspices of the European Union (EU) which responds more favorably to dominant financial interests than to the unity and social quality of life within the European societies themselves. While economic integration is often characterized as being capable of producing a semblance of political unity, the reality is that it often promotes factionalism and social strife both within and between nations (*Id.*, p. 308). If there is a genuine concern with advancing peace in First and Third World nations, then it will be necessary to acknowledge the fact that the 20th century ended with the development of entrenched rights for global corporations and financial institutions at the expense of the excluded, poor, marginalized, and dispossessed. The 21st century may, if this trend is not reversed, see "how economic restructuring backlashes on national societies, leading to the collapse of institutions and the escalation of social conflict" (*Id.*, p. 311).

In order to avoid the consequences of this trend, the deepening of democracy in First and Third World nations and regions will have to effectively embark upon building up international law instruments and courts that are capable of sustaining the rights of a global civil society. The rights of a global civil society, built on already existing covenants, treaties, norms of human and civil rights, constitutions, and the Nuremberg principle, can formulate an international charter to defend the rights of the excluded, poor and marginalized. I am suggesting that such an international charter would be a globalization of the European Social Charter (59 UNTS 89, entered into force Feb. 26, 1965).

The European Social Charter is a very inclusionary document with detailed and specified rights and protections well-entrenched within its four corners. It will be the responsibility and opportunity for the international community in the first decade of the 21st century to fashion a similar instrument for global application and the global protection of those who are currently unable to protect themselves. In Article 38, the Appendix to the Charter, it states that "the appendix to this charter shall form an integral part of it." The scope of the charter is defined in terms of persons protected. In Part III of the appendix, it clearly states that "it is understood that the Charter contains legal obligations of an international character, the application of which is submitted solely to the supervision provided for in Part IV thereof." In light of the international implications of the Charter's protections, it can serve as an effective foundation from which to build, write, authorize and implement a global social charter that is protective of the rights of billions of poor, marginalized, and dispossessed human beings who now live at the edge of survival.

4. Questions of Fact and Law

From a legal perspective, the principle and right of self-determination remains threatened by the perpetuation of poverty, inequality, and the entrenchment of the exclusionary state in the international order. To whom does self-determination apply? The first truly serious effort to enunciate its applicable principles were undertaken by the 15th General Assembly in the annex to Resolution 1541 of December 15, 1960. It seeks to stipulate the test for determining whether a territory is non-self-governing within the meaning of Article 73(e) of the Charter. But there is a broader concept of a *universal* right of self-determination enunciated in Article 1 of the International Covenant on Civil and Political Rights (December 16, 1966, 999 UNTS 171). This treaty was ratified or acceded to by 113 states as of November 1991. It is probably binding on other states as customary law (Franck, 1992, p. 58, fn. #42). Its scope is found in its sweeping categorical assertion that: "All peoples have the right of self-determination. By virtue of that right they freely determine their political status and freely pursue their economic, social and cultural development." The categorical nature of this broad assertion has made this provision the "most controversial" in a document "created and steeped in considerable controversy" (*Id.*, p. 58).

The Western powers, in particular, maintained that the right was only a *"political"* principle. Yet when we combine the universality of the scope of the right of self-determination with the force of its being a political principle, it would follow that its proponents could justifiably insist that the norm of self-determination was fundamental, and a precondition, to the enjoyment of other enumerated individual rights and freedoms (*Id.*, p. 58). As a consequence, the principle was given pride of place among the designated entitlements. More significantly for the long term (in the view of the Human Rights Committee), the majority—including states that had opposed the inclusion of the right—utterly rejected the notion that the entitlement applied to only colonial "peoples," declaring rather "that if included, it must apply to peoples anywhere, whether in a politically independent state or a dependent territory" (*Id.*, p. 58). The inclusionary dimensions of governance, undertaken relative to the mandate of the Covenant, provides the concept and practice of *inclusionary governance* with a firm legal basis from which to make other normative claims on behalf of the poor and excluded, on both a national and international basis.

The application of this principle has tremendous importance for the articulation of inclusionary governance and its promise of bringing the lives and concerns of the poor, the dispossessed and the marginalized into sharper focus and at the top rung of any new developmental agenda that calls itself "democratic." On this point, Makinda has noted: "As the Commission on Global Governance has observed: 'Sovereignty ultimately derives from the people. It is a power to be exercised by, for, and on behalf of the people of a state.' The Commission on Global Governance has also argued that the exercise of sovereignty must be linked to the will of the people, which basically means that political leaders must seek legitimacy through democratic processes. In this sense, sovereignty would be respected only if the people of a state had opportunities to exercise their political, economic, and cultural rights. As one analyst has observed, 'Increasing numbers of people are willing to act on what must be an implicit belief that sovereignty does not reside with an abstraction called the state, and certainly not with self-appointed military or civilian dictatorships, but with the people of a country themselves.'" (Makinda, 1996).

Dissenting views of this perspective have emerged, however, in spite of the acknowledgement that "it is easy to sympathize with the values underlying this statement" (Roth, 1999. p. 429). Brad Roth, in his book, *Governmental Illegitimacy in International Law*, argues that the term "Westphalian" is now "an historical reference intended to connote 'outmoded' rather than 'venerable'—and does not accurately describe the conception of sovereignty embodied in the United Nations system, as inaugurated by the Charter and developed through the series of declarations, resolutions, and concrete acts associated with decolonization and enhanced Third World participation in world affairs" (*Id.*, p. 429). Roth contests Makinda's interpretation because, in Roth's view, "the assertion that sovereignty should reside, not with 'an abstraction called the state', but with 'the people of a country themselves', fails to recognize that the latter is nearly as much an abstraction as the former" (*Id.*, p. 430). He cannot contest that the notion of sovereignty is historically predicated on "the will of the people," but he maintains that "the question is how concretely to respect popular will." He maintains that "although this question has an empirical component, it is not strictly an empirical question." Therefore, he concludes that "the criteria for determining the will of the political community . . . are highly contestable ideological propositions" (*Id.*, p. 430). With this conclusion, he simply argues that the "will of the people" is not unlike the will of God, insofar as it is revealed to different observers in different ways.

Roth's critique is itself contestable on several grounds. First, it is contestable because it ignores the nature, scope, and autonomous nature of the processes of democratic decision making on a national and international level. The realization that determining the will of the political community involves contestable ideological propositions points to the nature of democratic governance and decision making. The principle of autonomy, the notion of a democratic legal state, and the concept of cosmopolitan democracy, all form the backbone of a cosmopolitan model of democracy insofar as "the principle of autonomy is at the core of the democratic project and has to be grasped if the *raison d'etre* of democracy is to be understood" (Held, 1995, p. 145). In turn, the principle of autonomy is complemented and given practical expression by the right and principle of self-determination.

Second, Roth's critique is contestable because it ignores the unequal status of Western versus non-Western states in the international system. Consider the first human right, given in Article 1 of the two main human rights covenants: "All peoples have the right of self-determination. By virtue of that right they freely determine their political status and freely pursue their economic, social and cultural development" (International Covenant on Civil and Political Rights, 999 UNTS 171, 6 ILM 368 (1967), Art.1; International Covenant on Economic, Social and Cultural Rights, 993 UNTS 3, 6 ILM 360 (1967), Art. 1). There is sufficient historical evidence to show that, contrary to Roth's contention, the Third World, since 1945, has not enjoyed equal status with First World states in the process of determining the respective development of the economic, social, and cultural rights of the peoples contained within those regions. In fact, a more persuasive case may be made for the proposition that "while it is generally regarded as a positive, empowering term in discussion of state sovereignty and international law, recognition may be linked to specific cultural practices, resulting in the delegitimation of claims to authority made on behalf of territories and peoples with non-Western cultural traditions" (Biersteker and Weber, 1996, p. 12).

The very fact that many nations and their peoples are non-Western has made cosmopolitan democracy and inclusionary governance an exception to previous forms of governance. This also holds true for the practice of power and establishment of justice on an international scale. Understood in this way, the growth of rates of poverty, the increases in political marginalization, and the unequal distribution of wealth, have largely been the consequence of a system of sovereignty in which the recognition of the legitimtate claims and rights of non-Western peoples and nations have been historically and systematically denied credence. The exclusion of an ethical consideration of a right to wealth is among the casualties of the old Westphalian system and even the UN Charter system. However, such a right to wealth "may ultimately be necessary if sovereignty is ever to be fully realized by Third World states" (*Id.*, p. 12).

While ex-colonial states have been internationally enfranchised with juridical statehood, at the same time many have not been empowered domestically and lack the institutional features of sovereign states as defined by classical international law, thereby disclosing the fact that they enjoy limited empirical statehood (Jackson, 1990, p. 21). These limitations are disclosed in many states having grave deficiencies in their political will, institutional authority, and organized power to protect human rights or provide socioeconomic welfare for all of their peoples. Because these states are primarily juridical constructions, with the benefits of sovereignty denied to the citizenry at large, they have been termed "quasi-states" (*Id.*, p. 21).

Third and finally, Roth's critique is contestable because it ignores the negative effects of neo-liberalism, neo-colonialism, and neo-imperialism. While Roth and other commentators may applaud decolonization, they too easily ignore the effects of the negative sovereignty regime that replaced the old order imposed by colonialism and imperialism. Alternative institutional arrangements which might have better served the needs of particular colonial populations were ruled out with the triumph of legal uniformity, in the form of juridical sovereignty. This was the historical result of continued domination by the Western powers (through other means) in an emerging world of states that was highly pluralistic in many respects (*Id.*, p. 198). Power asymmetries have continued, even after the collapse of the Cold War paradigm and with the extension of those processes of financial expansion which come under the rubric of "globalization." In this regard, "violations of the basic rule of Westphalian sovereignty have occurred more frequently than violations of the basic rule of international legal sovereignty and have been more explicitly justified by alternative principles" (Krasner, 1999, p. 9).

In sum, a point should be made regarding the connection between the basic rule of Westphalian sovereignty on the one hand, and the international institutions and actors which impinge on it in the name of globalization on the other. According to Ian Clark, "those difficulties with which the contemporary democratic state is apparently beset are symptomatic of the way in which state transformation and the international order are reshaping each other" (Clark, 1999, p. 165). It is Clark's contention that there is a dialectic in international relations. While some critics of the international order posit that "the democratic shortcomings of the contemporary state have arisen because of the growth of globalized forces that disempower it from the outside," it is Clark's contention that "such an analysis fails to take due account of the reciprocal manner in which democratic deficits on the inside have been the necessary accomplices of globalization" (*Id.*, pp. 165–166). I argue, along these lines, that many democracies are hampered by a democratic deficit that needs to be overcome. That is why I argue, in Chapter 2 and elsewhere throughout this book, that inclusionary governance is the antidote to these exclusionary impulses. It is my contention that even states that are labeled "democratic states" may, in fact, be exclusionary states by virtue of their policies, by how they treat their domestic constituencies in the name of "majoritarian" or "representative" democracy because many millions are left effectively excluded from participation in the actual decision making processes that affect their lives. Hence, the deepening of democracy demands inclusionary states with inclusionary policies, procedures, and remedies that are constitutionally guaranteed.

As we contemplate the deepening of democracy on a global basis, in this kind of world order, we are struck by the way in which political and economic elites that insist on carrying out the Social Darwinian mandates of the international financial community (G-7, IMF, World Bank, GATT) serve to make the realization of new forms of inclusionary democracy increasingly unlikely. Yet neither can these states attempt to be democratic and carry out the World Bank's economic cure, a cure "which generally includes cutbacks in already miserly social spending, freezing already low wages, encouraging massive layoffs, and letting prices find their 'natural' level" (Denitch, 1996, p. 28).

In this environment, it is increasingly recognized that the international system is dramatically changing. James Rosenau suggests in *Turbulence in World Politics* that the scope of activities over which states can effectively control is declining. New issues have emerged such as "atmospheric pollution, terrorism, the drug trade, currency crises, and AIDs" which are the product of either interdependence or new technologies. Because these issues are transnational rather than national, states can no longer provide solutions for them. (Rosenau, 1990, p. 13). Hence, the limits of sovereignty are exposed as the capacity of individual nation-states to successfully address their domestic challenges diminishes.

E. COVENANT FOR A NEW DEMOCRATIC ORDER

The decline of state capacity should not merely become a requiem for sovereignty. Rather, pursuant to the legal tradition and normative thrust of the International Covenant on Civil and Political Rights, the Covenant may serve as the grounding for a new democratic order of international dimensions, capable of making the right of self-determination applicable to the citizens of all nations. Employed in this manner, the Covenant transforms the dimensions of citizenship by empowering citizens and civil society to confront the injustices of the international system. This is clearly the intention of the Covenant insofar as it entitles citizens to determine their collective political status through democratic means (Franck, 1992, p. 58). In this context, duties and moral obligations transcend the historical boundaries, prohibitions and axioms of older forms of world order. The international justice aspects of the growth/equity dilemma now are issue areas that can be transformed because they "relate to the duties to alleviate distress, which are specified as economic and social rights of those so victimized, and to the moral obligation to adopt policies that diminish inequities between countries, regions, races and civilizations" (Falk, 1999(c), p. 432). The idea of distributive justice, from this point of view, signifies that there is a growing recognition of the duty of the rich to ensure distribution sufficient to meet the basic needs of the poor, on a global level (Beitz, 1979, pp. 129–176).

In this connection, distributive justice concerns are intimately linked to the right of self-determination, for self-determination creates rights for all citizens (inclusively), entitling them to determine not only their collective political status through democratic means, but also raise issues regarding the accountability of those sites and forms of power which presently operate beyond the scope of democratic control (Held, 1999, p. 449). The cosmopolitan model of democracy is an attempt at specifying the principles and institutional arrangements for making unaccountable sites and forms of power subject to democratic control. In so doing, the cosmopolitan model of democracy is "not a theory of the state, or a theory of the international order, but a theory of the changing place of the democratic state within the international order" (Held, 1991, p. 223). In sum, cosmopolitan democracy recognizes that "the meaning and place of democracy have to be rethought in relation to a series of overlapping local, regional and global structures and processes" (*Id.*, p. 222). In this respect, democracy shares some of the characteristics and challenges of globalization itself.

Insofar as globalization is neither a singular condition nor a linear process, "it is best thought of as a multidimensional phenomenon involving diverse domains of activity and interaction, including the economic, political, technological, military, legal, cultural and environmental" (Held, 1998, p. 13). Similarly, the institutional framework for a new democratic international order cannot be properly conceived without the means of law enforcement coupled with a new institutional framework. This means that the achievement of democratic autonomy "must be conceived as based on the multiple lodging of the rights and obligations of democratic law in the organizational charters of the agencies and associations which make up the spheres of politics, economics and civil society" (Held, 1995, p. 277). With this challenge acknowledged, there is the concommitant realization that "an expanding democratic network of states and societies is incompatible with the existence of powerful social relations and economic organizations which can . . . systematically distort democratic conditions and processes" (*Id.*, p. 277).

In this regard, the great task will be to embark upon reconciling the promotion of economic growth with concerns about equity, and especially with the protection of those who are most economically disadvantaged or vulnerable (Falk, 1999(c), p. 430). Falk has argued that this rethinking is already under way on the part of Bretton Woods institutions which "may well point toward a new balance between a purely economic view of growth and a more normative concern with overcoming human suffering and inequality" (*Id.*, p. 433). In this task, both textually and in practice, it seems that the international system is moving toward a clearly designated democratic entitlement, "with national governance validated by international standards and systematic monitoring of compliance" (Franck, 1992, p. 91). In terms of its ultimate achievement, some have optimistically declared that "the entitlement now aborning is widely enough understood to be almost universally celebrated" (*Id.*, p. 90).

F. BUILDING THE INSTITUTIONAL AND LEGAL FRAMEWORK FOR A NEW DEMOCRATIC INSTITUTIONAL ORDER

The right to an entitlement requires the legal and institutional capacity to claim the right. The right to the "democratic entitlement" is no exception. In other words, rights without remedies are neither salutory in judicial rulings nor in the arena of political life. In the case of an emerging right to democratic governance, the transition from the articulation of the right to the consolidation of it is a long path. Its promotion and protection will be by means of a collective international process (Franck, 1992, p. 46). The emerging right to a functional democratic entitlement needs to be located within the matrix of political legitimacy and legal consent in an emerging international system of rules. At the dawn of the 21st century, it may be argued that the democratic entitlement has acquired a sufficient degree of legitimacy to undergird such an entitlement by virtue of its association with a much broader panopoly of laws pertaining to the rights of persons vis-a-vis their governments.

The nature of legitimacy is measured by four indicators: *pedigree, determinancy, coherence and adherence*. In this context, "*pedigree* refers to the depth of the rule's roots in a historical process; *determinancy* refers to the rule's ability to communicate content; *coherence* refers to the rule's internal consistency and lateral connectedness to the principles underlying other rules; and *adherence* refers to the rule's vertical connectedness to a normative hierarchy, culminating in an ultimate rule of recognition, which embodies the principled purposes and values that define the community of states" (Franck, 1992, p. 51). The legal hypothesis that follows from this list of indicators of legitimacy (in reference to the emerging right to democratic governance) is that the degree to which a rule, or a rulemaking process, exhibits these four qualities will determine the degree to which the rule or the process has matured and is perceived to be legitimate.

One such rule or principle would be the concept of *pacta sunt servanda*, the notion that promises should be kept. Unless states have first accepted this principle, it would be next to impossible to regard any treaty as binding. Similarly, the notion of authoritative state practice (even in the absence of a formal agreement) constitutes a key element of customary international law (Arend, 1999, p. 52). In principle and practice, international law can be seen as customary law, for the international legal system is one that has developed so as to accommodate itself to the fact that for much of its history "nothing remotely resembling a central law-applying institution has existed" (Nardin, 1983, p. 166). Even in the 20th century, with the establishment of the United Nations (whose various branches, committees, and associated agencies provide a forum for the application of international law) and the International Court of Justice, centralized law-application exists only in rudimentary form. In the absence of a central law-applying institution, the question becomes: How can the international community build a legal framework for a new democratic institutional framework that is global in its scope? Related to this question is the following: How can we measure whether the democratic entitlement has acquired a degree of legitimacy sufficient enough to connect it to a broader collection of rights, already existent in international law, which would pertain to the rights of persons via-a-vis their governments?

To begin with, the "basic norm" of international law has appears to be little more than the principle, itself a part of customary international law, that states are legally obligated to obey customary international law. International customary law has evolved to encompass rights—human rights, civil rights, minority rights, and even the right to democratic governance. Of all the international declarations of rights, the European Convention on the Protection of Human Rights and Fundamental Freedoms (1950) is especially noteworthy in this regard. It stands in marked contrast to the Universal Declaration of Human Rights and the subsequent UN Covenants of Rights. What makes it unique is embodied in its preamble: "to take the first steps for the collective enforcement of certain of the rights stated in the Universal Declaration." According to Held, "the European initiative was and remains a most radical legal innovation: an innovation which, against the stream of state history, allows individual citizens to initiate proceedings against their own governments" (Held, 1999(b), p. 101). What this innovation signifies is a major shift away from the absolute principle that state sovereignty must be safeguarded, irrespective of its consequences for individuals, groups, and organizations. Insofar as specific entitlements of rights have been accruing to individual citizens through various international law instruments throughout the 20th century, then, it follows that the emerging democratic entitlement may have played a dual role. First, it has undercut the principle of sovereignty as an absolute and inviolable norm. Second, it has correspondingly opened up the public, political, legal, and economic space for citizens to rely on these instruments in claiming rights to free and equal participation in governance.

In short, this innovation is seen as legitimate insofar as the various texts and instruments of international law that encompass rights speak of similar goals and deploy, for the most part, "a similar range of processes for monitoring compliance, several of which have already become common usage in connection with the democratic entitlement" (Franck, 1992, p. 79). The emerging legitimacy of the democratic entitlement, in other words, meets the criteria embodied in the four indicators of legitimacy—pedigree, determinacy, coherence, and adherence.

The application of these indicators to the innovations involved in the European Convention on the Protection of Human Rights and Fundamental Freedoms is reflective of the fact that, to a signficant extent, international law exists in the practice of states "because it exists in the minds of a class of legal professionals." In fact, it is because of what these professionals understand as international law that this understanding is accepted by others as a rule of customary international law. In this regard, "as this acceptance varies, so does the reality of international law as a factor in the relations of states" (Nardin, 1983, p. 173). Acceptance and understanding in this legal arena reflects the fact that customary international law has evolved to a point where "international law recognized rights of peoples and communities which transcend state authority and traditional conceptions of sovereignty. And, the international community as a whole has transgressed sovereign borders in the name of human rights, or at least with a recognition that human rights issues do not fall within 'domestic jurisdiction'" (Mills, 1998, p. 194). Similarly, David Held has noted that "there are significant areas and regions marked by cross-cutting loyalties, conflicting interpretations of rights and duties, interconnected legal and authority structures . . . which displace notions of sovereignty as an illimitable, indivisible, and exclusive form of public power" (Held, 1999(b), p. 103). This trend in international law means that "cosmopolitan law would demand the subordination of regional, national, and local sovereignties to an overarching legal framework, but in this framework associations would be self-governing at different levels" (*Id.*, p. 107).

In this view, the cosmopolitan model of democracy arises as "a legal basis of a global and divided authority system, a system of diverse and overlapping power centers, shaped and delimited by democratic law." This model, at its core, recognizes that the nature and quality of democratic relations among communities are interlocked and that "new legal and organizational mechanisms must be created if democracy is to prosper" (*Id.*, p. 107). Cosmopolitan governance recognizes that people would embark upon multiple citizenships and participate, as members, in the diverse communities which significantly affect them. The prospects for a sustainable democratic practice would, in large measure, become increasingly *inclusionary*.

As in the Europe of the 16th to 17th centuries, in the midst of civil wars, religious strife, and fragmented authority, at the dawn of the 21st century a new concept of the state and citizenship is emerging. At the close of the 20th century, the idea of global citizenship and the emerging right to democratic governance is revelatory of the need to make a comparable transition. The UN is one institutional source, among others, around which other innovative structures and strategies may be designed to incorporate the claims associated with the democratic entitlement. From issues of participation and equality, to issues of rights and basic human needs, the scope of the UN's work can assist in the task of institution-building, design, and creation, so as to incorporate the ideals and claims of the entitlement into global practice. Also, as a normative resource, it has the capacity and the emerging vision to fashion forums through which nations might better cooperate to resolve common challenges and common problems. This is especially the case with the management of inequality between unequal sovereign states.

The whole history of 20th century international law reflects the engagement of customary law in the management of inequality in traditional sovereignty-based accounts of international law. Throughout the 20th century, strategies for reconciling the sovereign equality system with existing inequalities has been at the center of a paradigm shift in international law. Still, the principles of self-determination and minority rights, while formulated as universal principles, have been applied only selectively in practice. At the close of the 20th century, however, these principles have gained greater significance as advances have been made in humanitarian law, humanitarian intervention, and self-determination. These developments underscore the reality that external sovereignty is being eroded by the facts of interdependence, as well as by international norms for the protection of human rights. The widening and overlapping of spheres of interdependence expose a new frontier of human experience where globalization, in spite of its predatory components, may also unleash the potential for greater humanization vis-a-vis international law and new institutions designed to specifically promote democratic and inclusionary forms of governance.

With respect to the principle of sovereignty and its historical claims, Stanley Hoffmann has identified a workable resolution to this problem with his observation that "we need to move to a situation in which it is clearly understood, and enshrined in international law, that sovereignty is justified by and limited to the protection of the polity from outside threats and interference and to the provision of order, justice, welfare, and self-government"

(Hoffmann, 1999, p. 232). Beyond this, he argues that sovereignty should be subject to "the authority of international and regional organizations with the right and power to enforce these restrictions, to ensure collective security, and to protect human rights both through collective interventions and through a system of international criminal justice" (*Id.*, p. 232).

Already, the international community has established the Rwanda Tribunal and the Yugoslavia Tribunal, pursuant to the Nuremberg principle, to deal with human rights violations and genocide. In terms of the legal basis for its establishment, the Rwanda Tribunal was established by the Security Council, acting under Chapter VII of the United Nations Charter, at the request of Rwanda, in contrast to the circumstances that led to the establishment of the Yugoslavia Tribunal (Morris and Scharf, 1998, p. xvi). These tribunals are, in many respects, the products of the emergence of a transnational civil society in which "states should be seen simply as important loci of power and authority within a transnational civil society which permeates their borders" (Kingsbury, 1999, p. 80). In this new global arena, international law can be seen as the law of an emerging transnational society. In sum, international law is increasingly seen as "regulating states, but not dependent entirely on states for its existence, content, or implementation" (*Id.*, p. 80).

With respect to international legal rules, the depth and density of rules promulgated by inter-governmental organizations is certainly increasing. These organizations are becoming more assertive visa-a-vis individual sovereign states in rulemaking as well as in implementation. In this new arena of legal development, progress toward equality (as an aspect of the democratic entitlement) has been almost continuously anticipated in international law: in Wilsonian or Leninist versions of self-determination, in the Class "A" mandates of the League of Nations, in the provisions for trusteeship and decolonization under the UN Charter, in the hopes for general and complete disarmament in various UN documents (Kingsbury, 1999, p. 77).

When inevitable shortcomings appear in the attainment of equality, they are explained by the relative infancy and weakness of international law in this arena. Therefore, the fact that enduring inequalities among sovereigns still exist, such as the structural inequalities in the UN Charter, the Nuclear Non-Proliferation Treaty, or voting arrangements in the IMF, are simply characterized as either functional exceptions or as temporary accommodations to the realities of power (*Id.*, p. 77).

At the dawn of the 21st century, the rules and processes for realizing self-determination, freedom of expression and electoral rights constitute a bright line which is linked to the concept of democratic entitlement and a corresponding effort to undertake the issues associated with structural inequalities within the international system. A common purpose has emerged for all persons to assume responsibility in the shaping of the kind of civil society in which they live and work. This common purpose is buttressed by a large normative canon for promoting that objective: the UN Charter, the Universal Declaration of Human Rights, the International Covenant on Civil and Political Rights, the International Convention on the Elimination of All Forms of Racial Discrimination, the International Convention on the

Suppression and Punishment of the Crime of Apartheid, the Declaration on the Elimination of All Forms of Intolerance and Discrimination Based on Religion or Belief, and the Convention on the Elimination of All Forms of Discrimination Against Women. Additionally, these universally based rights are supplemented by regional instruments such as the European Convention for the Protection of Human Rights and Fundmental Freedoms, the American Convention on Human Rights, the African Charter on Human and People's Rights, the Copenhagen Document, and the Paris Charter.

Each of these instruments "recognizes related specific entitlements as accruing to individual citizens" and "constitutes internationally mandated restraints on governments." As such, "they embody rights of free and equal participation in governance" with the result being "a net of participatory entitlement." Thus, "the democratic entitlement has acquired a degree of legitimacy by association with a far broader panoply of laws pertaining to the rights of persons vis-a-vis their governments" (Franck, 1992, p. 79).

The ramifications of this entitlement reverberate around the globe. The advent of democratic forms of government is expected to increase political participation, as well as widen the scope for public involvement in the public policy process (Robinson, 1999, p. 180). As this trend proceeds, however, this relationship should not be viewed as axiomatic, as the socioeconomic conditions prevalent in many developing countries limit the extent to which the poor and socially marginalized groups can effectively play an active role in shaping public policy. The central problem, in this regard, is that access to the public policy-making and decision-making processes remains largely confined to groups with wealth, power, and resources who are able to more effectively represent their members' entrenched concerns (*Id.*, p. 180). Hence, while democratization widens the scope for popular participation in formal politics, participation remains by and large restricted to campaigning and voting in periodic elections, while the public policy domain remains relatively impervious to popular influence.

The task of opening the domain of public policy to the poor, marginalized, excluded, and dispossessed is a challenge that inclusionary governance, as a concept and as a mandate, is specifically designed to overcome. Based on the evidence so far, there is every indication that "attempts to design institutions that promote political participation are fraught with difficulty. Entrenched inequalities in the rural power structure and scarce educational and organizational resources on the part of poor and marginalized groups limit the effectiveness of such reforms" (Robinson, 1999, p. 181). However, democratic structures can create the institutional space for political parties and popular organizations to function as effective intermediaries on behalf of poor and socially marginalized groups. At the same time, however, "the pervasiveness of structural and organizational constraints on autonomous participation throws into sharp relief the limitations of institutional innovation in the absence of political mediation and more fundamental socio-economic reforms" (*Id.*, p. 182). This obervation is not new. In 1936, John Maynard Keyes stated that "the outstanding faults of the economic society in which we live are its failure to provide for full employment and its arbitary and inequitable distribution of wealth and incomes" (Keynes, 1936, p. 372).

The task of *inclusionary goverance*, as will be argued throughout this book, is to identify those areas in national and international life where areas of political mediation may be opened up and created so as to assist people in engaging in fundamental socioeconomic reforms as an aspect of the "democratic entitlement." In other words, *inclusionary governance*, in concept and in practice, recognizes that institutional design *"from above"* must be complemented by political intervention *"from below."* The thrust and purpose of *inclusionary governance* is to facilitate this dual movement and interchange between people in the task of governance. For without a coordination between institutional design *"from above"* with political intervention *"from below,"* efforts at democratization will remain hollow, incomplete, and never reach full consolidation. In short, "democratization" (understood as a process) should not be confused or conflated with the "democratic entitlement" (as a body of legal rights, located within the matrix of international law covenants, charters, and UN instruments).

G. CONCLUSION

The end of the 20th century has led to a plethora of viewpoints and interpretations on the subject of global governance. Among these interpretations, one comes in the form of a question: "Is there a Third World?" (Martin, 1999, p. 355). There are many nuances to the question insofar as "the concept of a monolithic third world not only conceals differences in basic economic and social development, but also hides the transformation experienced by different poor countries over the past several decades." Yet, after all is said and done, there comes the recognition that "while it is relatively easy to dismantle an intellectual contruct like the third world, it is much harder to devise suitable alternatives. And alternative designations are sorely needed if we are to grasp a global geography where divisions are continually being produced and reproduced between wealthy people and places, and between poor people and places" (*Id.*, p. 358). In a world constituted by such radical divisions, it is no longer tenable to make the mistake of regarding any particular civilization as the centerpiece for the drama of human history. Yet, this tendency characterizes Western triumphalism in the post-Cold War era in a manner similar to Britain's 19th century triumphalism in the era of Queen Victoria.

In spite of triumphalism, there is the persistent reminder that great powers rise and fall, that "progress" is not inevitable, that there is no such thing as an "unchanging East," that Spengler's assumption that there is "only one river of civilization" and that "all others are either tributary to it or lost in the desert sands" is inherently flawed (Spengler, 1926–1928), that there need not be a predetermined "clash of civilizations" (Huntington, 1996). Rather, the 20th century is testimony to the evolution of a "multi-centric world" in which many actors transcend the authority networks of the "state-centric world" (Rosenau, 1990, pp. 250–251). In short, "the frequency of anomalies seems too great to ignore or rationalize. Each might be explicable by a particular set of historical circumstances, but taken together as a series of exceptions, they culminate to a pattern that is not easily explained" (*Id.*, p. 93). In recognition of the fact that one explanatory framework cannot suffice, "one is moved to investigate the possibility that world politics has become a turbulent field, that the complexities and dynamism unleashed by postindustrial technologies are so extreme as to have shattered the primary parameters of the global system" (*Id.*, p. 100).

We find ourselves not at "the end of history," but at the beginning of history—a history that concludes ages of exclusionary governance and opens paths to an inclusionary future that is global in its dimensions. The global dimensions of inclusionary governance expose the dimensions of an age that strives toward new normative priorities. In this connection, "even under ideal conditions, where the depredations of wild capitalism are controlled and the economy achieves a certain self-regulation, markets have a limited capacity to generate what a society needs" (Barber, 1995, p. 239).

The old world of exclusionary governance, based on the preservation of nation-state sovereignty immune from the claims of the democratic entitlement, is in the process of being replaced by the processes of inclusionary governance as the expansion of outcomes favoring human rights, justice, and an equitable distribution of wealth emerges. As early as 1981, Amir Jamal asserted that man was at the center of economic purpose. As such, he asked: "Should not the North ask the South to draft a charter for a new IMF which would receive constructive scrutiny and which could lead to the beginning of a deliberative process of change? Why not accept that the world is a vastly different place from the time of Bretton Woods, and that the most needed structural change today is in the Bretton Woods institutions themselves?" (Jamal, 1981, p. 120). Two decades later, as if in response, Amartya Sen, winner of the Nobel Prize in Economics, declared: "Development requires the removal of major sources of unfreedom: poverty as well as tyranny, poor economic opportunities as well as systematic social deprivation, neglect of public facilities as well as intolerance or overactivity of repressive states" (Sen, 1999, p. 4).

Significantly, the idea that "freedom is central to the process of development" was authoritatively posited for two congruent reasons: "(1) the evaluative reason: assessment of progress has to be done primarily in terms of whether the freedoms that people have are enhanced; (2) the effectiveness reason: achievement of development is thoroughly dependent on the free agency of people" (Sen, 1999, p. 4). Both rationales for centralizing the practice of freedom in the process of development underscore the importance of inclusionary governance, conceived of as a means of expanding, widening, and deepening the avenues that lead towards the realization of the democratic entitlement. At its most basic level, the idea of development of freedom finds its starting point in the principle of "protective security." According to Sen, protective security is needed "to provide a social safety net for preventing the afflicted population from being reduced to abject misery, and in some cases even starvation and death." In order to implement this principle, "the domain of protective security includes *fixed* institutional arrangements such as unemployment benefits and statutory income supplements to the indigent as well as ad hoc arrangements such as famine relief or emergency public employment to generate income for destitutes" (*Id.*, p. 40).

Conceived in the broader terms of history and international law, these aspects of an emergent normative framework for inclusionary governance resonate with the claims of the Universal Declaration of Human Rights. The radical nature of the Universal Declaration's norms, agreed upon and periodically affirmed, "can be appreciated by reference to Article 25 . . . which promises every person 'the right to a standard of living' sufficient to satisfy basic human needs, and Article 28, which insists that everyone 'is entitled to a social and international order in which the rights and freedoms set forth in this Declaration can be fully realized'." (Falk, 1999(b), p. 174).

International law and economic thinking are progressively moving toward a point of convergence (Marshall, 1995, pp. 50–68). As these instruments of governments move toward this point, the outlines of inclusionary governance come into sharper focus (Kapstein, 1999). As the practice and concept of civil society have been spurred by the revolutionary events in Eastern Europe, South Africa, and several Latin American countries, where well-ensconced authoritarian regimes crumbled after failing to sustain resistance movements of ordinary citizens in voluntary associations, there has been greater movement toward incorporating the norms of international human rights law and those of inclusionary governance.

The injustice of domination and oppression, which had inhibited or prevented people from participating in decision-making processes that affected their lives, could not sustain the systematic institutional processes that have artificially buttressed these exclusionary states (Young, 1999, p. 142; Dandler, 1999, pp. 116–151; Reis, 1996, pp. 121–137; Weeks, 1995, pp. 109–135; Vilas, 1995, pp. 137–163; Loveman, 1999, pp. 253–285). In both First and Third World arenas, the thrust of the democratic entitlement has met with measured success. One major lesson to be drawn from this trend is that, while "those who value democracy should recognize that there is nothing inevitable about its survival," they should also recognize that "there will always be forces that stand to lose from democracy's advance. They will oppose it. They will usually be powerful and they will sometimes prevail. But not always. Hence, the importance of working to achieve democracy, and to entrench it" (Shapiro, 1999, p. 239; see also White, 1999, pp. 17–51).

As inclusionary forces and impulses progressively become participatory, their procedural, juridical, and political institutionalization will remake world order and transform the nature of global governance. The relationship between democracy and public policy, for example, can escape the boundaries of purely instrumentalist terms and move toward a point where cosmopolitan democracies incorporate features which are a blend of the technical and procedural practice of democracy with its normative and substantive claims. In so doing, the interconnections and emergent properties of the democratic entitlement and inclusionary governance will be empowered to generate more humane outcomes (Jervis, 1997). While such a future is not guaranteed, it at least has positive implications for new regional and institutional alignments, such as the European Union (EU) (Falk and Szentes, 1997). The classic example is Ernst Haas's analysis of the spillover processes of regional integration in which "decisionmakers seek limited cooperation but the policies they adopt for this purpose trigger changes in laws, incentives, interest group strategies, and eventually loyalties that lead to much greater integration" (Jervis, 1999, p. 59).

The possibilities for greater integration lead to greater possibilities for realizing inclusionary governance. In this regard, "numerous studies have drawn attention to the importance of the character of the political system as a key determinant of the form and character of the public policy process, which refers to the manner in which government policy is deliberated, formulated, and implemented" (Robinson, 1999, p. 163). The character of inclusionary governance is found in its capacity for and adherence to policy deliberations and political outcomes which reflect the totality of the global village. As such, inclusionary governance transforms the democratic entitlement from a mere chimera to the incarnation of freedom in practice.

BIBLIOGRAPHY

Gabriel Almond, "Capitalism and Democracy," *PS: Political Science and Politics*, 24:467–74.

Anthony Clark Arend, *Legal Rules and International Society*, Oxford University Press, 1999.

Giovanni Arrighi and Beverly J. Silver, *Chaos and Governance in the Modern World*, University of Minnesota Press, 1999.

Benjamin R. Barber, *Jihad vs. McWorld*, Time Books, 1995.

Charles R. Beitz, *Political Theory and International Relations*, Princeton University Press, 1979.

Waldon Bello, *Dark Victory: The United States, Structural Adjustment and Global Poverty*, Pluto Press with Food First and Transnational Institute, 1994.

Thomas J. Biersteker and Cynthia Weber, *State Sovereignty as Social Construct*, Cambridge University Press, 1996.

Ken Booth, editor, *Statecraft and Security: The Cold War and Beyond*, Cambridge University Press, 1998.

Michael E. Brown, "The Causes and Regional Dimensions of Internal Conflict," *The International Dimensions of Internal Conflict*, edited by Michael E. Brown, The MIT Press, 1996.

Manuel Castells, *End of Millenium—The Information Age: Economy, Society and Culture*, Volume III, Blackwell Publishers, 1998.

Catherine Caufield, *Masters of Illusion: The World Bank and the Poverty of Nations*, Henry Holt and Company, 1996.

Antonia Handler Chayes and Abraham Chayes, "Mobilizing International and Regional Organizations for Managing Ethnic Conflict," *International Law and Ethnic Conflict*, edited by David Wippman, Cornell University Press, 1998.

Micel Chossudovsky, "Global Poverty in the Late 20th Century," *Journal of International Affairs*, Volume 52, No. 1, Fall 1998.

Ian Clark, *Globalization and International Relations Theory*, Oxford University Press, 1999.

Charles Covell, *Kant and the Law of Peace: A Study in the Philosophy of International Law and International Relations*, St. Martin's Press, Inc., 1998.

Robert W. Cox, "Towards a Post-Hegemonic Conceptualization of World Order: Reflections on the Relevancy of Ibn Khaldun," *Governance Without Government: Order and Change in World Politics*, edited by James N. Rosenau and Ernst-Otto Czempiel, Cambridge University Press, 1992.

Jorge Dandler, "Indigenous Peoples and the Rule of Law in Latin America: Do They Have a Chance?," *The (Un)Rule of Law in Latin America*, edited by Juam E. Mendez, Guillermo O'Donnell, and Paul S. Pinheiro, University of Notre Dame Press, 1999.

Bogdan Denitch, "Democracy and the New World Order: Dilemmas and Conflicts," *Social Justice*, Vol. 23, Nos. 1–2, Spring-Summer 1996.

Larry Diamond, *Developing Democracy: Toward Consolidation*, The Johns Hopkins University Press, 1999.
Giuseppe Di Palma, "Market, State, and Citizenship in New Democracies," *Inequality, Democracy, and Economic Development*, edited by Manus I. Midlarsky, Cambridge University Press, 1997.
John Dunn, "Democracy and Development?," *Democracy's Value*, edited by Ian Shapiro and Casiano Hacker-Cordon, Cambridge University Press, 1999.
Richard A. Falk, *The Status of Law in International Society*, Princeton University Press, 1970.
Richard A. Falk, *A Study of Future Worlds*, The Free Press, 1975.
Richard Falk, *Human Rights and State Sovereignty*, Holmes & Meier Publishers, Inc., 1981.
Richard A. Falk, *Explorations at the Edge of Time: The Prospects for World Order*, Temple University Press, 1992.
Richard Falk, Robert C. Johansen, and Samuel S. Kim, editors, *The Constitutional Foundations of World Peace*, State University of New York Press, 1993(a).
Richard Falk, "Democratic Disguise: Post-Cold War Authoritarianism," *Altered States: A Reader in the New World Order*, edited by Phyllis Bennis and Michel Moushabeck, Olive Branch Press, New York, 1993(b).
Richard Falk, *On Humane Governance: Toward a New Global Politics*, The Pennsylvania State University Press, 1995.
Richard A. Falk and Tamas Szentes, editors, *A New Europe in the Changing Global System*, United Nations University Press, 1997.
Richard Falk, "The United Nations and Cosmopolitan Democracy: Bad Dream, Utopian Fantasy, Political Project," *Re-Imagining Political Community: Studies in Cosmopolitan Democracy*, edited by Daniele Archibugi, David Held and Martin Kohler, Stanford University Press, 1998(a).
Richard Falk, *Law in an Emerging Global Village: A Post-Westphalian Perspective*, Transnational Publishers, Inc., 1998(b).
Richard Falk, "World Orders, Old and New," *Current History*, Vol. 98, No. 624, January 1999(a).
Richard A. Falk, *Predatory Globalization: A Critique*, Polity Press, 1999(b).
Richard Falk, "The Pursuit of International Justice: Present Dilemmas and an Imagined Future," *Journal of International Affairs*, Vol. 52, No. 2, Spring 1999(c).
Richard Falk, "The New Interventionism and the Third World," *Current History: A Journal of Contemporary World Affairs*, November 1999(d).
Thomas M. Franck, "The Emerging Right to Democratic Governance," *American Journal of International Law*, Vol. 86, 1992.
Thomas M. Franck, *Fairness in International Law and Institutions*, Clarendon Press, Oxford, 1995.
Johan Galtung, "Global Governance for and by Global Democracy," *Issues In Global Governance: Papers written for the Commission on Global Governance*, Kluwer Law International, in association with The Commission on Global Governance, 1995.
Manuel Antonio Garreton, "Social and Economic Transformations in Latin

Preface to Inclusionary Governance 47

America: The Emergence of a New Political Matrix?," *Markets and Democracy in Latin America: Conflict or Convergence*, edited by Philip Oxhorn and Pamela K. Starr, Lynne Rienner Publishers, 1999.

Jiom George, *Discourses of Global Politics: A Critical (Re) Introduction to International Relations*, Lynne Rienner Publishers, 1994.

Peter Gowan, *The Global Gamble: Washington's Faustian Bid for World Dominance*, Verso, 1999.

Graham Hancock, *Lords of Poverty: The Power, Prestige, and Corruption of the International Aid Business*, The Atlantic Monthly Press, 1989.

Andreas Hasenclever, Peter Mayer, and Volker Rittberger, *Theories of International Regimes*, Cambridge University Press, 1997.

David Held, "Democracy, the Nation-State and the Global System," *Political Theory Today*, edited by David Held, Stanford University Press, 1991.

David Held, "Democracy: From City-States to a Cosmopolitan Order?," *Prospects for Democracy: North, South, East, West*, edited by David Held, Stanford University Press, 1993.

David Held, *Democracy and the Global Order: From the Modern State to Cosmopolitan Governance*, Stanford University Press, 1995.

David Held, "Democracy and Globalization," *Re-Imagining Political Community: Studies in Cosmopolitan Democracy*, edited by Daniele Archibugi, David Held and Martin Kohler, Stanford University Press, 1998.

David Held and Anthony McGrew, David Goldblatt and Jonathan Perraton, *Global Transformations: Politics, Economics and Culture*, Stanford University Press, 1999(a).

David Held, "The Transformation of Political Community: Rethinking Democracy in the Context of Globalization," *Democracy's Edges*, edited by Ian Shapiro and Casiano Hacker-Cordon, Cambridge University Press, 1999(b).

Louis Henkin, "International Law: Politics, Values and Functions," 216 *Recueil des Cours* (Hague Acad. Int'l L.) 22 (1989–IV), as quoted in, Burns H. Weston, Richard A. Falk, Hilary Charlesworth, *International Law and World Order*, A Problem-Oriented Coursebook, Third Edition, West Group, 1997, p. 23.

Stanley Hoffmann, *World Disorders: Troubled Peace in the Post-Cold War Era*, Rowman and Littlefield Publishers, Inc., 1998.

Samuel P. Huntington, *The Clash of Civilizations and the Remaking of World Order*, Simon & Schuster, 1996.

Andrew Hurrell, "Security and Inequality," *Inequality, Globalization, and World Politics*, edited by Andrew Hurrell and Ngaire Woods, Oxford University Press, 1999.

Naeem Inayatullah, "Beyond the Sovereignty Dilemma: Quasi-States as Social Construct," *State Sovereignty as Social Construct*, edited by Thomas J. Biersteker and Cynthia Weber, Cambridge University Press, 1996.

Robert H. Jackson, *Quasi-States: Sovereignty, International Relations and the Third World*, Cambridge University Press, 1990.

Michael Jacobs, "Sustainable Development as a Contested Concept," *Fairness And Futurity: Essays on Environmental Sustainability and Social Justice*, edited by Andres Dobson, Oxford University Press, 1999.

Amir M. Jamal, "Man at the Centre of Economic Purpose," *Third World Quarterly*, Volume 3, No. 1, January 1981.

J. Craig Jenkins and Bert Klandermans, "The Politics of Social Protest," *The Politics of Social Protest: Comparative Perspectives on States and Social Movements*, Volume 3, edited by J. Craig Jenkins and Bert Klandermans, University of Minnesota Press, 1995.

Robert Jervis, *System Effects: Complexity in Political and Social Life*, Princeton University Press, 1997.

Robert Jervis, "Realism, Neoliberalism, and Cooperation: Understanding the Debate," *International Security*, Volume 24, No. 1, Summer 1999.

Hank Johnston and Bert Klandermans, "The Cultural Analysis of Social Movements," *Social Movements and Culture*, Volume 4, edited by Hank Johnston and Bert Klandermans, University of Minnesota Press, 1995.

Mary Kaldor, *New and Old Wars: Organized Violence in a Global Era*, Stanford University Press, 1999.

Ethan B. Kapstein, *Sharing the Wealth: Workers and the World Economy*, W.W. Norton & Company, 1999.

Robert F. Kennedy, *To Seek a Newer World*, Doubleday & Co., Inc., 1967.

John Maynard Keynes, *The General Theory of Employment, Interest, and Money*, Harcourt Brace, 1964; orig. 1936.

Benedict Kingsbury, "Sovereignty and Inequality," *Inequality, Globalization, and World Politics*, edited by Andrew Hurrell and Ngaire Woods, Oxford University Press, 1999.

Stephan D. Krasner, *Sovereignty: Organized Hypocrisy*, Princeton University Press, 1999.

Hanspeter Kriesi, Ruud Koopmans, Jan Willem Duyvendak, and Marco Giugni, *New Movements in Western Europe: A Comparative Analysis*, Volume 5, University of Minnesota Press, 1995.

Martin W. Lewis, "Is There a Third World?," *Current History*, Vol. 98, No. 631, November 1999.

Arend Lijphart, *Pattern of Democracy: Government Forms and Performance in Thirty-Six Countries*, Yale University Press, 1999.

Brian Loveman, *For la Patria: Politics and the Armed Forces in Latin America*, A Scholarly Resources, Inc. Imprint, 1999.

Samuel M. Makinda, "Sovereignty and International Security: Challenges for the United Nations," 2 *Global Governance* 149, 151 (1996), quoting respectively Commission on Global Governance, *Our Global Neighborhood* (New York: Oxford Univ. Press, 1995), p. 69, and Bsarry M. Blechman, "The Intervention Dilemma," 19 *Washington Quarterly* 63, 64, Summer 1995.

Ray Marshall, "The Global Jobs Crisis," *Foreign Policy*, No. 100, Fall 1995.

Kurt Mills, *Human Rights in the Emerging Global Order: A New Sovereignty?*, St. Martin's Press, Inc., 1998.

Helen V. Milner, *Interests, Institutions, and Information: Domestic Politics and International Relations*, Princeton University Press, 1997.

Virginia Morris and Michael P. Scharf, *The International Criminal Tribunal for Rwanda*, Volume 1, Transnational Publishers, Inc., 1998.

Terry Nardin, *Law, Morality, and the Relations of States*, Princeton University Press, 1983.

James Petras and Chronis Polychroniou, "Rethinking Globalization: From the

Future to the Past," *Socialism and Democracy*, Vol. 12, Nos. 1–2, 1998.
Luiz Carolos Bresser Perira and Yoshiaki Nakano, "The Missing Social Contract: Governability and Reform in Latin America," *What Kind of Democracy? What Kind of Market?: Latin America in the Age of Neoliberalism*, edited by Philip D. Oxhorn and Graciela Ducatenzeiler, The Pennsylvania State University Press, 1998.
Fabio Wanderley Reis, "The State, the Market, and Democratic Citizenship," *Constructing Democracy: Human Rights, Citizenship, and Society in Latin America*, edited by Elizabeth Jelin and Eric Hershberg, Westview Press, 1996.
Brue Rich, *Mortgaging The Earth: The World Bank, Environmental Impoverishment, and the Crisis of Development*, Beacon Press, 1994.
Mark Robinson, "Democracy, Participation, and Public Policy: The Politics of Institutional Design," *The Democratic Developmental State: Politics and Institutional Design*, edited by Mark Robinson and Gordon White, Oxford University Press, 1998.
William I. Robinson, *Promoting Polyarchy: Globalization, US Intervention, and Hegemony*, Cambridge University Press, 1996.
James N. Rosenau, *Turbulence in World Politics: A Theory of Change and Continuity*, Princeton University Press, 1990.
James N. Rosenau and Ernst-Otto Czempiel, editors, *Governance Without Government: Order and Change in World Politics*, Cambridge University Press, 1992.
James N. Rosenau, *Along the Domestic-Foreign Frontier: Exploring Governance in a Turbulent World*, Cambridge University Press, 1997.
Brad R. Roth, *Governmental Illegitimacy in International Law*, Clarendon Press, Oxford, 1999.
Amartya Sen, *Development as Freedom*, Alfred A. Knopf, 1999.
Ian Shapiro, *Democratic Justice*, Yale University Press, 1999.
The South Commission, *The Challenge to the South*, Oxford University Press, 1990.
James Gustave Speth, "Poverty: A Denial of Human Rights," *Journal of International Affairs*, Volume 52, No. 1, Fall 1998.
Sidney Tarrow, *Power in Movement: Social Movements, Collective Action and Politics*, Cambridge University Press, 1994.
UNDP, *Human Development Report*, 1997, Oxford University Press, 1997.
John A. Vazquez, *The War Puzzle*, Cambridge University Press, 1993.
Carlos M. Vilas, "Economic Restruturing, Neoliberal Reforms, and the Working Class in Latin America," *Capital, Power, and Inequality in Latin America*, edited by Sando Halebskt and Richard L. Harris, Westview Press, 1995.
Carlos M. Vilas, "Latin America and the New World Order," *Social Justice: A Journal of Crime, Conflict and World Order*, Vol. 23, Nos. 1–2, 1996.
Carlos H. Waisman, "Civil Society, State Capacity, and the Conflicting Logics of Economic and Political Change," *Markets and Democracy in Latin America: Conflict or Convergence?*, edited by Philip Oxhorn and Pamela K. Starr, Lynne Rienner Publishers, 1999.
John Weeks, "The Contemporary Latin American Economies: Neoliberal Reconstruction," *Capital, Power, and Inequality in Latin America*, edited

by Sandoe Halebsky and Richard L. Harris, Westview Press, 1995.

Burns H. Weston, Richard A. Falk, and Hilary Charlesworth, *International Law and World Order: A Problem-Oriented Coursebook*, Third Edition, West Group, 1997.

Gordon White, "Constructing a Democratic Developmental State," *The Democratic Developmental State: Politics and Institutional Design*, edited by Mark Robinson and Gordon White, Oxford University Press, 1998.

Iris Marion Young, "State, Civil Society, and Social Justice," *Democracy's Value*, edited by Ian Shapiro and Casiano Hacker-Cordon, Cambridge University Press, 1999.

CHAPTER 2

OBSTACLES AND OPPORTUNITIES: NUCLEAR DISARMAMENT AND THE ABOLITION OF THE GLOBALIZATION OF MILITARIZATION

There is no room for illusion, not least when they mislead us over deep-seated conflicts of interests and convictions. But do we not find the dangerous illusion-mongers where an outworn realism is cited as an argument for letting the breakneck arms race rush on, while world hunger is ignored? A new kind of realism is called for, one that takes our responsibility for our own heritage and a common future equally seriously. One can no longer claim with a clear conscience that more armaments automatically mean more security. One can no longer dispute the fact that, on the contrary, humanity is in real danger of arming itself to death.

Willy Brandt, Arms and Hunger,
1986, p. 166

Violations of human rights are the expression of deep structural problems; they are inherent in certain kinds of political regimes and in certain kinds of economic systems in many parts of the world. . . . Therefore, to deal with human rights is to deal with epiphenomena; and yet, given what these violations reveal and given their reasons, this is sufficiently inflammatory to poison the international atmosphere all by itself.

Stanley Hoffman, Duties Beyond Borders,
1981, p. 138

War is war; it obeys no principle but its own and uses even the noblest ideologies as means to forward its own ends. Every student of history knows this, and every man of intelligence is able to understand it. Once the war is over, the internal struggle for civilization and liberty will have to be waged within every single nation, whether victor or vanquished. . . . War cannot be avoided by the use of force; its prevention requires that man's spirit be attuned to peace, concord and the dignity of human labor. "Tongues have power to stay swords," as an old Italian philosopher put it.

Albert Einstein, *Einstein on Peace*, 1981, p. 329

A. INTRODUCTION

The nuclear age has given birth to new forms of global consciousness which, perhaps, might not have existed without the bomb. Not only have weapons of mass destruction altered our thinking about war, but also about what constitutes genuine "security." Are there alternative paths to security which go beyond reliance on nuclear weapons? What are the dynamics and ramifications which stem from man's own technological genius? Are nuclear weapons actually "totalitarian tools" insofar as they are a metaphor for omnipotence? Ultimately, do not "totalitarian tools" become the means to embark upon antidemocratic rule?

These questions are all interconnected. Each question, significant in itself, also presents us with a thousand tributaries by virtue of the potentials, possibilities, and ramifications inherent in each. For example, the so-called "security dilemma" is not the prisoner of the military mind, unless it is allowed to be so narrowly defined. A genuine appreciation of human security can and should encompass every aspect of human life, from the economic to the ecological. In the name of "security," nuclear weapons have produced a nation-state civilizational structure which is premised upon insecurity. The spiraling effects of the arms race are testimony to the "reponse/counter-response" syndrome born of fear matched to nuclear technology and testing. The economic costs are borne by depleted economies in North and South, East and West.

The "technological society," as Jacques Ellul has described it, has implications for humanity's psychology of fear and the political ideologies used to rationalize the fear. Yet both fear and ideology find their rationale in the role played by "technique" insofar as "technique tolerates no judgment from without and accepts no limitation . . . Morality judges moral problems; as far as technical problems are concerned, it has nothing to say. Only technical criteria are relevant. Technique, in sitting in judgment on itself, is clearly freed from this principal obstacle to human action . . . The power and autonomy of technique are so well secured that it . . . has become the judge of what is moral, the creator of a new morality" (Ellul, 1964, p. 134). The technological society and the "totalitarian tools" produced by it promote the ideology of total control over nature, consciousness and meaning (Schwartz, 1984, p. 261). Yet, as totalitarian meanings are produced as a consequence of this expression of a technological civilization, the political meanings transform even democracies into antidemocratic cultures.

The inclusionary promise of democracy has been sacrificed upon the altar of technological expediency and rationalization, promoting instead the exclusionary state with a "technofascist vision" of the future as the legal, political, and economic establishments become hostage to the "national security state." The interests of the state ("for reasons of state") predominate over and against the interests of people within states and between states. Hence, marginalization and exclusion are the direct product of the "national security state"—a state that is, for all intents and purposes, largely divorced from the claims and force of international law.

In the arena of war alone, the technological breakthroughs of the first half of the 20th century served witness to the "significant erosion of the principle that there should be specified limits governing the conduct of billigerent parties engaged in hostilities" and in this way "war became characterized by an increasing element of totality; the unconditional surrender of the enemy was the goal of the largest, most representative wars of the era" (Falk, 1980(a), p. 578). Falk attributes two critical developments to the *de facto* repudiation of the legal framework that had been earlier constructed to restrain the conduct of warfare: "the growth of 'mass society' among the northern industrial nations, and the rapid pace of technological breakthroughs that aggravated the unavoidable tensions between a normative framework of civilized restraint in warfare and the pressures to do whatever would be helpful to the military effort" (*Id.*, p. 578). In short, mass societies could be influenced and controlled by a mass media. In turn, technological breakthroughs could be heralded as "advancements" for humankind when, in point of fact, such breakthroughs were, more often than not, breaks in the wall of democratic protections and the safeguards of international law.

The United States which emerged from World War II was a different nation, transformed by global obligations and responsibilities it had not shouldered before. The new globalism of the post-1945 era became the first "new world order" of many other "new world orders" that would follow. All of these orders were constructed in the name of "security," but true human security—security from hunger, poverty, disease, war, and environmental degradation—were not a part of this particular security-calculus. And so the emerging task of defending "the Free World" brought both a new set of responsibilities and perceived threats which led to "an unprecedented peacetime allocation of resources to the military arm of the state, and to the creation of powerful government agencies that had not existed before . . . These transformations provoked a stormy debate over the degree to which national security needs might endanger the basic values and institutions associated with American democracy" (Hogan, 1998, p. 464).

This transformation of the state was augmented by the development of "mass societies" combined with "the possibility of governmental control over communications (a function of the the second factor, technological development)" thereby making "the survival of the state concomitant with the survival of the nation" (Falk, 1980(a), p. 579). In other words, mass propaganda became interlinked with the mass participation of society in the task of carrying out the idea of "total war" between supposedly "implacably hostile and mutually exclusive cultures" (*Id.*, p. 579). What I have termed the *"exclu-*

sionary impulse" had come to dominate mass society, mass media, and the governments of nuclear states. As a result, "the capacity of the international legal system to adopt suitable new norms responsive to the new military technology was rapidly outstripped by the political and military exigencies of the two world wars" (*Id.*, p. 579). Democracy was transformed by this ideology and practice when the United States entered an era of "total war" in which the line between citizen and soldier, civilian and military, war and peace, disappeared forever (Hogan, 1998, p. 465; Huntington, 1957).

The transformation of democracy by the doctrine of "total war" turned governance into governance by the experts, thereby rendering it inherently exclusionary. I call the "national security state" that emerged after 1945 an example of the "exclusionary state" (ES), insofar as it claimed for itself, in almost Platonic terms, the idea that "foreign policy was no place for mass opinion and that the public should be guided by the judgment of professional experts" just as in law and medicine (Huntington, 1957, pp. 383–384). Yet, as this process has crossed the decades and spanned the globe, the nuclear threat (through proliferation), as well as a cascade of conventional arms (for use in "low-intensity conflicts" throughout the Third World), has made an unstable global environment even more unstable, insecure, hungry, malnourished, unemployed, underemployed, and subjected to mass-media propaganda as the monopoly of a global media has expanded in conjunction with the guardians of the nuclear monopoly.

By introducing these weapons into an already unstable world, already encumbered with numerous global conflicts, the destabilizing effects of totalitarian tools have increased the perils of proliferation. In this unstable environment, it is not hard to argue that "equal access to totalitarian tools will not lead to human liberation" (Schwartz, 1984, p. 263). In place of the promised liberation and emancipation of humankind from the crucible of war, the entire population of the world's people has been forced to pay for a worldwide military-industrial complex. The argument for this assertion can be articulated at many levels. At the center of the argument is the fact that "Western technology is inherently periphery-forming" (Galtung, 1979, p. 291). This is a conclusion that can be reached by starting an analysis of technology at that point where it is demonstrable that technology is not merely a mode of production and therefore neutral. It loses its supposed "neutrality" at those points in the evolution of capitalist "progress" where it is recognized as having embedded in itself a code of structures—economic, social, cultural, and cognitive.

The economic code carries with it the mandate, inherent in Western technology, which demands that industries be capital-intensive. On the social level, the code creates a "center" and a "periphery," thereby perpetuating a structure of inequality. On the cultural level, the code of capitalist reproduction throughout the Third World demands that the Third World is recast in the image of the West, but subordinate to it. Practically, the course of this trajectory of "progress" means that "patterns of exploitation no longer possible in the First World countries can be perpetuated in the Third World through the international division of labor." It is, in this sense, that Western technology is "inherently periphery-forming" and that, as a result, "the Third

World needs to have a fourth world to exploit." While it can be argued that Third World elites in the capitals of exclusionary states (ES) use the rest of the country as the country, this raises the question: "Who can the fourth-worlders exploit?" The answer is nobody (Galtung, 1979, p. 290). That is because there is no "fifth world around: the process runs out of worlds" (*Id.*, p. 291).

In the context of global militarization and emergent nuclearism, it is clear that, like technology, militarization "is also related to the hierarchical structures by which powerful states exert varying degrees of hegemony over weaker states" (Falk, 1980(b), p. 340). The hegemonic enterprise is the structure which results from the periphery-forming process. Emergent nuclearism is a hegemonic project which is sustained by an antidemocratic premise—the maintenance of the exclusionary state (ES) throughout the Third World. Yet the antidemocratic premise in the Third World has, in point of fact, reflected the antidemocratic premise of nuclearism in the First World's center.

The political anatomy of emergent nuclearism was exposed early in the atomic age when "the antidemocratic premise was tacitly adopted—that crucial decisions bearing on nuclear weapons development and strategic doctrine should be determined within the Executive Branch on the basis of secret and technical information" (Lifton and Falk, 1982, p. 205; see also, I.M. Destler, 1986, pp. 226–242). The culture of secrecy combined with the cult of the technocracy to produce the "national security state" and all the vestiges of an antidemocratic culture which accompany it. Consequently, no aspect of life within the United States was left unaffected (Hogan 1998, pp. 7–10, 58, 178–9, 181, 298–9, 465–6; Leffler, 1992; Leffler, 1994; Leffler and Painter, 1994).

As automated warfare and nuclear weapons have evolved, they have reshaped human consciousness "through the agency of what can be called 'armament culture'" (Luckham, 1984, p. 1). Both nuclear weapons and conventional weapons make up the armament culture. This culture has not been confined to the orginal centers of its development, in the United States and the former Soviet Union. Now, "armament culture" has become truly global (Foltz and Bienen, 1985; Pierre, 1997; Krause, 1992; Klare, 1997; Weston, 1990; Cassidy and Bischak, 1993; Klare, 1984; Vargas, 1985; Weston, 1984; Falk and Kim, 1980; Stockholm International Peace Research Institute (SIPRI), 1971; Barnett, 1992; Tuomi and Vayrynen, 1982; McKinlay and Mughan, 1984; Katz, 1984).

The global dimensions of this "armament culture" have also relied on the media to protect its inhumane and antidemocratic nature from being exposed. The media has often depicted the armament culture as necessary to security and survival. The media has adopted the phrases and verbage of nuclear justification, such as "deterrence," as if the mere invocation of the terminology designed to rationalize the use, deployment and investment in these weapons possessed an inherent explanatory feature as well. Military spending and national budgets, on a global basis, have incorporated their rationales into the political jargon and media-hype of each fiscal year while, simultaneously, disguising or hiding the true costs. The connections between investments in weapons and the socioeconomic costs which deplete nations and exclude millions of people from having their basic needs met is often lost and left unexamined. Both emergent nuclearism and the conventional arms trade have created a global culture of poverty for billions of people, costing billions of dollars. One explanation for this result is that "militarization diverts world production away from meeting basic human needs toward the overproduction of weapons. Moreover, by redistributing income in favor of the rich, both within and between nations, it reduces the purchasing power of the masses, thereby reducing effective demand" (Szentes, 1984, p. 67).

The fact remains that the growth of the military sector in developing countries negatively affects their economic equilibrium. In large measure, this is a consequence of the exclusionary and antidemocratic features of global militarization which intensify and deepen the very structural distortions that produce disequilbria in the first place. In this critical respect, a growing military sector often "reinforces the developing nation's dependence upon foreign economies, which is accompanied by a regular income drain, balance of payment problems, and increasing indebtedness" (Szentes, 1984, p. 59). The growth of the exclusionary state (ES) is, in large measure, a consequence of these converging disequilibria. The growth of the ES reflects the deepening patterns of a symbiosis among political, military and business leaders in advanced capitalist countries (Halliday, 1983, pp. 172–202). The antidemocratic consequences which result are economic, political and social—all at the same moment in time. This is because "the growth of the military sector . . . implies a reinforcement of *monopolistic tendencies* along with state intervention at the expense of nonmilitary business and particularly the tax-paying working masses" (*Id.*, p. 60, italics mine).

As the globalizing tendencies of the armaments culture have spread to developing nations, the linkages between the advanced nuclear states and the developing countries exposes a pattern of exclusionary governance which, in turn, exposes a web of interconnected patterns of dominance, omnipotence, and exploitation. These developments, in turn, serve to generate widespread patterns of multi-dimensional exclusion, poverty, hunger, conflict, violations of human rights, and socioeconomic decline coupled with sociopolitical disempowerment. An entire global system of exclusionary states is reinforced by the war system insofar as it is a process engaged in purposely "diverting natural and human energies to sustain the war system" and "locks into place the effects of economic and cultural structures of dominance," which leads to the conclusion that "the governing process in sovereign states has become more militaristic, making the abuse of human rights a conventional and central feature of the operation of a modern state" (Sakamoto and Falk, 1980, p. 2). The combined effects of these trends converge in a global network of anti-democratic and exclusionary states, founded and maintained through monopolies—monopolies of terror, on the one hand, conjoined with media monopolies for the convergence of legitimating news coverage and "analysis," on the other.

When viewed together, the nuclear monopoly complements the media monopoly. Both are antithetical to a deepening of inclusionary democracy. Both provide the necessary framework for large-scale exclusion from decision making. Both require low levels of participation because both fear the power of social movements to stir democratic action and democratic forms of empowerment through media outlets, or through national and international courts, through the auspices of democratic action and representation. Understood from this perspective, both the nuclear monopoly and the media monopoly represent the embodiment of the "exclusionary impulse" insofar as both are driven by: (1) the profit motive; (2) the desire to increase their national and global monopoly by technological advances; (3) the need to legitimate, rationalize, and justify the expenditure of billions of dollars to support exclusionary governance (which, by definition, is to say, "exclusionary monopolies"). It is on the basis of this analysis, that this chapter purposely links the discussion of the nuclear monopoly with that of the media monopoly. We shall begin with an analysis of the nuclear monopoly.

B. BUILDING EXCLUSIONARY MONOPOLIES: GLOBAL INTERDEPENDENCE AND POWER UNDER EMERGENT NUCLEARISM

By the end of World War II, the development of the atomic bomb signaled the birth of the nuclear age. The devastation which descended upon Hiroshima and Nagasaki echo today, over a half century later. American relief at the war's end has given way to uncertainty and regret. Yet, in the Hiroshima context, the degree of uncertainty was minimized, as in all wars, under the rubric of geopolitical greatness and war's own inherent pretensions to a supposed mandate to inflict atrocities on enemy societies in order to make a point (Lifton and Falk, 1982, p. 196).

Historians, in the mid-1990s, recently discovered documents that have been devastating to the traditional idea that using the bomb was the only way to avoid an invasion of Japan that might have cost many more lives (Alperovitz, 1995). Even before the recently declassified documents came out, there was the recognition that Hiroshima and Potsdam were early examples of "atomic diplomacy" (Alperovitz, 1965, 1985, 1995). One centerpiece of the "atomic diplomacy" argument is that there was a belief, among those who advised President Truman, that the atomic bomb had the potential to place the United States in a position to dictate terms at the end of the war—and beyond (Alperovitz, 1995, p. 32).

On January 31, 1950, President Truman announced the historic decision to develop the hydrogen bomb. At the same time, he explicitly ordered the State and Defense departments to undertake "a reexamination of our objectives in peace and war and of the effect of the objectives on our strategic plans in light of the probable fission bomb capability and possible thermonuclear capability of the Soviet Union" (as quoted in Harper, 1994, p. 291). From this order, the resulting study culminated in NSC 68, completed in early April. These actions were taken against the backdrop of a perceived weakening the the US position after the fall of China and the Soviet atomic test in September-October 1949. The US Secretary of State, Dean Acheson, pointed out that while the loss of China had been "expected," that was not the case with the loss of the *atomic monopoly*. The loss of the *atomic monopoly* was more serious "since the bomb had compensated for America's conventional inferiority. The United States had seven active divisions in 1949; the Soviet Union was thought to have 175" (*Id.*, p. 292).

With the loss of America's atomic monopoly, the Joint Chiefs of Staff warned the NSC 68 study group, under the direction of Paul Nitze, of the potential for a new kind of Pearl Harbor attack. As early as 1945, Acheson himself had predicted that the US atomic monopoly would end within five years. Nitze had assumed that the monopoly and its "strategic significance" would "progressively decline" (as quoted in Harper, 1994, p. 292). While neither believed that the Soviets would attack Western Europe in the near future, "both believed in the overwhelming actual and potential economic and technological superiority of the United States" (*Id.*, p. 292). In order to maintain this "superiority," the whole face of the post-war world was changed in ways that went well beyond conventional military doctrine and a narrowly defined "national security." The doctrine of militarism changed under emergent nuclearism from Truman's "NSC-68" to Eisenhower's "massive retaliation," Kennedy's inherited policy of "mutually assured destruction" (augmented by his own program of "counter-insurgency" to combat Moscow's "wars of national liberation"), Nixon's "flexible counter-force," Carter's "countervailing strategy," and Reagan's "star wars" coupled with the largest military build-up in human history.

To maintain the potential economic and technological superiority of the United States around the globe, various elites—euphemistically referred to as the "wizards of Armageddon" and "guardians of the arsenal"—decided to make Third World states modern "vassal states" (my term). They were vassal states because of their socioeconomic and sociopolitcal position within the international hierarchy, which left them on the periphery with the United States and the Western Alliance (NATO), and the Soviet Union and the Warsaw Pact, sharing the center. In this bipolar world, the Third World was seen as a vast ground for competition between two superpowers seeking "spheres of influence." Third World nations who sought to opt out of the sphere-of-influence-game attempted to do so under the banner of the "Non-Aligned Movement" (NAM). Yet, the economic, political, military/strategic interests of the superpowers, combined with the political ideology and rationale of the Cold War era, would not allow for such attempts at claiming sovereign evasion of the struggle.

In the early 1960s, many Afro-Asian states established NAM as a response to the Cold War's pressures and also as an expression and embodiment of their collective aspiration to safeguard their freedom and independence from hegemomic pressures. By so doing, NAM sought to enlarge the opportunities for self-determination offered by that freedom. It was a defining moment. Considered by the Western powers as little more than an idle construct of the political left, "the NAM marked the emergence of Third World countries into the international system" (Grant, 1995, p. 568). As its founders intended, the NAM was neither monolithic in its organization nor homogeneous in its ideological orientation. Rather, the NAM "meant safeguarding the right to adopt positions that were informed by national interest, irrespective of whether those positions coincided with those of one power bloc or the other" (*Id.*, p. 568). Hence, it transcended the temptation to limit its goals to merely achieving political equidistance from the rival power blocs and sought, instead, to assert the internal empowerment of the states who had joined the NAM.

While the Westphalian model of "sovereignty," under the rubric of international law, would be invoked on behalf of the non-aligned movement and its claimants, the force of global political and economic power disallowed adherence to the claim and protection of sovereignty (Kaldor, 1990). In fact, the logic of the Cold War and the presence of nuclear weapons necessitated Third World participation in order to turn Third World states into a strategic theatre or "low-intensity" battleground for conventional military bloodbaths, civil wars, and ethnic conflict, in order that such conflicts would help to avoid a direct confrontation between the superpowers, which could lead to a nuclear exchange (Kaplan, 1983; Nolan, 1989; Gaddis, Gordon, May, and Rosenberg, 1999).

These perspectives on the configuration of power, as envisioned by US officials, were "increasingly defined in ways that distorted the importance of the Third World, underestimated the local sources of conflict, and exaggerated the relevance of strategic arms and the conventional military balance in Europe to developments on the periphery" (Leffler, 1992, p. 506). Hence, some historians have concluded that Truman administration officials, like policymakers everywhere, made important errors because they attributed an excessive strategic value to the Third World. For example, base sights in Egypt and raw materials from Saudi Arabia and Iran became defining points for foreign policy decision making and focus. In this context, the industrial core areas of Eurasia were viewed as potential targets for Soviet "expansion" if they were not effectively integrated with markets and resources on the periphery. As a result, throughout the Third World, the United States established linkages with discredited elites who would work with American elites as they had done with British and French elites (*Id.*, p. 509). A global network of exclusionary states was reinforced by the logic of Cold War struggles for spheres of influence, regardless of the cost to millions of economically, socially, and culturally excluded peoples around the world. Building exclusionary monopolies through global interdependence was the consequence of interconnected efforts: establishing military and economic spheres of influences; using the threat of nuclear weapons to back up diplomatic initiatives; supporting dictatorships and the exclusionary states which they ruled over. In this period, Truman administration officials "foolishly concluded that the United States had to become the world's policeman as well as its financial hegemon" (*Id.*, p. 509).

While the development experience of Third World countries has been influenced by their position on the periphery, that does not mean that their historical experiences can be collapsed into an explanatory scheme within the sole context of North-South relations. The experience has not been a uniform one. Indeed, South Korea has enjoyed a path of economic performance that has transformed it into a newly industrialized country (NIC). Its status has been recognized by multilateral financial intitutions. Yet NICs have not abandoned the rest of the Third World or disassociated themselves from one another. They remain at the periphery of the capitalist world, much as they did in the Cold War era, because the end of the Cold War has not been accompanied by a fundamental alteration of the international economic system. Understanding this means that, historically, "the NAM . . . encompasses countries whose political viewpoints often diverge, whose voting patterns place them on both sides of some political issues, and whose economies range from robust to weak, from promising to unpromising" (Grant, 1995, p. 569).

Still, when viewed in its totality, the essential features of the NAM are to be found in "its positive stand for peace, its respect for sovereignty, regardless of power or size, and its belief in an economically just world which, by inference, means the rejection of relationships that involve sacrifice of the national interest by perpetuating injustice and inequity" (*Id.*, p. 569). Hence, the NAM remains as an emerging group of inclusionary states, attempting to build an inclusionary hegemon which promotes the ideals of inclusionary governance.

In this respect, it may be asserted that the transition from a bipolar world does not render the NAM anachronistic. Neither does the end of a bipolar world justify the removal of the concept of the Third World from the arsenal of conceptual tools for the purpose of understanding international politics. On the contrary, as an analytical concept, the categorical concept of the Third World "is likely to retain its usefulness so long as the world continues to be riven by serious economic and political disparities" (Grant, 1995, p. 569). This argument is underscored by a widening scholarship on the false promise of the market, as the market-driven social policies of the 1980s have been proven to bring increasing hardship to all mankind. For example, the number of people around the world presently living in absolute poverty reached 1.4 billion in 1994—a 40 percent increase from less than two decades ago (Vale, 1995, p. 284).

As the differentials between rich and poor have widened between North and South, so have disparities in representation in the United Nations. Currently, the UN, while offering the services of its specialized agencies as platforms for dialogue, fails to incorporate the Third World in a process of economic restructuring promised by the Declaration on International Economic Cooperation, adopted May 1990, during the 18th Special Session on International Economic Cooperation (Declaration on International Economic Cooperation, in Particular the Revitalization of Economic Growth and Development of the Developing Countries, UN, GAOR, 18th Special Sess., Supp. No.2, at 5–7, UN Doc. A/S 18/15 (1990)). The significance of this document is that it called for a more favorable attitude by the major economic powers toward the developing world (Vale, 1995, p. 285).

Instead of engaging the Third World in a global process of economic restructuring, old thinking about military security has served to preclude innovative legal, political, and economic thinking about the many different dimensions of human "security." In this respect, "the attitudes that sustain large and deadly military machines did not fall with the Berlin Wall." Rather, the world is still divided into a complex of sovereign nation-states where each still largely attempts to improve its position vis-a-vis an anarchic international system. With few opportunities for cooperation, each state still insists upon maintaining the right to be free from the scrutiny and intervention of other states in its internal affairs. In this environment, "each nation is surrounded by danger and must protect itself to survive, which gives rise to a preoccupation with power, particularly military power" (Felice, 1998, p. 32). The problem with this trajectory of thought and action is that an acute sense of danger allows for a greater citizen susceptibility to acccept high taxation in order to pay for militarization at the expense of social development.

Ironically, engagement in the process of militarization in the name of security and peace often produces contradictory results, such as conditions of insecurity and conflict. In turn, expenditures for militarization deplete and undermine the ability of nations to fulfill international human rights obligations (especially economic and social rights). Hence, when "security" is defined solely "as the heavily armed defense of one's borders" then there is a subversion of efforts to secure the lives of those living within those borders (*Id.*, p. 33). It is on this basis that we may conclude that "arms control and disarmament and the demobilization of armed forces are prerequisites to providing the institutional framework within which nations may pursue implementation of the corpus of international human rights law" (*Id.*, p. 35). A whole new definition of what constitutes a "security community" can emerge from this analysis.

The old preoccupations with "balance of power" and outmoded notions of "realpolitik" which usually exacerbate insecurities can be replaced by human rights policies that can do more to provide the "realist" objectives of security and stability. The economic and social changes that have been witnessed in the recent past resemble what Andre Gunder Frank has called "dependent development" or the "development of underdevelopment." The new task for the 21st century is to re-channel history by advancing efforts which meet the full potential of autonomous development. This will mean breaking the cycle of dependency. In turn, this means that LDCs (lesser developed countries) need to generate the political ability to challenge not merely the terms under which they are allowed access to Western science, technology, and trade but, even more fundamentally, the power relationships that allow the developed countries to set the terms of global trade (GATT, NAFTA, WTO, IMF, World Bank).

Viewed in this light, Professor Falk has noted that "what we require minimally are visions of the present and future that can better encompass reality than 'realism,' as well as proposals and tactics for bridging the normative and ideological gaps between the ascent of economic globalization and the descent of human well-being in established societies" (Falk, 1997(b), p. 136). Part of that task will involve building security communities which foreclose on building up dangerous nuclear weapons regimes. This will necessitate, at the same time, a deepening of democratic norms, institutions, practices, procedures and avenues for broad-based citizen participation through a revitalized civil society.

C. BEYOND REALISM: BUILDING "SECURITY COMMUNITIES" FOR A SUSTAINABLE PEACE

It may well be that, in the tradition of Karl Deutsch's sense of a "security community," peace can become a predictable commodity among a group of states (Booth and Vale, 1995, p. 290). In Deutsch's conception, as articulated almost 40 years ago in his pioneering work *Political Community and the North Atlantic Area*, a security community grows out of: the mutual compatibility of values; strong economic ties; social, political, and cultural transactions; a growing density of institutionalized relationships; mutual responsiveness; and mutual predictability of behavior (Deutsch, 1957). One such example of this process can be identified in the nuclear confidence-building regime between Argentina and Brazil in the period of 1985–1988, following transitions to civilian democratic rule (Barletta, 1999, pp. 19–38; Hurrell, 1998, pp. 228–264). The changes that took place during the period from 1985 to 1988 constituted nothing less than a genuine metamorphosis.

Democratically elected officials were empowered to transform nuclear affairs from an expression of regional rivalry into a means to advance regional tension reduction, political solidarity, and economic integration (Barletta, 1999, p. 21). Within a four-year period, the Alfonsin Administration in Argentina and the Sarney Administration in Brazil established a comprehensive regime to organize bilateral nuclear relations. While building on longstanding cooperative practices, as well as the precedent set by the 1980 accords, the creation of this regime ultimately reflected impressive changes in the scope, sensitivity, institutionalization, and importance of bilateral nuclear cooperation. In this historical experience, relations between Brazil and Argentina improved as nuclear confidence-building followed transitions to democracy. But the question that arises is: How did democratization lead to the emergence of a nuclear regime? There are dissenting explanations.

The fact that democratic transitions were occurring in both countries is of great importance. Hurrell has suggested four major reasons for the importance of the transitions to democracy. First, democratization involved the shift in bureaucratic power away from the military. This shift was important for the sake of regional foreign policy. Second, democratization laid the political foundation for increased transparency on which more specific confidence-building measures were later to to built. Third, this process is not an example of a "democratic peace" between two consolidated democracies but should rather be seen within the context of contested processes of democratization. Fourth, and finally, the processes of democratization provided a shared sense of common purpose between a small group of politicians and government officials. This led to the overt use of foreign policy as a means of protecting a fragile democracy. This was especially the case with respect to Argentina (Hurrell, 1998, p. 244). Insofar as the leading actors on both sides believed democratization was vital in the task of redefining the interests of the two states by reshaping their identities and sense of common purpose, the process serves to establish one of Deutsch's conditions for a security community—namely, the compatibility of major values.

Hurrell's analysis maintains that "a simple Kantian account is difficult to reconcile with the relative pacificism of both civilian and military governments in the region." Further, inherent in the nuclear issue, there are many "cross-cutting pressures and relationships" (*Id.*, p. 245). Barletta offers a dissenting viewpoint, arguing that "the Alfonsin Administration framed its approach to nuclear and security affairs in terms of a Latin American variant of Kantian idealism" and, as a consequence of this orientation and conceptual framework, the Alfonsin government understood nuclear and bilateral affairs "as a question of democratic security" (Barletta, 1999, p. 24). In sum, then, they viewed nuclear confidence-building and cooperation as a means to reduce regional tensions and also as a means to "undercut the threat scenarios of their armed forces." Therefore, by taking this approach, they created what may be called a "diversionary peace"—a peace which "would eliminate one rationale for military autonomy and claims on state resources, and thereby contribute to democratic consolidation at home and abroad" (*Id.*, p. 24). In this sense, the Argentine decision makers rejected power politics in part as immoral, but also because they saw it as a threat to democratic consolidation and civilian control over the armed forces (*Id.*, p. 25). At least, on this point, Barletta is in agreement with Hurrell's fourth point—in the Argentine case, the processes of democratization led to the overt use of foreign policy as a means of protecting its newly established democracy.

Expanding on the motivations of the Alfonsin government's framing of the issues regarding nuclear and bilateral affairs touches on three interrelated points: the Argentine civilian-led government's (1) sense of identity, (2) its ideology, and (3) the agenda they confronted on assuming office. First, Alfonsin and other *Union Civica Radical* (UCR) Party leaders were human rights activists. As such, they were strong advocates for constitutional democratic rule. Second, UCR thinking about international relations was strongly shaped by Kantian idealist thought. UCR officials had come to reject "realist principles" which resulted in repression at home and a futile diversionary war abroad. Third, upon assuming office, UCR officals found themselves surrounded by non-democratic states, facing high inflation and a growing debt, and acutely aware that civilian leadership has not often survived for long in Argentina. Faced with this triple dilemma, their overriding imperative was to consolidate democratic rule. In this way, foreign policy converged with domestic policy in order to augment and help sustain the processes of Argentine democratization.

In terms of establishing a "security community," the process of nuclear confidence-building between Argentina and Brazil demonstrates that nuclear cooperation is possible between states, that it did diminish fears in both countries, and that bilateral confidence-building and joint efforts have the capacity to provide a legitimate basis to promote nonproliferation. Further, the establishment of a security community was, in part, the product of the emergence of democratic rule in Brazil and Argentina. While processes of democratization led to positive and consequential changes, it was not because these processes altered the balance of power or the distribution of material resources. Neither did the processes of democratization create domestic structures which could have impeded conflict, nor did they advance the cause of economic interdependence. Rather, in Argentina, these processes ultimately mattered because it brought officials to power whose identity and ideology allowed them to frame nuclear development and bilateral relations in a new way. In short, the redefinition of the nuclear confidence-building regime was placed in the context of building democratic security.

The redefinition and reorientation of policy may be further appreciated by the realization that "another leadership oriented by a different understanding—or the same one with less effective control over policy making—would have entailed quite different behavior in Argentine foreign policy and Argentine-Brazilian relations" (Barletta, 1999, p. 27). The fact that effective control over policy making by Argentina's civilian leadership became possible serves to demonstrate that the Argentine military was marginalized in foreign and military matters throughout the Alfonsin government (*Id.*, p. 35). As a result of this situation, the idea of democratic security, which came to be the predominant view that oriented the group that came to power in Argentina, was effective insofar as it allowed the civilian leadership to undertake successful negotiations in dealing with its Brazilian counterparts, thus becoming the key to the transformation of bilateral nuclear relations in the late 1980s. In this regard, it is critical to recognize that "positive change in Argentine-Brazilian nuclear relations was not a necessary product of democratic rule, of transitions to democracy, nor of the democratization process itself" (*Id.*, p. 27). In fact, the central lesson to be learned from this case-study is that the Argentine-Brazilian experience fits with the observation that expectations about other states, while not empirically grounded, if shared, can become self-confirming.

So the answer to whether democracy favors international peace and security seems to be that it depends on the democrats. In this case, the civilian leadership of Argentina brought with it a firm conviction in Kantian ideas and the opportunity to implement them. Overall, the 1980s will be remembered as a period when transitions to democracy in South America mattered primarily because they brought to power a community of like-minded Kantians who, in the process of governing, deliberately sought to alter and transform the regional security environment in correspondence with Kantian precepts.

D. THE CONVERGENCE OF WAR, POLITICS, AND INTERNATIONAL LAW IN THE POST-1945 WORLD

What the Second World War and the atomic bomb altered was not merely military in nature and scope. In addition to increasing mankind's destructive capacity, human consciousness was dramatically transformed as well. In this respect, historian Gabriel Kolko notes the nature of this transformation when he notes that "modern wars retain, as before, their traditional military and diplomatic dimensions, but their outcomes are also defined increasingly in the changes they provoke in individual and national consciousness. This additional change obligates us to to give far more consideration to war's impact on social systems in the largest sense—their economies, the new moods they encourage among the people, and changing political and class structures" (Kolko, 1968, 1990, p. 627).

The conventional view of historians, shaped through methodologies which emphaize diplomatic and military matters, "are less able to capture accurately the richly textured dimensions of the human experience in the modern era. In the twentieth century war telescopes 'social time' within nations . . . producing deep crises that in earlier periods might have taken many decades to gestate, crises that affect those individual values and commitments that are . . . essential to mobilizing parties and movements of change and opposition. The social, economic, and ideological problems that emerged from World War II have produced the dominant legacies that shape, in some great measure, the postwar world as well" (*Id.*, pp. 627–628). Kolko's assessment is vital for our understanding of how to comprehend the atomic monopoly in the nuclear age as being more than just a technological "advance" in destructive capacity. There is no arena or area of human life that has been left unaffected by the development, use, or threatened use of the atomic bomb, as well as technological innovations and their evolving impact (Dickson, 1984). When viewed in combination, however, Western-dominated technological innovation did not proceed without political blessing, economic support, and a great deal of propaganda.

Western domination has been occasionally challenged, however, as in the late 1970s. The LDCs, negotiating through the Group of 77, started with the proposition that global inequity in the distribution of science and technology was a reflection of broader economic and political inequalities. Eliminating the former, it was argued, would ultimately be achieved by addressing the latter. One of the clearest statements on this position emerged from the report of a symposium held for African scientists and science policy makers in Arusha, Tanzania, in January of 1978. The report stressed the fact that, by virtue of their position on the periphery, African states remained on the low rungs of the global economic hierarchy, dependent upon the centers of monopoly capitalism. This situation left them with no option but to accept the terms and conditions set by the center.

Those in attendance at the Tanzanian conference demanded "a new International Science and Technological Order" which would be capable of ensuring "an optimal application of science and technology in its broadest and most forward-looking sense." The viewpoint was further expounded in one of its most controversial passages. The Arusha Declaration stated: "It must be accepted universally, for a start, that technological knowledge is the common heritage of mankind" (*African Goals and Aspirations*, January 30 to February 4, 1978). In sum, the Arusha Declaration was a call for inclusion—the inclusion of Third World states in the global scientific enterprise and its universal and inclusionary promise for human fulfillment and advancement. It was a call to put an end to exclusionary global governance in science, politics, and economics. The implications of the Arusha Declaration remain far-reaching, for they point in the direction of treating science and technology as the "common heritage of mankind"—an idea initially used to refer to the exploration of outer space and the oceans. The claims contained in the Arusha Declaration were not to be realized.

By the early 1980s, the United Nations Conference on Science and Technology for Development (UNCSTD) effectively relinguished its advocacy for the sentiments contained in the Arusha Declaration and yielded to the growing effort of the private sector to defend its privileged access to scientific knowledge. In particular, the private sector's interest in scientific knowledge that had become the key to corporate competitiveness was held sacrosanct. In this regard, government action—"whether exercised domestically through federal agencies or internationally, in collaboration with other advanced nations, through the UN"—was supported "only to the extent that it helped corporations exploit knowledge without giving away any control over it. The result was to strengthen the patterns of control over science in the hands of private-sector institutions in the industrialized nations," thereby ensuring "the continued dominance of the core over the periphery in the global economy" (Dickson, 1984, pp. 201–202). The monopoly power of this form of exclusionary global governance is just one aspect of the ES and an international regime based upon old patterns of dominance, hierarchy, exclusion, coercion, and exploitation. The expression of this monopoly of power is just as evident in the global military-industrial complex, which also augments its power through concentrated economic-corporate-banking monopolies. The nexus of this power is protected through the interconnected auspices of law and politics, mutually interdependent and mutually reinforcing. It is to this issue, involving the monopoly over nuclear weapons and the question of their legality, that we now turn.

E. THE LEGALITY OF NUCLEAR WEAPONS: INTERNATIONAL LAW AND THE WORLD COURT AT THE CROSSROADS OF AN HISTORIC ENCOUNTER

Originally published in 1939, Edward H. Carr's book, *The Twenty Year's Crisis, 1919–1939: An Introduction to the Study of International Relations*, underscored what Kolko's account, *The Politics of War: The World and United States Foreign Policy, 1943–1945*, stressed over three decades later. Both works underscore the fact that law and politics are inseparable. As set forth by Carr, "every system of law presupposes an initial political decision, whether explicit or implied, whether achieved by voting or by bargaining or by force, as to the authority entitled to make and unmake law. Behind all law there is this necessary political background. The ultimate authority of law derives from politics" (Carr, 1964, p. 180). In this fundamental respect, nuclear weapons and the nuclear weapons culture is no exception.

In fact, Carr's insight is as current as the recent actions of the International Court of Justice, with its issuance of an advisory opinion of great weight on the legality of nuclear weapons (Legality of the Threat or Use of Nuclear Weapons, General List No 95—Advisory Opinion of July 8, 1996, hereinafter Nuclear Weapons). It was the first time in human history that an international tribunal had directly addressed the nuclear weapons issue as an unresolved threat to humanity, "forging a consensus that lends strong, yet partial and somewhat ambiguous, support to the view that nuclear weapons are of dubious legality" (International Court of Justice Statute Art. 55 (2), and:

Falk, 1997(a), p. 64; Ginger, 1998; Kauzlarich and Kramer, 1998; Nanda and Krieger, 1998).

The common ground forged by those elements of the *dispositif* that enjoyed the unanimous or near-unanimous support of the 14 judges is found in the advisory opinion's unanimous conclusion that "neither customary law nor conventional international law" contains "any specific authorization of the threat or use of nuclear weapons" (Nuclear Weapons, para. 105 (2) (A)). Yet, as noted by Falk, "in a somewhat more contested fashion, the judges voted eleven to three that 'neither customary nor conventional international law' contains 'any comprehensive and universal prohibition of the threat or use of nuclear weapons as such'" (Falk, 1997(a), p. 65). The reluctance of the court to rule on this aspect of the issues shows, at least in part, a deference to the political leadership of the national-security states involved who are not prohibited from employing nuclear weapons in a situation involving "self-defense." Yet, the terms and conditions of what constitutes self-defense are left rather unclear. What is clear is that, as mentioned earlier, the nexus between politics and law is a very close one—interconnected, intertwined, and intermingled.

The political ramifications of this legal decision expose the close nexus between law and politics, as both Carr and Kolko suggest, more generally, from the standpoint of history and the perspectives of political science. Falk concurs with their interpretations of what is at stake with his observation that "states are habitually resistant to legal challenges directed at their national security policies, and powerful states are especially so." However, this does not obviate the fact that "it would be a mistake to confine inquiry to short-term intergovernmental impact. The decision is likely to have a consciousness-raising effect on informed public opinion around the world, which might at some point result in renewed and intensified antinuclear pressures" (Falk, 1997(a), p. 74). Such pressures have been successfully mounted before as attested to by the history of the World Nuclear Disarmament Movement (1954–1970), and by the linkages between domestic society and international cooperation as evidenced by the impact of protest on US arms control policy (Knopf, 1998; Wittner, 1997).

From the days of Eisenhower and the emergent test ban movement to the the decision to begin SALT, as well as the opposition to Reagan's nuclear build up and the nuclear freeze movement, recent history has demonstrated that state preferences are not only set by political leaders, but also constrained by society's pressures. Alternatively, ordinary citizens can also serve as a direct stimulus to the development of a state interest in cooperation (Knopf, 1998). Given the dual forces of global civil society, as expressed through both constraint and stimulus, Falk has recognized that "the endeavors of global civil society with respect to nuclear weaponry were seeking an outcome in the World Court that minimized geopolitical influences and maximized the impact of the conscience of humanity as expressed by activist anti-nuclear forces . . . A global law of peoples is emergent, and it is time for jurists to provide a suitable framework for its comprehension and assessment" (Falk, 1998, p. 185).

In this new context, the various political, legal, economic, and social ramifications which emanate from this decision are enormous. For the fact remains that "the language and reasoning of the court provides strong encouragement to antinuclear social and political forces to push for abolition, with respect to both existing security and nuclear disarmament" (*Id.*, p. 74). In other words, the court's language and reasoning can contribute to what I have termed the "inclusionary impulse"—the impulse contained in a global and collectively shared consciousness (whose dimensions include religious traditions, political interests, legal reasoning, and the evolving mandates of a global civil society) to undertake inclusionary protective measures for the advancement of peace as a human right.

Such encouragement has already been produced by the issuance of *Report by the Canberra Commission on the Elimination of Nuclear Weapons* (August 14, 1996). The Canberra Commission is an idependent body which consists of 17 eminent persons, appointed by the Australian Government (in November 1995). Also in 1995, *The Report of the Commission on Global Governance* set forth its own position by declaring that the citizens of nuclear-weapon and threshold states would be immeasurably more secure in a world without nuclear or other weapons of mass destruction. A summary of its conclusions is set forth in Table 2.1.

There are numerous legal precedents to support the recommendations of the Commission on Global Governance with respect to nuclear weapons. The Commission itself cites relevant international agreements which, for over three decades have made substantial progress towards controlling the spread and use of weapons of mass destruction, which now include: the 1963 Partial Test-Ban Treaty, the 1967 Treaty for the Prohibition of Nuclear Weapons in Latin America (the Treaty of Tlatelolco), the 1968 Treaty on the Non-Proliferation of Nuclear Weapons (NPT), the 1972 Anti-Ballistic Missile Treaty, the 1972 Biological Weapons Convention, the 1979 SALT II Treaty, and the 1985 South Pacific Nuclear-Free Zone Treaty.

Even before these legal advances, the first half of the 20th century had posited a variety of international legal norms which support the conclusion that the use, threat, and perhaps even the possession of nuclear weapons is prohibited. In this regard, "the law of war as a whole is jeopardized to the extent that nuclear weaponry is to any extent legitimated" (Falk, 1980(a), p. 584). Nuclear weapons and nuclear strategy, when evaluated within the context of the Nuremberg Principles, reveal that the Nuremberg standard can be applied in such as manner as to make their very existence a crime against peace and a crime against humanity. The principle that individuals have international duties which transcend absolute obedience to the nation-state has emerged as the most principal principle of the Nuremberg Tribunal. This principle, when coupled with the other achievements of Nuremberg, such as the determination that violations of restraints upon the use of force in international relations constitute a crime against humanity, serves to create an entirely new conceptual framework for the evaluation of the illegality of nuclear weapons. It was not until Nuremberg that it could be argued that the intentional destruction of a group of people because of their race, religion or nationality was recognized as a crime under international law.

Appreciation of this principle was reiterated by the 1996 Advisory Opinion of the I.C.J. when it quoted the view that "recourse to nuclear

TABLE 2.1 Summary of Proposals for Ending the Threat of Mass Destruction (Report of the Commission on Global Governance)

Security for a New Era
1. The security of people and the security of the planet should be goals of global security policy, along with the security of states.
2. The Charter of the United Nations should be revised to allow the Security Council to authorize action in situations within countries, but only if the security of people is so severely violated as to require an international response on humanitarian grounds.

Anticipating Crises
3. The preventive approach to security should be strengthened, with the UN improving its capacity to anticipate and resolve crises and to respond early to armed conflict.
4. The United Nations should develop a more comprehensive system to collect information on trends and situations that may lead to violent conflict or humanitarian tragedies; all states should share with the UN information on such trends and situations.
5. Adequate resources should be provided to enable the Secretary-General to make full use of fact-finding missions as part of efforts to promote peace and security.

Responding to Crises
6. Both the Security Council and the Secretary-General should make more use of the mechanisms for peaceful settlement listed in Chapter VI of the UN Charter.
7. In peacekeeping operations, the integrity of the UN command should be respected, and consultative committees should be formed for each operation, which should include countries providing troops.
8. The Security Council should use a more precise, targeted approach to sanctions.
9. All nations need to live up to their obligation under the UN Charter to make armed forces available to the Security Council.
10. The Military Staff Committee provided for in the UN Charter should be revitalized to provide military information and expert advice to the Security Council.
11. A United Nations Volunteer Force should be formed and be available for rapid deployment under the authority of the Security Council.
12. The international community needs to make significantly increased funds available for peacekeeping operations.
13. The cost of peacekeeping operations should be progressively integrated into a single annual budget, and financed by assessed contributions by all UN members.

TABLE 2.1 *(continued)*

The Threat of Mass Destruction
14. The international community should reaffirm its commitment to eliminate nuclear and other weapons of mass destruction from all nations, and initiate a programme to achieve that goal in ten to fifteen years.
15. The Nuclear Non-Proliferation Treaty should be be renewed for an indefinite period.
16. Negotiations on a comprehensive ban on the testing of nuclear weapons should be successfully concluded in conjunction with the 1995 Nuclear Non-Proliferation Review Conference.
17. Nuclear-weapon-free zones should be created as a means of confining the spread of nuclear weapons.
18. The Biological and Chemical Weapons Conventions should be signed and ratified immediately by all nations that have not already done so, and their provisions rapidly put into effect.
19. Demilitarization should be given increased priority by the international community.
20. Governments should jointly adopt a concrete goal for lower levels of global defense spending.
21. A Demilitarization Fund should be established to help developing countries reduce their military commitment.
22. States should undertake early negotiation on a convention on the curtailment of the arms trade that should, among other things, make the reporting requirements under the existing Arms Register mandatory; meanwhile, arms-exporting contries should exercise restraint in arms sales.
23. There should be a world-wide ban on the manufacture and export of land-mines.

SOURCE: *Our Global Neighborhood: The Report of the Commission on Global Governance*, Oxford University Press, 1995, pp. 132–134.

weapons could never be compatible with the principles and rules of humanitarian law and is therefore prohibited. In the event of their use, nuclear weapons would in all circumstances be unable to draw any distinction between the civilian population and combatants, or between civilian objects and military intentions. . . . Such weapons would kill and destroy in a necessarily indiscriminate manner. . . . The use of nuclear weapons would therefore be prohibited in any circumstance, notwithstanding the absence of any explicit conventional prohibition. That view lies at the basis of the assertions by certain States before the Court that nuclear weapons are by their nature illegal under customary international law, by virtue of the fundamental principle of humanity" (Section 92, found in Weston, Falk, and Charlesworth, *Basic Documents*, 1997, pp. 1265–1266). In the Court's conclusion to its opinion, while it failed to rule out the use of nuclear weapons in self-defense, did state that "it follows from the above-mentioned requirements that the threat or use of nuclear weapons would generally be contrary to the rules of international law applicable in armed conflict, and in particular the principles and rules of humanitarian law" (Section 105, *Id.*, p. 1269).

Yet nuclear weapons have been used as a threat throughout the entire post-1945 era. The history of the Cold War era reveals that the restraints of the Cold War in Europe did not apply to the Third World. Throughout the Third World, both superpowers (the US and USSR) continually used and sponsored violence, even as they themselves moved toward direct confrontation on a variety of occasions. In this history, we find them, "in some cases, waging tense crises, making nuclear threats, preparing nuclear weapons for use, and even considering whether or not to cross the nuclear brink" (Schwartz and Derber, 1990, p. 82). In recognition of this history, E.P. Thompson revisited the concept of "deterrence" and noted that "deterrence is not a stationary state, it is a degenerative state. Deterrence has repressed the export of violence toward the opposing bloc, but in doing so the repressed power of the state has turned its back upon its own author. The repressed violence has backed up and worked its way into the economy, the polity, the ideology, and the culture of the opposing powers" (Thompson, 1981, p. 44). In this regard, deterrence has become a doctrine reflective of what has been called "the nuclear seduction" for it has the capacity to rationalize the irrational. Yet how can planetary suicide be rational? How can the superpower interventions in Lebanon, Vietnam, the Persian Gulf, Cambodia, Nicaragua, Angola, Afghanistan, and other Third World flashpoints be rational given their potential to have triggered a nuclear cataclysm? It can be argued "from either a moral or international law perspective, it is virtually impossible to vindicate reliance on nuclear weaponry" (Lifton and Falk, 1982, p. 137). Of course, moralists and legalists can be found who endorse nuclearism, but "their positions are so tortuous or their identities so bound up with state interests as to be unconvincing" (*Id.*, p. 137).

In response, it can be asserted that the lack of democratic accountability, in the superpower states, led to the crisis of nuclearism. As far as the United States is concerned, it has argued that "we can ensure that leaders are not free of public pressure when plotting aggression, intervention, and adventurism throughout the world. These are the real challenges for democracy in the nuclear age" (Schwartz and Derber, 1981, p. 236). But the question remains: How can a democracy be placed under public pressure when the public is lied to by the state and the media, acting as exclusionary monopolies?

Irrespective of their particular ideology, both superpowers, during the Cold War (and in its aftermath), have acted as exclusionary states (ES) in defense of exclusionary systems. The ES system is indeed global, transcending ideology and becoming interlinked through technology, profits, a proclivity for secrecy, and the protection and expansion of nuclear and media monopolies. In nuclear states, the corrosive effects of these trends upon the legitimacy of political power has created a condition of "tarnished legitimacy" which is "linked to the passion for secrecy, the official control and management of news" and the manipulation of public opinion (Lifton and

Falk, 1982, p. 138). This approach to world order has reinforced the exclusionary impulse by the reinforcement of hierarchy in all states, social fragmentation, tremendous disparities of wealth and power, an anti-democratic approach to both national and international life, as well as exacerbating national and global poverty, debt, unemployment, underemployment, and a failure to create avenues of participation on behalf of the excluded which could have influenced decision making.

The ES approach to world order violates the Nuremberg Principles as well as the conclusions and arguments most recently cited in the 1996 I.C.J.'s Advisory Opinion. The ES approach to world order also violates established principles of international law as embodied in the Convention on Genocide, passed by the UN General Assembly in 1948, and finally approved by the United States Congress in 1988. These instruments, however, fail to capture the psychological dimensions of resurgent militarism and its dangers. Legal instruments alone are not a substitute for democratic accountability and the engagement of the national and international public (the global civil society) in the consideration of the multidimensional aspects of this problem.

The distinguished legal scholar Raphael Lemkin fought hard to establish the importance of the concept of genocide, as defined by the United Nations General Assembly in 1946, as "a denial of the right to existence of entire human groups." In view of this history, psychologist Robert Jay Lifton and sociologist Eric Markusen wrote in their book *The Genocidal Mentality: Nazi Holocaust and Nuclear Threat* that: "We believe that our efforts here to explore common patterns in Nazi genocide and potential nuclear genocide are in the spirit of Lemkin's work . . . Both Nazi and nuclear narrative are crucially sustained by certain psychological mechanisms that protect individual people from inwardly experiencing the harmful effects, immediate or potential, of their own actions on others. These mechanisms. all of which blunt human feelings, include dissociation or splitting, psychic numbing, brutalization, and doubling" (Lifton and Markusen, 1990, pp. 12–13).

Further, the domination of technology, as already noted, with reference to the concept of "totalitarian tools," is found throughout "various bureaucratic procedures, by divesting the individual of a sense of responsibility for destructive collective bahavior" and "could greatly enhance numbing and doubling as well as brutalization. In the nuclear case, the domination of technology makes the numbing all the easier" (*Id.*, p. 13). The national security bureaucracy of the United States since the days of President Truman is testimony to this phenomenon. The blending of bureuaucracy with technology has been transubstantiated in "technocracy." The nature of the technocracy leads to a culture of "apocalyptic concealment." The culture underlies not only the armaments culture, but lies at the center of the nuclear state, the embodiment of the most deadly form of an ES. Its exclusionary nature corrupts the political process as well as the media which reports on it. In place of a sense of anguish there is a deterioration of public discourse.

With respect to Hiroshima and Nagasaki, the culture of the ES, with its reliance upon nuclearism, increasingly relied upon concealment. While it is true that "secrecy and concealment are used almost interchangeably," the reality is that "the latter suggests more active steps to suppress actual knowledge and is related in its derivation to the idea of covering, hiding, and (as a concealed place) 'the underworld.' From this standpoint, we can say that the bomb sequence has been from the *secret* to that which is *actively concealed*, and finally, to *falsification*" (Lifton and Mitchell, 1995, pp. 329–330, italicized in the original). When viewed from this perspective, the national security state not only becomes the national "insecurity" state, but also the exclusionary state (ES), for it actively works to exclude all the moral, economic, political, and social ramifications of the nuclear weapons enterprise.

In the nexus of its military and economic dimensions, the dynamic ramifications of the enterprise have created a kind of "military state capitalism," a condition wherein "the central government has primary control over capital resources and carries out the most important industrial management functions. In military state capitalism, military activity—building and operating armed forces and their industrial base—is the primary activity of the government" (Melman, May 20, 1991, p. 649). The financial cost of operating this ES has been astronomical. The United States has been operating under "military state capitalism" since 1945. From 1949 to 1989, the total budget of the Defense Department (in 1982 dollars) was $8.2 trillion. That sum was greater than the monetary value of civilian industry's plant equipment and of the nation's infrastructure in 1982, a total of $7.3 trillion. Put differently, the US government invested more capital in its military account than would be required to replace most of the human-made machines and structures in the country (*Id.*, p. 666).

The spill-over effect of this spending has affected both the corporate-controlled media and the ideology it expounds. It is revealed in a continuing state of affairs where "American state managers, with support from the education and media industries . . . teach that the US government should be the policeman of the world. Our racial inferiors of the Third World must be occasionally whipped into line by the application of American high-tech military power" (*Id.*, p. 668).

Melman's acerbic depiction of a dominant ideology which promotes the idea that Americans have "racial inferiors" throughout the Third World is a classic insight into the mentality of the ES and its denial of the principles outlined in the Nuremberg Charter. This is especially relevant with respect to the genocidal implications of nuclearism. There are many substantive prohibitions regarding state conduct found in the Nuremberg Charter. These prohibitions are outlined in Table 2.2.

The text of Principle VI of the Nuremberg Principles sets forth crimes which are punishable, under international law, as crimes against peace. These crimes involve the planning, preparation, initiation or waging a war of aggression in which there could be a violation of international treaties, agreements or assurances. These crimes against peace, pursuant to Principle VI, also involve participation in "a common plan or conspiracy for the accomplishment of any of the acts" previously cited. This standard affords an opportunity for the legal community to examine the role of the national security and its bureaucracy relative to the bomb.

In an article entitled "Bureaucracy and the Bomb: The Hidden Factor Behind Nuclear Madness," Fred Kaplan explained that shuttling MX missiles

> **TABLE 2.2 Substantive Prohibitions Found in the Nuremberg Charter**
>
> The following acts are crimes falling within the jurisdiction of the tribunal for which there shall be individual responsibility.
>
> a. *Crimes Against Peace:* namely, planning, preparation, initiation, or waging a war of aggression, or a war in violation of international treaties, agreements, or assurances, or participation in a common plan or conspiracy for the accomplishment of any of the foregoing;
>
> b. *War Crimes:* namely, violations of the laws or customs of war. Such violations shall include, but not be limited to, murder, ill-treatment, or deportation to slave labor or for any other purpose of civilian population or in occupied territory, murder, or ill-treatment of prisoners of war or persons on seas, killing of hostages, plunder of public or private property, wanton destruction of cities, towns, or villages, or devastation not justified by military necessity.
>
> c. *Crimes Against Humanity:* namely, murder, extermination, enslavement, deportation, and other inhumane acts committed against any civilian population, before or during war, or prosecutions on political, racial, or religious grounds in execution of or in connection with any crime within the jurisdiction of the tribunal, whether or not in violation of the domestic law of the country where perpetrated.
>
> SOURCE: A. Roberts and R. Guelff, *Documents on the Law of War*, Oxford: Clarendon Press, 1982, and reprinted in David Kauzlarich and Ronald C. Kramer, *Crimes of the American Nuclear State—At Home and Abroad*, Northeastern University Press, 1998, p. 32.

around the United States on an underground racetrack, or digging foxholes to protect against a nuclear blast, have not been the product of Dr. Strangelovian scientists, but of very ordinary government officials, adhering to some very common rules of bureaucratic behavior (Kaplan, 1983, pp. 49–59). In fact, bureaucratic jealousies within the US national security state have been a major force behind the irrational proliferation of nuclear weapons. Starting with the inter-service rivalry over nuclear strategy between the Air Force and the Navy in 1949, the bureaucratic struggle in the United States government continued through the times of General Tommy White, Air Force chief, who enthusiastically endorsed the concept of limited nuclear war two years after he had publicly denounced it. The reason? The Navy's new Polaris missile. Such actions demonstrate that uncontrolled bureaucracies guide, or at least dramatically affect, the decision making and policy making of states.

The logic of the bureaucracy of the national security state, as it relates to nuclear weapons policy and strategy, is diametrically at odds with international law's mandate in which there exists a legal duty to accord respect to international agreements seeking to establish peace. These agreements constitute part of a wider legal duty to refrain from the use of force in modern international relations, except in cases of self-defense or under the authority of the United Nations.

The precedent for this interpretation may be traced back to the General Treaty for the Renunciation of War, also known as the Treaty of Paris or the Kellogg-Briand Pact, signed on August 27, 1921. The political and legal nexus of arms control, the use of force, and the legality or illegality of nuclear weapons may be traced back to international legal precedents which were in place decades before the atomic bomb was developed and used. The historical significance of the Kellogg-Briand Pact is revealed through recognition of the fact that it is a treaty shaped by American diplomacy and validly ratified in accordance with United States constitutional requirements. Article I of the treaty reads as follows: "The High Contracting Parties solemnly declare in the names of their respective peoples that they condemn recourse to war for the solution of international controversies, and renounce it as an instrument of national policy in their relations with one another" (Friedman, 1972, p. 468). Article I is stunning when applied to an examination of the nuclear weapons question of the 1990s, insofar as it reveals two vital international principles: (1) that states are acting "in the names of their respective peoples" and (2) that recourse to war for the solution of international controversies is to be renounced "as an instrument of national policy." In the 1990s, both principles are violated in the policies and strategic conclaves of the nuclear states. Therefore, the restoration of the force and validity of international law norms, in the field of nuclear weapons, must restore these two principles into state practices and state policies. Doing so would accomplish the establishment of two major new trajectories for international law and the international community as whole.

First, the application of these principles would democratize the antidemocratic decision making of nuclear states. Subjecting these nuclear states to strict adherence to these norms would require the inclusion and incorporation of their respective peoples into the debate, as well as issues of taxation and funding which are necessary for the maintenance of these nuclear arsenals. So inclusionary governance, by demonstrating fidelity to the democratic principles of representation and participation, would force disclosure, the dismantling of a bureaucratic culture of secrecy, and the implementation of new forms of accountability to the peoples of the states individually, and the global commons collectively, as international law standards are finally given full force.

Inclusionary governance in the area of nuclear disarmament is not merely normative, for the normative aspects of inclusionary governance are as much derivative from principles of international law as a source for their inspiration. Further, the demands of inclusionary governance force its claims upon the processes associated with the negotiation of nuclear disarmament insofar as the International Court of Justice, in its Advisory Opinion of July 8, 1996, concluded with an examination of the duty of states to negotiate with a view to reaching an agreement on nuclear disarmament.

The relevant treaty obligation is found in Article VI of the Nuclear Non-Proliferation Treaty (NPT), which provides: "Each of the Parties to the Treaty undertakes to pursue negotiations in good faith on effective measures relating to cessation of the nuclear arms race at an early date and to nuclear disarmament, and on a treaty on general and complete disarmament under strict and effective international control" (Treaty on the Non-Proliferation of Nuclear Weapons, July 1, 1968, 21 UST 483, 729 UNTS 161). Based on this provision, the I.C.J. found unanimously that "[t]here exists an obligation to pursue in good faith and bring to a conclusion negotiations leading to nuclear disarmament in all its aspects under strict and effective international control" (Legality of the Threat or Use of Nuclear Weapons, Advisory Opinion of July 8, 1996, 35 ILM 809 & 1343, 1996, para. 105 (2) (F)).

The I.C.J. expounded on the phrase "and bring to a conclusion" as follows: "The legal import of that obligation goes beyond that of a mere obligation of conduct; the obligation involved here is an obligation to achieve a precise result—nuclear disarmament in all its aspects—by adopting a particular course of conduct, namely, the pursuit of negotiations on the matter in good faith" (*Id.*, para. 99). The significance of the I.C.J.'s additional language is to underscore the obligation which exists to pursue negotiations in good faith toward a particular result—namely, a duty to make all reasonable efforts to reach the result of disarmament through the negotiating process.

The problem is that the Court's finding does not dictate any timetable or negotiating forum for reaching this result. As a consequence, real US security interests (not to mention global interests) were probably damaged by the US Senate's rejection of the Comprehensive Test Ban Treaty (CTBT), in October 1999. Raymond Garthoff, former counselor to the US mission to NATO and former US ambassador to Bulgaria noted that "the Senate's action goes a long way toward telling the world that the United States places not only its own parochial interests, but even domestic partisan interests, above its responsibilities in the world" (Garthoff, *Los Angeles Times*, October 31, 1999, at p. M2). In this regard, Garthoff concluded, "the most dedicated opponents of the test-ban treaty saw its defeat as the first major step in rolling back the existing arms-control regime . . . The Anti-Ballistic Treaty is next. If so, then strategic arms limitations: the Strategic Arms Limitations Treaty of the 1970s, through the Strategic Arms Reduction Treaty I, the START II Treaty still awaiting Russian ratification and, prospectively, a START III Treaty" (*Id.*, at p. M2). Given the domino effect of the US Senate's demonstration of "bad faith," the treaty obligations of the NPT and the admonitions of the I.C.J.'s July 1996 ruling have been effectively ignored. Hence, the challenge for inclusionary governance, at the national and international levels, is to take up the disarmament task where the Court left off—by dictating a timetable for negotiations leading to nuclear disarmament and, at the same time, establishing a negotiating forum for reaching this result.

Second, by eliminating recourse to war as a means for settling international controversies, the leadership of nuclear states will be deprived of any legitimate justification to engage in planning, preparation, or participation in a common plan or conspiracy for nuclear war, in violation of both the Nuremberg Principles and the Treaty of Paris. In this regard, Article II of the Pact of Paris is quite explicit in its admonitions, as it recites the agreement of the contracting parties: "That the settlement or resolution of all disputes or conflict of whatever nature or of whatever origin they may be, which may arise among them shall never be sought except by pacific means" (Friedman, 1972, p. 469).

The "pacific means" currently available to the international community involves not only the United Nations, but also international organizations, NGOs, and security communities. In this regard, "we may conceive the habits and practices of the peaceful resolution of conflicts, and the shared norms on which they are based, as a crude governance structure" (Adler and Barnett, 1998, p. 35). Governance can best be defined as activities backed by shared goals and intersubjective meanings that "may or may not derive from legally or formally prescribed responsibilities and that do not necessarily rely on police powers to overcome defiance and attain compliance" (Rosenau, 1992, p. 4). The shared goals and intersubjective meanings attached to negotiations for reaching an agreement on nuclear disarmament are also strengthened by the norms and force of international law when that law is recognized and acted upon by the states. What the US Senate's October 1999 rejection of the CTBT reveals, however, is the fact that individual nuclear states, when left unaccountable to the requirements of even a strong legal mandate, will, in all probability, ignore the promises and requirements inherent in treaty obligations at the peril of not only their domestic constituencies, but the international community as a whole.

To leave a regime of nuclear arms control in abeyance, leading to its possible disintegration, is the zenith of political irresponsibility. The problem and the challenge was acknowledged by Karl Jaspers in his classic book, *The Future of Mankind*, when he noted that "the reality of the rational community cannot be proved, but mankind's fate depends upon its prevalence in the reality of politics. Its success is uncertain. What cannot be done by compulsion, only by the freedom of reason, will still thrive only when this freedom can guide itself" (Jaspers, 1961, p. 225). This problem is further acknowledged by the observation that "the content of international law is overwhelmingly associated with norms generated by intergovernmental behavior. The Nuremberg approach represented itself as an innovative attempt to insist that the idea of accountability extended to political leaders. However, in retrospect, the Nuremberg claim has not induced a law-making process capable of restraining or apprehending governmental leaders who exceed the bounds of normative authority. Similarly, the United Nations, as a mechanism of the global community, has been unable to make any serious inroads on state sovereignty vis-a-vis war-making discretion" (Falk, Meyrowitz, and Sanderson, 1980(a), p. 592).

The challenge that presents itself to the international community and international law is that of effectively challenging discretionary lawlessness when law-making claims have not been assimilated into the operational code of sovereign state behavior. This is especially troublesome when there is neither the will nor the capability at the intergovernmental level or the United Nations level to effectively challenge the proclivity of nuclear states to engage in discretionary lawlessness, as exemplified in the 1999 rejection of the CTBT by the United States Senate. It is to this challenge that we now turn.

F. INCLUSIONARY MEASURES FOR ADVANCING PEACE

The promise of inclusionary governance is the practical promise of filling in the gaps between the claims and aspirations of international law, sovereign nation-states, and an emerging global civil society. This book makes the argument that inclusionary governance, in its various forms, is a path toward peace which make the difference between the effective enforcement and adherence to international law standards and principles or, in the alternative, to their violation. Inclusionary governance constitutes a perspective which argues that a creative space must be established in the struggle against emergent and unconstrained nuclearism and its expression in resurgent militarism.

In the early 1980s, Professor Falk advocated the idea that it was necessary to take into account the political structures and restraints of different polities. He articulated the perspective that normative initiatives could so dramatically challenge the root assumptions of militarization that these challenges could ultimately culminate in the global linkage of social movements and forces working for principled demilitarization. He identified three systems in this task: the First System (the state system and its support infrastructure); the Second System (the UN and regional international institutes); and the Third System (represented by people acting individually and collectively through voluntary associations). In the interrelationship between these three systems, he argued that the Third System is the primary system because the First System is supportive of the underlying logic of militarization while the Second system is merely a dependency of the First System and, therefore, unable to sustain or implement demilitarization initiatives. Hence, it is left to the Third System to sustain normative initiatives of consequence to demilitarization (Falk, 1980(b), pp. 339–356).

The demilitarization perspective is framed by the dialectic which exists between a militarized global system, on the one hand, which stands in contrast to the goal of demilitarization, on the other. In the vortex of this tension exists a creative space which I call "inclusionary governance." It is inclusionary because of its capacity to incorporate the entire normative heritage of humankind into perspectives, policies, and institutions designed to enhance peace while, at the same time, refusing to participate in the legitimation of ideologies, practices, regimes, and behaviors which undermine the search for peace. Those civilizational norms which are supportive of human survival and cooperation constitute the normative basis of inclusionary governance. In contrast, norms of the global war system seek to rationalize and justify what Edward Thompson has termed "exterminism"— the idea of the bomb as the object of a new social order which has shaped and structured the societies out of which it grew, thrusting them inexorably towards extermination (Kaldor, 1982, p. 262).

Thompson makes the argument that "weapons are things and strategies are instrumental plans for implementing policies which orginate elsewhere. Thus what we must do is examine the ruling elites and their political intentions" (Thompson, 1982, p. 5). He proceeds to argue that "politics itself may be militarized: and decisions about weaponry now impose the political choices of tomorrow. Weapons, it turns out, are political agents also" (*Id.*, p. 7). To recognize the inherently *political* nature of nuclear weapons is the beginning of wisdom on the subject, for "the common tendency to identify the *problem of nuclear war* with the *nuclear arms race* is a logical fallacy that dangerously distorts nuclear politics by promoting technical fixes to what is overwhelmingly a political problem" (Schwartz and Derber, 1990, p. 19, italics in the original).

Overkill in itself did not make the arms race irrelevant. The arms race mattered only if it produced either (1) a way to defend society against nuclear weapons, or (2) a way to control nuclear war and prevent escalation to all-out carnage. The fact that it can do neither points toward the realization that "all that matters is the possibility of uncontrolled escalation once the nuclear shooting begins" (*Id.*, p. 18). This reality is the only reality that confronts the actual political leadership of nuclear states, not the abstract models of nuclear strategists. By giving inordinate attention to the supposed significance of the size and technical characteristics of the superpower's stockpiles is to fall into the logical fallacy of "weaponitis" (*Id.*, p. 13). In this respect, perhaps as early as 1955 and no later than the early 1960s, both the US and USSR had acquired so much destructive power that "only secondary importance would attach to any further quantitative or qualitative improvements in the leading weapons of the day. . . . The weapons paradigm was already obsolete" (*Id.*, pp. 14–15).

In recognition of this situation, on September 20, 1961, John J. McCloy and Valerian A. Zorin, on behalf the the United States and the Soviet Union respectively, submitted to the UN General Assembly a "Joint Statement of Agreed Principles for Disarmament Negotiations" (US–USSR Report to the General Assembly, UN Doc. A/4879). Popularly known as the "McCloy-Zorin Agreement," this joint statement, adopted unanimously by the General Assembly, called for multilateral negotiations to design and implement an internationally acceptable program of general and complete disarmament that would lead to the eventual dissolution of national armed forces and the establishment of effective and reliable mechanisms for the peaceful settlement of international disputes.

The "Joint Statement" was historic. Never before the Kennedy administration, or after it, has there been such a formal recognition that the numbers of nuclear weapons are irrelevant and that disarmament and abolition of the weapons was the only really sane political path to take. For example, in Kennedy's assessment of the strategic balance it is clear that he recognized that the very existence of a Communist Chinese bomb would alter the Chinese leadership's self-perception of its security and military capabilities. The possession of nuclear weaponry would, to some extent, affect and influence the Chinese state's behavior. Yet Kennedy's interpretation also reflected his view that while the possession of such weapons was relevant to Chinese perceptions, at the same time a mere change in the numbers of weapons would not necessarily be relevant (Nash, 1999, p. 138).

In fact, a review of JFK's overall view of nuclear weapons reveals that "Kennedy never went beyond almost ritualistically assigning nuclear weapons equal weight among other sources of force and influence. And in practice, Kennedy reduced their relative role in his foreign policy" (*Id.*, p. 139).

In this critical respect, "Kennedy's reliance on non-nuclear 'assets' overshadowed his reliance on nuclear weapons, just as nuclear restraint eclipsed any nuclear recklessness" (*Id.*, p. 140). Restraint and negotiation characterized the Kennedy approach to the nuclear question.

On the issue of the resumption of nuclear testing, JFK made a decision that was at least as much political as technical. He was forced to deal with internal political pressures for testing from the military and the weapons laboratories, reinforced by the fact that the Russians were learning from their tests (Kaysen, 1999, p. 103). Yet, there were continuing negotiations and discussions in a new forum through the tripartite Conference on the Discontinuance of Nuclear Weapons. The outcome of this process was that, "as a result of bilateral discussions between the United States and the Soviets in the summer of 1961, an Eighteen-National Disarmament Committee had been created under the auspices of the United Nations. Transferred to this new committee, a further discussion of a test ban began in March 1962" (*Id.*, p. 105).

On June 10, 1963, in a commencement address at the American University in Washington, D.C., JFK made the necessity of peace the central theme. Acknowledging the impossibility in the nuclear age of resolving conflicts by war and the futility of the arms race, he emphasized the need for coexistence and a complete reevaluation of US relations with the Soviet Union. He concluded his address with the announcement that high-level discussions would shortly begin in Moscow looking toward early agreement on a comprehensive test-ban treaty and that the United States would not conduct further tests in the atmosphere so long as other states refrained from doing so. Kennedy's efforts culminated in the signing of a "Treaty Banning Nuclear Weapons Tests in the Atmosphere, in Outer Space and Under Water," concluded in Moscow, August 5, 1963 and entered into force on October 10, 1963 (Text in Westen, Falk, Charlesworth, *Basic Documents*, 1997, pp. 213–214). One month later, Kennedy was assassinated in Dallas, Texas. With his death, the course of nuclear negotiations, relative to disarmament, changed as well. In the aftermath of Kennedy's assassination, "the KGB chose to ignore Johnson's promises to continue the Kennedy approach to foreign policy" (Fursenko and Naftali, 1997, p. 347). Within the government of the United States, dramatic changes were made both with respect to the nuclear issue and Vietnam (Kaiser, 2000).

From the late 1960s, the US and USSR regotiated the control and reduction of nuclear arms only intermittently. The manner in which these new discussions were conducted made resort to nuclear weapons more acceptable than unacceptable as a policy option in a variety of confrontational contexts, including Vietnam. Between the 1970s and the 1980s, two different sets of negotiations were pursued. The first was the Strategic Arms Limitation Talks (SALT I). The focus of these negotiations concentrated on the "control" of nuclear weapons, rather than on their reduction or elimination. The second set of discussions, the Strategic Arms Reduction Talks (START) began in the early 1980s, mainly in reaction to the collapse of SALT II. Regardless of how significant the advances and achievements made under these nuclear regimes, they are glaringly deficient when compared to the the broad principles of the McCloy-Zorin Agreement and the 1963 Test Ban Treaty. Further, they are deficient in terms of both the quantity and increased sophistication of nuclear arms in the world of the 1990s.

The Reagan administration's initiatives on START and the Strategic Defense Initiative (SDI) both revealed the sophisticated nature of the "rightwing" arms control posture of the United States since the 1980s. The initiatives were "sophisticated" in the sense that the major reason for right-wing advocacy of offensive arms reductions was designed to establish US nuclear superiority (Bodenheimer and Gould, 1989, p. 136). It was and remains premised on the view that US superiority in technology "may allow for a new generation of offensive weapons, making the current weapons obsolete over the next decades . . . Arms control agreements also may take many years to design, negotiate, and sign. By the time an offensive weapons reduction agreement is in place, the weapons to be eliminated might already be obsolete for the United States" (*Id.*, p. 137). What this means, in practice, is that it is to the advantage of the military-industrial complex of the United States to reduce current weaponry so that both sides would have to start their arms buildup anew—a situation which favors the nation with the more advanced technology (in the context of a bipolar world).

With the end of the Cold War, the US has had to go in search of new enemies to justify an SDI program. It has settled on "rogue states" that might get the bomb as well as the economic benefits that accrue from allowing a regime of nuclear proliferation among the Third World's "rogue states" to constitute a potential hazard and threat. After all, some credible military threat has to justify military spending, even though all the rogues are armed with largely obsolete Soviet weaponry (Klare, May 26, 1997, p. 23). Under either scenario (advances in technology or perceived threats from "rogue states"), the profit margins for the military-industrial complex and nuclear weapons production and technology continue to escalate. These political decisions, however, ignore both the real logic of the nuclear arms race, including SDI, and its scientific realities. Professor Carl Sagan observed that SDI would let enough Soviet warheads through to destroy the US anyway, making it "The Leaky Shield." He noted that "such a shield is not better than nothing; it is worse than nothing, because it might well engender a false sense of security, bringing on the very event it was designed to prevent . . . If there are no technological 'fixes' to the nuclear arms race forthcoming, then it seems that we should consider agreement on equitable, bilateral, verifiable and massive cuts in the nuclear arsenals. If properly devised, such a treaty might be one of those endeavors in which both parties, and eveyone around them, would win" (Sagan, December 8, 1985, p. 17). The same perspective was endorsed in other related contexts, such as nuclear proliferation (Spector, 1984); the flawed scientific basis of star wars in a nuclear world (Zuckerman, 1987; Union of Concerned Scientists, 1983), the environmental implications of Chernobyl (Hawkes, et al, 1986), the advent of the new nuclear nations (Spector, 1985).

Both the reoccurrence of calls for investment in the SDI program (euphemistically dubbed "Star Wars"), as well as the expansion and rearmament of NATO, reflect this profit-driven equation, employing through the corporate-controlled media the rationalization of "deterrence" and playing to irrational fears of Russian "expansionism" (Sanders, 1983; Mokhiber and Weissman, 1999, p. 32; Hartung, March 1998, p. 9; Hartung and Washburn, March 2, 1998, pp. 11–16; Hartung, May 1998, pp. 22–24). Europeans, since the days of the Reagan administration, were concerned for the economic harm that SDI might do to Europe. In fact, European leaders were "concerned about a growing 'technology gap' between Europe, the United States, and Japan. If the United States infused $26 billion into the high-technology sector of the US economy over five years, Europe might find itself even further behind" (Lakoff and York, 1989, p. 227). The logic behind such a conclusion was established by historical experience, in which Europeans knew that US firms would keep the lion's share of such contracts for themselves and treat the European firms as subcontractors (Thompson, 1985; Knelman, 1987).

In addition to the profit motive there is also the myth of technological determinism. As the arsenals of warfare have grown more elaborate, indeed baroque, there has been a corresponding temptation to buy into the myth that a limited nuclear defense project to protect against even a small-scale attack, such as might be launched by a terrorist group or "rogue state," is desirable. However, "the danger with this approach is that it can become an alternative to other means of addressing the problem and can foster costly illusions" (Lakoff and York, 1989, p. 340). Alternatives to the myth of technological determinism and its variants can be found in the fact that most nations around the globe have accepted the CTBT, and condemned the US Senate's rejection of it in 1999. Also, as pragmatists are coming to power in Third World states as well as First World states, there is a growing recognition of the need to pursue foreign policies of accommodation rather than of an unsupportable expansionism or outright belligerence. In short, there is growing appreciation of the need to achieve political understanding. The elements of such an understanding can begin with differentiating between a negative peace and negative security system versus positive peace and a positive security system.

Negative peace and negative security rely on the concept of "deterrence" and adopt the "realist" power-politics paradigm. Alternatively, positive peace and positive security stress the "desire to eliminate the threat by addressing its cause" (Felice, 1998, p. 33). The source of the solution to the problem is the realization that "central to positive peace is not just the absence of war and violence, but also the protection of human rights and social justice" (*Id.*, p. 33). The International Bill of Human Rights, for example, acknowledges human needs of survival, well-being, identity, and freedom. These rights are now cosmopolitan in nature, reflected in emerging forms of humane governance, in accord with the newly emerging right to democratic entitlement, and are exemplified by inclusionary states (IS) and inclusionary values, policies, and goals. In this task, arms control and disarmament, and the demobilization of armed forces within which nations may pursue implementation of the corpus of international human rights law, are increasingly critical elements of an alternative agenda (*Id.*, p. 35). These are a few of the necessary future steps that need to be taken if inclusionary governance is to be realized.

The realization of inclusionary governance, in the nuclear context, is also dependent upon the following factors: (1) the dismantling of structures and policies which allow for the continued investment in and expansion of nuclear and non-nuclear assets (Johansen, 1994, pp. 372–397); (2) a recognition of the fact that spending on nuclear and non-nuclear assets depletes the economy which pays for their production and is simultaneously destructive of the creation of norms which can lead to a deepening of democracy (Lifton and Falk, 1982; Schell, 1998); (3) the necessity to realize that accumulated scientific evidence is sufficient to ensure that the exchange and/or detonation of just a few nuclear bombs have the capacity to create a global condition known as "nuclear winter" which could lead to climatic catastrophe, agricultural collapse, and world famine (Sagan and Turco, 1990; Ehrlich, Sagan, Kennedy, Roberts, 1984); (4) the history and evolution of international law is moving in the direction of disarmament and has the capacity to build a global institutional structure which supports an alternative security system (Weston, 1990, pp. 78–106); (5) the historical experience of war and conflict, which has proven that a failure to recognize the influence of pre-existing beliefs has implications for decision making and that, therefore, the processes of decision making must become more inclusionary so as to overcome a history and practice of concealment, secrecy, distortion through propaganda, and bureaucratic and media manipulation (Jervis, 1976, pp. 181–202); (6) a perception that genuine security and a peaceful world order cannnot be premised upon notions of "deterrence" and "balance of power" because a spiral of violence is created by these concepts so that the exercise of power is self-defeating (Jervis, 1997, pp. 174–176); (7) the recognized need for a global security policy which places an emphasis upon non-military incentives to channel government's behavior, thereby giving support to an expanded role for international organizations or security regimes to facilitate cooperation and to regulate intergroup conflict (Johansen, 1983, p. 28; Adler and Barnett, 1998, pp. 3–28).

The seven points constitute the sustaining norms of nuclear restraint and the the core perspectives from which a security regime, reflective of the norms and values of inclusionary governance, may be achieved. The realization of inclusionary governance, in the nuclear context, is dependent upon the realization of all seven of these perspectives and the combined force of the political, legal, economic, social, cultural, and religious mandates to take the global community to that point of historical transition, perception, and transformation. These seven points will be discussed, in turn, in the summary, *"Sustaining Norms of Nuclear Restraint."*

At the dawn of the 21st century, the path to inclusionary governance, in these seven arenas, is blocked by the fact that America's peacetime foreign policy is dedicated to over-preparation for regional conflicts which may make the Pentagon's prophecy of a need to fight an endless succession of Third World adversaries a self-fulfilling prophecy (Klare, 1972; Lens, 1987; Hartung, 1994; Klare, 1995). At present, the emerging world security environment reflects a world inhabited by "tectonic forces" that are "reshaping human society and sharpening conflicts among various groups, tribes, peoples, and states" (Klare, 1995, p. 209). In this new world security environment there are two alternatives. The first is the path which acknowledges that human rights is the core domestic and foreign policy which has the capacity to provide a route for the achievement of peace and stability. The second path is the the dominant one which is now in vogue, the one that is still preoccupied with the "balance of power," "the balance of terror," "deterrence," profit maximization. The consequence of following this path has led to increased friction and conflict around the globe.

Michael T. Klare has identified five major forces which appear to be responsible for intensifying intergroup friction along social fault lines. First, the globalization of the market economy has produced increased competition between older and newer centers of capitalist production, contributing to a widening gap between rich and poor. Second, with the diminishing allure of multiethnic state systems there has been a corresponding increase in the assertion of ethno-nationalist loyalties. Third, the emergent popularity of Western consumer culture has served to exacerbate a resurgence of traditional mores and religion. Fourth, with a substantial rise in the world's population (to over 6 billion people), there is a dangerous combination of resource scarcities coupled with deteriorating environmental conditions. Fifth, a growing loss of faith in the ability of existing state structures to cope with these multiple pressures has created a global crisis of credibility (*Id.*, p. 210). Throughout this book, I attribute the existence of this global crisis of credibility in existing state structures to those qualities associated with the ES and the exclusionary impulse which emanates from its policies in every arena of decision making and policy making. Nowhere is this more recently apparent than in the context of the United States Senate's rejection of the CTBT.

In the following summary of my discussion of the role of inclusionary governance in the nuclear context, and the capacity of this approach to overcome the obstacles outlined by Klare, I seek to identify the mutually reinforcing nature of the issues involved and their interrelationship to one another. In so doing, the "sustaining norms of nuclear restraint" may be understood as emerging from paths of inclusionary governance.

G. SUSTAINING NORMS OF NUCLEAR RESTRAINT

Thompson's perspective on the relationship between weapons and political choices is very applicable to the politics of the CTBT defeat at the hands of the United States Senate of 1999. In the immediate aftermath of the Senate's action on the CTBT, David Sanger published an article in *The New York Times* entitled "The Real Power Struggle Isn't Just About Nukes" (Sanger, NYT, October 17, 1999). Sanger contended that Washington is split over whether to wield American power alone or with others. So "the test ban treaty was only the latest of a number of divisive issues in the capital that share a common subtext: an argument not over whether the United States is strong, but over how it should use its power. Should it strut the global beach alone, or leverage that power by accepting restraints on its freedom to act?" (*Id.*, October 17, 1999). Given this perspective, Thompson was probably correct over two decades ago by asserting that politics itself may be militarized. Yet the impact that these politics have on the status of international law and the global civil society are just as important.

Sustaining norms of nuclear restraint takes the dedication and commitment of what Falk called the Third System, where individuals and groups can act collectively through voluntary associations to bring the force of the global public's opinion back into the corridors of power and into the centers of decision making. These centers are not only military, legislative, and presidential; they also involve international courts of law. So, as inclusionary governance embraces a strategy that looks beyond the global hegemon of US power, it raises an argument that can be jurisprudentially formulated in natural law terms and benefit by being reinforced by the consensus of the global community. In this regard, to some extent, "individuals and grassroots groups, alive to these concerns, have claimed the responsibility and right to impose 'the law' on the state" (Falk, Meyrowitz, and Sanderson, 1980, p. 593). Such a role for global civil society and individuals within states corresponds well with David Held's notion of "cosmopolitan democracy"—a view which places individuals in a position to sue their respective states for violations of international law, human rights violations, and the pursuit of policies which violate the Nuremberg Principles. In all of these venues, the claims of inclusionary governance and its grounding in international law confronts the hierarchical structures of militarized states which, in varying degrees, exert hegemony over weaker states.

The global processes associated with a deepening of democracy demand accountability and an end to imperial intentions, politics, and norms. In this regard, at the heart of the US Senate's vote against the CTBT was a surrender to the imperial temptation, to unilateralism, which is ultimately commited to preserving America's ability to use its power unchallenged. Such a stance not only violates the mandates of international law and the aspirations of global civil society, but also constitutes an endorsement of traditional notions of deterrence. In the case of the rejected CTBT, that means "retaining an ability to go back to traditional deterrence, constantly improving America's nuclear arsenal and forcing a resurgent Russia or an ambitious China to fear a financially ruinous arms race" (Sanger, NYT, October 17, 1999).

By contrast, "demilitarization implies a comprehensive restructuring of world order and international security" for it "involves an assault on fragmentation and hierarchy" and thereby it entails "a shift away from violence to sustain the organized political life on the planet" (Falk, 1980(b), p. 340). I maintain that the violence in the current order of power is a global reflection of exclusionary states and exclusionary practices which have embraced militarization as a means of maintaining not only international hierarchy, but also the power which comes from the maintenance of class, ethnic, religious and regional cleavages. In short, the violence of the current order is the very antithesis of inclusionary governance and its mortal enemy. This assertion may be supported by numerous examples. I choose the "Delhi Declaration" of 1978 as a key example of the inclusionary impulse expressing itself as a political and legal mandate to engage in the renunciation of nuclear weapons as legitimate instruments of war.

The "Delhi Declaration" called for the entire world to be made into a nuclear weapons-free zone. The Declaration proposes the immediate negotiation of a Nuclear Disarmament Treaty, outlining its principal features and insisting that serious negotiations to make it happen be held. Such an approach needs to be resurrected in the aftermath of the 1999 defeat of the CTBT. In this way, the mandate of "good faith" in the processes leading to negotiations for global disarmament can be effectively resurrected. Its resurrection will be grounded in international law, treaties, covenants, the involvement and participation of individuals and groups throughout the entire global civil society. It will have the normative, legal, political, and ideological capacity to move humankind toward the fulfillment of the promises inherent in cosmopolitan democracy, humane governance, and inclusionary governance. To achieve this goal, the seven factors associated with the realization of inclusionary governance, in the nuclear context, are presented.

(1) *Structures and policies which allow for the continued investment in and expansion of both nuclear and non-nuclear-assets shall be dismantled and replaced with peacekeeping and monitoring institutions.* The history of the Cold War reveals high levels of investment in nuclear and non-nuclear assets within the United States and the former Soviet Union (Gaddy, 1996; Odom, 1998; Mead, 1987). An "atomic audit," undertaken by the Brookings Institution, estimates the cost to be in trillions of dollars (Schwartz, 1998). A precise calculation is impossible because between 1943–1951 there was no current, systematic accounting for atomic costs since, with few exceptions, no effort was made to distinguish these from other budget categories of which they formed a part. Insofar as defense efforts were funded in reference to the concept and doctrine of deterrence, a fully comprehensive view of the atomic audit would have to take into account the ways in which such spending preserved the strength inherent in the US economy (Kunz, 1997, Yarmolinsky, 1971; Grieder, 1998).

What the US experienced was insufficient public and congressional scrutiny which would have allowed it to be compared to other uses of national resources. The penalty paid by the US for procuring nuclear forces in this manner was substantial (Schwartz, 1998, p. 542). From this spending, Cold War communities emerged within the US creating what has been called "the rise of the gunbelt," which resulted in the military remapping of industrial America (Markusen, Hall, Campbell, Deitrick, 1991). The benefits of the gunbelt shaped regional income differentials and generated diverse new industries. The drawbacks were a lack of investment in regional infrastructure and a loss of creative talent (Markusen and Yudken, 1992, pp. 199–202).

The economic costs were associated with the political costs for democracy as a democratic deficit was also incurred. Largely, both the public and the Congress were left out of the debate and decisions on nuclear policy and investment. The ES state which emerged, calling itself the "national security state," remained the preserve of a small, self-interested elite (Hartung, 1994, p. 298). The anti-democratic nature of the nuclearized ES resulted in exclusionary effects that not only distorted the domestic politics of US democracy, but its foreign policy as well. Anti-communist rebels were armed around the world by every US administration from Truman to Bush. When the American "nuclear umbrella" was unfurled, it protected a vast arms trade which reached into many Third World countries and eventually escalated to hundreds of billions of dollars per year. The human cost of America's arms trade has led to the American-Islamic confrontation in the late 20th century and has the potential to duplicate the same situation elsewhere (Tirman, 1997). Preventive diplomatic action still remains merely an adjunct to the power politics of national security thinking (*Id.*, p. 286).

In the alternative, inclusionary governance seeks to de-emphasize limited and self-limiting concepts of national security (which emphasize threats to the nation-state) and re-conceptualize security as something that is both common and comprehensive. As the Independent Commission on Disarmament and Security (the Palme Commission) concluded in 1989, the very destructiveness of modern war, even in its conventional forms and derivations, has become so terrible that war has lost its meaning as an instrument of national policy. Further, it leaves the root causes of conflict unresolved. Hence, the need for replacing traditional notions of security with notions of "inclusionary security" and "common security" is more apt to address the root causes of conflict and serve to obviate reliance on force or weapons. This is especially important in the case of the Middle East where, with respect to conventional arms, the five major suppliers—the United States, China, France, Britain, and Russia—have failed, so far, to exercise "collective self-restraint" and have continued to export "destabilizing" weapons to nations in the region. And, in that regard, the Middle East is not alone (Keller, 1995; Klare, 1997, pp. 43–71). Latin America has experienced a "scourge of guns" as the diffusion of small arms and light weapons has made violence a pervasive part of the culture of the region (Klare, 1996; Klare, September/October 1997, pp. 19–21).

Inclusionary governance stresses decreasing the role of military power and, in its place, developing reliance on peacemaking and monitoring institutions. Increasing the effectiveness, representative capacity, and inclusionary potential and auspices of the UN Security Council, establishing an international disarmament agency under UN auspices, and encouraging the supportive efforts of governments that seek to institutionalize their peacekeeping responsibilities through the fulfillment of Article 43 of the UN Charter are all important components of an inclusionary security regime. Such a regime can act at the national and international level to dismantle the structures and policies of exclusionary states and regimes which have historically contributed to the invesment in and expansion of nuclear and non-nuclear assets. In its place, under the guidance of legal mandates from a strengthened International Court of Justice (ICJ), a timetable for negotiations leading to global disarmament may be put in place. Further, the transfer of funds from military to social accounts should be directed to alleviate the burdens of poverty, debt, unemployment, and destitution which continue to characterize the lives of the excluded. By generating broader political support for these constituencies, the claims of inclusionary governance can advance an agenda for peace which augments demilitarization as it also creates new institutional and social channels for inclusion.

(2) *In recognition of the fact that spending on nuclear and non-nuclear assets depletes First and Third World economies, it shall be the task of inclusionary governments and inclusionary regimes to embark upon the deepening of democratic norms, practices and policies so as to alter current spending priorities.* The end of the Cold War has presented humanity with a political

windfall. Because political assets such as the promise of disarmament and the abolition of nuclear weapons are not likely to increase with time, it is vital to move rapidly toward their realization. Otherwise, new military buildups, geopolitical crises and technological innovations may close shut the window of opportunity for a more peaceful and inclusionary world order (Schell, p. 11). This is especially critical in light of two important factors: (a) the 1999 defeat of the CTBT by the US Senate, and (b) the fact that during the Clinton administration the US has emerged as the world's premier arms-trading nation, exceeding or equaling the years of the Nixon/Kissinger weapons export boom of the 1970s (Hartung, 1995, pp. 25–35).

Spending on arms must be made subject to democratic controls at the national and international level. To facilitate this task, the publics of First and Third World nations must be included in deliberations, debates, and decision-making centers that make the final determinations on budgetary priorities. In this regard, the values, principles, policies, and goals of inclusionary governance can be combined with the drive toward the emerging right of democratic governance to make political and legal claims against elites and arms dealers who continue to promote genocide through the violation of the Nuremberg Principles, as in Rwanda, Bosnia, and East Timor. By deepening democratic principles of inclusion, national and international forums can be used to begin to place restrictions on investment in further nuclear testing (through passage of the CTBT) and begin the legal processes to control and eventually halt the international arms trade in conventional weapons. In this task, Edward Carr's historical analysis of international relations becomes more relevant: he noted that "politics and law are indissolubly intertwined; for the relations of man to man in society which are the subject-matter of the one are the subject-matter of the other. Law, like politics, is a meeting place for ethics and power" (Carr, 1964, pp. 177–178).

Law and politics should be made accountable to ethical demands and the exercise of power in relation to inclusionary norms, values, policies, and goals. This process can begin through the deepening of democracy when "we draw a contrast between *rulers security*, whereby elites employ military and paramilitary means to secure narrowly based hierarchical relationships and structures of privilege" and "*peoples security*, whereby the protection of general interests in autonomy and development are upheld in the least destructive manner" (Falk and Kim, 1982, p. 27, italics in the original). Peoples security addresses the problem of the "inclusion/exclusion dilemma" (my term) by advocating through legal and political mandate the right to participation in decision making on issues which affect basic human needs, survival, and the articulation of new concepts of security and community. Peoples security also represents the forging of a coalition of interests opposed to the status quo of exclusionary state practices (which exacerbate hierarchy, fragmentation, and democratic disempowerment). The boundaries of such a coalition transcend the national and become global. In fact, an inclusionary coalition, of necessity, must become global in an age of globalization insofar as "the projected model of globalism and 'world order' seeks to perpetuate international hegemonies within and between nations, and structures of governance that are repressive and inhumane" (Kothari, 1980, p. 23).

This task involves a global coalition that must confront an order that is "designed to ward off movements from below of exploited classes, peoples and nations and the assertion of their rights, including the right of national sovereignty and 'collective self-reliance' by countries whose economies and polities are affected by an international structure of domination and exploitation" (*Id.*, p. 23). It is in view of this opposition of the forces of "globalization from above" that a global coalition for inclusionary governance and democratic empowerment must engage in combative self-assertion. This will mean that exploited nations, "tied closely to movements for structural change within nations," must be transformed into inclusionary states (IS) that are democratic in practice so as to be positioned to more effectively combat "predatory globalization." Only in this manner can more hopeful scenarios emerge which "depend upon the greening of global civil society and its capacity to overcome modernist preoccupations of a territorially constituted system of world order" (Falk, 1999, p. 20). Without a global movement/coalition for structural change, globalization and the ideology of the new world order "will remain a recipe for management of the globe through an oligarchy of governing elites" (Kothari, 1980, p. 23). Such a result would solidify the ES and exclusionary regime structures.

The deepening of democracy, therefore, requires two parallel processes. One process is a global coalition for structural change within and between nations (largely the product of Falk's "Third System" involving global civil society). The other process involves the transformation of the state itself, especially in developing countries where the state performs at least six developmental functions: (1) director in guiding the course of economic development, (2) protector or gatekeeper between intrasocial and extrasocial flows of action, (3) provider of an industrial infrastructure, (4) a financier, (5) a producer, and (6) a consumer (Ross, 1997, pp. 104–105).

Third World initiatives are vital, for the main impetus to such a social movement of global proportions must reflect the inclusionary claims of billions of people who have borne the brunt of over two hundred years of planned underdevelopment (planned by the West and its capitalist centers). While Third World nations are vulnerable individually, they are collectively formidable. This would especially be the case in a reformed UN system where representation was matched to greater participation and inclusion in decision-making and policy-making processes involving human security issues (from the atomic bomb to problems of hunger and famine, from socioeconomic rights to human rights). Further, as states undergo the domestic transformation of their respective civil societies, the exclusionary bulwarks of hierarchy and elite privilege will begin to weaken and eventually collapse. This process can be globally replicated as a global alliance for a new international order takes shape with the birth of inclusionary states and inclusionary security regimes which promote cooperation and a reordering of North-South economic relations.

In fact, such a movement can link the respective civil societies of the North with those of the South insofar as it constitutes a dialogue and a logic that should make sense to those in the Western countries who have waged and continue to wage a struggle for equity at home. Some examples of this potential are already recognizable in Scandinavia and the Netherlands (Kothari, 1980, p. 29). Under the auspices of such an undertaking, a global social movement for global peace and disarmament may unite the First and Third Worlds in the struggle against militarism within both worlds. At that point, it would be possible to relate all of these efforts to the more generic movement for a just world with deepening democratic norms, practices, and aspirations (*Id.*, p. 36).

Practically, building such an alternative world security system, which gives credence to democratic claims, will require the creation of more representative and inclusionary institutions. Hence it may be argued that "the most reliable path for implementing reciprocity in world affairs is to move toward a more just representation of all people in increasingly effective international institutions" where many people also have "a strong (though seldom acknowledged) self-interest in securing balanced representative procedures in international organizations and courts, where reciprocity can be impartially defined" (Johansen, 1994, p. 378). Yet, these courts, if still controlled by the privileged or governed by the laws of a hierarchical system, may still yield an unjust result. Therefore there is still the need to build a new political order, such as cosmopolitan democracy, on a global scale. As Edward Carr observed: "Once . . . it is understood that law is a function of a given political order, whose existence alone can make it binding, we can see the fallacy of the personification of law implicit in such phrases as 'the rule of law' or 'the government of law and not of men'" (Carr, 1964, p. 178).

(3) *The necessity to embark upon a path toward inclusionary governance and demilitarization is supported by accumulated scientific evidence, which provides sufficient proof that the exchange and/or detonation of just a few nuclear bombs will have the capacity to create a global condition known as "nuclear winter" that could lead to climatic catastrophe, agricultural collapse, and world famine.* By 1982, it had become clear to a select group of scientists that had been studying the potential climatic changes which would result in the event of nuclear war that the consequences might be far worse than had been acknowledged or understood by the civilian and military establishments of the contending nation-states. Their calculations revealed the possibility of of a global climatic catastrophe, even from a "small" nuclear war.

In 1990, Carl Sagan and Richard Turco published *A Path Where No Man Thought: Nuclear Winter and the End of the Arms Race*, in which they argued that the end of the Cold War signaled the advent of an historical window of opportunity in which improved relations between the US and USSR made it "the optimum time to work to reassess military doctrine and policy, to reconsider weapons system on order, to reverse the arms race." To that end, the authors stated: "We believe that nuclear winter provides a compelling incentive for reversing the arms race—an incentive embracing not only the nuclear-armed nations, but the entire human community." To effectuate that goal, the perspective they set forth made the argument that "on issues of this importance it is not enough for citizens and policymakers to rely on experts . . . they need to inform *themselves*. There is no other way to make responsible decisions" (Sagan and Turco, 1990, pp. xviii–xix, italics in the original).

As early as 1983, Professor Sagan wrote an article for *Foreign Affairs* entitled *"Nuclear War and Climatic Catastrophe: Some Policy Implications,"* in which he outlined the central point of the new findings—that the "long-term consequences of nuclear war could constitute a global climatic catastrophe" (Sagan, Winter 1983/84, p. 259). Recognizing what was at stake, he introduced his essay by noting that "apocalyptic predictions require, to be taken seriously, higher standards of evidence than do assertions on other matters where the stakes are not as great. Since the immediate effects of even a single thermonuclear weapon explosion are so devastating, it is natural to assume—even without considering detailed mechanisms—that the more or less simultaneous explosion of ten thousand such weapons all over the Northern Hemisphere might have unpredictable and catastrophic consequences" (*Id.*, pp. 257–258). Addressing the political implications facing policymakers on this issue, Sagan explicitly warned that "for policymakers there is another concern: if it turns out that nuclear war could end our civilization or our species, such a finding might be considered a retroactive rebuke to those responsible, actively or passively, in the past or in the present, for the global nuclear arms race" (*Id.*, p. 258). Sagan's remarks anticipate the recent 1996 ruling of the International Court of Justice on the illegality of nuclear weapons and are as old as the international law concerns articulated in the Genocide Convention and within the framework of the Nuremberg Principles. Furthermore, his admonition resonates in a series of treaties and resolutions where the UN has recognized that the survival of the environment which sustains human existence must also be a consideration in formulating a prohibition against the use and possession of nuclear weapons.

As early as 1960, the Antarctic Treaty denuclearized that continent (402 UNTS, 71). Article V of that Treaty specifically prohibits nuclear explosions. Activities of States in Exploration and the Use of Outer Space including Celestial Bodies was adopted by the General Assembly, creating a nuclear "free zone" in outer space (610 UNTS, 205). Finally, the installation or testing of nuclear weapons has been banned from the world's oceans by the Treaty Banning Nuclear Weapons from the Sea Bed and Ocean Floor (23 UST, 701, TIAS No. 7337, reprinted in 10 ILM 146 (1971)). The recognition that the use of nuclear weapons has the potential to destroy the environment, as well as the human species, has also been acknowledged in General Assembly Resolutions. In 1971, Resolution 2849 (XXVI) deciared "that the rational managment of the environment is of fundamental importance for the future of mankind" (G.A. Res. 2829, UN GAOR 26th Sess., Suppl. no. 29). In specfiic terms, Resolution 3246 (XXIX) of 1974 deplored all efforts to influence the environment and the climate for military purposes because those kinds of efforts "were incompatible with the maintenance of international security, human well-being and health" (G.A. Res. 3246, UN GAOR 29th Sess., Suppl. no. 31, vol. 1). Another expression of ecological awareness is embodied in Resolution 3154 (XXVIII) of 1973 which denounced "environmental pollution by ionizing radiation from testing of nuclear weapons" (G.A. Res. 3154, UN GAOR 28th Sess., Suppl. no. 30). In other words, since its inception, the United Nations has continuously demonstrated an awareness that the use of nuclear weapons could terminate human existence.

With respect to nuclear winter, Professor Sagan set forth the possible strategic and policy implications of the new findings by emphasizing "the necessity of moving as rapidly as possible to reduce the global arsenals below levels that could conceivably cause the kind of climatic catastrophe and cascading biological devastation predicted by the new studies. Such a reduction would have to be to a small percentage of the present global strategic arsenals" (Sagan, *Foreign Affairs*, Winter 1983/1984, p. 259). In 1990, there were 60,000 nuclear weapons in the world (Sagan and Turco, 1990, p. xviii). Yet as early as 1983 it was recognized that "a threshold exists at which climatic catastrophe could be triggered, very roughly around 500–2,000 strategic warheads." Given this estimate, "a major first strike may be an act of national suicide, even if no retaliation occurs. Given the magnitude of the potential loss, no policy declarations and no mechanical safeguards can adequately guarantee the safety of the human species." And because "no national rivalry or ideological confrontation justifies putting the species at risk . . . there is a critical need for safe and verifiable reductions of the world strategic inventories to below threshold" (Sagan, Winter 1983/84, p. 292).

In early 1984, The Conference on the Long-Term Worldwide Biological Consequences of Nuclear War published its findings under the title *The Cold and the Dark: The World After Nuclear War* (Ehrlich, Sagan, Kennedy, Roberts, 1984). The authors relied on the year-long work of more than 200 scientists from around the globe. They found that the biological and climatic changes that would occur in the advent of a nuclear exchange would be so drastic that the survivors would envy the dead, for the collapse of societal systems would be coupled with the end of human civilization as we know it. An unprecedented competition for drastically reduced resources would make it highly uncertain what specific courses societal systems would follow, "but clearly the intense competition for limited resources would lead to an additional and consequential human toll" (*Id.*, p. 124). In recognition of this fact, Sagan and Turco concluded that massive reductions in the nuclear arsenal and in the conventional forces they deter are the only way to prevent nuclear winter. For "like the assault on the protective ozone layer and global greenhouse warming, nuclear winter is a looming planetwide catastrophe that is within our power to avert. It teaches us the need for foresight and wisdom as we negotiate our way through technological adolescence. And nuclear winter also reminds us of an ancient truth: When we kill our brothers, we kill ourselves" (Sagan and Turco, February 4, 1990, p. 13). From this perspective, Sagan concluded that "the problem cries out for an ecumenical perspective that can rise above cant, doctrine and mutual recrimination . . . What is urgently required is a coherent, mutually agreed upon, long-term policy for dramatic reductions in nuclear armaments, and a deep commitment, embracing decades, to carry it out . . . It is nowhere ordained that we must remain in bondage to nuclear weapons" (Sagan, Winter 1983/84, p. 292).

From the perspective of inclusionary governance, pursuant to the 1996 advisory ruling of the I.C.J. and in light of the 1999 rejection of the CTBT by the United States Senate, a new approach is required which legally mandates the following: (1) a timetable for negotiations to be concluded between all nuclear states leading to the reduction of nuclear arsenals below levels which could produce "nuclear winter;" (2) a cross-cultural and cross-civilizational dialogue capable of articulating and embracing those inclusionary features of our common humanity so that the moral, religious, normative levels of global civilization move beyond the "clash of civilizations" model, as formulated by Huntington, and embark upon a path which embodies the centrality of "humane governance" as formulated by Falk and the inclusionary aspects of civilizational dialogue which can emerge from the globalization of inclusionary governance; (3) the passage and endorsement of a Non-Proliferation Treaty by all nuclear states; (4) the conclusion of a Comprehensive Test Ban Treaty to end all nuclear testing indefinitely; (5) at the UN level and throughout all international organizations and NGOs, an ending of the political subordination of Third World states so that their inclusion in all decision making and policy making on nuclear issues (as well as socioeconomic issues) makes them equal partners in the global dimensions of inclusionary governance, as opposed to being consigned to a status of subordination that has been historically in place since the days of colonization. With these steps, aspirations to the global dimensions of inclusionary governance and building effective security regimes may be released from their current bondage to exclusionary practices and ancient doctrines.

(4) *The history and evolution of international law is moving in the direction of disarmament and has the capacity to build a global institutional structure which supports an alternative security system. Such a system must lead toward the effective subordination of the military establishments of the nation-states under the rubric of the values, principles, policies, and goals of inclusionary governance.* The emerging consensus in the arena of international law is that "what is needed is the development of a foundation for both nuclear disarmament and the elimination of the institution of war, a set of possibilities for rendering war itself, not the weapons and technologies that are its symptoms, obsolete. Law can and must play a critical role in this context. In fact, the materials of such a foundation can be none other than a set of effective international legal processes and institutions for resolving international disputes peaceably. Ultimately . . . the appeal of legal and normative arguments in the context of the nuclear debate is overwhelmingly simple. Law represents both a reflection of the aspirations of international society and an essential and concrete element of the kind of security system that will be necessary to convert the normative consensus into significant practice" (Arbess and Sahaydachny, 1987, p. 104).

International legal instruments have been used to condemn the use or threat of nuclear weapons (as with the 1996 I.C.J. Advisory Opinion). Yet, these instruments have yet to force states to effectuate a timetable for negotiations leading to disarmament and eventual abolition. Without a set date for the achievement of these goals, nuclear states have already demonstratred a pattern of non-compliance with the mandate and purpose of international law in the field of nuclear disarmament. To rectify this problem is, in my judgment, the next great challenge for international law and for nuclear states. The challenge has been a persistent one, widely appreciated by international law scholars and practitioners. For example, international law's struggle with non-compliance by states demonstrates that however much international law may interdict any planned use of nuclear weapons in theory (Weston, 1983; Arbess, 1984; Boyle, 1986; Meyrowitz, 1988), the fact remains that it is usually all too ineffective in practice. While it may be argued that, regardless of the sophistication and maturation of any particular legal system, such a legal regime remains impotent to politically volatile or otherwise intractable issues of public policy (Weston, 1990, p. 80), to deny its possible realization is to abdicate the field of decision making to elite-centered exclusionary states and exclusionary security regimes which remain beyond the rule of law and accountability to the people.

However, even E.H. Carr admonished international relations scholars to recognize that "it is profitless to imagine a hypothetical world in which men no longer organize themselves in groups for purposes of conflict" (Carr, 1964, p. 231). Part of the reason for skepticism is that "international law has no agents to enforce observance of the law" (*Id.*, p. 171). It is, therefore, left to the states themselves to produce the results mandated by international law. In the praxis of the late 1990s, scholars have returned to the work of realists like Carr, Han Morgenthau, and Kenneth Waltz to point out that their contribution to international relations theory "sought to highlight the manipulation, accumulation, and balancing of power by sober unsentimental statesmen, focusing above all on the limits imposed on states by the international distribution of material resources." It is from this perspective and for this reason that "they viewed realism as a bulwark against claims about the autonomous influence of democracy, ideology, economic integration, law, and institutions on world politics" (Legro and Moravcsik, 1999, p. 6).

Carr, in particular, had convinced the scholars of his generation that the central debate in international relations theory should be between "realists" (who believed in rationality and the national self-interest), and "idealists" (who believed in the uniform harmony of state interests, the power of altruistic motivations, or the possibility of world government). Whether this was a useful way to frame the question 50 years ago remains an open question. Today, some scholars argue, its unsuitability "should be obvious to all" because these two categories "are too vague, too broad, too open-ended, too normative, and too dismissive of contemporary nonrealist theory to be much use as a guide to social scientific theory and research" (*Id.*, p. 54).

Since the 1970s, rationalist theories and variants of liberal, epistemic, and institutionalist theories have become the competitors to realist claims. It is argued they should be recognized as such because "any categorization of international relations theories that fails to accord these a central and distinct place is profoundly misleading" (*Id.*, p. 55). One possible solution to the dilemma is not to simply jettison the term "realist" altogether but rather to give it greater precision by looking beyond the assumptions of and beliefs in state rationality. The dilemma may be overcome by making a commitment to "a particular rationalist theory of state behavior" (*Id.*, p. 55).

Applying this proposed solution to the task of making international law standards binding on state practices and security regimes in the context of nuclear disarmament means translating a rationalist theory of state behavior into a workable institutional structure that also benefits from the inclusion of national and international publics (the global civil society or "global village") in the framework of elite decision making. Such inclusion and practical incorporation into the resolution of the nuclear disarmament question would have the capacity to force democratic governments to take seriously the aspirations of their respective publics for the development of an alternative security regime. Such an approach would be able to dismantle the bulwark that realists established against the prospect of the autonomous influence of democracy and, at the same time, remove the exclusionary barriers and impediments to democratic claims, as exemplified in patterns of manipulation and balance of power calculations which have characterized the exclusionary practices of unsentimental statesmen.

The conversion of normative consensus into significant practice in the area of nuclear disarmament demands adherence to what Franz Neumann called "the concept of political freedom" (Neumann, 1953, reprinted in *The Rule of Law Under Siege: Selected Essays of Franz L. Neumann and Otto Kirchheimer*, 1996, pp. 195–230). The concept of political freedom is legally linked to civil liberties, insofar as "civil liberties establish a presumption in favor of the rights of the individual and against the coercive power of the state" (Neumann, p. 198). In Neumann's view, the state may intervene in the exercise of the individual's liberty "but first it must prove that it may do so." The proof for this "can be adduced solely by reference to 'law,' and it must, as a rule, be submitted to specific organs of the state: courts or administrative tribunals." Following this scheme, there are three statements which Neumann views as inherent in the analysis of civil rights: (1) the burden of proof for intervention rests always with the state; (2) the only means of proof is reference to a law; (3) the method by which a decision is to be reached is regulated by the law.

Neumann's analysis is important when applied to nuclear states insofar as they have constructed a "national security state" which denies citizens their civil rights when seeking to oppose or uncloak the veil of secrecy that allows for the concealment of the truth regarding these weapons, while at the same time propagating the mythology that the security of the nation (and freedom itself) is directly related to its control of the "nuclear monopoly." The inherently undemocratic character of these claims is further cloaked by the ideology of "progress." On this specific point, Neumann asserts that "technological progress (the *conditio sine qua non* of cultural progress) is used today largely for armaments." The problem arises when there is no set time-table for ending the union between technology and arms production. On this matter, Neumann wrote that "no threat to the political system of democracy can arise if the fruits of advancing technology are diverted from normal use for a relatively short time. But our historical experience tends to show that a long-range postponement of expectations is possible only in a wholly repressive system" (*Id.*, p. 222).

Between 1945 and 1999, the United States government produced a repressive system in the name of "national security," not unlike Latin American versions of *La Patria*, which have justified the suspension of constitutional norms, the imposition of a "state of siege," and anti-democratic initiatives that have reflected the "politics of anti-politics" (Loveman and Davies, 1989). Throughout Latin America, the defense of the "fatherland"— *La Patria*—meant that the military "sought to reserve a residual 'sovereignty' to sustain its virtually totemic status: feared and revered, quasi-sacred protectors of *la patria*" (Loveman, 1999, p. 215). The implications for the restoration of democratic politics and accountability are ominous insofar as "democracy is not simply a political system like any other; its essence consists in the execution of large-scale social changes maximizing the freedom of man" (Neumann, 1996, p. 222).

Large-scale social changes, such as nuclear disarmament, constitute a transition from an undemocratic security regime (which has escaped a fully accurate atomic audit) to an alternative security system governed by laws which are binding, enforceable, and accountable to democratic norms. Such an alternative security system would have the capacity to maximize the "freedom of man" from fear and the concept of the "enemy." This conclusion is vital for understanding the dimensions of the task of disarmament and the potential for an alternative human future. As Neumann stressed: "If the concepts 'enemy' and 'fear' do constitute the 'energetic principles' of politics, a democratic political system is impossible, whether the fear is produced from within or from without. Montesquieu correctly observed that fear is what makes and sustains dictatorships. If freedom is absence of restraints, the restraints to be removed today are many; the psychological restraint of fear ranks first" (*Id.*, p. 223).

The dictatorship of "decisionary exclusion" has marked the history of the Cold War/US paradigm and the expansion of the military-industrial complex. In order to remove the lingering vestiges of the national "insecurity" state and its dictatorship of exclusion, it will be necessary to transform the undemocratic politics of the nuclear state. The replacement of the ES with the inclusionary state (IS), dedicated to freedom instead of fear, makes a new kind of progress achievable and operative. According to Johansen, "progress toward the demilitarization of all societies is an important goal of global policy because nothing less can fulfill the human need for security. Moreover, demilitarization facilitates the realization of other preferred values, such as fair distribution of world resources, a lifting of military repression, and a respect for the environment" (Johansen, 1983, p. 29). These preferred values are already embodied in international law (Weston, 1990, pp. 81–82).

To make these values part of the practice of states will lead toward the objective realization of inclusionary governance. McDougal has asserted, in this regard, that "national law, like international law, may be most usefully regarded not as a mere body of rules but as the whole of a specialized process of authoritative decision" (McDougal and Reisman, 1981, p. 446). From this perspective, an inclusionary politics has the potential to emerge as states begin to recognize that "inclusive policies, relating to all values and of the greatest importance for both common and particular interests, are today being continuously prescribed and applied in external arenas for the effective regulation of both external strategies and internal policies of states" (*Id.*, p. 448).

Inclusion, in this context, overcomes the old fears of the "realist" school which posits a sharp divide between realism's perception of a need for a "balance of power" to maintain the international distribution of material resources and the "idealist" claim that the autonomous influence of democracy has the capacity to remake national and international institutions so that their respective practices accord with the normative claims of law and interpersonal justice. Inclusionary governance and demilitarization heal the divide between realism and idealism by establishing a rationalist framework for state behavior which can transcend the artificial divisions. On both the national and global levels what this means is moving beyond a singular focus on security for one nation state to a view of the peoples of the human race as the beneficiaries of security policies.

From the national level of governance to the emerging international level of governance, we find, as McDougal and Reisman predicted, that "many inclusive policies are designed to make easier the processes of persuasion and agreement" (*Id.*, p. 456). In no other area is this legal capacity more needed than that of nuclear weapons issues and efforts at establishing a timetable for disarmament negotiations between nations. What remains encouraging is the recognition that "the important decision-makers of the world arena have . . . been able to clarify a long-term common interest in the enforcement of many inclusive prescriptions . . . For other prescriptions, such as the community prohibition of unauthorized violence, common interest has not yet been clarified in comparable degree" largely because "effective elites are not yet fully convinced that in destroying others they will destroy themselves, and expectations of enforcement are accordingly low. The task of enhancing the effectiveness of inclusive prescription in the world arena remains, in measure, a task of enlightenment" (*Id.*, p. 458).

A sense of species solidarity and global citizenship may begin to coexist with realist notions of traditional national identity. There is, in other words, an increasing convergence between the national interest and the human interest. This is what makes the path to an alternative security system one of inclusion. It actively displaces the exclusionary methods of power wielding, power application, and power paradigms which represent the protection of elite interests at the expense of various classes and groups of people. In this regard, inclusionary governance unites prudence with ethics because concern with the security of one state becomes concern with the security of all states. Ethically, the security of one nation should result in the security of all nations.

The historical obstacle to this ethical prescription in practice is found in the old realist paradigm which seeks to preserve the largest possible domain for unilateral decision. Given this perspective, "state officials have commonly insisted upon distinguishing nonjusticiable or 'political' disputes and justificiable or 'legal' disputes" (*Id.*, p. 461). This distinction is a false one, however, insofar as "the distinction lies rather in the willingness or unwillingness of states to submit to inclusive decision" (*Id.*, p. 461). A corrective to this dilemma, from the standpoint of international law, is to counterbalance this historical unwillingness of states to submit to inclusive decision making by applying international standards where national standards favoring inclusionary paths are not yet evolved. What this implies for the 21st century is already prefigured in the last years of the 20th century by the observation that what may be even more "propitious for the effectiveness of inclusive policies . . . is the growing acceptance of the view that states may not in conformity with international law impose defects and inadequacies in their own constitutions and practices against others as defenses to obligation under either customary international law or agreements apparently authoritatively concluded" (*Id.*, p. 465).

Insofar as the history of the international system has been an exclusionary, hierarchical war system, the mandate provided by international law to move toward inclusionary governance restores to human beings the freedom to transform exclusionary states into inclusionary states. Greater degrees of inclusion have the capacity to transform governance by deepening democracy within and between nations. Such a transformation can be undertaken with the understanding that the late 20th century has borne witness to an interpenetration of multiple processes of authoritative decision making which cross the lines between traditional conceptions of national or municipal law and conceptions of international law. The legal environment may be more precisely understood, as McDougal suggested, as one where "the rules commonly referred to as international law and national law are but perspectives of authority—perspectives about who should decide what, with respect to whom, for the promotion of what policies, by what methods—which are constantly being created, terminated, and recreated by established decision makers located at many different positions in the structures of authority of both states and international governmental organizations" (*Id.*, p. 487).

When the bifurcation between municipal law and international law is recognized as contending perspectives of authority, it is possible to reorder their respective relation to one another. In other words, we can recover the inclusionary potential in each by recognizing the complementary potential of both in advancing inclusionary solutions. This is an objective possibility for placing transnational law on a new trajectory with the laws and practices of nation-states because "people demand values for particular identities, with various levels of inclusiveness. Changing perspectives of demand and expectation bring about changes in conceptions of the self" (McDougal, Lasswell, Chen, 1980, p. 115).

The problem and the challenge posed by bringing about changes in conceptions of the self and the group is the result of the following paradox: while some peoples are genuinely dedicated to a world public order of human dignity, "not all the aspiring world public orders exhibited in the contemporary world arena are equally dedicated, beyond rhetoric, to the values of human dignity" (McDougal, 1981, p. 489). Therefore, the rational alternative is to strike a balance "between the inclusive competence of the general community of states and the exclusive competence of particular states most economically designed to further their long-term basic goal values" (*Id.*, p. 490). In striking this balance, it will be necessary to assure the incorporation of civil society at the national and international levels in decision making. As this process moves forward, civil society is constantly empowered to bring pressures on government to make sure that its capacity to govern is directly tied to the issue of whether or not its mandate preserves the legitimacy given it to effectuate inclusionary forms of governance capable of sustaining disarmament and the building of an alternative security system which incorporates the security of the entire human species.

(5) *The historical experience of war and conflict has proven that a failure to recognize the influence of pre-existing beliefs has implications for decision making and that, therefore, the process of decision making must become more inclusionary so as to overcome a history and practice of concealment, secrecy, and distortion through propaganda as well as bureaucratic and media manipulation.* The failure to recognize the influence of pre-existing beliefs and the effects in international politics has led to a situation where "not being aware of the inevitable influence of beliefs upon perceptions often has unfortunate consequences" (Jervis, 1976, p. 181). Simply put, "it is common to find actors believing that strong evidence, if not proof, for their views is supplied by data that, they fail to note, also supports alternative propositions" (*Id.*, p. 181). Nowhere is this result more evident than in the arena of nuclear weapons and their use, production, and source of threat.

To cite one example from among many, consider the *Shimoda* case. It arose out of an action of five individuals who, in May of 1955, instituted legal action against the Japanese Government to recover damages for injuries allegedly sustained as a consequence of the atomic bombings of Hiroshima and Nagasaki. It gave occassion to consider how best to assess the legal status of nuclear weapons, assuming that some kind of effective standards governing their use could be arrived at. In general, two dominant modes of thinking were relied on in exploring this issue, taken from the international law of war. The first mode, used in connection with poison gas, is to deal with *the instrinsic legal character* of the weapon. The second mode, in some respects a residual of the first, is to assess legality exclusively by reference to *the context in which the weapon is used.* The *Shimoda* opinion is an amalgam of both modes (Falk, 1965, p. 787). This case embodies the dilemma referenced by Jervis, where the same data can be referenced and relied upon to reach alternative propositions.

Within the framework of military strategy itself, the problem of an unawareness of the influence of beliefs upon perceptions, combined with evidence without proof, can easily lead to strategic choices with diametrically opposed propositions being set forth which have little relevance to the actual state of affairs. For example, bureaucratic manipulation affected the planning guidance that was established by US leaders in 1947–1948 and resulted in the establishment of broad parameters for subsequent approaches to the contruction of war plans that allowed for the incorporation of nuclear weapons (Cimbala, 1994, p. 74). Considerations ranging from a first-strike capability to the tensions associated with bipolarity dominated discussions which rarely assessed the intrinsic nature of the weapons and the possibilities for building an institutional culture of restraint, negotiation, and eventual disarmament. In the decades before 1990, and certainly after, perceptions about nuclear weapons altered dramatically in response to the dangers of proliferation and the growing perception that they are little more than elaborate and expensive anachronisms. Coupled with a moratoria on nuclear testing by four nuclear weapon states and the fuller accounting of the "hidden" costs of the nuclear competition, there has been a further movement toward a paradigm shift, which has resulted in delegitimating this type of military force (Reiss, 1995, pp. 2–3). In 1996 this preceptual trend culminated the Advisory Opinion of the I.C.J. regarding the illegality of nuclear weapons.

Yet, of all the factors influencing the behavior of countries relative to nuclear weapons, by far the single most important one is the quality of political leadership. In this regard, "choosing the right goal is only the first element of good leadership" insofar as the real challenge is in finding the means to achieve desired ends. This is because "how close a country comes to actually achieving its objectives is the final measure of leadership" (Reiss, 1995, p. 329). In the early 1990s, while de Klerk (South Africa), Memem (Argentina), Collor (Brazil), and Nazarbayev (Kazakhstan) did well by this measure of leadership, "they were good leaders not because they chose to codify their countries' nonproliferation obligations but rather because they realized that their countries' nuclear ambitions impeded the achievement of political and economic goals that they valued more highly" (*Id.*, p. 329). Altered perceptions at the nation-state level expose an even more fundamental policy issue for international law: What is the impact of international law upon national law?

The question was addressed in 1981 by Myres S. McDougal in his essay, "The Impact of International Law Upon National Law: A Policy-Oriented Perspective" (McDougal and Reisman, 1981, pp. 437–492). From a comprehensive global perspective, he argued that it is possible to observe that "of the effective decisions which constitute the world power process, some are taken inclusively, in the sense that several or many or all states participate in the making of such decisions, and others are taken exclusively, with only a few issues" (*Id.*, p. 437). He argued that each state has an interest in developing what he called "inclusive competence." First, it was necessary to maintain democratic access to participation, "thus ensuring that peoples in fact primarily affected by decisions have a voice in determining such effects." Second, "in requiring wide assumption of responsibility for such competence, thus ensuring that decisions inclusively taken from community perspectives . . . will actually be put into effect by . . . particular states" meant that "each state has . . . an interest in its own freedom . . . because of contemporary interdependences" and "reciprocally an interest in the freedom of others" (*Id.*, p. 438). This leads to the conclusion that "the most general interest of all states and people, adhering to the values of human dignity, is . . . in a world public order" seeking to strike a balance between "the inclusive competence of the general community of states and the exclusive competence of particular states which best promotes the greatest total production, at least cost, of their shared values" (*Id.*, p. 438). In the examples cited, nuclear nonproliferation obligations (an expression of "inclusive competence") reflected and supported the municipal goals of nation-states seeking to maximize the welfare of their peoples with respect to their particular economic and political goals (an expression of the "exclusive competence" of states). The interplay of these two types of competences suggests that the path to inclusionary governance, in the field of nuclear disarmament, is attainable and within reach.

As suggested by my fifth point, an appreciation of the historical experience of war, as well as investment in the bomb and the ramifications associated with its proliferation in the nuclear age, have led to a reexamination of pre-existing beliefs. The processes of decision making, when they become more inclusionary (as through the auspices of international law), can fundamentally alter the domestic behavior of individual states. As such, individual nation-states, by participating in a more inclusionary international legal regime, are empowered to alter their domestic decision making and move their military policies and investment choices in the direction of compliance with the principles of inclusionary governance, thereby democratizing the actual decision-making process which leads to policy alternatives becoming new directions at both the level of individual nation states and the international global community at large. The transformation of perceptions is, in part, the benefit of living in "a world of ever-accelerating interdependence in all value processes" and, as a consequence, "it may also reasonably be expected that decisions with *inclusive effects* will similarly accelerate in range, frequency, and intensity of impact" (*Id.*, p. 444, italics mine).

(6) *Genuine security and a peaceful world order cannot be premised upon notions of "deterrence" and "balance of power" because a spiral of violence is created by these concepts so that the exercise of power becomes self-defeating.* The historical emphasis upon deterrence and balance of power concepts as ordering principles of nation-state power, strategy, and international relations theory is flawed by the resulting forms of global violence which are part of what Jervis has identified as "the spiral model of conflict." According to the spiral model of conflict, "states can be caught in a cycle of reinforcing hostility, arms, and conflict driven by the security dilemma and ancillary psychological dynamics, including the failure of decision makers to understand the dilemma" (Jervis 1997, p. 174).

The process that is identified by the spiral model of conflict is associated with the characteristics I have attributed to the leadership and policies of exclusionary states. The proclivity of the ES to define needs, beliefs, and goals in relation to hierarchical orderings of social, political, and economic exclusion makes the world more hostile and aggressive. In other words, sociopolitical instability (SPI) is a product of the spiral model of conflict. The reason for this result is that the ES seeks to suppress internal dissent of the excluded while, externally in its foreign policy, it seeks to "Finlandize" its neighbors so as to avert the building up of hostile regional alliances by other states in response to ES policies and their perceived threat to the security of surrounding states. Part of this phenomenon is associated with the fear of surprise attack. In the nuclear age, this fear has reached dangerous proportions, especially when rumors of war can easily be translated into self-fulfilling prophesy (*Id.*, pp. 174–175).

In large measure, the spiral model of conflict is associated with a divided world order, made up of exclusionary states and exclusionary security regimes which exhibit pervasive expectations of violence. These expectations generate chronic anxiety and personal insecurity. Governing elites of the ES can use these fears as propaganda weapons through the media and governmental announcements in order to justify military buildups and investments in "defense." The problem for world order which results from this practice is that many individuals and groups rely on strategies of violence more than strategies of peaceful cooperation. On this matter, it may be noted that "many governing elites, preoccupied with the consolidation and expansion of power, are determined to exclude most of the population from participating effectively in important value processes. They continue to impart a distorted worldview to their people. Not infrequently, they mobilize the masses in ways that encourage docility despite persisting circumstances of deprivation and nonfulfillment. They cultivate internal tension as a means of deflecting latent hostility toward foreign targets" (McDougal, Lasswell, Chen, 1980, p. 118).

While the Cold War did not produce preemptive strikes, that does not mean that they were not contemplated by contingency planners or feared by the opposing parties as real threats. In the 1990s, as India and Pakistan confronted the reality of how to govern their atomic arsenals, as well as their relations, the dangers associated with the spiral mode of conflict and fears associated with a preemptive strike led to a mutual reluctance to contemplate signing a CTBT. In 1997, one year before atomic tests were undertaken, one author observed that "while the likelihood of another war between India and Pakistan is low, the two states have fought three wars—in 1947, 1965, and 1971—and came close to military conflict in 1986–87 and again in 1990" (Holum, 1997, p. 266).

In the case of India, balance of power concerns continued to dominate the logic associated with national security. India's decision not to sign the CTBT in 1996 was based both on its traditional approach to nuclear disarmament and its national security concerns (Ghose, 1997, p. 239). Several factors made the position taken by India almost inevitable, including its general approach to nuclear disarmament, its perception of a potential threat from the existence of nuclear weapons, its strategic circumstances, and the unanimous rejection by the Indian Parliament of what was perceived as an unequal and coercive treaty (*Id.*, p. 260). Whatever the exact reasons for this result, it can easily be asserted that preferences for hostile policies may be the product of the difficulty of gaining mutual security. The real challenge for building a regime of nuclear restraint is to make mutual security an achievable goal so that limited wars do not escalate (Perkovich, 1999).

A feasible starting point for a regime of nuclear restraint was proposed in the 1996 Advisory Opinion of the I.C.J. where the Court finds "a growing awareness of the need to liberate the community of States and the international public from the dangers resulting from the existence of nuclear weapons," and to establish "a comprehensive and universal conventional prohibition on the use or threat of use, of those weapons as such" (Nuclear Weapons, para. 73). The Court's analysis supports the proposition that genuine security and a peaceful world order cannot be premised upon notions of "deterrence" and "balance of power" concerns because a spiral of violence is created by these concepts which eventually becomes self-defeating. Under these circumstances, the movement of states and the evolution of international law standards, which augment developing inclusionary systems of deliberation, create the preconditions for both inclusionary governance and disarmament.

(7) *The recognized need for a global security policy which places emphasis upon non-military incentives to channel governments' behavior empowers the international system to give added support to an expanded role for international organizations or security regimes to facilitate coopera-*

tion and to regulate intergroup conflict. Transnational public organizations have the potential to lay the basis for establishing a global authority to enforce arms reduction and prohibit the use of force. Such a direction has already been endorsed by the spirit, if not the letter, of the 1996 Advisory Opinion of the I.C.J., but it is also a direction which is prefigured in states comprising a security community.

States comprising a security community retain their sovereignty in a formal legalistic sense. Yet their sovereignty, authority, and legitimacy is contingent on the security community in two respects. First, "while a security community does not erode the state's legitimacy or replace the state, the more tightly coupled a security community is the more the state's role will be transformed" (Adler and Barnett, 1998, p. 36). In other words, in a presocial environment the state's role is limited to a Hobbesian construct of "protector of the national good" while, in the alternative, the "emergence of a transnational civic community will expand the role of the state as it becomes an agent that furthers the various wants of the community: security, economic welfare, human rights, clean environment, and so on" (*Id.*, p. 36). Second, when a state is viewed as part of a security community, its conception and practice of its rights, obligations, and duties is transformed by and dependent upon "its ability to abide by the region's normative structure" (*Id.*, p. 36). The conclusion to be drawn from these two interconnected points is that "states in a tightly coupled arrangement, while retaining their juridical sovereign status toward the outside world, can be seen as agents of the transnational community" (*Id.*, p. 36).

The dual nature of the security community as respective of juridical sovereignty on the one hand, and yet acting in compliance with the region's normative structure on the other, is a late 20th century step in the evolution of the mid-20th century distinction regarding the application of inclusive policies in arenas both external and internal to particular states (McDougal, 1981, p. 490). The balance to be struck between "inclusive competence" and "exclusive competence" acknowledges that while peoples have a common interest in the establishment and maintenance of "an exclusive competence adequate to protect particular peoples from arbitrary interference and oppression," there is a corresponding interest in "the establishment and maintenance of interacting competences." It is the processes of interaction and mutual obligation which allow free peoples to express their common interest through the processes associated with techniques designed for securing more democratic and inclusive prescriptions for policies that exhibit predominantly inclusive effects (McDougal, 1981, p. 490).

More concretely, this means that securing the rights and basic needs of all peoples becomes as important as securing the institutions of the state. This goal lies at the heart of the model of inclusionary governance. It provides an objective framework out of which states and security regimes can effectively work to eliminate the causes of violence, such as poverty and economic inequity, while working toward building the institutions of an enforceable peace. This would include an effective global monitoring agency for all nuclear reactors and fuel processing centers in the world. In the past, these more fundamental security goals have been relegated to a second-class status and subordinated to balance of power considerations and short-term geopolitical advantage (Schell, 2000, pp. 41–56). The model of inclusionary governance inverts the old paradigm.

The model of inclusionary governance recognizes that progress toward the demilitarization of all societies is a vital goal of global policy and humane governance because nothing less can fulfill the human need for security. At the same time, the model of inclusionary governance represents a quantum leap toward a more fair distribution of the world's resources, a lifting of military repression, and a growing respect for the environment. In this task, "there are many different kinds of world public order—involving many different interrelations of international and national law or of inclusive and exclusive decision" (McDougal, 1981, p. 492). The idea of a security community allows for more inclusionary paths to be taken because the full acceptance of inclusionary principles and policies means that states can no longer invoke their own constitutional inadequacies as a defense to international law and international obligation reasonably expected by others.

BIBLIOGRAPHY

Emanuel Adler and Michael Barnett, "A Framework for the Study of Security Communities," *Security Communities*, edited by Emanuel Adler and Michael Barnett, Cambridge University Press, 1998.

African Goals and Aspirations (report of symposium, Arusha, Tanzania, January 30 to February 4, 1978). See also *Science and Technology and the Future: Nairobi Declaration* (adopted at African Regional Symposium, Nairobi, Kenya, July 10–12, 1979).

Gar Alperovitz, *Atomic Diplomacy: Hiroshima and Potsdam: The Use of the Atomic Bomb and the American Confrontation with Soviet Power*, Pluto Press, 1965, 1985, 1994.

Gar Alperovitz, "Hiroshima: Historians Reassess," *Foreign Policy*, Summer 1995.

Gar Alperovitz, *The Decision to Use the Atomic Bomb and the Architecture of an American Myth*, Alfred A. Knopf, 1995.

Daniel J. Arbess, "The International Law of Armed Conflict in Light of Contemporary Deterrence Strategies: Empty Promises or Meaningful Restraint?," *McGill Law Journal*, Volume 30, 1984.

Daniel J. Arbess and Simeon A. Sahayachny, "Nuclear Deterrence and International Law: Some Steps Toward Observance," *Alternatives: Social Transformation and Humane Governance*, Volume XII, No. 1, January 1987.

Michael Barletta, "Democratic Security and Diversionary Peace: Nuclear Confidence-Building in Argentina and Brazil," *National Security Studies Quarterly*, Volume V, Issue 3, Summer 1999.

Michael N. Barnett, *Confronting the Costs of War: Military Power, State, and Society in Egypt and Israel*, Princeton University Press, 1992.

Thomas Bodenheimer and Robert Gould, *Rollback: Right-Wing Power in US Foreign Policy*, South End Press, 1989.

Francis A. Boyle, "The Relevance of International Law to the 'Paradox of Nuclear Deterrence," *Northwestern University Law Review*, Volume 80, 1986.

Willy Brandt, *Arms and Hunger*, Pantheon Books, 1986.

Edward H. Carr, *The Twenty Years' Crisis, 1919–1939: An Introduction to the Study of International Relations*, Harper Torchbooks, Harper & Row, Publishers, 1964.

Kevin J. Cassidy and Gregory A. Bischak, *Real Security: Converting the Defense Economy and Building Peace*, State University of New York Press, 1993.

Stephen J. Cimbala, *Military Persuasion: Deterrence and Provocation in Crisis and War*, The Pennsylvania State University Press, 1994.

The Report of the Commission on Global Governance, *Our Global Neighborhood*, Oxford University Press, 1995.

Karl W. Deutsch et al, *Political Community and the North Atlantic Area*, Princeton University Press, 1957.

David Dickson, *The New Politics of Science*, Pantheon Books, 1984.

Albert Einstein, *Einstein on Peace*, edited by Otto Nathan and Heinz Nordon, Avenel Books, 1981.
Jacques Ellul, *The Technological Society*, Vintage Books, 1964.
Paul R. Ehrlich, Carl Sagan, Donald Kennedy, and Walter O. Roberts, *The Cold and the Dark: The World after Nuclear War*, The Conference on the Long-Term Worldwide Biological Consequences of Nuclear War, W.W. Norton & Company, 1984.
Richard Falk, "The *Shimoda* Case: A Legal Appraisal of the Atomic Attacks Upon Hiroshima and Nagasaki," *American Journal of International Law*, Vol. 59, 1965.
Richard Falk, Lee Meyrowitz, and Jack Sanderson, "Nuclear Weapons and International Law," *The Indian Journal of International Law*, Volume 20, 1980.
Richard Falk, "Normative Initiatives and Demilitarization: A Third System Approach," *Alternatives: A Journal of World Policy*, Volume VI, No. 2, July 1980.
Richard Falk and Samuel S. Kim, editors, *The War System: An Interdisciplinary Approach*, Westview Press, 1980.
Richard Falk and Samuel S. Kim, *An Approach to World Order Studies and the World System*, World Order Models Project—Working Paper No. 22, 1982.
Richard Falk, "Nuclear Policy and World Order: Why Denuclearization?," *Toward Nuclear Disarmament and Global Security: A Search for Alternatives*, edited by Burns H. Weston, Westview Press, 1984.
Richard Falk, "Nuclear Weapons and the End of Democracy," *Toward Nuclear Disarmament and Global Security: A Search for Alternatives*, edited by Burns H. Weston, Westview Press, 1984.
Richard Falk, "Nuclear Weapons, International Law and the World Court: A Historic Encounter," *The American Journal of International Law*, Vol. 91, No. 1, 1997.
Richard Falk, "State of Siege: Will Globalization Win Out?," *International Affairs*, Vol. 73, No. 1, January 1997.
Richard Falk, *Law in an Emerging Global Village: A Post-Westphalian Perspective*, Transnational Publishers, Inc., 1998.
Richard Falk, *Predatory Globalization: A Critique*, Polity Press, 1999.
William Felice, "Militarism and Human Rights," *International Affairs*, Vol. 74, No. 1, January 1998.
Bernard J. Firestone, "Kennedy and the Test Ban: Presidential Leadership and Arms Control," *John F. Kennedy and Europe*, edited by Douglas Brinkley and Richard T. Griffiths, foreword by Theodore Sorensen, Louisiana State University Press, 1999.
William J. Foltz and Henry S. Bienen, editors, *Arms and the African: Military Influences on Africa's International Relations*, Yale University Press, 1985.
L. Friedman, editor, *The Law of War: A Documentary History*, Volume 1, Random House, 1972.
Aleksandr Fursenko and Timothy Naftali, *One Hell of a Gamble: Khrushchev, Castro, and Kennedy, 1958–1964*, W.W. Norton & Company, 1997.

John Lewis Gaddis, Philip H. Gordon, Ernest R. May, and Jonathan Rosenberg, *Cold War Statesmen Confront the Bomb: Nuclear Diplomacy Since 1945*, Oxford University Press, 1999.
Clifford G. Gaddy, *The Price of the Past: Russia's Struggle with the Legacy of a Militarized Economy*, Brookings Institution Press, 1996.
Johan Galtung, "Towards a New International Technological Order," *Science, Technology and the Social Order*, edited by, Ward Morehouse, Transaction Books, 1979.
Raymond Garthoff, "A Loss for the US in World," *The Los Angeles Times*, October 31, 1999, M2.
Arundhati Ghose, "Negotiating the CTBT: India's Security Concerns and Nuclear Disarmament," *Journal of International Affairs*, Volume 51, No. 1, Summer 1997.
Norman A. Graebner, editor, *The National Security: Its Theory and Practice, 1945–1960*, Oxford University Press, 1986.
Cedric Grant, "Equity in International Relations: A Third World Perspective," *International Affairs*, Vol. 71, No. 3, July 1995.
William Greider, *Fortress America: The American Military and the Consequences of Peace*, Public Affairs, 1998.
Fred Halliday, *The Making of the Second Cold War*, Verso, 1983.
John L. Harper, *American Visions of Europe: Franklin D. Roosevelt, George F. Kennan, and Dean G. Acheson*, Cambridge University Press, 1994.
WIlliam D. Hartung, *And Weapons for All: How America's Multibillion-Dollar Arms Trade Warps Our Foreign Policy and Subverts Democracy at Home*, Harper Collins Publishers, 1994.
William D. Hartung, "Nixon's Children: Bill Clinton and the Permanent Arms Bazaar," *World Policy Journal*, Volume XII, No. 2, Summer 1995.
William D. Hartung, "Pentagon Welfare: The Corporate Campaign for NATO Expansion," *Multinational Monitor*, March 1998.
William D. Hartung and Jennifer Washburn, "Lockheed Martin: From Warfare To Welfare," *The Nation*, March 2, 1998.
William D. Hartung, "NATO Boondoggle," *The Progressive*, May 1998.
Nigel Hawkes, et al, editors, *Chernobyl: The End of the Nuclear Dream*, Vintage Books, 1986.
Stanley Hoffmann, *Duties Beyond Borders: On the Limits and Possibilities of Ethical International Politics*, Syracuse University Press, 1981.
Michael J. Hogan, *A Cross of Iron: Harry S. Truman and the Origins of the National Security State, 1945–1954*, Cambridge University Press, 1998.
John D. Holum, "The CTBT and Nuclear Disarmament—The US View," *Journal of International Affairs*, Volume 51, No. 1, Summer 1997.
Samuel P. Huntington, *The Soldier and the State: The Theory and Politics of Civil-Military Relations*, Harvard University Press, 1957.
Andrew Hurrell, "An Emerging Security Community in South America?," *Security Communities*, edited by Emanuel Adler and Michael Barnett, Cambridge University Press, 1998.
Karl Jaspers, *The Future of Mankind*, The University of Chicago Press, 1961.
Robert Jervis, *Perception and Misperception in International Politics*, Princeton University Press, 1976.

Robert Jervis, *System Effects: Complexity in Political and Social Life*, Princeton University Press, 1997.
Robert C. Johansen, *The Disarmament Process: Where to Begin*, Institute for World Order, 1977.
Robert C. Johansen, *Toward an Alternative Security System: Moving Beyond the Balance of Power in the Search for World Security*, World Policy Paper, No. 24, World Policy Institute, 1983.
Robert C. Johansen, "Building World Security: The Need for Strengthened International Institutions," *World Security: Challenges for a New Century*, Second Edition, Michael T. Klare and Daniel C. Thomas, editors, St. Martin's Press, 1994.
David Kaiser, *American Tragedy: Kennedy, Johnson, and the Origins of the Vietnam War*, Harvard University Press, 2000.
Mary Kaldor, *The Baroque Arsenal*, Hill and Wang, 1981.
Mary Kaldor, "Warfare and Capitalism," *Exterminism and Cold War*, edited by New Left Review, Verso, 1982.
Mary Kaldor, *The Imaginary War: Understanding the East-West Conflict*, Basil Blackwell, 1990.
Fred Kaplan, *The Wizards of Armageddon*, Simon and Schuster, 1983.
Fred Kaplan, "Bureaucracy and the Bomb: The Hidden Factor Behind Nuclear Madness," *The Washington Monthly*, May 1983.
James Everett Katz, editor, *Arms Production in Developing Countries: An Analysis of Decision Making*, Lexington Books, 1984.
Carl Kaysen, "The Limited Test-Ban Treaty of 1963," *John F. Kennedy and Europe*, edited by Douglas Brinkley and Richard T. Griffiths, foreword by Theodore Sorensen, Louisiana State University Press, 1999.
William W. Keller, *Arm in Arm: The Political Economy of the Global Arms Trade*, Basic Books, 1995.
Michael T. Klare, *War Without End: American Planning for the Next Vietnams*, Vintage Books, 1972.
Michael T. Klare, *Supplying Repression: US Support for Authoritarian Regimes Abroad*, Institute for Policy Studies, 1977.
Michael T. Klare, *Beyond the "Vietnam Syndrome": US Interventionism in the 1980s*, Institute for Policy Studies, 1981.
Michael T. Klare, *American Arms Supermarket*, University of Texas Press, 1984.
Michael T. Klare, *Rogue States and Nuclear Outlaws: America's Search for a New Foreign Policy*, Hill & Wang, 1995.
Michael T. Klare and David Anderson, *A Scourge of Guns: The Diffusion of Small Arms and Light Weapons in Latin America*, Arms Sales Monitoring Project—Federation of American Scientists, 1996.
Michael T. Klare, "The Subterranean Arms Trade: Black-Market Sales, Covert Operations and Ethnic Warfare," *Cascade of Arms: Managing Conventional Weapons Proliferation*, edited by Andrew J. Pierre, Brookings Institution Press, and the World Peace Foundation, 1997.
Michael T. Klare, "The Growing Traffic in Arms," NACLA—Report On The Americas, Vol. XXXI, No. 2, September/October 1997.
Michael T. Klare, "Beyond The Rogues' Gallery," *The Nation*, May 26, 1997.

F.H. Knelman, *America, God, and the Bomb: The Legacy of Ronald Reagan*, New Star Books, Vancouver, B.C., 1987.

Gabriel Kolko, *The Politics of War: The World and United States Foreign Policy, 1943–1945*, Pantheon Books, 1990.

Rajni Kothari, *Towards a Just World*, World Order Models Project—Working Paper Number Eleven, 1980.

Jeffrey W. Knopf, *Domestic Society and International Cooperation: The Impact of Protest on US Arms Control Policy*, Cambridge University Press, 1998.

Keith Krause, *Arms and the State: Patterns of Military Production and Trade*, Cambridge University Press, 1992.

Diane B. Kunz, *Butter And Guns: America's Cold War Economic Diplomacy*, The Free Press, 1997.

Sanford Lakoff and Herbert York, *A Shield in Space?: Technology, Politics, and the Strategic Defense Initiative—How the Reagan Administration Set Out to Make Nuclear Weapons "Impotent and Obsolete" and Succumbed to the Fallacy of the Last Move*, University of California Press, 1989.

Melvyn P. Leffler, *A Preponderance of Power: National Security, the Truman Administration, and the Cold War*, Stanford University Press, 1992.

Melvyn P. Leffler and David S. Painter, editors, *Origins of the Cold War: An International History*, Routledge, 1994.

Melvyn P. Leffler, *The Specter of Communism: The United States and the Origins of the Cold War, 1917–1953*, Hill and Wang, 1994.

Jeffrey W. Legro and Andrew Moravcsik, "Is Anybody Still a Realist?," *International Security*, Vol. 24, No. 2, Fall 1999.

Sidney Lens, *Permanent War: The Militarization of America*, Schocken Books, 1987.

Robert Jay Lifton and Richard Falk, *Indefensible Weapons: The Political and Psychological Case Against Nuclearism*, Basic Books, Inc., 1982.

Robert Jay Lifton, *The Genocidal Mentality: Nazi Holocaust and Nuclear Threat*, Basic Books, Inc., 1990.

Robert Jay Lifton and Greg Mitchell, *Hiroshima in America: Fifty Years of Denial*, Grosset/Putnam, 1995.

Brian Loveman and Thomas M. Davies, Jr., editors, *The Politics of Antipolitics: The Military in Latin America*, Second Edition, University of Nebraska Press, 1989.

Brian Loveman, *For la Patria: Politics and the Armed Forces in Latin America*, A Scholarly Resources Inc. Imprint, 1999.

Robin Luckman, "Armament Culture," *Alternatives: A Journal of World Policy*, Volume X, No. 1, Summer 1984.

Myres S. McDouglal, Harold D. Lasswell, and Lung-chu Chen, *Human Rights and World Public Order: The Basic Policies of an International Law of Human Dignity*, Yale University Press, 1980.

Myres S. McDougal, "The Impact of International Law Upon National Law: A Policy-Oriented Perspective," *International Law Essays: A Supplement to International Law in Contemporary Perspective*, by Myres S. McDougal and W. Michael Reisman, The Foundation Press, Inc., 1981.

R.D. McKinlay and A. Mughan, *Aid and Arms to the Third World: An Analysis of the Distribution and Impact of US Offical Transfers*, St. Martin's Press, 1984.

Ann Markusen, Peter Hall, Scott Campbell, and Sabina Deitrick, *The Rise of the Gunbelt: The Military Remapping of Industrial America*, Oxford University Press, 1991.

Ann Markusen and Joel Yudken, *Dismantling The Cold War Economy*, Basic Books, 1992.

Walter Russell Mead, *Mortal Splendor: The American Empire in Transition*, Houghton Mifflin Company, 1987.

Seymour Melman, "Military State Capitalism," *The Nation*, May 20, 1991.

Elliot L. Meyrowitz, "The Opinions of Legal Scholars on the Legal Status of Nuclear Wepons," *Stanford Journal of International Law*, Volume 24, 1988.

Russell Mokhiber and Robert Weissman, "US Embarks on Massive Military Buildup," *Third World Resurgence*, No. 102, 1999.

Philip Nash, "Bear Any Burden?: John F. Kennedy and Nuclear Weapons," *Cold War Statesmen Confront the Bomb: Nuclear Diplomacy Since 1945*, edited by John Lewis Gaddis, Philip H. Gordon, Ernest May, and Jonathan Rosenberg, Oxford University Press, 1999.

Franz L. Neumann, "The Concept of Political Freedom," *Columbia Law Review*, Volume 53, No. 7, 1953, reprinted in *The Rule of Law Under Siege: Selected Essays of Franz L. Neumann and Otto Kirchheimer*, edited by William E. Scheuerman, University of California Press, 1996.

Janne E. Nolan, *Guardians of the Arsenal: The Politics of Nuclear Strategy*, Basic Books, Inc., 1989.

William E. Odom, *The Collapse of the Soviet Military*, Yale University Press, 1998.

George Perkovich, *India's Nuclear Bomb: The Impact on Global Proliferation*, University of California Press, 1999.

Andre J. Pierre, editor, *Cascade of Arms: Managing Conventional Weapons Proliferation*, Brookings Institution Press and the World Peace Foundation, 1997.

Mitchell Reiss, *Bridled Ambition: Why Countries Constrain Their Nuclear Capabilities*, published by the Woodrow Wilson Center Press and distributed by The Johns Hopkins University Press, 1995.

James Rosenau, "Governance, Order, and Change in World Politics," in James Rosenau and Ernst-Otto Czempiel, editors, *Governance Without Government: Order and Change in World Politics*, Cambridge University Press, 1992.

Andrew L. Ross, "Developing Countries," *Cascade of Arms: Managing Conventional Weapons Proliferation*, edited by Andrew J. Pierre, Brookings Institution Press and The World Peace Foundation, 1997.

Carl Sagan, "Nuclear War and Climatic Catastrophe: Some Policy Implications," *Foreign Affairs*, Vol. 62, No. 2, Winter 1983–84.

Carl Sagan, "Star Wars: The Leaky Shield," *Parade Magazine*, December 8, 1985.

Carl Sagan and Richard Turco, *A Path Where No Man Thought: Nuclear*

Winter and the End of the Arms Race, Random House, 1990.
Carl Sagan and Richard Turco, "Too Many Weapons in the World," *Parade Magazine*, February 4, 1990.
Yoshikazu Sakamoto and Richard Falk, "World Demilitarized: A Basic Human Need," *Alternatives: A Journal of World Policy*, Volume VI, No. 1, March 1980.
Jerry W. Sanders, *Peddlers of Crisis: The Committee on the Present Danger and the Politics of Containment*, South End Press, 1983.
David E. Sanger, "The Real Power Struggle Isn't Just About Nukes," *The New York Times*, October 17, 1999.
Jonathan Schell, *The Gift Of Time: The Case for Abolishing Nuclear Weapons Now*, Metropolitan Books, 1998.
Jonathan Schell, "The Unfinished Twentieth Century: What We Have Forgotten About Nuclear Weapons," *Harper's Magazine*, January 2000.
Daniel Schwartz, "Totalitarian Tools: Preface to a Theory," *Alternatives: A Journal of World Policy*, Vol. X, No. 2, Fall 1984.
Stephen I. Schwartz, editor, *Atomic Audit: The Costs and Consequences of US Nuclear Weapons Since 1940*, Brookings Institution Press, 1998.
William A. Schwartz and Charles Derber, *The Nuclear Seduction: Why the Arms Race Doesn't Matter—And What Does*, University of California Press, 1990.
Leonard S. Spector, *Nuclear Proliferation Today*, Vintage Books, 1984.
Leonard S. Spector, *The New Nuclear Nations*, Vintage Books, 1985.
Stockholm International Peace Research Institute (SIPRI), *The Arms Trade with the Third World*, Humanities Press, Inc., 1971.
Thomas Szentes, "The Economic Impact of Global Militarization," *Alternatives: A Journal of World Policy*, Volume X, No. 1, 1984.
E.P. Thompson, "A Letter to America," *Protest and Survive*, E.P. Thompson and Dan Smith, editors, Monthly Review Press, 1981.
Edward Thompson, "Notes on Exterminism, the Last Stage of Civilization," *Exterminism and Cold War*, edited by New Left Review, Verso, 1982.
E.P. Thompson, editor, *Star Wars*, Pantheon Books, 1985.
John Tirman, *Spoils of War: The Human Cost of America's Arms Trade*, The Free Press, 1997.
Marc Trachtenberg, *A Constructed Peace: The Making of the European Settlement, 1945–1963*, Princeton University Press, 1999.
Helena Tuomi and Raimo Vayrynen, *Transnational Corporations, Armaments and Development*, St. Martin's Press, 1982.
Union of Concern Scientists, *The Fallacy of Star Wars—Based on Studies Conducted by the Union of Concerned Scientists*, edited by John Tirman, Vintage Books, 1984.
Peter Vale, "Engaging the World's Marginalized and Promoting Global Change: Challenges for the United Nations at Fifty," *Harvard International Law Journal*, Volume 36, No. 2, Spring 1995.
Augusto Vargas, *Militarization and the International Arms Race in Latin America*, Westview Press, 1985.
Burns H. Weston, Richard A. Falk, and Hilary Charlesworth, *Supplement of Basic Documents to International Law and World Order: A Problem-*

Oriented Coursebook, West Group, 1997.
Burns H. Weston, "Nuclear Weapons Versus International Law: A Contextual Reassessment," *McGill Law Journal*, Volume 28, 1983.
Burns H. Weston, editor, *Toward Nuclear Disarmament and Global Security: A Search for Alternatives*, Westview Press, 1984.
Burns H. Weston, "Law and Alternative Security: Toward a Just World Peace," *Alternative Security: Living Without Nuclear Deterrence*, edited by Burns H. Weston, Westview Press, 1990.
Lawrence S. Wittner, *The Struggle Against the Bomb.* Volume Two: *Resisting The Bomb: A History of the World Nuclear Disarmament Movement, 1954–1970*, Stanford University Press, 1997.
Adam Yarmolinsky, *The Military Establishment: Its Impacts on American Society*, Harper & Row, Publishers, 1971.
Lord Zuckerman, *Star Wars in a Nuclear World*, Vintage Books, 1987.

CHAPTER 3

THE GLOBALIZATION OF MEDIA AND THE MEDIA OF GLOBALIZATION

The construct of national security is being deconstructed, perhaps more rapidly by mass publics than by political elites. . . . Will modern communications make it easier or more difficult to mobilize mass publics to support war?

David Bell, "Global Communications, Culture, and Values: Implications for Global Security," 1993, p. 173

So long as the media are not entirely monopolized, the individual can play one medium off against another; he can compare them, and hence resist what any one of them puts out. The more genuine competition there is among the media, the more resistance the individual might be able to command. But how much is this now the case? . . . The answer is: generally no, very few do: (1) We know that people tend strongly to select those media which carry contents with which they already agree. . . . (2) This idea of playing one medium off against another assumes that the media really have varying contents. It assumes genuine competition, which is not widely true.

C. Wright Mills, *The Power Elite*, 1956, p. 313

UNESCO's interest in communication has intensified in recent years, gradually reaching the current level of discussion during a Geneva Conference. As indicated by an approved plan of activities for 1977–1982, this interest is now firmly established: "Communication . . . is an essential component of a new social and economic order, and equal access to information sources and flows between and within societies is necessary for its establishment."

Bryan J. Holzberg, "The New World Information Order: A Legal Framework for Debate," 1987, p. 602

A. INTRODUCTION

The global media are the channels through which the messages of a global corporate culture, predicated upon the values of centralization, commercialism, and Westernized varieties of consummerism, shape national and international perceptions, images and discourses. They engulf the mind as they seeks to engage the individual as a consumer. Yet these values mainly function as justifications and rationalizations of entrenched inequalities. In this endeavor, the global media promote exclusionary policies in both governance and economics. They are also adept at creating new obstacles for inclusionary social movements which seek new forms of democratic accountability through emerging forms of, and experiments with, social democracy, the articulation of submerged discourses, and the reinvigoration of the democratic project.

The reinvigoration of democracy, however, is a task which is more daunting at the end of the 20th century. This is largely because "power itself is being redistributed, taking new forms and new characteristics. The rules of the game in international relations are changing and the origins of an extraordinary number of those changes can be traced to the Information Revolution" (Rothkopf, 1998, p. 325). The "information revolution" presents a clear and present danger to traditional avenues of citizens' participation in public affairs and understanding public issues, and thus to the effective working of democracy (Herman and McChesney, 1997, p. 1).

Information technologies, once believed to be avenues to enhanced forms of participation and knowledge helpful to the practice of inclusionary forms of democracy, have proven to be largely antithetical to the democratic task and its associated challenges. In large measure, technology can help democracy, but only if programmed to do so and only in terms of the paradigms and political theories that inform the program. Left to the market, technology is likely merely to reproduce the vices of politics as usual. Historically, politics as usual has meant maintaining inequality, inegalitarian power arrangements, the negation of efforts to bring about an equitable distribution of wealth, and the employment of inherently exclusionary practices. In this task, the media have been partners to corporate interests. The media's complicity with the interests of corporate capital is apparent in advertising brand names and marketing techniques. According to some observers, "what has become clear is that corporations aren't just selling their products on-line, they're selling a new model for the media's relationship with corporate sponsors and backers" (Klein, 1999, p. 43). The media giants "claim that their market power and conglomeration make them more efficient and therefore able to provide a better product at lower prices to the consumer. There is not much evidence for these claims" and "in view of media's importance for democratic politics and culture, they should not be judged by purely commercial criteria" (McClesney, 1999, pp. 312–313). By allowing legal, political, cultural, and social discourse to remain bounded by purely commercial criteria, it is possible to obscure the hidden "truths" of corporate control and its negative effects upon efforts to build a democratic political culture which is also inclusionary. Examples of these negative effects abound.

Commercial criteria can easily ignore the numerous forces which shape mainstream thought. For example, "the economics of the rich evolves over time in accord with changing conditions. As the rich develop new wants, and find earlier structures and policies obsolete, economists make appropriate adaptations" (Herman, 1997, pp. 19–20). A case in point is the growth of the military-industrial complex (MIC). If powerful corporate interests seek to expand the MIC of the United States and also sponsor an entire series of National Security States throughout the Third World (in order to provide a favorable investment climate abroad), then "the economists will not object, but will take these as policy givens, necessary and proper responses to external factors, like the Soviet threat" (*Id.*, p. 20). Correspondingly, the mainstream corporate media will take heed and reflect the ideological bias of this kind of investment in its portrayal of the news. The effect of this corporate influence on both government and media shapes the interaction between government and media. It also shapes the consciousness of the citizenry at large, because it shapes the nature of the "issues," debates, and discourse. The phenomenon is captured by the title of Mark Hertsgaard's book on the press and the Reagan presidency: *On Bended Knee* (Hertsgaard, 1988). Newspaper and television coverage of such "stories" as the Iran-Contra Affairs, the invasion of Grenada, the arms talks, and Reaganomics, all reflected a dynamic of power and exclusionary governance in which the press, both through government manipulation and through voluntary self-censorship, abdicated its responsibility to report on what was really happening.

More than forty years have passed since the publication of C. Wright Mlll's classic book, *The Power Elite*, one of the most vital and insightful critiques of the dynamic forces in US political culture. Mills addressed the dilemma of ordinary people seemingly driven by forces they could neither understand nor govern. Aptly, he noted that "'great changes' are beyond their control, but affect their conduct and outlook nonetheless" (Mills, 1958, p. 3). Such is the condition of people trapped in mass society, feeling that they are "without purpose in an epoch in which they are without power" (*Id.*, p. 3). Mills' argument is as appropriate for the dawn of the 21st century as it was applicable to the situation of the mid-20th century. In large measure this is the case because the new global media are representative of a small world of big conglomerates. The close of the decade of the 1990s leaves the media on the brink of a profound transformation. Whereas previously media systems were primarily national, these systems are now a part of a global commerical media marketplace.

Technology, media concentration, and commercialism have melded into one, creating, in political terms, a "depoliticized" society. In this context, the commercial media have come to play a major role in maintaining the socioeconomic and sociopolitical order. The global media market is now largely dominated by the same eight transnational corporations (TNCs) that rule the US media: General Electric, AT&T/Liberty Media, Disney, Time Warner, Sony, News Corporation, Viacom, and Seagram, as well as Bertelsmann, the Germany-based conglomerate. At the global level, as in the United States, this media complex (media monopoly) is a highly concentrated industry. For example, Time Warner, the largest media corporation in the world, enjoyed $27 billion in revenues in 1998. This figure is fifty times larger in terms of annual sales than the world's fiftieth-largest media firm. In terms of its cultural impact, the power and influence of the Time Warner empire is even more ominous.

Mills' critique explains this result as part of the four-part project of the media. First, the media tell the individual in mass society who and what to be. Second, the media supply aspirations for the individual in mass society. Third, with the goal of life supplied, the media supply the technique of how to become what the individual aspires to. Fourth, the media reassure the individual that his or her identity has been achieved, whether it has been incarnated in reality or not. In this way, the individual has been provided with an "escape" from the predicament of being human, in spite of the fact that "as a formula, it is not attuned to the development of the human being" (*Id.*, p. 314). The influence of the global media is an influence which reaches into many different areas. The contexts in which the media operate provide and suggest new approaches to understanding and interpreting mass media and communications.

The new media also include some non-corporate channels of communication such as the Internet, law journals to which non-jurists contribute, the popular cinema, the use of the phone for political networking, and religious tracts and educational material. The ability of the state or religious authorities to either control or filter this information has been on the wane for decades, not only in the First World, but in the Third World as well. For example, the new media complex inspires renewed attention to the social organization of communication. Further, the new media complex inspires the creation of new public space beyond conventional broadcast media, and face-to-face communications among people who trust one another. In this new world, "just as anonymous pamphlets in colonial America and newspapers in colonial Latin America fostered new senses of identity and community, today's new media contribute to the creation of new public spaces and identities different from the public square of democratic theory and based on bonds of trust and normative understandings that often are at odds with those of state and conventional religious authorities" (Eickelman and Anderson, 1999, p. vii).

In the event that central features of the corporate-induced media facade are broken, the apologists of the establishment's power-elite, both corporate and governmental, will probably declare, as they did in the decade of the 1970s, that a "crisis of democracy" threatens the social order. What does such a response reveal? How do the media fit into this arrangement designed for the legitimation of capitalism's consumer culture? In the vortex of it. As far as the state itself is concerned, "the modern state, among other things, is an engine of propaganda, alternatively manufacturing crises and claiming to be the only instrument which can effectively deal with them" (Lasch, 1967). Under these conditions, government and a corporate-controlled media can easily mislead and misdirect people. For example, "the word 'economy' has an all-inclusive sound, and policies improving the 'economy,' 'productivity,' and the 'growth in GDP' sound uncontroversial . . . But this is misleading in a trickle-down system. As the evidence of the last 25 years shows, productivity can increase and the GDP can grow while a majority of the population loses out and the gains of growth are skimmed off by the elite" (Herman, 1997, pp. 20–21).

In January 2000, the US Federal Reserve released its study showing that those on society's bottom rungs were actually losing wealth instead of gaining. Other studies of the growing gap between rich and poor focused exclusively on income. They found that the wages of the poorest segments of the nation were growing, although significantly less than the earnings of the middle class. The Federal Reserve's survey confirmed this trend, but did so not only by measuring Americans' annual incomes but also also their accumulated wealth or net worth, in inflation-adjusted terms, over the 1995–1998 period. By that standard, the nation's most disadvantaged were not just falling behind the more fortunate—they were clearly worse off (Walsh, *Los Angeles Times*, January 19, 2000, p. A-1). By January 2000, even US conservatives were acknowledging that the most important gap was not in income, but in wealth. Therefore, "in this view, the nation is becoming divided between people who are unable to save, invest and build wealth over the long run and those who are not" (Stevenson, *New York Times*, January 23, 2000, p. wk-3).

In the task of placing limits on the public sphere or the dynamics of a genuinely open democratic dialogue, the media's role is especially critical. Despite the rhetorical nuances associated with democratic politics and the creed of equality, both a nation's history and culture can potentially be viewed as a living testimony to the preservation of inequality. From this perspective, "the analyst of social inequality cannot fail to perceive the strength of factors that condition an individual or a group to contribute to social inequality as soon as he attains even a slight advantage. In a changing world community we are provided with innumerable exemplifications of the fundamental importance of the proclivity to turn an advantage into a special interest and to nullify or ignore, where possible, a common interest" (McDougal, Lasswell, Chen, 1980, p. 426). Early 21st century studies on growing gaps in income and disparities of wealth do not, in and of themselves, constitute grounds for optimism with respect to the future of inclusionary governance or an inclusionary media discourse.

Without the inclusion and incorporation of alternative viewpoints, the answers provided in response to the crisis of socieconomic inequality will be answers which emerge out of an elite-centered discourse, dedicated to minor alterations of the status quo. Conservatives, for example, continue to argue for minor steps in making adjustments to the Social Security system to create private investment accounts for all workers. Theoretically, such a step would give everyone a chance to own capital and have a direct stake in the system. But this proposal, as with so many others, ignores the objective consequence of declines in union membership and a future of lousy jobs that pay only minimum wage. Meanwhile, the stock market soars out of control, bringing the real profits (based on speculation) with it. In this environment, "the media gravitate naturally toward economists who speak elite truths that the media understand and favor and to which the public has already been conditioned. These economists are also given credibty as 'experts' by their affiliation with corporate-funded think tanks" (Herman, 1997, p. 20). Hence, exclusionary governance continues to dominate over and against inclusionary democratic governance. Yet, some members of conservative think tanks, such as Michael Tanner, director of health and welfare studies at the Cato Institute, note that: "The movement toward becoming one nation that can invest and one nation that cannot invest has potential consequences for social and political stability down the road" (as quoted in Stevenson, New York Times, January 23, 2000, p. wk-3). Recognition of a common interest in inclusion is occasionally noted by think tank representatives in the media. Yet, such admissions do not constitute the foundation for a genuine political consensus which can inaugurate an inclusionary democratic project in either governmental policies or news media coverage.

While the identification of a common interest is linked to an inclusionary democratic project, that is not to say that such a project is in the interest of elites who have benefited from inequality and the exclusionary socioeconomic structures, laws, and institutions which are an embodiment of it (Mintz and Cohen, 1971; Mintz and Cohen, 1977; Parenti, 1998; Zweigenhaft and Domhoff, 1998; Ferguson and Rogers, 1981; Nader and Smith, 1996; Vogel, 1989; Vogel, 1996; McQuaid, 1982; Schwartz, 1987; Parenti, 1995; Dye, 1995; Domhoff, 1998). Access rights to media are exclusionary and elitist in their political, social, and economic effect. Access rights constitute a real threat to inclusionary democracy for these rights can easily threaten media entities' capacity for partisan mobilization. Inclusionary democracy demands free and open access to media. In fact, an inclusionary democratic project is antithetical to the interests of "the power elite" which benefit from access rights insofar as an inclusionary project would remove the hegemony of the dominant elite-controlled discourse and open the path toward "complex democracy" which "seeks a political process that promotes both fair partisan bargaining and discourses aimed at agreement" (Baker, 1998, p. 344).

An inclusionary democratic project, in the context of a complex democracy, stands for the proposition that "society needs partisan media that are constitutive of groups and that promote group mobilization—and rights of access can undermine such media." (Id., p. 397). Developing a partisan media is to undertake the development of an inclusionary approach to media, civil society, and the regulatory role of government. In this context, Herman and McChesney have argued that "the central question is whether the various media activist groups can generate support from sympathetic larger aggregations such as religious bodies, labor, and educators, coalesce, and work to mobilize public opinion in favor of media reform" (Herman and McChesney, 1997, p. 204). The incentive for such a mobilization resides in the fact that "the ultimate goal must be the establishment of a global, non-profit sphere to replace, or at least complement, the global commercial media market" (Id., p. 204). The struggle between for-profit media versus non-profit media is a defining one because international groups such as the WTO, IMF, and World Bank, which have pressed for the creation of a global commercial media and communications system, have worked exclusively in the service of the transnational corporate community and its agenda—regardless of the social and political costs borne by the excluded majority. Within the framework of this analysis, "the battle for democratic communication is part and parcel of the battle for a more just and democratic economy" (Id., p. 204).

The un-democratic nature of the current communication and media structure lends itself to rationalizing both the aim of macro-policy and the criterion of progress, as embodied within corporate ideology. In turn, an un-democratic economy is preserved as the goal of economic growth, isolated from other values and priorities, and placed at the center of media and political adulation as the ultimate measure of a society's "progress." What this focus ignores is the exclusion from this schema of issues concerned with the distribution of income or improvement in the condition of the poor (Id., p. 36). The problems generated by this gap between progress and poverty have become global in scope because transnational corporations can move between states, working to bargain for host government aid in further improving the climate of investment (Id., p. 34). The developed countries of the First World are no more immune from this anti-democratic power than those of the Third World. In the context of the First World, "downsizing" and "outsourcing" continue while, at the same time, unemployment and underemployment expand incrementally. No longer does a rising tide lift all of the boats. Studies have been produced which demonstrate that while the upper classes have gained, those living at the bottom of society have lost ground, resulting in an unequal expansion for all (Stevenson, New York Times, January 23, 2000). Those at the bottom of the economic ladder have not benefited from the US prosperity boom of the 1990s and, by some measures, have fallen behind.

In the United States, the poverty rate in 1998, according to the Census Bureau, stood at 12.7 percent. While down from 15.1 percent in 1993, it was virtually the same as at the peak of the last expansion, in 1989. Further, it was worse than 1969, the year the previous record-setting expansion ended, when 12.1 percent of Americans lived in poverty. These facts and figures present the reality of a crisis of exclusion where, in an era of abundance, there are continuing disparities—disparities which serve as a means to focus upon the question of how to deal with inequality. Despite the economic boom, US poverty rates have dropped only by a fraction while the number of people living in extreme circumstances (less than $6,750 a year for a family of three), has actually increased from 13.9 million in 1995 to 14.6 million in 1997. In fact, one in every five chidren is still poor, compared with one in seven in the 1970s (Gergen, 1999, p. 64). Even the Council On Foreign Relations, an elite bastion of economic privilege, has at least addressed the causes and consequences of global wage inequality as free trade has come under attack and as the plight of the excluded becomes more apparent in the global market economy (Fishlow and Parker, 1999).

The role of media coverage in addressing issues associated with wage inequality and the dimensions of poverty in the United States and around the globe has been, as far as the commercial media are concerned, muted at best. Part of the reason for this, it may be surmised, reflects the fact that the corporate control of and influence on media is determinative of content. Power is not only economic, but political and ideological as well. Given this fact, it may be asserted that "to no small extent the stability of the system rests upon the widespread acceptance of a global corporate ideology" (Herman and McChesney, 1997, p. 35).

Certainly there is a vested interest among the CEOs of corporations to take the media's focus off the fact that over the course of the 1990s, corporate profits rose 108 percent, supporting an S&P 500 Index increase of 224 percent. Who gained? According to the Institute for Policy Studies, after nearly two decades of real wage declines, workers' pay has risen 28 percent in the 1990s, while CEO pay has risen 481 percent (Anderson, et al., 1999, p. iii). From a perusual of the "Top Ten" lists from *Business Week's* annual pay surveys since 1990, the IPS identified eight CEOs who stood out as some of the most overpaid executives of the decade. In addition, they were men who ranked among the top ten earners in the country while leading corporations that were: (1) committing crimes such as fraud, price-fixing, and toxic-dumping; (2) exploiting oppressed workers or slashing jobs in the United States; (3) pushing products that kill millions; (4) charging loan-shark-level interest rates to low-income Americans; or (5) using government funds to pad their pay packages (*Id.*, p. 10). Simply put, in response to the effort to expose these power-constellations and their inherently anti-democratic and exclusionary effects, "the global media is better understood . . . as one that advances corporate and commercial interests and values, and denigrates or ignores that which cannot be incorporated into its mission" (McChesney, 1999, p. 103).

Depending upon which variation of democratic theory one subscribes to, there is a corresponding linkage to that particular theory's relationship to the press clause. In the United States there are at least four different theories of democracy which have their own unique and corresponding press clause interpretation. The differences between these contending theories of democracy and their respective press clause interpretations provide a window on how to begin to conceptualize the differences between an inclusionary democratic approach to media versus an exclusionary approach to media. A tentative formulation is offered to outline these differences in Table 3.1.

In viewing the relationship between democracy, the political left, and the media, the evidence strongly suggests that "when the conditions of democracy are fruitful there will be considerable pressure to reduce economic inequality" (McChesney, 1999, p. 283). Under the theory of complex democracy, a more inclusionary media regime would be empowered to set forth and articulate submerged claims and discourses regarding socioeconomic inequalities in the body politic. The emergence and inclusion of previously suppressed claims and discourses constitute a form of political pressure which will demand that the profit motive be drastically curtailed. However, wealthy interests have historically worked and will work "resolutely to limit the capacity for informed self-government, through, among other things, maintaining corrupt campaign finance and lobbying systems, elite-dominanted economic policy making, distorted electoral systems, weakened educational systems, and commercial media" (*Id.*, p. 284). When viewed in combination, this cluster of interests is supportive of exclusionary governance. Its anti-democratic character is obvious. What is less obvious is how

TABLE 3.1 Tentative Formulation

Theories of Democracy	Press Clause Interpretation
Elite Democracy	Hands-off
Pluralist Democracy	Prohibit access rights; allow structural regulations that promote partisan media
Republican Democracy	Allow or mandate access rights; disfavor laws that promote more partisan media
Complex Democracy	Allow, but not mandate, access rights and legislation that promotes partisan media or that makes some media more inclusive
All Democratic Theories	Rule out censorship and legislation or practices aimed at suppressing media

SOURCE: C. Edwin Baker, "The Media That Citizens Need," *University of Pennsylvania Law Review*, Volume 147, Number 2, December 1998, p. 398.

private systems of media control pose a threat to the public sphere. Yet these threats can be discerned by identifying the narrow class interests which are represented by these private media centers, how they compete for advertiser attention, and how they are ideologically positioned to oppose the cultivation of the public sphere.

It has been suggested that "to counter these inequalities, a democratic regime might provide for (1) multiparty or proportional representation in citizen-financed elections, (2) equal public funding for diverse, issue-oriented committees to contest referenda, and (3) alteration of communications media to become, with regard to major issues, a public trust" (Gilbert, 1999, p. 201). Countering inequalities, however, demands that the oligarchic conception of wealth, privilege, wealth, and sociopolitical exclusion be challenged. The fact remains that "unless communication and information are biased toward equality, they tend to enhance social inequality, whether the society happens to be democratic or otherwise" (McChesney, 1999, p. 288). Developing a bias toward equality constitutes an inclusionary aspiration which admits that there are submerged discourses which ought to see the light of day if the practice of democracy is to become more "democratic." The incongruity of the situation is that democratic discourses which aim at dislodging the status quo are viewed as too threatening to entrenched economic elites (cultural and corporate). The antithetical nature of contending discourses about a capitalist economy dedicated to mega-mergers, privatization, and a reduction of the sphere of government's regulatory powers effectively delimits the range of ideas that are released to the civil society of individual nations. The shaping of cultural consciousness becomes one of the dominant tasks of the media where a corrective or alternative to the dominant discourse is absent or lacking.

The means for the shaping of economic and political culture, East and West, North and South, is the common-denominator for evaluating the inclusionary and exclusionary forms of the media's potential to shape the cultural consciousness of societies around the globe. In the context of Central and Eastern Europe, it was once assumed that that transition to democracy and a market economy would happen quite naturally. It was assumed that this process would be significantly advanced by the "Westification" or "Europeanization" of their media systems. The problem or downside with this set of expectations is that while the media of the Baltic countries were capable of applying Western journalistic practices and integrating seamlessly with Western media, they could not escape a reification of its perils, such as yellow journalism, deteriorating ethical standards, and the impact of big money on reporting (Jakubowicz, 1999, pp. 52–53). In short, it has now been at least acknowledged that "we know now that there is nothing preordained about the direction, pace or ultimate result of change in postcommunist countries and their media; and that Western-style capitalism or media systems cannot simply be transplanted to Eastern Europe" (Id., p. 53). In this critical respect, "no medium is an island." Therefore, in times of accelerated change the media can report on great transformations and "serve as a battering ram to accelerate the demise of a system when it collapses or is overthrown." In the alternative, however, "the prospects of the media depend largely on the social, political and economic context within which they operate" (Id., p. 54). Table 3.2 provides an outline of the processes of media change as determined by change in key areas of social life.

The social, political, and economic context in which the media operate exposes the fact that "democracy in general and freedom of the press in particular are not luxuries that only affluent Western societies can afford . . . but rather necessary conditions for sustaining equitable economic growth" (Adhikari, 2000, p. 61). Support for this proposition has been articulated by Amartya Sen, winner of the 1998 Nobel Prize in Economics. Sen was one of the few major economists of the 20th century to recognize the crucial links which exist between freedom and well-being, between democracy and growth. Freedom, in this context, includes freedom of the press to galvanize public opinion in favor of a rapid governmental response to natural disasters in countries with relatively poor economies, such as India and Botswana. Press freedom also has been employed to help avert famines and expose governmental corruption insofar as press freedom established the link between voice and accountability.

The linkage between voice and accountability is a media function which is correlative with a fully functioning democracy. Without it, the practice of democracy becomes an anachronism of its stated ideals. In short, "this protective power of a free press operating within a democratic political structure is vital for the poor and disadvantaged in developing countries no less than in

TABLE 3.2 Processes of Media Change as Determined by Change in Key Areas of Social Life

I. *Depending on political factors, the media can:*
   Be liberalized
   Become pluralistic and open
   Be deregulated
   Promote professionalism of journalists

II. *Politics, economy determine whether the media can:*
   Gain autonomy
   Decentralize
   Achieve diversity of content
   Address minority groups
   Internationalization

III. *Economy market mechanisms favor or hinder:*
   Abolition of media monopoly
   Commercialization
   Concentration
   Globalization

IV. *"Cultural change" is required for:*
   Depoliticization of media
   Rule of law
   Ability to define and serve the public interest
   Role for public opinion
   The media to serve as impartial watchdogs

SOURCE: Karol Jakubowicz, "The Genie Is Out of the Bottle: Measuring Media Change in Central and Eastern Europe," Media Studies Journal, Volume 13, Number 3, Fall, 1999, p. 55.

affluent ones" (*Id.*, p. 61). Hence, inclusionary governance requires press freedom if inclusionary democracy is to succeed in First and Third World contexts. As World Bank president James D. Wolfensohn noted: "A free press is not a luxury. A free press is at the absolute core of equitable development, because if you cannot enfranchise poor people, if they do not have a right to expression, if there is no searchlight on corruption and inequitable practices, you cannot build the public consensus needed to bring about change" (Wolfensohn, 1999, p. A-39). Indeed, as Wolfensohn suggests, the absence of a free press is the foundation of exclusionary governance, for it absents the poor and disadvantaged from enfranchisement while, at the same time, it debilitates democracy from its inclusionary impulse by failing to enable the civil society to build a consensus against corruption and inequitable practices. Insofar as inclusionary democracy requires the development of public avenues leading toward consensus, the absence of a free press is the death-knell for inclusionary governance in the sphere of civil society and the realization of governmental accountability to that civil society.

The so-called "culture industry" of mass society and the media actively exploits a combination of irrational susceptibilities and neurotic symptoms, "ever present within most human beings," making individuals in mass society open to exploitation by the mass media (Held, 1980, p. 93). The exploitation of mass society was recognized, before Mills' critique, by the main thinkers who comprised the Frankfurt School of Critical Theory, such as Erich Fromm, Herbert Marcuse, and Max Horkheimer. Their respective analyses of the growth and ordering of mass society was followed with a dire prediction by one of the architects of the economic and political order of the Third Reich, Albert Speer.

Speer, acting as a key player in the technocracy of the Third Reich, was uniquely positioned to appreciate the linkage between technology and the media in maintaining a large state, whether fascist or democratic. As a preeminent representative of a technocracy which had, without compunction, used all of its resources in an assault on humanity, Albert Speer understood that "Hitler's dictatorship was the first dictatorship of an industrial state in this age of modern technology, a dictatorship which employed to perfection the instruments of technology to dominante its own people . . . By means of such instruments of technology as the radio and public address systems, eightly million persons could be made subject to the will of one individual. Telephone, teletype, and radio made it possible to transmit the commands of the highest levels directly to the lowest organs where, because of their high authority, they were executed uncritically. Thus, many offices and squads received their evil commands in this direct manner. The instruments of technology made it possible to maintain a close watch over all citizens and to keep criminal operations shrouded in a high degree of secrecy. To the outsider this state apparatus may look like the seemingly wild tangle of cables in a telephone exchange; but like such an exchange it could be directed by a single will. Dictatorships of the past needed assistants of high quality in the lower ranks of the leadership also—men who could think and act independently. The authoritarian system in the age of technology can do without such men. The means of communication alone enable it to mechanize the work of the lower leadership. Thus the type of uncritical receiver of orders is created" (Speer, 1970, pp. 520–521).

In the post-1945 world, the uncritical receiver of orders may be the citizenry at large. On a global basis, the global citizenry of nations is exposed to a new kind of information order. The transnational corporate influence over information has redefined media distribution and content within nations by virtue of increasing transnational control over media (McChesney, 1999, p. 80). As of January 2000, the merger of American Online and Time Warner has created a situation that has negative consequences for consumers and citizens. It has effectively put the last nail in the coffin of the argument that the Internet will democratize the media by giving ordinary citizens the ability to compete in the marketplace against the media giants. Conglomerates such as AOL-Time Warner's have effectively established a global control capability vis-a-vis its control of commercially viable journalism and entertainment in the digital future. The efficiency and convenience which it promises will be costly as a handful of media executives set the agenda for the planet's information diet. The AOL-Time Warner, merger, the largest in history, represents the culmination of a wave of concentration of ownership in media and communication industries over the decade of the 1990s. While there were 12 major telecommunications companies in 1996, as of January 2000 there are six. What this effectively means is that the media system is dominated by eight or fewer massive firms, with an additional 12 to 15 rounding out the system of control and ownership. With approximately two dozen profit-drive companies owned and managed by billionaires in barely competitive markets, the assumption that the US media culture can advance the notion of a free press in a democratic society has evaporated (Leibovich, January 17, 2000, p. 6).

In place of a democratic society there is emerging, within the United States, what has been termed a "republic of denial" in which a deepening public alienation from the modern condition of politics and journalism has led to a loss of substance and structure in public life as well as citizen connection to it (Janeway, 1999). In short, what Speer observed about technology and media control in the Third Reich is no less compelling in its significance when applied to the United States at the dawn of the 21st century. Democracy triumphed over fascism not by arms alone, but rather by words, ideas, and modern mass media as well. Hence, the media were "no less instrumental to the leaders of the democracies in turning back the fascist tide" (*Id.*, p. 1). But what of the incorporation of anti-democratic norms into a democratic culture?

In the last decades of the 20th century, the quality of American democracy has been the subject of widespread despair. Michael Sandel has argued that the despair could be characterized as "democracy's discontent" and that government seemed helpless to respond to it. Sandel has asserted that "times of trouble prompt us to recall the ideals by which we live. But in America today, this is not an easy thing to do. At a time when democratic ideals seem ascendent abroad, there is reason to wonder whether we have lost possession of them at home" (Sandel, 1996, p. 3).

It is necessary, according to republican political theory, to recognize that self-rule involves more than participation in politics—"it means deliberating with fellow citizens about the common good and helping to shape the destiny of the political community." Still, deliberation requires more than the capacity to choose one's own ends and to to respect the other's right to do the same—"it requires a knowledge of public affairs and also a sense of belonging, a concern for the whole, a moral bond with the community whose fate is at stake" (*Id.*, p. 5). In short, self-rule requires inclusionary democracy and an inclusionary media to shape the discourses, debates and dialogues.

Liberal political theory has argued for a broader and more inclusionary democracy, insofar as it has historically emphasized toleration and respect for the individual. However, in recent decades, the civic or formative aspects of American politics have "largely given way to the liberalism that conceives of persons as free and independent selves, unencumbered by moral or civic ties they have not chosen" (*Id.*, p. 6). In this sense, modern liberalism and the modern media have built an exclusionary democracy together, creating an environment for a rich media and a poor democracy. In this context, the very nature of the corporate media system defends itself on the ground that "communication markets force media to 'give the people what they want'; that commercial media are the innate democratic and 'American' system; that professionalism in journalism is democratic and protects the public from nefarious influences on the news; that new communications technologies are inherently democratic since they undermine the existing power of commercial media; and . . . that the First Amendment to the US Constitution authorizes that corporations and advertisers US media without public interference" (McChesney, 1999, p. 7). Yet, these claims are myths "which are either lies or half-truths to strip citizens of their ability to comprehend their own situation and govern their own lives," leading McChesney to characterize this situation as "dubious" times (the subtitle of his book is: "Communication Politics in Dubious Times") (*Id.*, p. 7).

How can people govern their own lives when the unequal distribution of resources means that some citizens can raise their voice louder in political debate than others? Insofar as the US Supreme Court has interpreted the constitutional guarantee of free speech in a manner that effectively thwarts most government efforts to regulate the role of money in politics, it is hardly surprising that "the American public increasingly believes that their government is dominated by concentrations of wealth and special interests at the expense of ordinary citizens, and public trust in government has plunged" (Galston, 1998, p. 75). In a special-investigation cover story entitled, "Big Money & Politics: Who Gets Hurt," *Time* magazine published the work of two investigative journalists who disclosed the various ways that powerful interests have showered Washington with millions in campaign contributions and lobbying, leaving America's citizenry divided into two groups: first- and second-class citizens (Bartlett and Steele, 2000, pp. 38–39).

Second-class citizens, ostensibly the beneficiaries of a democratic system of representation, pay a disproportionate share of America's tax bill, pay higher prices for a broad range of products, are compelled to abide by laws while first-class citizens are granted immunity from them, must pay debts that are incurred while others do not, and are barred from writing off money on necessities while first-class citizens can deduct the cost of their entertainment. The special status of first-class citizens affords them the luxury of being bailed out of bad business decisions, hiring workers at below-market wage rates, benefiting from extensions of time in order to pay off debts which are not discharged, ignoring rules that their competitors must comply with, and killing legislation that is intended for the public good (*Id.*, pp. 39–40). Whether in the halls of Congress or in political campaigns carried on in the news media, the reality of democratic exclusion is apparent in the emergence of two classes of citizens. Equal citizenship has been effectively unraveled by unequal divisions of wealth, creating a divide between the two groups, which is an ever-expanding gulf (Strobel and Peterson, 1999; Petterson, 1994; Bartlett and Steele, 1996; Bartlett and Steele, 1992; Wolff, 1995; Nelson, 1995; Ryscavage, 1999; Danziger and Gottschalk,1993; Isaac, 1998; Danziger and Gottschalk, 1995).

Given this perspective, some have reached the conclusion that "if the promise of equal citizenship is to be realized, the Constitution must be amended to make it clear that freedom of speech does not entail the untrammeled right to amplify one's voice at the expense of one's fellow citizens"

(Galston, 1998, p. 75). In other words, the dangers of democratic exclusion and of exclusionary democracy have increasingly been recognized as antithetical to constitutional protections of equal citizenship and as abridgments of the right to free speech and free access to the public forum. This new situation has also led to the assertion that "deliberative processes within interest associations can help create effective social cooperation as participants affirm or alter their social identifications, place limits on their own and others' options through agreed procedures and work out or reinforce their obligations to neighbors, colleagues, opponents and other participants in the political process. When participants appeal to public values, deliberative forums within interest groups help create a larger public citizenship . . . Today, few interest associations in the United States or Europe institutionalize any formal deliberative processes among their membership, let alone deliberative processes designed to promote identification with the public good" (Mansbridge, 1995, pp. 143–144). The failure of citizens to institutionalize deliberative processes has resulted in the abdication of traditional approaches to practicing "democracy." The glaring absence of an inclusionary democratic forum allows us to focus attention on the exclusionary nature of speech and politics vis-a-vis a rich media and a poor democracy.

B. RICH MEDIA, POOR DEMOCRACY

The division between a rich media and the phenomenon of a poor democracy finds a common denominator in the ideology of global corporate capital, as expressed through unquestioned adherence to its core element and centerpiece—the market. The dogmatic adherence to the market as the primary means through which resources are to be allocated "provides *the* means of organizing economic (and perhaps all human) life" (Herman and McChesney, p. 35, italics in the original). Another related element of corporate ideology is the assumption that government intervention and regulation tend to impose unreasonable burdens on the conduct of business which ultimately undermines and impedes economic growth (*Id.*, p. 35). Corporate ideology also encompasses the belief that there must be sustainable economic growth, but "what is excluded from this schema of objectives is progress in the distribution of income or improvement in the condition of the poor" (*Id.*, p. 36). Hence, as already alluded to, even studies by the Federal Reserve now confirm what has been acknowledged in the United States for decades: a widening gap between the haves and have nots, the growth of democratic exclusion.

For its part, the corporate media largely uncritically applauds the growth of communication as central to the global market economy. Business wanted, needed, and required high-speed communication networks to manage global operations. In this context, the move toward embracing privatized communication was the key to admission to the global economy (*Id.*, p. 111). After all, there was no other alternative within the existing set of social relations. Social relations predicated upon the maintenance of inequality and exclusion could not afford to take the risks associated with a democratized media or an inclusionary democratic project. It is also true that the global commercial media is more developed in some parts of the world than in other places because, "as a profit-oriented enterprise, it devotes most of its attention to the wealthier sectors. In the so-called developing world, the system is accordingly oriented toward middle- and upper-class consumers" (McChesney, 1999, p. 101).

The Third World's pockets of poverty, as well as the ghettos of the First World, remain zones of social, political, and economic exclusion. In the case of India, for example, while the commerical media aims at an audience of 300 to 400 million, the number is really not overwhelming in a nation of almost one billion people. Hence, exclusionary governance is effectuated through a profit-driven media which relies on the dogma of privatization to justify the socioeconomic and sociopolitical exclusion of the majority of people. Further, another aspect of privatization is that it can easily lead to reduced competition. As private oligopolists collude, the danger of public firms disturbing collective private market arrangements recedes into the background (Herman, 1995, p. 21). The danger is that "journalism can be lost to the private sphere as surely as it can be crushed by public power" (Rosen, 1999, p. 120). According to Rosen, "among the lessons we should retain is the importance of 'civil society,' an idea—and a reality— that pointed the way to democracy's rebirth in the East, while illuminating its troubled condition in the West . . . One example is the movement for public (or civic) journalism." In this context, civil society is an "in-between territory—neither state in its official capacity nor citizens in their private affairs. It is the middle ground between the two." In short, while civil society "may be guaranteed by law . . . it is not the equivalent of the rule of law. Governments rise and fall against its backdrop. Politics flows into it and feeds off it. Journalism finds its audience there, and much of its purpose" (*Id.*, p. 117).

There are lessons for journalism, from East to West, that can be gleaned from the "Spirit of 1989," when Eastern European nations began their own quest for democracy and the journalism that is done in service to it. After all, journalism in a democracy is supposed to play a special role. In the parlance of American democratic theory, the press is the "Fourth Estate," supposedly designed to keep public power in check and governmental accountability to the people in place. The problem is that the "Fourth Estate" now constitutes its own private sphere. It remains beyond the control, scope, and influence of politicians and the public. As a result, the civil society that it is supposed to serve has become the victim of a disservice—a betrayal of democratic discourse. According to some, this disservice of the Fourth Estate is the consequence of the media's attitudes in the way that issues are presented mainly as arenas in which politicians can fight. The press is often referred to as the Fourth Branch of Government, which means that it should provide the information we need so as to make sense of public problems.

Far from making it easier to cope with public challenges, the media often make it harder. By choosing to present public life as a contest among scheming political leaders, all of whom the public should view with suspicion, the news media helps bring about that very result (Fallows, 1996, p.

7). In a similar vein of analysis, it has been argued that a "Washington Punditocracy" has led to the decline and collapse of American politics by virtue of the fact that "objective" reporting in the print and broadcast media has been reduced to doublespeak, depriving individual citizens and the civil society at large a viable context in which to make an informed judgment about any given issue. Political pundits have become authoritive opinion-makers, capable of disabling critical thought and destroying genuine democratic discourse. As a result, "our economy, our security, and most particularly our democracy are imperiled by the decrepit state of our national political discourse. We lack the ability, as a nation, to conduct a simple, sensible, and civil conversation about the choices we face" (Alterman, 1992, p. 4). This state of affairs reveals the duality of the media's power as well as its vulnerability—it can be lost to the private sphere of a "punditocracy" as surely as it can be crushed by intrusive governmental power. Therefore, the conclusion to be reached, as far as inclusionary democracy is concerned, is that journalism "thrives in a middle space, the civil sphere—but only when this territory is healthy, active, strong enough to draw people in as citizens" (Rosen, 1999, p. 119).

Failing to draw citizens into the discourse demonstrates that the middle space once occupied by civil society has been either lost or severely damaged. For, in the alternative, civil society, as the middle space between the state and private life represents "a *moral space* from which leaders emerge with their authority earned. A *free space* for art, politics, culture—and journalism. A *social space* where churches, unions and other voluntary associations flourish. A *civil space* on which elected governments stand. A *cognitive space* where people come back to think of themselves as citizens, able to live together despite stresses and strains. And finally, an *imaginative space*, where nations are formed or reformed in response to historic events" (*Id.*, p. 119; italics are mine). Given these understandings, it may be asserted that "professional journalism is arguably at its worst when the US upper class—the wealthiest 1 or 2 percent of the population, the owners of most of the productive wealth, as well as the top corporate executives and government officials—is in agreement on an issue . . . In such cases . . . media will tend to accept the elite position as revealed truth and never subject the notion to questioning" (McChesney, 1999, p. 50). It is for this reason that a vast majority of Americans have virtually no voice in the conduct of US foreign policy. In his book, *Who Speaks for America?: Why Democracy Matters in Foreign Policy*, Alterman concludes that with policymakers answerable only to a small coterie of self-appointed experts, corporate lobbyists, self-interests parties, and the elite media, US foreign policy operates not as the instrument of a democracy, but of a "pseudo-democracy"—that is, a political system with the trappings of democratic checks and balances but with little of their content (Alterman, 1998). The pseudo-democracy is the best evidence of the presence of a rich media with, correspondingly, a poor democracy.

A poor democracy cannot be enriched by a more "informed media" if that media does little more than supply pre-authorized news clips that have been sanctioned by a power-elite and their governing corporate ideology.

The challenge for small media is still full of possibility provided that its practitioners can turn the trends of globalization and digitalization to their own advantage. In this regard, "those with the ability to produce locally and distribute globally will enjoy a key advantage, for in the future it is networks that will matter most—but networks of people, not of machines and wires" (O'Connor, 1999, p. 33). The idea of networks of people rather than of mere machines and wires is a vital concept to grasp insofar as it exposes the nature of shifting power-relationships in the new media environment, which is reflective of the redistribution of power elsewhere. According to Castells, "in a world of global flows of wealth, power, and images, the search for identity, collective or individual, ascribed or constructed, becomes the fundamental source of social meaning . . . Our societies are increasingly structured around a bipolar opposition between the Net and the Self" (Castells, 1996, Vol. 1, p. 3). In short, the identity of individuals and their respective societies will reflect increasingly inclusionary or exclusionary trends and impulses in economic, social, cultural, and political endeavors, thereby altering and fundamentally transforming current power arrangements and relationships.

In this new environment, "the inclusion/exclusion in networks, and the architecture of relationships between networks, enacted by light-speed operating information technologies, configure dominant processes and functions in our societies" (*Id.*, p. 470). For example, while in the United States the trend is toward smaller government and the democratizing effect of new information technologies, there are other emerging models. In the case of Singapore, "a high-technology state is being engineered that is based on strong government control, active censorship of the Internet and close monitoring of media and human behavior" (Rothkopf, 1998, p. 357). The age-old battle between the quest for stability versus the quest for freedom is not over; it has merely been transferred to new battlefields. In this sense, the "Information Age" has not resolved the battle, but rather "the rules have been been changed and traditional power redistributed to new actors" (*Id.*, p. 357). In assessing these trends we must turn to an analysis of the rise of network society, a global society in which networks encompass more than technology-changing modes of communication, as they also involve state intervention as it embarks "on an accelerated process of technological modernization able to change the fate of economies, military power, and social well-being in a few years" (Castells, 1996, Vol. 1, p. 7).

C. THE RISE OF NETWORK SOCIETY

Networks and the new economy complement one another. One the one hand, the new economy is organized around global networks of capital, management, and information. These networks are essential to the efficient functioning of this particular system insofar as technological know-how is at the basis of productivity and competitiveness. On the other hand, networks are the perfect instruments for a capitalist economy which has come to be based on innovation, globalization, and decentralized concentration (Castells, 1996, Vol. 1, pp. 470–471). According to Castells, there are three primary arenas affected by the capitalist economy in its new form: work, the polity, and social organization. For work, networks are important because they affect the degree of flexibility and adaptability on which workers in firms rely. For a polity, networks are important in assisting the polity to prepare itself for the instant processing of new values and public moods. Finally, for a social organization, networks are important because they assist in overcoming the constraints of space and time. Yet, hidden beneath these three arenas is the realization that "the network morphology is also a source of dramatic reorganization of power relationships" (*Id.*, p. 471). For example, when America Online (AOL) bought Time Warner for $183 billion in the largest corporate merger in history, there were the predictable announcements of what it would mean, both from spokespersons for the beneficiaries of the deal as well as its critics. However, lost in the "merger big think was the one issue about which government can actually do something: access to cable lines." While most people enjoy access to the World Wide Web via telephone lines, over the next decade most consumers will begin to take advantage of the use of high-speed broadband systems that use the cable lines that bring television into homes. The problem is that "the public doesn't own the cable lines on which broadband depends. Those lines are currently owned by private companies, and under current law companies can dictate which Internet providers use their lines—thus denying consumers a choice" (*The New Republic*, January 31, 2000, p. 9).

The central issue to emerge from this aspect of network society is the fact that cable owners have the power to dictate the content that comes across computer screens. The question is: Would it not be better for the government to ensure that cable owners do not have the power to dicate the content that comes across the computer screens of its citizens? The question has many aspects to it. Long before the AOL-Time Warner merger, the intersection of global communications, culture, and values was investigated and the following questions emerged: (1) Does communication have the ability to transform international consciousness: i.e., is it likely to lead to a world that is less nationalistic, or more? (2) Are some technologies likely to be more conducive to consciousness transformation than others? (3) How genuinely global is the spread of integrated communications networks and systems? (4) Has the communications revolution empowered citizens vis-a-vis their states, or states vis-a-vis their citizens? (5) Are there any breakthrough technologies in communications that might have a major impact on international security in the coming decade? (Bell, 1993, p. 159). Whatever the particular responses, arguments, and counter-arguments to each of these questions, there is a common implication which arises from each of them, individually and in combination. The common implication is that a power shift has been in the process of occuring vis-a-vis communications and that access to electronic knowledge and networks, more than wealth or military might, has become the key factor in the new world order. In this critical regard, "new structures have appeared at levels both above and below that of the nation-state. The idea that territoriality is a defining characteristic of political association . . . may be overtaken by new types of political associations based on shared communications (no longer dependent on geographical propinquity)" (*Id.*, p. 175). In many respects, the AOL-Time Warner merger signals the inauguration of new types of political associations based on shared communications as being the most significant aspect of a financial deal which has far reaching significance for either the fortification of exclusionary governance or for the advance and extension of forms of inclusionary governance.

The aforementioned trend begs the question: "Will the development of global markets, global actors, global structures, and global problems be accompanied by a new global consciousness?" In answer to this question, it has been suggested that "the rise of a global commercial media system is closely linked to the rise of a significantly more integrated 'neoliberal' global capitalist economic system. To some extent, the rise of a global media market is encouraged by new digital and satellite technologies that make global markets both cost effective and lucrative. It is also encouraged by the institutions of global capitalism—the World Trade Organization (WTO), the World Bank, the International Monetary Fund (IMF)—as well as those governments, including that of the United States, that advance the interests of transnational corporations (TNCs)" (McChesney, 1999, p. 79).

In other words, the usual suspects—representative of the practices of exclusionary governance—emerge as the forces and the beneficiaries of this new information order and its global reach. As to their future success in solidifying their past gains by virtue of their dominance, it can at least be deduced that their dominance is more than an economic matter; "it also has clear implications for media content, politics, and culture" (Id., p. 79). In practical terms, the emerging global media system shares many of the attributes of the US hypercommerical media system and operates on the same profit-maximizing logic. Yet, beyond this point, there are other political and social factors to be assessed, such as the many governments and regional and international organizations that have a voice in the regulation of media. Further, language and cultural differences disallow any kind of immediate informational hegemony, making the establishment of a global version of the US system less than a guaranteed proposition. In spite of these further observations, however, the trajectory established by events such as the AOL-Time Warner merger do not promise easy times for inclusionary forms of governance when faced with the greater integration of a handful of transnational media conglomerates.

Increasingly, around the world, activists are making use of the Internet to create virtual communities of supporters within their countries and internationally. These efforts are the first steps toward inclusionary democracy within the context of the global communications arena. In Burma, for example, democracy advocates have networked with each other and the world via the new "network of networks despite government regulations prohibiting ownership of unregistered computers, fax machines, modems and software" (Rothkopf, 1998, p. 353). In many respects, the hope for the future lies in the possibility that the 21st century will produce for elites and masses a cultural mutation that will lead to a new global consciousness. But the hope for such a creative transformation remains slight at best. Part of the reason for skepticism is the historical reluctance of the powerful, rooted in forms of exclusionary governance, to subscribe to the inclusionary mandate of UNESCO's Declaration on the mass media.

In 1978 a new element was added to the media and communications debate with the passage of a UNESCO Declaration on the Mass Media (Resoution 4/19, adopted by the Twenty-first Session of the UNESCO General Conference, Belgrade, 1980). It was the product of six years of negotiation to achieve a consensus text. It carried the title, *The Declaration of Fundamental Principles concerning the Contribution of the Mass Media to Strengthening Peace and International Understanding, to the Promotion of Human Rights and to Countering Racism, Apartheid and Incitement to War*. It was regarded by the Non-Aligned Nations as furthering a new order movement, one which I have identified as inclusionary governance. It was the very first international instrument referring directly to moral, social, and professional responsibilities of mass media in the context of "the universally recognized principles of freedom of expression, information, and opinion." Once again, however, hovering over the debate, was the old issue regarding the role of government. The final version of the resolution failed to include—because of Western demands—proposals to make national governments responsible for the actions of communications companies working within their jurisdictions. This failure is underscored by the maintenance of media monopoly status quo in the United States in the aftermath of the AOL-Time Warner merger. It has prompted two suggestions to make sure that cable owners do not have the power to dictate the content of what comes across computer screens. The first involves having the Justice Department rule against mergers between companies that provide content (such as AOL), and companies that own the means to distribute content (such as Time Warner). There is precedent for such an action in the 1948 Supreme Court decision that forced movie companies to divest themselves of their theater chains. The second suggestion involves the action of the FCC to require that all cable companies provide full and equal access to all Internet providers. If such a direction was undertaken, one result would be inevitable: Americans could get decent Internet access at a fair price (*The New Republic*, January 31, 2000, p. 9).

Still, on an international scale, a problem remains with respect to the "flow of information"—a term that seems to subsume the proposition that ideas and attitudes follow a one-way direction from rich countries to poor countries. Another aspect of this "flow of information" may be delineated in the international flow of advertising, under multinational controls, that has promoted not only products and services but a way of life that is centered upon the acquisition of consumer goods. Some have criticized this trend as having the effect of diverting attention from necessities to luxuries and, in the process, becoming a threat to the integrity of indigenous peoples in particular and inclusionary governance in general. This trend was exacerbated in the early 1980s when differences in political systems came into sharper focus and, in the developed nations, a trend toward deregulation of information media and the privitization of public-sector enterprises was gaining momentum. The trend that began in the First World would soon spill over into the Third World. These trends effectively severed the efforts undertaken pursuant to the nonaligned summit held in Algiers in 1973, which adopted a resolution calling for a "new international economic order" (which was endorsed by the UN General Assembly a year later). The resolution became precedent for a similar resolution focusing on information, which was articulated at a 1976 nonaligned new symposium in Tunis. At the symposium, the existing communication systems were depicted as the vestiges and enduring legacy of a colonial past. The same year, UNESCO's General Conference in Nairobi discussed information issues, thereby pitting the interests of the First World against those of the Third World. An outcome of this 1976 UNESCO meeting was the selection of Sean MacBride of Ireland to study the totality of communication problems in modern societies. The final report, known as the MacBride Report, was submitted to the 1980 UNESCO Conference in Belgrade. Its findings are outlined in Table 3.3.

The work of UNESCO, as demonstrated by the findings contained in the MacBride Report, also evidences the fact that UNESCO is dedicated to the promotion and extension of human rights (UNESCO Const., entered into force November 4, 1946, 61 Stat. 2495, T.I.A.S. No. 1580, 4 U.N.T.S. 275, Preamble). As an institution engaged in the extension of human rights, it has become a primary forum for discussion about a New World Information Order. In terms of its structure and policy, the legal basis for UNESCO's involvement with human rights, and with the debate on communication, is its constitution. In particular, UNESCO is charged with the duty of "promoting collaboration among the nations . . . . in order to further universal respect for justice, for the rule of law and for the human rights and fundamental freedoms" of the UN Charter (*Id.*, at article 1, paragraph 1). Additionally, UNESCO is authorized to achieve this purpose by recommending "such international agreements as may be necessary to promote the free flow of ideas by word and image" (*Id.*, at article 1, paragraph 2(a)). UNESCO's responsibilities in this area are particularly important for Third World nations insofar as a majority of UNESCO's member states may be classified as developing states. These nations are critically aware of grave imbalances that arise in their culture and value systems as a result of the foreign origin and manufacture of information and communication channels.

The responsibility and charge given to UNESCO and elaborated upon by the MacBride Report, by virtue of its adherence to human rights as being effectuated and respected vis-a-vis the promotion of the free flow of ideas, is antithetical to what Herman and Chomsky have referred to as the "propaganda model"—a model for understanding and analyzing how the mainstream US media work and why they perform as they do (Herman and Chomsky, 1988). The distinct difference between the political implications of the propaganda model and mainstream scholarship of liberal and conservative analysts is found in the assertion that "if structural factors shape the broad contours of media performance, and if that performance is incompatible with a truly democratic political culture, then a basic change in media ownership, organization, and purpose is necessary for the achievement of a genuine democracy" (Herman, 1996, p. 116). Fundamentally, what the propaganda model exposes that "crucial structural factors derive from the fact that the dominant media are firmly embedded in the market system" (*Id.*, p. 116).

Insofar as the market-driven media are profit-seeking businesses, they are largely funded by advertisers who are also profit-seeking entities who

TABLE 3.3 Resolution 4/19 Adopted by the Twenty-First Session of the UNESCO General Conference, Belgrade, 1980

The General Conference considers that:

a. this new world information and communication order could be based, among, other considerations, on:
   i. elimination of the imbalances and inequalities which characterize the present situation;
   ii. elimination of the negative effects of certain monopolies, public or private, and excessive concentrations;
   iii. removal of the internal and external obstacles to a free flow and wider and better balanced dissemination of information and ideas;
   iv. plurality of sources and channels of information;
   v. freedom of the press and of information;
   vi. the freedom of journalists and all professionals in the communication media, a freedom inseparable from responsibility;
   vii. the capacity of developing countries to achieve improvement of their own situations, notably by providing their own equipment, by training their personnel, by improving their infrastructures and making their information and communication media suitable to their needs and aspirations;
   viii. the sincere will of developed countries to help them obtain these objectives;
   ix. respect for each people's cultural identity and for the right of each nation to inform the world about its interests, its aspirations and its social and cultural values;
   x. respect for the right of all peoples to participate in international exchanges of information on the basis of equality, justice and mutual benefit;
   xi. respect for the right of the public, of ethnic and social groups and of individuals to have access to information sources and to participate actively in the communication process;

b. this new world information and communication order should be based on the fundamental principles of international law, as laid down in the Charter of the United Nations;

c. diverse solutions to information and communication problems are required because social, political, cultural, and economic problems differ from one country to another and, within a given country, from one group to another.

SOURCE: Sean MacBride and Colleen Roach, "The New International Information Order," *The Globalization Reader*, edited by Frank J. Lechner and John Boli, Blackwell Publishers, 2000, p. 288.

want their ads to appear in supportive selling environments. In turn, the media are also dependent upon both government and major business firms as information sources. The net effect of these relationships is the creation of a structure for the transmission of information, values, and news that is ideologically filtered for the sake of both political and efficiency considerations. Overlapping interests cause a certain degree of ideological hegemony to prevail which has exclusionary implications for both the coverage of news and the evolving nature of governance. In short, the collusion of media, government and business has led to the promotion of inherently exclusionary practices in media coverage which has led to the manufacturing of consent. It is to this process that we now turn.

D. THE ELECTRONIC REPUBLIC AND THE MANUFACTURE OF CONSENT

Until the 1970s, large telecommunications corporations and media entertainment conglomerates could be found in most nations, but they were for the most part national corporations engaged in servicing domestic markets and working in separate sectors. Since the 1970s, both the national and international regulation of telecommuications and media industries has been transformed. While some domestic markets have become either ultracompetitive or saturated, there has been a trend toward relying on distinct technologies which have become increasingly fused together. As a result of this trend, there have been five major changes in corporate organization and activity: (1) the increasing concentration of ownership; (2) a shift from public to private ownership; (3) the increasingly transnational structure of the corporations that survive through the establishment of subsidiaries or through the purchase of local firms, titles, and so forth; (4) general corporate diversification across different types of media products; and (5) an increasing number of mergers of cultural producers, telecommunications corporations and computer hardware and software firms (Held, McGrew, Goldblatt, and Perration, 1999, p. 347).

These trends have been converted into a rationale used by media giants around the world to justify changes in their nations' media laws so as to allow more concentration of ownership. Corporate media giants, under this approach, have been able to play one nation's government off against others, for the greater influence and power of megamedia. These development are leading precisely where the head of Time Inc., predicted: "There will emerge on a world-wide basis, six, seven, or eight integrated media and entertainment conglomerates" that will dominate mass communications (Quoted in Ken Auletta, 1991, p. 86). The effect of this trend upon the prospects for inclusionary governance is grim. In this new context, a "genuine diversity of voices, a commitment to making major contributions to the democratic dialogue, and local control are clearly in serious retreat" (Alger, 1998, p. 216).

Within the United States, problems associated with helping democratic dialogue to keep pace with media trends is further exacerbated by the political shift of focus to single issues that require only yes or no votes. In this respect, the initiative process and the growing reliance on propositions to determine public policy has further undermined the process of compromise and the ability to form political coalitions. Political coalitions and popular mobilization are essential to building a complex and collaborative democracy which can reach consensus through interaction and dialogue. Building such coalitions is necessary if inclusionary governance is to be realized as a force that questions the power of the status quo and is capable of making claims upon decision making and decision makers. The absence of processes leading to conditions and circumstances for coalition formation weakens inclusionary democracy as it correspondingly strengthens democratic exclusion. Marginalized and dispossessed constituencies are left to the mercy of the sound-bite and the ideological bickering of elites.

In this new political/media environment, the information age has created an electronic republic in which initiatives and propositions "discard the traditional system of checks and balances of representative government. They close out the opportunity for careful deliberation and considered discussion by experts and experienced legislators. They greatly increase the role and influence of the mass media, especially the new electronic media, in translating initiative questions in ways the public can understand. They let through occasionally ill-conceived, rash, or poorly drafted schemes for the general electorate to consider. They leave voters overwhelmed by the number and complexity of measures on the ballot. They offer little protection against heavily financed, one-sided campaigns and special interest propaganda efforts. And major political issues are often decided on the basis of very low voter participation" (Grossman, 1995, p. 142). Given these trends, the democratic deficit experienced in many Third World contexts has come home to First World democracies. Throughout the First World, weak and low-intensity democracies are registering lower voter turnout and dwindling citizen participation as the corporate-controlled media bemoans growing citizen apathy, alienation, and non-involvement.

In short, a recipe for exclusionary governance lurks within and behind the media of the electronic republic as it effectively leaves out of its coverage the concerns of the excluded, the poor, the dispossessed and the "politically incorrect" groups and individuals who do not support the ideological presuppositions of the dominant discourse. Further, the electronic republic's media not only distorts the electoral process through countless initiatives and propositions, but also through the watershed of money from corporations to candidates for public office who buy commercial and debate time, thereby creating a bipartisan infomerical for corporate America's candidates (Raskin, 2000, pp. 21–24). The deflation of democracy in debates would not have come to such a juncture "if the Federal Election Commission (FEC) had not itself been captured by the campaign industry" for, in the alternative, "it could have blown the whistle on this outrageous corporate subsidization and promotion of two parties over the others" (*Id.*, p. 23). Additionally, campaign politics in the year 2000 has raised the question: How has politics, which is supposed to be the business of the entire society, become the preserve of a professional class? In response, Jonathan

Schell has described a phenomenon he calls "virtual primaries" as the result of what has become "technically possible" (Schell, 2000, p. 12). Whereas the Constitution in earlier times provided for direct political participation on election day, there is now "an entrenched new system" which "has grown up alongside the constitutional one," resting on three pillars: media, money, and public opinion polling (*Id.*, p. 12). In this new environment, elections themselves become the certification that the polls were accurate. In a real sense, the manufacturing of consent, once primarily dedicated to shaping public support for US foreign policy interests, has doubled back to reshape the domestic landscape of American electoral choice.

With respect to shaping the public's perception of international affairs, the US corporate-controlled media "serve as a system for communicating messages and symbols to the general populace . . . In a world of concentrated wealth and major conflicts of class interest, to fulfill this role requires systematic propaganda" (Herman and Chomsky, 1988, p. 1). As Albert Speer suggested with regard to Hitler's dictatorship, the shaping influence of a propaganda system is to control the opinions and viewpoints of the citizenry by virtue of the centralized control of information. Hence, in the context of the Cold War, the great discovery of the power elite was that "a propaganda system will consistently portray people abused in enemy states as *worthy* victims, whereas those treated with equal or greater severity by its own government or clients will be *unworthy*" (*Id.*, p. 37, italics in the original). With regard to US interventions in El Salvador, Nicaragua, the Philippines, Iran, Iraq, Vietnam, Cambodia, Chile, and Guatemala, the media largely gave differential treatment to those associations so as not to bring into question the legality or legitimacy of US government actions and policies.

The end of the Cold War did not bring a respite from the dominant media's coverage and spin on what was now euphemistically called "humanitarian interventions" in Haiti, Bosnia, and Kosovo (Chomsky, 1999). In large measure, preventive diplomacy was consistently ignored by US policymakers and corporate-controlled media coverage of these situations. Why, for example, if the humanitarian impulse of US foreign policy was so strong, did the US not become engaged in efforts to end the genocide in Rwanda? In fact, several years after mass killings in Bosnia, Somalia, and Rwanda, the United States is still searching for a comprehensive policy to address deadly communal conflicts (Kuperman, 2000, p. 94). One explanation for the inaction on prevention is that the world failed to halt the carnage of Tutsis by Hutus in Rwanda because the reporting was so poor that it was nearly over before most people knew what was happening (*Id.*, pp. 94–118). According to some analysts, "although US intelligence reports from the period of the genocide remain classified, they probably mirrored those of the international news media, human rights organizations, and the UN: because US intelligence agencies committed virtually no in-country resources to what was considered a tiny state in a region of little strategic value" (*Id.*, p. 101). Yet, to speak of strategic value in making policy judgments while failing to include moral considerations in the policy making equation only serves to expose the economic and strategic nature of exclusionary governance at the highest levels of governmental decision making and a corresponding disjuncture of that policy with moral considerations. The on-again/off-again nature of the invocation of "humanitarian intervention" demonstrates the congruence between the media's coverage and its connection with its respective governmental sources of information.

Another explanation for inaction and the lack of effort aimed at conflict prevention involves what has been termed "compassion fatigue." As the media careen from one trauma to another, covering an array of human tragedies from genocide and conflict to disease and death, the viewing public becomes inured to the suffering it views through the lens of the media. Behind this general critique is a larger question: "Are the media merely following marketplace demands for tabloid-style international news or are they creating an audience that has seen too much—or too little—to care?" Moeller argues that "perhaps if the coverage of crises were not so formulaic or sensationalized or Americanized we wouldn't lapse so readily into a compassion fatigue stupor" (Moeller, 1999, p. 53). In any event, "compassion fatigue, and even more clearly, compassion avoidance are signals that the coverage of international affairs must change" (*Id.*, p. 313). Some of the lessons of compassion fatigue, therefore, involve putting an end to the formulaic coverage of crises, "the if-it's-Tuesday-it's-time-to-wrap-this-all-up coverage of deaths and assassinations" because this approach to coverage "shoehorns crises into a preordained time slot, ignoring the inevitable slop of a crisis beyond its formulaic moments" (*Id.*, p. 313). In short, there must be a follow-up. This points back to Kuperman's review of Rwanda and Washington's lack of effective response. Kuperman noted that "during the genocide's early phases, the US government actually received most of its information from nongovernmental organizations. A comprehensive review of such international reporting—by American, British, French, Belgian, and Rwandan media, leading human rights groups—strongly suggests that President Clinton could not have known that a nationwide genocide was under way in Rwanda until about April 20" (Kupermann, 2000, p. 101). The genocidal violence began on April 7, 1994, and most foreign journalists had left before that date. It was not until April 20 that Human Rights Watch made the first correct guesstimate when it said that as many as 100,000 people may have died.

A retrospect on the Rwandan genocide also provides a glimpse into the possibilities for preventive diplomacy and a new United Nations role, provided that the media do more to help governments, and non-governmental organizations better anticipate such situations. Jonathan Power has argued that if there was a time to have intervened on a large scale, it was, in fact, way back in January of 1994, "when the moderate Hutu government was still in power, desperately trying to keep Hutu militants in check" and the government along with its old colonial power, Belgium, were arguing for a major UN intervention" (Power, 2000). While the United States and Britain quashed the idea, "arguing that the cost was prohibitive and that peacekeepers would be endangered . . . we have to better anticipate such situations . . . The intervention debate has become impaled on the horn of multiple dilemmas. If the UN needs to beef up anything, it needs to beef up its preventive diplomacy. That means developing a large cadre of people—not just a lone troubleshooter who flies to meet the president—which can go into a situation of conflict, stay a year or two or more and work at every level of society, not just the very top" (Power, 2000). This retrospect provides new guidance for needed changes in media coverage, governmental procedures, UN policies, and the agenda of non-governmental organizations.

As far as bringing about changes in media coverage are concerned, however, there are entrenched obstacles to change. Three major obstacles to reforming media coverage are the practices of: (1) agenda-setting; (2) priming; and (3) framing. First, agenda-setting reflects the impact of news coverage on the importance accorded to issues. This effect is made clear by the manner in which issues enter and leave the center stage of American politics with considerable speed. Agenda-setting effects are captured for all forms of media coverage ranging from suvey-based studies to open-ended indicators in which respondents identify the "most important problems facing the country" (Iyengar and Simon, 1994, pp. 168–170). Second, priming is an extension of agenda setting. It is used to address the impact of news coverage on the weight assigned to specific issues in making political judgments. Third, research on "framing" has been used to study the effects of alternative news "frames" on the public's attributions of responsibility for issues and events. Typically, the networks frame issues in either "episodic" or "thematic" terms. The episodic frame serves to depict public issues in concrete instances or specific events. Alternatively, the thematic news frame is used to place public issues in a general or abstract context (*Id.*, pp. 170–172).

In sum, public opinion may be shaped thematically when the media "frame" a problem according to its general societal factors, including cultural norms, economic conditions, and the actions or inactions of public officials. Public opinion may also be shaped by episodic framing, in which viewers are guided to attribute responsibility for national and international problems not to societal or structural forces but to the actions of particular individuals or groups. A prime examples of episodic framing is the Western media's treatment of Saddam Hussein in the Gulf War (Sifry and Cerf, 1991; Bresheeth and Yuval-Davis, 1991; Bennis and Moushabeck, 1991; Clark, 1992; Cockburn and Cockburn, 1999) . The effect of episodic framing is also distinguishable in the Western media's approach to Slobodan Milosevic (Thomas, 1999; Lituchy, 1998; Veljanovski, 2000).

In the case of the NATO powers and the Balkan tragedy, the demonization of Milosevic was used to cover the fact that "Western powers usually legitimize military interventions in terms of a proclaimed commitment to some universalist norm or to some goal embodying such a norm" (Gowan, 1999, p. 83). The reality, however, was that the break-up of Yugoslavia might have been a possibility without conflict and death "if clear criteria could have been established for providing security for all the main groups of people within the Yugoslav space" (*Id.*, p. 90). Certainly, the employment of inclusionary governance, as a strategy of peace, would have been effective in providing such an outcome. Instead, the effect of US intervention served the purpose of playing the Bosnian card against an emerging German sphere of influence. During 1991, the United States stood back from the Yugoslav crisis with the Bush administration preoccupied with ensuring that Western Europe remained firmly subordinated to the Atlantic Alliance under US leadership (*Id.*, p. 93; see also Mousavizadeh, 1992/1995; Human Rights Watch, 1995; Said, 1999; Fromkin, 1999; Burg and Shoup, 1999; Blackburn, 1999; Ray and Schaap, 1999).

In the case of Milosevic, the demonizing of him as a symbol allowed the US government, NATO, and the Western media the opportunity to never engage or include the citizens of the United States or Europe with an inclusionary dialogue. Rather, the filtering of news combined with distortion and misrepresentation reflected a latent hostility within elite governing circles that excluded the people from becoming genuine participants in the Balkan debacle, from the Bush administration through the Clinton administration. The exclusionary effects upon American democracy have effectively crippled independent opinion in the mainstream press and in political discourse. The reason for taking this exclusionary path was articulated by Samuel Huntington, writing for the Trilateral Commission's report, *The Crisis Of Democracy*, in which he noted: "The vulnerability of democratic government in the United States . . . comes not primarily from external threats . . . nor from internal subversion from the left or the right . . . but rather from the internal dynamics of democracy itself in a highly educated, mobilized, and participant society" (Huntington, 1975, p. 115). A contrary view is articulated in Richard Barnett's book, *Roots Of War: The Men And Institutions Behind US Foreign Policy*, in which he noted that "the national security managers believe that the public is so passive that it can be aroused to give positive support to a foreign policy initiative, particularly if it is a risky one, only if it is presented in the context of a crisis and then only if the crisis is deliberately oversold" (Barnett, 1972, p. 270). The "over-selling" of crises has been a permanent feature of the US foreign policy establishment and the mainstream media. It has been effectively employed as a means to help men of power keep it (*Id.*, p. 306).

In the electronic republic, the United States has witnessed its democratic political culture virtually transformed into what has been called "imperial democracy" (Barnett, 1972, pp. 239–332), as well as "friendly fascism" (Gross, 1980). Inherent in "friendly fascism" are two conflicting trends. The first is a drift toward "greater concentration of power and wealth in a repressive Big-Business/Big-Government partnership" while "the other is a slower and less powerful tendency for individuals and groups to seek greater participation in decisions affecting themselves and others" (Gross, 1980, p. xi). Certainly, the centralization, concentration, and monopolization of the media exhibit the first tendency of friendly fascism insofar as they have created a situation where "what seems lost is media material that meaningfully contributes to a recognition of common interests as members and citizens of our communities and general societies. Instead, media fare more and more seems to impoverish the realm of public discussion and interaction that is central to the democratic process" (Alger, 1998, p. 221). Yet if we halt analysis at this point there is the danger of missing another trend inherent in the process—the trend of concentrated power promoting genuine participation in decision making. As Gross has noted: "The process of concentration may have the unintended consequence of nurturing demands for genuine participation" (Gross, 1980, p. 347). In other words, inclusionary democracy may become the by-product of contradictions inherent in exclusionary governance. Such an outcome would have the capacity to liberate the inclusionary and participatory impulses of democracy—of which Huntington warned in his report for the Trilateral Commission.

BIBLIOGRAPHY

Gautam Adhikari, "From the Press to the Media," *Journal of Democracy*, Volume 11, No. 1, January 2000.

Dean Alger, *Megamedia: How Giant Corporations Dominate Mass Media, Distort Competition, and Endanger Democracy*, Rowman & Littlefield Publishers, Inc., 1998.

Erich Alterman, *Sound and Fury: The Washington Punditocracy and the Collapse of American Politics*, Harper Collins Publishers, 1992.

Erich Alterman, *Who Speaks for America?: Why Democracy Matters in Foreign Policy*, Cornell University Press, 1998.

Sarah Anderson, et al., "A Decade of Executive Excess: The 1990s," Sixth Annual Executive Compensation Survey, Institute for Policy Studies, September 1, 1999.

Ken Auletta, *Three Blind Mice: How the TV Networks Lost Their Way*, Random House, 1991.

C. Edwin Baker, "The Media That Citizens Need," *University of Pennsylvania Law Review*, Volume 147, No. 2, December 1998.

Benjamin R. Barber, *A Passion for Democracy: American Essays*, Princeton University Press, 1998.

Donald L. Barlett and James B. Steele, *America: What Went Wrong?*, Andrews and McMeel, 1992.

Donald L. Barlett and James B. Steele, *America: Who Stole the Dream?*, Andrews and McMeel, 1996.

Donald L. Barlett and James B. Steele, "Big Money & Politics: Who Gets Hurt," *Time*, February 7, 2000.

Richard J. Barnett, *Roots of War: The Men and Institutions Behind US Foreign Policy*, Penguin Books, Inc., 1972.

David V.J. Bell, "Global Communications, Culture, and Values: Implications for Global Security," *Building a New Global Order: Emerging Trends in International Security*, edited by David Dewitt, David Haglund, and John Kirton, Oxford University Press, 1993.

W. Lance Bennett and David L. Paletz, editors, *Taken by Storm: The Media, Public Opinion, and US Foreign Policy in the Gulf War*, The University of Chicago Press, 1994.

Phyllis Bennis and Michel Moushabeck, editors, *Beyond the Storm: A Gulf Crisis Reader*, Olive Branch Press, 1991.

Robin Blackburn, "Kosovo: The War of NATO Expansion," *New Left Review*, No. 235, May/June 1999.

Haim Bresheeth and Nira Yuval-Davis, editors, *The Gulf War and the New World Order*, Zed Books Ltd., 1991.

Steven L. Burg and Paul S. Shoup, *The War in Bosnia-Herzegovina: Ethnic Conflict and International Intervention*, M.E. Sharpe, 1999.

David Callahan, *Unwinnable Wars: American Power and Ethnic Conflict*, A Twentieth Century Fund Book, Hill And Wang, 1997.

Manuel Castells, *The Information Age: Economy, Society and Culture, Volume I: The Rise of Network Society*, Blackwell Publishers, 1996.

Manuel Castells, *The Information Age: Economy, Society and Culture, Volume II: The Power of Identity*, Blackwell Publishers, 1997.
Noam Chomsky, *World Orders Old and New*, Columbia University Press, 1994.
Noam Chomsky, *The New Military Humanism: Lessons From Kosovo*, Common Courage Press, 1999.
Ramsey Clark, *The Fire This Time: US War Crimes in the Gulf*, Thunder's Mouth Press, 1992.
Ramsey Clark, et al., *NATO in the Balkans: Voices of Opposition*, International Action Center, 1998.
Andrew Cockburn and Patrick Cockburn, *Out of the Ashes: The Resurrection of Saddam Hussein*, Harper Collins Publishers, 1999.
Jeff Cohen and Norman Solomon, *Through the Media Looking Glass: Decoding Bias and Blather in the News*, Common Courage Press, 1995.
David Croteau and William Hoynes, *By Invitation Only: How the Media Limit Political Debate*, Common Courage Press, 1994.
Michel J. Crozier, Samuel P. Huntington, Joji Watanuki, *The Crisis of Democracy: Report on the Governability Of Democracies To The Trilateral Commission*, New York University Press, 1975.
Sheldon Danziger and Peter Gottschalk, editors, *Uneven Tides: Rising Inequality in America*, Russell Sage Foundation, 1993.
Sheldon Danziger and Peter Gottschlk, *America Unequal*, Russell Sage Foundation and Harvard University Press, 1995.
G. William Domhoff, *Who Rules America?: Power and Politics in the Year 2000*, Third Edition, Mayfield Publishing Company, 1998.
Thomas R. Dye, *Who's Running America?: The Clinton Years*, Sixth Edition, Prentice Hall, 1995.
Dale F. Eickelman and Jon W. Anderson, "Preface," *New Media in the Muslim World: The Emerging Public Sphere*, edited by Dale F. Eickelman and Jon W. Anderson, Indiana University Press, 1999.
Richard Falk, *Law in an Emerging Global Village: A Post-Westphalian Perspective*, Transnational Publishers, Inc., 1998.
James Fallows, *Breaking The News: How the Media Undermine American Democracy*, Pantheon Books, 1996.
Thomas Ferguson and Joel Rogers, *The Hidden Election: Politics and Economics in the 1980 Presidential Campaign*, Pantheon Books, 1981.
Albert Fislow and Karen Parker, editors, *Growing Apart: The Causes and Consequences of Global Wage Inequality*, A Council on Foreign Relations Book, 1999.
David Fromkin, *Kosovo Crossing: American Ideals Meet Reality on the Balkan Battlefields*, The Free Press, 1999.
William A. Galston, "Political Economy and the Politics of Virtue: US Public Philosophy at Century's End," *Debating Democracy's Discontent: Essays on American Politics, Law, and Public Philosophy*, edited by Anita L. Allen and Milton C. Regan, Jr., Oxford University Press, 1998.
David Gergen, "To Have and Have Less—Don't look now, but the gap between rich and poor is widening," *US News & World Report*, July 26, 1999.

Alan Gilbert, *Must Global Politics Constrain Democracy?: Great-Power Realism, Democratic Peace, and Democratic Internationalism*, Princeton University Press, 1999.
Peter Gowan, "The NATO Powers and the Balkan Tragedy," *New Left Review*, No. 234, March/April 1999.
Bertram Gross, *Friendly Fascism: The New Face of Power in America*, South End Press, 1980.
Lawrence K. Grossman, *The Electronic Republic: Reshaping Democracy in the Information Age*, A Twentieth Century Fund Book, Viking, 1995.
David Held, *Introduction to Critical Theory: Horkheimer to Habermas*, University of California Press, 1980.
David Held, Anthony McGrew, David Goldblatt and Jonathan Perraton, *Global Transformations: Politics, Economics and Culture*, Stanford University Press, 1999.
Edward S. Herman and Noam Chomsky, *Manufacturing Consent: The Political Economy of the Mass Media*, Pantheon Books, 1988.
Edward S. Herman, *Beyond Hypocrisy: Decoding the News in an Age of Propaganda*, South End Press, 1992.
Edward S. Herman, *Triumph of the Market: Essays on Economics, Politics, and the Media*, South End Press, 1995.
Edward S. Herman, "The Propaganda Model Revisted," *Monthly Review*, July/August 1996.
Edward S. Herman, "The Economics of the Rich: The 'Natural Order' of Money," *Z Magazine*, July/August 1997.
Edward Herman and Robert W. McChesney, *The Global Media: The New Missionaries of Corporate Capitalism*, Cassell, 1997.
Mark Hertsgaard, *On Bended Knee: The Press and the Reagan Presidency*, Farrar Straus Giroux, 1988.
Bryan J. Holzberg, "The New World Information Order: A Legal Framework For Debate," *Third World Attitudes Toward International Law: An Introduction*, edited by Frederick E. Snyder and Surakiart Sathirathai, Martinus Nijhoff Publishers, 1987.
Human Rights Watch, *Slaughter Among Neighbors: The Political Origins of Communal Violence*, Yale University Press, 1995.
Samuel P. Huntington, "The United States," *The Crisis of Democracy*, New York University Press, 1975.
Jeffrey C. Isaac, *Democracy in Dark Times*, Cornell University Press, 1998.
Shanto Iyengar and Adam Simon, "News Coverage of the Gulf Crisis and Public Opinion: A Study of Agenda-Setting, Priming, and Framing," *Taken by Storm: The Media, Public Opinion, and US Foreign Policy in the Gulf War*, edited by W. Lance Bennett and David L. Paletz, The University of Chicago Press, 1994.
Karol Jakubowicz, "The Genie Is Out of the Bottle: Measuring Media Change In Central And Eastern Europe," *Media Studies Journal*, Volume 13, No. 3, Fall 1999.
Michael Janeway, *Republic of Denial: Press, Politics, and Public Life*, Yale University Press, 1999.
Mary Kaldor, *New and Old Wars: Organized Violence in a Global Era*,

Stanford University Press, 1999.
Naomi Klein, *No Logo: Taking Aim at the Brand Name Bullies*, Picador-USA, 1999.
Alan J. Kuperman, "Rwanda In Retrospect," *Foreign Affairs*, January/February 2000.
Mark Leibovich, "A Match for the Media Age: Why AOL and Time Warner Need Eachother to Survive," *The Washington Post National Weekly*, Volume 17, No. 12, January 17, 2000.
Robert W. McChesney, *Rich Media, Poor Democracy: Communication Politics in Dubious Times*, University of Illinois Press, 1999.
Myres S. McDougal, Harold D. Lasswell, and Lung-chu Chen, *Human Rights and World Public Order: The Basic Policies of an International Law of Human Dignity*, Yale University Press, 1980.
Kim McQuaid, *Big Business and Presidential Power: From FDR to Reagan*, William Morrow and Company, Inc., 1982.
Sean MacBride and Colleen Roach, "The New International Information Order," edited by Frank J. Lechner and John Boli, Blackwell Publishers, 2000.
Jane Mansbridge, "A Deliberative Perspective on Neocorporatism," *Associations and Democracy: The Real Utopias Project—Volume I*, edited by Joshua Cohen and Joel Rogers, Verso, 1995.
C. Wright Mills, *The Power Elite*, Oxford University Press, 1956.
Morton Mintz and Jerry S. Cohen, *America, Inc.: Who Owns and Operates the United States?*, A Dell Book, 1971.
Morton Mintz and Jerry S. Cohen, *Power, Inc.: Public and Private Rulers and How to Make Them Accountable*, Bantam Books, 1977.
Susan D. Moeller, *Compassion Fatigue: How the Media Sell Disease, Famine, War and Death*, Routledge, 1999.
Nafdar Mousavizadeh, editor, *The Black Book of Bosnia: The Consequences of Appeasement*, A New Republic Book/Basic Books, 1992/1995.
Ralph Nader and Wesley J. Smith, *No Contest: Corporate Lawyers and the Perversion of Justice in America*, Random House, 1996.
Joel I. Nelson, *Post-Industrial Capitalism: Exploring Economic Inequality in America*, Sage Publications, 1995.
The New Republic (by the editors), "Crossing Lines: What To Do About the AOL-Time Warner Merger," January 31, 2000.
Rory O'Connor, "How Independent Journalism Can Survive Globalization," *The Nation*, November 29, 1999.
Michael Parenti, *Democracy for the Few*, Sixth Edition, St. Martin's Press, 1995.
Michael Parenti, *America Besieged*, City Lights Books, 1998.
Wallace Peterson, *Silent Depression: Twenty-Five Years of Wage Squeeze and Middle-Class Decline*, W.W. Norton & Company, 1994.
Jonathan Power, "Could the UN Have Saved Rwanda?," *The Los Angeles Times*, January 24, 2000.
Jamin B. Raskin, "Let's Take Back the Debates: They've Become a Bipartisan Infomerical for Corporate America's Candidates," *The Nation*, February 7, 2000.

Ellen Ray and Bill Schaap, "NATO and Beyond: The Wars of the Future" *Covert Action Quarterly*, No. 66, Winter 1999.

David Reynolds, *One World Divisible: A Global History Since 1945*, W.W. Norton & Company, 2000.

Steven A. Rosell, *Renewing Governance: Governing by Learning in the Information Age*, Oxford University Press, 1999.

Jay Rosen, "Civil Society and the Spirit of 1989: Lessons for Journalism, from East to West," *Media Studies Journal*, Volume 13, No. 3, Fall 1999.

Theodore Roszak, *The Cult of Information: A Neo-Luddite Treatise on High Tech, Artificial Intelligence, and the True Art of Thinking*, University of California Press, 1986 and 1994.

David J. Rothkopf, "Cyberpolitik: The Changing Nature of Power in the Information Age," *Journal of International Affairs*, Volume 51, No. 2, Spring 1998.

Paul Ryscavage, *Income Inequality in America: An Analysis of Trends*, M.E. Sharpe, 1999.

Edward Said, "Protecting the Kosovars?," *New Left Review*, No. 234, March/April 1999.

Michael J. Sandel, *Democracy's Discontent: America in Search of a Public Philosophy*, Harvard University Press, 1996.

Jonathan Schell, "Our Virtual Primaries," *The Nation*, February 7, 2000.

Michael Schwartz, editor, *The Structure of Power in America: The Corporate Elite as a Ruling Class*, Holmes & Meier, 1987.

Richard E. Sclove, *Democracy and Technology*, The Guilford Press, 1995.

Andrew L. Shapiro, *The Control Revolution: How the Internet Is Putting Individuals in Charge and Changing the World We Know*, A Century Foundation Book, Public Affairs, 1999.

Micha L. Sifry and Christopher Cerf, editors, *The Gulf War Reader: History, Documents, Opinions*, Times Books, 1991.

Albert Speer, *Inside The Third Reich: Memoirs by Albert Speer*, translated from the German by Richard and Clara Winston, Galahad Books, 1970.

Richard W. Stevenson, "In a Time of Plenty, The Poor Are Still Poor," *The New York Times*, January 23, 2000.

Frederick R. Strobel and Wallace C. Peterson, *The Coming Class War and How to Avoid It: Rebuilding the American Middle Class*, M.E. Sharpe, Inc., 1999.

Robert Thomas, *The Politics of Serbia in the 1990s*, Columbia University Press, 1999.

Rade Veljanovski, "Turning the Electronic Media Around," *The Road to War in Serbia: Trauma and Catharsis*, edited by Nebojsa Popov, Central European University Press, 2000.

David Vogel, *Fluctuating Fortunes: The Political Power of Business in America*, Basic Books, Inc., 1989.

David Vogel, *Kindred Strangers: The Uneasy Relationship Between Politics and Business in America*, Princeton University Press, 1996.

Mary Williams Walsh, "Boom Time a Bad Time for Poorest, Study Finds," *The Los Angeles Times*, January 19, 2000.

James D. Wolfensohn, "Voices of the Poor," *Washington Post*, November 10, 1999.

Edward N. Wolff, *Top Heavy: The Increasing Inequality of Wealth in America and What Can Be Done About It—An Expanded Edition of a Twentieth Century Fund Report*, The New Press, 1995.

Richard L. Zweigenhaft and G. William Domhoff, *Diversity in the Power Elite: Have Women and Minorities Reached the Top?*, Yale University Press, 1998.

Part II

PATHS TO AND FROM INCLUSION

CHAPTER 4

MOVING TOWARD INCLUSION: OVERCOMING THE DYNAMICS OF DEMOCRATIC EXCLUSION

> There is perhaps no more fundamental political right than the ability to have a say in how one is governed. Healthy political systems reflect a shared contract between the people and their government . . . Effective participatory government based on the rule of law reduces the need for people to take matters into their own hands and resolve differences through violence.
> Carnegie Commission—Final Report,
> *Preventing Deadly Conflict,* 1997, p. 94

A. INTRODUCTION

Building a culture of peace depends on many interrelated factors. Primary among these factors is the fundamental political right of people to have a say in how they are governed. The implications of this right revive the Hobbesian notion of a vibrant commonwealth, and the Lockean notion of a social contract. The articulation of this right demands that people are included in the political, economic and social decisions that affect their lives individually and serves the cause of building a culture of peace. In that sense, the articulation of this right is hundreds of years old.

However, the embodiment of this right is yet to be fully realized. Even in nations that call themselves democratic, many groups, classes, and discrete and insular minorities have been and continue to be deprived of a right to have a say in how they are governed. This reality is the reality of political exclusion. And political exclusion, by virtue of the fact that it precludes effective participatory government based on the rule of law, also contributes to peoples' reliance on violence as a means of settling differences. Therefore, political exclusion is antithetical to the task of building a culture of peace.

In the alternative, political inclusion provides the normative and constitutional channels through which people are empowered to have a voice in how they are governed. Further, political inclusion is a universal principle of governance that has the capacity to transcend the limitations which are inherent in political categories and labels, such as democratic, authoritarian, totalitarian. Every political regime is subject to evaluation by the criteria of inclusion and the degree to which a regime does or does not practice inclusionary policies, provides for inclusionary avenues for popular participation, or fails to do so. In this manner, political inclusion provides both a normative and objective basis on which to evaluate current institutional arrangements in politics, economics, and social life. It is also a concept which provides a means to articulate new institutions for governance and new avenues to articulate normative concerns and rights-claims. Because it is a concept that is dynamic, not static, political inclusion is a new way to conceptualize how to proceed in building a culture of peace.

The purpose of this chapter is explain why the normative and objective criteria of political inclusion are essential to building a culture of peace at both the national and international levels. My analysis necessarily involves an historical analysis of the process of nation-building and the exclusionary practices that stem from it. Only by explicating the dynamic of what makes the practice of democracy exclusionary can we ever hope to discover the dynamics that makes its ideals achievable. It is only by engaging in this task that we can begin the process of moving toward inclusion—toward an understanding and a practice of inclusionary governance.

This chapter will examine three interrelated issues. First, I shall discuss how political exclusion, in general, and "democratic exclusion," in particular, divide different interests and communities within nations and create a dynamic that pushes toward exclusion. Second, I will discuss the separation between the ideal and practice of democracy in both First and Third World settings. I will offer explanations as how politically exclusionary practices fill the gap between the ideal and practice of democracy. Third, and finally, I shall discuss the relationship between state and civil society. The interplay and mutual dependence of the state on civil society for legitimacy and the dependence of the civil society on the state for promoting equity, tolerance, and a social contract are vital for overcoming dualities in the form of political, economic, and social exclusion.

By setting forth the problems and the challenges which are associated with political, economic, and social exclusion, I seek to evaluate how it is possible, even in a supposedly democratic society, to experience the perpetuation of economic and social dualism. The dynamic and evolving nature of these dualities further exacerbate the phenomenon of political exclusion. In turn, I seek to explain how these dualities lead to violence and are antithetical to building a culture of peace.

After articulating the problems presented by political exclusion, I shall have laid the foundation for a further elaboration of what constitutes political inclusion. The implications for this new direction encompass an increase in the participation and empowerment of previously marginalized groups by increasing the number of persons in the civil society and the state working on structuring and articulating inclusionary political and economic demands, reinforcing the kinds of economic activity which would advance more favorable terms for employment and a reduction in poverty.

The implications of this new direction also allow for addressing the issue of governmental accountability and the responsibility of the state toward all of its people. In short, the normative and objective criteria of political inclusion lays a theoretical and practical foundation for meeting basic human needs, actualizing the ideals of democracy in practice, protecting human rights, and then expanding on this foundation in the task of building a culture of peace.

1. The Current Situation

In both First and Third World nations, governance has often been characterized as a clash between the power of the state versus the power of the market. In the First World states, the decline of the welfare state has led to political, social, and economic trends characterized by an increasing reliance on privatization and deregulation as the optimal political and economic strategies for governance (Ruggie, 1996; Spulber, 1997; Grieder, 1997; Yergin and Stanislaw, 1998; Kuttner, 1997; Luttwak, 1999). Yet the benefits of these strategies have failed to reach marginalized groups and individuals, including the poor, the unemployed, and the underemployed (Giddens, 1998; King, 1995; Krieger, 1986; Gaffikin and Morrissey, 1992; McFate, Lawson and Wilson, 1995). Similarly, in Third World states, development theory has continued to largely ignore the status of the poor and other marginalized groups (Gurr, 1993; Richmond, 1994). Hence, in both First and Third World settings, the promise of democracy, as an ideal, has been eclipsed in the name of efficiency and profit.

Throughout the developing world there is broadening agreement on the need to overcome the old strategies and practices associated with economic populism and nationalist industrialization. Both breed exclusion. The question is what should replace them. The Bretton Woods institutions, the IMF and the World Bank, as well as the leading economic powers and the ruling currents in economics all press upon the developing countries the suggestion that they need to imitate the arrangements which are dominant in the North Atlantic world. This set of arrangements is presented as the necessary sequel to the failed program of economic nationalism and populism which has preoccupied most of the Third World for decades. However, this will require the implementation of the neoliberal program.

The neoliberal program mandates that current versions of representative democracy, the market economy, and civil society as currently constituted in the North Atlantic democracies are sufficient models for emulation. This argument fails to address the fact that this view represents a mere section of a much broader range of institutional, political, economic, social, and cultural possibilities. The argument also fails to take into account the fact that when we transport these models (and the assumptions underlying them) to societies more divided, desperate, or hierarchical, then there is less of a chance for these particular kinds of arrangments to flourish because they are historically specific and do not often meet the real needs of people in the situations into which they are transported and upon which they are imposed (Unger, 1999, p. 27 and p. 88).

In fact, the counter-productive nature of this attempt at transplanting the neoliberal model is revealed in a variety of ways. First, the neoliberal program amounts to "a realignment of economic practices compatible with the interests of most most preexisting elites" (Id., p. 82). By reinforcing preexisting patterns of domination, the neoliberal model reinforces exclusion. Whether or not these developing nations are called democratic, the fact remains that the effect of the model is exclusionary. Paradoxically, the neoliberal model suffers from the same fundamental flaws as the economic program it is intended to replace. It suffers from the perpetuation of economic, political, and social dualisms of past exclusionary practices and policies. Second, the state itself is made subservient to market considerations—foreign and domestic—thereby protecting the practice of political exclusion at every level in many spheres of activity. As a direct consequence, nothing is fundamentally transformed for the better as far as the lives of semiskilled and low-wage workers are concerned. They remain trapped in the vortex of export-oriented production. Because of the vesting of exclusionary dynamics throughout their nation and its place in the international hierarchy of states, they remain among the ranks of the politically, economically, and socially marginalized, disempowered, disenfranchised, and dispossessed.

Hence, the reinforcement of privilege when combined with the states' subservience to the market allows the neoliberal program to preserve political exclusion in all major realms of power and human relationships. In short, it protects inequalities and disparities between individuals and groups in terms of ideological rationalizations. The neoliberal program seeks to justify political exclusion, thereby making political exclusion a hegemonic reality.

The structural adjustment programs (SAPs) of the neoliberal program confront an intractable dilemma. One of the program's major achievements is to produce massive unemployment, as in the case of the Argentina of the 1990s (over 20 percent) while, at the same time, accelerating internal dualism: "the divison of the country between a minority of beneficiaries and a majority of victims" (Unger, 1999, p. 57). It leaves the government without either the resources or capabilities to invest in either people or infrastructure (Id., p. 57).

The net result of this pattern is that social needs go unattended while, simultaneously, bottlenecks in the production system build up. The policy becomes self-defeating as domestic and foreign investors lose confidence because they fear social violence will erupt from social unrest (Id., p. 57). Still, the ultimate consequence is that of the victory of political exclusion as a social, political, and economic policy. Exclusionary governance and exclusionary states, throughout Latin America, can be clearly seen by virtue of the fact that "inequality of access has been embedded in an approach to social services delivery that encourages exclusion, segmentation, and inefficiencies. Traditional vertical bureaucratic systems for organizing schooling and other services have been inefficient and have failed to serve the poor" (Birdsall and Londono, 1998, p. 139).

In light of the foregoing discussion, the primary issue that this chapter seeks to address is: why it has been so difficult to move toward inclusion in governance, in political practice, in economic practice, and in relations between the various classes and groups that constitute civil society. In order to do this, in my judgment, it will be necessary to begin with an examination of the defects in the practice of democracy that have made the attainment of its ideal so difficult, if not impossible. Of course, the practice of democracy is reflected in history. Much of that history has, until recent times, remained neglected. The various reasons for neglect emanate from considering the uncomfortable truths about nation-building, including, but not limited to, racism, genocide, and slavery, as well as inegalitarian policies and outcomes for subordinated and economically deprived classes and groups.

The intent of this analysis and discussion is not to detract from those qualities and characteristics of the democratic ideal that reflect inclusion, respect for the human rights of individuals and groups, or concerns with the equitable distribution of wealth and resources. Rather, the intent is to explicate and identify those areas of group interaction and participation where the practice of democracy denigrates the ideal of democracy by creating exclusionary practices in social relations, governmental practice, and economic relations.

My analysis necessarily involves an historical analysis of the process of nation-building and the exclusionary practices that stem from it. Only by explicating the dynamics of what makes the practice of democracy exclusionary can we ever hope to discover the dynamics that make its ideals achievable. It is only by engaging in this task that we can begin the process of moving toward inclusionary governance. With this in mind, I have divided the chapter into three main parts.

In Part B, I discuss the dynamics of "democratic exclusion" by engaging in a comparative examination of nation-building in the United States, South Africa, and Brazil. In particular, I will examine the role that political parties have played in reinforcing a two-party majoritarian-based system which excludes blacks and other minorities from effective participation and genuine representation. Because political exclusion has economic repercussions, disparities in income and employment in the marketplace will illustrate the extent and scope of "democratic exclusion."

The presence of double standards also implies second-class citizenship which affects rights-claims. This insight has international significance for other nation-states with ethnic and racial divides, as may be seen in the rise of the communitarian states of Afghanistan, Serbia, and Croatia. Yet, in a social and cultural context, the United States has itself fostered ascriptive themes in spite of the legal effects of formal equality. The defense of inegalitarian principles has served to perpetuate what I term the "inclusion/exclusion dichotomy." This dichotomy is replicated in both First and Third World states. It has come in the form of labor subordination, racial subordination, and socioeconomic segregation, thereby allowing for what could be termed a kind of "democratic apartheid."

In short, class, race and ethnicity continue to reinforce, preserve, and perpetuate political exclusion in a variety of forms. When these exclusionary trends are translated onto the economic plane, at the international level, international financial lending institutions such as the IMF and World Bank actually reinforce political exclusion and social hierarchy, and create the conditions for violence and deadly conflict as social unrest inevitably develops in response to these exclusionary practices (Veltmeyer, Petras and Vieux, 1997). Even as globalization proceeds, the emergence of more exclusionary governments may be seen, at the international level, as the growth of anti-developmental states. They are anti-developmental in not merely economic terms, but moral, cultural, social, and political terms. As grievances rise there is a corresponding reinforcement of conflict and violence. Obviously, these exclusionary trends mitigate against building a culture of peace.

In Part C, I discuss the separation between the ideal of democracy and the practice of democracy in both First and Third World settings. By analyzing this separation, it is possible to better appreciate the separation between the state and the civil society as a partial explanation for rising levels of conflict, violence, and political instability. If a state is exclusionary, then it serves only certain elites and classes while, at the same time, engaging in the formal and informal marginalization of others. Instead of building a culture of peace, such practices build a culture of violence, for exclusion itself may be seen as a form of violence. It is structural violence, for it deprives people of their human rights, dignity, and access to services and resources that should be attainable by them in terms of the social compact between the civil society and the state.

The importance of consensus building is discussed in terms of building a culture of peace and inclusionary governance as opposed to promoting the reinforcement of the "predatory state" or "conquest state" which has characterized Zaire, Rwanda, and Serbia. Examples of inclusionary states are South Africa and South Korea, which have built "efficacious states." They are efficacious because these states are noted for their inclusionary approach to all groups and classes within the civil society. Further, they are progressive and inclusionary states because of the congruence of human rights norms with values associated with mutual cooperation, reflecting a shared consciousness and discourse on human rights which serves to advance human dignity and a culture of peace. Part C ends with a discussion of state powerlessness as a reflection of repression and exclusionary governance. The role of tolerance, equitable distribution, and continuity in decisionmaking is analyzed with respect to the inclusionary state (IS) as opposed to the exclusionary state (ES).

Finally, in Part D, I discuss the state and civil society relationship as it relates to the task of development and the challenges associated with building a culture of peace. The liberal democratic development model is not a practical or transferable model to Third World settings that fails to institutionalize constitutional guarantees through the rule of law. That is why the neoliberal program has often produced illiberal democracies in Third World settings. Properly understood, inclusionary governance is a program of development which centralizes the importance of the individual and the need to incorporate the excluded, the poor, and the marginalized into the process of decision making and policy making at the regional and national levels.

Through this practice of constitutional incorporation of the previously excluded, the (IS) enhances the power of the state as it practices inclusionary governance through the channels of mediation, arbitration, and negotiation. This process strengthens the linkages that are necessary in creating a culture of peace. By uniting the agendas of the state and the civil society, an analogy is produced which stands for the proposition that: *Just as markets must be "embedded" in social relations if they are to work properly, so too states must also be "embedded" in civil society if they are to be truly effective.* In this manner, the new direction forged by inclusionary states (IS) allows for the participation and empowerment of previously marginalized individuals and groups. The result of these forms of participation and empowerment allow for the building of a culture of peace.

2. What Is Inclusion?

In the final analysis, inclusion remains a question of degree. What is the ultimate degree of inclusion versus exclusion from the centers of power and decision making? To what degree may the previously voiceless have their voices heard? And, if their voices are heard, will it matter? If the state and the forum for public debate on economic issues does not allow for greater economic inclusion, the result is a corresponding movement toward greater political exclusion for more and more persons. For nations that call themselves democracies, the very ideal of democracy is thrust into question. Such a result is antithetical not only to inclusionary governance, but to the realization of a political and economic commonwealth of persons capable of creating a community of mutual cooperation and respect. In short, the civic order itself is endangered when the economic and political realms of life freeze out the marginalized.

A prime example of this phenomenon is found in the United States itself. While the United States proclaims itself to be a "beacon of liberty," there is still a great deal of approximating going on with regard to inclusion. Compared to many European nations, US political parties are more weakly organized and lack a strong programmatic orientation. In other words, US parties suffer from unarticulated policies which, if articulated, would mobilize a larger constituency of voters. From such a mobilization, new channels of democratic participation could potentially open up, thereby leading toward the establishment and articulation of a common conception of the national interest.

Instead, US parties have not promoted mass mobilization. They have failed to enable to poorer strata to counterbalance through their large numbers the resource and wealth advantages of smaller elites and special interests (Verba, Nie, and Kim, 1978, chap. 7; Shattschneider, 1975, chap. 6). Therefore, the American state remains the prototypical case of rampant bureaucratic politics. The negative effect this has on any inclusionary project or policy is enormous. For, as elite groups effectively advance their narrow agendas, persistent state fragmentation prevents top-down reform and, instead, provides incentives for maintaining low levels of political organization throughout American society.

In a study on race and party competition in America, Paul Frymer has argued that two-party competition in the United States leads to the marginalizing of African-Americans and the subversion of democracy. Frymer argues that party competition is centered around racially conservative white voters, and that this focus on white voters has dire consequences for African-Americans. As both parties struggle to attract white swing voters by distancing themselves from blacks, black voters are often ignored and left with less than satisfactory alternatives. In this regard, African-Americans are the leading example of a "captured minority." The two-party system itself bears much of the blame for this state of affairs because the party system itself represents a genuine form of institutional racism. This situation largely exists because, in their efforts to win elections, "party leaders often resist mobilizing and incorporating blacks into the political system, and at times will go so far as to deny completely black Americans their democratic rights" (Frymer, 1999, pp. 6–7).

Unlike political parties in other democratic societies, the party system in the United States exacerbates the marginalized position of an historically disadvantaged group that was introduced, at the nation's founding, into slavery—not citizenship. With the passage of time, and despite a national civil war and subsequent amendments to the national constitution, the United States still maintains a majoritarian-based system in its electoral politics. In other racially and ethnically divided nations, two-party majoritarian-based systems are rarely an adequate solution. Unfortunately, even though democratic in name, they fail to include and represent the groups that find it difficult to enter majority-based coalitions (Lijphart, 1977; Grofman and Lijphart, 1986). Thus, the politics of democratic exclusion are reinforced by the two-party majoritarian-based system.

The United States has failed to deal with many of the problems associated with democratic exclusion. Specifically, it is notable that the United States does not have a political system that represents groups proportionate to their votes, even if their votes fall short of a majority (Singer, 1990; Frymer, 1999, p. 197). In the national governing systems of Israel, Iceland, Germany, Belgium, Finland, and South Africa, minority groups that are both politically and ethnically based have achieved a degree of consistent representation that is simply not comparable to what is available in the United States (Lijphart, Rogowski and Weaver, 1993; Rokkan, 1970). Most of these other nations offer greater political voice to the excluded, thereby making their states more inclusionary. Given this perspective, Joseph Schwartz has acknowledged that "one of the remaining challenges facing democrats in relatively open but flawed democratic societies is how to achieve relatively equal power among different interests and communities when society is presently characterized by significant socio-economic, political, and cultural inequalities among groups" (Schwartz, 1995, p. 233).

Another part of the explanation for low levels of political organization and low levels of inclusion in the United States has been attributed to the Constitution itself. The Constitution did not establish a government with a level of public authority adequate to the requirements of a modern democratic state. The result was a mismatch between the demands of civil society and the competence of state institutions. In a democratic society, where legitimate authority can only come from elections, the lack of institutions that can make elections meaningful has led to a displacement of public authority (Griffin, 1991, pp. 659–710).

Public authority no longer derives its expression from the national party-legislative process. Rather, there has been, in the history of 20th century America, a shift of authority to institutions that are not electorally accountable. There is a price that is paid for inadequate state authority and democratic accountability. Part of that price is the alienation of a majority of citizens from government. Another part of the price to be paid for the absence of democratic accountability is found in the marginalization of more and more people. Political marginalization has led to severe economic marginalization.

Political exclusion has economic repercussions. Disparities in wealth and income have translated into a lack of representation in the halls of government. For example, legislation promoting a national health insurance, which would include many people outside of the realm of the current scope of coverage, has been effectively blocked. As a direct consequence, powerful interest groups who would have risked a reduction in their monopoly in the marketplace remain protected with their profit margins intact. The net result of the work of various unaccountable forces and the absence of fully functioning systems of representation and inclusion has created an increasing incidence of policy difficulties that serve to erode the ability of the United States to fulfill the promises of the preamble of the Constitution: to provide justice and promote the general welfare of the people.

Thus, it may be argued that "despite enormous economic, social, and cultural differences, political organizations in the United States have had low levels of organizational scope, like their counterparts in Third World democracies" (Weyland, 1996, p. 221). The net result of this institutional fragmentation is an imposition of numerous obstacles on redistributive reform efforts in all these nations. If, in the alternative, these nations were more inclusionary in their policies, there would be greater distributive justice and political equality. The reality is that, because there are so many obstacles to inclusionary principles and policies, poverty and income inequality throughout the United States have worsened along with rising levels of political inequality (Kuttner, 1996; Raskin, 1986; Piven and Cloward, 1997). It is for this reason that we must now contemplate what Charles Taylor has called "the dynamics of democratic exclusion" (Taylor, 1998, pp. 143–156).

B. THE DYNAMICS OF DEMOCRATIC EXCLUSION

Taylor acknowledges that liberal democracy is "a great philosophy of inclusion" because it is premised on the rule of the people, by the people, and for the people. While contemporary liberal democracy seems to provide an inclusive politics, there is something in the dynamic of democracy that "pushes toward exclusion" (*Id.*, p. 143). Taylor argues that the source of the thrust toward exclusion is the by-product of a need, in self-governing societies, for a high degree of cohesion. What this need for cohesion translates into is a common identity. In fact, a modern democratic state demands a "people" with a strong collective identity. It is this need for a common identity that generates exclusion.

For example, in societies with a high degree of historic ethnic unity, the sense of a common bond is reinforced by a common language, history, and ancestry. This commonalty may lead to discomfort about accommodating fellow citizens of other origins. This situation need not automatically lead to exclusion, but it does mean the bases of mutual trust and the shape of the mutual commitment all have to be redefined or reinvented (*Id.*, p. 146). It is the redefinition and reinvention of citizenship that poses the challenge to deal with both the inclusionary and exclusionary tendencies of democracy. Accordingly, Taylor asserts that "the struggle to redefine our political life in order to counteract the dangers and temptations of democratic exclusion will only intensify in the next century" (*Id.*, p. 156).

To speak of definition and redefinition, invention, and reinvention, is to acknowledge that our conception of social reality is, in fact, a social "construct." Peter Berger wrote an entire book entitled *The Social Construction of Reality*. Still, he was not the first to identify the creative impulse that lies behind any particular political community. For example, Karl Mannheim, the famous German sociologist, wrote a classic work on the dynamics of how people see, conceptualize, and define their social reality entitled *Ideology and Utopia*. The central thesis that Mannheim elaborates is that most people, in any given culture or society, basically accept the world as it appears. This acceptance of "what is" remains an uncritical and unexamined cohabitation with the existing order of things. Only a few people are able to think "critically," which is to say that they can look beyond that which is to the possibility of the "not yet." Mannheim observes that "it is not men in general who think, or even isolated individuals who do the thinking, but men in certain groups who have developed a particular style of thought in an endless series of responses to certain typical situations characterizing their common position" (Mannheim, 1936, p. 3).

Those uncritical of power relationships within a nation support an ideology or belief system which endorses the dominant power system and the power relationships within it. These power relationships are either explained as part of the natural order or, in the alternative, the product of the will of God. Both explanations serve as a convenient hegemonic doctrine which undergirds the maintenance of the status quo and the elites who benefit from it. It is appreciated for its simplicity of explanation and allows the majority of people to remain undisturbed in their private pursuits, regardless of the cost that this system imposes on others. For example, from the very founding of the United States, African-Americans have been denied their full civil and political rights. A constitution emerged in 1787 that allowed for the protection of slavery (Brandon, 1998).

Even five years of civil war and an emancipation proclamation could not negate the effects and scars of the dominant white's accommodation to slavery (Xi Wang, 1997). Even a century after the American civil war, during the so-called "second reconstruction" of the 1960s, civil rights legislation and affirmative action failed to bring closure to the problems of what had become "second class" citizenship. This reality is mirrored in the socioeconomic marginalization of African-Americans as a group. In light of this history, we must include consideration of the often neglected socioeconomic dimension (Paupp, 1993; Brown, 1999).

For much of American history, two approaches to racial politics have contended for dominance. One is the color-blind approach, which purports to treat persons equally without reference to race. The second is the race-conscious approach, which treats people of different races differently, either to discriminate or to compensate for the effects of discrimination (Liberman, 1998, p. 227).

Significantly, the history of American social policy demonstrates that apparently color-blind, race-neutral policies can have seriously imbalanced racial consequences. A social policy that is oblivious to culture and a history of racial subordination is not well-equipped to overcome the dualities and divisions that encumber people of color in such societies. Further, those who argue that toying with the mechanisms of the capitalist marketplace is adequate to redress the social, economic, and political imbalances between different races and classes are destined to be disappointed in the long run if not the short run as well. History provides sufficient evidence that the market itself is incapable of addressing (and redressing) problems associated with social exclusion and undemocratic practices.

As to why discrimination has persisted in the United States, Carnoy has argued that "racist economic behavior has to be politically and legally sanctioned (or at least not condemned) by government institutions for discrimination to work in a competitive market. For much of US history, state and federal governments were more than willing to provide such sanctions, ignoring both democratic and market ideals. The practice of capitalism and democracy incorporated racism and segregation; private labor markets and public resource allocation, whether they fit market theory or not, internalized discriminatory behavior" (Carnoy, 1994, p. 174).

In fact, policies and political arrangements that appeared to be neutral with respect to race have often had racial divisions "built in," whether through imbalances in the position of African-Americans in politics and society or through institutions that translate color-blind laws into race-conscious effects (Liberman, 1998, pp. 227–228). On this same point, Anthony Marx also acknowledges that state actions were "highly consequential in shaping the template of modern race relations" and also that "elites encoded racial domination in pursuit of nation-state building, selectively enforcing earlier prejudice" (Marx, 1998, p. 267). Hence, the role of the state itself is important in understanding the protection and furtherance of racial discrimination and the formulation of policies of exclusion. Recognizing the role of the state in promoting social, political, and economic exclusion goes a long way toward understanding the process of nation-building in the United States as well as many Third World nations, despite the fact that these countries claim to adhere to the ideal of democracy.

Public policy makers who wanted to move social policy away from exclusionary tendencies and adopt more inclusionary approaches to governance sought to place the courts and the Congress into the social, political, and economic matrix of American society. One such approach has been "affirmative action." The primary practical and ideological goal of affirmative action has been to effectuate greater inclusion into the economic opportunities of the nation (Bowen and Bok, 1998, pp. 285–286). Yet the extent and degree of this inclusion is still a matter of questionable achievement. For while the black middle-class has expanded, the fact is also that slums and urban ghettos persist while the rate of black male incarceration in America's prisons continues to skyrocket (Lazare, 1996 and1998).

In spite of a host of laws and public policies advancing an affirmative action agenda, the years since 1964 have seen limited and partial success with regard to the track record of affirmative action. Part of the reason for this is that affirmative action was never designed to bring about a structural transformation of the system itself. Yet if the issue of democratic exclusion is ever to be effectively addressed and the deficiencies it brings about redressed, it seems to me that some structural transformations of the system, as it currently exists, are in order.

By leaving American capitalism as an economic system basically unaltered, the subordination and marginalization of large masses of people, especially women and minorities, has been allowed to expand, despite the fact that such expansion of inequality and exclusion has led to a corresponding crisis of legitimacy for the system as whole (Harris and Curtis, 1998; Lieberman, 1998; Danziger and Gottschalk, 1993, 1995; Rich, 1993; King, 1995). The "war on drugs," for example, inaugurated in the Reagan years, began a process of exacerbating social exclusion and economic marginalization for black America that has continued through the Clinton years (Miller, 1996; Cole, 1999; Reed, 1999; Miranda, 1998; Miller, 1996).

In fact, by the 1990s the affirmative action agenda was under attack and in retreat. As a legal mandate for social, political, and economic inclusion, it was eviscerated by the success in California of the so-called "Civil Rights Initiative," euphemistically referred to by its opponents as a "Civil Wrongs Initiative." If nothing else, it is a good example of why the experience of a full democracy—an inclusionary democracy— eludes citizens within the United States.

The democratic ideal is not something that can be fully experienced so much as aimed at as a goal. Democracy is more of a destination than a final point of arrival (Foner, 1998, p. 332). But the question remains: Why are racial discrimination, exclusion, and subordination still so prevalent within the United States? Christopher Lasch suggested that "common standards are absolutely indispensable to a democratic society. Societies organized around a hierarchy of privilege can afford multiple standards, but democracy cannot. Double standards mean second-class citizenship" (Lasch, 1995, p. 88). Second-class citizenship has, by and large, defined the historical experience of African-Americans within the United States. Racial subordination and exclusion are vested within the fabric of the nation's practices and institutions and certain exclusionary values and ideologies because second-class citizenship is still a part of the democratic project of the United States (Brown, 1999; Paupp, 1993).

Double standards continue to haunt and plague the American social, political, and economic landscape. The presence and persistence of double standards aid and abet the practice of exclusion in every arena of social, economic, and political life. The persistence of second-class citizenship carries with it other baggage—the baggage of barriers to building a fully integrated society. Because the goals associated with full integration have not been achieved or even viewed as accessible, the social dialogue has continued to be mired in the dualistic framing of the debate as a choice between integration and separation (Brooks, 1997).

1. Integration or Separation?

In the new world order of the 1990s, it is a question that resonates beyond the borders of the United States and into troubled Third World regions such as Rwanda and Europe's own underbelly in the Balkans, in Kosovo: Integration or separation? Self-determination or sovereignty? The dynamics of inclusion versus exclusion are the dynamics of both domestic politics and international relations at the dawn of the 21st century.

Whereas the Enlightenment state of the 18th century identified itself with reason and the acquired the rights of an enlightened despot, the emerging democratic nation-state became the first great modern example of the recognition of the autonomy of the political system. The democratic nation-state, as conceived of in Great Britain, the United States, the Netherlands, France, and the countries that adopted their models, recognized the political system as autonomous both from a state preoccupied with its own construction and from the struggles of societies still dominated by local and community life. The problem that emerged was that the political system enjoyed such a high degree of autonomy and power that it became detrimental to the state and the civil society alike. In the world of the late 20th century, the fragile balance between state, political society, and civil society has been destroyed.

With globalization of markets, the construction of the European Union, and the demise of the politics of the Cold War, there has been a corresponding decline in the ability of the political system to make decisions. In its place is the state, which has exacerbated both the decline of formal democracy even as it raises new barriers to the inclusion of people. Hence, both citizenship and the rights of minorities are threatened globally. At the dawn of the 21st century we are witnessing the rise of the communitarian state, as in Afghanistan, Serbia, and Croatia. The defining features of the communitarian state are the suppression of the political system and the quest for political homogeneity. In its most brutal form, it becomes "ethnic cleansing," as in the case of the Kosovo of 1999. The communitarian state rejects both minority rights and even the idea of citizenship. In this regard, it has been argued that "one can readily accept that the Serbs and Croats have the right to self-determination, to secede from the decomposed Yugoslav federation and to build a nation-state, but that right is conditional on that state's recognition of the basic rights of citizens, especially of minorities" (Touraine, 1997, pp. 194–195).

Again, I argue that the essential issue is one of the pursuit of inclusionary or exclusionary practices in government, in markets, in civil society, throughout the culture, norms, and values of nations. The triumph of the "exclusionary impulse" (my term) can only lead to democratic exclusion at best, and genocide at worst. In the alternative, the "inclusionary impulse" overcomes both democratic exclusion and communitarian fanaticism. The inclusionary impulse is the servant of political pluralism, because it approximates the democratic ideal of political participation, with belonging to a community, thereby protecting and advancing the rights and duties of citizenship.

The inclusionary impulse overcomes the fragmentation of the polity by uniting the polity. This is essential because a system of checks and balances is of no help against the evil of a fragmented polity which is the expression of exclusionary and elite pacts (Selznick, 1992, p. 535). In the final analysis, at the dawn of the 21st century, democracy must be a new idea. As Touraine has observed: "It cannot exist without a respect for negative liberty or without the ability to resist authoritarian power; but it is not reducible to that defensive action. Democratic action is equidistant from aggressively communitarian theories of difference and from the apolitical liberalism that is indifferent to inequalities and exclusions" (Touraine, 1997, p. 197).

I have been arguing that the practice of democratic exclusion is flawed precisely by its indifference to the suffering, marginalization, subordination, and dispossession of large segments of its citizens. It is for that reason that the "inclusionary impulse," attuned to the democratic ideal, is the most appropriate means to effectuate the new idea of a new democracy—a democracy without constitutionally protected exclusionary practices, a democracy without a two-party majoritarian-based system of representation that fails to incorporate and represent the interests of all.

2. Accommodating Inequality and Exclusion: South Africa and the United States

In the project of nation-building, racial domination was originally embraced or allowed because it served an economic and social function. It was powerful enough to gradually integrate the white populations that were already in violent confrontation and conflict with each other. Had ethnic or sectional conflicts continued, sociopolitical instability would have risen substantially. Neither capital nor labor could be so excluded because, if they were, the required prosperity that business and labor produced would have evaporated. Prosperity required both business and workers (Marx, 1998, p. 13). In this task, elites encoded racial domination in the legal, social, and cultural constructs of national life as they pursed state-building, selectively enforcing earlier prejudice. This was the common experience of both the United States and South Africa, and it was pursued in the name of white unity and nationalist loyalty to the state (Marx, 1998, p. 267).

However, the gradual decline of intrawhite conflict did not, in and of itself, bring an end to either apartheid or Jim Crow. With the decline of intrawhite conflict, the task of racial reconciliation served to provoke black assertions of solidarity and protest against past injustices. It was only after this above-and-below process—when elite domination from above ended and protest from below had played itself out—that the dynamics of race began to ease somewhat with the achievement of formal legal inclusion in both the South African and US contexts (Marx, 1998, p. 269). Despite the accomplishments and advances that came with formal legal inclusion, the covert practices of racial subordination have persisted (Brooks, 1997).

In the economic context, segregation had placed a high price on the establishment, due to the associated costs of sociopolitical instability (SPI) coming from black protest, industrialization, sanctions, civil rights, and human rights claims (which translated into boycotts and strikes), and lost opportunities for market growth. Still, the scars of race remain embedded. In the United States these scars are still salient reminders of a past clouded with practices leading to the subordination and humiliation of millions of people, simply because of the color of their skin. As a consequence of these scars, the mere practice of formal democracy has not brought equality (Carnoy, 1994, pp. 195–220; The National Urban League, The State of Black America, 1998; Frederickson, 1997, pp. 98–116); Wilson, 1996, pp. 111–146; Marx, 1998, p. 272; Smith, 1997, pp. 470–506).

New forms of exclusion and hierarchy have emerged, and continue to emerge, which deplete the salutary legal effects of formal equality. In the social and cultural context, US elites have always fostered ascriptive themes, which means that neither the possession nor the fresh achievement of greater equality can guarantee against later losses of status due to renewed support for various types of ascriptive hierarchy (Smith, 1997, p. 471). In the United States, many individuals have defended inegalitarian principles of social ordering far more enthusiastically than any doctrines of universal human rights or republican government. Such a history creates major difficulties for democratic governance, especially when viewed in light of our inclusion/exclusion dichotomy.

Practically speaking, the defense of inegalitarian principles and exclusionary practices may easily lead to a situation where citizens feel that their ultimate commitments belong to a racial, ethnic, religious, regional, national, or voluntary subgroup. If this becomes the case for large numbers of citizens, the broader society's leadership may find that their government lacks sufficient support to perform some functions effectively (Smith, 1997, p. 480).

Ultimately, the issue of what people feel committed to deals with the question of what constitutes the national identity. Inegalitarian principles coupled with exclusionary practices lead to a disintegration of the national fabric. This represents a disintegration and disappearance of the civic republican spirit because it negatively affects the national identity, national consciousness, nationalism, and national unity. In short, debates about multiculturalism and the persistence of the "American Dilemma" with respect to race have led to arguments and concerns about the degree of cohesion within America as a nation.

The arguments and debates about the degree of America's national cohesion are also important in understanding how America views other nations caught in the midst of ethnic conflict, civil strife, and political divisions. In his 1973 book *Liberal America and the Third World*, Thomas Packenham maintained that America's peaceful development gave it unrealistic expectations about the prospects for peaceful change and the building of liberal societies abroad. A whole school of historical interpretation emerged reflective of this assumption and it was placed under the rubric of "American exceptionalism." American exceptionalism presents the view that the United States was blessed with political stability, economic plenty and social well-being. Given this history, the exceptionalists argue, American foreign policy failed to set realistic standards for other countries and societies.

Reflecting on this debate in the 1990s, Benjamin Schwarz has presented an alternative view. Schwarz holds that America's view of the world is hampered not by the reality of its harmonious, liberal past, but by the myth. Schwarz argues that "taken without illusion, our history gives us no right to preach—but should prepare us to understand the brutal realities of nation-building at home and abroad" (Schwarz, 1998, p. 69). The brutal reality of America's nation-building includes slavery for blacks, the subjugation, extermination, and genocide of its native Indian population, and the domination of an Anglo elite dedicated to stamping its image on other peoples coming to this country.

Given this history, Schwarz concludes that, for better or worse, "the current fragmentation and directionlessness of American society is the result, above all, of a disintegrating elite's increasing aversion and inability to impose its hegemony on society as a whole" (*Id.*, p. 72). If this is the case, the United States is hardly an inclusionary democracy. Rather, the United States may exhibit many of the same traits it ascribes to other societies, such as the labels: "divided societies" and "failed states." If that depiction is accurate, it serves to explain why America's anxiety over the fragmentation of foreign states, such as the former Yugoslavia, arises from our sense that American society is fragmenting, culturally and ethnically (*Id.*, p. 76). Such fears reflect the old adage: "What you what, you will become."

Currently, electoral contests in the United States engage only about 40 percent of the eligible number of voters. The underclass has largely refused to take part in these contests because its members, especially weaker social groups, have felt a growing lack of confidence in traditional political parties and their ability to solve social problems. Yet this growing apathy towards conventional politics does not so much reflect a general indifference regarding social issues, but rather points to the fact that both political actors and settings are perceived as being exclusionary in character. This perception, in turn, puts into question the whole practice of liberal democracy when it operates as a system that allows a social minority (professional politicians) to determine the quality of life for each citizen (Fotopoulos, 1998, pp. 144–145).

What these trends expose is that the old liberal concept of formal legal and political equality, which is supposedly capable of producing an "equality of opportunity," is actually operating as a force designed for accommodating class inequalities. For that reason, it presents no fundamental challenge to either capitalism or its system of class relations. In fact, the whole focus of liberal democracy, as it has been practiced in the United States, has allowed for the artificial separation of political and legal principles and procedures from issues involving the actual disposition of social or class power (Wood, 1995, p. 259). The same critique, which has just been presented of the United States and its practice of liberal democracy, may be applied to the processes of political practices and democratic forms of institutionalization throughout the Third World.

3. Democratic Exclusion in First and Third World States

I shall argue that regardless of the category/label used (i.e., democratic, authoritarian, communist, capitalist), two basically different models of authority have emerged within the context of the Third World: inclusionary states (IS) and exclusionary states (ES). In this respect, it is important to note that some so-called dictatorships (i.e., South Korea, post-1961), have been more inclusionary in their political practice than some so-called democratic states, such as Mexico (Dominguez and McCann, 1996, p. 7).

Because inclusionary practices do not automatically equate with the practice of democracy, in either the First or Third Worlds, it serves to underscore the point that mere labels are not sufficient analytical substitutes. As we move from labels to identifying the characteristics of states and their practices of decision making, conflict prevention, resolution, and mediation, it is possible to discern a basic and fundamental point which is generally overlooked in the deliberate engineering of political order: that pieces of social and political systems must fit with other pieces, and an overall aim must be the fashioning of a certain congruence among the pieces (Eckstein, 1998, p. 281).

The great variety of exclusionary states throughout the Third World may be partially explained by their historical differences—as, for example, between Latin America's models versus Africa's models. But what characterizes all of these exclusionary states is their inability to create congruence between the state, the civil society, and the market.

The ES in Africa and throughout Latin America serves elite interests at the expense of ignoring millions of people outside of the inner circle of power and privilege. Because such regimes represent oligarchic elites, their self-defined governing task is one that remains dedicated primarily to the furtherance of the goals of an elite and the concomitant exclusion of all other potential claims from competing classes and marginalized social groups. In this regard, the exclusionary practices of states and the elites that control them make the apparatus of the state the central prize for control of the social order. Jorge Nef has noted, on this point, that "beyond the ceremonial transfer of office by electoral means and the absence of direct military rule, democracy in Latin America has not been consolidated. It is suffering a continuous erosion. Political elites throughout the continent have shown a remarkable continuity. The old formula of presidential continuity has resurfaced, as with presidents Alberto Fujimori of Peru and Carlos Saul Memem in Argentina and their efforts to push through constitutional reforms that would extend their tenure in office" (Nef, 1995, p. 99). This is necessarily the case, for it is the state itself that is the embodiment and incarnation of coercive power, military force, judicial decree, and the final arbiter of decision making.

The state's power has often been employed to effectuate labor subordination, enforce racial categories and employment opportunities or the lack thereof, suppress protest, and exclude dominated groups because of race, gender, or national origin. Take, for example, the case of Argentina. Like its counterparts in the Southern Cone, the Argentine junta sought to perpetuate itself, from 1976–1983, by its appeals to both the national security doctrine and market-oriented economics. The junta applied the national security doctrine against the labor movement. In so doing, the junta effectively removed labor as an obstacle to its own economic program. From the vantage point of the armed forces, many laborers were linked to subversives and married to state activism—both of which the military opposed in the name of order and growth (Drake, 1996, p. 158).

Intervention in the marketplace by the state, while needed to effectuate social justice for all groups and classes, is antithetical to classical free market and neoliberal assumptions about the proper role of the state. In the context of both First and Third World states this debate raises an important point. For free market purists decry the interference of the US federal government in hiring practices, but ignore the numerous ways that federal policies have always shaped and continue to shape both the size and composition of the domestic labor market. There is something disingenuous about employers who call for the cessation of state involvement when it comes to hiring practices, but never object to such "interference" when they perceive it as advancing their own economic interests (Jones, 1997, p. 387).

The central point is that politics are not separate from markets. This is especially true in a democracy where politics is the arena where social groups contest both the vision and direction of the economy (Carnoy, 1994, p. 55). Recognizing the domino effect of issues such as the distribution of income, wage policy, social investment, the treatment of poverty and property rights leads to the conclusion that politics play a central role in the determination and shaping of civil society's attitude toward markets and their effects on people (*Id.*, p. 55). Hence, because the intervention of the state in the marketplace is unavoidable, the non-inclusionary perspective of classical free market and neoliberal assumptions become irrelevant and superfluous to the goal of moving toward the greater inclusion of classes, races, and groups in the life of the nation.

4. Brazil and South Africa: A Comparative View

In both Brazil and South Africa, the 1980s witnessed the growth of militant labor movements throughout civil society that articulated visions of a transition to democracy and also incorporated popular aspirations. Unions were organized at the factory, but the organizations and larger labor movement were reliant upon community support throughout the civil society. The development of these labor organizations and the community support which they engendered represented opposition to the state. In particular, the opposition was aimed at an elite that had seized control of the state apparatuses and acted in an exclusionary manner in the formulation of policies which directly affected the lives of workers and the communities in which they lived. By the early 1980s, both labor movements and popular movements allied with trade unions had become important political actors in their own right.

The state and the market became arenas for contest. Why is this the case? Peter McDonough has argued that "the developmental priorities of the elites reflect their fundamental values. They represent not only abstract causal models but also basic commitments to options implying gains and losses for specific interests as well as for the nation as a whole" (McDonough, 1981, p. 131). Having proposed the hypothesis that the state and market are areas for contest for elites and their unique developmental priorities, with understandable implications of loss or gain for the elite and the specific interests that they represent, we are led to the next logical question which bears on the issue of inclusion versus exclusion. Specifically, if the interests of the nation as a whole are subordinated to an elite, even in the context of a formal democracy, how can it be argued that a legitimate democracy exists when it effectively excludes so many other people and interests? In other words, are we looking at a formal democracy that is also an exclusionary democracy?

Larry Diamond has argued that "democratic regimes will not be stable and secure until they are considered legitimate by all sections of their population" (Diamond, 1996, p. 74). He has argued that a distinction has to be made between democracy and semidemocracy. He defines semidemocracy as a regime in which the effective power of elected officials is limited and political party competition is restricted. The result is that the fairness of elections is so compromised that even competitive elections have outcomes that deviate significantly from popular preferences. Because of these outcomes, Diamond concludes that "semidemocracy has often been the empirical reality in countries whose formal constitutional structures look quite democratic" (*Id.*, p. 56). Placed in terms of my thesis, the formal structure of democratic constitutional structures may still deliver exclusionary outcomes. A formal democracy may still be considered an ES.

In the case of Brazil, the "new unionism" had convinced both critics and skeptics that key elements of Brazilian labor had successfully escaped the narrow confines which the Brazilian elite had laid out for them (Seidman, 1994, pp. 15–16). Still, even the much-hailed economic miracles failed to produce lasting development. Tragically, the combination of entrenched elite interests, the neoliberal agendas, and the structural adjustment policies of the era all left a lingering legacy of poverty in the form of political, economic, and social exclusion for the great majority of Brazilians. Since the close of the 1970s, Brazil's most enduring feature has been the most unequal income distribution in the entire Western Hemisphere (Nef, 1995, pp. 96–97). Brazil suffers from widespread poverty despite the fact it has had a democratic government since 1990 that has, at least, arrested the velocity of impoverishment. Still, the distributional profile is extremely skewed, in spite of the fact that the nation enjoys an annual growth rate of about 10 percent.

Similarly, throughout the 1960s and 1970s in South Africa, a white minority state had used apartheid to systematically exclude the nation's black majority from significant participation and inclusion in the decision and policy-making processes of the state. The crises of the system escalated to the point where the early 1980s found an apartheid state facing a mobilized domestic opposition in combination with international sanctions against the apartheid government and calls for the redistribution of power and wealth.

In both Brazil and South Africa, the demands that were placed on the state by labor went far beyond political change per se. The demands encompassed calls from popular movements to redefine the nature of citizenship itself. Citizenship was, from the perspective of these movements and labor unions, meant to include access to social resources and to their country's wealth. In the final analysis, the unions and popular movements argued that the authoritarian state had been so exclusionary, in the service of a very narrow elite, that the benefits of industrialization only accrued to this small elite and, as such, created an intolerable situation that was no longer acceptable. In the case of Brazil, for example, whereas "business elites' demands for political participation are not necessarily inconsistent with democratic values, unchecked business power can make the democratic system a hostage to private sector interests. Business elites can easily undermine the public interest, threatening the rights and safety of workers and consumers, as well as social welfare, education, environmental protections, and access to health care" (Payne, 1994, pp. 155–156). From this perspective of evaluation, Brazil fits the model of an ES. While exhibiting the formal traits of democracy, the empirical measures of how it practices democracy are inherently exclusionary and quite undemocratic in their outcome for large numbers of people. The system is, in short, restricted. As such, it is resistant to inclusionary claims, values, policies, and agendas.

Some of the restrictions characteristic of these exclusionary regimes ranged from limitations on the right to vote all the way to limiting access to governmental bodies. A revolt of the excluded and marginalized was taking place in the late 1970s and early 1980s in both Brazil and South Africa. In both countries, unions and popular movements challenged the very social and economic inequality that had characterized their countries' histories.

Certainly, nation-states exhibit differences in their capacity to rule, in their autonomous power, and in their particular forms. Yet what remains common to all states is their proclivity to restrain and contain challenges to their authority and legitimacy. Why? Put simply, it is because nation-states cannot afford expressions of instability which may undermine their vested social order and the benefits of particularistic economic growth. As a result, quite often nation-states have engaged in the practice of allowing ruling elites to structure relations between the state and the civil society. This practice usually involves the shaping of norms and reinforcing of social and political identities which are exclusionary in nature. In this regard, it should be understood that this task is primarily undertaken to avoid internal conflict (Marx, 1998, p. 4). The result of this historical trend, in contrast to the image of the nation-state as an inclusive "imagined community," is the reality of state-imposed exclusion (Marx, 1998, p. 25). In other words, the task of nation-state building has involved building an ES.

The nature of this state-imposed exclusion, in the cases of South Africa, Brazil, and the United States, has taken the form of the state-imposed exclusion of a specified internal group. The exclusion of a specified group of persons (often chosen along racial lines) was used to reinforce the allegiance and unity of a core constituency. This has been the pervasive pattern in all three of the aforementioned nations. Of course the criteria of exclusion is as varied as are examples of exclusionary states, encompassing not only racial differences but also ethnicity, class, and other cleavages (Marx, 1998, p. 25). The present international system reflects this tendency toward fragmentation. For example, in response to the policies of exclusion, the excluded have increasingly claimed their rights, under international law, to the norm of self-determination. Self-determination has emerged as a threat to territorial states in the form of secessions—Ukraine, Central Asia, Georgia, Azerbaijan, Eritrea. The principle of self-determination also has the potential to collide with other norms of international law, such as human rights protections, whether individual or (in the case of minorities) collective. In whatever form the collision takes place, the central question remains the one that troubled 19th century thinkers: What constitutes a nation? (Hoffmann, 1998, p. 223).

What remains important, for our analysis of inclusionary versus exclusionary states, is to recognize the fact that even in supposedly inclusive nations and democracies, we find that formal assimilation often rested on informal distinctions and hierarchy. And while formal assimilation may have been legally undertaken by elites to remove the dangers associated with social protest and rising levels of sociopolitical instability, such assimilation did not often result in actual inclusion into the centers of power or the decision-making processes of the society and nation-state.

In the experience of the 20th century United States, for example, two great advances took place in the generations following the New Deal. The first advance was in the Kennedy-Johnson period of the early to mid-1960s, when a second wave of entitlement programs was superimposed upon those that were part of Roosevelt's legacy. The second major advance involved the construction of an alliance between the Democratic party, the civil rights movement, and the federal judiciary. Emerging from the alliance came a far-reaching body of civil rights laws which provided formal protection and redress for violations of civil liberties, employment discrimination, and housing discrimination, and constituted an attack on the remnants of formal segregation.

Having cited these two major trends, it must be noted, however, that these advances remained tragically disconnected from any broader effort to promote the democratization of the market (Unger and West, 1998, pp. 51–52). As a consequence of this omission, no serious efforts were made to curtail corporate power or to fundamentally alter the nature of democratic politics as it had been practiced since the Civil War. It is for this reason that some scholars have concluded that "these two advances proved fragile to the point of being reversible. Each has turned out inadequate to its professed objectives" (Unger and West, 1998, p. 52). Part of the reason for the gulf between objectives and their realization is the failure of democratic practices to effectively consolidate the democratic ideal of inclusion into institutionalized channels and build a cultural consensus which would demand the presence and practice of inclusionary ideals. In short, such claims would have meant an articulation of an American creed for the 20th century which would reflect inclusionary objectives to correct the defects of the past.

Equipped with this historical perspective on selective nation-state building, we can at least comprehend how and in what form the nation-state was built and later challenged— as an arena for social contest, the matrix for creating or ameliorating violence, the center of decision making, and the forum in which the ultimate determinations for social inclusion or exclusion would eventually reside. With this understanding of nation-state building and its intimate connection to inclusionary and/or exclusionary practices, procedures, and institutional and cultural trends, we can finally begin to appreciate the significance of what differentiates the inclusionary state from the exclusionary state and, further, how trends of exclusion continue to reinforce cleavages and exacerbate rising levels of sociopolitical instability and political fragmentation.

Brazil stands apart from the historical experience of both South Africa and the United States primarily because it did not establish explicit rules of desegregation and categories of exclusion. Rather, Brazil advanced a myth— the myth of racial democracy. It did so by constraining racial identity and by not establishing formal rules of racial domination. As a consequence, without a fully consolidated, formal and assertive racial identity in place, Brazil was able to establish a nation-state that was both relatively unchallenged and without redress (Marx, 1998, p. 262). Following this path, the Brazilian state allowed formal inclusion while, simultaneously, retaining patterns of significant informal discrimination (Marx, 1998, p. 275).

What this path achieved for Brazil was two-fold. First, while Brazilian elites projected the image of a more inclusive nation-state, the actual practice of state-formation still rested on informal discrimination by advancing the myth of democratic inclusion. Second, general inequality has characterized Brazil since its creation. While practices of informal discrimination may be characterized as "Brazil's pact of silence," the presence of general inequality has consistently followed race lines, which were exposed only along lines of informal discrimination and segregation. While an assimilationist trajectory was followed by Brazil, nevertheless the nation was marked by both discrimination and inequality which, in turn, led to class tensions. Given this analysis, we now turn to the distinct but inseparable issue of "class."

5. Class, Race, and Ethnicity

Class is different from race or ethnicity (*Id.*, p. 277). Class and the economic cleavages it produces does not usually lead to conflict and violence. But we can establish the fact that conflict in this century has often emerged in situations where and when a class divide has coincided with and been aggravated by ethnic, racial, or religious differences. The literature on conflict reveals that ethnic, racial, and religious/cultural differences are contributing factors to deadly violence, political instability, and exclusion (Brown, 1996, pp. 1–31).

Moving Toward Inclusion 173

The issue of "who" is included in the nation and able to effectively use their democratic citizenship will, in large measure, determine substantive outcomes. This is an important point. For, in a democracy, citizens may be granted formal equality, but persistent informal discrimination may effectively deny some citizens full equality of opportunity, as well as equal protection under the law, because substantive outcomes are never actualized due to a failure to realize full civic inclusiveness. Insofar as specified exclusion was the predominant logic of nation-state building, where the predominant logic was one of ensuring political and social stability while, at the same time, expanding the national capacity for economic growth, the issue of equitable growth under the framework of an inclusionary state was subordinated to this hegemonic project. The result has been that racial and ethnic distinctions of identity have been institutionally reinforced by both the state and the culture of dominant elites in the civil society. This legacy brings with it associated costs, such as the costs of resurgent conflict and hatred, which are still being paid (*Id.*, p. 278).

In practice, South Africa, the United States, and Brazil have acted as exclusionary states by virtue of the manner in which official boundaries were purposefully (as well as informally) defined and enforced, in determining who was part of the nation and who was not. In cases of specified exclusion, a critical reference point was established for the social demarcation of those who were to be included and those who were not. In these cases, the state itself entrenched patterns of group formation and contributed to the formulation of identities, ideas, and social categories. Also, the processes of inclusion worked to solidify loyalty among those who were officially incorporated into the life of the nation. In either instance, that of inclusion or exclusion, citizenship remained as a key institutional mechanism for determining the boundaries of inclusion or exclusion in the nation-state (Marx, 1997, p. 5). In this way, state power is made manifest as it allocates distinct civil, political, and economic rights. This phenomenon represents the power of allocation, and the allocation of power, between classes and their economic interests.

Those who benefited from inclusion would give their loyalty. Those who were excluded and lived outside the community of citizens would, eventually, give their protest as a response to the state that made them objects of domination. Protest against exclusion would become a unifying issue for the excluded, allowing them to mobilize resistance against the structures of formal and informal domination that kept their lives in a condition of subordination.

It is necessary, at this point, to define exactly what I mean by my reference to the structures of formal and informal domination. For only by explaining what these structures are can we understand the role of popular aspirations for inclusion and the violent or non-violent expression of those aspirations throughout history. When referring to the structures of formal and informal domination, I am locating the matrix of state, market, and civil society within a capitalist economic framework.

Since the 16th century, the advent of capitalism has meant that the domestic economies of North and South have alternated between global and regional markets. The formal and informal structures of domination are those state institutions captured, by capitalist forces that have defeated the endogenous small-business political forces of peasants and the working class. In the 20th century, these capitalist class forces, after capturing the state, have enforced anti-welfare policies and depressed the living standards of millions of people in First and Third World nations. In economic terms, these elites have promoted exclusionary policies which have promoted export strategies (of commoditized capital). This process has been euphemistically called "globalization."

This economic victory was the product of the capture of the state by elite interests with a vested interest in pursuing exclusionary policies designed to subordinate labor, eviscerate the middle class, and erode participatory forms of democratic practice and organizations, while directing the political powers of the state to repress rising popular power and aspirations. In short, the economic victory of capitalist forces was the victory of exclusionary powers and policies designed to enforce the domination of multinational corporations and international banks (i.e., the IMF and the World Bank). This strategy has resulted in the determination of capitalist classes and ruling elites of First and Third World nations to abandon national development in favor of "globalization" (Petras and Polychroniou, 1998, p. 193).

The resulting levels of sociopolitical instability, and lack of democratic representation in countries that were ostensibly democratic, has served to expose the fact that there are "government-impoverishing" as opposed to "government-enriching" versions of fiscal adjustment, economic policies and political practice (Unger, 1998, p. 119). What this means in terms of the evolution of exclusionary states (ES) and exclusionary policies is that "no democratic politics can accommodate the pitiless economics of selective neoliberalism or its government-impoverishing fiscal adjustment" (Unger, 1998, p. 119). In fact, such an economic project becomes feasible only if the politics responsible for imposing it are sufficiently authoritarian (*Id.*, p. 119).

It is interesting that political authoritarianism can be expressed under the auspices of the politics of democratic exclusion. What this realization exposes is that, whatever the political label, the policies and practices of exclusion result in the demoralization of civil society and the creation of passive subjects, not the empowerment of active citizens. The role of politics and political decision makers is to advance and further the economic power elites of the market. Recognizing this dynamic exposes the fact that it is nonsense to speak of the notion of "market demands." For there are no axiomatic rules that mandate, in a predetermined fashion, the so-called "logic of capitalism." There is no "logic." What the market reflects is economic preferences that are articulated and justified through state action or state inaction. In this sense, the basic questions related to the behavior of markets are essentially *political* questions that find their ultimate resolution by and through state policy.

Now we have come full circle. Economic classes, reflective of elite interests, not citizens, capture the state. In turn, the state creates policies and conditions that answer the question of how open or closed an economy will be in relation to the market. These policies will also provide points of entry

Moving Toward Inclusion 175

which shall determine how elites may insert themselves into the market, when to enter markets and which markets. In the final analysis, political decision makers call the shots (Petas and Polychronious, 1988, p. 193). To understand this process is to understand the process of democratic exclusion and/or authoritarian subordination. In either case, it explains much about the political-economy of the ES. It also explains the failure, among the excluded, of popular aspirations for inclusion.

Historically, popular aspirations for inclusion could take violent or nonviolent form, but whatever form protest took, it promised protracted contest. And what remains interesting and important for us is the realization that in the cases of South Africa, Brazil, and the United States, democracy did not and has not brought equality, in spite of the fact that democracy allows for expressions of racial and class discontent (Marx, 1997, p. 272). While the achievement of equality remains a far distant ideal, it still represents a present and powerful common value that is recognized around the globe as worthy of pursuit. It is worthy of pursuit because of its inclusionary potential. And with inclusion comes the benefits of full citizenship.

6. Globalization and the Promotion of Common Values

As globalization evolves, the aforementioned examples from East Asia, the United States, Brazil, and South Africa all serve to underscore the fact that the process of globalization serves to promote common values across nations. In turn, this process can make foreign problems, conditions, issues and debates as vivid and as captivating as national, state, and local issues. In sum, globalization has created the conditions for a sense of world community and laid the foundation for the birth of the IS. An emerging human rights consciousness has transformed abstract statistics of deaths, poverty, and suffering into ethical and moral issues that affect the practical aspects of governing and economic policy and decision making. In sum, we are witnessing, in the 1990s, the fruition of a consciousness of the global dimensions of human rights (Paupp, 1981).

Gurr argues that, in the 1990s, disadvantaged peoples have won powerful allies, including some members of dominant groups who oppose discriminatory barriers on pragmatic and principled grounds. Additionally, both public and private organizations, such as NGOs (non-governmental organizations), are committed to the expansion and promotion of group rights. Generally speaking, challenges based on coalitions of minorities and their supporters have greatly increased in the second half of the 20th century (Gurr, 1993, p. 37).

Increasingly, scholars from a variety of disciplines have begun to comment upon the emerging idea of "one human race" in which nationality, while still the predominant political modality, must incorporate as a close second the idea that "the second most important social group is the human race and not a person's racial, religious, or ethnic group" (Seita, 1997, p. 462). This emerging consciousness is supportive of the values and principles of inclusionary governance and the emergence of the IS, because it is a consciousness which stresses common interests and bonds. In other words, as the formation of societies throughout the Third World undergoes change in response to globalization, there is a corresponding recognition of an essential commonalty of interests and shared fundamental values (*Id.*, p. 462).

Citizens of nation-states, then, are beginning to identify themselves as members belonging to the same community on the basis of a number of common ties, which include shared fundamental values. This, in turn, has created the foundation for a consciousness of the universality of rights by which members expect that all persons must be entitled to the same rights as well as charged with the same responsibilities to ensure that these rights are protected. Hence, there is increased consciousness at the national level and the international level regarding the importance of self-determination and the protection of minorities against the tyranny of the majority or some elite which operates along the lines of an exclusionary criteria of governance and economic decision making (Bose, 1995, pp. 21–26; Manby, 1995, pp. 27–52; Kymlicka, 1996, pp. 22–30).

It is also possible to re-examine current conceptions of the present state system in this new light so that the present system can be seen as a system of clubs. Ideally, everyone is a member of exactly one club from which they must get everything they need. But this does not preclude membership in other clubs. In this regard, Euro-citizenship can be conceived of as a system of clubs. What this implies is that the emerging European Union looks like a system of multiple, overlapping "sovereignties." This system operates at different levels and, as such, "we could be members of many different clubs, drawing on them and contributing to them in turn for many different purposes and many different kinds of support and assistance" (Goodin, 1996, p. 364).

However, "Europe's Monetary Union" may be creating what has been called a "democratic deficit" (Martin and Ross, 1999, pp. 171–175). While not denying that there are overlapping "sovereignties," some have argued that European integration appears to be increasingly undermining the political conditions for European democracy. In this interpretation, the economic and monetary union of Europe is simply the latest and most far-reaching step in a form of socioeconomic and sociopolitical integration that has deepened the democratic deficit. Some have alleged that the institutions of the European Union have been used to circumvent national democratic processes and insulate the key instruments of monetary policy from democratic control (*Id.*, p. 172). These issues will be dealt with in greater detail in the ensuing chapters.

Whatever the legitimacy of criticisms of the European Union in creating a "democratic deficit," there is still no question but that it is a grand experiment in social, economic, and political integration that demands the formulation of a viable social compact. The degree to which that compact will correspond to the ideals of democracy is what remains open to debate, question, and analysis. For example, Esping-Andersen has argued that "new disadvantaged strata, such as contingent workers, single mothers, long-term unemployed, and welfare dependents, appear too amorphous to coagulate into a viable collective force" (Esping-Andersen, 1999, p. 293). As far as the issue of political exclusion is concerned, however, there is no question but that continental western Europe is producing an ever deeper divide between a privileged employed core and a swelling mass of excluded and probably marginalized outsider strata (*Id.*, p. 295). This has already been confirmed and discussed by scholars who have started to investigate the problems associated with combating poverty and social exclusion in Europe and the need to formulate serious and precise proposals for addressing the issues of social protection and social quality in Europe (Beck, van der Maesen, and Walker, 1997).

I argue that the IS is a truly developmental state, as opposed to being a breeding ground for violence. Therefore, the degree to which people are excluded or marginalized, whether in the First World or Third World, is a vital question. The issues associated with the social quality of life cannot be divorced from those of economic development or political inclusion in the policy-making and decision-making apparatus of any society or nation. This is especially important when discussing the criteria, normative and value concerns, and objective conditions of an inclusionary state (IS) and the nature of inclusionary governance. This is because the IS recognizes citizenship for all in at least one club.

As the boundaries of inclusion are expanding, in concert with globalization, understood as a harmonization of common interests and not just another arena for competition and contention over limited resources, the realization of the IS and inclusionary governance become more of a possibility. In fact, as the principles of mutual cooperation, social bargaining, negotiation, and compromise become more acceptable and practiced, these trends become mutually reinforcing channels for the expression of a new consciousness of conflict resolution through non-violent means. The principles and practices of inclusionary governance may provide many of the solutions needed to overcome the "democratic deficit." In both First and Third World states, the principles and practices of inclusionary governance can potentially generate a culture of peace.

7. Exclusionary States as Anti-Developmental States

In the case of the ES, the delimiting nature of their political competition does not allow for the serious consideration of the alternative and submerged agendas of the larger civil society. In this connection, the ES rarely establishes a regime structure with dense public-private ties. Hence, the political process is both delimited and constricted by its non-inclusionary nature. Also, its use is delimited by the process so that a clearly defined, comprehensive national interest can never be formulated for the long run. A clear example of this is South Africa under apartheid (Massie, 1997).

Apartheid provides us with the textbook case of legal violations of legitimacy by denying the majority population equal political rights. The result of apartheid rule was that, with an ethnic minority in power, the majority were left disfranchised and illegitimacy became the norm. According to some scholars, this means that a legitimation crisis was being institutionalized (Adam and Moodley, 1986, p. 129).

South Africa's apartheid state represented an ES where legality became a substitute for legitimacy. What this means is that the separation of legality from legitimacy made it possible to rule illegitimately with the aid of law. When an ES is thus grounded, it is "divorced from substantive ideals with universal content" and "normative regularity becomes a reified faith in procedures, so that in the end legitimacy interests can succeed only by illegal means" (Id., p. 129). Obviously, ideals without a universal content become the particularistic domain of an elite. The particularistic character of these ideals makes them into tools of oppression that rationalize exclusion, separation, and subordination. When these kinds of ideals are adopted by the state, they are usually used to co-opt participation of major groups and classes that do not share in such a limited viewpoint. Accordingly, "apartheid ideology . . . advanced the scope of state activity while subordinating the major elements in civil society. . . . The state emerged as an instrument and realization of the volk, capturing and nationalizing the capitalist order and taking control of chaotic market processes. In the end, the state superseded the market as the arbiter of social forces" (Greenberg, 1987, p. 137).

South Africa's apartheid state, or an ES in general, is characterized by its non-inclusionary nature as well as its internal weaknesses and contradictions. These are qualities that lead to discontinuity in both political as well as economic decision making. Further, there is a corresponding discontinuity in inter-group dialogue, if there is any dialogue at all, because the civil society remains fragmented. As a result, it may well be that sociopolitical instability (violence) may emerge from conditions of fragmentation and social cleavages that have turned violent and conflictual. These cleavages may reflect political and/or material inequalities. The point is that they lead to SPI. As violence and SPI rise, these phenomena serve to perpetuate exclusion.

Gurr has identified the continuing tension between the communal desire for cultural recognition and governmental pressures for assimilation as constituting a perpetual tension that reinforces conflict which may arise from both political and material inequalities (Gurr, 1993, p. 71). He has stressed how the coincidence of cultural and material conflicts shapes the grievances and demands expressed on behalf of communal groups. On the basis of observations about the kinds of issues raised by groups surveyed in his study *Minorities at Risk*, he identified four general dimensions of grievances and a number of more specific issues for each dimension. The dimensions and issues are outlined in Table 4.1.

As exclusionary institutions and practices remain in place, we find that some groups and classes in the civil society are able to maintain linkages to the State/Regime structure, while, at the same time, other classes and groups are excluded. The failure of the State/Regime structure to build State/Society linkages contributes both to its own lack of legitimacy and often results in rising levels of political violence and deadly conflict. It is for this reason that the Carnegie Commission's Final Report, *Preventing Deadly Conflict*, argues that "effective participatory government based on the rule of law reduces the need for people to take matters into their own hands and resolve their differences through violence" (Carnegie Corporation, 1997, p. 94). There is, in other words, the need for inclusionary governance, principles and practices

> **TABLE 4.1 The Dimensions of Grievances That Reinforce Conflict (SPI)**
>
> 1. *Political Autonomy:*
>   General concern, explicit objectives not clear
>   Union with kindred groups elsewhere
>   Independence
>   Greater regional autonomy
>
> 2. *Political Rights Other Than Autonomy:*
>   Diffuse political grievances, explicit objectives not clear
>   Greater political rights in own community or region
>   Greater participation in politics and decision making at the central state level
>   Equal civil rights, status
>   Change unpopular local officials or policies
>   Other grievances about political rights
>
> 3. *Economic Rights:*
>   Diffuse economic grievances, explicit objectives not clear
>   Greater share of public funds, services
>   Greater economic opportunities (better education, access to higher status occupations, resources)
>   Improved working conditions, better wages
>   Protection of lands, jobs, resources from alienation to others
>   Other economic grievances
>
> 4. *Social and Cultural Rights:*
>   Freedom of religious belief and practice
>   Recognition or toleration of own language, culture
>   Protection from threats and attacks by other communal groups
>   Other social and cultural grievances
>
> SOURCE: Ted Robert Gurr, *Minorities At Risk: A Global View of Ethnopolitical Conflicts*, United States Institute of Peace Press, 1993, pp. 71–72.

if nations are to move away from exclusionary practices, justified under the norm of "rule by law" (which is authoritarian in nature) and, instead, move toward the "rule of law" (which means adherence to constitutionally stable procedures and protections).

C. THE SEPARATION BETWEEN THE IDEAL AND PRACTICE OF DEMOCRACY IN FIRST AND THIRD WORLD SETTINGS

Monarchs and dictators throughout Europe's early history, as well as in Third World contexts, were usually protectors of the upper classes (Ertman, 1997, pp. 317–324). As such, they were incapable of ushering in democracy in either its institutional or procedural forms. Therefore, they often found themselves incapable of ushering in either growth or development. Democracy—as it has been practiced in both Europe and the Third World—demonstrates that the separation between the ideal of democracy and the practice of democracy has been the rule more than the exception. This finding suggests, as already noted, that political labels do not suffice in determining degrees of inclusion or exclusion in the life of the nation, the quality of life that citizens enjoy, or the extent to which basic human needs are met or go unmet.

In this regard, the future of nations of the world, including both First and Third World, will be largely determined by whether they follow a path of inclusion or exclusion. This is, however, more than just a political observation. It is also an economic observation in the sense that if the inequality gap is too egregious, if the market's benefits are regarded as exclusive rather than inclusive, there will be a backlash (Yergin and Stanislaw, 1998). The backlash, as events in Indonesia proved in late 1997 and early 1998, with the removal of President Suharto, involved rising levels of SPI. By the middle of 1998, events in Russia also underscore the point that reliance solely upon market-oriented schemes is not enough to transition to a democratic state, much less consolidate one.

The tasks of democratic transition and ultimately the promise of democratic consolidation are premised upon the emergence of a reasonably strong state with a clear hierarchy of laws and implementation of the policies of the new democratic government (Linz and Stepan, 1996, p. 390). Indeed, the rights of democratic citizenship can only be realized if there is a *coherent* state. This *coherence* makes possible an enforceable rule of law that is combined with a usable state apparatus.

The centrality of the state in this project becomes clear when it is recognized that the state is uniquely positioned to formulate and install a clear regulatory framework which allows for the emergence of a law-based economic society. It is this achievement that makes possible the realization and institutionalization of a state's capacity to govern and, eventually, be consolidated. Therefore, the political restructuring of the state is essential for the eventual triumph of some kind of expression of democracy. To achieve this result, it is necessary that the state be restructured so as to give new expression to *consensually* and constitutionally based powers. The crafting of a consensual constitution makes possible both the restructuring of federal relations and the restructuring of the economy.

In the case of Russia, it had become clear by the late 1990s that, in the vertical relations of the federation, Russia faced the need to undertake tasks which had to be effectively addressed before it could become a coherent democracy (Linz and Stepan, 1996, p. 391). These tasks revolved around, as noted, first the establishment of a coherent state and second the emergence of a law-based society that gives expression to consensual forms of decision making. With coherence and consensus, the transition to a consolidated democracy becomes possible. Without coherence and consensus in the reformulation of the state and its regulatory and legal apparatus, democratic consolidation is not only unlikely, it is impossible. For the absence of coherence and consensus reveals discontinuity in state structures and economic policies, as well as in the state's relationship to the civil society and the market.

The net result of such discontinuity, both at the State/Regime level and throughout the larger civil society, is the eventual disintegration of the civil society. Moreover, the State/Regime, as a "Regime of Exclusion," loses the capacity to rule with legitimacy. Hence, oppositional posturing arises among groups that are excluded. This phenomenon results in State/Regime structures which are incapable of carrying forward any genuine developmental program. Such incapacity is attributable, in large measure, to their exclusionary policies and practices, as well as the discontent that these policies and practices generate. In these nation-states, groups are set against groups, classes are set against classes, either by acts of omission or as a deliberate policy.

In other words, the State/Regime preys on its peoples and classes. Such policies only serve to strengthen the exclusionary characteristics of the Russian states as well as most of Africa's ES. Africa's ES include, for example, Zaire, Nigeria, and Rwanda. These states differ radically from South Africa's IS, in the sense that the precondition of "participatory inclusion" of all groups and classes has not been met by the ES. (The distinction between state and regime is that regimes come and go, depending on who is in power, while the institution of the state itself remains constant, for it is the formal apparatus of governance.)

South Africa, in 1994, was able to move away from the edge of civil war because both Mandela and De Klerk had only one precondition to participation: the renunciation of violence as a method of obtaining objectives. In South Africa, supporters of Black Power and White Power were included in the negotiation processes which culminated in the South African election of 1994. With Mandela's election, all major groups became included in the Government of National Unity (GNU).

South Africa stands as an example of an IS, and also as an example of national reconciliation. Yet, on this point, I stress that policies have to go beyond "power-sharing" at the top, in order that nations can "build consensus" from the bottom up. In other words, power-sharing is really only partially curative of violence and exclusionary practices. The actual prevention of conflict and the introduction of inclusionary practices in both the state and the civil society requires building a consensus within the civil society.

Building consensus requires institutional reforms that will dismantle the "predatory state" or, as some scholars term it, the "conquest state." In its place, South Africa and South Korea have built "efficacious states," noted for their inclusionary approach to civil society. Indeed, they have combined their well-developed, bureaucratic, and technocratic organizations with dense public-private ties. These ties are also supportive of the market. But these ties, more than anything else, mirror the dynamics of a vibrant civil society that exhibits mutual respect for all, recognizes the values associated with mutual cooperation, and reflects a shared consciousness and discourse of human rights that is supportive of the dignity and worth of the individual.

What becomes clear from the cases of South Korea and South Africa, when juxtaposed with the cases of Zaire and Rwanda, is that the recipe for developmental success only works if both elements are present—that is, the state must always seek to combine the evolution of a strong bureaucratic organization with dense public-private ties. In this approach, the State/Regime structure becomes linked to the larger civil society, as the state goes about the process of articulating the national interest and welfare.

In contrast, Zaire and Rwanda remain as the archetypes of the predatory state. They have little capability of transforming the economy and social structure over which they preside. They are, therefore, what the literature has called "weak" states. Zaire and Rwanda are isolated in the sense that their goals are not shaped by societal forces which can act in conjunction with an IS. They are states that lack the capacity to formulate collective goals. Zaire is the type of state in which the majority of the incumbents are simply out for themselves. It is a situation that is not unlike many Latin American states. As a result, in Zaire, there is the unfortunate coincidence of repressive violence with a market that is captured by an elite and special interests. This union results in the formation of the ultimate expression of self-interested "rent-seeking." At the same time, the ES of both Zaire and Rwanda work to ensure that coherent interest groups, organized at the national level, which might compete for power, are disrupted before they emerge.

In sum, insofar as a "predatory state," or ES employs a coercive instead of consensual program for social and economic transformation, it does so because it is always threatened by the potential of new and emerging agendas for reform from the larger civil society. After all, while coercion may secure order by raising the costs for those who engage in social conflict and take violent action against the government, consensual power reduces violence and conflict because it works to encourage voluntary compliance through the grants or promises of moral and material benefits. This is what separates the ES from the IS, in the most fundamental sense. The IS is capable of building strong consensual institutions, which lead to durable and stabilized patterns of power, complemented by both shared moral purposes, clear expectations about leaders' authority and, hence, political order (Andrain and Apter, 1995, p. 136).

The ES, in contrast, as in the cases of Zaire and Rwanda, are examples of weak states that block the processes of capital accumulation as well as the formation of inclusionary ties between their State/Regimes and civil society. As a consequence of these actions, these types of states fail to produce a set of policies reflective of a national interest that could lead to the development of distributional equity. Their primary goal remains singular: the strengthening of their power-position by violence, repression, force, and intimidation. The result is rising levels of social violence. At that point, capital accumulation is discouraged and development is foreclosed upon and a de-legitimation of political institutions creates a crisis for the regime which will only increase until it is overthrown, replaced, or transformed by the political pressures which inaugurated the crisis in the first place. Indonesia under Suharto and the Philippines under Marcos serve as salient examples of this phenomenon.

1. State Powerlessness as a Reflection of Repression and Exclusionary Governance

The ES is intolerant of classes and groups in the civil society that are not part of an elite pact. The ES promotes divisiveness, is elite-centered and beholden to certain select groups and parts of particular class interests. This elite-centered approach relates with low rates of human capital formation and is plagued by varying levels of social conflict. As a result, it is forced to rely on coercive aspects of state power and various forms of intimidation as the chief means of repression.

The ES engages in repression and coercion because it lacks moral authority and political legitimacy among broad segments of the population. In this context, then, the use of the term "state power" is the wrong term to use, insofar as repression is actually an expression of "state-powerlessness."

Under the regime of an ES, there is no clear definition of what constitutes the national interest and welfare. Civil society remains in crisis and the state's legitimacy is in decline. The State/Regime structure under the auspices of an ES is increasingly isolated from broad social strata, which leads to a "state of siege" mentality. Throughout Latin America, this "state of siege" mentality has justified the suspension of constitutional rights in the name of preserving the nation (Loveman, 1993). In reality, all that was preserved were the interests of an oligarchy that sought to maintain its power in the face of agrarian transformation, technological change, urbanization, and industrialization, all of which had served to create new types of conflict (*Id.*, pp. 23–24).

Reliance on a non-inclusionary approach throughout Central and South America resulted in an entire series of constitutional tyrannies throughout the hemisphere. When the fundamental legitimacy of the government or of the constitutional order was called into question by emergency conditions or internal disorders, as it was in 19th century Latin America, it is easy to understand how these events gave way to class antagonisms and ideological struggles in the 20th century (Loveman, 1993, pp. 30–31). Violent conflict over the control of resources and shares of a growing economic surplus intensified class cleavages. This phenomenon was accompanied by the erosion of traditional values and established patterns of social deference. As a result, new types of conflict emerged in addition to more traditional sources of political unrest which ranged from contests over regional autonomy to the exploitation of religious, ethnic and racial cleavages.

When it is forced to rely upon the full measure of the state's coercive mechanisms, the ES exposes its own inherent weaknesses and contradictions. This was certainly the case in Chile under the military regime of General Augusto Pinochet. Years of repression, however, ignited a democratization process which began when Pinochet was defeated in the 1988 plebiscite and ended with the inauguration of the new democratic government headed by President Patricio Aylwin on March 11, 1990. Unfortunately, the transition was an incomplete one. The Aylwin government lacked a *coherent* strategy of political leadership. Because it has failed to produce a coherent strategy for the political management of the state, it has failed to overcome authoritarian enclaves and failed to create the institutional capacity that would allow it to govern on the basis of its electoral majority (Garreton, 1994, p. 224). The Aylwin government's lack of coherence is exemplified in its pursuit of a series of one-shot negotiations without strategic objectives. This situation left the government at the mercy of the opposition (*Id.*, p. 224). Such is the fate of governments that lack coherence and have failed to adequately define a consolidation strategy for democratic inclusion.

The ramifications of the Aylwin government's lack of coherence in political management extended to a failure to address tax, labor, judicial, and constitutional reforms, despite their intrinsic importance. The government's failure in these areas was reflective of a broader set of weaknesses—a lack of political leadership, the absence of a coherent strategy of institutional democratization that was necessary to complete the transition, and a fear the of the Right. In fact, negotiations with the Right were avoided on grounds that such a dialogue would be interpreted as a signal of the government's intention to effect real changes and that, in turn, could be interpreted by military and business sectors as destabilizing.

The government's reluctance to negotiate with the Right was surprising in light of the government's announced fidelity to the principle of action, as characterized by the terms, a "democracy of agreements" or a "democracy of consensus." If these terms were to have any practical application or any historical, political, or theoretical meaning, then these terms would have to refer to basic or fundamental agreements, not transitory project-by-project accords (Garreton, 1994, p. 226). This is a case where a democracy was neither consolidated or inclusionary. Because it lacked the principle of coherence, the government had, de facto, given mere ideological support to inclusionary principles, but in practice had followed an exclusionary path of governance for the sake of expediency. In doing so, the government's failure to embrace all major groups and confront the contradictions between state policy and the influence of the Right had effectively allowed for the marginalization of vast sectors from the sociopolitical realm. In short, the government has failed to become an IS because it has not created the political and cultural space for debating new challenges and alternatives to the status quo.

In Latin America, as a whole, the 1980s and 1990s have witnessed a movement by civilian interests away from authoritarianism. This movement springs from many sources, but mainly from the economic failures and the exclusionary tendency of these regimes. The state's forceful exclusion of labor was all too obvious in previous decades. Many of these regimes also acted in conjunction with closed circles of military and technocratic decision makers that effectively denied regularized channels of access to other groups. Hence, many groups that originally supported the new authoritarianism turned against them because of the erratic patterns of access offered to them and the impact upon them of policies that were formed with little or no counsel from them. A prime example of this phenomenon is the Brazil of the late 1970s and early 1980s.

Moving Toward Inclusion *185*

2. The Case of Brazil in the Late 1970s

In mid-1978, after 14 years of military rule, eight leading industrialists in Sao Paulo had publicly declared that only democracy absorbs social tensions. They argued that it was no longer possible to avoid or ignore "screaming needs" in health, sanitation, and education. They called on the state to modernize labor laws and allow wages to keep pace with inflation. While they considered business and the state the major protagonists in policy making, the businessmen nevertheless declared: "We believe that economic and social development, such as we know it, will only be possible within a political system that permits full participation by all. And there is only one regime capable of promoting the full expression of interests and opinions with at the same time enough flexibility to absorb tensions without transforming them into an undesirable conflict—a democratic regime. More, we are convinced that the system of free enterprise and the market economy are viable and can be long lasting, if we can construct institutions that protect the right of citizens and guarantee liberty." (Bardella, 1978, p. 20).

In this environment, the Brazilian industrialists were critical of their loss of influence, but were grateful that they retained the protection of private property under the regime. They had adapted to the regime, in part, because they derived benefits from the regime's effective economic management and enforcement of social order. Hence, social conflict concerns played a conscious role in the calculus. They also lauded the military regime's protections for the private sector. Yet despite these important advantages most of these industrialists neither actively endorsed the regime nor passively acquiesced to it. Instead, they criticized it for not allowing business groups to have a significant voice and directing influence over policies that affected them. There is no evidence to confirm that the industrialists played a role in designing or shaping the policies of the military regime. Instead, their very exclusion from the regime's policy decisions suggests the opposite.

The very diversity of the business community prevented a genuine consensus from emerging. The only strong endorsements of the military regime came from a small minority of reactionary industrialists. They were primarily motivated by fears of subversion and were totally unconcerned about democratic rights and liberties, so they were comfortable in defending the regime's repressive policies. In contrast, another small group within the business community opposed the authoritarian regime. While they had initially endorsed the coup against Goulart, it was only because they believed that, as in the past, the military would restore order and then call for new democratic elections. When the military failed to carry through and instead imposed an authoritarian regime, these business leaders withdrew their support. The clear fact, however, is that the majority of business leaders were uncommitted either to democratic or to authoritarian rule. If a government, whether democratic or authoritarian, provided investment stability, business elites accepted it and used their significant political resources to influence it from within the system (Payne, 1994, pp. 53–54).

Still the fact remains that the 1978 manifesto, coming from leaders of the consumer durables industry, challenged the very basis of Brazil's economic growth. It criticized the military's centralized control over the economy, the closure of political channels, and the inequality that had come to mark Brazil's industrialization strategy. Leading up to the events of 1978, there had been discernible changes in the international economic climate and the domestic political climate which had exacerbated tensions that were latent even during the peak years of Brazil's "economic miracle."

Business leaders had become frustrated by contradictory state policies and by increasing conflict over state resources. It was this frustration that led business leaders to challenge both state control over the economy and the national security priorities that had justified authoritarian practices. By 1978, social conflict was a looming threat due to the increasing militancy of the labor movements and a state that no longer seemed responsive to the private sector's immediate needs. It was in this context of threat and uncertainty that some members of the business community announced their belief that democracy offers a system of both control and self-defense (Seidman, 1994, pp. 99–101).

Brazil's military regime had made many significant errors in its exclusionary style of governance that affected substantive political and economic policy making. The regime had: (1) failed to consult with large segments of the business community; (2) ignored free market principles by engaging in attempts at command economy; (3) refused to build state/society linkages for dialogue in order to determine how best to incorporate claims about what the goals and policies of a national welfare agenda should embody; and (4) repressed organized labor and created the conditions for rising levels of political violence and deadly conflict.

In the alternative, an IS engages in a dialogue with all social groups, classes and interests in its effort to formulate a vision of the national interest and welfare as the primary point of reference. The individual elements which characterize the IS are as follows: tolerance, high integrity, a focus on "national interest," centered, and continuity in its decision-making processes and procedures.

In the case of Brazil in the late 1970s, it is clear that in order to have investment stability, business elites believed that, in addition to government competence and legitimacy, they also required access to needed information about government policies affecting the private sector or that, at the very least, they were made participants in the making of those policies. Many new Latin American democracies have enjoyed a fortified democratic stability because of the inclusionary characteristics of their respective states.

On the one hand, newly formed State/Society linkages have formalized channels of communication. These channels have been used by business and elites and other social sectors to influence political outcomes. On the other hand, business elites have maintained traditional informal channels of access to government officials. It is the maintenance of these informal channels that undermines the integrity of the state and an inclusive national welfare agenda. For the fact remains that business elites can easily undermine the public interest as well as threaten the rights and safety of workers and consumers, social welfare policies, the availability of education, environmental protections, and even access to health care.

It is the primary task of an IS to consult with all major classes, groups and interests and, at the same time, to effectively insulate a well-educated state bureaucracy from the aforementioned dangers of having the national welfare agenda undermined by some dominant group or class. The difficult balance that an IS must maintain is one that, on the one hand, allows the inclusion of all groups into the discussion and debate on national goals and objectives while, on the other hand, removing that political influence from the process of policy making, which must remain as uncontaminated as possible from the domination of particular class and group interests. For example, while it is widely acknowledged that the redistribution of wealth and power throughout most of Latin America is long overdue, business elites have historically viewed any such attempts as a threat to private property and have blocked reforms. If an IS is to bring about necessary changes for the national welfare, such resistance to basic reforms must be dealt with by state power.

Hence, while the IS governs in an inclusionary manner there is also a corresponding independence of action that the IS retains to implement binding reforms, regardless of powerful domestic opposition. An IS must provide clarity and consistency in the formulation and implementation of the redistribution policies that are adopted.

3. Tolerance, Equitable Distribution, and Continuity in Decision Making

Having compared and contrasted some of the traits and elements of the ES with those of the IS, it would be beneficial to outline, in more specific detail, three general areas of emphasis where IS and ES styles of governance diverge. The first is in the area of tolerance as opposed to intolerance. The second is in the critical distinction between pursuing a reasonable distribution of income, once growth and development have taken off. This is where my definition of inclusionary development comes in. The third is the presence or absence of continuity in decision making. We shall examine each in turn.

First, the IS is characterized by tolerance. By tolerance we mean an ability to be inclusive in the practice of politics, in the way in which decisions are made and reached. Tolerance is to be understood as a trait of an IS because it shows that, by inviting all groups, classes and interest groups to the bargaining table, no one group possesses a monopoly on the state and its power. Therefore, there is no need to "fight for control" of the state. That is because the integrity of character that the IS possesses convinces all groups that its primary concern is the advance of the national welfare and the national interest over the long run.

This approach was successfully used by President Park of South Korea throughout the 1960s and has been used by President Mandela of South Africa throughout the early to mid-1990s. In contrast, the ES, by focusing upon narrow, short-range goals, reflective of the interests of small parts of various classes and their elites, serves to contribute to growing levels of social conflict as the State/Regime faces a loss of legitimacy.

The second area which characterizes an IS is its emphasis upon a reasonable distribution of income once economic growth and development are under way. For example, this has been the case in South Korea and Taiwan. The IS seeks a reasonable distribution of income for a variety of reasons. A reasonable distribution of income strengthens the legitimacy of the state. It also serves to unite the groups and classes of the larger civil society insofar as all groups and classes are the beneficiaries of the national interest having been successfully pursued. It is also the result of greater capital formation, as well as high investments in human capital. By demonstrating, in practice, a reasonable distribution of income, the IS exhibits a leadership which encompasses economic development and growing social cohesion. This results in a reduction of social conflict and the development of stronger State/Society linkages which also facilitates the growth of dialogue, the level of trust throughout the society at all levels, and enhances the bargaining, mediating and negotiating posture of the IS in all future undertakings.

The third and final area which differentiates an IS from the ES is in the area of continuity or discontinuity in the decision-making process. The IS engages in political decision making with an eye to realizing the long-range interests of the nation in terms of economic growth and development as well as the maintenance political stability as the nation progresses. At the same time, it leads and empowers an educated, bureaucratic, and technocratic elite, isolated from political pressures, while mediating at the same time between all of the major classes, groups and interests of the civil society.

In this manner, state and civil society linkages are strengthened. The IS coerces reluctant parties by invoking the state's coercive power while, at the same time, it engages in articulating a national interest through which a national consensus can be built. This allows the nation to effect solutions to long-term problems concerning political evolution, economic growth and development, and income distribution. South Korea, under Park, as well as Taiwan and Singapore from the 1960s onward, are prime examples of this.

By refusing to allow the State/Regime and the educated bureaucrats to be used by an oligarchy, the IS embodies an integrity of character that results in political loyalty from all sectors of the civil society and within the government itself. What the IS is able to create, therefore, is a new social consensus, in practice, which also reflects the nature of a new social contract. Hence, the realization of the nation's welfare is not empty rhetoric. Rather, it is the embodiment of the success of a project undertaken by the entire society, guided by the IS and carried out under the guidance and auspices of an educated and efficient bureaucracy.

After all, the bureaucracy received its mandate for action from the combined efforts of the IS and the larger civil society, in a preliminary period of mediation, bargaining, and negotiation. The new social consensus is characterized, therefore, by an increased demand for investments due to social and political stability, because all groups had been invited to the bargaining table and conferred on the developmental project their approval. Thus, the state enjoys greater legitimacy.

In contrast, the ES finds that its decision-making processes exclude many groups and classes altogether. State/Society linkages are either weak or non-existent because policy choices reflect the interests of governmental, business and labor elites who have placed short-run considerations first, at the expense of the larger national interest. Of this path, Mexico is a prime example. In Mexico, it is the struggle for control over the state that characterizes the real nature of politics. Under these circumstances, there is no real social contract. The ES may vacillate between explicit authoritarian structures or remain disguised under so-called democratic regimes.

The political label which a regime is given actually matters little. As in the case of Mexico, the mere fact of elections does not mean that a democracy is alive and strong enough to include the masses or to represent the interests of all the classes and groups. It follows, therefore, that whether democratic or authoritarian in name, the ES is incapable of a type of governance that can produce the kind of social cohesion and agreement which is a prerequisite for growth and development. Hence, there is a resulting discontinuity of policy choices from election to election, and regime to regime.

Further, the implementation of policy is crippled by the exclusionary nature of the regime. Such a regime never undertakes the bargaining, negotiating, and mediating process necessary to gain a political mandate which would make the economic plan successful when the state begins to act. Therefore, the goal of continuity of policy and continuity of policy implementation are crippled by the exclusionary nature of the ES and the oligarchy which it represents.

D. THE STATE/SOCIETY RELATIONSHIP REVISITED

In reviewing the options that the literature on development presents us with, we really have only two choices. On the one hand, we can accept the liberal model of development, which posits that poverty is the primary source of social conflict. The liberal model also stands for the proposition that democratic institutions are enough, in and of themselves, to make a State/Regime legitimate, popular, and inclusionary. On the other hand, we can accept the view that social conflict and civil violence are the product of the twin forces of economic and social modernization, which lead to widening circles of political and exclusion. I believe that the socioeconomic and sociopolitical weight of evidence support the second choice.

How can the forces of economic and social modernization be addressed and resolved by the artificial imposition of Western democratic norms, as derived from the liberal model of development? The resolution of this problem cannot be found in the liberal model of development because of the resulting forms of democratic exclusion inherent in the model and its application in practice. Therefore, a new form of governance, which I call the IS, is required to guide the developmental processes of Third World nations.

Greater attention needs to be given to what political theory has termed the "State/Society" relationship. Additionally, we need to inquire as to how this relationship should effectively be forged under the auspices of a truly strong, centralized, decision-making authority, the purpose of which is to act as an effective arbitrator between groups and social classes. Existing conflict theories have paid little attention to the objective developmental requirement of each nation being able to forge and to articulate a long-range national interest and have that interest guided by the hand of an IS (Huntington, 1987, pp. 13–14).

In fact, as Erich Nordlinger pointed out, it was not until the year of 1968, with the publication of Samuel Huntington's book, *Political Order in Changing Societies*, that scholarly attention was drawn back to the political realm by focusing upon the extent to which the state and other political organizations and their procedures are institutionalized as "stable and valued patterns of interaction" (Nordingler, 1987, p. 355). My criticism of what I have called the "limitations of democracy" centers upon the realization that the practices and ideals contained in past traditions are negated by their failure to realize a democratically defined set of "rights" leading to the recognition of "individual dignity."

The liberal democratic developmental model provides no practical alternative to societies that have neither achieved an adequate level of economic development nor a certain level of political institutionalization. Without such an objective foundation, and without an alternative specific enough to engender a general consensus within either the State/Regime structure or the civic order, it is no wonder that social conflict supplants growth. In fact, such a lack of consensus on what constitutes the national interest, as well as differing perceptions on what is required to meet the demands of the nation's welfare, results in revolutions.

The failure of State/Regime structures to form basic linkages with the civil society, as well as rising levels of social conflict, does not allow for the creation of societal space and political ingenuity to construct institutions, practices and procedures that are capable of sustaining a developmental state. Hence, the open-endedness of the democratic tradition becomes little more than a formal structure of visionary aspirations into which various groups, classes, and interests can deposit their own content and meanings. For example, they can deposit their own vested interests and claims without having gone through a process of arriving at a consensus with other groups and classes, or with the centralized authority of the State/Regime structure— a process which involves negotiation, arbitration, bargaining, compromise and a mitigation of differences and conflicts of interest.

Mexico's historical efforts to develop have failed because its state has essentially been a weak authoritarian state that is neither sufficiently embedded in civil society nor capable of acting as an autonomous IS by including all groups, classes and interests at the bargaining table. In fact, Mexican history, with regard to the state's treatment of labor, serves to exemplify a politics of co-optation which has often led to the exclusion of those elements of labor and the peasantry that failed to adopt the party line. This is what constitutes the paradox of organized labor in Mexico (Mainwaring and Scully, 1995, p. 265).

Hence, the problem for both Mexico's political crisis, as well as its economic crisis, can be found in how both conservatives and the left agree that the nature of the crisis arises from a situation where the conservative side of the society could not accept the changes insisted on by the left, and the left could not accept the kind of society insisted on by the conservatives

(Sheahan, 1987, p. 187). This observation has already been made in reference to Brazil as an explanation as to why Brazilian democracy was demolished in 1964. Therefore, it is vital to note, once more, that the characterization of a particular regime as being either "democratic" or "authoritarian" is not as important, per se, as the policies it pursues and the manner in which a particular State/Regime helps to organize the interests of the society.

What matters is how the State/Regime works to arbitrate among contending interests, groups, and classes. It is necessary to look at the defining characteristics of how the state acts, as opposed to being preoccupied with its form or labels that are attached to it. If it is an IS, it must guide the State/Regime structure so as to include all affected parties, classes, groups, and interests, as well as work to mediate whatever differences remain so that a cohesive program and set of policies can be pursued for the long run. It is not necessary, therefore, to label an IS as either "democratic" or "authoritarian."

What matters is how this IS exercises its power, its moral suasion, and its ability to mediate and arbitrate as a sovereign, seeking only the pursuit of the national interest. For elite pacts do not a democracy make. Neither do elections and voting registration make for a democracy. What matters most is that an IS be established that sees itself as leading the enterprise of development under the auspices of an inclusionary developmental state. To that end, whether the IS possesses an ability to effect real transformation depends on State/Society relations.

1. Beyond Dictatorship and Democracy

The IS must be simultaneously "embedded" in the civil society, by virtue of its mediating role between classes and groups, and also "autonomous" from the pressures of any one group or alliance of classes. For the fact remains that autonomous states that are completely insulated from society may be very effective predators. Hence, the IS must become a state that immerses itself in a dense network of ties that binds it to social allies with transformational goals (Evans, 1995, p. 248). *Transformational goals are goals which are inclusionary*. They are inclusionary because they reflect what needs to be accomplished by the union of the State/Regime and the civil society in effectuating and realizing what is in the national interest. In this way, the ultimate goal is the realization of the national welfare along with correct policies and programs to sustain growth and development.

In contrast, the ES seeks to maintain the status quo. It refuses to adopt transformational goals. In its refusal to do so, it becomes, de facto, both the protector and apologist of the narrow interests of specific classes. In place of a dense network of ties between all segments of the civil society, the resulting class formations reflect high degrees of social stratification which, in turn, are reflected in the marketplace. Economic stratification means that various sectors of the economy are de-coupled from each other, with the result that beneficial shocks that occur in one sector of the economy are not transmitted to other sectors in the economy as a whole. This de-coupling is exacerbated in dual economies.

This stratification is common to all ES. Such stratification spans the continuum of the social, political, cultural, and economic life of such societies. Politically, the State/Regime structure of exclusionary states maintains their exclusionary policies, patron-client relationships, and favoritism. In turn, the absence of strong State/Society linkages, across all classes, serves to effectively exclude major classes, interests, and groups from the social bargaining process. Hence, a national interest is neither formulated by the nation's guiding political institutions nor implemented by a politically insulated bureaucracy.

In contrast, the IS makes explicit efforts to "de-stratify" their societies and economies, allowing, thereby, the energy of one social or economic sector to be transmitted to other sectors. We need not identify any particular class as the engine of the transformation, so long as communicative channels are open. Therefore, the primary task of an IS is to guide an inclusionary process of social bargaining between the groups, classes and interests that make up the civil society, thereby creating a social environment of de-stratification, in terms of political influence. As the inordinate power of some classes and groups declines, there is a corresponding de-stratification of economic power in the marketplace.

The sacrifices that are made to achieve this growth and development should also be undertaken with the promise that once the necessary levels of economic growth and development have been achieved, there will be a reasonable distribution of income. Understood in this way, the "embedded autonomy" of the IS gives the developmental project of the state its efficacy (Evans, 1995, p. 248).

2. Enhancing State Power Through Inclusionary Governance: Arbitration, Mediation, Negotiation

The best State/Regime structure for the developmental project of a Third World nation is an IS that has put away bayonets as the ultimate form of coercive authority and relies more upon its state power, state capacity, moral suasion, and the "rule of law" as it acts as an arbitrator and mediator. Many items of this agenda, that entail serious structural and behavioral reforms, are long-run problems that democracy is neither inclined to address nor, more often than not, capable of solving. Income distribution is such a long-run problem. In the short run it can frustrate expectations and result in increased levels of social conflict. Even in advanced Western democracies, after the votes are cast and elections are held, shifting coalitions and political re-alignments often produce only gridlock. A real consensus on what constitutes the national interest is rarely achieved. Hence, the national welfare suffers and legitimacy is subject to further erosion.

Even an IS, at the start of its stewardship, may have problems in its task of becoming "embedded" in the civil society. Frequently, the general support given by the civil society, at the outset, is limited. Therefore, periods of transition may require a degree of force before the IS engenders enough support to sustain its claim of political legitimacy. The nature of the force to which I refer is the force of the rule of law. Of critical importance is institution-building. European integration and the evolution towards the European Union (EU) provides a key example of unification through law. Legal instruments, rather than spending or taxing powers, will be the key forces in the establishment of European unification at the dawn of the 21st century (Leibried and Pierson, 1995).

Unlike political parties in democratic systems, always seeking out the realization of their narrow interests on contested political terrain, the IS pursues a politics of inclusion which works to neutralize the dangers of segmentation, dualities, and short-run goals. Hence, gridlock is immediately overcome as consensus is arrived at through the mediating and bargaining processes that take place under the direction of an IS. If differences still remain, final negotiations can lead to a settlement of differences, thereby diffusing the dangers of sociopolitical instability (Gupta, 1990, pp. 123–173).

As the inclusionary politics of an IS set the stage for full-scale negotiations between all parties, the dangers associated with elite-pact making (as in the case of Mexico) are removed. Further, full-scale negotiations between all groups, interests, and classes not only define the ways in which the civil society may be linked to the regime structure in realizing the national interest, but also such negotiations allow the various constituents of civil society to dialogue with one another, build mutual respect, and out of this respect create a more vibrant and cooperative civil-order.

Such an outcome was exactly the process of negotiation that allowed Nelson Mandela to work with the apartheid government of De Klerk in moving toward the dismantling of the apartheid state and creating a Government of National Unity (GNU). Both Mandela and De Klerk were armed with the power to incite civil war if either side felt that a satisfactory solution was not forthcoming.

As the various components and groups of civil society begin to authorize the national agenda, there are two things that happen almost concurrently. First, the previously segmented and fragmented components of civil society build mutual respect for one another's interests. Second, individual class and group interests are subordinated to a common national agenda to promote the national welfare over the long run. This allows for the bureaucracy of the IS to formulate policies and engage in decision making that is isolated from political pressures. This autonomy creates the space for more informed and educated decisions to emerge from the State/Regime structure while, at the same time, the IS retains the power and force to keep the respective groups and classes on board with respect to the bargains and compromises that were negotiated under its auspices.

3. Uniting the Agendas of the State and Civil Society

The IS, by invoking its legitimacy and power, can produce, in the long run, truly democratic results through its all-inclusive national agenda. Park himself referred to his regime as an example of "administrative democracy." Therefore, I propose a new definition of what constitutes political legitimacy in a developing country. If development is to be inclusive, the State/Regime must encompass all aspects of the larger civil society in the service of and in transition to new institutions, new social bargains, and, finally, new ways for individuals and institutions to relate to one another.

In this emerging culture of mutual respect, the new associational forms that develop within the civil society will augment behaviors of cooperation and reduce levels of conflict and violence. As the entire society moves toward non-violent resolutions to disputes and becomes more familiar with the processes and patterns of social bargaining and negotiation, both political stability and economic growth will become mutually reinforcing. This pattern has had universal success in Taiwan, South Korea, Japan, Singapore and, we hope, South Africa.

In this way, conflict can be reduced, and a dialogue with the civil society can be increased and made more efficient and effective. The IS works to create new State/Society linkages in which channels of communication clarify what form and expression the national interest ought to take. At that point, it relies upon its authority and power to enforce the articulation of that interest. This is essential for there is certainly little guarantee that such outcomes will represent some kind of harmonious mesh. It is just as likely to be the sum of ill-fitting responses which arise out of the different components of the state as these components respond to various pressures within the state and from the broader environment (Jacobs, 1985, p. 17).

This state, as already noted, must be equipped for and capable of bargaining through its institutions. It must arbitrate. It must mediate. It must advance a national interest which incorporates and includes all classes and groups, as opposed to being the spokesman for, or the apologist of, one class. Otherwise, the adoption of one political system over another might reflect the biases of intellectual imperialism and not the best interests of the country. In its task of defining and defending what is in the best interests of the country, the IS always works to both expand and widen its channels to and linkages with the larger civil society.

On this matter, Cohen and Arato have argued that with the collapse of the two dominant paradigms of the Cold War era, pluralism and neo-Marxism, there has been a tendency to over-emphasize the notion of "bringing the state back in." While it is important to have a state-centered perspective, it is equally vital to include "all that is non-state." For although we cannot afford to leave the state and the economy out of consideration, "the concept of civil society is indispensable" (Cohen and Arato, 1992, pp. 1–2). Cohen and Arato have also noted that social movements "in the East and West, the North and South have come to rely on various and interesting, albeit eclectic, syntheses inherited from the history of the concept of civil society" (Cohen and Arato, 1992, p. 199).

Cohen and Arato are not alone in reviving interest in the theoretical and practical aspects of the role of civil society as it relates to governments and economic policy choices. Evans has noted that the idea that states somehow operate more effectively when their connections to society are minimized "is no more plausible than the idea that markets operate in isolation from other social ties" (Evans, 1995, p. 41). In fact, an analogy may be made between markets and civil society. *Just as markets must be "embedded" in social relations if they are to work properly, so too states must also be "embedded" in civil society if they are to be truly effective.* While states, such as the IS, must act autonomously in carrying out long-term developmental policies and decisions, these same states must effectively combine this "autonomy" with "embeddedness" because states and social structures shape each other.

Arguing that the State/Regime structure of the IS must form linkages and channels of communication with the larger civil society requires the recognition that the state and society are neither monolithic nor organic entities. There are areas of overlap, but they also must be "disaggregated" so that their dynamics can be traced and understood. In this regard, Chazan has noted that "civil society is separate from the state but relates to the state . . . State organs and social groups continually engage each other in multiple settings that are arenas of struggles for domination and accommodation" (Chazan, 1994, p. 256).

Insofar as the struggle for domination has historically led to increasingly high levels of sociopolitical instability, it is clear that one of the primary tasks of the IS is to stand in the midst of this struggle in order to maintain stability, using its powers of moral suasion on behalf of reconciling different classes and groups so that both state and civil society can work in concert to advance an national agenda. The IS does not, however, play this role once or twice in the course of the nation's developmental take-off. Rather, in the constantly changing interactions that occur in the structural and institutional spaces between the state and social groups, there is the constant need to redefine the nature of state structures and social forces. It is this process of redefinition that accounts for what generates an ongoing and mutually transforming dynamic (Chazan, 1994, p. 256).

In this regard, Migdal has asserted that "it is impossible to understand the term 'society' without the state. The formation of the state has created and activated society. If society is the outermost limits with which people identify, then it is the state that initially determines those limits or boundaries" (Migdal, 1994, p. 23). What is of primary importance in this statement is that, relative to our paradigm, the state leads, the state serves to shape the national interest, and, having completed its work, the state then unites the civil society behind its program for the advancement of an inclusive national interest.

The modern state possesses a distinctive ideology and organization. When looking at the common core of ideology among the leaders of transformative states, their primary purpose has been to create a hegemonic presence, "a single authoritative rule—in multiple arenas, even in the far corners of society" (Cohen and Arato, 1994, p. 23). On this point, it is possible to go as far back as Hegel, who argued that social integration moves through six steps, the first three of which are developed as parts of his theory of civil society (Cohen and Arato, 1994, p. 100). Hegel maintained that non-economic propositions of economy, such as law and contract, have implications that go far beyond the economy, per se. Furthermore, he believed that the publication of the legal code and the publicity of the legal proceedings are changes of universal significance and validity for they serve to make possible the emergence of a universalistic sense of justice (*Id.*, p. 101).

In other words, Hegel sought to identify the unity between state action on the one hand and autonomous cultural processes on the other. For him, the realization of universal rights can occur only through a process of education (Bildung) that has become possible in civil society (*Id.*, p. 101). It is through the autonomous cultural processes of the civil society that these rights acquire validity and recognition. Yet there are also acts of the state and its organs which are vital if a systematic relation to other rights is to become possible. Therefore, Hegel concludes that it is only the combination of the efforts of the state, in conjunction with the civil society, that imparts to rights their obligatory force (*Id.*, p. 101).

The significance of the relationship between the state and civil society cannot be over-emphasized. The historical emergence of civil society has been credited with having had crucial political consequences throughout history. This is because civil society actually is the means through which citizens can limit the power of the state and transform it. One such direction for that transformation is that of liberal democracy (White, Howell, and Xiaoyuan, 1996, p. 1). Simply put, civil society has become a convenient analytical tool for explaining part of the dynamic behind periods of historical transition. After all, the term can be put to many uses. It can be used, for example, to criticize the post-colonial developmental states of the Third World. It can be employed to identify newly emergent social movements. It has been identified as being the responsible force and political agent for bringing about the collapse of authoritarian regimes and ushering in some kind of democratic-like practice.

Regardless of the emphasis one places on these interpretations, when viewed in combination the common denominator is that civil society is a force that plays a vital role in the decline or enhancement of the legitimacy and political capacity of states, as well as the political institutions and ideology which undergird them. Correspondingly, civil society can buttress the legitimacy of a state, assist the state in coming to terms with social changes by either participating in the co-opting of dynamic social forces or, in the alternative, building bridges of cooperation. In either capacity, the role played by civil society can ameliorate or rein in social growing tensions between state and society. In so doing, the civil society can channel pressures for participation and avert rising levels of sociopolitical instability by halting a decline in "governability."

For example, it was hoped that the return to civilian government in Argentina, and then in Brazil in 1985, would eventually permit the broader interests within civil society to be expressed in the formulation of economic policies. The crucial question was whether the new social openings could be used to bring conflicting social groups closer to new forms of mutual acceptance. If so, such openings could be used to spur the evolution of new forms of negotiation that would be necessary if the various groups and classes of civil society were to live together without state repression (Sheahan, 1987, p. 199–200). The larger hope was that a more open political process would give greater credence to the preferences of workers and the poor in the formulation of economic policy. Such a development would be a crucial step on the road to governing by inclusion.

What this means is that such an opening of the political process would support the kinds of changes in social investment, tax structures, and factor input requirements which would be favorable to creating a more sustainable pattern of growth. The implications of this new direction encompass an increase in the participation and empowerment of previously marginalized groups by increasing the number of persons in the civil society working on structuring political and economic demands and reinforcing the kinds of economic activity which would advance more favorable terms for employment and a reduction in poverty.

BIBLIOGRAPHY

Herbert Adam and Kogila Moodley, *South Africa Without Apartheid: Dismantling Racial Domination*, University of California Press, 1986.
Philip Alston, "The Fortieth Anniversary of the Universal Declaration of Human Rights: A Time More for Reflection Than for Celebration," *Human Rights in a Pluralistic World*, edited by Jan Berting, Meckler Ltd., 1990.
Charles F. Andrain and David E. Apter, *Political Protest and Social Change: Analyzing Politics*, New York University Press, 1995.
Claudio Bardella, et al., "So democracia absorve tensoes socias: Manifesto de oito empresarios paulistiias," *Folha de Sao Paulo*, June 26, 1978, 20.
Robert H. Bates, "Modernization, Ethnic Competition, and the Rationality of Politics in Contemporary Africa," in *State Versus Ethnic Claims: African Policy Dilemmas*, edited by Donald Rothchild and V.A. Olorunsola, Westview Press, 1983, pp. 152–71.
Wolfgang Beck, Laurent van der Maesen, Alan Walker, editors, *The Social Quality of Europe*, Kluwer Law International, 1997.
Nancy Birdsall and Juan Luis Londono, "No Tradeoff: Efficient Growth Via More Equal Human Capital Accumulation," *Beyond Tradeoffs: Market Reforms and Equitable Growth in Latin America*, edited by Nancy Birdsall, Carol Graham, and Richard H. Sabot, Inter-American Development Bank and Brookings Institution Press, 1998.
Sugata Bose, "Safeguard for Minorities Versus Sovereignty of Nations," *The Fletcher Forum of World Affairs*, Volume 19, No. 1, Winter/Spring 1995.
William G. Bowen and Derek Bok, *The Shape of the River: Long-Term Consequences of Considering Race in College and University Admissions*, Princeton University Press, 1998.
Mark E. Brandon, *Free in the World: American Slavery and Constitutional Failure*, Princeton University Press, 1998.
Michael Bratton and Nicolas van de Walle, *Democratic Experiments in Africa: Regime Transitions in Comparative Perspective*, 1997.
Albert Breton, Gianlugi Galeotti, Pierre Salmon, Ronald Wintrobe, *Understanding Democracy: Economic and Political Perspectives*, Cambridge University Press, 1997.
David Brown, "Democratization and the Renegotiation of Ethnicity," *Towards Illiberal Democracy in Pacific Asia*, edited by Daniel A. Bell, et al, St. Martin's Press, 1995.
Michael E. Brown, "Introduction," in *The International Dimensions of Internal Conflict*, edited by Michael E. Brown, The MIT Press, 1996.
Michael K. Brown, *Race, Money, and the American Welfare State*, Cornell University Press, 1999.
Carnegie Commission Final Report, *Preventing Deadly Violence*, Carnegie Corporation, 1997.
Martin Carnoy, *Faded Dreams: The Politics and Economics of Race in America*, Cambridge University Press, 1994.
Douglas A. Chalmers, et al., editors, *The New Politics of Inequality in Latin America: Rethinking Participation and Representation*, Oxford University Press, 1997.

Naomi Chazan, "Engaging the State: Associational Life in Sub-Saharan Africa," *State Power and Social Forces: Domination and Transformation in the Third World*, edited by Joel S. Migdal, Cambridge University Press, 1994.
Jean L. Cohen and Andrew Arato, *Civil Society and Political Theory*, The MIT Press, 1994.
David Cole, *No Equal Justice: Race and Class in the American Criminal Justice System*, The New Press, 1999.
Giovanni A. Cornia and Sheldon Daniger, *Child Poverty and Deprivation in the Industrialized Countries, 1945–1995*, Oxford, 1997.
Harold Crouch and James W. Morley, "The Dynamics of Political Change," *Driven by Growth: Political Change in the Asia-Pacific Region*, edited by James W. Morley, M.E. Sharpe, 1993.
Sheldon Danziger and Peter Gottschalk, *America Unequal*, Russell Sage Foundation, 1995.
Sheldon Danziger and Peter Gottschalk, editors, *Uneven Tides: Rising Inequality in America*, Russell Sage Foundation, 1993.
Francis M. Deng, Sadikiel Kimaro, Terrence Lyons, Donald Rothchild, and I. William Zartman, *Sovereignty as Responsibility: Conflict Management In Africa*, The Brookings Institution Press, 1996.
Frederic C. Deyo, *Beneath the Miracle: Labor Subordination in the New Asian Industrialism*, University of California Press, 1989.
Frederic C. Deyo, "Coalitions, Institutions, and Linkage Sequencing—Toward A Strategic Capacity Model of East Asian Development," *The Political Economy of the New Asian Industrialism*, edited by Frederic C. Deyo, Cornell University Press, 1987.
Larry Diamond, "Democracy in Latin America: Degrees, Illusions, and Directions for Consolidation," in *Beyond Sovereignty: Collectively Defending Democracy in the Americas*, The Johns Hopkins University Press, 1996.
Giuseppe Di Palma, "Why Democracy Can Work in Eastern Europe," *The Global Resurgence of Democracy*, edited by Larry Diamond and Marc F. Plattner, The John Hopkins University Press, 1993.
Jorge I. Dominguez and James A. McCann, *Democratizing Mexico: Public Opinion and Electoral Choices*, The John Hopkins University Press, 1996.
Anthony Downs, *An Economic Theory of Democracy*, Harper and Row, 1957.
Pual W. Drake, *Labor Movements and Dictatorships: The Southern Cone in Comparative Perspective*, The John Hopkins University Press, 1996.
Harry Eckstein, "Lessons for the Third Wave from the First: An Essay on Democratization," *Can Democracy Take Root in Post-Soviet Russia?: Explorations in State-Society Relations*, edited by Harry Eckstein, et al., Rowman & Littlefield Publishers, Inc., 1998.
Miriam F. Elman, "The Need for a Qualitative Test of the Democratic Peace Theory," *Paths to Peace: Is Democracy the Answer?*, Miriam Fendius Elman, editor, The MIT Press, 1997.
Thomas Ertman, *Birth of the Leviathan: Building States and Regimes in*

Medieval and Early Modern Europe, Cambridge University Press, 1997.

Milton J. Esman, *Ethnic Politics*, Cornell University Press, 1994.

Gosta Esping-Andersen, *The Three Worlds of Welfare Capitalism*, Cambridge: Polity Press, 1990.

Gosta Esping-Andersen, "Politics Without Class?: Postindustrial Cleavages in Europe and America," *Continuity and Change in Contemporary Capitalism*, edited by Herbert Kitschelt, Peter Lange, Gary Marks, and John D. Stephens, Cambridge University Press, 1999.

Peter Evans, *Embedded Autonomy: States and Industrial Transformation*, Princeton University Press, 1995.

William F. Felice, *Taking Suffering Seriously: The Importance of Collective Human Rights*, State University of New York Press, 1996.

Erich Foner, *The Story of American Freedom*, W.W. Norton & Company, 1998.

Takis Fotopoulous, *Toward an Inclusive Democracy: The Crisis of the Growth Economy and the Need for a New Liberatory Project*, Cassell, 1997.

Raymond S. Franklin, *Shadows of Race and Class*, University of Minnesota Press, 1991.

George M. Fredrickson, *White Supremacy: A Comparative Study in American and South African History*, Oxford University Press, 1981.

George M. Fredrickson, *The Arrogance of Race: Historical Perspectives on Slavery, Racism, and Social Inequality*, Wesleyan University Press, 1988.

George M. Fredrickson, *Black Liberation: A Comparative History of Black Ideologies in the United States and South Africa*, Oxford University Press, 1995.

George M. Frederickson, *The Comparative Imagination: On the History of Racism, Nationalism, and Social Movements*, University of California Press, 1997.

Paul Frymer, *Uneasy Alliances: Race and Party Competition In America*, Princeton University Press, 1999.

Frank Gaffikin and Mike Morrissey, *The New Unemployed: Joblessness and Poverty in the Market Economy*, Zed Books, Ltd.,1992.

Manuel A. Garreton, "The Political Dimension of Processes of Transformation in Chile," *Democracy, Markets, and Structural Reform in Latin America: Argentina, Bolivia, Brazil, Chile, and Mexico*, edited by William C. Smith, Carlos H. Acuna, and Eduardo A. Gamarra, Transaction Publishers, The North/South Center of the University of Miami, 1994.

Barbara Geddes, *Politicians Dilemma: Building State Capacity in Latin America*, University of California Press, 1994.

Anthony Giddens, *The Third Way: The Renewal of Social Democracy*, Polity Press, 1998.

Hermann Giliomee, "South Africa's Emerging Dominant-Party Regime," *Journal of Democracy*, October 1998, Vol. 9, No. 4, pp. 128–142.

Bernard Gofman and Arend Lijphart, editors, *Electoral Laws and Their Political Consequences*, Agathon Press, 1986.

Richard Goodin, "Inclusion And Exclusion," *European Journal of Sociology*, 37, No. 2, 1996.

Luis W. Goodman, et al., editors, *Lessons of the Venezuelan Experience*, The John Hopkins University Press, 1995.

Duncan Green, *Silent Revolution: The Rise of Market Economies in Latin America*, Cassell and LAB, 1995.
Stanley B. Greenberg, *Legitimating the Illegitmate: State, Markets, and Resistance in South Africa*, University of California Press, 1987.
William Greider, *One World, Ready or Not: The Manic Logic of Global Capitalism*, Simon & Schuster, 1997.
Stephen M. Griffin, "Bringing the State into Constitutional Theory: Public Authority and the Constitution," *Law & Social Inquiry*, Volume 16, No. 4, Fall 1991.
Merilee S. Grindle, *Challenging The State: Crisis and Innovation in Latin America and Africa*, Cambridge University Press, 1996.
Dipak K. Gupta, *The Economics of Political Violence: The Effect of Political Instability on Economic Growth*, Praeger, 1990.
Ted Robert Gurr, *Why Men Rebel*, Princeton University Press, 1970.
Ted Robert Gurr, *Minorities At Risk: A Global View of Ethnopolitical Conflicts*, United States Institute of Peace Press, 1993.
Stephan Haggard and Robert R. Kaufman, *The Political Economy of Democratic Transitions*, Princeton University Press, 1995.
Fred Harris and Lynn Curtis, editors, *Locked in the Poorhouse: Cities, Race, and Poverty in the United States*, Rowman & Littlefield Publishers, Inc., 1998.
Stanley Hoffmann, *World Disorders: Troubled Peace in the Post-Cold War Era*, Rowman & Littlefield Publishers, Inc., 1998.
Donald L. Horowitz, *Ethnic Groups in Conflict*, University of California Press, 1985.
Donald L. Horowitz, *A Democratic South Africa?: Constitutional Engineering In A Divided Society*, University of California Press, 1991.
Donald L. Horowitz, "Democracy in Divided Societies," in Larry Diamond and Marc F. Plattner, editors, *Nationalism, Ethnic Conflict, and Democracy*, The John Hopkins University Press, 1994.
Jennifer L. Hochschild, *Facing Up to the American Dream: Race, Class, and the Soul of the Nation*, Princeton University Press, 1995.
Samuel P. Huntington, *Political Order in Changing Societies*, Yale University Press, 1968.
Samuel P. Huntington and Joan M. Nelson, *No Easy Choice: Political Participation in Developing Countries*, Harvard University Press, 1976.
Samuel P. Huntington, "The Goals of Development," *Understanding Political Development*, edited by Myron Weiner and Samuel P. Huntington, Little Brown & Company, 1987.
Samuel P. Huntington, *The Third Wave: Democratization in the Late Twentieth Century*, University of Oklahoma Press, 1991.
Samuel P. Huntington, *The Clash of Civilizations and the Remaking of World Order*, Simon & Schuster, 1996.
Norman Jacobs, *The Korea Road to Modernization and Development*, The University of Chicago Press, 1985.
Helio Jaguaribe, *Political Development: A General Theory and a Latin American Case Study*, Harper & Row, Publishers, 1973.
Jacqueline Jones, *The Dispossessed: America's Underclasses From the Civil War to the Present*, Basic Books, 1992.

Jacqueline Jones, *American Work: Four Centuries of Black and White Labor*, W.W. Norton & Company, 1998.
Mark P. Jones, *Electoral Laws and the Survival of Presidential Democracies*, University of Notre Dame Press, 1995.
Sidney Jones, "The Impact of Asian Economic Growth on Human Rights," *Fires Across The Water: Transnational Problems in Asia*, edited by James Shinn, A Council on Foreign Relations Book, 1998.
Tony Judt, "The Social Question Redivivus," *Foreign Affairs*, September/October 1997.
Colin H. Kahl, "Population Growth, Environmental Degradation, and State-Sponsored Violence: The Case of Kenya, 1991–93," *International Security*, Fall 1998, Vol. 23, No. 2, p. 90.
Desmond King, *Separate and Unequal: Black Americans and the US Federal Government*, Clarendon Press, Oxford, 1995.
Desmond King, *Actively Seeking Work?: The Politics of Unemployment and Welfare Policy in the United States and Great Britain*, The University of Chicago Press, 1995.
Arthur Kleinman, Veena Das, and Margaret Lock, editors, *Social Suffering*, University of California Press, 1997.
Hans-Dieter Klingemann and Dieter Fuchs, *Citizens and the State*, Oxford University Press, 1995.
Atul Kohli and Vivienne Shue, "State Power and Social Forces: On Political Contention and Accommodation in the Third World," *State Power and Social Forces: Domination and Transformation in the Third World*, edited by Joel Migdal, et al., Cambridge University Press, 1994.
Hagen Koo, "The Interplay of State, Social Class, and World-System in East Asian Development: The Cases of South Korea and Taiwan," *The Political Economy of the New Asian Industrialism*, edited by Frederick C. Deyo, Cornell University Press, 1987.
Andrew Koppelman, *Anti-Discrimination Law and Social Equality*, Yale University Press, 1996.
Walter Korpi, *The Democratic Class Struggle*, London: Routledge, 1982.
Stephen D. Krasner and Daniel T. Froats, "Minority Rights and the Westphalian Model," *The International Spread of Ethnic Conflict: Fear, Diffusion, and Escalation*, edited by David A. Lake and Donald Rothchild, Princeton University Press, 1998.
Joel Krieger, *Reagan, Thatcher and the Politics of Decline*, Oxford University Press, 1986.
Robert Kuttner, editor, *Ticking Time Bombs: The New Conservative Assaults on Democracy*, The New Press, 1996.
Robert Kuttner, *Everything for Sale: The Virtues and Limits of Markets*, Alfred A. Knopf, 1997.
Will Kymlicka, editor, *The Rights of Minority Cultures*, Oxford University Press, 1995.
Will Kymlicka, "The Good, the Bad, and the Intolerable: Minority Group Rights," *Dissent*, Summer 1996.
David A. Lake and Donald Rothchild, editors, *The International Spread of Ethnic Conflict*, Princeton University Press, 1998.

Christopher Lasch, *The Revolt of the Elites and the Betrayal of Democracy*, W.W. Norton & Company, 1995.
Daniel Lazare, *The Frozen Republic: How the Constitution Is Paralyzing Democracy*, Harcourt Brace & Company, 1996.
Daniel Lazare, "America The Undemocratic," *New Left Review*, No. 232, November/December 1998.
S. Leibfried and P. Pierson, editors, *European Social Policy: Between Fragmentation and Integration*, Brookings Institution Press, 1995.
Robert C. Lieberman, *Shifting the Color Line: Race and the American Welfare State*, Harvard University Press, 1998.
David A. Leblang, "Political Capacity and Economic Growth," *Political Capacity and Economic Behavior*, edited by Marina Arbetman and Jacek Kugler, Westview Press, 1997.
Arend Lijphart, Ronald Rogowski, and R. Kent Weaver, "Separation of Powers and Cleavage Management," in R. Kent Weaver and Bert A. Rockman, editors, *Do Institutions Matter? Government Capabilities in the United States and Abroad*, Brookings Institution Press, 1993.
Arend Lijphart, *Majority Rule Versus Democracy in Deeply Divided Societies*, 4 Politikon, 113, 114, 1997(a).
Arend Lijphart, *Democracy in Plural Societies*, Yale University Press, 1997(b).
Juan Linz, *The Breakdown of Democratic Regimes: Crisis, Breakdown and Re-Equilibration*, The John Hopkins University Press, 1978.
Juan Linz and Alfred Stepan, *Problems of Democratic Transition and Consolidation: Southern Europe, South America, and Post-Communist Europe*, The John Hopkins University Press, 1996.
Brian Loveman, *The Constitution of Tyranny: Regimes of Exception in Spanish America*, University of Pittsburgh Press, 1993.
Edward Luttwak, *Turbo Capitalism: Winners and Losers in the Global Economy*, Harper Collins Publishers, 1999.
Peter McDonough, *Power and Ideology in Brazil*, Princeton University Press, 1981.
Katherine McFate, Roger Lawson, and William Julius Wilson, *Poverty, Inequality, and the Future of Social Policy: Western States in the New World Order*, Russell Sage Foundation, 1995.
Scott Mainwaring and Timothy R. Scully, editors, *Building Democratic Institutions: Party Systems in Latin America*, Stanford University Press, 1995.
Scott Mainwaring and Matthew Soberg Shugart, editors, *Presidentialism and Democracy in Latin America*, Cambridge University Press, 1997.
James Mally and Mitchell A. Seligson, editors, *Authoritarians and Democrats: Regime Transition in Latin America*, University of Pittsburgh Press, 1987.
Bronwen Manby, "South Africa: Minority Conflict and the Legacy of Minority Rule," *The Fletcher Forum of World Affairs*, Volume 19, No. 1, Winter/Spring 1995.
Karl Mannheim, *Ideology and Utopia*, Harcourt Brace Jovanovich, New York and London, 1936.
Jose Maria Maravall, *Regimes, Politics, and Markets: Democratization and Economic Change in Southern and Eastern Europe*, translated by Justin Byrne, Oxford University Press, 1997.

Anthony W. Marx, *Making Race and Nation: A Comparison of the United States, South Africa, and Brazil*, Cambridge University Press, 1998.
Robert K. Massie, *Loosing the Bonds: The United States and South Africa in the Apartheid Years*, Doubleday, 1997.
Joel S. Migdal, "The State in Society: An Approach to the Struggles for Domination," *State Power and Social Forces: Domination and Transformation in the Third World*, edited by Joel S. Migdal, Atul Kohli and Vivenne Shue, Cambridge University Press, 1994.
Jerome G. Miller, *Search and Destroy: African-American Males in the Criminal Justice System*, Cambridge University Press, 1996.
Richard L. Miller, *Drug Warriors and Their Prey: From Police Power to Police State*, Praeger, 1996.
Charles W. Mills, *The Racial Contract*, Cornell University Press, 1997.
Joseph Miranda, "War or Pseudo-War?," *Social Justice*, Vol. 25, No. 2 (Summer 1998).
National Urban League, *The State of Black America*, 1998.
Jorge Nef, "Demilitarization and Democratic Transition in Latin America," in *Capital, Power, and Inequality in Latin America*, edited by Sandor Halebsky and Richard L. Harris, Westview Press, 1995.
Joan Nelson, "Participation," *Understanding Political Development*, edited by Myron Weiner and Samuel P. Huntington, Little Brown, 1987, pp. 103–159.
Charles Norchi, "A Pivotal States Human Rights Strategy," *The Pivotal States: A New Framework for US Policy in the Developing World*, edited by Robert Chase, Emily Hill, and Paul Kennedy, W.W. Norton & Company, 1988.
Erich Nordlinger, "Taking the State Seriously," *Understanding Political Development*, edited by Myron Weiner and Samuel P. Huntington, Little Brown & Company, 1987.
Mancur Olson, "Dictatorship, Democracy and Development," *American Political Science Review*, Vol. 87, No. 3, September 1993.
Michael Omi and Howard Winant, *Racial Formation in the United States: From the 1960s to the 1990s*, Second Edition, Routledge, 1994.
Terrence E. Paupp, "The Planetary Dimensions of Human Rights," *The Inter-American Congress of Philosophy*, Florida State University, 1980.
Terrence E. Paupp, "Building the Third Reconstruction Society: A Proposed United Charter of Socioeconomic Rights," *The Urban League Review*, 1993.
Leigh A. Payne, *Brazilian Industrialists and Democratic Change*, The Johns Hopkins University Press, 1994.
James Petras and Chronis Polychroniou, "Rethinking Globalization: From the Future to the Past," *Socialism and Democracy*, Vol. 12, Nos. 1–2, 1998.
Frances Fox Piven and Richard A. Cloward, *The Breaking of the American Social Compact*, The New Press, 1997.
Samuel Popkin, *The Rational Peasant*, University of California Press, 1979.
Marcus G. Raskin, *The Common Good: Its Politics, Policies and Philosophy*, Routledge & Kegan Paul, 1986.
Adolph Reed Jr., editor, *Without Justice for All: The New Liberalism and Our Retreat From Racial Equality*, Westview Press, 1999.

Michael J. Rich, *Federal Policymaking and the Poor: National Goals, Local Choices, and Distributional Outcomes*, Princeton University Press, 1993.

Anthony H. Richmond, *Global Apartheid: Refugees, Racism, and the New World Order*, Oxford University Press, 1994.

Cedric J. Robinson, *Black Movements in America*, Routledge, 1997.

Stein Rokkan, *Citizens, Elections, Parties: Approaches to the Comparative Study of the Processes of Development*, Oslo: Universitetsforlaget, 1970.

Donald Rothchild, *Managing Ethnic Conflict in Africa: Pressures and Incentives for Cooperation*, Brookings Institution Press, 1997.

Douglas Rueschemeyer, Evelyne Huber Stephens, and John D. Stephens, *Capitalist Development and Democracy*, University of Chicago Press, 1992.

Mary Ruggie, *Realignments in the Welfare State: Health Policy in the United States, Britain, and Canada*, Columbia University Press, 1996.

Elmer E. Schattschneier, *The Semisovereign People*, Dryden, 1975.

Michel Schudson, *The Good Citizen: A History of American Civic Life*, The Free Press, 1998.

Joseph M. Schwartz, *The Permanence of the Political: A Democratic Critique of the Radical Impulse to Transcend Politics*, Princeton University Press, 1995.

Benjamin Schwarz, "Exporting The Myth of a Liberal America," *World Policy Journal*, Volume XV, No. 3, Fall 1998.

Benjamin Schwarz, "Perspective on Kosovo: We Forget Our Own Cruel Past," *The Los Angeles Times*, March 30, 1999.

Gay W. Seidman, *Manufacturing Militance: Worker's Movements in Brazil And South Africa, 1970–1985*, University of California Press, 1994.

Ann and Robert Seidman, *State and Law in the Development Process: Probelm-Solving and Institutional Change in the Third World*, St. Martin's Press, 1994.

Alex Y. Seita, "Globalization and the Convergence of Values," *Cornell International Law Journal*, Vol. 30, No. 2, 1997.

Philip Selznick, *The Moral Commonwealth: Social Theory and the Promise of Community*, University of California Press, 1992.

Amartya Sen, "Freedom and Needs," *New Republic*, January 10 and 17, 1994.

John Sheahan, *Patterns of Development in Latin America: Poverty, Repression, and Economic Strategy*, Princeton University Press, 1987.

Marshall Singer, "Prospects for Conflict Management in the Sri Lankan Ethnic Conflict," in Joseph V. Montville, editor, *Conflict and Peacemaking in Multiethnic Societies*, Lexington Books, 1990.

Timothy D. Sisk, *Democratization in South Africa: The Elusive Social Contract*, Princeton University Press, 1995.

Timothy Sisk, *Power Sharing and International Mediation in Ethnic Conflict*, United States Institute of Peace, 1996.

Helene Slessarev, *The Betrayal of the Urban Poor*, Temple University Press, 1997.

Rogers M. Smith, *Civic Ideals: Conflicting Visions of Citizenship in US History*, Yale University Press, 1997.
William Smith, Carlos H. Acuna, and Eduardo A. Gamarra, editors, *Latin American Political Economy in the Age of Neoliberal Reform: Theoretical and Comparative Perspectives for the 1990s*, Transaction, 1994.
Lewis W. Snider, "Political Capacity, Growth, and Distributive Commitments," *Political Capacity and Economic Behavior*, edited by Maria Arbetman and Jacek Kugler, Westview Press, 1997, pp. 235–266.
James Gustave Speth, "Poverty: A Denial of Human Rights," *Journal of International Affairs*, Columbia University School of International & Public Affairs, Vol. 52, No. 1, 1998.
Nicolas Spulber, *Redefining the State: Privatization and Welfare Reform in Industrial and Transitional Economies*, Cambridge University Press, 1997.
Paul Streeten, "Beyond the Six Veils: Conceptualizing and Measuring Poverty," *Journal of International Affairs*, Columbia Univeristy School of International and Public Affairs (Special issue: "The Multiple Faces Of World Poverty: Conceptions, Manifestations and Responses"), Vol. 52, No. 1, Fall 1998.
Charles Taylor, "The Dynamics of Democratic Exclusion," *The Journal of Democracy*, Vol. 9, No. 4, October 1998, pp. 143–156.
Alain Touraine, *What Is Democracy?*, Westview Press, 1997.
Roberto Mangabeira Unger and Cornell West, *The Future of American Progressivism—An Initiative for Political and Economic Reform*, Beacon Press, 1998.
Roberto Mangabeira Unger, *Democracy Realized: The Progressive Alternative*, Verso, 1998.
Juhana Vartianinen, "The State and Structural Change: What Can Be Learnt From the Successful Late Industrializers?," *The Role of the State in Economic Change,* edited by Ha-Joon Chang ad Robert Rowthorn, Oxford, 1995.
Sidney Verba, Norman H. Nie, and Jae-on Kim, *Participation and Political Equality,* The University of Chicago Press, 1978.
Henry Veltmeyer, James Petras, and Steve Vieux, *Neoliberalism and Class Conflict in Latin America: A Comparative Perspective on the Political Economy of Structural Adjustment,* St. Martin's Press, 1997.
Sidney Verba, et al., *Elites and the Idea of Equality: A Comparison of Japan, Sweden, and the United States,* Harvard University Press, 1987.
Xi Wang, *The Trial of Democracy: Black Suffrage and Northern Republicans, 1860–1910,* The University of Georgia Press, 1997.
Gordon White, Jude Howell, and Shang Xiaoyuan, *In Search of Civil Society: Market Reform and Social Change in Contemporary China,* Clarendon Press Oxford, 1996.
Linda Weiss, *The Myth of the Powerless State,* Cornell University Press, 1998.
Kurt Weyland, *Democracy Without Equity: Failures of Reform in Brazil,* University of Pittsburgh Press, 1996.
William Julius Wilson, *When Work Disappears: The World of the New Urban Poor,* Alfred A. Knopf, 1996.
Howard Winant, *Racial Conditions: Politics, Theory, Comparisons,* University of Minnesota Press, 1994.

Ronald Wintrobe, *The Political Economy of Dictatorship*, Cambridge University Press, 1998.
David Wippman, "Practical and Legal Constraints on Internal Power Sharing," edited by David Wippman, *International Law and Ethnic Conflict*, Cornell University Press, 1998.
Ellen M. Wood, *Democracy Against Capitalism: Renewing Historical Materialism*, Cambridge University Press, 1995.
Daniel Yergin and Joseph Stanislaw, *The Commanding Heights: The Battle Between Government and the Marketplace That Is Remaking the Modern World*, Simon & Schuster, 1998.

CHAPTER 5

BACK TO THE FUTURE: HOBBES'S VISION OF SOVEREIGNTY, COMMONWEALTH, AND ANARCHY

Europe not only needs a new social order, it requires a common moral order to sustain new forms of societal networks, based on the modern conception of citizenship. The social rights of citizenship will sustain social freedom in order to defend and to develop forms of social cohesion.
Wolfgang Beck, et al.,
The Social Quality of Europe,
1997, p. 275

People must and do give priority to the material conditions that affect their lives. This Hobbesian premise is especially important in the realm of political morality.
Philip Selznick, The Moral Commonwealth: Social
Theory and The Promise of Community, 1992, p. 532

In truth, rights are never the bottom line in moral or political theory—or practice. They are conclusions, end-results of long chains of reasoning from commonly accepted premises. Rights have little authority or content in the absence of a common ethical life. They are conventions that are durable only when they express a moral consensus. When ethical disagreement is deep and wide an appeal to rights cannot resolve it. Indeed, it may make such conflict dangerously unmanageable.
John Gray, False Dawn: The Delusions of Global
Capitalism, 1998, p. 109

A stable social order is possible where there exists great diversity of basic beliefs and values, even if religious, ethnic, and other differences are often associated with conflict and civil war . . . It is the existence within a society of a habit of deference to

common rules of mutual accommodation that helps to keep such differences from leading to civil war or other kinds of social dissolution.
>   Terry Nardin, *Law, Morality, and the Relations of States*, 1983, p. 315

A. INTRODUCTION

Hobbes's great work, *Leviathan*, is now almost 350 years old. Yet it still has much to teach us. The relevance of his work stems from the fact that he not only identified a number of enduring problems regarding political life and social behavior, but he also provided some provisional and feasible solutions for them. In particular, Hobbes was preoccupied with the civil wars that wreaked havoc on the England of his day and generation. The lessons and challenges of those times persist into the 20th century.

In the post-Cold War world we have come to learn, to our dismay, that the increasing integration of states does not necessarily integrate their nations. For the state is only a formal juridical and political structure. A nation is composed of peoples who are united under the common rubric of culture, race, philosophy, and multicultural or ethnic ties. A nation is, after all, composed of people, and every "people," which is the product of a national process of ethnicization, is forced to find its own evolutionary path of going beyond exclusivism or identitarian ideology. This is especially the case in a world of transnational communications (Balibar, 1991, p. 105).

Take, for example, the crisis in Kosovo in 1999. Once again, civil war has erupted to scar the politics and peoples of Europe. Similar to the civil wars that wrecked the England of the 17th century, the situation of the former Yugoslavia in Bosnia and Kosovo will not find final resolution on the basis of either a return to pre-civil war provincial borders established by the great powers and NATO or in the context of ethnic equity. Rather, the ultimate resolution of this conflict will, in large measure, probably be the product of the balance of military forces. As early as 1995, the Croats and Muslims have come to understand—and are applying—the great lesson of the Yugoslav war. It is the same lesson which the Serbs demonstrated in their own time of military supremacy: "that in the post-Cold-War world there is no collective security, no international will to protect the weak against the strong." The tragedy and the lesson is that "to win freedom and security for one's people requires neither a sound argument nor a good cause but a big army. Victory in former Yugoslavia will fall not to the just, but to the strong" (Silber and Little, 1996, p. 372).

In conformity with Hobbes's 16th century analysis of how conflicts get resolved, the resolution of Kosovo conflict of the late 1990s will probably come about as a result of a redivision of the area into sovereign states with unequal economic conditions, military resources, and political power. This is not to argue, however, that conflict-resolution necessarily follows the

Hobbesian prescription of centralized authoritarian states in an anarchic world. Rather, such an interpretation is a recognition of the prevalent need for the institutionalization of authority and the need to find legitimate norms, values, and institutions to effectuate that authority as a means of securing peace. The institutionalization of authority must involve reestablishing the legitimacy of the state. For, as Delmas has argued, "the economic factors favoring integration may be powerful and active yet they do not favor political or social order" (Delmas, 1995, p. 143). The period of the Cold War allowed for the power of security concerns and political slogans to mask the underlying reality of the difference between integration and order. That mask is now removed in the post-1990s. In its place is the grim reminder that without a legitimate state, the perils of genocide and ethnic cleansing are a part of modern history once again. In the African states of Rwanda, Mauritania, Sudan, and Angola, ethnic legitimacy prevails to justify massacres. In the former Yugoslavia, Bosnia and Kosovo have emerged to compete in their horror with the killing fields of Cambodia.

In *Leviathan*, Hobbes sought to emphasize the institutionalization of authority in a legitimate state. In the late 20th century, the wars in Bosnia and Kosovo are the real harbinger, because they are war without a state, "a battle for survival where each side's very existence is seen as incompatible with that of the others" (*Id.*, 1995, pp. 149–150). While current Western nationalisms are benign, many Eastern European nationalisms have many, although not all, of the attributes that make nationalism dangerous. It is for this reason that the risk of large-scale violence stemming from a rising tide of European nationalism has made Kosovo the most recent expression of the malignant nationalisms of earlier times in Europe's history (1870–1945).

Commenting on this phenomenon, Tismaneanu has noted that, "there is nothing intrinsically wrong with national pride. The tragedy occurs when this natural sentiment ceases to mean just 'love for the little platoon we belong to in society' (Edmund Burke), and is exacerbated into an ideology of hostility, hatred, and envy" (Tismaneanu, 1998, p. 157). Similarly, Nardin has maintained that "it is not differences of language, religion, or nationality alone that lead to civil war, but their existence along with doctrines that hold that such differences are intolerable. Conversely, a pluralist social order is most likely to prevail where the ideas of toleration and mutual accommodation have emerged and become rooted in custom, morality, and law" (Nardin, 1983, p. 315). On the ideological level, doctrines of exclusion emphasize differences and a lack of tolerance for those differences. Alternatively, doctrines of inclusion emphasize a common humanity with common needs, interests and the inherent worth of the individual. It is a moral and cultural viewpoint with direct political ramifications. For the recognition of human worth is a recognition of human dignity which, ultimately, leads to the political demand for the recognition and protection of human rights by the state, the law and the national and international society.

1. The Purposes of This Chapter

The main purpose of this chapter is to explicate those legitimate norms, values, and institutions that will be capable of effectuating moral, political, and economic authority in the service of peace, justice, and human rights at the dawn of the 21st century. By juxtaposing this discussion with a new analysis of Hobbes's vision in his classic work, *Leviathan*, I hope to present a more balanced and comprehensive view of the nation-state system, the role of nationalism and war, and what the implications of these elements portend for international relations and the possibilities for peace, conflict prevention and conflict resolution at the dawn of the 21st century.

In Part B, I discuss the relationship between nationalism, war, and the emerging international legal culture of the 20th century. I shall explain why there is a need to create a new legal culture that is more attuned to dealing with the enduring conflict between sovereignty and human rights. Instead of being conflicting domains of law, there needs to be a greater complementarity between them. Such a congruence within the international legal culture could dispel many of the difficulties associated with humanitarian intervention as a strategy to deal with extreme claims to sovereignty, which often act as a cover to human rights abuses, genocide, and ethnic cleansing. Further, the issue and the right to self-determination is another component in the international legal equation that needs to be addressed if we are ever to overcome those justifications of governance which rely on "rule by law" in place of the "rule of law."

Additionally, the argument in this section will stress the significance of a restored and maturing international legal culture. Such a culture will facilitate, within and between nations, solutions associated with the problems of global exchange and global exploitation. After all, these problems have stimulated an escalating crisis between the task of building a global commonwealth, on the one hand, while protecting private enclaves of power in the pursuit of private wealth, on the other. Private wealth exposes the corruption of the processes of democratic inclusion by introducing the rule of an elite ("polyarchy") and imposing on Third World states a limited juridical application of the doctrine of sovereignty which has compromised their independence by making them "quasi-states." The resulting problems for these states exposes the challenge of weak state-power under democracy. The failure of these states to attain greater power and independence within the international system re-opens the Hobbesian dilemma. The articulation of this continuing dilemma underscores the relevance of Hobbes with respect to nationalism, war, and the emerging need for a revitalized legal culture at the dawn of the 21st century.

In Part C, I discuss the international and national dynamics of democracy in conflict with globalization under capitalism. Insofar as capitalism develops unevenly and capitalist growth is often the product of forcible extraction and class warfare, the ramifications of globalization may be depicted as antithetical to building a culture of national and international peace. The Hobbessian dilemma is reinforced by the combination of capitalist expansion and exploitation. Recognizing these interrelated trends allows me to argue that geopolitical conflict and scarcities make Hobbes and Malthus more relevant to the late 20th century than Adam Smith or Friedrich van Hayek.

In Part D, I revisit the Hobbesian dilemma and its implications. Specifically, I discuss Hobbes's prescriptions for forging an inclusionary social compact as a model for dealing with current geopolitical dilemmas and national challenges to equitable development, a culture of peace, and the promise of inclusionary governance. Forging an inclusionary compact that is sensitive and responsive to human needs and the social quality of life exposes a crisis of citizenship in the emerging European Union (EU) with the multiplication of membership categories. The growing resistance to new waves of immigrants has resulted in a crisis of citizenship. A crisis of citizenship, in turn, raises issues and challenges which impact upon the task of forging an inclusionary social compact. As long as such a compact remains elusive, the Hobbesian dilemma remains an ever-present problem for individual nation-states and the international community as a whole.

In Part E, the distinction between the "rule of law" and "rule by law" is more fully examined. Exclusionary states that "rule by law," as Indonesia, Mexico, the Philippines, Zaire, Rwanda, and Yugoslavia have discovered, demonstrate that there cannot be meaningful political inclusivity without socioeconomic and cultural inclusivity. Where the phenomenon of "rule by law" predominates, it is there that what Hobbes called "the negligent government of princes" destroys the basis of civil peace, creates the conditions for civil wars, and negates the value and force of inclusionary governance.

In Part F, I discuss the founding of the Hobbesian state. Its founding is predicated upon the possession of territory, for without a territorial base it is doubtful whether political authority can be exerted over sets of institutions or issues that are part of an enduring system. Within an enduring system, negotiations between parties (agents), as understood within the framework of the Hobbesian social contract, are composed of three major elements or sets of considerations: (1) the nature of the negotiations; (2) the rules for negotiations; (3) appreciation of a "no-agreement point" (what happens if agreement is not reached?). Each of these sets of considerations are examined in detail.

In Part G, I discuss the legacy of Hobbes, as an intellectual point of departure, for creating a global commonwealth and an international culture of peace. In this regard, special attention will be given to an examination of the nature of the state and the limits of governmental action. The elements of these limitations will be discussed in detail. This will lead to the final section of the chapter: an analysis of how civil society shapes national commonwealths and the international commonwealth. Further, the precise tasks of civil society are explicated with respect to its relationship with the state and dealing with the limits of governmental action.

In Part H, the specific tasks of civil society in the shaping of the national and international commonwealth will be discussed. Understood as an arena of autonomous action from the state, the civil society provides a source for the revitalization of nations, a source for the reconfiguration of international relations in the pursuit of peace, a source for the mitigation of deadly conflict, and a source for the mediation of differences which could potentially lead to deadly conflict. In all of these endeavors, civil society serves as a source of countervailing power and influence that can mitigate many of the difficulties associated with national and international trends that lead toward a resurrection of the conflictual and violent potentialities locked within the Hobbesian dilemma.

B. THE ROLE OF NATIONALISM, WAR, AND INTERNATIONAL LEGAL CULTURE

The character and consequences of nationalism are not written in stone (Van Evera, 1998, p. 261). Recognizing this fact allows us to appreciate the fact that the Western powers have some capacity to influence the character and consequences of Eastern nationalist movements, and efforts have been made to channel the energy of these movements in more benign directions. Yet, beyond political efforts to influence Eastern nationalist movements, Western powers would find their energies put to more productive use in seeking to promote full respect for minority rights, extending the reach of inclusionary democratic practices, and building new institutions to mediate conflicts and differences.

I am advocating the view that there is a great need to create a new legal culture. This is because just as a concept of law is not a constant, neither is a legal culture a constant. Montesquieu observed long ago that knowledge enables societies to choose among a variety of different concepts of law and different legal cultures. In this sense, both concepts of law and legal cultures are variables and, as such, are always embedded in a general thought guiding society (Schmidt, 1996, p. 174). The rule of law can be a way of resolving conflicts more effectively, peacefully and cooperatively (Seita, 1997, p. 430). This view of the rule of law stands in sharp contrast to the reality of many post-communist societies that have retained the primordialist perspective. The primordialist perspective prevails throughout many of the Eastern nationalist movements because it "perceives the fact of national belonging as a genetic determination and culture is simply reduced to a dispensable appendage" (Tismaneanu, 1998, p. 157).

In contrast, I shall argue, throughout this chapter, that national belonging, under the rule of law, is the most effective antidote to ethnic conflict and virulent nationalisms. For, as Nardin has argued, "law understood as a framework of restraint and coexistence among those pursuing divergent purposes presupposes diversity and the toleration of this diversity" (Nardin, 1983, p. 324). I contend that it is the toleration of this diversity that trumps the Hobbesian dilemma that depicts people as merely self-interested rational calculators who require a ruler with unlimited power in a predatory and/or oppressive state.

1. Overcoming the Hobbesian Dilemma

Overcoming the Hobbesian dilemma involves a recognition that the legitimacy of the political order is two-sided. One side can be thought of as the propensity of groups and individuals living under it to adhere to it voluntarily and to defend it out of mutual interest as well as self-interest. On the other side, however, the legitimacy of the political order can be questioned and undermined when it is under assault from the very officials responsible for administering it. Now, because every political order claims to secure a specific set of values, its citizens accord it legitimacy only insofar as the order works to incorporate those values into practice and they can see, in turn, that the political order does indeed honor and respect them (Becker, 1999, p. 142).

Between the extremes of complete peace and the military doctrine of all-out war, there lies an answer. In his book, *The Rosy Future of War*, Philippe Delmas observed, as early as 1995, that "the comeback of all-out wars has shown us in five years what we had forgotten for over fifty: force alone does not create any shared concept of rationality" (Delmas, 1995, p. 190). We have, he argues, created a false equivalency between military force and politics. We should acknowledge that the two are separate and that that realization leads to the acknowledgment of the importance of the role of doctrine. The very purpose of doctrine is to help decide when the stakes are worth the use of force and how much force is justifiable to defend them (*Id.*, p. 190).

The doctrines of statehood and sovereignty confer rights attendant to the status of citizenship. The doctrines of statehood and sovereignty create a geographical space in which the moral and normative imperatives of human and civil rights may be either recognized or violated. It is doctrine which establishes ends and means. In the absence of statehood and sovereignty, stateless nationalisms rely on nationalist myths to justify ethnic cleansing, genocide, and separatist politics in violation of human rights norms and values. After all, it is a well-tested hypothesis that stateless nationalisms pose a greater risk of war if they have the strength to reach for freedom and the state has the will to resist their attempt (Van Evera, 1998, pp. 257–291). In contrast to stateless nationalisms, democratic regimes are less prone to the myth-making phenomenon that are a large component of stateless nationalisms, "because such regimes are usually more legitimate and are free-speech tolerant; hence they can develop evaluative institutions to weed out nationalist myth" (Van Evera, p. 285).

So, if the end result of the conflict in Bosnia and Kosovo is to be peace, then the means to that peace may be, some have argued, reliance upon the traditional doctrine, sovereign statehood as an appropriate international institution (Keohane, 1995, p. 182). Whether the doctrine of sovereign statehood can institutionalize the channels to accommodate diversity, pluralism, and democracy and, at the same time, can effectuate a sense of justice, develop a moral community or help to create a viable civil society is still open to debate. There are a great variety of nationalisms that are most likely to cause war, including both civil war and inter-state war. In Table 5.1, Stephen Van Evera identifies the causes of these dangerous varieties of nationalism and the conditions that govern the size of the dangers they produce. Table 5.1 sets forth twenty-one hypotheses—nine main hypotheses and twelve sub-hypotheses. Some focus on the environment that surround these movements while others focus on the ideology and character of the movements themselves, for the internal character of a nationalist movement can help to determine its general inclination toward peace or war.

What prescriptions follow from this delineation of nationalisms and the risk of war inherent in them? First, that current Western European nationalisms are benign while, in contrast, many Eastern European nationalisms run the risk of large-scale violence, as in the case of Bosnia and Kosovo. Second, that the Western powers retain the capacity to influence some aspects of the character and consequences of Eastern nationalist movements. Third, that the doctrine of sovereignty is still alive and that a revived international legal order should place greater emphasis upon building mediating institutions that can effectuate and promote full respect for minority rights, the principle of self-determination, human rights in general, more democratic institutions that are inclusionary, and set forth courts and tribunals to deal with war crimes and war criminals.

Yet, other vital questions remain: what are the boundaries, limitations, potentials of sovereign statehood in an age of globalization? Also, what are the demands which stem from the legal, moral, and normative aspects of human rights and self-determination? Can these demands and legal covenants be institutionalized at the domestic and international levels? A comprehensive answer to these questions is beyond the scope of this chapter. Yet, some tentative answers must be provided. In this regard, the doctrine of sovereignty is a good place to begin this discussion.

2. Of Sovereignty and Sovereigns

The doctrine of sovereignty has been much maligned in the post-cold war world—and for good reason. Governments that have relied on sovereignty as an established norm of international law have often abused its protective precepts as an argument against humanitarian intervention when genocide and massive human rights violations have accumulated within sovereign borders. After all, "in an ideal Westphalian order, political relations between rulers and ruled are territorially bounded and not subject to any external authority" (Krasner and Froats, 1998, p. 226). But all that is now largely changed, at least to a significant degree, because of the evolution of human rights norms and covenants, along with international institutions backed up by alliances and powerful nation-states willing to enforce them.

What has transformed both the role of the doctrine of sovereignty, in particular, and international relations, in general, is the international law of human rights and minority rights. What this means is that the principle of human rights is now empowered as an independent legal standard. Because individuals and groups are now endowed with inherent rights, the implica-

TABLE 5.1 Hypotheses on Nationalism and War: Summary

I. *Immediate Causes*
1. The greater the proportion of state-seeking nationalities that are stateless, the greater the risk of war.
2. The more nationalities pursue the recovery of national diasporas, and the more they pursue annexationist strategies of recovery, the greater the risk of war.
3. The more hegemonistic the goals that nationalities pursue toward one another, the greater the risk of war.
4. The more severely nationalities oppress minorities living in their states, the greater the risk of war.

II. *Causes of the Immediate Causes and Conditions Required for Their Operation*
   Structural Factors:
   1. Stateless nationalisms pose a greater risk of war if they have the strength to plausibly reach for freedom, and the central state has the will to resist the attempt.
   2. The more densely nationalities are intermingled, the greater the risk of war.
       a. The risks posed by intermingling are larger the more local (house-by-house) rather than regional (province-by-province) the pattern of intermingling.
       b. The risks posed by intermingling are larger if the rescue of diasporas by homelands is difficult but possible; smaller if the rescue is either impossible or easy.
   3. The greater the defensibility and legitimacy of borders, and the greater the correspondence between these political borders and communal boundaries, the smaller the risk of war.
       a. The less secure and defensible the borders of emerging nation-states, the greater the risk of war.
       b. The greater the international legitimacy of the borders of emerging nation-states, the smaller the risk of war.
       c. The more closely the boundaries of emerging nation-states follow ethnic boundaries, the smaller the risk of war.

   Political/Environmental Factors:
   4. The greater the past crimes committed by nationalities toward one another, the greater the risk of war.
       a. The better these crimes are remembered by the victims, the greater the risk of war.
       b. The more that responsibility for past crimes can be attached to groups still on the scene, the greater the risk of war.
       c. The less contrition and repentance shown by the guilty groups, the greater the risk of war.
       d. The coincidence of power and victimhood, the greater the risk of war.

> **TABLE 5.1** *(continued)*
>
> 5. The more severely nationalities oppress minorities now living in their states, the greater the risk of war. (This restates Hypothesis No. I.4; I list it twice because it operates both as a direct and a remote cause of war.)
>
> *Perceptual Factors:*
> 6. The more divergent are the beliefs of nationalities about their mutual history and their current conduct and character, the greater the risk of war.
>   a. The less legitimate the governments or leaders of nationalist movements, the greater their propensity to purvey mythical nationalist beliefs, hence the greater the risk of war.
>   b. The more the state must demand of its citizens, the greater its propensity to purvey the mythical nationalist beliefs, hence the greater the risk of war.
>   c. If economic conditions deteriorate, publics become more receptive to scapegoat myths, hence such myths are more widely believed, hence war is more likely.
>   d. If independent evaluative institutions are weak or incompetent, myths will more often prevail, hence war is more likely.
>
> SOURCE: Stephen Van Evera, "Hypotheses on Nationalism and War," *Theories of War and Peace: An International Security Reader*, edited by Michael E. Brown, Owen R. Cote, Jr., Sean M. Lynn-Jones, and Steven E. Miller, The MIT Press, Cambridge, Massachusetts, 1998, pp. 260–261.

tion is that public authorities are no longer totally free to structure relations between rulers and ruled in any way that they wish and that the state is no longer the sole arbiter of proper conduct within a particular territorial expanse. Rather, it is subject to a wide variety of restrictions on its conduct, particularly with regard to the treatment of individuals and groups (Mills, 1998, p. 126).

The legal standard of self-determination in modern international law has emerged to circumscribe the behavior of states with respect to their treatment of individuals and groups. The law relating to self-determination in the post-1945 era was developed primarily in response to the growth of nationalism in the Third World, particularly in the states of Africa and Asia (Minogue, 1967; Kilson, 1975; Smith, 1979; Breuilly, 1982). Most of these states were former colonies and consequently the nationalism that emerged in those states had as a primary goal the termination of their colonial status and the attainment of independence. It was in this context that the concept of self-determination in these states became mostly associated with the process of decolonization (Musgrave, 1997, p. 91).

Embodied in the international legal instruments concluded by Western states, such as the Helsinki Declaration, is an understanding of self-determination which asserts that self-determination also involves the periodic exercise of popular sovereignty through democratic elections. Western states also maintain that United Nations General Assembly Resolution 2625 (XXV) embodies this particular understanding of self-determination. Third World states do not accept the construction that the language contained in Resolution 2625 (XXV) imports any particular obligation on states to engage in the building of representative governments or that they be elected in a democratic process. Alternatively, Third World states share the opinion that all that Resolution 2625 (XXV) requires of governments is that its government is not racist in composition (Musgrave, 1997, p. 125). In other words, most Third World states hold that the sovereignty and territorial integrity of the state is paramount in all situations. Obviously, this is the point where the principle of human rights collides with the doctrine of state sovereignty.

Yet, in the world of the 1990s, as claims to self-determination are increasingly put forward by ethnic groups, these claims, more often than not, involve secession from an existing state. While the post-1945 period was characterized by most states refusing to recognize entities which had seceded from independent states, the post-1990, post-Cold-War period appears to have changed that practice. A key case in point is that of Yugoslavia. With the dissolution of the Soviet Union, Yugoslavia has been transformed into a number of ethnically-based nation-states. These particular successor states have been recognized by the international community and accepted as member states of the United Nations. Yet this change in practice, custom, and norm, coupled with NATO's 1999 military intervention in Kosovo, calls into question the extent to which self-determination, based on a purely ethnic criteria, may now constitute an element of international law, and the circumstances in which it may apply.

The matter is far from resolved. For the doctrine of human rights collides with traditional notions of sovereignty in such a way that new mediating institutions have not yet fully emerged and internationally recognized norms have not evolved to a sufficient level of maturity so as to birth human rights accountability into effective governance. Fifty years after the Nuremberg and Tokyo trials, nations around the world are still grappling with the need to hold individuals accountable for human rights atrocities (Ratner and Abrams, 1997; Neier, 1998; Minow, 1998; Kochavi, 1998; Roht-Arriaza, 1995; The Report of The Century Foundation/Twentieth Century Fund Task Force On Apprehending Indicted War Criminals, 1998). Even when placed in the most optimistic of terms, it has to be acknowledged "it seems that while human rights has won the battle with sovereignty, it does not know what to do with the victory" (Mills, 1998, p. 194).

3. The "Democratic Peace Thesis" and the Crisis of Sovereignty

One of the most important empirical findings and theories to emerge from the studies of international relations in recent decades is the "democratic peace" thesis. According to the democratic peace thesis, the best explanation of a state's behavior lies in the nature of the state (Elman, 1997, p. 1). Strictly speaking, the democratic peace thesis is an empirical finding and not a theory. The empirical finding includes both evidence that democracies have rarely gone to war with each other (the dyadic finding) and evidence that they are less likely to use force in general (the monadic finding) (*Id.*, p. 1).

Associated with the democratic peace thesis are three central points which are relevant to this chapter's concern with the rule of law and the evolution of norms, values, and a cultural consensus that protects and respects diversity and tolerance: (1) that democratic states remain at peace because of democratic norms and institutions; (2) that democracies are predisposed to peaceful methods of international conflict resolution; (3) that non-democratic norms and institutions are obstacles to international peace.

I shall argue that a "democratic commonwealth," within and between nations, is the best means to overcome the problems of "democratic exclusion" (as discussed in Chapter 1). This idea will be explicated throughout this chapter by juxtaposing this view with the historical vision of Hobbes. Further, I shall argue that "governing-by-inclusion" makes democracy a proper subset of inclusionary practices and inclusionary governance.

4. The Struggle Between "Commonwealth" and "Private-Wealth"

At the beginning of the 20th century, dependency Marxists argued that world capitalism develops not progress, but rather shapes the dynamics of "underdevelopment" in the dependent economies of the Third World periphery—the "development of underdevelopment," to use Andre Gunder Frank's famous phrase (Lewellen, 1995; Munck, 1984; Inglehart, 1997; Eisenstadt and Roniger, 1984; Leys, 1996; Slater, Schutz and Dorr, 1993; Thomas, 1994). The reality of dependence for the nations of the poor South makes for the continuous replication of poverty in the periphery. The replication of poverty takes a variety of forms which range from "exploitative prices shaped by monopolized trading channels controlled by core economies, declining terms of trade between the raw material exports of the peripheries and the manufactured goods exports of the cores, restricted consumption by the impoverished peripheral laborers caused by the limited opportunities for increases in their wages . . . and lastly the monopoly of advanced technology held by the core economies" (Doyle, 1997, p. 486).

From this list of economic factors comes the opportunity to juxtapose the political weaknesses of these peripheral societies, which includes serious internal class divisions among landlords, merchants, workers and peasants. The result is what I have labeled the "exclusionary states" (ES) of the Third World. Others have called these states "weak states." But to depict these states as "weak" fails to explain why they are so weak. Further, by simply describing these states as "weak" simply ignores the deeper structural problems of these societies. The structural problems include but are not limited to the following: the marginalization, dispossession, repression and exclusion of significant classes, groups and interests that constitute the basis of a civil society. These exclusionary states are, therefore, incapable of effectively bargaining in such a manner that the interests of the poor and excluded members of their respective societies are also represented, *at the international level*, with the more integrated societies and powerful states of the core. What we find is that bargains are usually bargains among elites and between elites at the national and transnational levels.

There are three interrelated points that follow from this analysis. First, that most Third World states do not have a representative or inclusive form of democracy and are, therefore, more appropriately described as polyarchies. Second, that the so-called "weak" states of the Third World are really more appropriately understood as "quasi-states." Third, and finally, democratization is a particularly weak form of state power that opens up the state to a variety of private, confused, contradictory, and ultimately stalemated kinds of pressure. We shall discuss each point in turn.

First, most Third World states do not practice democracy but are, rather, polyarchies. Polyarchy refers to a system in which a small group actually rules, on behalf of capital. Further, it means that participation in decision making by the majority is confined to limited electoral contests in which choices are among competing elites in tightly controlled electoral processes (Robinson, October 1998–March 1999, pp. 120–121). The polyarchy is being promoted by the transnational elite in the poor South who service the needs of a neoliberal agenda, which includes promoting policies of "structural adjustment programs" which further exploit, marginalize, and exploit labor and other classes and groups. The various expressions of polyarchy, throughout the Third World, combine with the demands of global capital to make the promotion of inclusionary democracy and respect for human rights an impossibility. This is because the neoliberal model of development does not require an inclusionary social base (*Id.*, p. 122). Instead, the emphasis is placed upon maintaining a system of socioeconomic exclusion because capital accumulation does not depend upon a domestic market, internal social reproduction, or the inclusion of the majority in the decision-making processes of state that are designed to serve international capital, not the national interest.

Second, the so-called "weak states" of the these Third World nations are really "quasi-states." In many cases, the ex-colonial states have been internationally enfranchised and possess the same external rights and responsibilities as all other states, including judicial statehood. At the same time, however, many of these states have not yet been domestically empowered to act independently of the dictates of international global capital interests. Their internal institutions are weak and their democratic processes are inherently compromised and weak as a result. As Doule has noted, "the semipheriphery needs strong states in order to mobilize savings into growth and thereby onto a path that is equalizing rather than one that perpetuates and reinforces global capitalist hierarchy" (Doyle, 1997, p. 488). Political violence and socioeconomic instability characterize these "quasi-states" on the periphery because capitalism develops unevenly and capitalist growth is the product of both forcible extraction and class warfare. Therefore, it is not just the ethnic strife in Kosovo of 1999 which qualifies as an example of "ethnic cleansing." Throughout the Third World, there are many examples of "social cleansing," such as the murder of street children in Guatemala, Brazil, and elsewhere in Latin America. Death squads hired by businessmen and local politicians operate to kill and remove thousands of poor people (Robinson, October 1998–March 1999, p. 122). These "quasi-states" have governments that are deficient in the political will, institutional authority, and organized power to protect human rights or to provide their people with socioeconomic welfare. The benefits of sovereignty accrue to a narrow elite while the citizenry, at large, have not seen their lot improved since independence and are, therefore, subject to the whims of "quasi-states" (Jackson, 1990, p. 21).

Third, and finally, it follows from the above-referenced discussion of polyarchy and the nature of "quasi-states" that democracy is an extremely weak form of state power, in practice. For if the ideal of democracy connotes a respect for human rights, the inclusion of the majority of citizens, as well as "discrete and insular minorities," then we know that democracy does not really exist in the quasi-states of the Third World. In its place are exclusionary states and practices that foster worldwide inequality. Recognizing this reality, then, we can comprehend that what is called "democracy" is simply a form of permanent structural violence against the world's majority. In turn, this structural violence fosters protest among the victims of state repression. In this way, "the structural violence of the socioeconomic system and violations of human rights are different moment of the same social relations of domination" (Robinson, October 1998–March 1999, p. 123).

The combination of these political and economic factors does not create a fruitful ground for democracy or for inclusionary governance *within the domestic frontiers* of these nations either. The implications of this crisis for the South has been identified by the report of The South Centre, in which the authors stress the point that "progress cannot be 'brought in from the outside,' but must be won by the people concerned." However, the peoples of the periphery are blocked by the objectives of the Western powers, for these Western objectives are exclusively preoccupied with the maintenance of the status quo, of which they are the beneficiaries (The South Centre, p. 137). In short, Western objectives depend and rely upon the persistence of exclusionary governance, whether in the form of authoritarian regimes or so-called democratic ones which seeks to identify capitalism with democracy. This underlying theme in the economic orchestration of the North's interventions in the South is nothing less than a deceitful trick. On the contrary, the reality is that in all of the peripheries, the progress of democracy implies and requires social measures that clash with the logic of capitalist expansion.

C. DEMOCRACY IN CONFLICT WITH GLOBALIZATION UNDER CAPITALISM

The accumulation of contradictions and social antagonisms has created a crisis of ungovernability of democratic regimes throughout the Third World and accelerated their delegitimation. This result runs the risk of an unexpected and undesirable installation of a military dictatorship of a new type. The fundamental point that I seek to stress is that these accumulated contradictions and social antagonisms reinforce the marginality of the excluded and fuels the growth of exclusionary states. Given this assessment, it may be argued that "democratization in this analysis is a particularly weak form of state power that opens up the state to all sorts of private, confused, contradictory, and ultimately stalemating kinds of pressure. The semiperiphery needs strong states in order to mobilize savings into investment into growth and thereby onto a path that is equalizing rather than one that perpetuates and reinforces global capitalist hierarchy. Capitalism develops unevenly, and capitalist growth is the product of forcible extraction and class warfare" (Doyle, 1997, pp. 487–488).

If capitalism in the periphery creates this kind of violence and instability through exclusionary practices and policies, then it can be argued that peace is automatically forfeited with its expansion. In its place, the politics of democratic and authoritarian exclusion violates human rights and sovereignty, for the sovereignty of the Third World's states are subjected to the West's neoliberal prescriptions which, in turn, exclude the majority of its peoples. Hence, the Hobbesian dilemma is reinforced by capitalist expansion and exploitation as the "war of all against all" returns to the historical stage triumphant. It is not really the triumph of the market that defines the post-Cold War world but, rather, the triumph of marginalization, exclusion and the subordination of human rights norms as well the integrity of the principle of state-sovereignty. In recognition of the renewed threats to global peace in the global village of the 20th century, John Gray has astutely acknowledged that "the lesson is clear. As presently organized, global capitalism is supremely ill-suited to cope with the risks of geo-political conflict that are endemic in a world of worsening scarcities . . . Thomas Hobbes and Thomas Malthus are better guides to the world that global *laissez-faire* has created than Adam Smith or Friedrick von Hayek; a world of war and scarcity at least as much as the benevolent harmonies of competition" (Gray, 1998, p. 207).

The key problem of world order now, it has been argued, is "to seek to devise institutional arrangements that are consistent with key features of the international relations and the new shape of domestic politics in key countries" (Keohane, 1995, p. 183). Of course, the construction of new institutions is the greatest challenge of all for the international community. But, before focusing upon the role played by international institutions, it is essential to not forget the role played by the domestic institutions, policies, and politics of each country. And, in remembering and assessing the politics of a nation's domestic life, we are returned to Hobbes and the Hobbesian vision of order, of what constitutes a commonwealth and what are the threats that remain to its realization. For this reason it is necessary to discuss and reflect upon the meaning of the Hobbesian dilemma, especially in an era of capitalist expansionism and exploitation.

D. REVISITING THE HOBBESIAN DILEMMA

The Hobbesian dilemma may be summarized in two propositions:

1. Since people are rational calculators, self-interested, seeking gain and glory, and fearful of one another, there is no security in anarchy.
2. But precisely because people are so self-interested and power-loving, unlimited power for the ruler implies a predatory, oppressive state.

Now, 350 years later, both critics and adherents of Hobbes concur that Hobbes's dilemma cannot be ignored. On the one hand, the realist school of international relations claims that pessimism is justified by history and that military conflict is inevitable, both between the great powers as well as their client-states in the form of "low-intensity conflicts." This is the case, the realists hold, because great powers are locked into a mutually destructive competition from which there is no escape. Attendant to this competition is Hobbes's often cited depiction of human life as the "war of all, against all." The law of self-defense and the rational desire for security combine to effectuate a strategy designed to ensure self-preservation. In this view, all human beings are characterized as little more than rational egoists, in the sense that their dominant concern is the satisfaction of their passions. On the other hand, others believe that humans may institute a commonwealth by institution-building and mutual contract. A Hobbesian commonwealth may be established by pledging to one another to cede all our rights except the right of self-preservation (Doyle, 1997, pp. 114–115). But that is an authoritarian political arrangement, not a democratic one. In either of these two scenarios, the state of nature and our assumptions about it predominate in shaping political views and the dominant political consensus.

Although various scholars (e.g., G. Kavka, 1986; J.W.N. Watkings, 1973; F.S. McNeilly, 1968) have pointed out a number of shortcomings in Hobbes's analysis and the methods used, nevertheless, a great deal of his thought remains fundamentally sound and, therefore, its philosophical structure and conclusions can fruitfully be used by both theoreticians of political life and social organization and policy makers. To appreciate Hobbes's vision of social organization, we must recover his basic argument about good governance and its fundamental elements.

Surprisingly, with the notable exception of those studies that address themselves to the entire philosophical structure of Hobbes's work, a great deal of scholarship has been very narrow, focusing only on the more coercive aspects of the sovereign. This interpretation, however, distorts the spirit of Hobbes's work in a variety of fundamental ways. In contrast to this reading of Hobbes, it may be argued that he placed his emphasis upon the establishment of the state and he provided a protocol for good governance. In other words, he outlined in his political works the necessary conditions for the formation of the *inclusionary state* (IS). In this endeavor, he sought to identify the nature of the relationship between a people and their government. He envisioned the realization of a social compact that was more inclusionary than his predecessors and contemporaries acknowledged.

1. Forming an Inclusionary Social Compact

This social compact was understood to be a compact within the borders of a sovereign nation-state. Such a compact may be understood as evolving within the context of well-developed constitutional institutions. By extrapolation, it can be argued that the world of the 20th century has produced many nations without well-developed constitutional institutions and that, as a direct consequence of that failure, these nations lie between anarchy and predation. It is for that reason that the Hobbesian dilemma persists.

Throughout parts of modern Europe, Asia, Africa, Latin America, and the Middle East, the state of nature has not been transcended in the post cold war world of the 1990s. Just the opposite has occurred. Rwanda, Haiti, Bosnia, and Kosovo are just a few examples of where the problems of anarchy versus order have been reborn. In these nations, the call to build *"democratic"* institutions remains largely empty because "democracy is a vessel that has to be filled with content" (Brezinski, 1993, p. 75). Understood in this way, the democratic political process may be seen as the conveyor of a vibrant constitutional system which protects the sovereignty of law, but "democracy by itself does not provide the answers to the dilemmas of social existence and especially to the definition of the good life. That role is played by culture and philosophy—which together generate the values that motivate and shape social behavior" (*Id.*, p. 75). It follows, then, that if culture and philosophy are responsible for providing democracy with its unique content—nation to nation—then the formation of a commonwealth of persons in a vibrant civil society, with strong political institutions capable of securing the peace, and a normative constitutional order, are the prerequisites for both peace and development in all of its forms.

Robert Keohane has acknowledged as much in his observation about the enduring importance of the concept of sovereignty in zones of conflict. He admits that sovereignty "in the zones of conflict may retain its traditional role, moderating the effects of anarchy by conferring supreme authority over delimited territories and populations and, as in the sixteenth- and seventeenth-century Europe, erecting barriers to intervention and universalization of strife" (Keohane, 1995, p. 182). Similarly, Mahmood Mamdani has stressed the fact that the history of Europe itself teaches us that a nation is a cultural community, living on a common territory and that "its self-determination requires that it create its own state." He also acknowledges that "we forgot that, in the making of nation-states, Europe went through an entire history of ethnic cleansing" (Mamdani, March/April 1996, p. 34). The eventual outcome, in most cases, was a situation in which the sovereign nation-state branded cultural minorities as permanent "national minorities" alongside the cultural majority of the nation. In this sense, what emerged was a series of multi-cultural and no uni-cultural, communities (*Id.*, p. 34).

2. In Search of a Commonwealth

Chapter XIX of *Leviathan* identifies three different forms of commonwealths: *monarchy, democracy, and aristocracy*. In explicating the difference between them, Hobbes states that: "the difference between these three kindes of Common-wealth, consisteth not in the difference of Power, but in the difference of Convenience, or Aptitude to produce the Peace, and Security of the people; for which end they were instituted." (Hobbes, *Leviathan*, Cambridge, p. 131). The very institution or inauguration of a Commonwealth is predicated on establishing "rules of the game" of statecraft that places the protection of the peace, for all classes of people within the nation, as a matter of first priority.

The standard by which the success of governance is to be judged, in Hobbes's vision, is by the way in which government effectuates a peace— that is, an *aptitude* to produce peace. The words "convenience" and "aptitude" are meant to emphasize Hobbes's sensitivity to the *culture* of the people and need of government to accommodate the *culture* so as not to violate the well-being of the subjects and the purposes for which government was instituted in the first place. Therefore, even when a Commonwealth is formed and the people submit to it, the formation of the Commonwealth does not create a dictatorship. Rather, Hobbes states that "what Liberty we deny ourselves" is the result of free will when political power is transferred to "the Man, or Assembly we make our Sovereign" (*Id.*, p. 150). Once the people submit to the authority of the Leviathan, whether in the form of an individual man or an assembly, a dialectic of power is created between leader and led. As Hobbes states: "For in the act of our Submission, consisteth both our Obligation, and our Liberty; which must therefore be inferred by arguments taken from thence." (*Id.*, p. 150).

The power of the state, as expressed by Hobbes, does not hold that only an absolute government has a claim on its subject's obedience. Neither does Hobbes suggest that subjects could be justified in resisting the commands of a mixed or limited government. What does this mean? It means that establishing an absolutist form of government is less central to Hobbes's theory of the power and authority of the state than establishing an unconditional obligation to obey any effective government, no matter what its form.

Put in its most basic terms, Hobbes argues that if a government is not effective, the citizens lose their moral reasons for obeying it (Lloyd, 1992, p. 293). Obligation on the part of the citizenry is to be expected from citizens, just as the effectiveness of government is to be expected from the state. Therefore, Hobbes's argument does not make political obedience conditional on the form of government at all (*Id.*, p. 293). Rather, what matters to Hobbes are the characteristics of good government— its effectiveness, its ability to protect the citizenry, and its maintaining its strength to effectuate the peace.

The characteristics of what constitutes good government in the 20th century involve a matrix of concerns, ranging from citizenship to immigration laws, asylum laws and border controls, dealing with the emerging crisis in unemployment rates and rising levels of poverty. Today, in the European Union, over 20 million citizens are unemployed and 55 million citizens are living in relative poverty (Beck, van der Maesen, and Walker, 1997, p. 274). In short, there is a fertile soil for social tensions. Some of those tensions are the product over the contested terrain of what constitutes citizenship and what rights are inherent in the idea and practice of citizenship.

Modern states identify a particular set of persons as their citizens, while labeling others as non-citizens or aliens. As a consequence of this, the legal debate on citizenship, throughout Europe, is closely tied to discussions of social and cultural policy, as well as societal tolerance. Citizenship is no longer simply a result of constructing a legal formula, but is more and more a salient social and cultural fact. As Lemke has noted: "The mutual inclusion of citizens of member states in the European Union, with its cross-cutting cleavages and multilayered foci of self- and group-identification, has simultaneously been accompanied by the exclusion of nationals from non-EU-members" (Lemke, 1997, p. 86). The phenomenon of political exclusion, even what I have called "democratic exclusion," haunts Western states. According to Christian Joppke, "The multiplication of membership categories, which goes along with the rise of post-national membership, and the resistance of immigrants to assimilate . . . point to a crisis of citizenship in Western states" (Joppke, 1998, p. 23).

Both the crisis of citizenship and the issue of what constitutes good government, beg the question: "How much concentration of power is rational for a large defensive group to adopt?" Hobbes lived in a time when seven major wars and a long civil war had devastated England's chances for peace. Therefore, Hobbes sought lasting security in his model for the state and the conditions he perceived as essential for bringing about an end to these wars and creating the basis for long-term stability. In the 20th century, humankind has learned that "security" per se is not enough if it is defined in purely military terms. For security involves the security of the person against governmental abuse and encroachment. True security involves the realization and enforcement of human and civil rights through laws, institutions, policies and practices. If we allow the notion of security to be too narrowly defined so that it never reaches escape velocity, we shall remain trapped within the narrow confines of the Hobbesian security dilemma.

Because Hobbes depicts people as forward-looking and guided by egoism, he believes that such individuals would opt for a concentration of power in three critical areas. According to Kavka, these three areas are: (1) the ability to field and support enough military forces to deter or repel foreign invaders; (2) the ability to authoritatively settle disputes within the group and to put down challenges to its own authority; and (3) the ability to provide citizens with sufficient security against one another so that they are not forced to engage in self-help actions which could lead to escalating cycles of violence (Kavka, p. 165). In all three of these areas, Hobbes believed that there had to be a concentration of power that would be substantial enough to meet any one of these challenges.

Therefore, Hobbes's foundation for the state is premised on what rational state-of-nature parties would opt for in terms of security arrangements. Hobbes's own historical circumstances led him to adopt the view that real and lasting security could only be obtained under the auspices of an absolute sovereign—that is, a single individual or an assembly with unlimited authority to act for all members of the group. The primary reason for reaching this conclusion was Hobbes's conviction that such a concentration of power is both necessary and sufficient to prevent civil war.

However, we find that as history unfolds from Hobbes's time such a view is disconfirmed. History disconfirms the efficacy of centralized governments and dictatorships (as well as aristocracy and monarchy) in effectuating the desired goals that Hobbes envisioned. In examining the political cycles of non-democracies and the problem of transition to democracy, Alberto Alesina has observed that "immediately before dictators are overthrown, they employ the worst opportunistic and self-interested policies." He cites two reasons. First, collapsing dictators realize they have no future so any consideration of good economic management is secondary to their interest in remaining politically viable. Second, if a dictator perceives his span of remaining time in power as short, he may steal the wealth for himself and his cadre of supporters (Alesina, 1994, p. 46).

Further, a closer examination of what Hobbes meant by absolute sovereignty shows that Hobbes differentiated between "powers of exercise" and "powers of selection" in the sovereign authority. Powers of exercise involved the powers to enforce laws, command troops, and collect taxes. Powers of selection are those powers which allow for choosing persons who shall or shall not be in positions of governmental power. This distinction is significant for, as Kavka notes: "Such an arrangement has the apparent advantage of precluding stalemates between branches of government which could lead to civil war, by having an ultimate authority who can break the deadlock by removing and replacing one (or both) of the contending parties, or threatening to do so" (Kavka, pp. 166–167). Therefore, Hobbes wrote retrospectively about his times. His reflections on the coercive aspects of government do not survive the scrutiny of time and history. We can, therefore, disavow the coercive aspects of his political theory as being antithetical to the demands and requirements of good governance.

I maintain, throughout this book, that good governance is best depicted as "governing by inclusion." The significance of governing by inclusion is borne out through decision-making processes which reflect the principle of equal participation and the recognition and inclusion of the poor and marginalized in making policies which impact on all major social groups within a society. In addressing the task of economic and political development, *democratic inclusion* in decision making is critical throughout the First and Third World. As Peter Berger has noted: "Development is not what the economic and other experts proclaim it to be, no matter how elegant their language. Development is not something to be decided by experts, simply because there are no experts on the desirable goals of human life. Development is the desirable course to be taken by human beings in a particular situation. As far as possible, therefore, they ought to participate in the fundamental choices to be made, choices that hinge not on technical expertise but on moral judgments" (Berger, 1976, p. 59).

Governing by inclusion is an approach to development that makes participation and inclusion the cornerstone of policy and practice. Governing by inclusion forces developmental states and developmental policies to recognize and to respect governing as more than "managing the tensions" and more than "containing participatory and distributive demands." Governing by inclusion transcends the language of manipulation and control. In this critical sense, democracy is, of necessity, a subset of inclusion because the resolution of ethnopolitical conflicts in institutionalized democracies depends most fundamentally on the implementation of universalistic norms of equal rights and opportunities for all citizens. Of course, this includes ethnoclasses and appreciates the need for the pluralistic accommodation of indigenous and regional peoples' desires for separate collective status (Gurr, 1993, p. 137).

Back to the Future 229

When we look back 350 years, hindsight allows us to appreciate Hobbes's preoccupation with coercive power, but that should not be divorced from the inclusionary elements of his theory which charted a different path. Although, at this point, an argument can be made in principle in favor of centralized government, as well as sequencing political and economic evolution, nevertheless this principle is not borne out by history. Coercive governments, throughout history, have turned dictatorial, cleptocratic and corrupt. In short, their long run efficacy is dubious, to say the least. We would need a long table to enumerate the evidence provided by history in support of this statement. In this sense, therefore, I do not subscribe to the coercive aspects of Hobbes's theory. I accept fully, however, the implicit and explicit aspects of inclusionary governance as the means by which long-run stability can be achieved. This was ultimately to be achieved through the virtues of limited government.

3. The Virtues of Limited Government

Within a generation of Hobbes, John Locke argued for the virtues of limited government. Locke saw the benefits of checks and balances as a means to avoid the pitfalls of absolute government. Absolute government, in his view, tended to blind, corrupt, and compromise its proper role toward all classes, interests and groups, thereby leading to an exclusionary form of governance. As a consequence of such exclusion, violence, civil wars and rebellions could jeopardize the prospects of developmental enterprise. Given this, Locke's critique demonstrates that it is necessary to qualify how Hobbes's view is correct.

Hobbes view of limited government must be counter-balanced with the realization that its limitations need not inevitably lead to civil war and rebellion. This is so for a number of reasons. First, in systems of limited government (with checks and balances), officials or bodies that share power in a system of divided government will be strongly motivated to compromise. As the compromise of differences moves ahead, these officials may, among themselves, develop the abilities to coordinate their actions to promote peace and defense, because all parties realize that they have much to lose. Among those things that may be lost are their present power, their status, their wealth, and potentially their very lives, in a civil war or a collapse of the state itself. So, in order to avoid war or governmental paralysis, power-sharing officials will probably be inclined to effectuate compromise and, in so doing, effect a politics of inclusion.

I argue that inclusionary governance is a prescription for peace and long-term stability and provides the framework for economic growth and development, as well as the framework for democratic inclusion by constructing legal rules and norms that can empower new constitutionally constructed institutions that promote social justice by dealing more effectively with the "social question." In this interpretation, long-term stability is achieved through a reconfiguration of citizenship and the advancement of those rights, through state, market, and civil society that can transcend narrowly defined, exclusionary and egoistic agendas.

On this matter, S.A. Lloyd's examination of Hobbes's argument has stressed that "Hobbes does indeed think an absolutist form of government is, for practical reasons, preferable to any other, but I don't believe he thought that only an unlimited and undivided government could be effective . . . The question is one, not of effectiveness at a time, or simpliciter, but of long-term stability" (S.A. Lloyd, 1992, p. 294). The key point, then, what is of crucial theoretical importance, is that citizens come to believe that they have sufficient reason to obey any effective government unconditionally (*Id.*, p. 294).

This view of Hobbes's theory of state power and the nature of government resonates with Hendrik Spruyt's historical review of the evolution of the sovereign state. Spruyt has argued that feudalism did not give way to any single successor institution in a simple linear fashion. The present international system, composed mainly of sovereign, territorial states, is not the inevitable outcome of historical development. In the aftermath of feudalism's demise there were many competing institutional alternatives ranging from urban leagues, independent communes, city states and sovereign monarchies.

According to Spruyt, "sovereignty need not imply absolutism. Even Hobbes recognized that sovereignty could take the form of parliamentary rule. But within sovereign states there existed a final decision-making structure which brooked no outside interference and which gradually claimed a monopoly on violence and justice. In addition, the sovereign state confined itself territorially. That is, sovereigns claimed hierarchy within borders and recognized no higher authority" (Spruyt, 1994, p. 153).

State power may be seen as emanating from three sources. First, under the notion of sovereignty and territorial boundaries, citizens within such boundaries were subject to the logic of territorial organization, which had replaced alternative modes of authority in Europe. This notion of sovereignty, then, is central to understanding Hobbes's political theory for his theory takes the notion of sovereignty as its starting point. Second, institutions that internally possessed such final decision-making authority were in a better position to overcome the feudal remnants of economic and legal particularism (*Id.*, p. 155). That is why Hobbes argues for the "effectiveness" of state power and requires a corresponding obedience of citizens/subjects to the commands of the state. Third, this newly emergent sovereign state now had evolved institutions that were, comparatively speaking, "more effective and more efficient in curtailing freeriding and defection, and hence they were better equipped at mobilizing the resources of their societies"(*Id.*, p. 155). This increased and enhanced capacity for mobilizing the resources of society led, naturally, to the state's power to claim a monopoly on violence and justice. Such a monopoly of power could, in the final analysis, produce the conditions for peace which, in turn, could lay the groundwork for more universal forms of prosperity and economic growth and development. This analysis, therefore, brings us full circle in understanding the nature of state power, as conceived in Hobbes's political theory.

In other words, the obligation that the people have toward their sovereign exists only insofar as he protects their liberty and property through maintaining the peace. After all, in the original state of nature, before this social contract was enacted with the Leviathan, people lived without any obligation toward one another or a central authority. In order to advance their protection and enjoy their liberty without fear of an untimely death or the random scourge of violence, the people are co-authors of a social covenant which contains "the rules of the game" and certain "protocol" which is enforced by the Leviathan (one man or an assembly).

Still, as Hobbes stresses, "The Obligation of Subjects to the Sovereign is understood to last as long, and no longer, than the power lasteth, by which he is able to protect them" (*Id.*, p. 153) Hence, the power of the Leviathan is to last only as long as that power can offer sufficient protection. Should the Leviathan fail to extend such protection, then the people may reclaim the liberty which they had voluntarily surrendered, "for the right of Nature to protect themselves, when none else can protect them, can by no Covenant be relinquished" (p. 153). Hence the protection of the people, in Hobbes's vision, within a particular institutional framework, leads to the perpetuation of the state.

Again, the perpetuation of the State should be understood to be under the rubric of "sovereignty," for "sovereignty simultaneously provides an ordering principle for what is 'internal' to states and what is 'external' to them. It presumes a system of rule that is universal and obligatory in relation to the citizenry of a specified territory but from which all those who are not citizens are excluded" (Giddens, 1985, p. 281). When sovereignty is defined in this way, it is easier to argue that the incorporation and inclusion of all citizens, groups, and classes into the political processes of the nation-state was intended by Hobbes's discussion on the duty of the sovereign to protect his subjects and that from such protection and the effectiveness of that protection a reciprocal political obedience was due to the state.

For Hobbes, the form of governance does not matter as much as the way in which government structures and enforces strategies for including all classes, interests and groups under a common rubric. To be sure, the common cultural values and religious principles forged by the Christian church in 17th century England made cultural inclusivity much more attainable. Still, the economic and political exclusivity of the Stuarts and Tudors tore apart any emerging cultural consensus until a central political authority, based on common principles, emerged. Hobbes's major contribution, therefore, is not found in his mediations concerning force and coercion.

Practical and efficient as force and coercion may be for bringing about short-term periods of peace, they only guarantee a respite between civil wars. In other words, enduring peace and sociopolitical stability demands adherence to a bond between and among subjects, as well as ruler and ruled, that is founded upon concepts of "fairness," legitimacy, and the protection of and respect for certain human rights. To put it differently, what is required is a government of laws and not mere men. Over 350 years later, at the close of the 20th century, the same challenges persists. The challenge is for societies in both the First World and the Third World to distinguish between the "rule of law" and "rule by law."

E. THE "RULE OF LAW" VERSUS "RULE BY LAW"

Hobbes's vision is informed by two central views on law. The first involves the unwritten laws of nature. The second involves the legitimacy of law itself as valid only when the people are able to acknowledge written laws as emanating from the Sovereign himself, in whom they have vested their faith and reposed their hope and aspirations.

As to the first point, Hobbes states: "The Laws of Nature therefore need not any publishing, nor Proclamation, as being contained in this one Sentence, approved by all the world, 'Do not that to another, which thou thinkest unreasonable to be done by another to theself" (p. 188). Hence, Hobbes argues for common principles of fairness and of a shared expectation among people, by virtue of their being human, as entitling them to a basic recognition of their common humanity and therefore deserving of certain basic dignities. In other words, good governance first emerges from the hearts of people. Nature, conceived of as man's natural "state," itself offers proof of what man's essence is and how, by extrapolation, it should be expressed in the context of a civil society. The notion of equal treatment, which Hobbes subscribes to, is premised on the "Golden Rule," but it also speaks to an inclusivity of persons in the sense that they are entitled to certain forms of treatment, by conduct, that reflect human mutuality and are an acknowledgment of our common condition.

As to the second point, Hobbes states: "Nor is it enough the Law be written, and published; but also that there be manifest signs, that it proceedeth from the will of the Sovereign" (*Id.*, p. 189). Hobbes's insistence on establishing the source and validity of the law proceeds from the fact that, in the inclusivity of governance established by the Leviathan, by "Man or by Assembly," such governance must always prove itself to be fair, and not arbitrary in a way that de-legitimates it in the eyes of those who are affected by virtue of their own self interest.

In some general sense, therefore, Hobbes introduces a contract theory which seeks to both justify and explain various social arrangements and institutions that rational people would adopt and create for specific purposes and under quite specific conditions. Hobbes's thoughts concerning this social contract should not be perceived as the foundation of a theory of social justice such as contemporary authors like John Rawls and David Gauthier have attempted to provide (Rawls, 1978; Gauthier, 1986). Instead, Hobbes's social compact theory attempts to identify the conditions a social organization called the state must satisfy so that individual agents (citizens) must feel obliged to obey its rules. To put it differently, Hobbes's social contract theory seeks to provide an understanding of the necessary and/or sufficient conditions for political obligation, thereby identifying the circumstances under which the state attains moral legitimacy.

Hobbes's insistence on establishing both the source and validity of the laws that are enacted and imposed still echoes down the corridors of history and into the praxis of 20th century Third World states. For example, many Asian governments, since the 1980s, have begun to modify laws and legal institutions which are primarily related to their commercial affairs. The extent and scope of these modifications has been extremely narrow insofar as these changes usually stop short of subordinating government's power to the law. In fact, from Malaysia to Taiwan and Indonesia, from South Korea to China, these limited efforts to modify the law while leaving governmental power to operate "above the law" has led to criticisms that these efforts "are better understood as efforts to achieve *rule by law* than the *rule of law*" (Carothers, 1998, p. 101).

1. Overcoming the "Negligent Government of Princes"

Society, as a collective endeavor and as a collective creation, exhibits different traits and is affected by different laws and limitations in its evolution and unfolding. In this respect, while man is a social animal and requires the society and interaction of other persons, the individual still remains an individual capable of unilateral decisions and unilateral actions. It is this rather one-sided dimension to man's being and character that creates the difficulties for the realization of political community that both Plato and Hobbes confronted in their political theories.

To be sure, both Plato and Hobbes sought the perpetuation of their political communities. But what makes Hobbes's idea of a Commonwealth different from Plato's stratified "Republic" is that the guardians of order and of the status quo are removed by Hobbes. In their place, Hobbes places principles and characteristics of "good governance." This is what I have identified as inclusionary governance. And, as noted in our introduction, inclusive governance for Hobbes means that obligations and liberties must achieve a certain balance under the Leviathan. This governing "balance" matters more than the form of governance or the label that one attaches to it. Hence, it matters little whether England is called a democracy or aristocracy or monarchy; what is crucial is that the peace is established for all groups. In some sense, Hobbes seems to argue that you cannot have social inclusivity without having political and economic inclusivity. Further, you cannot have political inclusivity without having economic inclusivity.

Inclusivity, in the last analysis, should be defined by including its economic, political, cultural, and social dimensions. As these dimensions are placed into proper relationship by balancing obligation with liberty, shared values and common principles emerge which, in turn, create a common practice that all social groups understand and are made to adhere to by the rule of law. The resulting peace among classes, groups, and interests allows for the flourishing and evolution of civil society, the stability of the state, and shared expectations regarding contract and property laws and the role of markets. From this it follows that peace provides the preconditions for economic growth and development as well as effective political institutionalization. Effective political institutionalization, of a democratic variety, was unique to Europe. According to Brian M. Downing, "Europe was . . . the first—and, unfortunately, virtually the last—to develop democratic political systems that featured institutional checks on political monopoly, varying but frequently increasing degrees of political representation, chartered rights of citizenship, and the rule of law" (Downing, 1992, p. 18).

As established rules of political and economic conduct are put into place, reflective of an emerging consensus of the society's aspirations and objective needs, the nature of inclusionary governance itself may be evaluated from an objective point of view. In other words, insofar as inclusionary governance is guided primarily by certain basic characteristics and principles, the practical effect is the removal of decision making, strategies, policies from the realm of greed and subjective application into the realm of identifying and pursuing the national welfare. As Marcus Raskin has noted: "By definition, modern democracy is committed to all people being active subjects of their own history. Democratic adherents accept the potentiality and the common sense of all people. The result is that a common good may be forged" (Raskin, 1986, p. 37). The pursuit of the common good establishes the goals for inclusionary governance. In turn, inclusionary governance is dedicated to the realization of the common good. In short, inclusionary governance itself becomes the acknowledgment of the mutuality of persons and a commonalty of purpose and allows the realization of the benefits of cooperation. It is only the failure to establish this mutuality of persons and commonalty of purpose that makes life ugly, brutish, and short. This realization is at the heart of the Hobbesian legacy of the Commonwealth. It is also the driving force behind inclusionary governance and the moral, political, social, cultural, and economic mandate to govern by inclusion.

The mutuality of persons and commonalty of purpose that I refer to is objectively grounded in the historical evolution of Europe during the period between the incomplete collapse of the Carolingian Empire in the 9th century and that of the Holy Roman Empire in the 13th. From the 9th to the 13th century a rough balance was struck between crown and nobility. From the 13th century onward, we see the reemergence of imperial or princely authority. This was then followed by contest between center and locality (Downing, 1992, p. 19). According to Downing, "from this set of circumstances emerged compromises, power sharing, and a climate of partial trust and partial mistrust, which informed much medieval constitutionalism before it settled into a stable system of consensual government" (*Id.*, p. 19).

The contest between center and locality provides the objective historical context in which to begin speaking of hierarchy, marginalization, and eventual inclusion into decision making as we analyze economic, social, cultural, and political development. For example, had the marginalization of the locality as compared to the center been reinforced, rising levels of violence could easily have halted the thrust of medieval constitutionalism. In the absence of such a marginalization, medieval constitutionalism contributed to the accelerated political institutionalization of not only the politically centralized state but also representative assemblies. Representative assemblies, in turn, allowed for the incorporation and inclusion of all major classes, interests, and groups which could affect the nation's welfare and the direction of its development in a multitude of contexts.

According to Gunner Lind, "the Eighteenth Century state was only modern to a limited extent by the standards of today. However, it differed greatly from what could have been found two or three centuries before." (Lind, 1996, p. 139). The modern state that evolved was, in Lind's view, the embodiment of three attributes. The first was found in the very nature of the state, the "Machtstaat" or "power state." The power state possessed a permanent army and was capable of quelling any internal opposition. Certainly, such a capacity was expressed, as we noted earlier, in Hobbes's vision for the Leviathan. Only in this way could the Hobbesian principle of preservation triumph and order, stability, and peace emerge from the chaos of civil wars and the "negligent government of princes." The second attribute of the modern state was to be found in its political centralization. According to Lind, "where they had not been swept away by royal absolutism, representative assemblies formed part of the center" (Id., p. 139). In other words, inclusionary governance, as exemplified by representative assemblies, made possible the legitimation of state activity, which included both regular taxation and law making. The twin forces of taxes and laws also helped to contribute to the three conditions which Downing has identified as providing Europe with a predisposition to democracy: "a rough balance between crown and nobility, decentralized military systems, and peasant property rights and reciprocal ties to the landlord" (Downing, 1992, p. 19). In combination, these three elements forced political centralization without producing a command economy. The third attribute of the modern state is to be found in the development of bureaucratic procedures. The state developed a cadre of servants for the state which made for a degree of professionalization in the arena of government service. The net result of all three of these attributes contributed to producing an environment where "patron-client relations had to be transformed by the change" (Lind, 1996, pp. 139–140).

With the expansion of the state through its increased power, its centrality, and the growth of a professional bureaucracy, the state had gained a monopoly on violence. What this meant in terms of political hierarchy and privilege was that the state could bring something new to the table in terms of patron-client relations. According to Gunner Lind, "changed notions of legitimacy enhanced the power of centrally placed patrons to the detriment of local ones" (Id., p. 140). This outcome created a lasting change. It was an enduring change in spite of the remaining opponents of centralization, because their disobedience was subdued by state power and their revolts could be easily defeated (Id., p. 140). The end result of this evolution was a narrowing of all patron-client networks, with the exception of the king's. In fact, the royal network broadened and changed. (Id., p. 141).

From the 13th century to the 17th century of Hobbes, there would be tension between clientelism and inherited privilege on the one hand, and the use of and legitimation by universalist principles on the other. Yet the tension was ultimately resolved as European states moved beyond the modernized monarchies of the 18th century. (Id., p. 145). Hobbes's vision had been critical for England's own transition insofar as he helped provide a governing vision which never exposed the nation to protracted warfare, with its requirement of large modern armies. In place of armies, constitutional government prevailed (Downing, 1992, p. 179).

Hobbes recognized that the collective maintenance, order, and stability of a given society will not be realizable if the individuals within that order are unrestrained and remain ungoverned or ungovernable by virtue of either the failure of an overriding principle of social organization or of the coercive force of a political power; i.e., a power that is not sufficiently equipped to control what would otherwise remain controllable. Restraint and control, order and stability, are the central tenets of concern that characterize the political philosophies of both Hobbes and Plato.

For Hobbes, the English Civil War took a similar toll on the possibilities for the realization of political community. His argument traced man's history from a brutal and brutish "state of nature" characterized by insecurity and misery, without government and without law, to the necessity for government formulated under Leviathan—the absolute Sovereign, in whom all political power, as a decisive power, would reside. This would enable the transitional leap from the state of nature to the state of a civil society, and guarantee the longevity of that civil society by ensuring compliance with a centralized rule which determined how elites as well as yeoman were to be held accountable in terms of advancing the national interest, as identified by the sovereign, under the rubric of the principle of preservation.

As I argued earlier, one of the major challenges for Hobbes was to determine the parameters of the Leviathan's rule. After all, the English Civil Wars exposed the corrosive dangers of having many different centers of power at odds with one another across the broad spectrum of society. How could English society be organized and ordered so as to avoid the violence that resulted from the conflicting claims of barons, dukes and other elites? Under the minimalist view of the sovereign's rights, the sovereign's powers were limited by his representative character. The representational aspect of the sovereign, as conceived by Hobbes, was not merely a reflection of his place and power, as subject to natural law.

I argue that the sovereign's representational character is also reflective of the inclusive nature of his governance. In fact, it is the very fact of its inclusivity that gave legitimacy to the sovereign's rights and prescribed the parameters of his power. As exemplified in *Leviathan*, Chapter 19, the preservation principle is expressly detailed as the "Convenience, or Aptitude to produce the Peace, and Security of the people" (*Id.*, p. 131). After all, the Commonwealth itself was "instituted" to achieve such a result. Correspondingly, it became the chief duty of the sovereign to make sure that the purposes for which the Commonwealth was instituted were realized in practice. In short, in the realm of rights and duties, a balance had to be struck.

Although I do not subscribe to the coercive aspects of Hobbes's theory, as mentioned earlier, it is worth recognizing that Hobbes reduced the sovereign's power below that which was traditionally acceptable. In Chapter 21 of *Leviathan*, Hobbes stressed that individual rights of resistance applied only to situations where the person's survival was in question. Hence, a sovereign in his capacity as representative of the people was entitled to enforce on his people only those things which he believed necessary for their preservation. If he went beyond this limit, his subjects would not have to accept his judgment. In fact, equipped with no natural right to do so, the sovereign would be breaking the law of nature. If the subject resisted the will of the sovereign, the subject would also act without benefit of right. Since Hobbes was primarily preoccupied with the realm of rights and duties, he concluded Chapter 31 with a somber observation on the consequences of the violation of rights by subject and sovereign by noting that punishment would come in the form of the "*Negligent government of Princes, with Rebellion; and Rebellion, with slaughter*" (*Id.*, p. 254). Such would be the consequence of serious violations of the principle of preservation.

The principle of preservation allowed England to subdue the internal challenges and pressures that were generated by social and political instability. The "Negligent government of princes" was, after all, the embodiment of England's civil discord. In turn, this discord, if allowed to continue, could lead to economic, social, and political implosion. In order to avoid this consequence, Hobbes presented a prescription to deal with political violence and discord which would help to create the peaceful conditions for England to grow internally while, at the same time, preparing itself to meet any external challenge that might confront it. Therefore, all other things being equal, it can be argued that the preservation of the state entails the ability of a state to meet challenges from within and/or outside the state. This dual capacity to govern effectively involves the ability of the state to centralize decision making on the one hand, while expanding participation through a widening of domestic inclusivity on the other.

Internal challenges are most effectively met by a centralization of decision making coupled with a broadening of political and social avenues of inclusivity. The combination of these factors should result in a reduction of political violence and deadly conflict. This, in turn, allows the economy to grow. This argument, however, should not be understood as an endorsement of an authoritarian or autocratic Leviathan. For a review of the historical landscape, both before and after Hobbes, reveals that, with few notable exceptions, Leviathans in general have abused their power. The adage that "power corrupts and absolute power corrupts absolutely" has been borne out time and again by history. Therefore, how a state meets its internal challenges, organizes the society, and forms links between itself and the civil society, involves varying degrees of "embeddedness" in and "autonomy" from the society itself.

What finally governs the degree of a state's embeddedness and autonomy are the principles of exclusive versus inclusive governance, particularistic values versus universalistic values. For example, the more particularistic the values of a state, the more likely it will be that the state will be intrusive on the civil society and seek the promotion and perpetuation of a limited constituency. Such a route will result in the various forms of aristocratic governance and absolutism that have disfigured and even halted the development and evolution of inclusionary societies and states. The exclusionary state, after all, is the kind of Leviathan that is involved in the practice of nepotism, the protection of a cleptocratic state, and is not concerned with the disfranchisement of the non-privileged classes who remain victimized by its particularistic agenda. In the long run, such states do not long endure. In Lincoln's phrase, a government "of the people, by the people, and for the people" is the basis for long-term inclusionary governance with universalistic values that fulfill aspirations for and expressions of political, social, economic and cultural freedom.

Further, the inclusionary state is better equipped to compete with external challenges. The conclusion that may be drawn is that whether external challenges will succeed often depends upon the ability of the state to answer its internal challenges. This, in turn, depends on the degree of inclusivity that the state practices. Hence, Hobbes's analysis is a prescription for reducing social and political violence and deadly conflict. It is a lesson whose relevance remains just as forceful at the close of the 20th century as it was in the middle of the 17th century.

2. Egoistic Man and the Absolute Sovereign

In response to his efforts, Hobbes was denounced on all sides, finding himself at odds with both constitutional royalists and Puritans who abhorred his completely secular premises. Characteristic of the Renaissance, his philosophy is oriented toward the secular realities of life in this world as opposed to seeking an other-worldly conformity with the transcendent possibilities contained within Revelation. Yet even his secular vision of power and the nature of man shared much in common with the Medieval vision of man as fallen, sinful, egoistic and turned inward on himself (Huntington, 1984, p. 218).

The egoistic man must be dealt with. The natural duty of the sovereign is to assure the safety of the people under conditions of anarchy. Therefore, we find that there exist two arguments for a Hobbesian pacification. According to Michael Doyle, "one is a matter of moral duty; the other, of rational egoism. A Hobbesian Realist could argue that peace could be the outcome of prudent diplomacy guided by effective moral duties." (Doyle, 1997, pp. 123–124). *Government, according to Hobbes, is charged with the making and execution of laws and using its power to enforce them. Without genuine strength the laws themselves become useless and the pursuit of justice is rendered powerless*. Law becomes a vital force in a civil society only when the institutional powers of government have power and are capable of using that power whenever the occasion requires. In fact, Hobbes argues that sovereigns have a natural duty not to act against "the reasons of peace . . . Dominions were constituted for peace's sake, and peace was sought for safety's sake" (Hobbes, *De Cive*, in *The English Works of Thomas Hobbes*, London: J. Bohn, 1874, vol. 2, pp. 166–167).

In Chapter 20 of *Leviathan*, Hobbes distinguishes between two forms of governance, or "dominion." One form is paternal and the other is despotic. He differentiates the two by noting that one form of Commonwealth exists by virtue of "acquisition" while the other form is created by "institution." In the first instance, Hobbes states that a Commonwealth by acquisition is "acquired by Force" and that a man or assembly "hath their lives and liberty in his power." In the second instance, the dominion or sovereignty of the Leviathan in a Commonwealth which exists by virtue of institution differs from that of acquisition in only one way: "That men who choose their Sovereign, do it for fear of one another, and not of him whom they Institute." (Hobbes, *Leviathan*, Cambridge, p. 138).

Does this distinction have any real effect upon the power of the sovereign? That is, does it matter whether the Commonwealth has been the product of either institution or acquisition? Hobbes answers: "But the Rights and Consequences of Sovereignty, are the same in both. His Power cannot, without his consent, be Transferred to another: He cannot Forfeit: He cannot be Accused by any of his Subjects, of Injury: He cannot be Punished by them: He is Judge of what is necessary for Peace; and Judge of Doctrines . . ." (*Id.*, p. 139). In short, because of the primacy that is placed upon establishing and maintaining the peace, Hobbes's sovereign is beyond reproach so long as he does not violate the preservation of his subjects. Again, it is because of the principle of preservation that the sovereign's power is absolute as between social forces and elites. After all, they do not trust each other, so they have vested all power and authority in the sovereign. That is why the rights and consequences of sovereignty are the same whether the Commonwealth exists by virtue of institution or of acquisition.

The egoistic man is made subject to the will of the sovereign both for the sake of the survival of the individual subjects and, by extension, for the sake of the survival of the society. What we see, then, is a two-pronged approach by Hobbes. One prong is that of enforcement. The absolute power of the Leviathan is derived from the consent of the governed so that subjects, who fear one another, may be protected from one another by virtue of having vested their very lives under the protective wings of their sovereign who (by institution or acquisition) guides, protects and sustains the Commonwealth. The second prong is found in the sovereign's ability to provide the conditions for peace so that a social compact between groups and classes and elites might be effectuated and sustained. Both the right of the sovereign to rule absolutely and the integrity of the commonwealth itself are established by the "covenant" that is made by all social classes, groups, and interests. It is not a situation of victor and vanquished, as would be the case in war. Hobbes is explicit on this point. He states: "It is not therefore the Victory, that giveth the right of Dominion over the Vanquished, but his own Covenant" (*Id.*, p. 141). It is consent, not victory as in war, that establishes the foundation of the covenant between groups and between groups and their sovereign.

In summary, the *first* prong of his prescription for governance, which is enforcement of all legitimate sovereign laws and powers, does not, in and of itself, yield great results for peace or the maintenance of the commonwealth. For if it were sufficient by itself, then any despotism or dictatorship would do. Hobbes goes beyond this limited view. Rather, he also intones the admonition that consent of the governed and limits upon the sovereign's own powers, by virtue of the principle of preservation, must be part of the governing equation. Therefore, the *second* prong of governance, premised upon consent, also implies the principle of inclusivity. For it is by the inclusion of all major social actors that consent is rendered and peace is made possible. These two prongs, therefore, combine to create a social compact that is inviolable and that is to be honored and respected by the governed, subject to laws that clearly emanate from the sovereign in whom they have vested their trust and to whom they have submitted authoritative decision making.

When Hobbes combines the power of the sovereign with the conditions born of consent and sustained by the principle of preservation, which forged the social compact in the first place, he effectively spells out the nature of inclusionary governance. Inclusionary governance is the union of centralized political power with consenting subjects, dedicated to a social compact that preserves the peace while advancing the interests of all in the service of the national welfare. The principle of preservation is also the prescription for the maintenance of the Commonwealth and, in turn, the Commonwealth is the embodiment of the power of a unified people who find their strength in a unity of purpose that exists by virtue of practicing a politics of inclusivity. Submission does not mean slavery in this context. Rather, submission vests power in a sovereign to remove fear, war, and anarchy so that a commonwealth can emerge and with it a civil society. Out of this bonding come the fruits of commerce and cooperation, the pleasures of common purpose through a shared vision of what this political association of persons can render the nation both individually and collectively.

Hobbes's formulation regarding the absolute rule of the sovereign is an attempt to bring warring parties to the bargaining table in a negotiating process under the auspices of the centralized rule and authority of the Leviathan. The personhood of the Leviathan as absolute sovereign is infused with an almost divine majesty for, in the Hobbesian formulation, he is above the law and need only command others to obey it. This practical rendering of secular authority has its theological counterpart in the Reformation thought of Luther insofar as Luther posits that princes and other political officials are put in place because God has placed them there and ought to be respected and obeyed on that account (Marius, 1999, pp. 364–371). But what are we to understand about the particular characteristics of the type of governance envisioned by Hobbes? We shall examine this question next.

F. THE FOUNDING OF THE HOBBESIAN STATE

As already noted, Hobbes begins his political theory by making a number of assumptions concerning the nature and character of human beings as being forward-looking, risk-adverse, and predominantly self-interested creatures. As such, these self-interested agents seek to emerge from the "state of nature" and will seek a particular form of social organization that can "defend them from the invasion of foreigners, and the injuries of one another, and thereby to secure them in such sort, as that by their own industry, and by the fruits of the earth, they may nourish themselves and live contentedly" (Hobbes, *Leviathan*, Chapter 17, p. 157).

However, as human beings emerge from the state of nature, Hobbes warns against anarchy in any form. He warns that neither non-state defense groups nor a system of individualist anarchy can perform any of the aforementioned functions in an adequate or reliable manner. Therefore, Hobbes completes his argument about social organization by showing that the state (or some kinds of state) is better equipped to carry out the functions of defense with respect to foreign policy on the one hand, and the tasks of building a fruitful domestic Commonwealth on the other. Only through the state can imposition of the worst deprivations on citizens be avoided. From this fundamental argument, Hobbes sets forth a number of propositions.

Hobbes's first proposition is that the state is best equipped to perform the function of protecting its citizens. This first proposition follows directly from the definition of the state as "an organized society with a territory and a government, that is, a subgroup possessing a substantial enough concentration of power to generally enforce domestic decisions, discourage self-help, and deter external aggression" (Kavka, 1986, p. 179). While no one definition of the State is really appropriate in all contexts, it can at least be stated with certainty that this definition serves adequately in the Hobbesian argument against anarchy. In fact, one of the primary benefits of this definition of the state is its emphasis upon the idea that there must be a sufficient concentration of power in the state to provide real security against both internal and external dangers. The idea of a sufficient concentration of power in the state is inseparable from the reality of territory.

Territory is important to political governance, at least in part, because it provides a locus for the exercise of political authority over a broad range of interests and initiatives. Despite all of the changes in the conception, management and defense of territory, over the 300 years from Hobbes's time to the late 20th century, since before the signing of the Peace of Westphalia, the notion of territorial control has remained at the heart of political thought and life. Without a territorial base, it is doubtful whether political authority can be exerted over sets of institutions or issues that are part of an eduring system. In short, both the survival and success of sovereignty as an organizing principle of the modern state owes its importance and status to its territorial underpinnings (Murphy, 1996, p. 110).

Again, the emphasis upon the concentration of authority in the state is not an argument to establish a dictatorship, but rather to elaborate on the nature of sovereignty. To explicate what Hobbes means by absolute sovereignty, it is necessary to evaluate his argument by distinguishing between two kinds of governmental powers. There are "powers of exercise" and "powers of selection." Powers of exercise are those powers which encompass the following: the powers to make and enforce laws, command troops, collect taxes, and distribute or redistribute property. Juxtaposed to this are powers of selection. Powers of selection are powers of choosing which persons shall possess power of exercise. This allows for the removal and replacement of those who are in positions of governmental power. Hobbes's view is that those who possess powers of exercise are ministers of the sovereign. Direct powers of exercise and selection lie in different hands. Hobbes makes it clear that an elective king for life is only sovereign if he retains the power to appoint his successor, otherwise sovereignty lies in whosoever else possesses that power (Hobbes, *Leviathan*, Chapter 19). It is this power of appointment which is central in Hobbes's vision of absolute sovereignty.

What the power of appointment creates is a state wherein there is a built-in arrangement that precludes stalemates between branches of government which could lead to civil war. The exercise of absolute power and authority that is capable of breaking the deadlock by removing or replacing certain people in particular positions within the government has a salutary effect. But, as Kavka reminds us, "even on this interpretation, Hobbesian absolute sovereignty is neither sufficient nor necessary for preventing civil war" (Kavka, 1986, p. 167). First, it is not sufficient because those that are at risk of being removed may resist. Further, if the sovereign is an assembly, there may be sufficient support from within that assembly to aid those who are resisting removal. Hence, there is not only a prescription for civil war in this scenario but also the risk of military officers staging a coup to prevent being fired. Second, such absolute sovereignty is not necessary, in Hobbes's view, to prevent civil war. The fact that constitutional limits on governmental power exist are consistent with lasting order. The very fact of a division of powers among distinct governmental bodies serves to maintain order "even if different constituencies select members of different branches by different procedures" (Kavka, p. 167).

Hence, a more balanced view of a Hobbesian vision for the state and groups that contend for state power allows us to reject Hobbes's extreme views about the concentration of power. What security and order require are a sufficient concentration of certain governmental powers of exercise, not a total concentration of the power to select exercisers of unlimited powers (Kavka, p. 168). So, in order to bring the Hobbesian argument against anarchy full circle, what remains is to demonstrate how a "sufficient" concentration of power is needed to carry out the various protective functions of the state.

In the legal realm—the protection of property, dispute resolution through courts and an independent judiciary, and the enforcement of contracts—we find expressions of how a sufficient concentration of state power is essential for both social organization and the long-run maintenance of economic and social cooperation between and among classes. Spruyt has argued that before and during Hobbes's time, sovereigns (acting as territorial rulers) were "recognized as political entrepreneurs who had vested interests in decreasing the remnants of feudal economies. In standardizing coinage, reducing the number of weights and measures, and creating more legal certitude, they reduced transaction and information costs. The greater degree of internal hierarchy was also more suited to control freeriding and defection" (Spruyt, 1995, p. 166). These are examples of the internal aspects of the protective functions of the state.

Further, there are external aspects of the protective functions of the state that need to be identified. These aspects are, more often than not, associated with trade and the interests of merchants. It has been argued by historians that sovereign authorities took it upon themselves to regulate trade. This was an essential protective function of the state on behalf of merchants who, without such assistance, would be left to rely on self-help. Hence, this demonstration of sufficient state power must also be shown to be sustainable for the long haul, without the danger of imposing on its citizens worse costs and harms that they could have suffered in the state of nature. The sufficiency of state power is revealed, at least on the foreign front, when a merchant is defrauded by an alien. In order to avoid a spiral of mutual retaliations, sovereigns start to create focal points for institutional redress. In this regard, "only their subjects would obtain benefits from such regulation, and likewise they would punish members of their own society who violated agreements" (Spruyt, 1995, pp. 168–69).

The concentration of power in the state was, from the early Middle Ages forward, designed to assist kings in their efforts to reserve the right to represent their subjects in foreign affairs. With the emergence of the sovereign nation-state, there came about an increased role for the heads of state to work out international laws, rules, and regulations for the amelioration of disputes which, if left unaddressed, could lead to war and other unintended consequences. Therefore, foreign affairs should be viewed as an arena of human endeavor which joined together commercial, legal, and political institutions and actors. By acting in concert, with the guidance of the state, social and political violence could be avoided at the internal level and war between sovereign nation-states at the international level. The bridge between anarchy and Commonwealth is to be found in the Hobbesian social contract. As already discussed, Hobbes states that a Commonwealth may arise by acquisition or by institution.

In the case of acquisition, a party achieves dominion by acquisition when its members, who are in its power, pledge obedience to its rule (Hobbes, *Leviathan*, Chapter 21). Hence, the conqueror acquires dominion over those that he conquers by having the conquered pledge obedience to his rule. By virtue of the fact that these united groups are strong enough to repel an invasion, we are left with a Commonwealth by acquisition.

In the case of Commonwealths formed by institution we find, as we saw earlier, that a number of individuals work to create a common power over themselves through mutual agreement. This is a state-creating pact, or social contract, as Hobbes envisions it. It is more complex than that of a Commonwealth by acquisition because of the fact that there is not just one mutual agreement. Rather, there is a set of bilateral agreements linking contractors with each other. In this case, a single party can rightly demand fulfillment of the agreement by each of the others (*Leviathan*, Chapter 18). In this situation, each of these bilateral agreements results in the surrendering of the individual's right to self-rule. It also authorizes all of the action of a sovereign person or assembly to be elected, at a latter point in time, by the parties through a majority vote. This is a two-stage process.

The process is similar to the process by which racial apartheid was ended in South Africa in the 1990s. First, there was a period of negotiations between the major parties. Second, a president and an assembly was elected by majority vote, thereby creating South Africa's Government of National Unity (GNU). The important principle, however, is that Hobbes's theory demands that "the actual sovereign is selected only after the parties are joined into a social union by overlapping mutual agreements. The parties bind one another to confer on whoever is elected their combined power and authority, in hopes thereby of achieving protection against foreigners and one another" (Kavka, p. 181). This analysis leads us to a discussion of the parties (agents) in the Hobbesian social contract.

1. The Negotiations of the Agents

There are a number of elements that must be clearly identified and delineated in order to fully appreciate the scope and inclusiveness of the Hobbesian state. The parties to the contract deserve special attention because it is necessary to consider and speculate about the plausible outcome of a social contract for all of the parties involved and the nature of the negotiations that lead to it. There are three major components to negotiations: (1) the "target" of the negotiations (what is being negotiated); (2) the "rules" for negotiation and the adoption of proposals; and (3) the nature of the "no-agreement-point" (what happens if agreement is not reached).

The first major concern of the Hobbesian social contract involves the security of the bargainers (Kavka, 1986, p. 236). The first barrier for the state-of-nature parties to address is how to negotiate a social contract when they distrust and fear one another. The solution to this security problem is readily available. In the social contract negotiating setting, the agents have a motive to come together in order to achieve a civil society that endures. Hence, each party is likely to apply, and expect the other parties to apply, Hobbes's 15th law of nature, which requires "that all men that mediate peace, be allowed safe conduct" (*Leviathan*, Chapter 15). The primary subject of the negotiations is to achieve a civil society and to establish an enduring Commonwealth.

Because the target of the social contract is probably a specific kind of state or Commonwealth, we can expect, at minimum, that the parties aim at adopting rules that create public offices with powers that are sufficient to perform security functions as well as establish procedures for selecting officials to fill those offices. Further, the parties may seek both substantive and procedural rules for governing or limiting the conduct of private individuals and/or public officials and institutions (Kavka, p. 189). We have already mentioned this task in regard to Constitutional rules and how Constitutional limits on governmental power are consistent with lasting order. For Hobbes, the main consideration is that whatever rules are ultimately adopted must be understood as binding on all. Further, these rules are to be selected with the goals of stability and permanence, and with the resulting system predominantly in mind. Should the parties reach a "no-agreement point," they remain in the state of nature.

An aside is necessary at this point. Insofar as the Constitutional limits that are specified are to be binding on all, the matter of inclusion comes in early in the process of formulating a Hobbesian social contract. In light of Hobbes's theory and our theme about inclusionary governance, it should be observed that the very process of establishing the social contract, which is the realization of a permanent state or Commonwealth, employs the principle of inclusion by virtue of the fact that it is held to be binding on all agents. Further, the inclusion or incorporation of all relevant agents is, in and of itself, testimony to the inclusionary nature of negotiations over a social contract. Finally, the desires, aspirations and goals of the agents all converge to achieve a mutual goal: that is, the kind and form of institutions that the state or Commonwealth will eventually include.

Next, as to the "rules for negotiations," all agents are included in the discussions and negotiations because there is an expectation that all parties are free to offer proposals on what will be necessary for the establishment of sufficient public power to constitute a state or Commonwealth. Further, proposals concerning the nature of the Commonwealth must be explicit and reasoned. And, by extrapolation, the rules and procedures agreed upon in negotiations and then translated into practice work to preclude political instability and, in its place, lay the groundwork for the necessary forms of political institutionalization, as well as the economic growth and development of the nation.

Some scholars have noted that one problem with the Hobbesian contract theory involves those nations that have an "insufficiency of social resources" and that it may be costly "in terms of social resources, to support the social, economic, and procedural arrangements required by the terms of the Hobbesian social contract" (Kavka, p. 237). This objection, however, would be valid only after comparing them with the costs associated with political violence and deadly conflict. The proposed solution to this dilemma is found when the social contract entails a balance between claims and available resources. In the case in which resource claims and availability are not balanced, it is necessary to prioritize claims. Such a prioritization should, in principle, reflect the claims of all social interests and classes. This is a very important point. For it helps us to identify why the Hobbesian approach to social contracting in establishing a state or Commonwealth, in an inclusionary manner, is an antidote to short-term agreements that may dissolve into anarchy or return parties to the state of nature, with the society fragmenting under rising levels of social and political violence.

The problems with democracy, as opposed to the aforementioned elements of Hobbesian social contracting, are rooted in competing conceptions of democracy in radically different contexts around the world. According to Richard S. Katz, "in trying to assess the degree to which various electoral systems promote democracy, it is similarly crucial to remember that democracy assumes different meanings for different people and that the evaluative standards vary accordingly. An institution that epitomizes democratic practice from one perspective may impede democratization from another. The democraticness of an institution can be judged only on the basis of a particular conception of democracy" (Katz, 1997, p. 106).

Insofar as conceptions of democracy vary, so too does the practice of democracy. In terms of my thesis on inclusion, what is at issue is the degree of inclusion available to the poor, the marginalized and the dispossessed. The less inclusive a democracy is, it is at that point we begin to travel down the slope toward "democratic exclusion" and the possibility of reinforcing the power of an exclusionary state. We can, then, differentiate between the benefits of Hobbesian social contract theory and those of democracy by looking at (1) the perspectives of the parties, (2) the differing and/or conflicting aspirations of the parties, (3) the meanings that the parties assign to particular goals and the order of priority to be given those goals, and (4) the relationship between the institutions of the state or Commonwealth in effecting the targeted goals, through agreed-upon procedures.

In a certain sense, the Hobbesian formulation for establishing the target for negotiations and then formulating rules for negotiation and the adoption of proposals may, in fact, yield more "democratic" outcomes then "democratic" elections. Indeed, not all democracies are inclusive and not all centralized governments are exclusive. We should understand that when we speak of inclusivity and exclusivity we refer to the extent of their application. It is a complex phenomenon which involves the interactions between institutions, the civil society, cultural norms and ethics, as well as economic expectations and goals. The nexus in which these considerations are resolved will determine the degree and extent to which these elements are experienced by the society. There are numerous reasons why this is the case.

To begin with, the perspectives of all of the agents are taken into account because of the inclusionary character of the Hobbesian contract negotiations. Second, differing and conflicting aspirations of the agents are shared with all of the other agents. Proposals from all of the parties are made a matter of public record and become, at the same time, alternative demands which can create alternative futures for the state or Commonwealth. Proposals under the Hobbesian formulation are subject to negotiations. This means that such proposals can be modified and changed as a result of compromises.

In Hobbes's view, the formation of coalitions and agreements among individuals and subgroups are not allowed during the negotiations. In contrast, democratic elections are premised upon building coalitions for the sake of obtaining an electoral majority and, once achieved, using its majoritarian power to win advantage over less organized coalitions with alternative agendas. If this is the case, then it follows that democratic elections are not only short-sighted but often premised upon exclusionary politics with potentially very narrow goals. The consequences of the type of democracy that is practiced may exhibit an inclusionary or an exclusionary tendency. As such, the prospects for ethnic accommodation, political stability and improved prospects for democratic consolidation are enhanced when the type of democracy that is practiced is parliamentary, consensual, or by proportional representation. In the alternative, the prospects for increased ethnic hostility, political instability, and threats to democratic consolidation are heightened when the type of democracy that is practiced is majoritarian, presidential or pluralist or majoritarian (as seen in Table 5.2 below).

Too often, democratic elections entail the manipulation of procedures so that advantages will adhere to those most adept at coalition building, irrespective of the needs and aspirations of the excluded. So the primary benefit of Hobbes's approach is that it allows us to take seriously the critical questions concerning the characterization of all of the negotiating parties. What do the other parties know? Kavka has suggested that, in order to deal with this question, we should artificially divide up things that the parties might want to know into five categories: (1) the negotiating circumstances, (2) general social knowledge, (3) their own particular views on society's characteristics, (4) individual characteristics, and (5) individual social position. It will be necessary to examine each in turn.

The "negotiating circumstances" are, as noted above, the target and rules of negotiations and the specific characteristics of the other parties

TABLE 5.2 The Consequences of Democratic Types

Democratic Type	Tendency	Prospects
Proportional Representation Parliamentary Consensual	Inclusion	Ethnic Accommodation Political Stability Improved Prospects for Democratic Consolidation
Plurality or Majority Presidential Majoritarian	Exclusion	Increased Ethnic Hostility Political Instability Democratic Consolidation Threatened

SOURCE: Andrew S. Reynolds, *Electoral Systems and Democratic Consolidation in Southern Africa*, Dissertation, UCSD, 1996, p. 555.

(Kavka, p. 191). Because it is assumed that the parties possess this information, it follows that they should know what they are doing in the negotiations and have the ability to reasonably argue, bargain and reach agreement.

"General social knowledge" is simply general knowledge about human psychology and social behavior. Such knowledge is inclusive of all subjects in the domain of the social sciences, including economics, sociology, political science, and so on. Insofar as it is the task of these parties to construct institutions and consider appropriate arrangements to successfully govern a society, all parties assume this information is available to themselves and to the other parties.

A "particular society's characteristics" are "its significant features not shared by human societies in general" (Kavka, p. 192). These features include effects of the vagaries of history, language, culture, geography, the economic system, and social and governmental institutions. Despite this recognition of the particularity of human societies, we must remember that we are attempting to employ Hobbes's theory so that we can develop general criteria of political legitimacy for institutions, as well as a general justification for the state, that can survive scrutiny across a large spectrum of societies. The fact that we have adopted general criteria for the accommodation and legitimation of institutions does not necessarily mean, as Hobbes reminds us, that we may not also include criteria that reflect the particular characteristics of a society.

The challenge of incorporating the particular characteristics of a society into a general criteria aimed at the legitimation of institutions means that the division between the institutions of state and a civil society must be bridged. Hobbes's legacy implies that linkages must be made between the agents of the state and agents of a civil society that can produce shared norms. In the case of Czarist Russia, the civil society was not suppressed. This changed with victory of the Communists in 1917. As the Communist Party took over control of the apparatus of the state, it also took over the policing and suppression of the civil society. With the demise of the Russian empire in the early 1990s, as state institutions were liberated from the vice grip of the Communist Party, previously repressed segments of Russia and its empire came to the surface (Illarionov, 1999, pp. 68–82; Fairbanks, 1999, pp. 47–53; Lukin, 1999, 35–40; McFaul, 1999, pp. 4–18). This entailed not only the resurfacing nationalistic and ethnic sentiments, but also demands to liberate the civil society from state supervision. At the same time, communicative links with the state were about to be sought by newly formed experiments with democracy, primarily in the area of elections.

In modern Russia, the purpose of elections, in accordance with Western precedent and theory, is to build linkages and bridges between the state and the civil society through representation in the Duma. Yet, with a new Constitution that gave some traditional legislative power to the president in order to deal with the chaos that emerged from the empire's collapse, and a faltering economy that was being re-worked into a market-style economy, the practice of democracy in Russia has rarely come near the ideal of democracy. Hence, with institutions and institutional practices suffering from a crisis of legitimacy, Russia has been thrown into economic uncertainty, a crime wave, and a state that is foundering between contending parties with conflicting agendas (Glinski and Reddaway, 1999, pp. 19–34). No real bridge has been built between the institutions of state and Russia's civil society, because they still operate in different normative realms.

The characteristics and features of each nation's civil society will differ because of the vagaries of history and experience. The civil society will have its own components, consisting of universal and particularistic elements. Cohen and Arato have identified the following components: "(1) Plurality: families, informal groups, and voluntary associations whose plurality and autonomy allow for a variety of forms of life; (2) Publicity: institutions of culture and communication; (3) Privacy: a domain of individual self-development and moral choice; and (4) Legality: structures of general laws and basic rights needed to demarcate plurality, privacy, and publicity from at least the state and, tendentially, the economy.

Together, these structures secure the institutional existence of a modern differentiated civil society (Cohen and Arato, 1994, p. 346). For example, concerning the issue of privacy, the expression of religious belief, as a dimension of moral choice, is universal to all societies. Religion reflects the ontological essence of human beings. On the other hand, the church, as an institution of organized religion and part of civil society, places different claims and mediates in a variety of different ways between the individual and the state, depending upon time and place.

In his own generation, Hobbes considered civil society from the standpoint of how parties in a culture evaluate "good and evil." Kavka's observation about Hobbes's theory puts it this way: "Goodness is not a feature of objects or states of affairs in themselves, but of their relations to standards of evaluation created and employed by people for human purposes. The standards or common rules of evaluation in civil society are those laid down by custom, tacit agreement, referees, private arbitrators . . . Outside civil society—and presumably within civil society in matters where public standards have not been laid down or agreed to—an individual is free to choose his own standards of evaluation and to treat objects or states of affairs as good or evil according to his desires or preferences" (Kavka, p. 295). These considerations must be taken to be part and parcel of "a particular society's characteristics" and are, therefore, important for parties to take into account when setting the general criteria of political legitimacy for institutions, and also for determining where the boundaries are between these institutions (their proper function) and the civil society.

There are two remaining features left to examine in reference to the characterization of the negotiating parties: a person's "individual characteristics" and "one's individual social position." As to a person's "individual characteristics," such items as gender, state of health, appearance, strength, traits of character, skills, level of knowledge, intelligence, goals, ideals, plan of life, all remain as elements that make up the totality of the individual. Still, we should remember that the individual is more than the sum of these elements. The final feature of the negotiating parties to recall is one's "individual social position." One's social position is characterized by one's social and economic status within society—occupation, level of wealth, and membership in groups with high or low status (Kavka, p. 192).

All of these features have been examined and defined for the primary purpose of effectuating a hypothetical contract theory that is "motivationally efficacious" (Kavka, p. 193). The reason for this is that for the social contract to be effective, "we want real people, who know their individual characteristics and social positions, to be persuaded that they should go along with the kind of social institutions and principles that would be agreed on in the hypothetical contract situation" (Kavka, p. 193). Hobbes's basic assumption is that if parties can see others in a situation similar to that situation in which they find themselves, they should be able to identify with the other parties, thereby facilitating agreement in order to avoid facing this trade-off between motivational efficiency and agreement facilitation. At least this is the case in the classical modern tradition concerning the nature of communication between agents.

The efficacy of the negotiating process has diminished considerably in the 20th century because the process of modernization has resulted in a proliferation of differences between groups. Indeed, modernization has, as a historical process, led to pluralization and social fragmentation, thereby increasing the number of subcultures and the possibility of conflict in Western European societies. Jurgen Habermas has recognized this.

In his book, *Between Facts And Norms*, Habermas depicts Hobbes as starting from a naturalistic conception of the struggle for self-assertion among individuals (Habermas, 1996, p. 2). He maintains that "in the classical modern tradition of thought, the link between practical reason and social practice was too direct" (*Id.*, p. 3). In the translator's introduction to Habermas's book, William Rehg discusses the emphasis that Habermas places on positive law in his theory of communicative action and the nature of modern societies. First, because modern societies "are pluralistic, conflict resolution must occur across a number of subgroups, each of which has a somewhat different self-understanding and set of shared background assumptions." (*Id.*, p. xvii). Second, modern pluralization has engendered a process that Max Weber called "the disenchantment of the world." For our purposes, this refers to the loss of the "sacred canopy," the fact that pluralization has undermined, or at least fragmented, common religious authorities and worldviews. (*Id.*, p. xvii). Third, and finally, "modern societies have developed a complex differentiation of functional spheres defined by specific tasks of social reproduction (economy, educational system, politics, and so on)" (*Id.*, p. xvii).

Rehg's evaluation of Habermas's work leads him to conclude that, in terms of developed Western European societies, Habermas's perception is that "modern societies witness an increasing variety of groups and subcultures, each having its own distinct traditions, values, and worldview. As a result, more and more conflicts must be settled by reaching explicit agreement on a greater range of contestable matters in which the shared basis for reaching such agreement is diminishing . . . That is, members are increasingly forced to separate different spheres of validity, for example, to distinguish scientific questions from those of faith, those of justice and morality from aesthetic judgments, and so forth, a development that Weber attempted to capture with his concept of the differentiation of 'value spheres'" (*Id.*, pp. xvii–xviii). This is why the role of law has come to have greater efficacy.

According to Habermas's argument, "modern law is meant to solve social coordination problems that arise under the above conditions, that is, where, on the one hand, societal pluralization has fragmented shared identities and eroded the substantive lifeworld resources for consensus and, on the other, functional demands of material production call for an increasing number of areas in which individuals are left free to pursue their own ends according to the dictates of purposive rationality" (*Id.*, p. xix). Habermas concludes that constitutional democracy "is becoming a project, at once the outcome and the accelerating catalyst of a rationalization of the lifeworld reaching far beyond the political" and, for this reason, he calls it "constitutional dynamics" (*Id.*, p. 489).

Differences in personal characteristics between the parties is to be understood as natural and influenced, at least indirectly, by the social position of the parties within existing institutional structures. Kavka reasons that "since these differences would remain at least partly as they are under various institutional arrangements, it is appropriate to view the institutions of the State as designed to accommodate these differences" (*Id.*, p. 195). This is achieved, in part, by allowing the parties to retain knowledge of their personal characteristics while they are in the process of negotiating the social contract. Such an approach is in opposition to Rawls's analysis, which assumes that a "veil of ignorance" exists concerning the amount of knowledge the respective agents have of one another.

In Kavka's reading, Hobbes views the institutions of the state as institutions designed to accommodate the differences which exist among the parties. This is a clear argument for inclusion. But the process of inclusionary negotiations returns us to Habermas who, like Hobbes, is at odds with the Rawlsian attempt to impose knowledge restrictions on the parties as to what the differences are that exist among the parties. Habermas explicitly argues that "every social interaction that comes about without the exercise of manifest violence can be understood as a solution to the problem of how the action plans of several actors can be coordinated with each other in such a way that one party's actions 'link up' with those of others. An ongoing connection of this sort reduces the possibility of clashes among the doubly contingent decisions of participants to the point where intentions and actions can form more or less conflict-free networks, thus allowing behavior patterns and social order in general to emerge" (Habermas, 1996, pp. 17–18).

Habermas's interpretation of social interaction is a ringing endorsement of Hobbesian contract theory on a variety of points. First, the very act of negotiation between parties automatically reduces or totally removes violence from the political equation while the parties are attempting to create a durable social contract that can effectively lift them out of the violence of the state of nature. Second, Hobbes, like Habermas, sees the possibility for coordination among the actors in the process of social contracting so that the very fact of this "connection" between the parties creates the objective conditions for conflict resolution and leads toward the formation of "conflict-free networks." Third, Habermas argues, like Hobbes, that behavior patterns can now develop in this context that allow new patterns of social order to emerge. Now, what does this process have to do with the inclusion of heretofore excluded groups, interests and classes?

According to Kavka, the problems associated with what I have called the "exclusion/inclusion dilemma" are dealt with by reasonable and prudent negotiators because "if they are reasonably prudent, even negotiators with favorable personal characteristics will see definite advantages to themselves in incorporating certain significant social insurance measures into the social contract" (*Id.*, p. 198). Why is this the case? Again, the threat of the alternative is either no agreement and a return to the state of nature, or "the establishment of a commonwealth that is unstable because the needs of the least advantaged are not met" (*Id.*, p. 198). It follows, then, that "one would expect that almost all those possessing favorable personal features could be persuaded to accept provisions concerning such measures as part of the found agreement" (*Id.*, p. 198).

In his chapter on "Citizenship and National Identity," Habermas has argued this very point, noting that: "The citizens want to regulate their own living together according to principles that are in the equal interest of each and thus can meet with the justified assent of all. Such an association is structured by relations of mutual recognition in which each person can expect to be respected by all as free and equal. Each and every person should receive a three-fold recognition: they should receive equal protection and equal respect in their integrity as irreplaceable individuals, as members of ethnic or cultural groups, and as citizens, that is, as members of the political community" (Habermas, 1996, p. 496).

There are, of course, numerous possibilities which some parties can or will embrace. Some parties who are especially favored in all the personal characteristics most associated with social and economic success may be so confident of success that in any competitive system they might rationally refuse to accept any proposal calling for a form of social insurance that will aid those members of the society who are the least advantaged. Similarly, some parties may be willing to accept the risks of failing in an uninsured social environment. Also, some dominators may, as a result of their own nature, be so enthralled with the love of conquest that they would prefer the state of nature to the security of the state. All of these possibilities present serious problems for those theories that require unanimous consent to the social contract. Yet, by not requiring unanimous consent, the Hobbesian theory, outlined here, avoids these difficulties by arguing for inclusion, social insurance, recognition, protection and respect as part of the social contract.

2. The Moral Minimum as an Antidote to Social/Political Violence

Hobbes's theory is an attempt to articulate the hope of reconciling group interest and duty. This is especially the case with regard to requiring rich and powerful groups to share with the weak and poor. The goal is not absolute equality. In fact, it is not even obvious that morality demands as much. But what morality does demand and require is that "the rich and powerful refrain from actively harming the poor and weak and that the former aid the latter when the costs of giving are small and the benefits great" (Kavka, pp. 440–441). This moral issue raises questions of justice and what constitutes the just society and a just government.

In particular: "Why should the rich and powerful groups of a nation seek to provide opportunities for the poor in the fields of education, employment, advancement and, at the same time, provide social welfare programs which benefit the poor?" Why, in other words, do we subscribe to such programs? First, we may argue that it is in the short as well as long-term interests of the rich and powerful to treat the domestic poor well. Second, we may argue that extending opportunities to members of all groups widens the pool of talent available to fill all of society's useful jobs which, in turn, should lead toward the realization of providing long-term term economic benefits to all groups. Third, we may argue, as have social theorists from Aristotle to De Tocqueville, from Hobbes to Rawls and Habermas, that meeting basic human needs and providing decent treatment to the marginalized classes promotes social stability and cohesion and discourages rebellion and revolution. Hence, social and political violence may be avoided by inclusionary governance, inclusionary policies, and inclusionary procedures.

What does this interpretation mean for the Hobbesian social contractors? It means that the Hobbesian contractors aim at creating and securing a decent life for all citizens which requires the protection of life and property, political freedom, and the satisfaction of at least the basic needs. Accordingly, the sovereign has to address these needs. In the alternative, the immiserized may be willing to reshuffle the social deck through various forms and degrees of social and political violence.

Hobbes is, in fact, an early exponent of inclusionary governance, over 300 years before Rawls and Habermas and Gauthier ventured this prescription for stable governance. It is possible to trace this emphasis in Hobbes back to his view of the social contract. It also is a view that fits better with Hobbes's idea that the state is an institution capable of ameliorating conflict, promoting cooperation among rational individuals and mediating the political interactions between the government and its challengers. For the fact is that violence does not merely follow because governments are inept. It is also true that violence cannot be totally avoided by governments which are capable. It has been argued, therefore, that domestic political violence "results from a complex relationship between the strength of a government vis-a-vis the opposition and the increase or decrease in relative capacity among the parties" (Kugler, Benson, Hora and Panasevich, 1997, p. 223). It is primarily for this reason that the strength of a government, by itself, is insufficient to ensure domestic stability. Indeed, it is possible for weak governments to survive for long periods when a viable opposition has not materialized. Conversely, a relatively strong government may face violent opposition if that opposition is organized and rejects attempts by the government to govern (*Id.*, p. 223).

In the final analysis, it may be argued with certainty that we need not be concerned with the type of political regime which emerges as a stable successor. For political violence should not be seen as simply the result of competition among authoritarian regimes versus democratic ones. Rather, properly understood, violence and deadly conflict may be seen as a competition among weak governments with strong oppositions which may find themselves challenged by a vast array of potential successors. When viewed from this perspective, a weak authoritarian regime may be replaced by a democratic one, as was the case in Argentina after the Falklands War (*Id.*, p. 223). This leads to a whole new appreciation of the viability of democracy in Third World settings. In light of my thesis on the need for democratic inclusion, it may be argued that "what preserves democracy is the general knowledge that assaults on it will be resisted, and such resistance can be provided by organizations whose members believe they have a stake in continued democracy . . . the survival of democracy does not depend on the benevolence of its leaders but on the calculation by them and by other political entrepreneurs that they cannot become autocratic rulers of the country" (Clague, Keefer, Knack, and Olson, 1997, p. 113). I would suggest, in this spirit, that democratic inclusion, the growth of an accountable and involved civil society in the processes of state decision making, serves to forge a social compact which, in turn, makes all parties accountable to the quality of the political outcome. The nature of the outcome should reflect the best features of inclusionary governance. Of necessity, this implies democratic inclusion in the social, political, cultural and economic realms of the nation's life.

Not to be confused with or mistaken for a Kantian kingdom of ends, I assert that Hobbes's approach is really a prescription to avoid social disaster. In this regard, the social contract purports to include as many social classes as possible in the discursive processes of negotiation. What does this have to do with the social contract's terms of agreement with respect to economic welfare? It means that the Hobbesian principle is at the heart of why inclusionary governance is good governance, in a variety of arenas. In fact, it is the very principle that the modern concept of guaranteeing the satisfaction of "basic needs" is based upon. This principle means that in practice, the poor must, of necessity, be included in the dialogues and decisionmaking arenas of public policy that affect their lives.

This perspective has recently been acknowledged even by the World Bank in its 1999 report, *Can The Poor Influence Policy?: Participatory Poverty Assessments in the Developing World* (Robb, 1999, pp. xii–xiii). The World Bank's report demonstrates that "participatory poverty assessments" (PPAs) demonstrate that poor people have a long overlooked capacity to contribute to the analysis of poverty and "without their insights we know only a part of the reality of poverty, its causes, and the survival strategies of the poor" (*Id.*, p. xii). The poor emphasize their experience as one of vulnerability, physical and social isolation, lack of security and self-respect, powerlessness, and a lack of dignity. Now the significance of the PPAs is that "where there is a broad policy dialogue on poverty that includes different civil society groups, the constituency for reform is widened, ownership is increased, and the resulting policy is more likely to be implemented" (*Id.*, p. xiii). This finding corresponds perfectly with Clague's argument that democracy is preserved when the members of a society believe they have a stake in continued democracy. Such an approach is what I have described by the term "democratic inclusion." It is a formula for social justice, social and political stability, regime legitimacy, and the evolution of more peaceful and cooperative means to achieve inclusionary policy results.

3. Widening the Constituency for Reform

Hobbes's idea of a guaranteed economic minimum is hinted at in his discussion of the fifth law of nature, which requires mutual accommodation. He exhibits a negative attitude toward those who would not aid the desperate, the needy, the poor, when he writes: "[A] man that by asperity of nature, will strive to retain those things which to himself are superfluous, and to others necessary; and for the stubbornness of his passions, cannot be corrected, is to be left, or cast out of society, as cumbersome thereunto. For seeing every man, not only by right, but also by necessity of nature, is supposed to endeavor all he can, to obtain that which is necessary for his conservation; he that shall oppose himself against it, for things superfluous, is guilty of the war that thereupon is to follow" (*Leviathan*, Chapter 15, p. 139).

Here, we see Hobbes's clear warning that political violence and instability and war are the inevitable result of social deprivation, of actual or perceived injustices or neglect toward the poor, the needy, the excluded. It is only by having an inclusionary state that such a disaster can be avoided. In this regard, he clearly argues that it is the duty of the state to ensure that those in need are cared for: "Whereas many men, by accident inevitable, become unable to maintain themselves by their labour; they ought not to be left to the charity of private persons; but to be provided for, as far forth as the necessities of nature require, by the laws of the Commonwealth" (*Leviathan*, Chapter 30, p. 334).

Hence, the Commonwealth is to ensure that a guaranteed economic minimum is extended to the excluded citizens who, by virtue of their poverty and the difficulties leading to it, cannot maintain or "conserve" themselves. So, the Commonwealth is the source of the means for their conservation though the auspices of the state—the inclusionary state. But, in the interdependent world of the later 20th century, there is also the recognition of a common well-being that transcends the nation-state, because advancement of the common well-being of humanity has become a task of international dimensions and international responsibility. As James G. Speth has argued: "In an interdependent world, international cooperation must be an integral part of public policy. Our common well-being will increasingly depend on factors, from the environment to the economy, that have already been globalized. The West in general and the United States in particular must increase their investment in less-developed countries. The costs of neglecting the rapidly growing international class divide will be immense, reaped in environmental harm, humanitarian disaster, and economic growth. The West must have the foresight to act now" (Speth, 1999, p. 17).

The international class divide, of which Speth writes, is the crisis of political, social and economic exclusion on a global scale. The dimensions of this divide have created ethnic conflict and environmental destruction throughout much of the Third World. In his recent book, *Environment, Scarcity, and Violence*, Thomas F. Homer-Dixon concludes "that scarcity of renewable resources," what he calls "environmental scarcity," can "contribute to civil violence, including insurgencies and ethnic clashes" (Homer-Dixon, 1999, p. 177). Increasingly, there is a growing consensus that the combination of mediation and inclusion between peoples can and does make a significant difference in enhancing the cause of peace and reducing violent and deadly conflict. For example, in the case of Slovakia, "the combination of mediation plus the prospect of greater inclusion in economic and political organizations that would enable improvements in the quality of life in a given state may provide a useful model of conflict prevention in other regions" (de Nevers, 1999, p. 169).

The key to overcoming the international class divide is to govern by inclusion. For inclusionary governance requires the building of new institutions for the mediation of disputes, the invocation of new norms and values that transcend the old concerns of power politics and narrowly conceived national interests. Inclusionary governance, after all, is in the human interest. And, in the final analysis, there can be a correspondence between the national interest and the human interest. In that spirit, Robert Johansen has stressed the notion that "the service of human needs should be the guiding principle for major economic and political decisions, rather than the maximization of national power or corporate profit" (Johansen, 1980, p. 21).

Of course, the articulation and implementation of such guiding principles, which demand political participation by the poor and excluded, will be influenced by the receptivity of already established political and economic elites. Historically, in First and Third World nations, at each step in the expansion of political participation, the ruling elites have found it hard to accept as legitimate the demands of their "social inferiors" or economic dependents

(Huntington and Nelson, 1976, p. 120). But changes in structural and institutional participation can be effectuated in the context of the broader system (*Id.*, p. 121). The role for new claims and the establishment of new institutions that are designed for the channeling of the claims of the previously excluded are impossible to overestimate. In strictly economic terms, the role for institutions in societies are what has been identified as the "underlining determinant of the long-run performance of economies." In fact, Douglas North has argued that "if we are ever to construct a dynamic theory of change—something missing from mainstream economics... it must be built on a model of institutional change" (North, 1990, p. 107).

Such a dynamic theory of change must begin, at the dawn of the 21st century, with the recognition that what is happening in most capitalist economies and countries throughout the world is comparable to the same processes that characterized the mid-19th century: large scale growth of capital accompanied by a rise in unemployment and/or low paying jobs, poverty, crime, and overall human suffering. By 1999, the official number of the unemployed in OECD countries remains at over 35 million and is growing, with another 15 million having given up on searching for a job altogether. In particular, the youth labor force among several OECD countries is 30 percent. Similarly, by the early 1990s, 15 out of the 18 "developing" countries had records of declining income growth with some nations—Nigeria, Argentina, and Venezuela—experiencing an absolute decline of gross domestic product in the double digit range. In summary, it may be observed that world inequality has reached new dimensions. The effects of global exclusionary governance combined with growing income disparities resulted in a North/South development gap between the GNP per capita in the less developed countries that has doubled since the 1970s (Petras and Polychroniou, 1999, pp. 199–200).

G. TO CREATE A GLOBAL COMMONWEALTH AND CULTURE OF PEACE

What are the consequences of these trends for global peace? Given the relationship between economic and social development, the prospects for peace are grim. From nation to nation, "failures of development can be seen as contributing to instability and the eruption of conflict. Experience demonstrates that penury, hopelessness, inequity and marginalization are often among the root cause of devastating conflict" (Speth, 1998, pp. 286–287). Social and cultural rights for the marginalized must be translated into real participation and inclusion within the counsels of government and national and international decisionmaking. Without such inclusion, citizens in North and South will be effectively deprived of the experience of the fair value of their rights. In this regard, Habermas has accurately depicted the stakes as best summed up in the recognition that "democratic citizenship can only realize its integrative potential—that is, it can only found solidarity between strangers—if it proves itself as a mechanism that actually realizes the material conditions of preferred forms of life" (Habermas, 1998, pp. 118–119). Democratic inclusion, ultimately, only has effective meaning when and if it transcends the limits inherent in systems of limited or divided government. It is to this issue we next turn.

1. The Nature of the State and the Limits of Government Action

Hobbes, for all of his theoretical genius, fails to show that systems of limited or divided government are maximally unstable. Even Hobbes implicitly acknowledges that absolute governments are not perfectly stable. Locke suggests that: "When the People are made miserable, and find themselves exposed to the ill usage of Arbitrary Power . . . [they] will be ready upon any occasion to ease themselves of a burden that sits heavy upon them" (Locke, *Second Treatise*, sec.224, p. 463, quoted in Kavka, p. 231). As we have already noted, modern history lends a degree of support to this point. Absolutist governments have not tended to be long-lived in recent centuries, certainly not longer-lived than less absolutist forms. Twentieth century examples of this phenomenon abound throughout the Third World. Take, for example, the Philippines under Marcos or Indonesia under Suharto. In the last analysis, Hobbes actively promotes a kind of government and governmental action that protects the personal liberty and well-being of its subjects: all subjects.

As to the issue of the substantive limits on government action, we must agree with Kavka that Hobbes's prescription is guided and framed by the primary idea that government action must be designed to protect the personal liberty and well-being of its subjects. In this sense, we may also see, at least implicitly, that Hobbes has laid the foundation for inclusionary governance. Kavka states that there are four points that we can adapt from what Hobbes says (Kavka, p. 232). They are as follows:

First, it is the responsibility of the government to enforce the laws of nature—moral laws protecting individuals from murder, cheating on contracts, and so on (Hobbes, *Leviathan*, Chapters 14–15; Chapter 26, p. 253; Chapter 30, pp. 322–23). The powers of protection and enforcement are, after all, what make a state powerful. Still, it is not power for power's sake, as in the case of that group called the "dominators." Rather, power is allied to principles that foster protection and stability. These are key ingredients to the formation of a durable Commonwealth. Its very durability prescribe the government's actions by employing state power and authority to protect the personal liberty and well-being of the subject—all subjects. Therefore, the protection extended by the state is inclusionary, and the benefits of it are extended to all groups and classes of persons regardless of their social status.

Second, Kavka argues that Hobbes stresses the idea that there is a requirement of equal status among citizens. This means that each subject possesses the same fundamental rights, including equal treatment under the law (this is implied in the second and eleventh laws of nature). This particular notion is embodied in Locke, the Federalist Papers, and the United States

Constitution. It is, in short, the proposition that what is being constructed is a government of laws, not of men. Hence, because law itself is supposed to be principled and follow certain procedural steps in conjunction with the concept and application of justice for all citizens, the role of law, as envisioned by Hobbes's notion of equal treatment under the law, is inclusionary in nature.

Third, Kavka maintains that Hobbes's thought maintains that individuals "possess freedom of action in matters permitted by the government because they do not infringe on the interests of the community. Hobbes lists as examples the freedoms to contract, to choose a profession, diet, and a place to live, and to raise one's children as one sees fit" (Kavka, p. 232). In all of these examples, the autonomy of the individual seems to be the kind of autonomy that one would expect to see in the sphere of civil society—that distinct sphere of human life which is separate from government and the market. Therefore, Hobbes does place substantive limits on government action so that arbitrary governmental power cannot legally or morally invade the realm of personal and social autonomy wherein the personal liberty and well-being of subjects is supposed to be allowed to flourish. After all, as long as the community is not harmed by the exercise of such autonomy, what legitimate reason exists for the government to invade and invoke its powers into this sphere? There is none. In fact, if such arbitrary power was invoked by the state, it could lead to political violence, revolt, and a loss of legitimacy for the government itself.

Fourth and finally, Hobbes does not recognize unrestricted economic freedom. For him property rights begin only with the establishment of the state. Therefore, such rights are within the authority of the government to regulate. The state creates and protects these rights. In this very sense, the state has a stake in generating and protecting wealth. According to Hobbes, the state, in effecting a viable Commonwealth, is willing to use some of its "share" to protect the needy, the marginalized, and the underprivileged. In this regard, as to the issue of taxation, Hobbes sees taxation as the means to support vital activities of the state, such as providing aid to the needy in order to promote an inclusionary agenda that benefits all classes, thereby avoiding political violence.

Hobbes's concern is to avoid extreme stratifications of society and not to generate a welfare state. In all of this, we should not read into Hobbes some kind of implicit intention, on his part, to regulate the market. The market was, indeed, beyond the confines of his theory. Yet, it should be recognized that Hobbes's analysis, by exhibiting concerns regarding the health of the society and addressing problems that, if left unattended, may result in political violence, could be viewed as a precursor to Adam Smith's theory of wealth creation.

2. A Prescription Against Anarchy

In summary, the Hobbesian social contract is a three-part argument against anarchy. The first stage of the argument outlines the miseries and problems of pure anarchy—the war of all against all. The second stage of the argument exposes how all groupings, apart from the state, fail to solve the individuals' security problems. The third stage of the argument serves to demonstrate how the state solves the security problems of individuals and effects a working Commonwealth. A satisfactory state is the result because it is realizable. Hobbes outlined conditions for a satisfactory state that are achievable, and these conditions are general enough to be met. In fact, in the 20th century, we argue that many states actually realize these conditions. What we add to the analysis, however, is that the inclusionary nature of governance and the characteristics of inclusionary governance make all the difference as to whether or not a satisfactory State is, in fact, achieved. As Kavka notes, "this demonstration that a realizable state is rationally preferred to the state of nature completes the Hobbesian argument against anarchy" (Kavka, p. 236).

3. Neo-Liberalism and the Un-Making of Civil Society

As a child of the Renaissance, Hobbes trusted man's reason to resolve disputes and fashion pathways to peace. Hobbes asserted that "we are not to renounce our Senses, and Experience; nor (that which is the undoubted Word of God) our naturall Reason. For they are the talents which he hath put into our hands to negotiate, till the coming again of our blessed Saviour" (*Id.*, p. 255). Hobbes reminds his readers that we are neither powerless nor defenseless against violence. For the benefits of natural reason have given us political purpose and direction to effectuate a tenuous peace, but peace nevertheless. The senses and experience we share, mediated through our reason and our ability to reason together, form "the talents which he hath put into our hands to negotiate"(*Id.*, p. 255).

The power to negotiate means that reasonable men, seeking a reasonable peace, have the power to create reasonable forms of governance that are inclusionary by virtue of the fact that nature itself has supplied us with not only the power to negotiate our differences but has been augmented by the Word of God, as delivered through the prophets, to give us guiding principles by which, through which, and in which we may develop a Christian politics. These principles point toward the value of negotiations and the promise of bringing about inclusionary solutions for all classes, groups, and interests by virtue of our common humanity.

The idea of the Leviathan as a rational unity actor is perhaps best described by Hobbes in Chapter 16 of *Leviathan*, in which he states: "A Multitude of men, are made One Person, when they are by one man, or one Person, Represented; so that it be done with the consent of every one of that multitude in particular. For it is the Unity of the Representer, not the Unity of the Represented, that maketh the Person one." (Hobbes, *Leviathan*, p. 114). Herein lies the essential notion of inclusionary governance. The distinction between the unity of the representer and the unity of the represented is critical. After all, Hobbes has vested in Leviathan, whether one man or an assembly, the ultimate power of the state through the centrality of power.

The difference can be seen in juxtaposing Hobbes with Rousseau's notion of the "General Will." Whereas Hobbes believes that in making a social contract, the contractee surrenders all claims of political independence, except the right to preserve one's own life, to the sovereign, Rousseau maintains that by personally willing obedience to the common good the citizen maintains his/her personal freedom. The difference between the Hobbesian formulation and that of Rousseau is that, in Hobbes's own words: "And because the Multitude naturally is not One, but Many, they cannot be understood for one; but many Authors, of every thing their Representative saith, or doth in their name; Every man giving their common Representer, Authority for himselfe in particular . . . " (Hobbes, *Leviathan*, p. 114). Hence, because the multitude is not one, of one mind or one will, Hobbes placed the consent of the governed under the rubric of the Leviathan for the sake of the entire civil society.

Because the surrender of final authority is to the state, the state has an obligation to protect every member of the Commonwealth. The notion of membership in a Commonwealth comes and goes according to whether or not one accepts the protection of a particular Commonwealth. For example, membership in a particular Commonwealth means that one is obliged to be obedient to it. Membership incurs obedience and obligation. However, should the Commonwealth fail to provide protection to the individual or to certain groups, then, when there is a threat to one's preservation that the Commonwealth cannot provide against (i.e., the power of a bandit or systematically marginalized), it is at that point that one's membership in the Commonwealth is suspended. Therefore, in Hobbes's political theory, the condition of obedience contained in his principle of political obligation is that the political authority of the Commonwealth, of which one is a member, is effective only if it can provide protection. There are three elements to this principle of obedience and the political obligation that comes with it: (1) that there be a Commonwealth, (2) that one be a member of it, and (3) that it be able to protect one. All of these elements must be present to obtain the condition of obedience.

The obligations of the state to society have undergone many transformations in the 20th century. With the rise of market society the battle for the "commanding heights" has theoretically placed the state in competition with the market. In the nation-state phase of capitalism, subordinate classes mediated their relation to capital through the nation-state. There was nothing which was either transhistoric or predetermined about this process of class formation worldwide. It is now being superceded by globalization (Robinson and Harris, 2000, p. 17). Globalization in the 1990s and early 21st century has produced three "globalist" factions (the free-market conservatives, the neoliberal structuralists, and the neoliberal regulationists) which speak for a transnational capitalist class (TCC) rather than for national capitals.

The globalist blocs of the TCC became politicized from the early 1970s into the 1990s as a class project of capitalist globalization. All three factions are neoliberal in that none question the essential premises of world market liberalization and the freedom of transnational capital. The first faction, comprised of free-maket conservatives, call for a complete global laissez-faire based on an undiluted version of the Washington consensus. The second faction, the neoliberal structuralists, seek a global superstructure capable of providing a modicum of stability to the volatile world financial system. It seeks to do this by adjusting the Washington consensus without interfering with the global economy. The third faction, the neoliberal regulationists, call for a broader regulatory apparatus that could effectively stabilize the financial system while working to attenutate some of the sharpest social contradictions of global capitalism. This process of attentuation is sought in the interests of securing the political stability of the system (*Id.*, p. 43).

Among the three factions, the neoliberal regulationists are the most aware of the dangers of sociopolitical instability (SPI) as a direct consequence of the neoliberal project. The recognition of SPI is also a late 20th century appreciation of Hobbes's 16th century depiction of the political authority of the Commonwealth as a social and political arrangement that must guarantee membership and protection to all within its jurisdiction. At the dawn of the 21st century, the jurisdiction of capitalism is global. Hence, the task that confronts First and Third World nations to build an inclusionary democratic commonwealth or, in the alternative, to surrender to the dictates of the exclusionary directions taken by the three factions of the globalist ruling bloc. Should the exclusionary path inherent in the neoliberal agenda of the structuralists be taken it will be distinguished by its adherence to neoliberal political and economic policies, its concern to build a stable and regualted environment for global accumulation, and its effort to protect world financial institutions from ruin and failure (*Id.*, p. 43).

In the context of the First World, neoliberal political and economic policies are embodied in the political configuration of a "Third Way." The predecessor of the Third Way, in its more dogmatic and ideological form, was launched by the Reagan and Thatcher regimes of the 1980s. Free market conservatives worked to dismantle diverse Keynesian welfare and developmentalist regimes around the world. But by the late 1990s it appeared that the most extreme aspects of the globalist project were being moved into a moderating phase in which structuralists and regulationists were starting to coalesce around a new political configuration called the "Third Way." In the United States and Great Britain, the Clinton and Blair regimes were joined by Chancellor Gerhard Schroder in Germany to make the "Third Way" or "Middle Way" the most recent project of global capitalism (Faux, 1999, p. 67–76; Ryan, 1999, pp. 77–80). In the case of Germany, "the 'crisis of democracy' . . . as in other advanced industrial democracies, is . . . more accurately termed a crisis of democratic party systems, in part the cause and in part the product of a crisis in democratic political culture. It is one of the ironies—and inconveniences—of history that that commuist successor parties became participants in newly competitive party systems at a time when established competitive party systems were in what many observers considered a crisis, and it is Germany's dubious privilege to be the only country simultaneously confronted by the challenges of democratization and by a 'crisis of democracy' otherwise typical of the advanced industrial democracies since the mid-1970s" (Saadah, 1998, p. 241).

The triumph of "Third Way liberalism" represents a hybrid of the project of the neoliberal structuralists and regulationists. It has allowed Third Way politicians to place the issues of poverty, unemployment, and inequality back on the economic policy agenda. In order to maintain the political viablility of the First World commonwealth it became necessary to address these problems insofar as they were no longer to be mediated through state interventionist mechanisms (Robinson and Harris, 2000, p. 49). An ideological rationale for this approach has been provided by Anthony Giddens, the Director of the London School of Economics and frequently referred to as Tony Blair's guru. Giddens has asserted that "it is often thought, even by some of the modernizers, that adopting a third way position means diluting a concern with inequality. It seems as though the modernizers are deserting the values of the left while the traditionalists are preserving them, or would do so if their policies were implemented. After all, the more traditional left wants existing welfare systems to stay intact, and to keep taxes and levels of welfare spending high, even if this implies large state deficits. But this view is false. We cannot tackle inequalities by further extending such policies, which have reached their limits. A different approach is needed. Sound fiscal and macroeconomic policies can reduce poverty and social exclusion as well as reverse trends toward increasing economic inequality more generally" (Giddens, 2000, pp. 166–167; see also, Giddens, 1998). Notwithstanding the reassurances offered by Giddens, his claims do not fit with the facts.

According to Third Way theory, "society will retain social inequalities but encourage equal opportunity; the goal accordingly is not to redistribute income but to increase income for all" (Petras, 2000, p. 21). On this trajectory we can begin to trace the makings of an inherently exclusionary project in First World states. According to Petras, "what is most striking about the connections between Third Way rhetoric and New Right politics is that where the ideology is most deeply implanted—in the United States and England—social programs have suffered the worst and capitalist class prosperity is greatest . . . Third Way theorists argue that their goal is a more competitive and open economy shaped by the market. In reality, Third Way regimes have approved and aligned themselves with the greatest merger movement in history—leading to greater concentration of economic power among a decreasing number of monopolistic giants" (Id., p.32). In this respect, the dynamics of exclusionary governance in First World states reflects the same trends exhibited in many Third World states. Exclusionary governance is reflected in the fact that "the frequent resort to executive decrees, the assumption of legislative, executive, and administrative powers by the presidents and prime ministers on questions affecting fundamental issues of property ownership, trade, and investments without any pretense of public consultation smacks of the powers exercised by third-world dictators" (Id., p. 34). Of this trend, John Gray asserts that "as in the thirties, a crisis of the global economy is unfolding at a time when the international community is effectively leaderless" (Gray, 1998, p. 18).

Global society is increasingly characterized by what has been depicted as a three-tiered social structure. According to Robinson and Harris, "the first tier is made up of some 30–40 percent of the population in core countries and less in peripheral countries, those who hold 'tenured' employment in the global economy and are able to maintain, and even expand, their consumption. The second tier, some 30 percent in the core and 20–30 percent in the periphery, form a growing army of 'casualized' workers who face chronic insecurity in the conditions of their employment and the absence of any collective insurance against risk previously secured by the welfare state. The third tier, some 30 percent of the population in the core capitalist countries, and some 50 percent or more in peripheral countries, represents those who structurally excluded from productive activity and completely unprotected with the dismantling of welfare and developmentalist states, the 'superfluous' population of global capitalism" (Robinson and Harris, 2000, p. 50). This the is background against which to assess the objective effects of the Third Way and neoliberal policies.

Neoliberal and Third Way policies represent a politics of exclusion which makes the problem of social control paramount. As already noted in Hobbes's political theory, the condition of obedience is contained within his principle of political obligation. Obedience and obligation are only effective if the Commonwealth is capable of providing protection. In neither First nor Third World contexts can neoliberalism provide the global commonwealth with a justification for either obedience or obligation. Both obedience and obligation presuppose inclusion and the provision of protection inherent within a viable Commonwealth. Absent the capacity of the state to provide the political, social, and economic aspects of inclusion and protection, there is a corresponding shift from the social welfare state to the social control of the police state, replete with "the dramatic expansion of public and private security forces, the mass incarceration of the excluded population (disproportionately minorities), new forms of social apartheid maintained through complex social control technologies, repressive anti-immigration legislation, and so on" (*Id.*, p. 51; see also, Huggins, 1998).

In the context of Latin America, while moves toward free-market economics and integration into the world economy signified important paradigm shifts they were not panaceas. Latin America's overall effort to prune the state's economic activities, privatize production and distribution, attract foreign investment, emphasize exports, and open itself to international competition, all represented major conceptual changes, but they could not, and did not, all have an immediate positive impact (Lowenthal, 2000, p. 45). Opposition from parties and leaders critical of the "Washington Consensus" on market-oriented macroeconomic reforms and pledging to alleviate poverty and expand social services won election in Argentina and Chile and came close to winning in Uruguay. Hence, the dynamics of exclusionary governance or what its critics call "savage capitalism" is under attack in many countries. Still, no broad agreement has been reached in an alternative policy framework. In this regard, "a wholesale reversion to statist approaches, demagogic populism, and fiscal irresponsibility is unlikely, but so is the unrelieved application of neoliberal orthodoxy" (*Id.*, p. 47). The inclusionary impulse is exhibited in new approaches which are beginning to emerge in market economies but including a stronger state role in both improving and extending education, public health, and social services, as well as in the tasks of alleviating poverty and reducing inequality. In other words, both inside and outside the Latin American region there is growing recognition of the need to focus on equity, education, and inclusionary governance as the 21st century's indispensable agenda. The movement toward inclusionary governance is an indispensable agenda in light of the regions recent history in which "unemployment and underemployment are up and real wages are falling. Labor conflict and social protests are expanding. Street crime, kidnapping for profit, and the sale of children are rising. Rejection of established authorities and institutions is growing, and the approval rating of many incumbent democratic leaders have plummeted" (*Id.*, p. 43).

Alternatively, inclusionary governance commands higher degrees of obedience and corresponding obligations by virtue of its embodiment of the mandates of a democratic commonwealth. In this global task, the UN has a role to play. But "it must be emphasized that democratization as a process comes down to people. Often international democracy is equated with the notion of sovereignty and equality of all states. That is not the meaning here. Rather, democracy refers to the practices of people in a national society that strive to provide free and fair elections, with respect for the civil and political rights of individuals, protected under the rule of law. This means that the concept of democracy at the global level must constantly give attention to the roles and actions of people in different countries. In sum, since 1990, the UN has acted openly to provide the ways and means for instituting democratic practices in various countries" (Joyner, 1999, p. 334). Significantly, "the practice of democracy is increasingly becoming regarded as essential for progress on a wide range of social-economic concerns and the protection of human rights" but, in the language of the UN Secretariat, "a culture of democracy" must be established to foster the process of democratization (*Id.*, p. 351). Therefore, while the UN can assist in establising democratic and inclusionary practices in accordance with the institutions and mechanisms of democracy, no less critically needed is the government-supported action to institute and sustain a culture of democracy through a developed civil society and A political culture grounded in practices supportive of popular participation, inclusion, and consultation.

Exclusionary governance is primarily mediated through markets defined by free trade agreements such as the General Agreement on Tariffs and Trade (GATT) and NAFTA, along with technologies like the Internet allow investors to negotiate these markets at electronic speed. These structures are created and maintained by governments through their public investment, regulatory efforts, and diplomatic coordination (Shakow and Irwin, 2000, p. 58). These facts highlight the interconnectedness between state and market that are discounted by conservative economists. It would not be wise, therefore, to accept the conclusion that markets have emerged as the ruling international authority, more significant and potent than any military or political power. Rather, "markets cannot control hate radio, arms smuggling, the spread of disease, economic inequality, or the passion of ethnic conflict and the havoc it produces. Markets alone can neither modulate the volatility of capital nor the deepening of economic inequalities" (Lyman, 2000, p. 96).

In the wake of the Asian and global financial crisis that began in 1997, neoliberal theories have increasingly come under attack both on the basis of their brutal consequences for the poor as well as their failure to deliver the benefits they promise for the non-poor. Insofar as neoliberals have followed exclusionary policies which are supportive of exclusionary governance, their policy prescriptions has been inherently anti-democratic. This is inspite of the fact that "democratic progress in East Asia was already creating pressures for greater attention to social policy as well as greater transparency in business-government relations, and the economic crisis of 1997–1999 has accelerated these trends. It has contributed to a change of regime in Indonesia, to a strengthening of political oppositions elsewhere, and to growing pressures for changes in regulatory regimes and in the social contract" (Haggard, 2000, p. 144).

Some have speculated that the long-run impact of the crisis may allow for "a reversion to political habits and institutions that bear a closer resemblance to the past than most observers had initially anticipated" (*Id.*, p. 144). If there is such a reversion then the dynamics of exclusionary governance will be reinforced. However, if the emerging social contract in East Asia has ignited democratic pressures for giving greater attention to social policy and inclusionary forms of governance it may be argued that the inclusionary impulse will force a change toward inclusionary forms of governance whether endorsed by the IMF or not. The point is underscored by Nelson Mandela's observation that "if overnight, as a result of turmoil on the financial markets, 17 million people in Indonesia fall back into poverty; if one million children in that region will not be able to return to school; if across the world 1.3 billion people live on less than $2 a day; 1.3 billion have no access to clean water; three billion no access to sanitation; two billion no access to power; if that is so, we certainly cannot go on with business as usual" (Mandela, 2000, p. 34). These realizations serve to underscore the enduring releance of Hobbes's concept of state responsibility toward the Commonwealth. Within this concept the relationship between the state and civil society was born.

Who or what will determine whether the state discharges its obligations concerning the maintenance of the Commonwealth? It became necessary to generate independent and autonomous institutions whose purpose would be the determination of whether the elements of the Commonwealth were there—this was the making of civil society. It is the task of the civil society to act as a separate sphere to bring claims upon the Commonwealth and its sovereign power to protect the excluded, those placed under danger and threat, those who are suffering by virtue of their vulnerability and lack of protection.

H. THE TASK OF CIVIL SOCIETY IN THE COMMONWEALTH

The civil society stands apart as a separate and distinct sphere of social life from the Commonwealth. For it may be the case that the Commonwealth and its politicians have tried, for example, to convince some groups and individuals that they are members of the Commonwealth, but they never really meant to let them in. Therefore, civil society is a realm of associational and communal life which exists independently of the market and the state. It exists as a countervailing force and a corrective for the political, social, and economic imbalances that have excluded some individuals and groups from participation in the protections and privileges that are afforded to other members of the commonwealth. The government, for example, may claim that farmers and peasants are part of the Commonwealth, but they allow them to be subjected to famine, or may initiate anti-farmer policies. Therefore, the state often does not extend protection to them. At that point, the civil society will intervene to make claims on behalf of the voiceless and insist upon the satisfaction of the conditions which make up a Commonwealth. The state will have to respond to these claims in some fashion.

It is the civil society that makes claims upon the Commonwealth and the state to include the excluded under the umbrella of its protections and promises so that the national welfare may be advanced without leaving individuals and groups isolated, for example, in enclaves of poverty and without political and social influence in the life of the Commonwealth. In short, civil society re-unites the richness of citizenship with the rewards of personal and group responsibility.

To return to Hobbes's concept of Commonwealth, it may be that if an association or Commonwealth fails to protect you, then it is either not a Commonwealth or you are not a member of it. In neither case are you obligated to obey its political authority. The dynamic nature of civil society is that it represents an autonomous realm which holds the state and the Commonwealth accountable for all citizens that exist under its domain and within its borders. Should it fail to include them in decisions which affect their lives, then they are put at risk and potentially placed in a subordinate position wherein they are acted upon, by force or threat of force, and left without recourse or protection. At that point, the formulation of Hobbes takes hold and exempts the unprotected, the vulnerable, and the victimized from the principle of political obligation to the Commonwealth.

It is necessary, therefore, to juxtapose the notion of the Commonwealth with the separate sphere of civil society. For example, when the Commonwealth fails to demonstrate inclusionary policies and harms excluded individuals and groups, it is at that point that the sphere of civil society acts as an advocate for the excluded by saying: "Take into consideration these individuals, associations, and communal groups that have been promised the protection and benefits and privileges inherent in being a member of the Commonwealth and yet still do not enjoy the fruits of those protections, benefits and privileges." A political claim is thereby lodged against the powers which govern the state and make up the entirety of the Commonwealth. The scope and extent of their power is called into question as their collective failure to protect and benefit all segments of the civil society is exposed.

By concentrating on the state's regulatory function with regard to the power to tax and the protection of property rights, Hobbes reminds us that civil society is distinct from the state and the market. It is only in recognizing these three spheres of human activity as distinct but interacting that we can begin to distinguish their linkages and relationship to one another. That understanding explains, after all, why citizens, classes, and groups give up a measure of individual liberty—it is for safety, security, and peace. As long as the sovereign delivers peace and creates rights, laws, and obligations that everyone considers obligated to obey, the Commonwealth may flourish. In conjunction with that power, however, there is the distinct and separate realm of civil society where all individuals, classes, and groups reside and interact. Civil society has continuously played its beneficial role and has never lost its relevance and salience.

In this regard, the market cannot play the role of a surrogate for the civil society. Cohen and Arato, in their analysis of Eastern Europe after the fall of Communism, have noted that: ". . . it will take more than the magic of the marketplace to restore the minimum for marginalized segments of the population. Finally, while only democratic movements and actors can today legitimately institute market economies that, initially at least, ask for great sacrifices from those who have been victims of the last phase of state socialism, their legitimacy can be maintained only if their goals include tangible improvements and political trade-off that the combination of liberal economy and elite democracy cannot provide." (Cohen and Arato, 1994, p. 490).

What Cohen and Arato have underscored about the marginalized serves to highlight the importance of what I call "inclusionary governance." I argue that it is foolish to rely on the state and market in isolation from key actors, classes, and groups within the civil society. If economic advances as well as political freedoms are to be expanded, the entire civil society must demand and find avenues for the free expression and participation of all of its members and check whether such demands find their satisfaction in the behavior of the state. It matters not whether the labels of elite democracy, social democracy, or democracy are attached to this endeavor. What matters is that objective and clear channels of access to centers of power, decision making, and dialogue are formally in place, constitutionally guaranteed, and frequently used by all members of civil society. Only in that way can inclusionary governance become real, become workable, and provide channels for avoiding violence and avoiding a crisis of legitimacy for the state.

1. Some Final Thoughts

Hobbes's thought in writing the *Leviathan* pre-dates the formation of the nation-state. In that regard, the "security dilemma" for Hobbes is primarily an internal dilemma, divorced from the external concerns of foreign policy. Yet internal chaos erodes the capacity of the nation and its state to answer external challenges. We discover, in Hobbes's vision, that the issue of mutual fear dominates his assessment of class interests and the need to centralize political power so as to bring about a workable social process of political legitimation.

It is Hobbes's contention that the legitimation of social policies and decisions by the Leviathan would insure the workings of law and respect for law. This, in turn, would render the legislative powers of government an integrative tool that would allow the maximization of the productive ability of the society, both in terms of the exploitation of natural resources and the efficient and productive use of social knowledge and individual skills. This becomes the road to a Commonwealth. In fact, it is the very foundation of the Commonwealth. In some real sense, therefore, Hobbes anticipated Adam

Smith in that their goals were not dissimilar.

Third World nations may either choose the path of a Commonwealth or the path of exclusionary governance. Exclusionary governance in the Third World wears many different faces. It may be the predatory face of Zaire or Rwanda, or it may be the authoritarian face of the Philippines or Chile of the past, the Indonesia or Pakistan of the present, or the supposedly democratic face of Mexico. I argue, like Hobbes, that an inclusionary social covenant constitutes the best path for Third World nations as they seek prosperity and social justice without having to face the debilitating consequences of political violence.

State power is essential, insofar as it exists to enforce a social contract. The social contract itself must be an inclusionary one. Because the combination of state power with an inclusionary social contract leads toward the possibility of an emergence of new forms of political consolidation, new avenues of social, economic, and political inclusion are created that are in harmony with each nation's unique history, goals, and hopes for the future.

Thus, in building such a framework, political consolidation would make for general social progress, for all would advance within the constraints of the social contract—enforced, as always, by the Leviathan. Understood in this way, Hobbes's "authoritarianism" should not be confused with having an essential connection to or with the doctrine of the "Divine Right of Kings." Hobbes certainly speaks as though the sovereign is in some sense the representative of God; but in the first place monarchy is not for him the only proper form of government and in the second place sovereignty, whether vested in one man or in an assembly of men, is derived from the social covenant, not from appointment by God.

It is precisely the issue of the state and the structure of the state that underlies the essence of Hobbes's thesis in *Leviathan* and its revolutionary potential. For contained within the prescriptive and descriptive elements of the Hobbesian formulation is the emphasis upon developing a political unity and building a state machinery that can allow for the mitigation of the nationalist aspirations of various classes, while working as a mediating agency for the channeling of their interests and drives. It is not so much an ideological construction as it is an institutional framework for the building up of an administrative entity that can allow for economic change, for a change in the social order and a change in the ideologies and institutions that support it.

The Hobbesian depiction of the social contract is a formulation that is based, in large measure, upon the elements of practical association. Practical association is grounded in the fundamental recognition that achieving consensus among disparate interests is virtually impossible. Given men's preference for conflict over cooperation and their tendency toward anarchy instead of society-maintaining behaviors, the category of practical association has contained within itself a unifying potential that directly addresses the selfish motives of individuals as well as nation—states in the struggle for survival and self-preservation. While ends and goals may radically differ, there are necessary practices, norms, and customs that must be taken as authoritative for the individuals within the praxis of the political community. While individual ends may be realized, collective ends must be achieved at all costs, and the protection and realization of these collective ends becomes the responsibility and domain of the Commonwealth.

The formation of the state enterprise, as Schlozer was to recognize in 1767, was such that "thousands of years may pass before the whole sum of its forces can be recognized . . . ," but that did not excuse the political theoreticians from devising new approaches to the subject, nor did it foreclose upon a growing popular desire and sense of individualism to realize a greater observance of those interests which were representative of the concerns of those at the bottom of the social ladder.

The old Medieval world that was crumbling in England and throughout the European continent in the 16th century was itself representative of a traditional order where a man was bound by ties attaching his status and a definition of his duties to forms of social life prescribed by the church. Tradition was the only form of social control, and these traditions stretched back into a past where man was assigned a relatively fixed place in society. The social universe of Hobbes, on the other hand, was a rather gruesome caricature of an age of individualism. As men shook off the ties of their guilds and local communities, a new natural philosophy was beginning to render the naturalistic foundations of the former worldview untenable. Vestiges would remain, but even the vestiges of the old order would be transformed in the transition to the new order.

The central concept to appreciate, concerning this historical moment, is the concept of transition as it relates to the political theory of Hobbes, for the question of primary importance for him was framed by the transitional nature of his times. What this implies is a set of historical circumstances where the old order is being swept away, and the question that needs to be immediately addressed is what other form or forms of social control could take its place so as to prevent the anarchy of a state of nature?

The answer was to be found in the emphasis placed upon an increased executive power in the state and in the growth of statute law. Together with the growth of individual conscience, the union of executive decision making matched to the increased emphasis upon secular law in combination with a reformation which granted greater authority to the individual's decision-making powers, resulted in a more secularized conscience (i.e., it was social in nature and less dependent upon external authority or sanctions). Hence, the decline of ecclesiastical authority allowed for the growth of state authority and the growing emphasis upon the liberty of the conscience, which was to culminate in the 18th century Enlightenment and the Age of Revolutions.

While Hobbes was content with the growing authority of the state and the apparatus of laws formulated by that authority, he was also enormously disquieted by the anarchic tendencies of the individual conscience. In this respect, the decline of religious authority is significant, for contained within its de-emphasis of the spiritual and the accelerated reliance on scientific inquiry and secular authority were the seeds of the Enlightenment's reliance upon the doctrine of "Reason." It was this doctrine which was to give energy and direction to the rising bourgeoisie in its struggle against the aristocracy (Stavrianos, 1981, p. 347).

Yet the stages of the evolution of states, in the nation-building process, differ radically in terms of emphasis. At one point the economic concerns will predominate over the military or political, while at another stage the opposite will be true. In some other periods, the cultural or regional dimensions will be of greater significance. Hence, given the relationship that exists at the various stages between the exercise of the coercive power of the state, economic integration, income redistribution, cultural standardization, and the extension of political participation, the question posed by authority is always central in political life as well as in the evolution of social institutions and the intellectual apparatus that legitimizes them. If the authoritative apparatus is lacking or in contention, the chances are that submerged social groups and alternative political orientations will undermine the old bases of traditional rule and create the conditions for revolutionary activity.

To return to a consideration of Hobbes's England on this point, the 1650s were characterized by an economic crisis in which the actions of Cromwell as Lord Protector (1653–8) meant that taxes had to be levied. The exactions by him made those of the old monarchs look modest. Yet the crisis was multidimensional, and it was precisely the multidimensionality of the crisis that made governance so difficult and Hobbes's prescription for the Leviathan so radical, yet so important.

Given the historical praxis of Hobbes's England, the emphasis upon authoritative political practice is not difficult to ascertain or its merits invisible to the critical eye. The project of nation-building, at certain levels of economic development, social integration, and political modernization is not a trivial task. Hence, the issue of authority is of central importance during particular stages of economic, social and political evolution.

Accordingly, in Hobbes's *Leviathan* we observe the undertaking of a number of tasks all of which are considered *sine qua non* conditions for both the establishment and the smooth evolution of the state. In the process, one has to answer questions regarding the coercive power of the state as well as its appropriate use regarding issues related to economic and social integration, allocation of resources and the attendant income distribution, the degree of openness of the market, private ownership, cultural standardization, and the form and nature of political institutions which are required to effect and serve the implied changes and decisions. The range of these tasks makes for the raising of the issue of authority an inescapable consideration. The authoritative and normative dimensions of law are preoccupied with how best to maintain and preserve society. This is as true today as it was in Hobbes's 17th century England.

The range of these tasks also has implications for democratic societies that are attempting to overcome "democratic exclusion" and govern by inclusion. Democratic societies are doomed, or at least predestined, to try to find compromises between the extremes of liberty, on the one hand, and complete social equality, on the other. As Jacques Thomassen has observed, "all democratic societies will find a compromise between the two extremes of unlimited liberty at the risk of extreme differences in the social condition of its people, and complete social equality which can only be achieved—and even in theory only—by an oppressive political system" (Thomassen, 1995, p. 388).

Authority may be depicted as a centralization of human strivings and efforts around a common focus point in order to preserve the disparate elements within and between groups and interests in the society. The centralization of authority is realized vis-a-vis the articulated linguistic structure of values, norms and mores. Hence, the production of authority in a political and social sense is connected with the demands and pressures of the human condition as interpreted by the various societies.

Braudel has pointed toward a societal accommodation to new economic forms of organization and production and the efforts undertaken by the establishment to integrate itself into the emerging scheme of capitalistic society. The ruling classes and the newcomers in the Europe of the 17th century began to work out patterns for centralization and accommodation in order to overcome the arbitrariness of pre-modern, hierarchical societies characterized by the absence of universalistic laws and centralizing governing structures. The alternative to centralizing institutions and value structures is segmentation.

Segmentation is a process of deepening chaos, disorder, and social disintegration and SPI. It is the explicit consequence of a society's failure to effectively reproduce itself over time and under changing circumstances and, more often than not, the result of exclusion. In this regard, the changes in the method of production in Europe accounted for a change in political practices, structures, and institutions, thus effectuating a broad-based social revolution which would eventually sweep away the coercion of old political structures and the monopolizing tendencies associated with pre-modern and pre-capitalistic economic practice.

The issue of a social contract, on the other hand, an element of the Hobbesian theory, may be argued along lines that do not correspond to an absolutist position. The social contract had its roots in both Roman and Medieval thought. We find the theory codified in the *Corpus Juris Civilis*. This codification contains the idea that all power and all rights of lawmaking resided in the Roman people themselves. There was a transfer of authority, however, effectuated vis-a-vis a *Lex Regia* in which these powers had been surrendered to the emperor. In Justinians' *CODEX*, I, 17, we find the statement: "All the rights and all the powers of the Roman people have been transferred to the Emperor. To him alone it is granted to make the laws and to interpret them."

In the Middle Ages, the Emperor and then the princes seized upon this interpretation as a weapon against the supremacy of the church. Such an act fitted very nicely into the medieval political ideas, according to which the relationship between the governed and the governor was one based on mutual obligations (i.e., tacit or explicit contracts between parties). This is the seed of the theory of the social contract that suggests all civil authority, initially resting in the people, has been transferred by them to the ruler so that he may perform more easily certain necessary functions (Skocpol, 1979, p. 47).

The historical function of the social contract model was nothing less than an attempt to rationalize political obligation, to work to substitute an intelligible bargain for mystifying appeals to tradition and divine rights. This is the strain of the tradition of contract theory that Hobbes elaborates upon in his conceptualization of the relationship between the Leviathan and the people. Significantly, however, his absolutist emphasis still represents a departure from the emphasis in the original theory of obligation.

Hobbes's England was too divided for certain processes of political legitimation to take off without the centralization of authority at that time. Yet this centralization of authority could not continue for long once the expansion of economic life made possible the political ascendancy of new classes, especially the bourgeoisie. For absolute monarchy could not permanently play the role of arbiter insofar as the process of arbitration implies the existence of a balance, in this case a balance between power and wealth. Between the 16th and 18th centuries there is a constant internal struggle both within and between the European nations with respect to the balance of influence and power to be enjoyed by the newly emergent bourgeoisie, the Kings, and the aristocrats.

Clearly, the history of the period of the 16th to 18th centuries is replete with numerous instances of insatiable competition and the drive for power. In this specific instance, both Hobbes and Machiavelli, two of the Renaissance's major intellectual voices, were overt in their arguments for the need to centralize authority given the way in which power was achieved. Indeed, consensus was difficult, if not impossible, to achieve. And competition for power, wealth, and status often led to wars and civil disorder, both within and between states, thereby disrupting any real hope for economic development and lasting economic prosperity. Therefore, in examining the processes associated with political and economic development, it is imperative that economic welfare issues are viewed in conjunction with the concerns associated with power and status. Such a linkage is necessary, in order to understand both the history that Hobbes writes and reflects as well as present day Third World developmental challenges.

Indeed, it is the establishment of public order that is needed to provide the necessary conditions for all other values to find some degree of realization and flourish. Hobbes's England was clearly such a divided and stratified society. That is why the absolutist order of hierarchy as a method of centralized control was so workable as a provisional solution to the problems associated with civil war and social chaos. As the competition for distribution and consumption was worked out between classes in the longer political struggle for power and wealth, the channels for a constructive engagement were built between the various groups and classes. This was the birth of what I have called "inclusionary governance" and the "inclusionary state."

The experiences of compromise and negotiation in this period established those necessary behavioral and attitudinal abilities which made the legal tradition more operative and workable. Along with this, the processes of modernization and institutionalization combined to create a parliamentary system in England that outstripped anything else that was remotely similar on the continent. As the scope of organizational membership was thus transformed we find, in the example of England, a situation where regime and dissident organizations do begin to merge and slowly start to overlap. This creates a movement toward social and economic integration that also serves to reduce competition and increase cooperation. The key point is that, in the Hobbesian world of the 17th century, and well into the early 18th century, the hierarchical tendency was no mere atavism. Rather, it was a faithful response to a fundamental social demand of the age.

The demand and challenges involved with the framework of practical association necessitated, for Hobbes, an emphasis upon the absolutist characteristics of the state and its ideological justification vis-a-vis a more limited rendering of the mandate contained in earlier visions of contract theory. Yet with the evolution of European states to a more refined realization of the nation-state concept, the evolution of the legal conceptualization of sovereignty, and the associated aspects of juridical evolution, the basis was laid for the birth of liberal bourgeois democracy.

The preconditions for social interaction and cooperation were forged in the mid-16th century to the later 17th century, when the requirements for military security, the mitigation of social differences, and the prevention of religious war were addressed. These various trends and partial resolutions of societal crises of transition represent stages of a multidimensional evolution that forged the very foundations of what would come to be called representative government.

Hobbes's *Leviathan* provides a short-run solution to the long-term dilemma of unrestrained anarchy and the dynamics of political contestation—the prestige of the Leviathan. Hobbes envisioned the prestige of the Leviathan as the initiator of a new kind of society because he saw the Leviathan as a political force who could invoke his political power and moral suasion to bring actors that had been trapped in conflict to the bargaining table. It was his belief that once brought to the table of negotiation, compromises and understandings would be forged that could lay the foundation for the long-term needs of a vibrant Commonwealth. With the creation of a Commonwealth would come the reduction of political violence and the end of civil anarchy. In short, the debilitating effects of anarchy would be replaced with the blessings of civil society in the Commonwealth.

Yet, we should question the validity of Hobbes's assumption that a Leviathan is beneficial to the evolution of inclusionary systems of governance, even if serving only as a transitionary stage in the developmental process. In reviewing the historical landscape we find that history is cluttered with the ruins of absolutist states and authoritarian states that failed to produce long-term stability. With very few notable exceptions, if any, Leviathans, in general, have abused their power and generated powerful and exclusionary constituencies. Too often the energy and focus of such states has been predominantly dedicated to the perpetuation of a type of governance which has involved nepotism, cleptocratic practices, and the marginalization of many social groups and classes from the decisionmaking practices of the state. Such social, political, and economic isolation has resulted in the immiseration of masses of people and a disregard for the general welfare.

In the long run, Hobbes argued that the Commonwealth was capable of taking care of itself. Hence, it depends less and less on the interventions and tutelage of a Leviathan. With the reduction of political violence, the rationale for an interventionary Leviathan fades because its power becomes more irrelevant. In fact, with the end of anarchy, political, and social peace enables commerce to flourish so that economic growth and development may take off. As this process takes on a life of its own the Leviathan is seen more and more as an anachronism and becomes an unacceptable presence in the new society, for the Leviathan's role is outlived as the commonwealth is secured, commerce and industry advance and generate their own powerful classes, and political compromise and bargaining takes precedence over anarchy.

It is important to emphasize the provisional role played by Leviathan, but the emphasis should be upon the *provisional* nature of its task and purpose. Too often, Hobbes's vision has been misrepresented and distorted by the assertion that the Leviathan was supposed to be a *permanent* institution that was always to play essentially the same role. That is not the case. Rather, Leviathan's provisional task was to act as an antidote to anarchy. Once having brought the major parties and social actors to the table, he kept them at the negotiating table by virtue of his prestige and sometimes the implementation of his coercive force. For it was by his own authority he could help provide solutions and forge a larger societal consensus. His method to ameliorate differences may have started with coercive force but it was not intended to remain as mere coercion. This is where is the emphasis upon institution-building and the rule of law, especially constitutional law, comes into play. In Hobbes's vision, the task of generating a Commonwealth is what gives Leviathan his actual legitimacy and ultimate purpose. In practice, however, we find that historical evidence leads to the conclusion that Leviathans, once in power, have stayed too long and have compromised the national interest in favor of their own constituencies.

According to Hobbes, the Leviathan is constrained by the social contract itself. Hobbes makes it very clear that sovereign power is made conditional on the Leviathan's ability to provide protection for all parties, to include them in the long-run decision-making processes of the state, and to forge a social consensus strong enough to overcome anarchy. In historical practice, many Leviathans have trespassed their jurisdictional activities and gone beyond the parameters envisioned by Hobbes.

In the process of suppressing anarchy, the Leviathans of history repressed, instead, various classes, interests, and groups. In this sense, modern Leviathans have only been caricatures of Hobbes's vision. Therefore, a correct reading of Hobbes should, at the outset, recognize the fact that he stressed that coercion only lubricates the process of negotiation. Coercion is not a substitute for leadership or for a vibrant Commonwealth. Neither should coercion be confused with what constitutes legitimacy. What modern Leviathans have in common with Hobbes are the coercive characteristics to the exclusion of his prescription for inclusionary governance that would result in a reduction of political violence in the long run. This bifurcated reading of Hobbes is a distortion. It distorts not only by what it emphasizes, but also by what it omits.

Inclusionary governance is, in my definition, a form of statecraft that is cognizant of the fine balance which exists between "embeddedness" and "autonomy." The inclusionary state is not an intrusive state. Because it seeks consensus to reduce anarchy, violence, and political instability, it also seeks to introduce universalistic values and political expectations.

In short, the inclusionary state provides a map for the developmental process. It maps those areas of governance to avoid, such as reliance on coercion, nepotism, and particularism. It also maps those areas of governance to attend to, such as negotiation, arbitration, and consensus-building between classes and between the state and the larger civil society. Therefore, the inclusionary state both negates and affirms what is essential for the long-term benefits of economic, social, cultural, and political development. By consciously choosing what to affirm and negate, it also provides the basis for long-term legitimacy.

Legitimacy is derived from two prongs. The first is the short-run prong, which seeks to overcome societal anarchy while the state provides security for all parties to meet at the same table for dialogue, to work out their differences through political bargaining, negotiation and therefore accommodation. The second prong is focused on the long run. The emphasis is upon the fruition of a vibrant Commonwealth that is capable of improving the welfare of all classes through a stable social and political environment.

As societies become more inclusionary, they take on modern and post-modern values that undermine the rationale that supported coercive Leviathans in the first place. The particularistic elements must ultimately yield to the universalistic ones. Universalistic values, such as democratic participation, negotiation and arbitration in place of civil war, and recognition of the debilitating effects of anarchy for all sides, all combine to serve as the ingredients for inclusionary governance and the legitimating principles that are required to support it.

A society will be prepared to dispense with its particular Leviathan as soon as its Leviathan is seen as anachronistic in the context of an emerging form of governance that I have called inclusionary. It is inclusionary because the universalistic values which emerge in developing societies are the product of many experiences of group interaction, negotiation, and arbitration which form bonds of trust. These bonds of trust automatically transcend particularistic expressions of power which are linked to coercion.

To be truly legitimate, a society, as well as its state, must evolve toward the recognition that particularistic values and practices lead back to anarchy and the state of nature. As Hobbes reminded us, it is essential to form a Commonwealth of mutual respect, where inclusionary practices foster inclusionary governance and lay the foundation for more universalistic principles and practices. In turn, these principles and practices support the long-run efficacy of inclusionary governance in the service of the Commonwealth as a whole.

BIBLIOGRAPHY

Bruce Ackerman, *We the People*, Volume 2—*Transformations*, Harvard University Press, 1998.
Bruce Ackerman and Anne Alstott, *The Stakeholder Society*, Yale University Press, 1999.
Alberto Alesina, "Political Models of Macroeconomic Policy and Fiscal Reforms," *Voting for Reform: Democracy, Political Liberalization, and Economic Adjustment*, edited by Stephan Haggard and Steven B. Webb, Published for the World Bank, Oxford University Press, 1994.
Etienne Balibar and Immanuel Wallerstein, "The Nation Form: History and Ideology," *Race, Nation, Class: Ambiguous Identities*, Verso, 1991.
Wolfgang Beck, Laurent van der Maesen and Alan Walker, "Social Quality: From Issue to Concept," *The Social Quality of Europe*, edited by Wolfgang Beck, Laurent van der Maesen and Alan Walker, Kluwer Law International, The Hague, London, Boston, 1997.
David G. Becker, "Latin America: Beyond 'Democratic Consolidation'," *Journal of Democracy*, April 1999, Volume 10, No. 2.
Peter L. Berger, *Pyramids of Sacrifice: Political Ethics and Social Change*, Anchor Books, 1976.
Walden Bello, *Dark Victory: The United States, Structural Adjustment and Global Poverty*, Pluto Press with Food First and Transnational Institute, 1994.
Walden Bello and Stephanie Rosenfeld, *Dragons in Distress: Asia's Miracle Economies in Crisis*, A Food First Book, The Institute for Food and Development Policy, 1992.
Jon Breuilly, *Nationalism and the State*, Manchester: Manchester University Press, 1982.
Zbigniew Brezinski, *Out of Control: Global Turmoil on the Eve of the 21st Century*, Charles Scribner's Sons, 1993.
Thomas Carothers, "The Rule of Law Revival," *Foreign Affairs*, March/April 1998, p. 101.
Antonio Cassese, *Self-Determination of Peoples: A Legal Reappraisal*, Cambridge University Press, 1995.
Robert Chase, Emily Hill, Paul Kennedy, editors, *The Pivotal States: A New Framework for US Policy in the Developing World*, W.W. Norton & Company, 1999.
Dimitris N. Chryssochoou, *Democracy in the European Union*, Tauris Academic Studies, 1998.
Christopher Clague, Philip Keefer, Stephen Knack, and Mancur Olson, "Democracy, Autocracy, and the Institutions Supportive of Economic Growth," *Institutions and Economic Development: Growth and Governance in Less-Developed and Post-Socialist Countries*, edited by Christopher Clague, The Johns Hopkins University Press, 1997.
Jean L. Cohen and Andrew Arato, *Civil Society and Political Theory*, The MIT Press, 1994, p. 346.
Joshua Cohen and Joel Rogers, *Associations and Democracy: The Real Utopias Project*, Volume I, Verso, 1995.
Dennis Davis, Matthew Chaskalson, and Johan De Waal, "Democracy And

Constitutionalism: The Role of Constitutional Interpretation," *Rights and Constitutionalism: The New South African Legal Order*, edited by Dawid Van Wyk, John Dugard, Bertus de Villiers and Dennis Davis, Clarendon Press, Oxford, 1995.
Philippe Delmas, *The Rosy Future of War*, The Free Press, 1995.
Renee de Nevers, "Slovakia," *The Costs of Conflict: Prevention and Cure in the Global Arena*, edited by Michael E. Brown and Richard N. Rosecrance, Carnegie Commission on Preventing Deadly Conflict, Rowman & Littlefield Publishers, Inc., 1999.
Brian M. Downing, *The Military Revolution and Political Change: Origins of Democracy and Autocracy in Early Modern Europe*, Princeton University Press, 1992.
Michael W. Doyle, *Ways of War and Peace: Realism, Liberalism, and Socialism*, W.W. Norton & Company, 1997.
S.N. Eisenstadt and L. Roniger, *Patrons, Clients and Friends: Interpersonal Relations and the Structure of Trust in Society*, Cambridge University Press, 1984.
Miriam F. Elman, "The Need for a Qualitative Test of the Democratic Peace Theory," *Paths to Peace: Is Democracy the Answer?*, edited by Miriam F. Elman, The MIT Press, 1997.
Charles H. Fairbanks, Jr., "The Feudalization of the State," *Journal of Democracy*, April 1999, Volume 10, No. 2.
Richard Falk, *On Humane Governance: Toward a New Global Politics*, The Pennsylvania State University Press, 1995.
Jeff Faux, "Lost on the Third Way," *Dissent*, Spring 1999.
Takis Fotopoulos, *Towards an Inclusive Democracy: The Crisis of the Growth Economy and the Need for a New Liberatory Project*, Cassell, 1997.
Geoffrey Garrett, *Partisan Politics in the Global Economy*, Cambridge University Press, 1998.
D. Gauthier, *Morals by Agreement*, Oxford University Press, 1986.
Alan Gewirth, *The Community of Rights*, The University of Chicago Press, 1996.
Anthony Giddens, *The Nation-State and Violence: Volume Two of a Contemporary Critique of Historical Materialism*, University of California Press, 1985.
Anthony Giddens, *The Third Way: The Renewal of Social Democracy*, Polity Press, 1998.
Anthony Giddens, *The Third Way and Its Critics*, Polity Press, 2000.
Dmitri Glinski and Peter Reddaway, "What Went Wrong in Russia?: The Ravages of 'Market Bolshevism'," *Journal of Democracy*, April 1999, Volume 10, No. 2.
John Gray, *False Dawn: The Delusions of Global Capitalism*, The New Press, 1998.
John Gray, "Not for the First Time, World Sours on Free Markets," *The Nation*, October 19, 1998.
Ted Robert Gurr, *Minorities at Risk: A Global View of Ethnopolitical Conflicts*, United States Institute of Peace, 1993.
Jurgen Habermas, *Between Facts and Norms: Contributions to a Discourse*

Theory of Law and Democracy, translated by William Rehg, The MIT Press, 1996.
Jurgen Habermas, *The Inclusion of the Other: Studies in Political Theory*, The MIT Press, 1998.
Stephan Haggard, "The Politics of the Asian Financial Crisis," *Journal of Democracy*, April 2000, Volume 11, No. 2.
Thomas Hobbes, *Human Nature and De Corporate Politico*, Oxford University Press, 1994.
Thomas Hobbes, *Leviathan*, edited by Richard Tuck, Cambridge University Press, 1992.
Stanley Hoffmann, *World Disorders: Troubled Peace in the Post-Cold War Era*, Rowman & Littlefield Publishers, Inc., 1998.
Thomas F. Homer-Dixon, *Environment, Scarcity, and Violence*, Princeton University Press, 1999.
Martha K. Huggins, *Political Policing: The United States and Latin America*, Duke University Press, 1998.
Samuel P. Huntington, *The Clash of Civilizations and the Remaking Of World Order*, Simon & Schuster, 1996.
Samuel P. Huntington and Joan M. Nelson, *No Easy Choice: Political Participation in Developing Countries*, Harvard University Press, 1976.
Ronald Inglehart, *Modernization and Postmodernization: Cultural, Economic, and Political Change in 43 Societies*, Princeton University Press, 1997.
Jeffrey C. Isaac, *Democracy in Dark Times*, Cornell University Press, 1998.
Andrei Illarionov, "The Roots of Economic Crisis," *Journal of Democracy*, April 1999, Volume 10, No. 2.
Robert H. Jackson, *Quasi-States: Sovereignty, International Relations and the Third World*, Cambridge University Press, 1990.
Robert C. Johansen, *The National Interest and the Human Interest: An Analysis of US Foreign Policy*, Princeton University Press, 1980.
Christian Jopke, "Immigration Challenges the Nation-State," *Challenge to the Nation-State: Immigration in Western Europe and the United States*, edited by Christian Jopke, Oxford University Press, 1998.
Christopher C. Joyner, "The United Nations and Democracy," *Global Governance: A Review of Multilateralism and International Organizations*, Volume 5, No. 3, July-Sept. 1999.
Richard S. Katz, *Democracy and Elections*, Oxford University Press, 1997.
Gregory S. Kavka, *Hobbesian Moral and Political Theory*, Princeton University Press, 1986.
Robert O. Keohane and Stanley Hoffmann, editors, *The New European Community: Decisionmaking and Institutional Change*, Westview Press, 1991.
Robert O. Keohane, "Hobbes's Dilemma and Institutional Change in World Politics: Sovereignty in International Society," *Whose World Order?: Uneven Globalization and the End of the Cold War*, edited by Hans-Henrik Holm and Georg Sorensen, Westview Press, 1995.
Martin Kilson, editor, *New States in the Modern World*, Cambridge, Mass.: Harvard University Press, 1975.
Jytte Klausen and Louise A. Tilly, editors, *European Integration in Social and Historical Perspective—1850 to the Present*, Rowman & Littlefield Publishers, Inc., 1997.

Bradley S. Klein, *Strategic Studies and World Order: The Global Politics of Deterrence*, Cambridge University Press, 1994.

Arieh J. Kochavi, *Prelude to Nuremberg: Allied War Crimes Policy and the Question of Punishment*, The University of North Carolina Press, Chapel Hill, 1998.

Stephen D. Krasner and Daniel T. Froats, "Minority Rights and the Westphalian Model," *The International Spread of Ethnic Conflict: Fear, Diffusion, and Escalation*, edited by David A. Lake and Donald Rothchild, Princeton University Press, 1998.

Jody S. Kraus, *The Limits of Hobbesian Contractarianism*, Cambridge University Press, 1993.

J. Kugler, M. Benson, A. Hira, D. Panasevich, "Political Capacity and Violence," *Political Capacity and Economic Behavior*, edited by Marina Arbetman and Jacek Kugler, Westview Press, 1997.

Hans Kung, *A Global Ethic for Global Politics and Economics*, Oxford University Press, 1998.

Percy Lehning and Albert Weale, editors, *Citizenship, Democracy and Justice in the New Europe*, Routledge, 1997.

Christiane Lemke, "Crossing Borders and Building Barriers: Migration, Citizenship, and State Building in Germany," *European Integration in Social and Historical Perspective: 1850 to the Present*, edited by Jytte Klausen and Louise A. Tilly, Rowman & Littlefield, Publishers, 1997.

Ted C. Lewellen, *Dependency and Development: An Introduction to the Third World*, Bergin & Garvey, 1995.

Colin Leys, *The Rise and Fall of Development Theory*, Indiana University Press, 1996.

S.A. Loyd, *Ideals as Interests in Hobbes's Leviathan: The Power of Mind Over Matter*, Cambridge University Press, 1992.

Gunner Lind, "Great Friends and Small Friends: Clientelism and the Power Elite," *Power Elites and State Building*, edited by Wolfgang Reinard, Clarendon Press, 1996.

Michael Lind, *The Next American Nation: The New Nationalism and the Fourth American Revolution*, The Free Press, 1995.

Michael Lind, *Up From Conservatism: Why the Right Is Wrong for America*, The Free Press, 1996.

Stephan Leibfried and Paul Pierson, "Semisovereign Welfare States: Social Policy in a Multitiered Europe," *European Social Policy: Between Fragmentation and Integration*, edited by Stephan Leibfried and Paul Pierson, The Brookings Institution Press, 1995.

Abraham F. Lowenthal, "Latin America at the Century's Turn," *Journal of Democracy*, April 2000, Volume 11, Number 2.

Alexander Lukin, "Forcing the Pace of Democratization," *Journal of Democracy*, April 1999, Volume 10, No. 2.

Princeton N. Lyman, "Politics and Diplomacy: Globalization and the Demands of Governance," *Georgetown Journal of International Affairs*, Winter/Spring 2000, Volume 1, Number 1.

Michael McFaul, "The Perils of a Protracted Transition." *Journal of Democracy*, April 1999, Volume 10, No. 2.

Mahmood Mamdani, "From Conquest to Consent as the Basis of State

Formation: Reflections on Rwanda," *The New Left Review*, No. 216, March/April 1996.
Nelson Mandela, "The Challenge of the Next Century: The Globalization of Responsibility," *New Perspectives Quarterly*, Volume 17, Number 1, Winter 2000.
Jose Maria Maravall, *Regimes, Politics, and Markets: Democratization and Economic Change in Southern and Eastern Europe*, Oxford University Press, 1997.
Richard Marius, *Martin Luther: The Christian Between God and Death*, The Belknap Press, Harvard University Press, Cambridge, Massachusetts, 1999.
Andre Martin and George Ross, "Europe's Monetary Union: Creating A Democratic Deficit?," *Current History: A Journal of Contemporary World Affairs*, April 1999.
Rex Martin, *A System of Rights*, Clarendon Press, Oxford, 1993.
Ralph Miliband, *The State in Capitalist Society: An Analysis of the Western System of Power*, Basic Books, Inc., 1969.
Kurt Mills, *Human Rights in the Emerging Global Order: A New Sovereignty?*, St. Martin's Press, Inc., 1998.
K. R. Minogue, *Nationalism*, London: Batsford, 1967.
Martha Minow, *Between Vengeance and Forgiveness: Facing History after Genocide and Mass Violence*, Beacon Press, Boston, 1998.
Ronaldo Munck, *Politics and Dependency in the Third World: The Case of Latin America*, Zed Books Ltd., 1984.
Alexander B. Murphy, "The Sovereign State System as Political-Territorial Ideal: Historical and Contemporary Considerations," *State Sovereignty as Social Construct*, edited by Thomas J. Biersteker and Cynthia Weber, Cambridge University Press, 1996.
Thomas D. Musgrave, *Self-Determination and National Minorities*, Clarendon Press, Oxford, 1997.
Terry Nardin, *Law, Morality, and the Relations of States*, Princeton University Press, 1983.
Aryeh Neier, *War Crimes: Brutality, Genocide, Terror, and the Struggle for Justice*, Times Books, Random House, 1998.
Michael Newman, *Democracy, Sovereignty and the European Union*, St. Martin's Press, 1996.
Douglas C. North, *Institutions, Institutional Change and Economic Performance*, Cambridge University Press, 1990.
Michael J. Perry, *The Idea of Human Rights: Four Inquiries*, Oxford University Press, 1998.
James Petras and Chronis Polychroniou, "Rethinking Globalization: From the Future to the Past," *Socialism and Democracy*, Vol. 12, Nos. 1–2, 1998.
James Petras, "The Third Way: Myth and Reality," *Monthly Review*, March 2000.
Kevin Phillips, *The Cousins' Wars: Religion, Politics, & The Triumph of Anglo-America*, Basic Books, 1999.
Paul Pierson and Stephan Leibfried, "The Dynamics of Social Policy Integration," *European Social Policy: Between Fragmentation and Integration*, edited by Stephan Leibfried and Paul Pierson, The Brookings

Institution Press, 1995.
Paul Pierson and Stephan Leibfried, "Multitiered Institutions and the Making of Social Policy," *European Social Policy: Between Fragmentation and Integration*, edited by Stephan Leibfried and Paul Pierson, The Brookings Institution Press, 1995.
Frances Fox Piven and Richard A. Cloward, *The Breaking of the American Social Compact*, The New Press, 1997.
Marcus G. Raskin, *The Common Good: Its Politics, Policies and Philosophy*, Routledge & Kegan Paul, New York and London, 1986.
Steven R. Ratner and Jason S. Abrams, *Accountability for Human Rights Atrocities in International Law: Beyond the Nuremberg Legacy*, Clarendon Press, Oxford, 1997.
John Rawls, *A Theory of Justice*, Harvard University Press, 1978.
The Report of The Century Foundation/Twentieth Century Fund Task Force On Apprehending Indicted War Criminals, *Making Justice Work*, With background papers by Marshall Freeman Harris, R. Bruce Hitchner, Michael P. Scharf, and Paul R. Williams and Diane F. Orentlicher, The Century Foundation Press, 1998.
Andrew S. Reynolds, *Electoral Systems and Democratic Consolidations in Southern Africa*, Dissertation, University of California, San Diego, 1996.
Anthony H. Richmond, *Global Apartheid: Refugees, Racism, and the New World Order*, Oxford University Press, 1994.
Thomas Risse-Kappen, "Structures of Governance and Transnational Relations: What Have We Learned?," *Bringing Transnational Relations Back In: Non-State Actors, Domestic Structures and International Institutions*, Cambridge University Press, 1995.
Caroline M. Robb, *Can the Poor Influence Policy?: Participatory Poverty Assessments in the Developing World*, The World Bank, Washington, D.C., 1999.
William I. Robinson, "Latin America and Global Capitalism," *Race & Class: A Journal for Black and Third World Liberation*, Vol. 40, October 1998–March 1999, No. 2/3.
William I. Robinson and Jerry Harris, "Towards a Global Ruling Class?: Globalization and the Transnational Capitalist Class," *Science & Society*, Volume 64, Number 1, Spring 2000.
Naomi Roht-Arriaza, editor, *Impunity and Human Rights in International Law and Practice*, Oxford University Press, 1995.
Alan Ryan, "Britain: Recycling the Third Way," *Dissent*, Spring 1999.
Anne Saadah, *Germany's Second Chance: Trust, Justice, and Democratization*, Harvard University Press, 1998.
Lawrence A. Scaff and Edward J. Williams, "Participation and the Primacy of Politics in Developmental Theory," *Political Participation in Latin America, Volume I, Citizen and State*, edited by John A. Booth and Mitchell A. Seligson, Holmes & Meier Publishers, Inc., 1978.
Joachim K. H. Schmidt, "Philosophical Roots of Totalitarianism in Twentieth-Century Germany," *Totalitarian and Post-Totalitarian Law*, edited by Adam Podgorecki and Vittorio Olgiati, The Onati International Institute for the Sociology of Law, Dartmouth, 1996.

Michael Schudson, *The Good Citizen: A History of American Civic Life*, The Free Press, 1998.
James C. Scott, *Seeing Like a State: How Certain Schemes to Improve the Human Condition Have Failed*, Yale University Press, 1998.
Philip Selznick, *The Moral Commonwealth: Social Theory and the Problems of Community*, University of California Press, 1992.
Aaron Shakow and Alec Irwin, "Terms Reconsidered: Decoding Development Discourse," *Dying for Growth: Global Inequality and the Health of the Poor*, edited by Jim Yong Kim, Joyce V. Millen, Alec Irwin, John Gershman, Common Courage Press, 2000.
Donald W. Shriver Jr., *An Ethic for Enemies: Forgiveness in Politics*, Oxford University Press, 1995.
Laura Silber and Allan Little, *Yugoslavia: Death of a Nation*, TV Books, Distributed by Penguin USA, 1995.
Theda Skocpol, *States and Social Revolutions: A Comparative Analysis of France, Russia and China*, Cambridge University Press, 1979.
Robert O. Slater, Barry M. Schutz, and Steven R. Dorr, editors, *Global Transformation and the Third World*, Lynne Rienner Publishers, 1993.
Anthony D. Smith, *Nationalism in the Twentieth Century*, Canberra: Australian National University Press, 1979.
Jens M. Sorensen, *The Exclusive European Citizenship: The Case for Refugees and Immigrants in the European Union*, Avebury, 1996.
The South Centre, *Facing the Challenge: Responses to the Report of the South Commission*, Zed Books, in association with South Centre, 1993.
James Gustave Speth, "Poverty: A Denial of Human Rights," *Journal of International Affairs*, Columbia University School of International and Public Affairs, Vol. 52, No. 1, Fall 1998.
James Gustave Speth, "The Plight of the Poor: The United States Must Increase Development Aid," *Foreign Affairs*, May/June 1999.
Hendrik Spruyt, *The Sovereign State and Its Competitors: An Analysis of Systems Change*, Princeton University Press, 1994.
Nicolas Spulber, *Redefining The State: Privatization and Welfare Reform in Industrial and Transitional Economies*, Cambridge University Press, 1997.
Julius Stone, *Visions of World Order: Between State Power & Human Justice*, The Johns Hopkins University Press, 1984.
Clive Y. Thomas, *The Rise of the Authoritarian State in Peripheral Societies*, Monthly Review Press, 1984.
Jacques Thomassen, "Support for Democratic Values," *Citizens and the State*, edited by Hans-Dieter Klingemann and Dieter Fuchs, Oxford University Press, 1995.
Vladimir Tisaneanu, *Fantasies of Salvation: Democracy, Nationalism, and Myth in Post-Communist Europe*, Princeton University Press, 1998.
Steven Van Evera, "Hypotheses on Nationalism and War," *Theories of War and Peace*, edited by Michael E. Brown et al., The MIT Press, 1998.
Frank Vibert, *Europe: A Constitution for the Millennium*, Dartmouth, 1995.
Spencer R. Weart, *Never at War: Why Democracies Will Not Fight One Another*, Yale University Press, 1998.

J. H. H. Weiler, *The Constitution of Europe: "Do the New Clothes Have an Emperor?" And Other Essays on European Integration*, Cambridge University Press, 1999.

Burns H. Weston, Richard Falk and Hilary Charlesworth, *International Law And World Order: A Problem-Oriented Coursebook*, Third Edition, American Casebook Series, West Group, 1997.

Gordon White, Jude Howell, and Shang Xiaoyuan, *In Search of Civil Society: Market Reform and Social Change in Contemporary China*, Clarendon Press, Oxford, 1996.

Franke Wilmer, "The Social Construction of Conflict and Reconciliation in the Former Yugoslavia," *Social Justice*, Vol. 25, No. 4, Winter 1998.

David Wippman, "Practical and Legal Constraints on Internal Power Sharing," *International Law and Ethnic Conflict*, edited by David Wippman, Cornell University Press, 1998.

Daniel Yergin, *The Commanding Heights: The Battle Between Government and the Marketplace That Is Remaking the Modern World*, Simon & Schuster, 1998.

Part III

THE BROKEN AND UNBROKEN PROMISE OF INCLUSION

CHAPTER 6

THE PROMISE OF INCLUSION: INCLUSIONARY VERSUS EXCLUSIONARY GOVERNANCE

If government fails to meet the increasing burdens put upon it by the process of social mobilization, a growing proportion of the population is likely to become alienated and disaffected from the state, even if the same language, culture and basic institutions were shared originally throughout the entire state territory by rulers and ruled alike . . . At bottom, the popular acceptance of a government in a period of social mobilization is most of all a matter of its capabilities and the manner in which they are used—that is, essentially a matter of its responsiveness to the felt needs of its population. If it proves persistently incapable or unresponsive, some or many of its subjects will cease to identify themselves with it psychologically; it will be reduced to ruling by force where it can no longer rule by display, example and persuasion and if political alternatives to it appear, it will be replaced eventually by other political units, larger or smaller in extent, which at least promise to respond more effectively to the needs and expectations of their peoples.

Karl W. Deutsch,
Tides Among Nations, 1979, pp. 104–105

Poverty increases insofar as freedom retreats throughout the world, and vice versa. And if this cruel century has taught us anything at all, it has taught that the economic revolution must be free just as liberation must include the economic. The oppressed want to be liberated not only from their hunger but also from their masters. They are well aware that they will be effectively freed of hunger only when they hold their masters, all their masters, at bay.

Albert Camus, "Bread and Freedom,"
Resistance, Rebellion, and Death, 1974, p. 94

> Every society provides the stage for certain hardened, recurrent ways of dealing among people. These enacted images of association translate the indeterminate idea of society into particular ways of living together. Each such image connects beliefs about the possible with beliefs about the desirable and both with practical arrangements. Each is at once a promise of happiness and a device of order.
>
> Roberto Mangabeira Unger, *Democracy Realized: The Progressive Alternative,* 1998, p. 125

A. INTRODUCTION

In both the First and Third World, social and political instability has been the primary cause of deadly conflicts. Additional causes are found in the combined forces of modernization and globalization which have further accentuated inequalities that are already present in nations. Coupled with the challenges brought by modernization and globalization are historically entrenched practices of exclusionary governance that are antithetical to the realization of peace, economic and social justice, a serious undertaking to reduce and eventually eliminate poverty, and an expansion of democratic inclusion.

Exclusionary practices and hierarchies of power have traditionally been employed by nation-states to maintain the status quo of domestic power arrangements. The resulting exclusionary practices and hierarchies have served to fuel deadly conflicts from the Balkans to Rwanda and Burundi (Weissman, 1998). The presence of these exclusionary hierarchies have also blocked genuine constitutional reform in Kenya and allowed the Nigerian military to suffocate civil society (United States Institute of Peace, December 1997; RFK Memorial Center For Human Rights, September 1998) .

In Latin America, the face of exclusionary practices, in the name of law and order, comes in the form of militarized democracy, sometimes referred to as "guardian democracy." In "guardian democracy" military power endures as a check against and counter-weight to popular majorities. The result of this trend is the latent threat of a military reaction that has the power to shape government decision making and inhibit popular participation (Mc Sherry, 1998, p. 16). So-called "transitions to democracy" have been characterized by an enduring authoritarian legacy of previous military dictatorships.

Both military rulers and their civilian business counterparts have collaborated in defining and negotiating the conditions of the "transition." As a result, most institutions of the state, including the police, the judiciary, and the military, have been able to keep the legacy of an authoritarian past intact. This authoritarian socioeconomic system is based primarily upon elite control of the mass media while, at the same time, the financial and productive systems remain unchanged. The "civilian neoliberal politicians" have largely maintained their political power through ruling by decree and have used the military to enforce their policies of privatization and adjustment. According

The Promise of Inclusion 289

to Veltmeyer, "the point of this continuity of authoritarianism is that it limits citizen activity, undermines political debate and forces politicians into the neoliberal framework" (Veltmeyer, 1997, p. 214).

The nature and requirements of the neoliberal approach to fiscal adjustment have been deadly to the realization of democracy in the context of both First and Third World states. But is has been worse in the Third World. The weakening of state institutions by too great a reliance on the neoliberal agenda reveals the fundamental flaw inherent in neoliberalism. The principal flaw, which is also neoliberalism's greatest mistake, is that its prescriptions "underestimate the role of state institutions in organizing both the public and the private life of groups and individuals. Without an effective state, there can be no democracy" (Przeworski, 1995, p. 110).

For example, in the First World context, the practice of democracy has been reduced to little more than a ritual in which "no policy alternative is offered to the electorate. As in the one-party state, the results of the ballot have virtually no impact on the actual conduct of state and economic policy. In turn, the state under the neoliberal policy agenda has become increasingly repressive in curbing the democratic rights of its citizens" (Chossudovsky, 1997, p. 25). The developed nations, from the United States to the European Union, are the new protagonists of "strong economic medicine," labeled under slogans such as: "we must reduce the deficit," "we must combat inflation," the "economy is overheating" so "put on the brakes."

In the Third World context, the International Monetary Fund (IMF) and the World Bank operate through a standard regime of reform packages or "austerity measures" which result in a consistent pattern of economic and social collapse. These austerity measures lead to an eventual disintegration of the state in which the national economy is remolded and destroy the entire fabric of the domestic economy (*Id.*, p. 69). The implications for democracy are grim. Why? Because democracy's grim future is the product of the five main tenets of neoliberal rule and an attempt at global governance through a process of exclusionary governance, under the auspices of exclusionary states.

1. From Commonwealth to "Private Wealth"

Neoliberal rule is composed of five main elements. The elements and their effects are as follows:

First, *the rule of the market* means liberating "free" enterprise or private enterprise from any bonds imposed by the state. This "liberation" is imposed no matter what the social costs, irrespective of massive human suffering. The de-unionization of workers and the subordination of worker's rights are at the heart of the neoliberal enterprise (Barry, 1995; Grinspun and Cameron, 1993; Warnock, 1995; Rosen and McFadyen, 1995).

Second, *removing or reducing the safety net for the poor has cut public expenditure for social services*. Government's role is reduced for the majority while, at the same time, its role has been effectively increased for the minority who enjoy the privileges of subsidies and tax benefits.

Third, *deregulation* has effectively removed government's hand from almost every conceivable avenue of activity that could impinge on business profits while, at the same time, failing to protect the environment and workers' safety on the job.

Fourth, *privatization* has allowed for the sale of state enterprises, goods and services to private investors, including banks, key industries, railroads, schools, hospitals, and even access to sources of fresh water. In the name of efficiency, wealth is more concentrated in a few hands and the "free" market becomes the reign of the monopolies. Hence, the cost to the public increases while the fortunes of the wealthy minority rise.

Fifth, and finally, *the elimination of fidelity to the concept and ideal of the common good or "commonwealth" is translated into an ideology for the expansion, concentration and protection of "private wealth."* Hence, the legacy bequeathed by neoliberalism is an elite-driven global system of "private wealth" that is at odds with the goals of a political and economic "commonwealth." It is in this exclusionary vortex that democracy discovers its contemporary predicament. These social, economic, and political trends have become the matrix of exclusion.

According to Unger, under these circumstances "no democratic politics can accommodate the pitiless economics of selective neoliberalism or its government-impoverishing fiscal adjustment." Why can't the state accommodate the neoliberal policies? Because "such an economic project would be feasible for a while if the politics that imposed it were sufficiently authoritarian, or the society that suffered it demoralized and passive enough" (Unger, 1998, p. 119).

However, the days of authoritarianism have passed with what Hungtington has called "the Third Wave." Between 1974 and 1990, transitions to democracy changed the political face of the globe. Beginning with the end of the Portuguese dictatorship in 1974, democratic regimes have replaced authoritarian ones in approximately thirty countries in Europe, Asia, and Latin America (Huntington, 1991, p. 21). Further, in other nations, there was a considerable liberalization which occurred in authoritarian regimes. In other countries, social movements in support of democracy gained momentum in spite of resistance and setbacks (*Id.*, p. 21). In Eastern Europe, in particular, the democratic gains were stunning. According to Maravall, the new democracies of Eastern Europe offer "no support for the thesis that markets can only be established by authoritarian regimes, or that the most viable sequences are those in which economic reforms come before political reforms" (Maravall, 1997 p. 125).

Still, there is a problem. Democratic gains are not enough, by themselves, to ensure democratic outcomes. While social scientists have invested a great deal of time and energy into trying to arrive at a parsimonious definition of democracy that can be used for measurement purposes, the definition remains elusive. Perhaps the attempt to measure and quantify a project such as "democracy" is impossible, at least in a purely scientific sense as something that is quantifiable and reducible to a mathematical calculus. That is not to say that political scientists have not tried.

Robert Dahl and Samuel Huntington have attempted to count the number of democratic advances in the period of the late 1910s and early 1920s. Dahl calculated that there were exactly twenty-two "polyarchies" (his term for institutionalized approximations of the democratic ideal), while Huntington found thirty-three incarnations of "democracy" (Dahl, 1989, p. 240; Huntington, 1991, p. 14). These discrepancies have been attributed to either a problem of definition or measurement. Therefore, the remedy that has been suggested by other political scientists has been to arrive at more precise definitions and more accurate measurements (Markoff, 1997, p. 54). This approach has only compounded the problem.

The embodiment, form, and practices of democracy are shaped by the matirix of culture, economics and markets, levels of social consciousness, and participation and debate. In the case of markets, the power of markets, especially those fashioned by international lending institutions under a neoliberal framework, has succeeded in creating divided societies, even when those societies are characterized as "democratic." A prime example is that of Mexico.

By mid-1999, Jorge Castaneda recognized that "the cleavages sundering Mexico have created not only two countries but two increasingly alienated societies." In differentiating between the two societies within one nation, he observed that "a booming export sector, concentrated in and looking to the north, has taken off. It is competitive, efficient, dynamic and outward-looking. Its inputs, credit output and standards are all US-based. The rest of Mexico—where more than 80% of the nation's 100 million inhabitants live and work—finds itself sinking into political fragmentation, economic stagnation and social dissolution" (Castaneda, May 10, 1999, p. B-5). The ranks of the excluded have increased. Social inclusion has been on the wane in spite of "democratic gains." Why?

Passivity has been turning into rebellion, as demonstrated by the rebellion in Chiapas. In a real sense, the Chiapas rebellion was a response to the logic of concentrating too much power in the state and its authoritarian policies, which only served to exclude civil society from economic and social policies. Coupled with the fact that there are no legal strikes in Mexico because the regime will not permit such democratic expressions of grievances, the absence of legal and peaceful channels for articulating the protests of the excluded and marginalized has juxtaposed Mexico's neoliberal regime with the demands of its own people. In this way, having deprived the excluded and civil society from articulating its peaceful demands from above, through formal legal channels, the Mexican state has forced significant sectors of the civil society to resist neoliberal and authoritarian policies by an armed struggle from below. Why?

The answer to many of the "whys" is found in the exclusionary practices of the Mexican state, operating under neoliberal guidelines. For example, more rigid labor legislation has provided protection and high incomes only to groups that are not poor while limiting the possibilities for job creation. These trends have tended to depress the incomes of temporary workers, the self-employed, and the rural classes. In fact, this neoliberal approach throughout Latin America has created rigid labor codes that have prompted governments to take further steps to make labor more flexible on the margins, thereby reducing protection for the more vulnerable groups (Lora and Londono, 1998, p. 81). Contrary to the predictions of orthodox economic theory, the high growth rates of the 1990s have not brought new jobs or higher wages. The new reality is forcing Latin American workers to work longer hours just to make ends meet. In political terms, what Latin Americans are experiencing are new policies which reflect dramatic changes between labor and capital.

The relationship between labor and capital is being restructured within the so-called neoliberal "reform state." This restructuring has brought about changes which would not have come about were it left to the actions of companies and private investors alone. Rather, the World Bank, the International Monetary Fund (IMF) and the Inter-American Development Bank (IDB) have worked together to dismantle labor legislation. The dismantling of labor legislation has been coupled with cuts within the public sector. The resulting privatizations and reductions in public spending have severely reduced public employment and led to a shrinking of the state's bureaucracy that has deprived the state of its most skilled and efficient public servants (Vilas, 1999, p. 19).

Along with the deterioration in the quality of employment are the associated cuts in health care, education, and a trend toward the inter-generational transference of poverty. All of these consequences are associated with a reduction of state spending in these areas. Why? Again, this is predominantly the result of following the model of the neoliberal reformers.

The contradictions which have emerged from the collapse of this neoliberal model have scholars working for the Inter-American Development Bank (IDB) talking out of both sides of their mouths. On the one hand, in assessing "where to go from here," they admit that "market reforms have been incomplete" and uneven because "market reforms have not advanced evenly in all areas or among the various countries" (Lora and Londono, 1998, p. 83). They admit that privatization has moved along unevenly from one country to another. On the other hand, they argue that "the greatest potential is found in the area of labor legislation, where market reforms have been meager despite the rigidities that hinder job creation in the region" (*Id.*, p. 83). Further, the IDB scholars acknowledge that markets not only have an impact on the inequality of income and opportunity throughout Latin America but also that "inequitable access to government services and to the decisionmaking bodies in government and other public institutions also influence the characteristics and persistence of inequality" (*Id.*, pp. 85–86). *In short, the prescription for social, political, and economic exclusion has been adherence to a neoliberal agenda.*

The conclusion to be drawn seems inescapable: *the persistence of inequality leads inexorably to the persistence of exclusion*. Market reforms, under a neoliberal framework, have created exclusionary regimes, whether they are labeled democratic or authoritarian. For the fact remains that market reforms have "not reduced the ranks of the unemployed or improved the uncertain incomes of specific population groups" (*Id.*, p. 86).

2. Outline of the Chapter

This chapter is divided into two main parts. The plan of Part B is to identify the major obstacles to realizing inclusionary goverance. The plan of Part C is to supply solutions for overcoming the obstacles to inclusionary governance and suggest the means for achieving it.

In Part B, the main obstacles that I have identified as blocking inclusionary governance are discussed in nine sub-sections. These subsections are: (1) the growing global inequalities which are, in part, a consequence of a reduced sovereignty among some nation-states relative to others; (2) the evolution of "quasi-states" throughout the Third World and their exclusionary tendencies; (3) a general discussion on the global dimensions of exclusion and how this translates into a vanishing welfare function in states and a greater reliance upon austerity programs and structural adjustment programs, which produce higher levels of social exclusion; (4) the idea of a global "Third Way" as a means to cushion the harsh effects stemming from the removal of the welfare function of the state and the imposition of austerity programs and structural adjustment programs; (5) how current trends reinforce, perpetuate and defend social, political and economic privilege, thereby acting as an obstacle to the promotion of inclusionary governance; (6) how social development needs to reject both the advances of polyarchy and neoliberalism if it is to embark on an inclusionary path; (7) why it is necessary to move social policy considerations from the background to the foreground of developmental thinking, institution-building, and the task of building an international culture of peace; (8) how the neoliberal program can be contested and opposed by demanding inclusionary governance be practiced in the realms of political decision making, economic practice, and social policy choices and investments; and (9) exposing the poverty of violence and the violence of poverty as interrelated obstacles to the achievement of peace, national and international equality, and the realization of an effective union between the advancement of human rights and legitimate forms of full state-sovereignty, both within and between nations. Having identified some of the major obstacles to inclusionary governance, Part C will examine the range of interrelated issues and solutions which can lead toward the achievement of and advancement toward inclusionary governance.

Part C is organized into three sub-sections that allow us to examine the various challenges to social, economic, political, and normative development. An examination of the interrelated nature of these challenges will be juxtaposed with proposed solutions. First, the interrelated factors of internal conflict are examined. Second, I propose five principles of inclusionary governance (the "Five C's"), which are presented as solutions to the crisis spawned by exclusionary governance. Third, and finally, I discuss the degree of effectiveness and efficiency with which the institutions of states ultimately determine successful or unsuccessful developmental outcomes. For, as I shall argue, ineffectiveness and inefficiency can be antithetical to both social development and inclusionary governance, thereby becoming contributing factors to wars, conflicts, and escalating violence. In order to end the trends toward conflict, war and violence, the five principles of inclusionary governance provide provisional solutions for overcoming exclusionary obstacles.

B. IDENTIFYING THE OBSTACLES TO INCLUSIONARY GOVERNANCE

1. Increasing Inequality and Reduced Sovereignty: The Dimensions of Exclusionary Governance

Latin America's corporative tradition has further accelerated the trend toward the exclusion of many social groups from the negotiating and decision-making process. Given the nature of exclusionary governance in this region of the world, the only real decisionmakers are those companies that belong to major business associations or workers who are tied to labor federations that are represented in bargaining social pacts (*Id.*, p. 86). For the great majority, however, the growth of poverty and high rates of unemployment are "combined with the increasing transformation of complex productive processes into simple operations" which have had the effect of reducing the returns on investments in training and education. In the final analysis, this process has "heightened the competition for available jobs and diminished the capacity of workers to bargain with capital" (Vilas, 1999, p. 20).

Between 1994 and 1995, the neoliberal model collapsed in Mexico. As a recent victim of so-called "structural adjustment policies" (SAP), Mexico's experience has vast implications for other nations on a global level. The implications include, but are not limited to, the realization that: (1) SAPs have stimulated crashes rather than take-off economies; (2) SAPs open the economy to massive trade deficits; (3) privatization has failed to produce increased levels of efficiency and, instead, resulted in higher concentrations of wealth in the form of new monopolies (with correspondingly higher levels of social, political and economic exclusion for the majority of people); (4) SAPs have created high-cost inefficiencies, through monopolies, which are the consequence of having eliminated competition. All of this has taken place in the name of the "free market" (Veltmeyer, 1997, p. 162). But the so-called "free market" is not free.

The state has not been turned into a consolidated democracy but has, instead, reverted back into a state-directed economy which is controlled by transnational corporations and banks. At stake have been Mexico's oil revenues and budget allocations, as well as the terms of trade. In short, the collapse of the Mexican model was a death-knell for the promises of neoliberalism. It represents the end of an illusion. The illusion is in two parts.

The first part of the collapsed illusion is that so-called free markets, of the neoliberal variety, could usher in an age of economic expansion, growth and development. What has been ushered in is a wide range of exclusionary economic and political practices that form an interlocking network of obstacles to any real efforts to bring about an inclusionary set of institutions and social practices. In the absence of mediating institutions to advance democratic inclusion, social conflicts have invariably arisen. Increased social and political conflict has led to rising levels of violence that has begun to shape a shared consensus—among both defenders and critics of the neoliberal model—that Latin America must develop institutions for handling social conflicts or expect more such conflicts in the absence of such institutions.

The second part of the collapsed neoliberal illusion is that some kind of viable or consolidated democracy would eventually emerge from this model of economic expansion, growth and development. Considering that what has developed is highly inegalitarian, in economic and social terms, it is next to impossible to imagine how egalitarian democratic politics and mediating institutions could evolve. The neoliberal expectation is especially problematic when we take into account the fact that the overall policy framework of neoliberalism has been in flux. In contrast, an attendant phenomenon of slow or stalled reform has allowed organized interest groups with strong stakes in the status quo more opportunities to protect their positions and to advance their exclusionary policies and practices (Graham and Naim, 1998, p. 349).

Out of this vortex of competing interests, we have reached a critical imperative in our thinking about the future of the democratic project in Latin America. That imperative is not to confuse the persistence of democracy, in name, with the genuine stability that flows from its actual consolidation. Further, it has been argued that "we should not confuse the absence of regime breakdown with the healthy persistence of democracy . . . corruption, human rights abuses, and institutional decay and inefficacy have already pushed a number of regimes below the threshold of democracy, and prolonged economic decay has played no small role in this" (Diamond, 1996, p. 76). In a similar vein of interpretation, Przeworski argues that "the ability of governments to compensate the losers and, more broadly, to manage social tensions is greatly curtailed, while the scope of decisions controlled by the democratic process is reduced by the international economic and political integration. And this combination of an increasing inequality with a reduced sovereignty is likely to exacerbate social conflicts and weaken the nascent democratic institutions" (Przeworski, 1995, p. 10).

The great challenges to development, effective statehood, the cause of peace, and the promotion of democratic norms are now multifaceted. We must move beyond the neoliberal illusion which has persistently distorted economic growth and development, and has stalled the creation of mediating institutions which could move the state, the market, and the civil society toward more inclusionary forms of governance and practice. We must also understand that the neoliberal project, on a global basis, distorts the reality presented in Hobbes's realism which centralizes the conception of sovereign statehood in both political theory and international law.

In a word, many states in Latin America, Asia, and Africa are not really sovereign states, but what Robert Jackson has called "quasi-states" (Jackson, 1990). What this means is that *democracy in Latin America is partial because sovereignty is partial*. Where sovereignty is partial, the state is not fully a state—it is a "quasi-state"—because the benefits of sovereign statehood have been limited to narrow groups of elites and not yet extended to the citizenry at large (*Id.*, p. 21).

The phenomenon of democratic exclusion or "guardian democracy" exists because the status of many Third World states is not co-equal with the status of the more economically advanced nations in the states-system, whose members have evidently decided that certain states shall remain as colonies and not be treated as co-equal sovereign states (*Id.*, p. 21). The demise of sovereign statehood for these nations has left them at the mercy of the dogmas and doctrines and neoliberalism that have turned Hobbes's views of sovereign statehood inside out. It is necessary to explain what this means before proceeding with an analysis of inclusionary versus exclusionary governance. For, as Chapter 5 on Hobbes's vision explained, the integrity of the sovereign state is essential to understanding all other attendant concepts of governance—authority, territory, population (society, nation), and recognition in a unique way and in a particular place (the state). If Hobbes's vision of governance has been turned into a paradox and is no longer consistent with his realist logic, it is now essential to explain why and how this is the case.

2. From Sovereign States to "Quasi-States": The Continuing Struggle for Inclusionary States

Hobbes's realism is founded on a conception of sovereign statehood. Chapter 13 of Hobbes' *Leviathan* calls direct attention to the frontiers of the state—internally and externally sovereign, protecting the inhabitants from not only one another but from an international state of nature. In terms of international relations, sovereigns are in the same condition as men in the state of nature. The task of national defense is carried out according to the sovereign's judgment and commands, thereby fulfilling the entire scope of the social contract which involves protecting the subjects of the sovereign from foreign threat. Should the sovereign fail the task of his office, which is to defend his subjects from external threats, the covenant with his people is dissolved and domestic civil society reverts to the state of nature. In this context, sovereignty is based on the sovereign's performance of his duty under the covenant. Ultimately, Hobbes's political theory is a constitutional theory of the sovereign state, with obligations involving the preservation of domestic peace as well as the maintenance of security against external threats.

With regard to Third World states, which Robert Jackson has called "quasi-states," the Hobbesian vision is transformed because "quasi-states possess arms but they usually point inward at subjects rather than outward at foreign powers which indicates that either no significant external threat exists or an internal threat is greater" (Jackson, 1990, p. 168). In quasi-states, the great majority of citizens are not defended against the external exploitation of political, economic, and social forces which rob them of the very guarantees and protections that sovereignty is supposed to provide them. Instead of a social contract, the excluded majority of peoples in Third World states experience the denial of human rights as they become subservient to national and international powers that create and acquire wealth at their expense. The price of exclusion results in profits for the few.

Within the quasi-sovereign jurisdiction of so many Third World states come the demands of international capitalism and Western powers and the internal compliance of their exclusionary states. All of this serves to reveal that the neoliberal agenda necessitates a sundering of the Hobbesian social contract, and that Third World states are not considered as "sovereign" states in the same manner in which Western states exercise their sovereignty. This is what makes many Third World states "quasi-states," for they exist in a different sovereign context—a non-Western sovereignty. What is the nature of this sovereignty? Looking inward at its expression, "there can hardly be a social contract since the ruler is threatening (at least some of) his subjects and evidently they him . . . The quasi-state is an uncivil more than a civil place: it does not yet possess the rule of law based on the social contract" (Jackson, 1990, p. 169). In the absence of the rule of law and a social contract, the populations of quasi-states constitute majorities throughout the Third World, subject to the predatory, cleptocratic and anti-democratic policies and procedures of exclusionary states.

From a Hobbesian realist perspective, this state of affairs means that quasi-states cannot logically collapse into a state of nature because their "sovereignty" is not derived internally from a social contract but, rather, is derived externally from the states-system, whose dominant Western membership has decided and resolved to uphold this arrangement. The consequence of this arrangement is one where the question is not: "Can international society influence state-building and the construction of positive sovereignty?" (which it certainly can), but the question is: "How ought it to influence this process?" (Inayatullah, 1996, p. 71).

The question of "ought" raises the ethical-normative question, in typical Kantian fashion. What is the "ethical ought" of international relations and the development of Third World states? Ought exclusionary states be reinforced? Ought there be greater degrees of political, social, and economic inclusion among the poor, the marginalized, and dispossessed? None of these questions have been seriously addressed by the Western-dominated neoliberal agenda because they raise a deeper and more fundamental question: "Do the excluded have a right to wealth?"

Behind the various theories of international relations and the legal regime of power relations and their legal status is the deeper question: "How ought states to create and acquire wealth within the global political economy?" This raises both normative and ethical issues which impinge on the smooth operations of a supposedly objective set of circumstances.

If we change the nature of the discourse on sovereignty to include the normative issues associated with the creation and acquisition of wealth—the equitable or inequitable distribution of economic wealth—then we must also raise corresponding questions about political structures, states, institutions and practices which systematically deny and exclude large numbers of groups, classes, and interests in every society and across the globe. If we change the nature of the discourse on sovereignty to be inclusive of these concerns, then we must see questions and issues of injustice, inequality, poverty, and indignity as the new ordering principles of global social life.

More precisely, such principles would invite new questions, such as:

"What role do wealth creation and acquisition play in constructing and challenging sovereignty?" Also: "What tacit principles have determined wealth creation and acquisition within the systems of sovereignty and capitalism?" Further: "Which principles ought to govern such wealth creation and acquisition?" (Inayatullah, 1996, p. 77). Returning to Robert Jackson's depiction of quasi-states is helpful at this point. For he reminds us that the quasi-state is upheld by an external covenant among sovereign states. This result "is not only ironical but also paradoxical in Hobbes's terms and inconsistent with his realist logic. Quasi-states turn Hobbes inside out: the state of nature is domestic, and civil society is international" (Jackson, 1990, p. 169).

Because the state of nature is now domestic, much social and political violence and instability in Third World states may be seen as imposed from the outside, disallowing the internal articulation of peaceful forms of discourse, bargaining, negotiation, and mediation between contending social groups, classes, and interests. The contagion of violence throughout the domestic politics of many Third World states may be seen as attributable to decisions made at the international level of power, on the level of a global civil society that is international in scope.

According to David Strang, this means that the "quasi-states," products of non-Western sovereignty, are not so much lacking in sovereign status as they are actively delegitimated in the eyes of the West. They are delegitimated because these non-Western states are located outside a rich Western framework of political meanings and a community of identities organized around those meanings (Strang, 1996, pp. 22–49). In a global perspective of international relations, what this interpretation implies is that sovereign recognition is embedded in a network of international political economy practices that, in their liberal form, exclude ethical considerations such as a right to wealth. Yet, such a right to wealth is ultimately necessary if sovereignty is ever to be fully realized by Third World states (Biersteker and Weber, 1996, p. 12).

The right to wealth is a right that can only be recognized and ultimately enforced by inclusionary states. That is because inclusionary states are not quasi-states, but sovereign states that are guided by inclusionary principles and practices, capable of acting as independent sovereign entities which are no longer susceptible to neoliberal manipulation or any other kind of manipulation that is beyond the scope of a rule of law which adheres to the protection and respect of the dispossessed, the poor, and the marginalized, around the globe. Yet, the realization of the inclusionary state is threatened because democratic citizenship is threatened by a rising tide of violence and deadly conflicts which emerge out of the vortex of exclusionary institutions, practices, and policies. In this connection, Przeworski has observed that "economic strategies have political consequences" (Przeworski, 1995, p. 111).

There are three categories which characterize the political consequences of economic strategies. Among these three categories are issues such as sovereignty, citizenship rights, and democractic deliberation, public expenditures and pro-market reforms. They are but a few of the political consequences that emanate from the articulation of economic strategies. The citizens of both the

First and Third World are deeply affected by these economic strategies. The three categories include:

First, the rapid internationalization of both economic and political relations has required nations, especially quasi-states, to alienate some traditional instruments of economic policy. Further, this status of reduced sovereignty restricts the scope of decisions that can be controlled by the democratic process. In other words, global finance has helped to short-circuit democracy's deliberative ideals and practices. In so doing, the process that leads to exclusionary governance has, de facto, limited the peoples' stake in political participation by constricting their range of choices and options (MacGregor, 1999, pp. 91–118).

Second, nascent representative institutions are undermined by a technocratic policy style that is deeply intertwined with pro-market reforms. This is now problematic for even First World states in the European Union for EU institutions have been used to "cicumvent national democratic processes and insulate the key instruments of monetary policy from democratic control" (Martin and Ross, April 1999, p. 172).

Third and finally, indiscriminate cuts in public expenditures serve to reduce the capacity of the state to guarantee the effective exercise of citizenship rights. This is especially the case in the areas of police protection, education, jobs, and income maintenance (Przeworski, 1995, p. 111; Anderson, July–September 1997, pp. 37–49); Keohance and Hoffmann, 1991; Leibfried and Pierson, 1995; Beck, Maesen and Walker, 1997; Newman, 1996; Joppke, 1998; Sorensen, 1996; Ucarer and Puchala, 1997; Vibert, 1995; Klausen and Tilly, 1997; Weiler, 1999; Chryssochoou, 1998; Lehning and Weale, 1997; Castells, 1998, Vol. III, pp. 310–334).

3. The Global Dimensions of Exclusion

In both the developing world and postcommunist transition countries, the hope of emulating the West's durable welfare state has vanished beyond the historical horizon of hope. The building of such a welfare state is another victim of the constant budgetary crises and austerity measures thrust upon developing nations and postcommunist transition countries by the IMF and global financial markets. Even the previously ascendant "Asian tigers" have collapsed, in a region that once believed in its own unique capacity to fashion an export-led growth plan into a proxy for welfare state policies. In the aftermath of the "Asian flu" that vision has evaporated like a dream. In its place, the contagion of IMF-imposed austerity programs and structural adjustment programs have replaced what was once considered to be irreversible dynamism.

From Korea to Indonesia, millions of newly unemployed have fallen into a deep cavern of misery, without social insurance of any kind. As the casualties mount, hopes diminish. The harbinger of the soon-to-be replicated crisis in Asia emerged earlier, in the Mexico of 1995. In 1995, the IMF and the United States arranged a fifty-billion dollar bailout for the Mexican economy. While investors were shielded from risks of economic catastrophe, the attendant social costs were high.

Mexico was to become one case, in a long line of cases, which would reveal the *exclusionary policies* of the IMF and how the IMF's "solution" was to become the cause of crisis. For example, wages in Mexico declined by 28 percent between 1995 and 1997. Social spending was dramatically slashed. Bank lending was cut to almost zero. Last, but not least, twenty-thousand small- and medium-sized businesses—one third of Mexico's commercial enterprises—went bankrupt and over two million people lost their jobs. The price of exclusionary governance, ultimately to be paid by millions of average people, was to be the astronomical social cost of, and tribute to, the IMF's structural adjustment programs and bailout in Mexico.

In Asia, as in Mexico, the primary aim of the IMF's program was to facilitate the return of foreign capital. The strategy is not a new one. Its history dates back to the era of Woodrow Wilson. In the aftermath of the the Great War, President Woodrow Wilson articulated a worldview which lay at the heart of Western progressive or enlightened liberalism. Specifically, this worldview held that the irrational and nationalist autocracies were ultimately reponsible for war and imperialism.

In the 1960s W.W. Rostow, in his influential work, *The Stages of Economic Growth*, set forth the first versions of modernization theory, accompanied by a variety of teleological representations designed to valorize the Western identity. At the core of the argument was the idea that underdeveloped countries remained particularly susceptible to social unrest in the first transition phase, from "traditional society" to the "preparation for take-off." It was here that the basic problem presented was one of the restructuring of long-standing work and life forms into *markets and exchange-oriented practices*. The result was that the ensuing dislocation of millions of people, now effectively excluded, often led to militant nationalism and had to be subordinated, repressed, held in place, lest it become the foundation for militant, radical oppositional social movements.

Rostow clearly understood that the processes of domestic change in Third World countries could not be carried out of their own accord. He was forced to concede that the internationalization of post-war capital and the construction of a truly international trading order require a strong political hand to lead developing nations through the first precarious stages toward "take-off." Additionally, investment capital would require more than charismatic leaders. The necessary infrastructure had to be built up in order to accommodate the needs of investment capital. Given this task, the most important goal during the first phase of the modernization process would have to be the establishment of more stable political institutions (Klein, 1994, p. 99)

The dominant model of modernization theory that emerged in the 1960s spawned contradictory imperatives that would eventually be imposed upon the governments of the newly industrializing countries. On the one hand, a nationalist orientation to reduce dependence on the rest of the world system was dedicated to developing both the economic and military self-reliance of individual nations through the full diversification of their economic activity. On the other hand, the opposing imperative was one of expanding the income and power of the state by developing linkages with the global economy and market capitalism which would increase interdependence along with increased specialization (Harris, 1986, p. 168).

In this emerging international matrix of power, the more successful governments of newly industrializing countries were pursuing growth as an end in itself, with little or no attention being given to the equitable distribution of the resultant economic benefits of that growth. Further, as private capital grew more powerful at home and the more closely integrated it became with external markets and world capital abroad, the more the power of government to shape the domestic economy declined. In other words, governmental power became increasingly less effective because its power was subordinated to the trends of the market (Harris, 1986, p. 169).

As to the Asian economies in the period of 1997–1998, we are now left to ponder the question of how the policies and trends spawned by modernization theory are now incarnated in the neoliberal prescriptions of the IMF for the purpose of accelerating the return of foreign capital. The late 1990s reveal the glaring inadequacies of the IMF prescription. First, a real program of recovery demands and requires a more diverse platform than merely waiting for the return of foreign investors. Second, even if we were to grant that focusing on foreign investors alone constitutes a valid strategy, the question that arises is: How can they be expected to return and make profitable investments in an economy where a recession is being engineered?

The severity of the Asian recession is stark in both its outline and its substance. Predictions were that in Thailand, where two million workers labor in service to capital's logic, 15 percent to 20 percent of the workforce would be left jobless between 1998 and 1999. In Indonesia, the economic free fall has increased the number of people in poverty from 22 million, at the beginning of 1998, to 58 million. At the same time, the ranks of the unemployed have swelled to over 15 million, or about 20 percent of the workforce.

In South Korea, unemployment reached around two million by the end of 1998, which is about 10 percent of the workforce. Throughout all of this, Asia's governments have been compliant with the IMF's bitter economic pills. Built on the foundation of exclusionary governance, these governments have constructed the legal framework in which these financial institutions operate. The governments of these nations have, in short, largely collaborated with the interests of international capital to build exclusionary states which no longer defend or promote the interests of their people but, rather, sacrifice their people's welfare and national interest to the demands of finanical institutions which seek to exact not only economic profit, but payment of the attendant social costs associated with such an extraction of profit as well. The effect of this trend is more than just "collateral damage" in the social arena. Its ultimate consequence is nothing less than an expanding pattern of social exclusion and marginalization in the name of profit, productivity, and efficiency. In this vortex, governments still retain the means to regulate the operation of the international money markets. All they lack is the political will to do so (Levinson, 1998, pp. 10–12).

4. A "Third Way" or "No Way"?

What would an alternative scenario look like? One such alternative has been called a "Global Third Way." A global "third way" has to be global, so the argument goes, because of the lessons which have emerged from the recent round of financial crises. In a global economy, a third way between traditional welfare states and IMF neoliberal policies cannot be forged by individual national governments working on their own. Rather, similar to the original post-war order of 1945, it must be the product of international cooperation and vision (Kapstein, 1998/1999, pp. 23–35).

By this logic, a viable "third-way strategy" represents the reconciliation of the logic of globalization with our moral sense of social justice. Under this scenario, we are reminded of the admonitions of John Rawls' classic work, *A Theory of Justice*, where he reminds us that increasing efficiency represents only one social concern among others. In contention for normative concern are the values of equality and justice—values that are of even greater ultimate consequence and must be taken into account by policy makers since, according to Kapstein, "an economic system that is widely viewed as unjust cannot, should not, endure" (Kapstein, 1998/1999, p. 31).

In thinking about third-way strategies, we are told that we must also think of third-way reformers. A third-way reformer would seek to promote and advance a more equitable economy. In fact, this reformer will seek to launch policies and programs on behalf of the least-advantaged citizens. This will, of necessity, involve the expansion of educational opportunities and retraining facilities. It will demand the provision of income transfers, health care, and social safety nets (*Id.*, p. 32). In all of this, a progressive "third-way" strategy must focus on two interrelated problems: "the renegade and destabilizing nature of mobile capital and the erosion of social safety nets" (*Id.*, p. 33). In making this argument, Kapstein comes to the conclusion that, taken together, these two measures "will mean a strengthening of the two Bretton Woods institutions, the Intenational Monetary Fund and the World Bank" (*Id.*, p. 33). On this point, I disagree.

I disagree because these institutions have promoted exclusionary governance around the globe in the name of efficiency. Also, much of the agenda of Kapstein's "third-way reformer" would be halted or destroyed by these institutions. Further, the social costs associated with the policy demands of the IMF and World Bank are, more often than not, antithetical to what I have called "inclusionary governance." The characteristics of an inclusionary agenda remain dedicated to eliminating poverty and unemployment while, at the same time, expanding the realm of democratic rights through more than mere reliance on formal elections. Hence, inclusionary governance, as an expression of state power, popular sovereignty, and adherence to democratic ideals would not be tolerated by IMF officials.

I argue that in place of the IMF and World Bank, inclusionary governments build "mediating institutions" so that the substance of the ideal of democracy begins to find a correspondence with the everyday reality of ordinary people. The actual substance of democracy, as an ideal, as well as the legal channels to realize and protect that ideal—through constitutionally protected inclusionary means—requires mediating institutions between the state and civil society. Such mediating institutions must act in conjunction with the norms of international law, which are complementary to inclusion. Western-dominated financial institutions, such as the IMF and World Bank, have not proven themselves capable of articulating, much less promoting, such a vigorous expression of social inclusion on a national or international basis. Therefore, inclusionary governance transcends the prescriptions of a global "third way," when such an approach merely leads to a strengthening of pre-existing modes of privilege through the continuing political and economic domination of countries and peoples. It is in this context that I turn to a discussion of the defense of privilege versus the promotion of inclusion.

5. The Defense of Privilege Versus the Promotion of Inclusion

In this chapter, I focus upon the need to adopt specific principles and practices which are the embodiment of what I call "inclusionary governance." The goals of governance can be associated with one of two different and distinct criteria. One criteria is dedicated to the defense of a privileged status quo. It seeks to advance the interests associated with privilege and hierarchy and exclusion, no matter what the human cost. It is the neoliberal agenda. The other criteria is the antidote to exclusionary governance, in all of its forms, because it vests its faith and effort into realizing and accomplishing the inclusion of all groups and classes within the nation into a social compact. The inclusionary social compact is one that produces equitable results as it opens channels for widespread participation in decision making and policy choices. The central criteria of inclusionary governance embodies the recognition that *it is vital to advance human development through peaceful means.*

I maintain that the means and institutions employed to effectuate and implement policies will directly affect the degree to which sociopolitical instability (SPI) inhibits or totally curtails economic growth and development, the pursuit of human rights, the institutionalization of democratic values and practices, as well as other significant values which are intimately associated with inclusionary governance. In this task, the state remains at the center for determining how inclusionary criteria are employed or ignored.

I view the means through which a state governs as important because violence, conflict, and social instability all operate to delay or disrupt development for both First and Third World states. Also, because the need for equitable and peaceful economic, political, social, and cultural development throughout the Third World is vital for the ultimate well-being and life opportunities of millions of people, I argue that the means should not be left to chance. After all, instead of transitions to democracy, the First and Third Worlds have seen transitions to polyarchy (an elite-based and undemocratic status quo), a system in which a small elite class rules on behalf of capital. This phenomenon is present from the European Union (EU) to the United States, from Asia to Africa, from Latin America to the Middle East.

6. Social Development: Beyond Polyarchy and Neoliberalism

Under polyarchy, participation by the majority is confined to virtually meaningless elections in which voters get to choose between competing elites. In the case of Latin America, the transitions from authoritarianism to polyarchy simply afford transnational elites the chance to reorganize state institutions so as to accommodate a framework for a deepening of neoliberal adjustment. In fact, under polyarchy, the practice of political inclusiveness is limited to the right to vote. This exposes polyarchy's "electoral fixation." For what political inclusivity fails to deliver under the framework of polyarchy leaves mass constituencies without formal institutional mechanisms or mediating institutions for holding elected officials accountable to them.

In fact, polyarchy, in its theory, makes the claim that democracy itself *requires* that the elected officials be "insulated," once they have taken office, from popular pressures, so that they may "effectively govern" (Robinson, 1996, p. 59). The result of this trend is what I call the establishment of "exclusionary states" and exclusionary governance. There is no equality of conditions that can result from such limited forms and expressions of electoral competition. As Robinson notes, "these conditions are decidedly unequal under capitalism owing to the unequal distribution of material and cultural resources among classes and groups, and to the use of economic power to determine political outcomes" (Robinson, 1996, p. 59). These are the adjustments made under political polyarchy and its economic twin, the neoliberal "structural adjustment programs."

Such adjustments do not constitute "development" if "development" is understood as inclusionary, participatory, comprehensive, equitable, and politically democratic in the broadest sense. In fact, what is being developed under the conditions of polyarchy and neoliberalism are new modalities of domination. As a new modality of domination, polyarchy is a structural feature of the emerging global society (i.e., "globalization") and as such it impacts both First and Third Worlds.

I seek to analyze the possibilities for a new kind of social, political, cultural, and economic development—one that is antithetical to the mandates of both polyarchy and neoliberalism. But what kind of "development" do I mean? If by the term "development" we mean that only the strictly economic aspects of development are emphasized, then too much has been omitted by that particular definition. For in conjunction with the need for economic "development" is the need to articulate and conceptualize the whole approach to *social* policy as well.

Social development should not be divorced from the complex matrix of economic development. Rather, development is the product of the union of social and economic development, in combination with social forces and movements, the evolution of civil society, the institutionalization of the state, and the degree to which a state is either embedded or autonomous from the civil society. It is this complex matrix which forms the basis for political development. And if political development is to be inclusionary, the nature of economic and social policies must be inclusionary as well.

If political development fails to be inclusionary and fails to attempt to approximate the democratic ideal, then we are left with what has been euphemistically called "low-intensity-democracy"—a form of political practice that is aimed at mitigating the social and political tensions which are the very product of an elite-driven and undemocratic status quo. This status quo is driven by the "exclusionary impluse" (my term). The *exclusionary impulse* works through social, political, cultural, economic institutions and practices to repress, de-politicize, subordinate, and suppress popular mass aspirations of the excluded, the marginalized, and dispossessed. The *exclusionary impulse* works to take social policy captive by depriving its shaping and formation of any voices other than those now occupying the vortex of power. And, again, it is a global process that affects both First and Third World peoples.

7. Reclaiming Social Policy from Background to Foreground

In conventional/traditional terms, social policy has been depicted as all that which is "non-economic"—areas such as social welfare, health, shelter, education, culture and all the rest. By adopting a limited view of development and by relegating "social policy" to the background, Rajni Kothari has noted that "social policy has . . . been accorded only residual attention and resources, after the demands of economic policy, which is the preoccupation of most governments, have been satisfied." That is not enough to fill out the terms, conditions and terrain of what really constitutes "development," however. For "the need today is for a social policy which cuts across sectors and levels in the government and encompasses all aspects, economic and non-economic, of governance. The need is for a social policy which clearly posits, before the nation, the social objectives which must guide all governmental action and must take predominance over merely sectoral interests" (Kothari, 1993, p. 143)

Kothari's view, once viewed by many economists and political scientists as being an "expendable" concern, or at least a subordinate concern, is now recognized by the United Nations as a top priority. In its *Human Development Report 1998*, the United Nations Development Program (UNDP) stated that "the human development perspective has moved into the mainstream of global debate"(Human Development Report 1998, p. 16).

The global *Human Development Report*, published annually since 1990, has triggered extensive national and international debate about the importance of "focusing on people and their capabilities and opportunities as the goal of development efforts" (*Id.*, p. 17). National teams have prepared these reports through a process of consultation with governments and its development partners. While the scope, nature, and processes for their preparation and follow-up have varied greatly from country to country, a review of their uses reveals four main impacts: (1) advocating human development; (2) highlighting critical concerns; (3) focusing on equity when planning for development; and (4) articulating people's perceptions and priorities (*Id.*, p. 19).

The overall result of these impacts has been to elucidate the idea that human poverty, as a concept, sees impoverishment as multidimensional. Since income is not the sum total of human lives, it follows that the lack of it cannot be the sum total of human deprivation. The authors of the UNDP report content that "more than a lack of what is necessary to material well-being, poverty can also mean the denial of opportunities and choices most basic to human development. To lead a long, healthy, creative life. To have a decent standard of living. To enjoy dignity, self-esteem, the respect of others and the things that people value in life" (*Id.*, p. 25). Because human poverty involves more than just income, as some economists would often have us believe, there is the growing recognition of the importance of what it means to be "included" or, alternatively, suffer the pangs of being "excluded" from the life of a community (*Id.*, p. 29). What are the implications of this new emphasis for social policy?

Returning to Kothari, he asserts that "a social policy must necessarily humanize governance, and be guided by concern for communities and individuals, however small and weak" (Kothari, 1993, p. 144). This concern serves to underscore my emphasis upon "inclusionary governance" as a more comprehensive approach to development, per se, and the challenges associated with the realization of human rights, the democratic ideal, social justice, the rule of law, the incorporation of the poor and dispossessed into the life of individual nations, and the recognition of their needs and rights throughout the international community as a whole.

Even the World Bank has recognized the importance of incorporating the previously excluded, marginalized, and poor into the development dialogue by helping to expand what it calls "participatory poverty assessment" (PPA). According to the World Bank, "PPAs use participatory research methods to understand poverty from the perspective of the poor by focusing on their realities, needs, and priorities . . . The principle of a PPA is to ensure that the intended beneficiaries have some control over the research process" (Robb, 1999, p. xiii). When it comes to moving toward strengthening policy implementation, the PPA needs to be designed to accomplish three main tasks: (1) use participatory techniques to diagnose both the policy environment and the ability and willingness of institutions to deliver the evolving policy; (2) build the capacity of institutions to use participatory methods in the formulation and implementation of the policy; and (3) initiate appropriate partnerships and linkages along and within formal and informal networks and institutions (*Id.*, pp. xv–xvi).

8. Contesting the Neoliberal Dogma by Demanding Inclusion

It is vital for both the international community and individual nation-states to begin to recognize and act upon the task of meeting the needs of the poor, the excluded, and the marginalized. In a real sense, the unmet needs of the poor, the excluded, and the marginalized are at the heart of what constitutes poverty and what lie behind "underdevelopment" in both First and Third World contexts. The relationship between poverty and development is so intimate that some have argued that "development cooperation is in crisis in the true medical sense: its condition will either improve or slide into terminal disease" (Speth, 1998, p. 277).

The countries of the North have left the poor and excluded masses of the South to drift away into economic oblivion. For example, during 1996, official development assistance from Organization for Economic Cooperation and Development (OECD) donor countries dropped in 11 of these 21 nations. What these numbers show is nothing less than a continuing pattern of benign (malign) neglect of the poor, the marginalized, the excluded, and the dispossessed. The numbers, ultimately, stand in sharp contrast to the goals expressed by OECD members, the world's most industrialized nations (*Id.*, p. 277).

The human cost of the Third World's debt crisis, ever since the 1980s, has been enormous. Economic restructuring and neoliberal reforms have deeply and negatively affected Latin America's working class. Under the leadership of capitalist governments, working under the umbrella of the Group of Seven (G-7), we find that multilateral institutions like the IMF and the World Bank have promoted a comprehensive globalization of economic, trade, and financial policies. As a result, it may be argued that any G-7 agreement on trade or interest rates may involve the difference between starvation and survival, life or death, for millions of Latin American workers and their families (Vilas, 1995, p. 161; Vilas, 1999, pp. 15–20). Millions of abandoned children, millions of unemployed, some of the lowest wages on earth, all have combined to make Latin America a continent in crisis, dominated by exclusionary forms of governance at both the national and international levels (Branford and Kucinski, 1988, pp. 24–34). The same may be said of the African continent.

While Africa has, for decades, required more accountable states to guide the path of its economic development in order to make it more inclusionary, the conditions which continue to prevail throughout much of sub-Saharan Africa are not conducive to creating them. Instead of grappling with the crisis and the implications of this dilemma, we find the World Bank and the IMF pushing the idea of the "liberal-democratic/minimalist state." Yet, what has this prescription done for Africa? It may be argued that, as far as the IMF and the World Bank are concerned, "democracy and the free market are the twin panaceas. The free market will provide the economic rationale the state has undermined. Democracy will serve to keep the minimalist state honest" (Sandbrook, 1990, p. 684). What is the result? According to a voluminous literature on the subject, the conclusion points to the fact that there is no determinate relationship between regime type and economic growth (*Id.*, p. 690). The international capitalist lending institutions hide behind an ideological smokescreen of their own construction.

The imporant point to stress is that democracy, the minimalist state, and the free market, still leave exclusionary governance and its associated practices in place. For, in the final analysis, "though congruent with growth, democracy is unlikely to eliminate unproductive allocations of public resources and poor public management stemming from patronage appointments" (*Id.*, pp. 691–692). Recognizing this phenomenon as anti-developmental, it is now possible to appreciate the persistence and preservation of underdevelopment as the dominant and dominating reality throughout Africa and Latin America, as well as other areas of the Third World along the capitalist periphery.

The basic problems that remain are those associated with the lack of equity and the absence of inclusion, political and economic. Because most, if not all, of Third World democracies fail to introduce equity and inclusionary social issues into their decision-making calculus, they render the World Bank's stated goal of "equitable growth" a utopian fantasy. In this respect, it may be argued that since the poor are the majority in most developing nations, this should mean that the poor should have even greater political clout to push for both popular amelioration programs and for more equitable patterns of growth. However, it is widely understood that "electoral democracies often fail to do this. This contradiction mirrors the tension inherent in the concept of liberal democracy" (*Id.*, p. 693). I have discussed this very point in Chapter 4 and will explicate its meaning in the context of this chapter as well. There are deeper causes and explanations for this phenomenon. To be precise, they are the outgrowth of exclusionary practices and the ramifications of the gap that exists between the despair of the excluded and the inability and unwillingness of modernizing elites to adopt inclusionary styles of decision making that could begin to heal this widening gulf in the body politic.

The ramifications of exclusionary practices has led to a situation where "the breakdown of governance structures in poor, crowded countries cannot be attributed directly to demographic pressures, but the presence of such pressures certainly seems relevant . . . these tendencies are themselves generally manifestations of popular despair induced by the inability of moderate and modernizing elites to bring about real improvements in human well-being" (Falk, 1995, p. 198). The chronic nature of high unemployment combined with poor human development records, a rapidly expanding population, "with the largest increases concentrated among the poorest sections of the population" (*Id.*, p. 198), has effectively enforced the mechanisms of what I have called "democratic exclusion." Where a formal democracy does not exist, the regime engages in even harsher repression of the inevitable rising levels of protest and violence. The poor and excluded feel they have nothing to lose.

In these circumstances the defense of the status quo, as mediated through exclusionary governance in all of its forms, threatens the integrity and political capacity of the state to deliver on its promises and to promote the necessary policies that are capable of guiding the course of development over the long term. It also relegates the meeting of basic human needs to a point of absolute neglect. Such neglect not only negates human rights, it sabotages development. Underdevelopment, as it deprives millions of people of their basic human needs, also contributes to the tragedies of our time—famines, war, and social and political instability.

These connections are not accidental. In fact, Susan George has an accumulated wealth of data which proves that debt and underdevelopment have actually caused wars. She has noted that "war has been a major cause

The Promise of Inclusion

of heavy debt in 12 states: El Salvador, Ethiopia, Guatemala, Israel, Mozambique, Morocco, Myanmar, Nicaragua, Somalia, Sri Lanka, Sudan and Uganda" (George, 1992, p. 148). Further, the assembled data shows 15 countries in which, during the late 1980s and early 1990s, "there was major violence which did not amount to war. In every case, large numbers of people were or are involved; the ensuing deaths numbered from a handful to several hundred . . . Every one of these countries has a serious debt problem; all have had to turn to the IMF or World Bank for the special agreements and attached conditions which are the fate of heavy debtors. In all, though to varying degrees, the economic conditions which grow from indebtedness are important factors in conflict" (George, 1992, p. 160).

We find that there is a direct connnection between political violence and economic austerity (*Id.*, pp. 162–163). Violence does beget violence. The consequence is higher levels of violence with a corresponding development of underdevelopment. A major reason for this is the pressure of debt. The pressure of debt is the result of pressure exerted by the IMF and World Bank. The pressure is placed on regimes and nation-states trapped in exclusionary patterns, practices, and institutional settings which preclude the development of more equitable patterns of political participation and the benefits of economic growth and development. Out of this matrix of exclusion, violence is inevitable and peace becomes increasingly elusive, if not impossible to grasp.

Ironically, the ideology of the "free market" serves to uphold and endorse new forms of state interventionism predicated on "the deliberate manipulation of market forces. Moreover, the development of global institutions has led to the developent of 'entrenched rights' for global corporations and financial institutions . . . Beneath the rhetoric of so-called 'governance' and 'free market,' neoliberalism provides a shaky legitimacy to those in the seat of political power" (Chossudovsky, 1998, p. 310). For these reasons, I conclude that neoliberalism enforces exclusionary governance and is antithetical to humane governance, equitable growth and development, and remains hostile to inclusionary forms of democratic practice. On this basis, neoliberalism's project has been a developmental disaster, on a global scale. It should be rejected without equivocation.

9. The Poverty of Violence and the Violence of Poverty

Historically, the phenomenon of war itself has been the primary organizing principle of states and human societies. *I maintain that the call to development and a collaborative effort to end the violence of poverty and the poverty of violence could and should be an alternative organizing principle*. Unfortunately, it is not. But it does have the potential to become such a principle for practice. Therefore, I have set forth, in Part C of this chapter, an outline of the causes of sociopolitical instability as documented by leading scholars and the Carnegie Commission's Final Report, *Preventing Deadly Conflict* (1997).

The purpose of this analysis is to accentuate the importance of looking at social violence, deadly conflict, and political instability as avoidable and not inevitable historical outcomes. My main argument is as follows: *The choices we make, the priorities we establish, the values we emphasize shall, in the final analysis, be the ultimate arbiters of human destiny and human fate.* That fate will be worked out in the interplay between the national and international institutions we build and the degree to which we move toward more humane and inclusionary forms of governance in our stated ideals and our corresponding practice.

C. SOLUTIONS FOR ACHIEVING INCLUSIONARY GOVERNANCE

Part C is organized so as to examine the various challenges to human, economic, and political development by concentrating on a number of interrelated issues. In Section (1), I review the primary literature which has identified the main underlying causes of internal conflict. In Section (2), I proceed to discuss the reasons why the presence of the state must, of necessity, be a pervasive presence in both national life and in the task of development, in all of its tasks. This involves an analysis of the five inclusionary principles that I have identified as the "Five C's": (1) consensus; (2) consistency; (3) congruence; (4) cohesiveness; and (5) coherence. In Section (3), I discuss the degree of effectiveness and efficiency with which the institutions of states determine successful or unsuccessful developmental outcomes, for ineffectiveness and inefficiency can be antithetical to development and a contributing factor to wars, conflicts, and escalating violence.

Any recognition of the values of efficiency and effectiveness leads us directly toward an examination of inclusionary states versus exclusionary states. I maintain that inclusionary states, by virtue of their emphasis upon the need to realize the principles of inclusionary governance—consensus, consistency, congruence, cohesiveness, and coherence—promote the reduction or elimination of social and political instability through inclusionary strategies that can only be implemented by an effective and efficient state combined with effective markets and a vibrant civil society.

In the alternative, exclusionary states are often predatory, cleptocratic, and not deeply embedded within their civil society. Further, they are not autonomous enough to effectuate an equitable distribution of wealth, nor are they capable of acting with integrity toward the excluded and marginalized sectors of their populations. As such, exclusionary states are anti-developmental, in the fullest sense of that term.

I distinguish between those particular characteristics, policies, and principles that adhere to inclusionary or to exclusionary approaches to governance. I conclude that the policies of the "Inclusionary State" (IS) are both identifiable and essential to realizing development. Inclusionary states do this by recognizing the urgency of development and by choosing the most appropriate means, principles, and policies to effectuate it. The policies of the IS include: the rule of law; the protection and extension of human rights; the ability of the state and the civil society to promote tolerance, mutuality and cooperation; distributive justice; and the maintenance of effective, efficient and inclusive state institutions.

In sum, inclusionary governance is a critical, yet still widely ignored and overlooked, element of national and international development. Inclusionary governance involves not only the structural components of government and the political capacity of government, but also the need to place greater emphasis upon the guiding principles of inclusion as the primary means through which the urgency of development is articulated and conflict prevention, mediation, and resolution are made primary goals and, ultimately, translated into effective and efficient policies that benefit all groups and classes in the nation.

1. The Underlying Causes of Internal Conflict

It has been argued that there a definite correlation between weak states and the underlying causes of internal conflict within nation-states. Some of the structural factors that make states weak are as follows: (1) some are born weak; (2) many states carved out of colonial empires in Africa and Southeast Asia are little more than artificial constructs; (3) many post-independence states lack political legitimacy and political institutions capable of exercising control over their own territory; (4) after the collapse of the Soviet Union, the majority of the resulting newly formed entities came into being with only the most rudimentary political institutions in place. (Brown, 1996, p. 14).

Weak states are hampered by internal problems such as endemic corruption (cleptocracy), administrative incompetence, and an inability to promote economic development. The common experience that all of these kinds of states face is the fact that when state structures weaken, conflict and sociopolitical instability (SPI) often follow, which further exacerbate their weaknesses .

State structures throughout the Third World have weakened for a variety of reasons. Among these reasons is SPI. SPI has been identified as an expression of the social violence which has emerged from a "revolution of rising expectations," brought on by modernization (Gurr, 1970; Nelson, 1987). As a consequence of modernization, the gap between achievements and aspirations has been widening, frustrating in the process any and all raised expectations.

Along with the pressures of modernization, additional social phenomena that have been cited for the rise in violent conflict and SPI include the rise of peasant movements in Asia as forces that have led to the breakdown of traditional authority systems, due largely to economic change (Popkin, 1979; Bates, 1983). Other social phenomena include the rise of ethnic conflict in Africa that may be traced directly to modernization (Bates, 1983). Nevertheless, by focusing on the need for viable political institutions to absorb the participatory upsurge, analytic attention has switched to an emphasis on the primacy of politics and the attendant requirement to give due attention to the political management of economic change. In short, many scholars have viewed the policies of governments and their ability to promote economic growth as one of the keys to the maintenance of political stability (Linz, 1978). Table 6.1 illustrates the underlying causes of internal conflict and the areas in which expectations are frustrated.

Table 6.1 reflects the fact that the literature on internal conflict has identified four main clusters of factors: (1) structural factors; (2) political factors; (3) economic/social factors; (4) and cultural-perceptual factors. Because these four main clusters have been identified as being central to an understanding of how internal conflicts arise, we shall briefly review the elements of each cluster. We can then proceed to identify how these areas of internal conflict can be mitigated by the inclusionary state (IS) and its five governing principles (consistency, consensus, congruence, cohesiveness, and coherence).

Structural Factors

Weak state structures are usually the starting point for various analyses of internal conflict (Zartman, 1995; Helman and Ratner, 1992–93). Some states are born weak due to their historical tutelage under colonial empires, as in Africa and Southeast Asia. Lacking political legitimacy as well as capable political institutions, these states could not demonstrate any kind of meaningful control over the territory placed under their supervision, much less formulate effective developmental goals and policies. In the 1990s, the new states that emerged from the collapse of the Soviet Union and Yugoslavia suffered the same difficulties and encountered similar obstacles. The fundamental reason that these states were weak is that they came into existence with only the most rudimentary political institutions. These states lacked the cohesiveness necessary to chart and coordinate a developmental agenda and failed to gain the political support required to sustain such coordination.

While some are born weak, others simply became weak over time. The African experience, as a whole, is a prime example of states weakening over time. Because Africa's problems involve building new institutional structures, inculcating new cultural norms within and throughout the civil society, and making market adjustments, the ultimate resolution of the continent's problems will, in the final analysis, depend on two major components: first, the directions and goals which are set for economic development and, second, the simultaneous creation of regimes that are responsive to all major classes, groups, and interests in the civil society. These regimes, along with the state-society linkages that develop in conjunction with them, must have the capabilities of taking on the tasks that modern states are expected to perform. In the alternative, states will continue to be weakened by internal problems that range from endemic corruption, administrative incompetence, and a general inability to promote economic development. Usually, the weakening of state structures leads to violent conflict. Power struggles between contending elites intensify. Ethnic groups that have suffered exclusion and repression by central authorities begin to assert themselves politically, often by seeking greater administrative autonomy or realizing the principle of self-determination by setting up their own state.

TABLE 6.1 Underlying Causes of Internal Conflict

Structural Factors	Economic/Social Factors
Weak states	Economic problems
Intra-state security concerns	Discriminatory economic systems
Ethnic geography	Modernization
Political Factors	*Cultural/Perceptual Factors*
Discriminatory political institutions	Patterns of cultural discrimination
Exclusionary national ideologies	Problematic group histories
Inter-group politics	
Elite Politics	

SOURCE: Michael E. Brown, editor, *The International Dimensions of Internal Conflict*, The MIT Press, 1996, p. 14.

In addition to weak state structures, the literature has also addressed intra-state security concerns. These concerns arise when states are so weak that individual groups within these states undertake to defend themselves. When states are incapable of assuring the safety and security of all groups within their borders, then citizens view themselves as no longer obligated to the original social compact. After all, as Hobbes noted, the social contract exacted citizen and group loyalty and obligation only so long as the state and its compact with its citizens was capable of providing security. In the case of intra-state security concerns, a perceived or actual threat from other groups triggers concerns about whether other groups pose genuine security threats.

Finally, following the structural factors of weak states and intra-security concerns, there is the area of ethnic geography—the structural factor that characterized states with ethnic minorities. These states are more prone to SPI than other states. While the ethnically homogeneous states are rarely problematic as to exhibiting a proclivity to internal conflict, it is also true that their number is relatively small. Of more than 180 states in existence in the 1990s, only 20 are ethnically homogeneous. The presence of ethnic factors, therefore, implies that democratization, as a political process, is complicated and may involve sequencing that differentiates between democratic transitions and democratic consolidations.

Because there are distinct normative, substantive, and political factors which separate democratic transitions from democratic consolidations, we often find that democracy is exceptional in severely divided societies. In fact, some have argued that democracy simply cannot survive in the face of serious ethnic divisions. Given these assertions, some have concluded that unless great precautions are taken, democratic arrangements tend to unravel with almost deterministic predictability in ethnically divided societies (David Horowitz, 1985, p. 681). This raises serious questions about exclusivity as a block to the realization of democracy, participation, and representation where ethnic divisions are deep and social grievances reflect divergent, if not contradictory, political, social, religious, and economic agendas and claims.

Claims about democratic arrangements in divided societies also raise questions about the possibility and viability of a cure or solution to healing such divisions through inclusionary principles and building inclusionary states that are designed to ameliorate divisions, resolve conflicts and lessen or eliminate tensions because of their capacity to engage in dispute resolution, mediation, negotiation, and striking social bargains.

Political Factors

The first political factor that may be cited as an underlying cause of internal conflict is the presence of discriminatory political institutions. I will define them as exclusionary states. It is clear that the prospects for avoiding deadly conflict in a country depend, in large measure, upon the type and fairness of its political system. Authoritarian regimes are over time the most likely forms of state structure to breed resentment because some classes benefit while other ethnic groups or classes have their interests ignored and trampled.

Even in the formal context of so-called democratic regimes, resentment can build if some groups are inadequately represented. So the adequacy of representation, as well as social, political, and economic inclusion, is critical in mitigating against the corrosive dangers of social instability and political violence. In other words, social and political violence and instability correlate more strongly with the exclusionary state than with the inclusionary state. This is, in part, because an ethos of inclusion leads to practical power-sharing arrangements in ethnically divided societies (for example, South Africa). To generalize this point is to understand that inadequate representation, as an expression of exclusion and constitutional arrangements that fail to provide for or enforce procedural norms of inclusion, produces a set of conditions in which political institutions are no longer viewed as legitimate. These conditions can (and have in the past) yielded growth but not development. As legitimacy declines, the tendency toward state repression rises and with it SPI, which leads to the deterioration or even the arrest of growth itself. The arrest of economic growth is often accompanied by the decline of political stability and legitimacy.

In 1997, the Robert F. Kennedy Memorial Center for Human Rights produced a report entitled *Kenya at the Crossroads: Demands for Constitutional Reforms Intensify* (RFK Memorial Center for Human Rights, 1997). Specifically, the report noted: "True stability cannot rest on a system that excludes large sectors of the population from meaningful participation in the political process, systematically denies freedom of association and assembly, limits freedom of expression, effectively bars grassroots participation,

The Promise of Inclusion

repeatedly violates the human rights of those regarded as opponents and fails to protect its citizens' human rights" (*Id.*, p. 27). True stability, therefore, requires constitutional inclusion and the establishment and enforcement of democratic processes and institutions to realize it. This did not happen in Kenya.

One year later, in 1998, the Robert F. Kennedy Memorial Center for Human Rights issued a second report on the situation, entitled, *Moving towards Constitutional Reform In Kenya?* (RFK Memorial Center For Human Rights, 1998). The report lamented the fact that "the reforms called for repealing some colonial-era legislation used to restrict freedom of association, expanding the composition of the Electoral Commission, and establishing a framework for a comprehensive constitutional review and reform process. *The reforms did not, however, establish any means to redress problems in voter registration procedures that left some two to four million Kenyans disenfranchised; nor did they lessen the constitutional powers of the executive.* This incomplete and belated reform process left the country ill prepared for truly democratic elections" (*Id.*, p. 1, italics mine).

The second political factor that can be identified as leading to internal conflict and rising levels of political violence is the reliance on exclusionary national ideologies. In nations where nationalism and citizenship are based upon ethnic distinctions, as opposed to the recognition of shared human rights and privileges, there is a drift toward exclusionary political, economic, and social practices. Further, these exclusionary national ideologies may be religious in nature. Ireland's bitter struggle between Catholics and Protestants is a clear example of this phenomenon. This is especially the case in theocratic states which divide society into two distinct groups: those who adopt the theologically derived political, social, and economic order and those who do not.

Hence, both religious belief and ethnicity can produce social and political violence when they are intentionally used to divide, separate and fragment the civil society. Additionally, both religious belief and ethnicity are both capable of dividing the state so that it sides with some classes, but not others. Thus, the ES may be the product of religious or ethnic differentiations that produce unequal political and economic consequences which reinforce an ethos of exclusion.

The third political factor that has been identified as an element leading to internal conflict and rising levels of political violence and deadly conflict is the presence of inter-group politics. Whether grounded in political, ethnic, religious, or ideological affiliations, there are certain groups that have ambitious objectives which are designed to promote and advance their own agenda, at the expense of the national welfare. Moreover, they often practice confrontational strategies which point the nation in directions opposite to a path toward conflict resolution.

In the absence of a strong state, these inter-group politics take the place of inclusionary state leadership and power-sharing constitutional arrangements in divided societies. The result is rising levels of political violence as opposing groups fear domination by other groups. Further, with continued fragmentation, as a consequence of various forms of incompatibility, the emergence of new groups may destabilize the situation, and disequilibrium comes to characterize the entire body politic.

The fourth political factor that has been emphasized as an element leading toward political violence is the emergence of elite politics. Elite politics are representative of tactics which are adopted by opportunistic politicians in times of economic and political turmoil. In practice, elite politics follow the logic of "divide and conquer" by provoking ethnic conflict in times of economic and political difficulty to fend off domestic challengers.

Economic and Social Factors

The third cluster of factors resulting in political violence is in the arena of economic and social problems. Here patterns of cultural discrimination persist and there are group histories which remain problematic. It is possible to identify three broad social and economic factors which present the potential for political violence: economic problems; discriminatory economic and social systems; and the pressures generated by modernization.

First, in the economic realm, if a nation is not growing fast enough—that is, has failed to achieve an economic "fast track"—it cannot keep pace with societal demands. This has been a particular problem for Eastern Europe, the former Soviet Union, and Africa, as nations move from centrally planned economies to market-based economic systems. Problems such as unemployment, inflation, income distribution, and lack of growth have contributed to growing levels of social and political violence in all of these regions.

As tensions grow, the potential for development diminishes. Further, the excluded groups and classes are even more marginalized from the state as state subsidies for food, basic goods and services, as well as social welfare benefits, are reduced or eliminated. For these reasons, the drift toward ES institutions and practices is a particular danger in these regions unless countervailing forces and principles are put into place to mitigate against these consequences. Because of the primacy of economic development in these states, the advent of economic slowdowns, deterioration of opportunities, and the collapse of prospects portend social and political violence while simultaneously contributing to dangerous anti-developmental trends.

Second, where economic systems discriminate on the basis of class or ethnicity, the foundation is laid for political violence and for repressive and exclusionary states. Unequal access to decision making, as well as resources, creates a situation where the disadvantaged and excluded members of society withdraw their support for the system and the legitimacy of the regime is called into question. But economic growth standing alone is not the solution. It must be coupled with inclusionary practices and principles that allow the previously excluded to be incorporated into the nation's social, economic, and political life and allow their voices to become a part of the calculus of what constitutes the nation's welfare.

Third, and finally, we may identify the process of economic development itself as a major contributor to political violence and internal conflict. The combined effects of industrialization, migration, and urbanization have resulted in the disruption of social patterns and the fragmentation of family at the micro-level as well as political life and institutions at the macro-level. At the same time, social awareness and political consciousness has been raised through higher literacy rates coupled with greater access to educational opportunities and communication media and information technology that span the globe. Correspondingly, these developments have placed greater strains upon existing political institutions as calls and demands for greater participation and inclusion have expanded and intensified throughout Second and Third World nations. For all of these reasons, instability and disorder have become greater problems at the close of the 20th century than they were at its inception.

Cultural and Perceptual Factors

The fourth cluster of factors which threaten political violence is in the area of culture and perception. To begin with, cultural discrimination against minorities has been an enduring challenge to maintaining peace and stability, as well as economic growth and development. The problems in this arena range from inequality in educational opportunities to legal and political constraints on religious freedom and on teaching of minority languages. Following cultural discrimination, a second factor is found under the broad heading of group histories and their perceptions of themselves and others. Genocide and "ethnic cleansing" have influenced the self-perception of the peoples of Bosnia, Rwanda, and Kosovo.

The weakening of state structures is due in large measure to the phenomenon of "exclusionary governance" and the growth of exclusionary states. The primary reason for this relationship is that the state remains the central forum and medium in which class and interest-group differences are dealt with and distributional equity is accepted or rejected. To mention one example, the Coase Theorem suggests that economic efficiency can be realized and attained in all mutually beneficial bargains that can be struck. Yet, such a suggestion amounts to an artificial separation between the market, the state, and the civil society and evolves in an institutionally vacuous environment.

To hold the view that economic efficiency should be the ultimate or primary goal in and of itself is suspect. Any generalization in the social and political spheres concerning benefits from the premise of efficiency is questionable. In my view, such an argument ignores the proper and necessary role of the state in sanctioning transactions, and protecting the rights of participants, protecting private property, in the process of deriving mutually beneficial bargains for the parties involved. Further, such a premise ignores the significance and the role of the civil society itself, not only in terms of the linkages that it forges with the state and the market, but also of the protection it affords to the parties in and by itself. Additionally, this premise fails to address the larger questions about the long-term goals of what is in the national interest, and how that national interest will be determined in the first place.

In short, the intellectual leap of faith that the economic efficiency argument requires leaves us to interpret Coase's result as an assertion that a decentralized economy can always attain efficient outcomes without state intervention. Even disregarding market failures, I still maintain that state intervention, in some form, is necessary. Indeed, it is too strong an assumption that, in the real world, the functioning of laissez faire economies can organize all bilateral and multilateral exchanges without the active involvement of mediating institutions and public bodies that are capable of organizing and sanctioning such exchanges. The fact remains that the state is there precisely because of the need to organize these socially necessary bargains.

Without the state's involvement, how can socially necessary bargains be made that are not only efficient, but also fair? And is it not precisely this issue of fairness and distributional justice that the primary focus upon efficiency ignores? For when we look at efficiency, it does not demand that the ideal of democratic participation be realized, or any other. Neither does it demand that the issues associated with distributional justice be addressed. The focus upon efficiency does not demand that social, political, and economic inequalities be addressed. It does not demand that we live in a pleasant society. If social, political, and economic inequalities are not addressed then, especially in ethnically divided societies, political violence will almost certainly result.

Economic and political disenfranchisement will often bolster one another. Under such conditions, the civil society will probably experience even greater fragmentation. Such a result is not efficient, much less humane, for it incites deadly conflict. Therefore, it is inhumane as well as anti-developmental. Pursuing efficiency, without requiring equity, results in political inequality and "political equality is important not only because it affects and is affected by economic inequality; it is important in its own right, it is a goal in itself, not merely a means to an end" (Verba, 1987, p. 157). Economic efficiency, when it becomes the primary goal and is practiced apart from distributive justice, as well as the principles of inclusionary governance, can become a destructive force to development.

I argue, therefore, that economic efficiency should not be the only goal or even the primary goal in the developmental equation. Rather, the IS demands that distributional justice should be a part of the developmental process. So the developmental agenda should have as one of its primary purposes distributional equity—*as a matter of policy*. Efficiency is not a goal, it is a means to an end. The task of the state, then, is to help to organize the resources of civil society and the market in such a way that the efforts of all of these realms may be coordinated toward goals that result in higher levels of political, social, cultural and economic inclusion.

When human and non-human capital formation, income distribution, and development are seen as intertwined, then we can appreciate the fact that much of East Asia's success, as in the case of South Korea and Taiwan, resulted from the fact that land reform effectuated growth. It also became a practical symbol of distributional justice. In the alternative, the lack of genuine land reform contributed to income inequality and the de-linking of growth and distribution throughout most of Latin America. The result of this divorce between development and distribution has resulted in social and political violence, supported exclusionary states and served elite interests, and engendered high levels of political inequality accompanied by widespread deprivation, poverty and human suffering. Latin America's history gives testimony to this proposition.

The Enduring Presence of the State and Its Role in Organization of Social Bargains

To effectuate and produce socially necessary bargains is one of the primary tasks of the state. This is the reason why, when looking at successful late industrializers, it can be argued that the state must step into the developmental process, for the ideal role of the state is in fact to act as a mediator. The challenge presented is to determine the extent of state intervention and where the state must intervene in the developmental process. The answer to this question remains unresolved and subject to debate.

Modern liberal democratic theories have consistently struggled with the challenge of how to justify the sovereign power of the state and, at the same time, justify limits on that very power. It constitutes a persistent dilemma for political theory since Hobbes's time, when the boundaries and balance between might and right, power and law, duties and rights became issues of both theoretical and practical contention.

On the one hand, the theoretical dilemma exists because states must retain a monopoly of coercive power. It is this monopoly on power that gives the state its special function in securing the general welfare and providing for domestic tranquillity. On the other hand, if the state was to be granted unrestricted regulatory and coercive capabilities, then its powers to intrude on the civil society could easily deprive citizens of their political and social freedoms. In response to this dilemma, liberal democrats constructed representative democracy as the institutional means through which this dilemma might be resolved.

The great values of liberal democracy encompassed an overriding concern with reason, law, and freedom of choice. Liberal democrats stressed the idea of equality as the overarching rubric underneath which these values could obtain practical significance. The assumption was that if all mature individuals were acknowledged as equal, then the recognition of this equality would serve to secure a social environment which would be protective of the individual's freedom to pursue his or her own private interests and activities. Still, the individual's freedom would be, in some respects, bounded by the state's authority, laws, and coercive powers so as to protect what was in the public interest.

Representative democracy through the use of representative assemblies has used elections to force a clarification of issues. In turn, elected representatives would attempt to strike a balance between competing interests and classes and, hopefully, become capable of discerning the national interest in the process. Parallel with this view, representative democracy was also designed to protect the civil society from an intrusive state that was capable of oppression. The representative state, then, was to protect citizens from the despotic use of state power and, at the same time, act as an umpire or referee in the civil society while individuals pursued their own narrow interests in the market. In combination, the free vote and the free market are both viewed as essential for the realization of the collective good. This argument is premised upon the assumption that the collective good can be achieved by the interaction of these two spheres with only minimal state interference.

However, there is another aspect to this argument. Arguments for the minimal state recognize that a need exists to maintain adherence to certain types of state intervention. Such state intervention is required to regulate not only trade and commerce, but to prosecute those who violate the laws. State intervention has a continuing task to reshape social relations and institutions, especially in the event that there is a failure of laissez-faire. Still, there are limits to what the state can do under the liberal democratic paradigm. This is where the principle of the minimal or limited state becomes important.

The principle of the limited state argues that there is a separation between the public and private spheres. The private sphere encompasses the autonomous civil society, the market, private property, and family and personal relations, as well as the free exercise of conscience. The public-private distinction is relevant to democracy in the sense that there exists an interrelated set of considerations: (1) that the practice of democracy demands an autonomous sphere of citizen will-formation which remains separate from the state; (2) that the practice of democracy requires the protection of a pluralism of power centers, so that one group or interest may not gain a monopoly of power and influence over the others, leading to various forms of exclusion; (3) that the practice of democracy requires that the state refrain and be restrained from taking as many forms of social coordination as possible under its own auspices; and (4) that the practice of democracy not allow all social relations to be politicized.

Together, these considerations imply that the democratic state has to be a limited state in practice, in spite of the fact that there is considerable room for disagreement about where the precise limits should be drawn. First of all, the limited state concept does not focus sufficiently on the relationship between democracy and equity. In the case of many Latin American states, for example, rapid industrialization has rested upon close cooperation between the state and private business, but has integrated only part of the populace into the formal economy. As a result, this incomplete integration has left the numerically substantial remainder marginalized and excluded.

In addition to the problems of divergent interests, various social strata differ greatly in both the form and effectiveness of their organizations. For example, the lower classes have been institutionalized by factors that keep them apart from each other and divide them internally. The result is that in spite of their large numbers, they have been unable to act as a united front. There are, in other words, organizational obstacles that have decisively aggravated the difference in power capabilities between the poor and elite. This problem of organizational fragmentation in society has made it difficult, if not impossible, for the lower classes to reverse social inequality (Weyland, 1996, p. 5). Such a fragmentation also exposes the limits of the liberal democratic model of representative government and the arguments for the minimal or limited state.

The Inclusion/Exclusion Dilemma

Organizational fragmentation in society and in the state has created crucial impediments to redistributive reform. Recognizing this dialectic exposes what I call the "exclusion/inclusion dilemma" as it relates to state organizations and their political capacity, the prospects for economic growth and development, the means through which political violence may be avoided or reduced, and the issues associated with distributional equity and social justice.

One of the main challenges to greater inclusion is revealed in associations of narrow scope which allows people of higher status to keep the poor divided and separated from potential allies. In turn, personalist networks and narrow associations have served to corrode the internal unity of the state. As a result, "bureaucratic politics" has undermined the state's ability to impose equity-enhancing reforms on reluctant elites. This has resulted in the "inclusion/exclusion dilemma," which affects both the integrity of the civil society and the state.

It is well-established that equity-enhancing reform has decisive implications for the inclusiveness and the long-term stability of states (Dahl, 1971, pp. 4–9). In countries with extreme inequalities, redistributive change is essential for the effective extension of citizenship to the poor. Universal citizenship, as the basic principle underlying democracy, (Schmitter, 1983, pp. 891–96), demands that all members of a political community have equal chances of being taken into consideration when public decisions are made (Dahl, 1971, p. 2). The reality of social inequality endangers this principle throughout the Third World. This state of affairs also exposes the problems associated with organizational fragmentation which makes effective interest representation difficult for the poor and excluded. Because the poor would especially benefit from equity-enhancing reforms, the fact of organizational fragmentation only strengthens their elite opponents by giving them privileged access to decision makers. This has resulted in the entrenchment of cleptocratic states and exclusionary states throughout large portions of the Third World.

The absence of equity-enhancing reforms and policies also exposes the dearth of redistribution under democracy in many Third World nations. Theoretically, through the mechanisms of democratization, states could bring about greater social justice. There are rational-choice and socioeconomic hypotheses concerning the dearth of redistributive measures. The primary difficulty we have with these explanations is that they neglect institutional factors. In this regard, organizational fragmentation in society, as well as within the state, combine to give elites, who command power capabilities, greater economic weight in decision making, special access to the center of decision making, and overwhelming influence on the actual implementation of these elite-made decisions.

According to the rational choice hypothesis, the dearth of redistributive outcomes in LDCs may be attributed to the fact that collective action becomes increasingly difficult as the number of potential actors increases (Olson, 1971, pp. 34–35). Olson argues that while small groups may be successful in reaching binding agreements, larger groups face greater problems in inducing their members to work toward a common goal. According to this line of thinking, redistribution is rare because the mass of poor people are unable to unite together in collective action. Therefore, they cannot compete with elite control, in spite of their large numbers, by pressing for equity-enhancing reforms. In contrast, a narrow elite has the capacity to easily organize itself to defend its privileges and organize its power capabilities.

Following this line of thought, the rational choice approach posits that one can explain the prevailing "urban-bias" in many Third World nations (Lipton, 1977). After all, since the urban masses are concentrated in the cities, they have a greater capacity to organize and are more threatening to elites than the more widely dispersed rural masses. Hence, the urban masses are able to extract more benefits than the poor in the rural areas (Bates, 1981, pp. 87–95).

The Legacy of European Social Democracy

While the rational choice approach does provide some significant arguments, it fails to account for important facts. For example, it ignores the historical successes of European social democracy, which serves to contradict the emphasis of rational choice authors on the difficulties of collective action, including the bottom-up pressure for redistribution (Weyland, 1996, p. 22). European social democracy achieved its successes through a process of sustained bottom-up pressure by creating an encompassing trade union movement and a political party which appealed to ever widening segments of the working population (Weyland, 1996, p. 38, Stephens, 1986, Przeworski, 1985).

In the end, European social democracy did not plead for special favors for only certain sectors of the working class. Rather, it sought to advance the interests of all of the poor, because its primary goal was the extension of rights and benefits to everyone. It was an openly inclusionary vision, defined by universalistic principles, and based on the notion of equal citizenship.

For these historically specific reasons—the nature of an encompassing organization, the idea of equal citizenship and the universalism that accompanied it, and redistributive reform efforts—the social democratic countries of Europe were able to establish congruence in their political, social and economic practices (Kingman and Fuchs, 1995; Giddens, 1998; Kitschelt, 1994; Janoski and Hicks, 1994; Esping-Andersen, 1996; Spulber, 1997; Garret, 1998; Berman, 1998). Such success has been blocked in the contemporary Third World by enduring social, political, and economic dualities, as well as the confinement of many of those that are excluded to clientelist networks and the limited scope of worker's organizations (Weyland, 1996, p. 39; Ascher, 1984, pp. 34, 40–41; Rosenberg and Malloy, 1978, pp. 159–163).

The pressures for redistribution throughout the contemporary Third World may be framed in terms of "bottom-up" pressure for redistribution, as well as "top-down" pressures. The directionality of "bottom-up" pressures reflects, under conditions of democratic practice, the role played by political parties. With electoral competition, political parties may be induced to advance the agenda and interests of the poor and excluded. If these same parties are elected to office, then they have the capacity to translate promises of redistribution into practice. In this way, partisan democracy may be capable of enacting equity-enhancing reform. In turn, redistribution may be effectuated through "top-down" reforms as well as autonomous state initiatives. On the other hand, the bureaucracy of the state, seeking to avoid bottom-up pressures, may seek to preempt bottom-up initiatives by introducing equity-enhancing reforms on its own initiative.

If a bureaucratic commitment is made to universalist principles, in response to elections and claims of political equality under democracy, then the process of democratization may serve to motivate state officials to impose redistributive reforms on their own. In this way, bottom-up pressures and top-down initiatives can reinforce each other. This was, indeed, the case in the creation of welfare states in Europe (Kraus, 1987, pp. 207–14).

Bottom-Up Pressures and Top-Down Initiatives

In many Third World states, the coincidence between bottom-up pressures and top-down initiatives for redistribution fails because of two factors. First, the persistence of personalism and segmentalism, at the popular level, hinders or blocks the formation of encompassing civil associations which can articulate a common interest. In this situation, social movements do not form or fail to generate sufficient momentum to mobilize bottom-up pressures for distribution. The second factor is found in the nature of bureaucratic politics. It may be that exclusionary organizational patterns reinforce interest conflicts within the bureaucracy itself, thereby inhibiting top-down state initiatives from being articulated or actualized. Similar exclusionary organizational patterns may exist among the popular sectors, thereby encouraging segmentalism and clientelism. This process can result in reinforcing social cleavages that deflect the attention of political parties and classes from broad collective goals and prevent the emergence of encompassing civil associations and social movements.

To effectuate redistribution, the state has to act as a mediator. There are a number of models that have been proposed regarding such a role for the state. Corporatism is such a system of organization. In particular, corporatism is that system which emphasizes the relationship of organized interests to the state. The state under corporatism acts in concert, for example, with banks, farmers, employers' and workers' federations, toward acceptable bargains on income distribution. Under these circumstances, the acts of the state have implications for the civil society and the market. For example, once decisions regarding income distribution are arrived at, the state serves to exercise its powers to implement compliance among all parties (Weiss, 1998, p. 24). Such a compliance, which can be seen as the essence of corporatism, is revealed less by the structure of political bargaining than by the mode of interaction with the state (Crouch, 1993). What is meant by the term "mode of interaction" involves power-sharing or the "sharing of public space." Yet these power-sharing arrangements may contribute to state capacity in ways that are unanticipated in the corporatist analysis.

Corporatist analysis focuses primarily upon the structure of political bargaining—that is, the power-sharing arrangements between business, labor, and the state (tripartism). By focusing upon tripartite arrangements, corporatist analysis narrows its focus to a study of the nature of these business, labor, and state relationships, giving little attention to the analysis of the organization of the state itself (Weiss, p. 25).

The organization of the state itself may contribute to state capacity and state effectiveness in ways that are unanticipated by corporatist analysis. For example, while corporatism focuses upon state capacity in terms of social bargaining, it fails to anticipate the possibility of state capacity being effectuated by coercive measures through the "strong state." Further, corporatism gives little attention to policy instruments, such as the role of national financial systems, as adding to the arsenal of tools that affects state capacity to affect transformative and developmental changes. Other unanticipated sources of state capacity include Peter Evans' model of "embedded autonomy," which emphasizes state-society linkages and the effectiveness of the state in bringing about social transformations.

The organization of the state itself is largely ignored by the corporatist perspective because its vision centers more upon how to explain state capacity in terms of economic outcomes, such as inflation or unemployment. The problem is that these particular subjects may be too narrow or fleeting for long-term or comparative analysis. That is the reason why corporatism's focus upon tripartite arrangements may be helpful in specific spheres of economic management, but deficient in explaining the full scope of what is involved in the larger processes of industrial transformation. So, explaining a state's capacity must take into account more than economic outcomes which are too narrowly focused on a short duration of time or very specific outcomes. In order to formulate long-term development policies, analysis needs to be broadened to encompass an analysis of how the organization of the state itself results in efficient or inefficient performance, effective or ineffective policy-formulation and outcomes.

The State as "Embedded" and "Autonomous"

An alternative analysis is found in Peter Evans' notion of "embedded autonomy," which examines the complementary interactions between the organization of the state and the civil society. Evans' work shifts the analytic focus from state structure and autonomy *per se* to the effectiveness with which the state carries out its transformative tasks. Hence, the concern with effectiveness explains the emphasis upon state-economy linkages.

The concept of embedded autonomy draws together two seemingly contradictory aspects: one aspect, embeddedness, provides both sources of intelligence and channels of implementation that enhance the competence of the state, while the second aspect, autonomy, serves to complement embeddedness by protecting the state from being captured by rival elites. If such a capture of the state were to be effectuated, the result would be the destruction of the cohesiveness of the state itself. In turn, such a result would eventually undermine the coherence of its social interlocutors (Evans, 1995, pp. 248–249). Evans contends that it is the state's corporate coherence which serves to enhance the cohesiveness of external networks with the civil society, while assisting groups that share its vision to overcome their own problems of collective action.

Furthermore, the strength and capacity of the state apparatus is inextricably linked with the fate of civil society. In particular, if there is a deterioration of state institutions there will be a corresponding disorganization of the civil society. It is for this reason that Evans stresses the importance of sustaining or regaining the institutional integrity of state bureaucracies for, in the last analysis, it is the integrity of the state which leads to "the possibility of mounting projects of social transformation" (Evans, 1995, p. 249). The institutional integrity of the state must be understood as united to the organization of the civil society. In the absence of this linkage the pressure to mount projects of social transformation, which involves all aspects of what we call "development," is foreclosed upon. The institutional integrity of the state is a precondition for development.

In delineating the delicate balance which exists between autonomy and embeddedness, Evans acknowledges that while autonomy is fundamental to the definition of the developmental state, it is not sufficient to define it in its totality. Most basically, the ability to effect transformation is seen as depending upon state-society relations as well. This means that a purely autonomous state is just as potentially anti-developmental as one that is in the service of particular elites, because fully autonomous states can become predatory states as easily as they can remain inefficient and ineffective. Therefore, he argues, developmental states must be immersed in a dense network of ties that bind them to societal allies who share transformational goals. In this way, autonomy and embeddedness work effectively in congruence with one another to effectuate coherence within the developmental state and throughout the entire society (Evans, 1995, p. 248). The state's corporate coherence is thereby achieved because it serves to undergird and enhance the cohesiveness of external networks and helps groups, classes, and interests which share in its vision to overcome the endemic problems associated with collective action. Yet, embeddedness and autonomy, although necessary, are not sufficient to produce socially desirable bargains.

Three major propositions emerge from this line of thinking: first, that the fate of the civil society is bound to the robustness of the state apparatus, so that if there is a deterioration of state institutions it will be reflected in the disorganization of civil society; second, that predation is not a function of state capacity, so that it is wrong to assume that eviscerating state bureaucracies will wipe out predators; and, third, that bureaucracy alone is not enough for development and so, therefore, the state-society linkages create connections that are essential to the realization of coherence and cohesion in the state and in the developmental process as a whole (*Id.*, p. 249). Moreover, the quality, organization and effectiveness of bureaucracy will affect, positively or negatively, in many ways, the developmental enterprise.

In my view, state power is enhanced as a result of both strong state institutions and adherence to the principles of inclusionary governance. What this means, in relationship to Evans' thesis, is that "embedded autonomy" is not sufficient, in and of itself, to build strong state-society linkages, or to effect targeted social transformations or social bargains. The concept of embedded autonomy may be extended by framing it within the larger context of state inclusionary principles and practices.

When speaking of inclusivity, I mean that inclusion is both procedural in nature and possesses institutional components as well. The IS and its *mediating* institutions are guided by inclusionary principles. This results in the union between a particular concept of development with policies which promote distributive justice. When viewed in its totality, a proper conception of the IS involves the degree to which key social groups are institutionally empowered to participate in, as well as influence, the decision making of the state. The presence of inclusive institutions guarantees membership to a broad spectrum of social groups in the decision-making tiers of the executive realm (i.e., cabinets, the civil service, the military, etc.). Also, in representative assemblies, the IS is affected by a national legislature as it works to influence and constrain executive policies. Associated with these structural and institutional components are the very ideals of a consolidated democratic state, which include elections, a bill of rights, free speech, etc.

These ideals are all parts of the substance of democracy and must be manifested if the ideal of democracy is to be realized. In practice, this state of affairs is not often realized. This is because some democratic states either do not have all of these substantive attributes or experience low levels of inclusivity. Highly inclusive institutions may also provide groups with mutual vetoes or require supra-majorities for policy decisions which have a significant impact on group rights. At the extreme, we have the ES, usually referred to as the authoritarian state, in which decisions are made by a narrow clique of state elites and their allies who enjoy the benefits of their actions (Kahl, 1998, p. 90; Lake and Rothchild, p. 59; Olson, 1993, p. 579; Horowitz, 1994, pp. 35–55).

The IS's developmental agenda is conjoined with the issue of distributive justice. Verba has implicitly pointed out why it is necessary to conceive of democracies as intersecting sets with the IS when he observed that "the one-person, one-vote policy aims at equality in political influence by creating a ceiling on the amount of political voice an individual can have. But many ways of exercising political influence circumvent that limitation, and most of those means depend on the political use of economic resources" (Verba, 1987, p. 157). In other words, there is a conflict between one-person and one vote versus one-dollar and one-vote, in the context of democracy.

Rule Obedience and the Rule of Law

Earlier it was noted that Evans' concept of "embedded autonomy" is not sufficient for the developmental project. What is also needed is an effective and efficient bureaucratic body. Because societies exhibit tremendous differences in their economic, social, and political institutions, there are some societies which are more effective than others in channeling individual's energies. While some societies have well-functioning institutions that can channel the energy of individuals into socially productive activities that lead to economic and social progress, other societies are burdened by the poor quality of institutional infrastructure which, in turn, frustrates attempts at reform and perpetuates stagnation.

What ultimately determines the quality of a society's human infrastructure depends on a variety of factors, including not only the actual content of rules and norms, but also the degree to which bureaucrats exhibit obedience and fidelity to such rules and norms. In this regard, it may be argued that many societies lack even a minimal level of rule obedience for a well-functioning infrastructure. Yet what is required is a high level of rule obedience (Clague, 1993, p. 393).

Where a high level of rule obedience is lacking, efficiency and effectiveness suffers. This point serves to explain why Evans' concept of embedded autonomy, although important, is not sufficient for explaining what makes bureaucracy effective or ineffective. For while a bureaucracy may be both autonomous and embedded, it is not necessarily efficient. To improve the prospects for development and the effective implementation of social bargains, institutional autonomy and embeddedness must be augmented by institutional efficiency and bureaucratic competence and compliance. In turn, institutional efficiency is made possible through the internalization of goals, a high level of rule obedience, and socially beneficial behavior which transcends mere external compliance with rules. On this point, it may be argued that "in societies which display more than this minimal level of rule obedience, institutional efficiency is supported by constructive kinds of internalization of goals, which leads to socially beneficial behavior that goes well beyond merely following the rules" (Clague, 1993, p. 393).

Because incentives and attitudes reinforce one another in a cumulative fashion, it is largely impossible to disentangle the effects of one upon the other. However, it can be argued that the level of rule obedience and the degree of organizational effectiveness in a society will ultimately affect many aspects of its economic development. More specifically, these aspects include the incentives for physical and human capital accumulation, the quantity and quality of public goods, the nature of the economy's comparative advantage, the rate of its technological progress, and many other factors (*Id.*, pp. 412–413).

What this discussion suggests is that current understandings on both rule obedience and organizational effectiveness require further research because this may lead to greater insight into the strategies that governments might follow to promote a more favorable evolution of institutions (*Id.*, p. 413). In the section that follows, I shall outline what strategies the IS should effectuate. I do this by defining and outlining five principles that promote stability and inclusivity in governance.

Inclusionary Versus Exclusionary States:
Principles Promoting Stability

Not unlike the conditions under which Hobbes introduced the concept of the Leviathan (as discussed in Chapter 5), many modern Third World states are characterized by high levels of sociopolitical instability. Sociopolitical instability is endemic to, and the result of, economic, political, and social modernization; that is to say, development. History itself provides the factual and empirical basis for this statement. After all, Hobbes's England was plagued by civil wars. Medieval institutions were not capable, in and of themselves, of sustaining the society. Therefore, a new institutional bridge had to be built between the past and the future.

In part, the embryonic fabric of medieval constitutionalism served to provide an inclusionary political ground from which a sovereign, acting with the different classes and interests of English society, could bring an end to the violence and embark upon a new developmental path. This very same set of circumstances may be seen in many 20th century Third World states. Yet, the vital question remains: In whose interest shall government govern? Or, put differently: Who shall be included and who shall be excluded in matters of policy choice?

Merilee S. Grindle has examined the 20th century states of Latin America and Africa. In that regard, she has specifically addressed the need to redefine states and their various capacities—institutional, technical, administrative, and political. She has developed a description of the "capable state" as one that can coordinate and maintain effective institutional, administrative, and political functions.

In other words, the politically "capable" state has political "capacity." Grindle defines political capacity as "the ability of states to respond to societal demands, allow for channels to represent societal interests, and incorporate societal participation in decision making and conflict resolution" (Grindle, 1996, p. 10). Political capacity includes the provision of law and order, the protection of public and private property rights, as well as the enforcement of other formal rules. But added to this list comes the assertion that the "focus of state action may change over time and across countries, but in order to implement its own objectives, the state must overcome the potential resistance of various groups, both inside and outside its national boundaries. State capacity, then, should indicate the power of government vis-a-vis these forces" (Leblang, 1997, p. 112).

My primary concern is to examine the ways in which a state may employ its full powers most effectively and, in so doing, reduce SPI as a major obstacle to economic growth. As I have argued, insofar as SPI has hindered economic growth and development, it has also served to block expressions of political institutionalization that are necessary if the society is to achieve a consensus on the national interest and support the state's efforts to realize that interest.

At the nation-state level, the marginalization of large segments of society contributes to SPI. The antidote to marginalization is inclusion. Therefore, I submit the proposition that an IS is the state that is best equipped to deal with the problem of SPI and its negative effects upon development. Further, the articulation of the functions of the IS serves to help conceptualize for policy makers and power brokers the ways in which development may be placed on a "fast track."

Without having to suffer needless impediments, the IS emerges as the most appropriate model to meet the Third World's developmental crisis. The reason for this assertion is that a primary purpose of the IS is to bring the disadvantaged into the mainstream of the nation's life. Yet, the nature of this inclusion may be merely "bare" inclusion, a situation in which it is just a matter of "getting over the line." As Goodin notes: "There is nothing in that notion which implies, or is even compatible with, insisting on getting all the way to the center." (*Id.*, p. 359).

Before proceeding to elaborate upon the five principles of inclusionary governance, it is necessary to add a significant caveat. While the state remains the primary agent of transformative change in society, there is always the danger that the power of the state can be so diminished by the social fragmentation of civil society that the state becomes weakened and unable to carry out its transformative task. So while it is vital to appreciate a state-centered approach to inclusionary governance, it is just as important to admit that many Third World governments have not been able to exercise their power effectively because the demands of various social forces and classes have exceeded the capacity of the state to satisfy them. As a result, the state has weakened. In such a situation, even if a state adheres to the five principles of inclusionary governance that we are about to examine, the state remains incapable of enacting them.

In almost dialectical fashion, the fragmentation of the society results in undermining the unity and power of the state. Under such conditions, attempts at democratization fail and the crisis of the state deepens while, at the same time, classes and factions increasingly gain veto-power. The further result of this trend is a profound impasse and political paralysis.

The state gains its power and legitimacy from its ability to satisfy demands from key constituencies. It also derives its political and moral authority from its ability to lead by transcending the limited scope of some demands and by its ability to incorporate individual and group demands into a broader definition of the national interest. The promotion of the national interest demands of the state that it be inclusive, that it promote distributional justice, and that it practice political inclusion in its decision-making processes. In the alternative, in states where narrow interests have successfully sustained and defended their privileges and independence against attempts at state-building and increasing state control, any attempt toward inclusion, democratization, and income redistribution invariably fails.

From Narrow to Inclusive Interests

In the first sections of this chapter, I have presented an analysis of the underlying causes of internal conflict and the enduring importance of the state in resolving and avoiding these conflicts through the social bargains it is able to effectuate. A number of tentative findings flow from this discussion. First, the overarching causes of political instability and violence are frustrated expectations that are the result of not only modernization but also the exclusionary policies of governments and elites. This, in turn, has created an ever-widening gap between practical achievements and popular aspirations in a variety of dimensions—social, economic, political. Second, in explicating the differences between inclusionary and exclusionary states, I have sought to affirm the need of an IS to overcome the dangers of deadly conflict and political instability. Third, inclusionary governance implies and necessitates inclusionary economic growth, for political inclusion implies economic inclusion. Fourth, and finally, constitutionally inclusive procedures and practices will have to be inculcated through law, mediating institutions, and governmental practices, so that inclusionary norms are advanced in the interactions between the state, the courts, and the civil society.

2. The "Five C's" of Inclusionary Governance

I now turn to five governing characteristics that promote sociopolitical stability while, at the same time, promoting an inclusionary posture for the state. These five characteristics are: consensus, consistency, congruence, cohesiveness, and coherence. I maintain that these characteristics of inclusionary governance enable a nation to embark upon a more equitable approach to economic development and growth, promote effective political institutionalization, serve to create a fair and just legal environment, provide the basis for inclusive constitutional adjudication and procedural due process, and evolve mediating institutions at the national level.

Consensus

Consensus entails bargaining, negotiating, and reaching compromises between parties. The goal of conflict resolution and the path to achieving it demands a dialogue between all classes and the state. Consensus, conceived in this manner, reduces previously high levels of SPI while also preventing SPI from emerging in the first place. The excluded status of marginalized and repressed groups and classes renders them powerless, both economically and politically. The consequence of this imposed powerlessness is that the conditions which foster exclusion, more often than not, make deadly conflict the only viable alternative through which the powerless and excluded can express their grievances. This, in turn, entails tremendous social suffering, waste of opportunities and missed goals (Kleinman, 1997; Felice, 1996).

It is for this reason that I stress the linkage between social suffering and political exclusion as being most problematic and universal. Social suffering and political exclusion have continued in the aftermath of formal independence in Africa, Latin America, and Asia. Due largely to political and economic exclusion, political systems on all of these continents have faced grave challenges to govern societies that were themselves torn by division and SPI. During the 1980s and 1990s, regime changes, civil wars, civic protest, demands for human rights, and accountable public officials have all escalated. These trends all serve to illustrate the lack of consensus and need for such a consensus if SPI is to be effectively dealt with. These crises, individually or in combination, exposed the weakness of state capacities to manage economic, political and social relationships (Grindle, 1996, p. 18).

Realistically or not, Africans who expected the post-1945 period of independence to bring both political freedom and higher standards of living have been frustrated. In practice, they obtained neither. Exclusionary state practices, in the name of democracy, have given African political elites an opportunity to consolidate their power by centralizing control over public life. For example, once an election was held, the usual scenario was that rulers sought to weaken parliamentary prerogatives, while, at the same time, granting themselves extended terms in office (Bratton, 1997, p. 99). Such trends were usually accompanied by the introduction of single-party constitutions. This allowed for the fostering of patterns of exclusionary governance. Exclusionary forms of governance arose due to the absence of consensus and while opponents of the regime were systematically intimidated and mass

The Promise of Inclusion

political activity was enclosed within state-sanctioned associations. The dividing line between the state and civil society was so blurred that political challengers were disallowed from making legitimate bids that could displace the holders of power. This resulted in arbitrary changes to the rules of political competition and had the corollary effect of allowing incumbent leaders to establish economic and political monopolies (Bratton, 1997, p. 99).

What Africa demonstrates is that a prerequisite for consensus is a shared vision. For example, mass participation, in Africa, proved itself to be an insufficient strategy in the absence of a clear program of political reforms and consensus-building (Bratton, 1997, p. 184). The elements of popular protest and plebiscitary precedents of mass mobilization, as well as national conferences, are no real substitute for a clearly articulated program of what reform is "for." To merely be "against" the status quo has created a situation, throughout the African continent, in which African citizens could confront the old regime but were left ill-equipped and unprepared to design new institutional forms with which to replace the old ones. Without a programmatic agenda of reform it is difficult if not impossible to create consensus. An IS requires consensus. Yet, there is a dialectic between consensus and a long-run agenda. The agenda is the ground on which a consensus can be forged. The absence of consensus reinforces or results in exclusionary states and exclusionary policies. In the alternative, inclusionary states and policies produce forms of consensual practice and decision making that reduce SPI and build new linkages between state, civil society and the market.

Where there is consensus, it is usually the result of bargaining. Bargaining is needed in order to create a set of fair political institutions. And bargaining is, after all, an example of inclusionary practices producing a shared consensus. All that is required is that the bargaining process be mutually perceived as fair (Sisk, 1995, p. 258).

The concept of "fairness" may be seen in two contexts: the first may be termed the "compromise context," the second may be termed the "uncertainty context." In the "compromise context," the course of negotiations on a democratization pact leads the respective parties through painful bargains in order to realize their overriding common interest. This ultimately leads to the conclusion of a settlement—a consensus. In the "uncertainty context," there is the presence of political institutions that are seen as arenas for ongoing bargaining, where bargaining is experienced as flexible and inherently fair under conditions of uncertainty. Although there is uncertainty, there is a shared commitment and a common interest in establishing a set of fair political institutions. This, then, becomes the basis for the IS. This is where there is a convergence between the compromise context and the uncertainty context which allows for a fair outcome which provides all parties with certain guarantees that minorities' vital interests (the previously excluded) will be protected and that a shared consensus can emerge.

The emergence of a shared consensus is, we argue, best achieved by the IS rather than either a democracy or a dictatorship, as historically understood. What we mean is that, in the case of dictatorships, there is a wider latitude and capacity for action—good or bad—because they are not really constrained by opposition groups in effectuating whatever policies that they wish to pursue (Wintrobe, 1998, p. 338). The problems for dictators arise when their policies, without general consensus, undermine their legitimacy and, as a result, SPI and domestic dissent rise in opposition to the policies and/or the means through which they are effectuated. Dahl has noted that dictatorships, even when they develop their economies, usually find it harder to survive politically (Dahl, *Polyarchy*, p. 78). On this same point, Maravall has noted that, in the case of Southern Europe, "economic development and its consequences ultimately favored democratization, despite the very different intentions of those who had promoted it" (Maravall, 1997, pp. 49–50).

Maravall also notes that a comparison of the experiences of Southern and Eastern Europe, involving Spain, Greece, and Portugal, reveals that democratization had important economic consequences for the states. In particular, the change of regime modified the functions of the state itself, rather than simply leaving these decisions to markets. In fact, "of these state functions, social policies were those which grew most in importance, and this affected the relations between citizens, governments and regimes" (Maravall, 1997, p. 124). Social policies exhibited the characteristics of what we have called the inclusionary principles of inclusionary governance. These policies reflected broad-based consensus. Yet, as we also point out, consensus is a necessary but not sufficient condition for the full effectuation of inclusionary governance. It is one of five elements.

The recent historical experience of Southern and Eastern Europe suggests that effective action in democracies is only possible when they can build support for their policies and are able to reach a critical mass of consensus that would allow them to put their developmental project forward. On the other hand, where gridlock is significant, politicians are left to hide their real program behind the curtain of ambiguity or be on all sides of all issues. In these circumstances, the resulting gridlock is even more serious when the pressures for political action on an issue are especially conflicting and there is no possible groundwork for consensus. If this is the case, the population may be left divided along racial or ethnic lines, or over the means and ends of contending policy alternatives.

Lacking the political capacity to act decisively, the democratic system, perhaps like the Weimar Republic of the 1920s and 1930s, may create a situation in which democratic rulers cannot rule (Judt, 1997; Beck, 1997; McFate, 1995; Corina and Danziger, 1997). In the alternative, however, where democratic governments demonstrate a capacity to manage their economies in hard times, their capacity to govern was strengthened by mandates and/or *consensus*. What is meant by *consensus*, is that democratic governments exhibit a capacity to forge agreements through the "complicity of their societies" and that this performance was not determined by a foreordained logic, but rather was largely the result of decisions made by governments, social groups and citizens themselves (Maravall, 1997, p. 125).

In contrast to both dictatorships and so-called democracies, the IS promotes and practices the values and norms of inclusion so as to overcome both formal and informal forms of discrimination (whether socioeconomic, racial and ethnic, or sociopolitical). This capacity of the IS to overcome both formal and informal discrimination is premised on the recognition that the resulting costs of exclusion at a point in time, or through time, are too high

The Promise of Inclusion   333

a price to pay—morally, economically, socially, and politically. For example, Maravall argues that exclusive societies . . . "often have the power to sacrifice entire generations in the name of a future paradise, whether under communism or the free market. However, dictatorships have no mechanisms to guarantee that these sacrifices will not simply lead to even more sacrifices" (Maravall, 1997, p. 73). We have found that the "sacrifices" which most dictatorships demand are closely associated with both formal and informal typologies of discrimination. And it is the phenomenon of formal and informal "discrimination" which exacerbate the "sacrifices" made by the excluded which, in turn, often lead to rising levels of SPI.

Racial identity, for instance, is not primordial, but a remnant of past institutional arrangements and ongoing informal social practice shaping and being shaped by those who establish institutional arrangements. Such institutional arrangements became the determinants of emergent racial orders—whether in South America, South Africa, or the United States (Slessarev, 1997; Fredrickson, 1981, 1995; Mills, 1997; Robinson, 1997; Franklin, 1991; Paupp, 1993; Omi, 1994; Winant, 1994; Koppelman, 1996; Hochschild, 1995; Schnudon, 1998; Smith, 1997).

Similarly, what currently remains as "cultural identity" in the United States is also tied to structure. In fact, until social discrimination ends, race will remain as an historical legacy which result in exclusionary practices. If political institutions do not reinforce contrary trends for the realization of racial justice, race conflict will inevitably continue to shake the very foundations of the constructions of social order (Marx, 1998, p. 274).

Whenever and whether a new consensus emerges in previously divided societies, it is the product of states that pursue the policies of an IS. These states recognize the advantages of unifying state action and civil society through inclusionary governance and social life. Such an approach to political institutionalization is essential to overcome the damaging effects of SPI, which often emerge in response to both formal and informal exclusion. After all, those classes who benefited from internal exclusion did so at the cost of also reinforcing social cleavages, inequality, potential mobilization, and conflict. While countering prejudice in order to build a more inclusive or "civic" nation confronts many obstacles and hazards, it is a task that nevertheless can end some of the major causes of social conflict which not only create the potential for SPI but also block the forging and formation of a more democratic consensus.

Consistency

Consistency entails going beyond a mere reliance on procedural democracy. Consistency means that the goals and policies of the state resonate with an inclusive national agenda. It also means taking long-term objectives into account. For this, it is necessary to empower the state with an autonomous bureaucracy that is free from narrow political pressures, to pursue those policies and advance those values that were arrived at through consensual bargaining, negotiating, and compromise.

Consistency is the result of substantive decision making that is not overturned by shifting electoral coalitions that may reflect a much narrower set of concerns than those concerns and goals that are embodied in the inclusionary agenda. What the principle of consistency implies, therefore, is that the national consensus on development and inclusionary practices is so strong that no party, class, elite or interest group would be able to challenge its basic tenets, and the state embarks upon a course that results in the attainment of such goals. Such a path has characterized the developmental states of East Asia, the northern European democracies, as well as the recent policies of South Africa's Government of National Unity (GNU).

The principle of consistency requires consensus. Although consensus may stem from ideology, consistency is a set of policies that resonates with such an ideology and purports to effectuate its goals. South Africa's ANC policies, for example, purport to achieve the realization of a consensus that was arrived at as of the late 1990s. Before this consensus could develop, there were certain steps or "sequences" that had to be undertaken at the institutional level, the societal level, and the juridical level. These steps resonate with the norms, values, practices, and procedures which are supportive of inclusionary and accommodative modes of governance in both the realms of state and civil society. In the case of South Africa, the challenge is that "deep ethnic or racial divisions compound the dangers, since questions of 'belonging' affect not only the distribution of material goods, but also the amount of prestige and identification with the state that various groups enjoy"(Gilomee, 1998, p. 132). It is the task of the IS to promote policies which endorse and support a sense of inclusionary "belonging" and, at the same time, provide the practical and procedural avenues which can enforce fidelity to inclusionary policies while effectuating and realizing inclusionary goals. The ideology of consensus should be accompanied by consistency in the pursuit of inclusionary goals.

The strength of this consensus is necessary but not sufficient for long-term policy making and planning. It should constitute a social contract which incorporates all major segments of the society. To use, once more, South Africa as an example, what this means is that while a new social contract will not totally eradicate identity politics in South Africa's long-term post-apartheid future, it will make sure that ethnicity is not made the basis of the national identity (Sisk, 1995, p. 259).

By removing ethnicity from the processes of state-building, Third World societies are able to concentrate upon building political, social, and economic institutions on the firm foundation of inclusionary principles and policies. By focusing upon inclusion, previous problems with ethnic differences are forced to subside because the state refuses to legally or politically mandate artificial barriers of exclusion. The primary challenge for the state, then, is to think about the matter of finding and establishing accommodative and inclusionary institutions in the beginning of the process of institutional change. In this way, it will be easier to urge apt institutions on the designers and, in the final analysis, to urge maximum incentives for the accommodation of everybody and at every level (Horowitz, 1991, p. 161).

So, understood in these terms, the real challenge for institution-building in LDCs (lesser developed countries), which has conflict prevention in mind, is to avoid becoming vulnerable to a plan for development and institution-building that caves in to the pitfalls of exclusion without possessing accommodative or inclusionary components. In other words, we may argue that major benefits accrue to polities that start out with accommodative and inclusionary institutions, rather than trying to build them later. A primary benefit of this approach is that we do not have to deal with SPI at a later time. This point allows us to see the importance of "sequencing" inclusionary attributes into institutional practices at the beginning of the political institutionalization process. For if accommodative and inclusionary ideals, values, norms, and procedures are present in the formation of the state and its relations with the civil society, there is a greater likelihood that the practice of consistency in implementing consensus will become more deeply rooted and more widely applied with the passage of time.

This is especially important in Third World nations where the twin pressures of development and exposure to the outside world lead their citizens to demand political freedoms that did not heretofore exist, including the right to participate in the political process and to have political equality. In these situations, the aspirations of citizens begin to outstrip the capacity of the state to deliver which, in turn, can lead to growing objective and subjective disparities. This is another manifestation of the phenomenon of "relative deprivation," which causes political violence (Gurr, 1970; Streeten, 1998, pp. 8–13).

Relative deprivation is the consequence of perceived concerns of both a material and psychological nature, which may be understood in terms of unequal access to opportunities and rights. This experience of relative deprivation is a universal one, affecting the lives of millions in the First, Second, and Third World. It is for this reason, for example, that political rights have become a highly salient theme for all types of disadvantaged groups (Gurr, 1993, p. 75). In fact, what is most significant in light of our description of the principles of the inclusionary state is that the demand for political rights is a universal theme among the disadvantaged and excluded because, in the modern state system, we find that political rights are usually held to be essential to the protection and promotion of all other group interests. Gurr has gone as far as to argue that the differences among world regions in the assertion of political rights are due mainly to cross-regional differences in human rights policies (*Id.*, p. 75). For example, we may delineate these differences by acknowledging that democratic states are more likely to protect the civil and political rights of minorities, whereas Marxist-Leninist states (both Cuba and China) tend to control the expression of these rights. In the cases of Middle Eastern and Asian regimes, we find the tendency is to deny these rights, while most Latin American regimes choose to ignore them altogether (*Id.*, p. 75).

The practice of the principle of consistency should result in a more equitable distribution of income and wealth, in conjunction with a greater respect for political and civil rights, thereby conjoining socioeconomic rights with sociopolitical rights. An equitable distribution of income increases aggregate demand for domestically produced commodities, resulting in economies of scale that, in turn, lead to the development of an outward-looking economy. This process must involve, also, an administrative bureaucracy, an independent judiciary, both of which enforce the principles and practices of inclusionary governance. These accomplishments exhibit governmental integrity. These accomplishments result in an IS which is capable of fostering a civil society which is more adept at cooperation, trust and mutual respect.

In this regard, the civil society is united to the market, not divorced from it. Civil society is instrumental in preparing the social, cultural, and associational terrain for a market (Di Palma, 1993, p. 265). Civil society provides the essential link between the emerging market and all other significant associations. Civil society and its development and evolution is the necessary component between state and market, for within civil society the triad of state, civil society and market converge to make possible the practice of consensus and consistency in both governance and development. Understood in this way, consensus and consistency furthers not only economic and political development, but internal peace as well.

Consensus and consistency are also traits which have been credited with building a "democratic peace" between nations. One of the most important empirical findings to emerge from studies of international relations in recent decades is the absence of war between democracies. Its importance for our discussion on the IS and the threats of SPI to development is that, according to the democratic peace thesis, the best explanation of a state's behavior lies in the nature of the state (Elman, 1997, p. 1). Because the focus on the state concentrates on the nature of the state, it allows us to present the five key characteristics which depict the IS as the best antidote to SPI and the most appropriate prescription for sustained development. To meet this challenge, the response of many states has been to adopt consociational or quasi-consociational practices in order to avoid SPI and to advance consistency and consensus in decision making that would enhance the legitimacy of the state (Rothchild, 1997, pp. 59–85; Deng, 1996).

Congruence

Congruence entails confronting the problems associated with displacements and transformations in the political, sociological, and economic arenas. Throughout the Third World, development entails displacements and fundamental structural transformations that invariably produce social, political, and economic difficulties and divisions which often give rise to SPI. The lack of state capacity to deal with these pressures becomes even more evident in the developmental process. The state has a crucial dual role to play during this process. First, it must cultivate the conditions for development. Second, it must act as a catalyst for development.

As to the first point, the state must bring the excluded and divided factions of civil society under one canopy. This is essential because civil society is either divided and fractured by political, social, and economic displacement, or non-existent. The state has to play the role of the ultimate social arbiter of disputes and conflicts. As such, the state should effect a high equality in income distribution. By doing this the state reduces or eliminates SPI, extending thereby the economic horizon of all actors concerning decisions in regard to savings and investments. It cultivates the formation of human capital, in general, while it aids the emergence of an entrepreneurial class, in particular. It also undertakes the task of providing the economy with the necessary infrastructure projects. By doing so, it encourages domestic investments and attracts foreign ones. This can be done only under the tutelage of an enlightened and autonomous bureaucracy. It becomes the task of the state, therefore, not only to create the conditions for generating a bureaucratic class, but also to guarantee the maintenance of its integrity, competence and efficiency.

At the same time, the state should address problems associated with refugees, human rights violations, and the potential for genocide. In short, in cultivating the condition for development, the state's concern should not be limited to economic considerations. Along with economic policies, the state must reconstitute the various classes of the civil society under a new developmental rubric that cultivates the conditions for development, that of conflict resolution.

As to the second point, the state should act as a catalyst to economic growth and development by improving the incentives for investments through fiscal means as well as reducing impediments to long-term capital movements. In this regard, what is important to realize for the pursuit of peace and the prevention of deadly conflict and political violence is that the state must constantly work to adjust the ever moving frontier between itself, the market, and civil society.

Conflict prevention, management, and resolution should be seen as operating at the edges of these frontiers to maintain peace and aid in bringing about the realization of inclusionary policies in all three of these aforementioned arenas of development. In this sense, the effort for development should be seen as an attempt which unites the market, the state, and the civil society together as related and mutually dependent spheres of activity. When this triad is operating in a coordinated manner, the chances for peace are enhanced. Alternatively, when this triad shows that the spheres are unbalanced, as with a fragmented civil society, a weakened state, or a few powerful forces dominating the market, then the proclivity for conflict and violence begins to rise.

Cohesiveness

Cohesiveness entails the coordination of developmental policies the political and social support that undergirds them. First, cohesiveness should be understood in terms of cultural, political, and social policies, reflective of inclusionary values that promote dialogue, communication, and cross-cultural understanding between people. These expressions of cohesion serve to give legitimacy to the state. Hence, inclusionary values have structural consequences in terms of allowing the state to develop its capacity to intervene in disputes in the civil society and conflicts regarding issues that are properly in its domain. Second, cohesiveness refers to the degree of complementarity and continuity that exists within the policies of the state which can effectuate peaceful forms of cooperation and communication between hostile factions, groups, and classes within civil society. Such cohesiveness is important so that massive contradictions do not erupt into conflict.

In short, values serve to create policies which are inclusionary in nature, thereby helping to foster behaviors of mutual trust and cooperation between groups. In other words, the state does not become the apologist for some ruling class alliance or coalition. Under these circumstances, the state's policies, goals and agenda by exhibiting continuity and complimentarity contribute to both its political legitimacy as well as promote economic growth and development. In addition, they make peace more attainable and conflict less likely.

In post-1917 Russia, for example, whatever the revolutionists' subjective goal commitment may have been at arriving at a conflictless—and therefore totally consensual society—they failed to achieve this goal in a double sense. First, the revolutionary means used to build a new society served to also increase the counterrevolutionary response of various sectors of the Russian society. This was the case because the ideology of the Soviet state was exclusive, non-cohesive and non-consensual. As a result, full support was never really achieved from more than a small group of militants. Second, the necessary sacrifices required by the Soviet ideology, were combined with unavoidable injustices which created discrepancies that actually disallowed the articulation of the national interest. Hence, conflict remained an inherent element of the Soviet experiment due to its non-inclusive nature, the exclusive ideology and incoherent policies of an elite nomenclature, and the inability of the party's leadership to maintain control over these conflicts (Jaguaribe, 1973, p. 216).

Coherence

Coherence means that, under the guidance of the IS, paths toward development and diminishing SPI involve new linkages between the state, civil society, and the market. In this way, strong developmental states emerge, that are enabled to satisfy the economic and political aspirations of their peoples. Without coherence, shifting governmental agendas reveal stark sociopolitical contrasts. Extreme shifts in governmental regimes and agendas also pave the path to conflict.

The principle of coherence represents the idea that the state, civil society, and the market must be understood as interconnected spheres of development. We should not allow any one of these spheres to dominate over the others. Coherence means focusing policies in a way that unites the state, civil society, and the market. To accomplish this, policies need to be developed that forge linkages between these three spheres. At the same time, as these linkages are being forged, the progress being made should discourage opposition to these policies.

Where a viable civil society does not yet exist, the state must act as a surrogate for the evolving role civil society is to play in the market. Under these circumstances, the state will initially play a greater role in the control of the market until the civil society is sufficiently developed to influence the market. Understood in this way, civil society becomes an arena where mutual cooperation, dialogue, and communication are characteristic of interactions between religious bodies, student groups, labor unions, and other civic groups. However, until the civil society reaches that level of maturity and is able to develop a coherent set of political values and claims upon the market, the state plays a more dominant role.

The role of the state in the market involves, as already noted, the enlargement and articulation of the market by building sectors and encouraging linkages with other economic sectors. The articulation and enlargement of the market necessitates the effectuation of an equitable income distribution that will support the increase in the domestically produced goods. At the same time, while the state organizes, expands and develops markets where they did not previously exist, labor and other groups within the civil society come into their own as powerful political and economic forces. As the civil society comes into its own, it can play a greater role in the market, a role previously dominated by the state. The state, then, may begin to recede as the civil society takes a more commanding role in the market.

The principle of coherence is necessary for development because it recognizes the linkages and interaction between the state, the civil society, and the market. The principle retains its theoretical and practical importance for governance in emphasizing the necessity of balancing these three spheres so that one sphere does not come to dominate another sphere at the expense of the others. Understood in this way, the state organizes the developmental task by simultaneously nurturing an autonomous civil society while working to enlarge and articulate the market.

It is the responsibility of the state to assure that the principle of coherence is maintained so that the development of the market is complemented by policies which encourage and effectuate equitable income distribution. The incorporation of labor and other groups from the civil society serves to keep the market in line with the rest of the society. Civil society should be seen as a countervailing force against the concentration of power in the market. The state should be seen as having the legal and political power to regulate and intervene only when the balance between these spheres is about to be lost. That determination will be made in accordance with the principle of coherence.

3. Promoting Effectiveness and Efficiency in Governance

Taken in combination, the aforementioned principles of inclusionary governance constitute mutually reinforcing principles, aspects and expressions of the IS in practice. Table 6.2 outlines the correspondence between the principles of the IS and the expression of these principles in practice.

Table 6.2 shows that the principle of consensus guides the IS to follow, in practice, conflict resolution through striking bargains between social groups and ameliorating differences through negotiation and compromise. These efforts are mutually reinforcing. They also produce a dialogue between clashing interests which allows the state to intervene as a mediator in preventing political conflict and violence from arising in the first place, and

TABLE 6.2	The Principles of the IS and Their Expression in Practice
Principles	*Practices*
Consensus	Bargains, Negotiations, and Compromises
Consistency	Procedures, Goals, and Policies
Congruence	Solving Problems of Political, Social, Economic Displacement, and Transformation
Cohesiveness	State/Society Linkages
Coherence	State, Civil Society, Market

establish a social space in which mutual cooperation, trust, and a history of interaction can provide the society with a track record which undergirds sociopolitical stability.

The principle of consistency strengthens the leadership and bureaucracy of the IS by mandating governmental compliance with established procedures, goals and policies. Such compliance undergirds the inclusive practices that complement the principle of consensus. Insofar as consensus is predicated upon bargains, negotiations and compromises, consistency is devoted to constitutionally inclusive procedures, goals, and policies which create state capacity through protecting the autonomy of the state to effectuate policies that are reflective of the agreements worked out in social bargains, negotiations, and compromises. Consistency and consensus work as an antidote to the phenomena of relative deprivation. While sacrifices may be required for the sake of development, at the very least those sacrifices should be more or less equitably shared.

Where development creates problems of social, economic, and political displacements and transformations, the principle of congruence guides the IS to seek to effectuate the attainment of developmental goals with a minimum of antagonism between the elements of the civil society. Congruence is a function of the IS because the principle demands that the state not only cultivate the conditions for development, but also aids the state in its task to be a catalyst for development. Understood in these terms, the principle of congruence gives the IS the ability to organize various developmental policies so that they reflect the nature of the original consensus.

Such a consensus reflects the Rawlsian concept of a well-ordered society, which is a three-part proposition. First, there is a publicly recognized conception of justice. Second, the effective regulation of this conception of justice is found in the structure of its main political and social institutions. Third, and finally, the citizens share a general sense of what is just and so they generally comply with the society's basic institutions (Rawls, 1993, p. 35). When these three concepts are viewed in combination, they individually explicate what the principle and practice of congruence means. For the principle of congruence guides the IS to effectuate a social consensus by constructing a social contract which reflects a conception of what is just, intervenes to regulate the manifestation of this concept in the basic structure of the nations' social and political institutions, and encourages compliance with its policies because it inspires by the integrity of its example.

The principle of cohesiveness is twofold. First, it refers to the internal cohesiveness of the state's policies and practices. Second, it refers to the external linkages of the IS to the civil society. Cohesiveness is a measure of the ideological coherence of the state and its developmental agenda. It is also a way of measuring the degree to which the state is embedded in the civil society and attendant to the messages that are filtered to it through formal and informal channels of communication. In this way, less conflict-prone societies can emerge because the state assures the previously marginalized access to the decision-making process. This communication should place pressure upon the state to actively work to effectuate an equitable sharing of the benefits of economic growth and development. This understanding complements the Rawlsian idea of a well-ordered society because "the publicly recognized conception of justice establishes a shared point of view from which citizens' claims on society can be adjudicated" (Rawls, 1993, p. 35).

Finally, the principle of coherence entails the guidance of the IS in developing linkages between the state, the civil society, and the market. The primary value of these linkages, from the standpoint of the IS, is to ensure equity in distribution, the maintenance of the public sense of justice in practice, and the avoidance of monopolistic market behaviors that could adversely affect development and the capacity of the state to govern effectively. Coherence is the principle that looks at the goal of equity and demands that state capacity be strong enough to keep social groups accountable to constitutionally inclusive practices while, at the same time, preserving a proper balance between market, civil society, and the state which promotes equitable distributions of wealth of power so that the primary principle of inclusion is maintained as development proceeds.

The IS can effectuate a political, social, and economic environment that is conducive to the evolution and development of democratic principles and practices. It is for this reason that we have argued that democracy is a subset of inclusion. The installation of an IS serves to inaugurate democratic practices and to perpetuate these practices through the periods of transition and then consolidation of democratic practices.

The only remaining nuance is that each state and society must develop its own version of what its model of democratic practice will be, for such a construction is a social construction and cannot be "transported," or imposed, or constructed from myopic or xenophobic perspectives which are merely derivative from the Western experience. Rather, democratic social models and social constructions for governance must be understood as endemic to the Third World nations in which they arise, a reflection of their aspirations and goals for the future.

BIBLIOGRAPHY

Bridget Anderson, "Servants and Slaves: Europe's Domestic Workers," *Race & Class: A Journal for Black and Third World Liberation*, Vol. 39, No. 1, July–September 1997.
Tom Barry, Harry Browne and Beth Sims, *Crossing the Line: Immigrants, Economic Integration, and Drug Enforcement on the US-Mexican Border*, Resource Center Press, Albuquerque, New Mexico, 1994.
Tom Barry, *Zapata's Revenge: Free Trade and the Farm Crisis in Mexico*, South End Press, 1995.
Wolfgang Beck, Laurent van der Maesen, Alan Walker, editors, *The Social Quality of Europe*, Kluwer Law International, The Hague, London, Boston, 1997.
Sheri Berman, *The Social Democratic Moment: Ideas and Politics in the Making of Interwar Europe*, Harvard University Press, 1998.
Thomas J. Biersteker and Cynthia Weber, "The Social Construction of State Sovereignty," *State Sovereignty as a Social Construct*, edited by Thomas J. Biersteker and Cynthia Weber, Cambridge University Press, 1996.
Nancy Birdsall, Caroll Graham, and Richard Sabot, editors, *Beyond Tradeoffs: Market Reforms and Equitable Growth in Latin America*, Inter-American Development Bank, Brookings Institution Press, 1998.
Sue Branford and Bernardo Kucinski, *The Debt Squads: The US, the Banks, and Latin America*, Zed Books Ltd., 1988.
Michael Bratton and Nicolas Van De Walle, *Democratic Experiments in Africa: Regime Transitions in Comparative Perspective*, Cambridge University Press, 1997.
Jeremy Brecher, John B. Childs, and Jill Cutler, editors, *Global Visions: Beyond the New World Order*, South End Press, 1993.
Jeremy Brecher and Tim Costell, *Global Village or Global Pillage: Economic Reconstruction from the Bottom Up*, South End Press, 1994.
Michel E. Brown, editor, *The International Dimensions of Internal Conflict*, The MIT Press, Cambridge, Massachusetts, 1996.
Harry Browne and Beth Sims, *Runaway America: US Jobs and Factories on the Move*, The Resource Center Press, Albuquerque, New Mexico, 1993.
Harry Browne, Beth Sims and Tom Barry, *For Richer, for Poorer: Shaping US Mexican Integration*, The Resource Center Press, Albuquerque, New Mexico, and Latin American Bureau, 1994.
Roger Burbach, Orlando Nunez, and Boris Kagarlitsky, *Globalization and Its Discontents: The Rise of Postmodern Socialisms*, Pluto Press, 1997.
Albert Camus, "Bread and Freedom," *Resistance, Rebellion, and Death*, Vintage Books, A Division of Random House, New York, 1974.
Carnegie Commission—Final Report with Executive Summary, *Preventing Deadly Conflict*, Carnegie Corporation of New York, December 1997.
Jorge G. Castaneda, "When Citizens Disagree on Even The Time of Day," *The Los Angeles Times*, May 10, 1999, Commentary, p. B-5.
Manuel Castells, *The Power of Identity—The Information Age: Economy, Society and Culture*, Volume II, Blackwell Publishers, 1997.

Manuel Castells, *End of Millennium—The Information Age: Economy, Society and Culture*, Volume III, Blackwell Publishers, 1998.
Catherine Caufield, *Masters of Illusion: The World Bank and the Poverty of Nations*, Henry Holt and Company, New York, 1996.
Michel Chossudovsky, *The Globalization of Poverty: Impacts of IMF and World Bank Reforms*, Zed Books Ltd., London and New Jersey, TWN—Third World Network, Penang, Malaysia, 1997.
Michel Chossudovsky, "Global Poverty in the Late 20th Century," *Journal of International Affairs*, Volume 52, No. 1, Fall 1998.
Dimitris N. Chryssochoou, *Democracy in the European Union*, Tauris Academic Studies, London and New York, 1998.
Frederic F. Clairmont, *The Rise and Fall of Economic Liberalism: The Making of the Economic Gulag*, The Other India Press—Third World Network, 1996.
Giovanni A. Cornia, Richard Jolly, and Frances Stewart, editors, *Adjustment with a Human Face—Volume I—Protecting the Vulnerable and Promoting Growth*, Clarendon Press, Oxford, 1987.
Bruce Cummings, *Parallax Visions: Making Sense of American-East Asian Relations at the End of the Century*, Duke University Press, 1999.
Robert A. Dahl, *A Preface to Economic Democracy*, University of California Press, 1985.
Kevin Danaher, editor, *Fifty Years Is Enough: The Case Against the World Bank and the International Monetary Fund*, South End Press, 1994.
Larry Diamond, "Democracy in Latin America: Degrees, Illusions, and Directions for Consolidation," *Beyond Sovereignty: Collectively Defending Democracy in the Americas*, edited by Tom Farer, The Johns Hopkins University Press, 1996.
Francis M. Deng, Sadikiel Kimaro, Terrene Lyons, Donald Rothchild, and I. William Zartman, *Sovereignty as Responsibility: Conflict Management in Africa*, The Brookings Institution Press, 1996.
Jack Donnelly, *Universal Human Rights in Theory & Practice*, Cornell University Press, 1989.
Milton J. Esman, *Ethnic Politics*, Cornell University Press, 1994.
Gosta Esping-Andersen, editor, *Welfare States in Transition: National Adaptations in Global Economies*, SAGE Publications, (Published in association with the United Nations Research Institute for Social Development), 1996.
Richard Falk, *On Humane Governance: Toward a New Global Politics*, The Pennsylvania State University Press, 1995.
William F. Felice, *Taking Suffering Seriously: The Importance of Collective Human Rights*, State University of New York Press, 1996.
Orlando Figes, *A People's Tragedy: A History of the Russian Revolution*, Viking, 1997.
Francois Furet, *The Passing of an Illusion: The Idea of Communism in the Twentieth Century*, The University of Chicago Press, 1999.
Geoffrey Garrett, *Partisan Politics in the Global Economy*, Cambridge University Press, 1998.
Susan George, *The Debt Boomerang: How the Third World Debt Harms Us All*, Westview Press, 1992.

Susan George, *A Fate Worse Than Debt: The World Financial Crisis and the Poor*, Grove Press, New York, 1988.

Alan Gerwirth, *The Community of Rights*, The University of Chicago Press, 1996.

Anthony Giddens, *The Third Way: The Renewal of Social Democracy*, Polity Press, 1998.

Carol Graham and Moises Naim, "The Political Economy of Institutional Reform in Latin America," *Beyond Tradeoffs: Market Reforms and Equitable Growth in Latin America*, edited by Nancy Birdsall, Carol Graham, and Richard H. Sabot, Inter-American Development Bank, Brookings Institution Press, 1998.

John Gray, *False Dawn: The Delusions of Global Capitalism*, The New Press, New York, 1998.

Duncan Green, *Silent Revolution: The Rise of Market Economics in Latin America*, Cassell, Latin American Bureau, 1995.

Ricardo Grinspun and Maxwell A. Cameron, editors, *The Political Economy of North American Free Trade*, St. Martin's Press, 1993.

Dipak K. Gupta, *The Economics of Political Violence: The Effect of Political Instability on Economic Growth*, Praeger, Westport, Connecticut, 1990.

Ted Robert Gurr, *Minorities at Risk: A Global View of Ethnopolitical Conflicts*, United States Institute of Peace Press, Washington, D.C., 1993.

Graham Hancock, *Lords of Poverty: The Power, Prestige, and Corruption of the International Aid Business*, The Atlantic Monthly Press, 1989.

Nigel Harris, *The End of the Third World: Newly Industrializing Countries and the Decline of an Ideology*, Penguin Books, 1986.

Donald L. Horowitz, *Ethnic Groups in Conflict*, University of California Press, 1985.

Donald L. Horowitz, *A Democratic South Africa?: Constitutional Engineering in a Divided Society*, University of California Press, 1991.

Samuel P. Huntington, *The Third Wave: Democratization in the Late Twentieth Century*, University of Oklahoma Press, 1991.

Samuel P. Huntington, *The Clash of Civilizations and the Remaking of World Order*, Simon & Schuster, 1996.

Naeem Inayatullah, "Beyond The Sovereignty Dilemma: Quasi-States As Social Construct," *State Sovereignty as Social Construct*, edited by Thomas J. Biersteker and Cynthia Weber, Cambridge University Press, 1996.

Inter-American Development Bank, *Facing Up to Inequality in Latin America: Economic and Social Progress in Latin America, 1998–1999 Report*, Distributed by The Johns Hopkins University Press for the Inter-American Development Bank, Washington, D.C., 1998.

Robert H. Jackson, *Quasi-States: Sovereignty, International Relations and the Third World*, Cambridge University Press, 1990.

Thomas Janoski and Alexander M. Hicks, *The Comparative Political Economy of the Welfare State*, Cambridge University Press, 1994.

Christian Joppke, editor, *Challenge to the Nation-State: Immigration in Western Europe and the United States*, Oxford University Press, 1998.

Peter Juviler, *Freedom's Ordeal: The Struggle for Human Rights and Democracy in Post-Soviet States*, University of Pennsylvania Press, 1998.

Colin H. Kahl, "Population Growth, Environmental Degradation, and State-Sponsored Violence: The Case of Kenya, 1991–93," *International Security*, Vol. 23, No. 2, Fall 1998.

Ethan B. Kapstein, "A Global Third Way: Social Justice and the World Economy," *World Policy Journal*, Volume XV, No. 4, Winter 1998/1999.

Robert F. Kennedy Memorial Center For Human Rights, "Kenya at the Crossroads: Demands for Constitutional Reforms Intensify," Washington, D.C., July 1997.

Robert F. Kennedy Memorial Center for Human Rights, "Moving Towards Constitutional Reform in Kenya?—An Update," Washington, D.C., September 1998.

Ann Kent, *Between Freedom and Subsistence: China and Human Rights*, Oxford University Press, 1993.

Robert O. Keohane and Stanley Hoffman, editors, *The New European Community: Decisionmaking and Institutional Change*, Westview Press, 1991.

Anatoly M. Khaanov, *After the USSR: Ethnicity, Nationalism, and Politics in the Commonwealth of Independent States*, University of Wisconsin Press, 1995.

Jytte Klausen and Louise A. Tilly, editors, *European Integration in Social and Historical Perspective—1850 To The Present*, Rowman & Littlefield Publishers, Inc., 1997.

Bradley S. Klein, *Strategic Studies and World Order: The Global Politics of Deterrence*, Cambridge University Press, 1994.

Arthur Kleinman, et al., *Social Suffering*, University of California Press, 1997.

Hans-Dieter Klingemann and Dieter Fuchs, editors, *Citizens and the State—Beliefs in Government* (Volume One), Oxford University Press, 1995.

Herbert Kitschelt, *The Transformation of European Social Democracy*, Cambridge University Press, 1994.

Rajni Kothari, *Poverty: Human Consciousness and the Amnesia of Development*, Zed Books Ltd., London and New Jersey, 1993.

David M. Kotz, Terrence McDonough and Michael Reich, editors, *Social Structures of Accumulation: The Political Economy of Growth and Crisis*, Cambridge University Press, 1994.

Tim Lang and Colin Hines, *The New Protectionism: Protecting the Future Against Free Trade*, The New Press, 1993.

Percy Lehning and Albert Weale, editors, *Citizenship, Democracy and Justice in the New Europe*, Routledge, London and New York, 1997.

Stephan Leibfried and Paul Pierson, editors, *European Social Policy: Between Fragmentation and Integration*, The Brookings Institution Press, Washington, D.C., 1995.

Mark Levinson, "The IMF in Asia: Its Solution Is the Cause of the Crisis," *Dissent*, Summer 1998.

Anatol Lieven, *Chechnya: Tombstone of Russian Power*, Yale University Press, 1998.

Eduardo Lora and Juan Luis Londono, "Structural Reforms and Equity," *Beyond Tradeoffs: Market Reforms and Equitable Growth in Latin America*, Inter-American Development Bank, Brookings Institution Press, 1998.

Patrice McSherry, "The Emergence of 'Guardian Democracy'," *NACLA-Report on the Americas*, Volume XXXII, No. 3, November/December 1998.
John Markoff, "Really Existing Democracy: Learning From Latin America in the Late 1990s," *New Left Review*, No. 223, May/June 1997.
Andre Martin and George Ross, "Europe's Monetary Union: Creating a Democratic Deficit?," *Current History: A Journal of Contemporary World Affairs*, April 1999.
Hans-Peter Martin and Harald Schumann, *The Global Trap: Globalization and the Assault on Prosperity and Democracy*, Zed Books Ltd., London & New York, 1996.
Christopher Merrett, *Free Trade: Neither Free Nor About Trade*, Black Rose Books, 1996.
Istavan Meszaros, *Beyond Capital: Towards a Theory of Transition*, Monthly Review Press, 1995.
Michael Newman, *Democracy, Sovereignty and the European Union*, St. Martin's Press, New York, 1996.
Geraldo Otero, editor, *Neo-Liberalism Revisited: Economic Restructuring and Mexico's Political Future*, Westview Press, 1996.
James Petras and Chronis Polychronious, "Rethinking Globalization: From the Future to the Past," *Socialism and Democracy*, Vol. 12, Nos. 1–2, 1998.
Anne Phillips, *The Politics of Presence*, Clarendon Press, Oxford, 1995.
Adam Przeworski, *Democracy and the Market: Political and Economic Reforms in Eastern Europe and Latin America*, Cambridge University Press, 1991.
Adam Przeworski, *Sustainable Democracy*, Cambridge University Press, 1995.
John Rawls, *A Theory of Justice*, Harvard University Press, 1971.
Andrew S. Reynolds, *Electoral Systems and Democratic Consolidation in Southern Africa*, dissertation submitted in partial satisfaction of the requirements for the degree of Doctor of Philosophy in Political Science, University of California Press, San Diego, 1996.
Bruce Rich, *Mortgaging the Earth: The World Bank, Environmental Impoverishment, and the Crisis Of Development*, Beacon Press, 1994.
Caroline M. Robb, *Can the Poor Influence Policy?: Participatory Poverty Assessments in the Developing World*, The World Bank, Washington, D.C., 1999.
William I. Robinson, *Promoting Polyarchy: Globalization, US Intervention, and Hegemony*, Cambridge University Press, 1996.
William I. Robinson, "Latin America and Global Capitalism," *Race & Class—A Journal for Black and Third World Liberation*, Volume 40, Nos. 2/3, October 1998–March 1999.
Fred Rosen and Deidre McFadyen, *Free Trade and Economic Restructuring in Latin America—A NACLA Reader*, Monthly Review Press, 1995.
Richard Sandbrook, "Taming The African Leviathan," *World Policy Journal*, Volume VII, No. 4, Fall 1990.
Vivien A. Schmidt, "The New Order, Incorporated: The Rise of Business and the Decline of the Nation-State," *DAEDALUS—Journal of the American Academy of Arts and Sciences*, Spring 1995.

Timothy D. Sisk, *Democratization in South Africa: The Elusive Social Contract*, Princeton University Press, 1995.
William C. Smith, Carlos H. Acuna, and Eduardo A. Gamarra, editors, *Latin American Political Economy in the Age of Neoliberal Reform: Theoretical and Comparative Perspectives for the 1990s*, Transaction Publishers, 1994.
Jens Magleby Sorensen, *The Exclusive European Citizenship: The Case for Refugees and Immigrants in the European Union*, Avebury, 1996.
James Gustave Speth, "Poverty: A Denial of Human Rights," *Journal of International Affairs*, Volume 52, No. 1, Fall 1998.
Nicolas Spulber, *Redefining the State: Privatization and Welfare Reform in Industrial and Transitional Economies*, Cambridge University Press, 1997.
Barbara Stallings, editor, *Global Change, Regional Response: The New International Context of Development*, Cambridge University Press, 1995.
David Strang, "Contested Sovereignty: The Social Construction Of Colonial Imperialism," *State Sovereignty as Social Construct*, edited by Thomas J. Biersteker and Cynthia Weber, Cambridge University Press, 1996.
Rosemary Thorp, *Progress, Poverty and Exclusion: An Economic History of Latin America in the 20th Century*, Distributed by The John Hopkins University Press for the Inter-American Development Bank and the European Union, 1998.
Emek M. Ucarer and Donald J. Puchala, editors, *Immigration into Western Societies: Problems and Policies*, Pinter, London and Washington, 1997.
Roberto Mangabeira Unger, *Democracy Realized: The Progressive Alternative*, Verso, 1998.
United Nations Development Programme, (UNDP), *Human Development Report—1998*, Oxford University Press, 1998.
United States Institute of Peace, "Special Report—Can Nigeria Make a Peaceful Transition to Democratic Governance?," Washington, D.C., December 1997.
Henry Veltmeyer, James Petras, and Steve Vieux, *Neoliberalism and Class Conflict in Latin America: A Comparative Perspective on the Political Economy of Structural Adjustment*, St. Martin's Press, Inc., 1997.
Frank Vibert, *Europe: A Constitution for the Millennium*, Dartmouth, 1995.
Carlos M. Vilas, "Economic Restructuring, Neoliberal Reforms, and the Working Class in Latin America," *Capital, Power, and Inequality in Latin America*, edited by Sandor Halebsky and Richard L. Harris, Westview Press, 1995.
Carlos Vilas, "The Decline of the Steady Job in Latin America," *NACLA—Report on the Americas*, Volume XXXII, No. 4, January/February 1999.
John Warnock, *The Other Mexico: The North American Triangle Completed*, Black Rose Books, 1995.
J. H. H. Weiler, *The Constitution of Europe: "Do the New Clothes Have an Emperor?" And Other Essays on European Integration*, Cambridge University Press, 1999.
Claude E. Welch, Jr. and Ronald Meltzer, editors, *Human Rights and Development in Africa*, State University of New York Press, 1984.

Ronald Wintrobe, *The Political Economy of Dictatorship*, Cambridge University Press, 1998.

Stephen R. Weissman, "Preventing Genocide in Burundi: Lessons from International Diplomacy," United States Institute of Peace, Washington, D.C., July 1998.

Kurt Weyland, *Democracy Without Equity: Failures of Reform in Brazil*, University of Pittsburgh Press, 1996.

I. William Zartman, *Ripe for Resolution: Conflict and Intervention in Africa*, Oxford University Press, 1985.

CHAPTER 7

BETWEEN POVERTY AND POLYARCHY: THE PRAXIS OF DEMOCRACY IN THIRD WORLD STATES

> The developmental priorities of the elites reflect their fundamental values. They represent not only abstract causal models but also basic commitments to options implying gains and losses for specific interests as well as for the nation as a whole.
>
> Peter McDonough,
> *Power and Ideology in Brazil,* 1981, p. 131

> The world has become more polarized, both between and within countries. The risk of a huge global underclass undermining international stability is quite real.
>
> James Gustave Speth,
> *"The Plight of the Poors:
> The United States Must Increase Development Aid,"* Foreign
> Affairs, May/June 1999, p. 13

> The successful transition to democracy may begin with the acceptable of rituals and mechanisms—elections and parties—but it will remain superficial and essentially irrelevant to those most victimized, until it addresses directly and effectively both state violence and minority grievances.
>
> Richard Falk, "Democratic Disguise:
> Post-Cold War Authoritarianism," *in Altered States:
> A Reader in the New World Order,* eds. Bennis and
> Moushabeck, 1993, p. 26

> Organization fragmentation makes effective interest representation difficult for the poor, who would benefit from equity-enhancing reforms, and strengthens their elite opponents by giving them privileged access to decision makers.
>
> Kurt Weyland, *Democracy Without Equity:
> Failures of Reform in Brazil,* 1996, p. 15

A. INTRODUCTION

Even in the First World of the 1990s, democracy is at risk. In the praxis of the Third World, it has only partially established itself with the procedural formality of elections. Its scope and its substantive content remain weak or non-existent. And so, democracy remains trapped between poverty and polyarchy. Poverty has left the majority engulfed in misery, socioeconomic deprivation, and political exclusion. Polyarchy, not democracy, dominates political and economic decision making processes throughout the Third World.

Polyarchy, as a form of elite rule, differs from authoritarianism and dictatorship because it is better equipped to control popular pressures and demands from within civil society. Polyarchy is a hegemonic form of social order. It is a system that seeks to process social demands for change by facilitating the advancement of demands that reproduce the existing social order. Polyarchy supports demands that operate to benefit the long-term interests of dominant groups, just as elites and their alliance structures act to preserve elite-dominated interests while actively working to advance narrow and particularistic agendas within a matrix of elite interests and the coalitions within it. Alternatively, those demands that challenge the social order are filtered out of the hegemonic discourse of this elite constellation of power (Robinson, 1996, p. 71).

Unlike the democratic ideal, the practice of polyarchy and its continuing institutionalization operates in defiance of the realization and articulation of greater representation for the marginalized and their suppressed claims. In this way, polyarchy opposes the inclusion of all classes, groups, and interests in the affairs of the nation. Polyarchy refuses to incorporate the demands of the excluded and marginalized classes, and opposes any perspectives that could emerge from a socially transformative agenda. The authentic aspirations of the oppressed and marginalized remain excluded from both social and elite discourse. As a result, democracy, throughout the Third World, is caught between the extremes of polyarchy and poverty.

The purpose of this chapter is to outline the dimensions of the democratic dilemma characterizing the Third World, as citizens and their governments remain trapped between poverty and polyarchy. The quality, scope, and substance of democracy, in the praxis of the Third World, is largely defined by the dialectic of poverty and polyarchy. While polyarchy preserves the hierarchical status quo of Third World states, the dynamic processes attendant on the deepening and widening of poverty, unemployment, and underemployment serve to create a fisure between the legitimacy of the state and the tolerance of the civil society. As the state's legitimacy declines with citizen's tolerance there is, as James Gustave Speth, Administrator of the United Nations Development Program, has observed, "the risk of a huge global underclass undermining international stability" and this risk "is quite real" (Speth, 1999, p. 13).

In every nation of the Third World, in every region, the social costs and consequences of the interplay between polyarchy and poverty mount and the price that is paid is calculated in terms of a "democratic deficit." *Polyarchy* is a system which allows for the aggrandizement of elite power and its supportive networks at the national and international levels of capital accumulation. *Poverty* is the measure of the social cost that each population pays for the maintenance and preservation of this process. It is predicated on widening circles of exclusion and diminishing circles of inclusion. In the midst of this process, democracy itself is moved further away from the implementation of its ideal claims and its inclusionary mandate. Being forced by the institutionalization of polyarchy to surrender its inclusionary mandate, democracy forfeits its promise. The form this forfeiture takes is found in the so-called "democratic deficit."

The persistence of poverty has, in large measure, allowed for "semi-democracy" or "low-intensity-democracy" to persist. The short-term military, political, and economic goals and interests of Third World elites account for the "democratic deficit." In turn, the democratic deficit allows for the virtual eclipse of the goals of poverty eradication and human development. With the demise of policies, programs, and a national commitment to combat poverty, Third World states abandon comprehensive strategies for human development. The future of individuals, groups and nations becomes mortgaged to exclusionary states that are increasingly forced to rely on elite choices ("polyarchy"), while masquerading as democracies.

Accompanying the persistent presence of poverty is the political curse of polyarchy. Polyarchy places enormous institutional restraints on popular pressures for democratization. While polyarchy allows for the formality of elections, it does not produce popular democratic outcomes. Rather, its actual effect is two-fold. First, it represents the political institutionalization of preexisting social relations, thereby limiting the accountability of the state to periodic elections. Second, in between these elections, it allows the groups who won control of the state to pursue their own exclusionary agenda, irrespective of the national welfare and ungoverned by any formal channels of accountability to or for the excluded and marginalized masses of its citizens. Polyarchy, in short, allows for the process of exclusionary governance to continue unabated because decision making is perpetually insulated from popular pressures.

Many exclusionary states have justified their exercise of power by reliance on the strength of their records of economic growth. As long as the government in power can show healthy growth statistics, its legitimacy is believed to be secure and sound, at least in a very narrowly defined political sense. However, such a political result ignores the fact that growth alone is not enough to allow all segments of the population to participate in the growth process (Gaiha and Kulkarni, 1998, p. 145). In fact, the impoverishment of some sections of the population has been attributed to this particular kind of growth and may be understood as a direct consequence of growth (*Id.*, p. 149). Why? Because growth is not equitable. It is not equitable because it is tied to the decisions of a national and international political polyarchy. In this analysis, it may be asserted that "given the inequality in endowments of both physical and human capital, as well as a rigidly hierarchical social structure, it is not surprising that some sections benefit while others lose when economic opportunities expand" (*Id.*, p. 150). This is, after all, the logical outcome of exclusionary governance and an aspect of its purpose and general design. Consequently, poverty persists despite growth.

It follows that the persistence of poverty is part of the praxis of the Third World not so much because of a lack of growth but as a consequence of the *exclusion* of some sectors of the poor from growth. In other words, the absence of equitable growth patterns and policies serves to perpetuate poverty. To avoid exclusion and marginalization, the poor must be participants in the development process. This includes their participation in the benefits of growth and their role as active beneficiaries of an equitable distribution of the nation's wealth.

Therefore, inclusionary states operate under the recognition that "growth alone will not accomplish much unless it is combined with measures designed to promote the participation of the poor" (*Id.*, p. 180). The evolution of such measures must be the product of community initiatives and not just governmental action. The practical implementation of such measures must be backed by a strong coalition of the poor. Such a coalition must have the active support of other sectors of the civil society, must be associated with the decision-making processes of the state, and be the product of an emerging normative framework of shared values and aspirations.

Taking a closer look at what kind of measures might be required involves being cognizant of the fact that growth can still have "varying degrees of efficacy in terms of its impact on poverty, depending on the 'structural' forms that poverty and growth take and on the political and social contexts in which the growth process unfolds" (Bhagwati, 1998, p. 35). A number of institutions may be called into play. A combination of governmental action with the efforts of Non-Governmental Organizations (NGOs) may be necessary to maximize the impact of governmental expenditures on social and economic programs that benefit the poor. Understood in these terms, it may become possible to comprehend the fact that growth, poverty, and social agendas are ultimately bedfellows in the larger developmental equation.

This combination is required especially for those peripheral groups who are still emerging, in some instances, from feudal social and political structures. And this is also the case where formal democratic practices may be in place. For democracy, by itself, does not assure or guarantee inclusion. To be even more precise, it may be argued that the great unanswered or elusive question of formal economics is: What allows one group to benefit from the labor of another? The answer to that question is that "at the heart of the matter, [it] is the failure of economics to adequately address the social and political dimensions of any economic issue" (Yunus, 1998, p. 53). This is not an isolated opinion. Celso Furtado, reflecting upon the historical transformation of Third World societies from feudal social and political structures, also emphasized the point that "it should be borne in mind that the desacralization of nature and the secularization of society were facilitated by social practices that reflected the demands of accumulation" (Furtado, 1983, p. 167).

The accumulation of capital, as an exclusionary process, has often been accompanied by the accumulation of political and social power. As power and capital merged into an incestuous relationship, the social cleavages that were engendered left each nation with its civil society divided and demoralized. Mutual cooperation was replaced by mutual distrust. And where distrust vested, it resulted in a high return in social and political instability, often leading to deadly conflict. The net result, at least for the cause of democracy, has been a deficit. Terms such as "weak democracy," "semi-democracy," and "low-intensity-democracy" reflect attempts to define and describe the nature of this democratic deficit and its distance from its ideal.

The demands of accumulation, under capitalism, are historically reliant on the principle of profit maximization. Because this principle of profit maximization is a feature of capitalism which seems to be permanently embedded in it, this has not only economic repurcussions but various political consequences as well. In economic theory, the individual entrepreneur is usually portrayed as one who actively works to ensure the optimal use of scarce resources to produce the greatest possible financial return. The problem with this scenario is that it often ignores or simply obviates the negative social consequences associated with this kind of financial return. In short, classical, liberal, and neoliberal economic theory ignores the fact that there are alternative scenarios which may be helpful in dealing with removing the blight of poverty.

By chosing to ignore alternative scenarios, economic theory reinforces those trends that perpetuate both poverty and exclusion. In this way, economic theory constitutes an apologetic and a dogma for accumulation, regardless of the harm done to people or to their environment. In this sense, economic theory enables violence to intercede where a culture of peace could have evolved. The violence begins as structural violence. It then finds its expression in multifaceted dimensions of human life. An alternative scenario is, therefore, important to articulate as an alternative discourse, capable of forging a new consciousness of what human development can and should embody.

Such an alternative scenario simply means that social goals can replace profit maximization as a powerful motivating influence (Yunus, 1998, p. 62). If, for example, enterprises are driven by goals to maximize social awareness, then such enterprises could present a tremendous challenge to enterprises based solely on profit maximization. The challenge is to create appropriate social and financial incentives for socially conscious enterprises which could be viable and effective forces in the marketplace. Such an alternative vision, however, is not only at odds with traditional economic theory, but also with the political structures of polyarchy at the national and international levels.

The structural power of transnational capital in the global economy is opposed to such an alternative vision. After all, the current arrangments in the global economy give political and ideological power to elites that are tied directly and indirectly to the benefit of the profit maximization principle of transnational capital. Transnational elites exercise their "veto power" over alternative visions when they are adopted by local states. This happened in the case of Cuba in the early 1960s, when it was captured by popular sectors.

The structural power of transnational capital seeks to combine its resources with the institutions of polyarchy and the exclusionary state in order to halt the democratization of social life and the practices and principles of inclusionary governance. For if inclusionary governance, in the form of inclusionary states, were to be triumphant, then the very economic, political, and social foundations for profit maximization and the predations of polyarchy would be removed as the structural supports of transnational capital. This is a logical conclusion insofar as the political and social foundations for inclusionary governance (as discussed in the Introduction) emphasize a wider approach to development than that which is so narrowly conceived under the profit maximization model of growth, now extended under the auspices of "globalization."

It is for this reason that, despite its avowed commitment to liberalism and democracy internationally, the United States has frequently chosen to actively support authoritarian regimes throughout the world. Right-wing dictatorships and exclusionary states, for the last five decades of the 20th century, have enjoyed the support of US foreign policy makers. Elite US foreign policy makers were largely compelled by a persistent concern for order, in support of the investment concerns of transnational capital, to maintain these kinds of anti-democratic regimes. Further, this support was also combined with a paternalistic racism that characterized non-Western peoples as vulnerable to radical ideas and ideals. Hence, support for dictatorships in Iran, the Philippines, El Salvador, and elsewhere forged alliances between international capital and Third World governmental elites who supported a favorable atmosphere for US trade (Schmitz, 1999; Rabe, 1999; Lowenthal, 1987; Munck, 1984; Joyce Kolko, 1988; Gabriel Kolko, 1988; Schoultz, 1998; Blachman, et al., 1986; Rabe, 1988; Bodenheimer and Gold, 1989).

Polyarchy, as a system of elite rule, has created what I have called the ES. It is more effective than authoritarianism because authoritarian regimes insulate state-structures and economic decision making from popular pressures, but remain unable to legitimate elite rule. The ES, or "polyarchic state," may legitimately employ repression against popular sectors that transgress the rules of established "legality," especially when the demands they place on the state are not met. Thus, while authoritarian states can insulate elite rule, they cannot legitimate elite rule, but polyarchy serves to perform both functions (Robinson, 1996, p. 61).

The primary function of polyarchy is to maintain social stability. Yet this function and goal of polyarchy collides with the entire neo-liberal project, which is dedicated to profit maximization, irrespective of the social costs. The transnational project of these two enterprises has resulted in the following: (1) under the pressure of globalization, the growth of socioeconomic inequalities and human misery in nearly all countries (First and Third World); and (2) a growing gap between the haves and have-nots within the framework of the new world order. These trends have led to a situation where "the tendency is for wealth to become concentrated in a privileged stratum encompassing some 20 percent of humanity, in which the gap between rich and poor is widening within each country, North and South alike, simultaneously with a sharp increase in the inequalities between the North and the South" (Robinson, 1996, p. 339).

These trends constitute the crisis of new world order. Such trends are reflective of the "exclusionary impulse" that poisons the praxis of democracy throughout the Third World. Hence, between polyarchy and poverty, the politics of the ES thrive. Concurrent with the rise of the ES is the decline of and opposition to the democratic ideal and its advance under and through the auspices of the model of the IS. The politics of the ES derives its sustenance from the maintenance and perpetuation of widespread socioeconomic misery through exclusion, growing elite power through popular disempowerment, and the escalation of private profit at the cost of socialized poverty.

The Outline of This Chapter

The main purpose of this chapter is to examine, analyze, and explain the nature of those national and international forces which continually disallow the embodiment of the democratic ideal in the praxis of Third World states. Within and between each of the (7) parts of this chapter there is one common denominator. The common denominator is the argument that *if groups, classes and interests are excluded, no amount of developmental success can rescue them from social and political instability and the corresponding danger of ever-increasing levels of violence and deadly conflict.* Insofar as exclusion eviscerates the benefits of development, so too it fuels the proclivity of groups and classes to indulge in the call to exacerbate the divisions which are endemic to ethnic strife. Inclusion, on the other hand, leads to accommodation and a shared culture of mutual cooperation instead of mutual hostility and distrust. Therefore, if individual nation-states and the international community is to build a culture of peace, it is a culture which must be predicated upon inclusion.

In a world of increasingly multicultural societies, I concur with Habermas's assessment that "multicultural societies can be held together by a common political culture, however much it has proven itself, only if democratic citizenship pays off not only in terms of liberal individual rights and rights of political participation, but also in the enjoyment of social and cultural rights. The citizens must be able to experience the fair value of their rights also in the form of social security and the reciprocal recognition of different cultural forms of life. Democratic citizenship can only realize its integrative potential—that is, it can only found solidarity between strangers—if it proves itself as a mechanism that actually realizes the material conditions of preferred forms of life" (Habermas, 1998, pp. 118–119). To realize the material conditions of preferred forms of life will necessitate the building of cultures and institutions that correspond with a common ideal. It is the ideal of inclusion.

Part B sets forth the argument that the socialization of poverty dooms the democratic ideal from even being approximated in the praxis of the Third World. For while the formal aspects of democracy, such as elections, may be operating, the substance of what democratic citizenship means and promises is effectively foreclosed upon in practice. It is foreclosed upon by the elite political structure of polyarchy, masquerading as democracy. The ramifications of its policies take concrete form in the embodiment of economic and social policies that ignore the basic human needs of large sectors of the population and relegate the distribution of growth and development to the vagaries of the market and the criteria of international lending institutions that have no interest in promoting an equitable distribution of wealth. The socialization of poverty is replicated in First and Third World states, thereby reinforcing, preserving and even expanding exclusionary practices, policies, and programs that create limited safety nets instead of embarking upon a fundamental redistribution of wealth and the benefits of development.

Part C outlines the growth of what has been termed "illiberal democracy," as opposed to constitutional democracy. Illiberal democracy is inherently exclusionary. Its expansion throughout the Third World serves to explain, in part, why demands come from some social classes and groups, but not others. Illiberal democracy is devoid of inclusionary zeal because it relegates the poor and groups outside traditional patronage and alliance structures to the nation's welfare as expendable appendages to the profit maximization potential for greater capital accumulation. In this way, I argue that the process of capitalist development is the causal variable in the relation between capitalism and polyarchy.

Part of the reason for the non-realization of the democratic ideal resides in the recognition that democracy itself does not refer to an "end-state" harmonious consensus, but rather to a commitment to the endless exploration of disagreements by political means. Exclusionary governance and polyarchy effectively remove avenues for disagreement and eliminate channels of communication between the state and the larger civil society. Once the state apparatus is captured, in a formal election, elites dispense with dialogue and foreclose upon building mediating institutions for genuine inclusion. Hence, governance by exclusion results. In turn, the results of exclusion create grounds for social conflict, instability, and a culture of rising levels of violence. In this situation, the state is no longer playing the role of the "Hobbesian protector" of the Commonwealth. The state's elites, operating in the name of democracy, repress the aspirations of the commonwealth while seeking to advance the interests of private wealth. These trends have created the "neoliberal cruel state."

Part D presents the argument that what development requires is a new approach to economic growth and development. The construction of inclusionary societies demands nothing less. In this respect, the people's physical, cultural, and social aspirations must all be addressed. Development must become holistic. The broadest measure of development, under this scenario, would centralize a comprehensive program for social well-being within the developmental equation. Six principles underlie such a program: (1) it must be comprehensive; (2) it must actively encourage productive activities that will guarantee enduring improvements in the lives of the poor; (3) it must be national in scope; (4) it must be participatory, which means that it mandates the inclusion of all affected parties, allow them to voice their concerns in the decision-making processes that affect their lives, and keeps them involved in the implementation and evaluation of all measures undertaken; (5) it must be decentralized; and (6) it must be unified, assuring solidarity among all participants and promoting the achievement of social rights.

All of these elements are necessary in the building of a developmental program for inclusionary societies, for inclusionary societies are well-ordered societies. As such, they must take into account considerations of constitution-making, human rights, and the articulation of class interests.

First, designing a new constitution for inclusionary states is important so that citizens have formal constitutional rights which not only place limits on state action, but also reflect the attitudes and beliefs of citizens as they are given expression through the emerging constitutional culture. Second, a developmental program for inclusionary societies must also articulate answers for the resolution of the human rights dilemma as it exists throughout the Third World. The issue of human rights is a substantive value in the practice of democracy. Democracy is a subset of inclusionary governance. And in nascent democracies which may be crippled by problems of illiteracy, corruption, ethnic or religious cleavages, and winner-take-all political systems, it is important to make sure that the losers in electoral contests maintain the formal recognition of their rights through inclusionary practices, laws, policies and procedures that are constitutionally undisputed. Third and finally, as the realignment of social classes and class perspectives move forward, developmental programs need to expand in order to adequately accomodate new demands.

Part E outlines how democracy operates in theory and in practice. Because the democratic ideal remains remote, it is necessary to investigate what forms it actually takes in practice. The phenomenon of "low-intensity" democracy helps to explain Latin America's enduring political and economic plight. The exclusionary features of low-intensity democracy are outlined so that criteria can be articulated that differentiate between left-wing and right-wing regimes. Similarly, an overview of Africa's experience with democracy allows us to understand the failure of protest-led reform and the limitations of electoral contests in bringing about genuine structural change. Lacking a sufficient heritage of political competition, democracy in Africa continues to be fragile, potentially transitory, and always threatened by reversal.

Part F outlines the relationship between the state, in the praxis of the Third World, and the plight of the extremely poor. The quality of citizenship itself becomes a critical issue for examination. This is especially critical for inclusionary developmental efforts when unsolved structural problems continue to undermine both the efficacy and the legitimacy of regimes that are not fully democratic and persist in promoting exclusionary practices.

Part G outlines the interrelated issues of statism, state autonomy and the dilemmas of development. It is clear that state autonomy is the hallmark of statism. In its most basic form, an autonomous state is an organizational entity that often acts in ways that do not reflect the aspirations of the majority. Yet inclusionary governance demands the inclusion and articulation of the demands and interests of all classes, interests, and groups in the process of policy formation. Too often, in the praxis of Third World states, the conduct of democratic elections allows for a zero-sum game in which the losers are not merely excluded from the government but also from the larger political community. Because this is a fact of life, the fear of permanent exclusion is not unreasonable. The fear of permanent political exclusion must be overcome if economic development is to proceed, and if political and social stability are to be actualized. Why? Because political and social stability are the primary conditions for economic development. In the absence of a broadly shared economic development, the prospects for inclusion diminish and the exclusionary impulse accelerates.

Should the exclusionary impulse become dominant, the prospects for democratic inclusion evaporate and the potential for social and political violence becomes more likely. Under these circumstances, exclusionary government results in shifting coalitions, short-terms policies, elite-led pacts, a fragmented civil society, and weak states. The challenge for inclusionary governance is one of constructing a cohesive civic bond. A cohesive civic bond is the guiding developmental force that accelerates the institutionalization of an inclusionary state by welding the normative aspects of civil society with the procedural practices of the state. It guarantees the state's conformity to established rules and allows for the proper and effective use of state power in the performance of its duties.

Part H offers a prescription that allows Third World states to successfully embark on building the praxis of a more ideal democratic future with political, social, and economic inclusion. Moving toward an equality of citizenship is at the center of inculcating democratic practices, because democratic policies in the state-making process are those that emphasize a broad and inclusive citizenship where all citizens are accorded equal individual rights. The guarantee of this kind of citizenship is intimately related to the state, thereby revealing the enduring importance of the state in the task of development. Whether the course of that development will be inclusionary or not depends on how the state either strengthens or weakens the civic bond.

I conclude by arguing that citizenship and the civic bond are related to each other positively. When one is denied the other is diminished, when one is enhanced, the other benefits. A strategy for inclusionary governance requires the building of a governing strategy of inclusion. It also means moving beyond the unilinear conception of progress. Overcoming the dualities of class-divided societies begins with a redefinition of progress. It must be progress for all citizens, and this means giving greater attention to the inclusionary impulse. Ultimately, the predominance of the inclusionary impulse promises the realization of the democratic ideal because it transcends formal distinctions between democracy and authoritarianism by placing emphasis upon the substantive characteristics of governance, citizenship, and the economy.

B.   THE SOCIALIZATION OF POVERTY AND THE FATE OF DEMOCRACY

The real problem is that democracy, as an ideal, demands that there be a "shared commitment" on the part of all groups, interests, and classes in the civil society to the democratic political process. This shared commitment must also be a commitment of the state. The democratic ideal entails a shared vision of and commitment to the principle of "inclusion." For only when a high degree of political inclusion exists can a civil society emerge which is dedicated to the practices and the principles of inclusionary governance. In both First and Third Worlds, this rarely happens.

The promise of a shared vision eludes classes and groups that remain snared in the political arena of contest over the actual control of the apparatus of the state. Given this scenario, the ensuing exclusionary practices and policies of whatever group lands in the seat of state power virtually guarantees the persistence of poverty, unemployment, and underemployment for the majority. In the praxis of the Third World, as well as the First World, poverty and unemployment remain the persistent nemesis of democracy's promise (Chossudovsky, 1997; Kothari, 1993; Thorp, 1998; Inter-American Development Bank, 1998).

Throughout the developing world, the problems associated with creating a shared vision within the political arena are compounded by the intervention of the IMF-World Bank reform package of structural adjustment. The IMF-World Bank package constitutes "a coherent programme of economic and social collapse" (Chossudovsky, 1997, p. 69). Why? Because the austerity measures that are imposed lead to the disintegration of the state. With the state effectively removed from its own civil society, channels of communication are broken off. The economy itself is remolded as the processes of production destroy the domestic market and redirect the production processes towards the world market. The net effect of this process results in the destrution of the entire fabric of the domestic economy.

The socialization of poverty becomes inevitable. An example of this process can be found in Mexico. The contradictory demands of economic survival and political survival collide. This is because Mexico's leaders have been dealing with established distributional coalitions (like the PRI) with legitimized claims to resources. During the Salinas administration, the Mexican state was forced by the IMF-World Bank interventions to adopt market-oriented reforms which resulted in selling off public assets and ending social welfare entitlements for privileged members of the populist-distributive ISI coalition. The ensuing process of coalition restructuring created an increased tension between economic strategy and political control. Mexico, under Salinas, had embarked upon a hybrid policy mix of neoliberalism and neopopulism. Its continued survival was predicated upon its sustainability to deliver on growth in the economy. Still, growth or no growth, the road was paved to greater exclusion for many individuals and groups who were already marginalized and newly excluded groups who would become the victims of privatization, layoffs, and other consequences of the neoliberal policy package (Dresser, 1994(a), p. 164).

Mexico's democratic system fits squarely within the parameters of presidentialism. Presidential democracy in Mexico proved to be both the key to the success of its neoliberal program and its Achilles' heel. The concentration of power in the hands of the executive may allow for effective discretion in policy making, but it also invites a great deal of arbitrariness and heavy-handedness. In short, presidentialism reinforces personalist politics at the expense of institution-building (*Id.*, p. 164; Mainwaring, 1990). It is the perfect prescription for establishing the ES. This process was replicated throughout Latin America during the neoliberal decade of the 1980s. Its exclusionary trappings remained throughout the 1990s.

The condition of democracy in Mexico is one where Mexican elections still lack credibility, a credibility that defines the dominant party democracies in (for instance) Japan, Italy, and Sweden. As long as Mexico's state elites lack the will and the vision to embark on an inclusionary path and begin to build mediating institutions for the construction of an inclusionary state (IS), Mexico will not only fail to move into the realm of exceptional democracies, but will continue to descend into the discredited category of exceptional authoritarianisms (Dresser, 1994(b), p. 144). Such a descent is already clearly visible in the retructuring of state-labor relations in Mexico.

The social-authoritarian style of development that practiced building state/working-class relationships (corporatism) was always a privileged arena for resolving disputes between labor and capital (Toledo, 1994, p. 196). With the advent of neoliberalism, corporatism and the requirements of the neoliberal package of the IMF appear to be virtually mutually exclusive. The emergence of neoliberal states has resulted in changes in corporatist arrangements and in the industrial relations system as a whole. It has resulted in the following: (1) a decline in the state's commitment to an activist social policy; (2) a decline in the bargaining power of unions; (3) a decline in the frequency of national accords and a rise in the defensiveness of unions; and (4) a growing gap between the state, on the one hand, and the working class, unions, and political parties, on the other (Toledo, p. 200). In short, the rise of the neoliberal agenda has inaugurated the birth of the ES as the governing model for the entire Third World. The replication of the IMF's agenda encompasses Latin America, Africa, and Asia with little or no variation. The consequence is that socialization of poverty is a worldwide phenomenon. It is disguised under the euphemistic title of "globalization."

1. Democratic Crises in First and Third World States

Beginning in the 1980s with the demise of the welfare state in Western Europe and the United States, the growing problem of poverty and unemployment in the midst of affluence has created a global pattern of exclusion that is no longer confined to the periphery of the world political economy. As of 1997 there were more than 18 million officially unemployed in the European Union. Further, 17 percent of the population of the EU live below the poverty line (defined as income less than 50 percent of the average in a person's country of residence). This situation constitutes a social crisis. According to Tony Judt, the social crisis ". . . concerns not so much unemployment as what the French call the 'excluded.' This term describes people who, having left the full-time work force, or never having joined it, are in a certain sense only partly members of the national community" (Judt, 1997, p. 98).

According to Judt, what distinguishes them from even the poorest within the unskilled workforce is not their material poverty, but "the way in which they exist outside the conventional channels of employment or security, and with little prospect of reentering these channels or benefiting from the social liaisons that accompany them" (*Id.*, p. 100). Within the context of supposedly democratic states, then, we find growing numbers of people who are excluded.

It is a social crisis because even social security can be seen as having a disciplinary effect on people in their day-to-day lives. A discourse which legitimates exclusion and labels the excluded as "failures" is the new political reality which has come to dominate the declining welfare states and their peoples. This disciplinary effect is not seen to stem so much from the pressure of external sanctions, such as the withdrawal of the social security benefit or the corresponding hardship, deprivations, and suffering that are attendant to it. Rather, "its disciplinary force emerges through the ways in which these discourses colonize claimants who, by internalizing their meanings, work to constitute themselves as 'docile,' compliant and obedient subjects" (Mizen, 1998, p. 42).

The dominant discourse establishes a norm—the norm of independence and self-reliance. The effect of this dominant norm is to stress the personal short-comings and "failures" of the poor. The disciplinary effect of this dominant norm is observable in those situations where the poor take on the identities of the dependent and begin to internalize its association with failure (*Id.*, p. 43). The relationship between growing poverty in the EU (along with "social exclusion") and the condition of Third World populations, under the tutelage of IMF-World Bank structural adjustment programs (SAPs), points to the global socialization of poverty.

The "Thirdworldization" of the First World is now under way. Its engine has been referred to by Luttwak as "turbo-capitalism" (Luttwak, 1999). Turbo-capitalism is private enterprise liberated from government regulation, unchecked by effective trade unions, unfettered by concerns for employees or investment restrictions, and relatively unhindered by taxation. This new economic path, led by the United States, closely followed by Britain, is spreading throughout the Third World. It is causing even greater societal upheavals and inequities. *It is the birth of the exclusionary state on a global basis*. Under its auspices is manifested increasing inequality: exploding incomes at the top, outright exclusion at the bottom (*Id.*, p. 94). The socialization of poverty is replicated in First and Third World states, thereby reinforcing, preserving and even expanding exclusionary practices, policies, and programs that create limited safety nets instead of embarking upon a fundamental redistribution of wealth and the benefits of development.

This dominant discourse, which legitimates exclusion and fosters a generalized sense of personal failure among the victims of this political, social, and economic exclusion, has the effect of *placing politics and principles beyond the rule of law*. In so doing, the rule of law is replaced by the *role* of law—as something that is designed to control, subordinate, and exclude the claims of the dispossessed and disenfranchised, whose ranks are swelling.

Part of the problem is that politics is taken beyond the rule of law and the role that constitutions are supposed to play in establishing a principled limit on power within a society and between a society and its state. On this point, Fareed Zakaria has noted that "democratically elected regimes, often ones that have been reelected or reaffirmed through referenda, are routinely ignoring constitutional limits on their power and depriving their citizens of basic rights and freedoms" (Zakaria, 1997, p. 22). Hence, elections alone are not enough to ensure democracy or the attendant promises of inclusion, representation and participation. In fact, elections are, more often than not, little more than window-dressing, placed on systems of privilege and prejudice.

C. TOWARD AN ILLIBERAL DEMOCRACY IN EXCLUSIONARY STATES

In the world of 1998, 118 of the world's 193 countries are democratic. Within these democratic nations lives a majority of the world's population (54.8 percent). Yet the practice of democracy in the Third World states remains distant and remote from the ideal of democracy. Zakaria eloquently expresses this fact in noting that "popular leaders like Russia's Boris Yeltsin and Argentina's Carlos Menem bypass their parliaments and rule by presidential decrees, eroding basic constitutional practices. The Iranian parliament—elected more freely than most in the Middle East—imposes harsh restrictions on speech, assembly, and even dress, diminishing that country's already meager supply of liberty. Ethiopia's elected government turns its security forces on journalists and political opponents, doing permanent damage to human rights (as well as human beings)" (*Id.*, p. 23). All of these examples serve to expose the rise of what Zakaria has termed "illiberal democracy."

He juxtaposes illiberal democracy with constitutional liberalism. The distinction is crucial. For illiberal democracy embodies the characteristics and practices of what I referred to in Chapter 1 as "democratic exclusion." Alternatively, constitutional liberalism allows for the evolution of inclusionary governance, by offering protection to discrete and insular minorities and marginalized groups and classes by incorporating them into the decision-making processes of the body politic in, under and through the rule of law. The global retreat from constitutional liberalism serves, in part, to account for the rise of exclusionary states and is testimony to the failure of liberal capitalist revolutions that are divorced from the rule of law, the principles of inclusionary governance, and the democratic ideal.

1. The Failure of Liberal Capitalist Revolutions and the Rise of Illiberal Democracy

Liberalism is best exemplified as either a conception of political liberty or a doctrine about economic policy. It coincides with the rise of democracy in the West. Constitutionalism, on the other hand, stands for the rule of law, a separation of powers, and the protection of basic rights ranging from liberties of speech and assembly to religion and property. In the world of the late 1990s, given the rise of illiberal democracy and the erosion and decline of constitutional liberalism, the failure of democracy to become more inclusionary often makes the actual practice of "democracy," as it is embodied in illiberal regimes, as inimical to inclusionary governance as some of the worst dictatorships (Bell, et al., 1995).

Economic growth is hardly an antidote to violence in and of itself. For the kind of political regime which is in place, whether it be a democracy or an authoritarian dictatorship, will have to demand sacrifices from some social classes and groups. The question of social sacrifices and costs is one that transcends the raw exercise of political power itself. It is a question that also involves the calculus of poverty and its effects on future generations. For, as Marazvall reminds us: "we all know that dictatorships often have the power to sacrifice entire generations in the name of a future paradise, whether under communism or the market. However, dictatorships do not have mechanisms to guarantee that these sacrifices will not simply lead to even more sacrifices" (Maravall, 1997, p. 73).

The continuation of political violence, as well as the persistence of deadly conflict throughout the world, seems to lead to the conclusion that even with an improvement in developmental prospects, regime choice alone is not a cure-all for the political, economic, and social crises that affect Third World and post-communist nations. Why? It is usually assumed that regime choice was primarily responsible for determining the direction that capital accumulation would take in the course of development. Yet, when we examine the nature of polyarchy in the Third World, as well as the First World, we find that "polyarchy is not the causal factor for the accumulation of wealth. Polyarchy emerged as a political requisite for the emergent capitalist system in Europe, and it was the emergence of capitalism in Europe that provides causal explanation for the current unequal distribution of wealth among the center and periphery in the world system" (Robinson, 1996, p. 362). Because capitalism develops unevenly, the "core" countries of the world system constitute the dynamic centers where accumulation is concentrated.

Contrast this concentration of wealth with the fact that among 4.4 billion people in the developing countries around the globe, about three-fifths live in communities lacking basic sanitation; about one-third go without safe drinking water; about one-quarter lack decent housing; about one-fifth are undernourished; and about 1.3 billion live on less than $1 a day. These are some of the statistical distinctions that separate North from South. Yet it is vital to recognize that these figures would probably not reflect such disparities were it not for the practice of capital accumulation and the logic, doctrines, and dogmas that justify its expanse around the globe, while ignoring the social and human costs of its continuing march.

Recognizing these disparities, it becomes possible to understand that *the process of capitalist development is the causal variable in the relation between capitalism and polyarchy*. In this situation, local class and social struggles emerge as protests against the processes of the international political economy. Given the nature of the process and the struggles it engenders, the persistent efforts to incarnate democracy in the Third World context are less than adequate to effectively deal with the persistence of poverty or with the process of building an end-state harmonious consensus. Both democracy and human rights, in their ideal form, represent constructs. As Habermas notes: "The concept of human rights does not have its origins in morality, but rather bears the imprint of the modern concept of individual liberties, hence of a specifically juridical concept. Human rights are juridical *by their very nature*. What lends them the appearance of moral rights is not their content, and most especially not their structure, but rather their mode of validity, which points beyond the legal order of nation-states" (Habermas, 1998, p. 190). Capitalism and polyarchy co-exist because they are anchored in legal orders which promote, preserve and protect exclusion. Thus, the ES is a product of the very nature of nation-states that exercise the legal mandates of legal orders that sanction privilege, hierarchy and discrimination (formal and informal). It is no wonder that inclusionary claims meet with resistance and disaster in these settings.

2. Capitalism, Polyarchy, and the Dynamics of Structural Change

Part of the reason for the non-realization of the democratic ideal resides in the recognition that democracy refers "not to an end-state harmonious consensus, but rather to a commitment endlessly to explore disagreements by political means" (Brown, 1995, p. 161). Additionally, many Third World nations have created social structures that are incapable of nurturing the kind of political trust and cooperation that the practice of democracy, in its ideal form, demands and requires for its sustenance and substance. In place of the *ideal of democracy* is the *mask of democracy*.

Behind the mask of democracy lies the reality of exclusionary governance, in all of its forms. Various forms of exclusionary governance find a common denominator in the historical resistance of elites to both innovation and structural change. For, as noted with regard to Habermas's discussion of human rights, the validity of human rights (as well as the ideal of "equality" in democracy) posits a moral claim that transcends the legal order of nation-states. In this regard, Richard Falk is correct in asserting that "democratization is not itself an assurance of decency or moderation, but can be both abusive and abused. The quality of a given democracy depends on the direction and orientation of civic life" (Falk, 1995, p. 111). Elsewhere, Falk has elaborated on this idea by noting that "capitalist Third World countries display a far lower capacity than do their socialist counterparts to provide jobs for their population" (Falk, 1981, p. 136).

Why do the Third World's capitalist experiments fail to approximate the democratic ideal of socioeconomic inclusion and exhibit such a lowered capacity to assist the poor, the marginalized, the dispossessed? And, associated with this question, why do the Third World's capitalist experiments usually create exclusionary states and oppose efforts to build inclusionary states? There are three major reasons.

The first is that is that there is *historical resistance to innovation and structural change*. Such resistance is usually associated with "relatively closed social structures, distrust of individualism and competition, and elite reliance on political privilege and ownership of resources rather than leadership toward economic change" (Sheahan and Iglesias, 1998, p. 51). Closed social structures are exclusionary structures. In the praxis of the Third World, closed

Between Poverty and Polyarchy 365

social structures set the state against the ideals of democracy.

Second, *the Third World's capitalist experiments are inherently exclusionary*. What the process of capitalist expansion and modernization has done is to create what Kothari describes as "the paradox of transformation" (Kothari, 1989, p. 55). Third World states have been overtaken by the combination of the dominant Western ideology of capitalism as expressed through technological innovation and a model of militarization that is essentially technological. The dominion of technology has had a pervasive impact on these states. Its ramifications include a massive erosion of the ecological basis of many Third World cultures, destroying the resource base of millions of rural, tribal and ethnic poor. The combination of these forces impinges on traditional societies by forcing them to fall in line and accept, unconditionally, the dominant mode and ideology of forced modernization. Neoliberalism is only the most recent economic variant on this particular theme. The effect it has had on Third World states and their respective governments is tragic, for it precludes the political inclusion of the poor and creates either an authoritarian state or polyarchy (masquerading as democracy). As for the fate of the people themselves, Kothari acknowledges that "as the state in effect withdraws from its responsibility and surrenders its autonomy, civil society in these lands is thrown to its own resources" (*Id.*, p. 57).

The withdrawal of the state as the "Hobbesian protector" of the people (see Chapter 5) leaves Third World societies vulnerable to two powerful impacts. First, the impact of modernization becomes "immanent in the aggressive thrust of ruthless technologism," which is advanced by capitalism. Second, social and ethnic conflicts are mitigated by formal electoral competition as long as it remains controlled by an alliance of elites elements. However, with rising expectations and participation of the masses, landed and industrial elites have often relied on their allies, in the apparatus of the state, to accomplish the twin goals of exclusionary politics: engage in the massive repression of the poor, on the one hand, and advance the promulgation of a depoliticized technocratic state, impervious to the social and political aspirations of the masses on the other (*Id.*, p. 57).

Elite reliance on political privilege has imbued many states with qualities that are exclusionary. In exclusionary states, decisions are made by a narrow clique of elites and their allies. Highly inclusive states and institutions, on the other hand, provide groups with mutual vetoes or require supramajorities for policy decisions which have a significant impact on group rights. In other words, the presence of highly inclusive institutions allows structurally disadvantaged groups input into national decision making (Kahl, 1998, p. 90).

Third, and finally, in order *to overcome and replace exclusionary forms of governance, social democracy must be combined with a strategy for inclusionary growth if genuine democratization is to have a chance of success*. According to Carlos Vilas, "to advance democratization, political democracy must be constructed as social democracy, in its broadest and most powerful sense. A democratization process so conceived must rest on a development strategy" (Vilas, 1995, p. 186). The fact that the union of a democratization process with an inclusionary development strategy is rarely achieved helps to explain the growth and expansion of illiberal democracy and the preservation of the ES throughout the praxis of most of the Third World.

In the absence of this union (a democratization process with an inclusionary development strategy), many Third World states, as in the case of Peru, have found that the state is experiencing increasing difficulty in monitoring and enforcing compliance with the law. This is largely because "any economic strategy that depends excessively on sophisticated monitoring methods and on government officials' discretion will most likely fail" (Cacere and Paredes, 1991, p. 104). It is a recurrent theme in nations that the most severe increases in poverty are caused by the prolonged economic crises that necessitate adjustment to neoliberal prescriptions—that is, "extensive macroeconomic distortions, such as inflation, causing fiscal deficits and regressively distributed subsidization of consumer goods and social services, which tend to hurt the poor more than other social groups" (Graham, 1994, p. 4).

In the absence of a broad social democracy combined with an inclusionary development strategy, Third World states are left in a precarious position. It is precarious for it has to be premised on the continued marginalization of the poor, the repression of labor and other popular movements, coupled with a polyarchy which works largely to effectuate accommodations with international finance capital at the expense of the nation's long-term welfare, broadly conceived.

The surrender of the possibility of embarking upon equitable development and distribution reinforces the tendency to try a fall back position—reliance on safety nets. However, "safety nets should not be confused with what the market or the state is expected to deliver; namely, economic growth and production in the first case and basic social services in the second" (Graham, 1994, p. 5). The failure of exclusionary states to deliver on economc growth and basic social services relegates the state to protecting the vested interests of private wealth, while sacrificing the possibility of realizing a social democratic commonwealth with inclusionary policies and channels for participation (see Chapters 4 and 5). By relying on safety nets, exclusionary governments have discovered, to their dismay, that safety nets cannot substitute for coherent macroeconomic management or the effective provision of basic services. Therefore, the challenge presented to governments is how to take responsibility for social well-being.

3. Restoring the Responsibility of the State Toward the Poor

According to the Carnegie Commission's Final Report, *Preventing Deadly Violence*, "there is perhaps no more fundamental right than the ability to have a say in how one is governed" (Carnegie Commission, 1998, p. 94). The hallmark of a healthy political system, in other words, reflects a "shared contract between the people and their government that, at its most basic, ensures the ability to survive free from fear or want" (*Id.*, p. 94). Such a shared contract has never become fully inclusionary under either communism or liberal capitalist revolutions.

Over the past 200 years there have been two great waves of liberal cap-

Between Poverty and Polyarchy 367

italist revolutions. The first such wave was in the 19th century. It was responsible for the sundering of the old ruling trinity of monarchy, church and nobility. While co-opting elements of all three parts of the old ruling trinity, it was able to dismantle, destroy or undermine the social and economic forms and cultural traditions of the both the peasantry and the urban artisans. The second wave of liberal capitalist revolutions has taken place since the 1970s when the modernizing processes of the modern era swept China in 1979 and the former Soviet bloc since 1989, as the dynamics of international capital and power politics culminated in active or passive revolutions against Communism.

In the case of China, the modernizing revolution of liberal capitalism was largely a state-led process while, in the case of the former Soviet bloc, it was a combination of elite-led changes with upsurges from below. Elsewhere, in Italy and Spain, as well as most of Latin America, the effect of liberal economics for the past 150 years has been to produce only weak, unstable, and unbalanced growth combined with some measure of social and political progress (Lieven, 1998, p. 150). The main lesson to be gleaned from this review of liberal capitalist revolutions (as well as the rise of illiberal democracy) is that these revolutions have generally produced more exclusionary states. Further, the various forms that exclusionary governance have taken have resulted in a combination of deadly conflict, violence, and instability with developmental failures. The most recent variant of this developmental failure is to be found in what Richard Falk has termed "the neoliberal cruel state" (Falk, 1999, p. 31).

What is required is a new approach to growth. A new set of priorities must address the population's physical needs as well as its social and cultural aspirations. Pursuant to these new priorities, the truest and broadest measure of development would be the achievement of minimal well-being in terms of nutrition, health, clothing, housing, and access to education, information and other basic services. In assessing the value and effectiveness of these endeavors, increases in GNP or per capita income, while still useful indicators, could no longer be accepted as comprehensive measures of development. This is because they remain limited by the fact that they reflect the indiscriminate accumulation of goods and services. Who benefits and who does not? We still do not know by this standard. Further, the GNP and per capita income tell us precious little about the composition of national product and nothing about its distribution. The issue of distribution is central for it goes to the larger issues of equity, social justice, inclusion, and meeting the needs of the poor and marginalized.

D. INCLUSIONARY STATES MEASURE DEVELOPMENTAL SUCCESS

The main point of this chapter is to highlight and underscore the argument that *if groups, classes, and interests are excluded, no amount of developmental success can rescue them from social and political instability and the danger of ever-increasing levels of violence and deadly conflict.* Hence, the exercise of state power, in the service of inclusionary practices, policies and procedures, is the important issue to be addressed, not the number of so-called "democratic procedures" that are used to give the cosmetic impression of political representation.

Those regimes which lack deep legitimacy depend precariously on current performance and are vulnerable to collapse in periods of economic and social distress. This constitutes a particular problem for democratic as well as undemocratic regimes in the developing world. A number of factors account for this finding, including the tendency of many Third World countries to experience an interaction of low legitimacy and low effectiveness (Diamond, Linz and Lipset, 1995, p. 10).

The combination of widespread poverty, when coupled with the strains imposed by modernization, creates a situation where regimes that begin with low levels of legitimacy consequently find it difficult if not impossible to perform effectively. Further, regimes that are lacking in effectiveness, especially in the area of economic growth, find it difficult to build legitimacy (Clague, 1997; North, 1990; Arbetman and Kugler, 1997).

Generally speaking, the experience of Third World regimes with democracy has been hampered by the prevalence of political corruption as the primary motive for the pursuit of political power because of the dominance of the state over economic life. This praxiological reality reduces the political process to one of constant struggle for power rather than a debate about policies. As the focus moves toward the attainment of power, long-term developmental policies and a debate upon the national interest are foreclosed upon. This, in turn, taints the electoral process while, at the same time, generating apathy and cynicism in the electorate at large. This is especially the case for those groups outside of the scope of the patronage networks (Diamond, Linz, Lipset, 1995, p. 11).

Sheahan and Iglesias maintain that perhaps the clearest changes, in the praxis of Latin America, have been movement "away from narrowly based political control to democracies that, with all their remaining weaknesses, have opened up a wider range of political voice; from societies in which majorities or near-majorities were illiterate and unaware of the ways in which social choices damage their interests to conditions of much greater literacy, organization and awareness; and from highly protected economic systems that did not force business to seek dynamic change to more open systems in which such effort comes closer to being necessary for survival" (Sheahan and Iglesias, 1998, pp. 51–52).

In the context of Mexico, a number of proposals can be offered for immediate action. In response to the social and economic dislocations inaugurated by modernization, there are new needs to be addressed. This is especially necessary with respect to the ramifications of the IMF's structural adjustment programs (SAPs). According to Carlos Tello, "the struggle against poverty cannot be viewed as a mere appendage to Mexico's development strategy. Rather, it must be made the axis on which the country's social and economic modernization turns" (Tello, 1991, p. 65). Success in this undertaking can be achieved only if the government's program for social well-being and inclusion incorporates the characteristics outlined in Table 7.1.

The implications of this program have the potential to dramatically alter the praxis of democracy in the Third World for the poor and excluded. Additionally, as a strategy for development, the program has the capacity to articulate new avenues and channels for the prevention and mediation of conflict, create new forums for policy and decision making within government, and mandate a dramatic shift in socioeconomic priorities and the macroeconomic oversight responsibilities of the state. In all of these endeavors, a framework of inclusion and for inclusion can and must take place.

In the final analysis, inclusionary societies are well-ordered societies. And well-ordered societies have the capacity to produce liberty for wider segments of their populations. It follows, then, if the praxis of democracy in the Third World is to emerge from its current status of being caught between the grinding effects of poverty and the elite-driven politics of polyarchy, the social democratic and inclusionary developmental strategy, as outlined here, should be the preferred starting point for reference, for guidance, and for initiative.

1. Inclusionary Societies Are Well-Ordered Societies

Principles are important for inclusionary governance because, in Rawlsian terms, the idea of a well-ordered society is predicated upon three central elements. First, there is a publicly recognized conception of justice in which everyone else accepts the same principles of justice. Second, the acceptance of these principles implies the idea of the effective regulation of such a conception through the structures of the society, such as its main political and social institutions and how they fit together as one unified system of cooperation. Third, and finally, compliance with the society's basic institutions is achieved by virtue of the perception that the institutions are just and that a publicly recognized conception of justice serves to establish a shared point of view, a consensus so to speak, from which citizens' claims on society can be adjudicated (Rawls, 1993, p. 35).

Rawl's emphasis upon the concepts of acceptance, regulation, and compliance, as applied to the democratic ideal, serve to help explain why the practice of democracy in the praxis of Third World has failed to establish the democratic ideal. The Rawlsian emphasis upon the need to establish a well-ordered society through a "publicly recognized conception of justice" resonates with the definition of consolidated regimes as the embodiment of a consensus, at both the elite and mass levels, on the rules of the democratic system. The point that needs to be stressed here is that "central to maintaining democracy is that it be in the interests of elected officials to abide by the limits on the state" (Weingast, 1997, p. 35). Insofar as these limits are usually transgressed in many Third World nations, we find the praxis of democracy is truncated from its ideal and the practice of politics dissolves into a struggle for power that leads to rising levels of SPI and a growing contempt for the vestiges of democratic practice.

To unite the ideal of democracy with its practice will require three complementary trends: (1) the advancement of formal constitutional rights and

> **TABLE 7.1 A Comprehensive Program for Social Well-Being**
>
> 1. It must be *comprehensive*; that is, it must view poverty in its totality and confront it simultaneously across all areas where basic needs exist: nutrition, health care, education, and housing. If a comprehensive strategy is not implemented, progress in one area—in health care, for example—may be offset by setbacks in another area, such as nutrition.
>
> 2. It must *encourage productive activities* which, along with federal social programs, will guarantee enduring improvements in the lives of the nation's poor and remove the legal obstacles which now impede the poor's efforts to improve their economic situation.
>
> 3. The program must be *national in scope*, able to satify the basic needs of all Mexicans.
>
> 4. The federal program must be *participatory*, such that all affected parties have a voice in decision making and in the implementation and evaluation of all measures taken.
>
> 5. It must be *decentralized*. Decentralization is essential both in defining the means by which to achieve program objectives and in distributing resources and administrative authority.
>
> 6. It must be *unified*. Solidarity among all participants will assure that social rights are achieved. If programs fall victims to the types of group interests which characterize many ongoing efforts to meet basic needs in Mexico, the initiative against poverty may fail.
>
> SOURCE: Carlos Tello, "Combating Poverty in Mexico," *Social Responses to Mexico's Economic Crisis of the 1980s*, edited by Mercedes Gonzalez de la Rocha and Agustin Escobar Latapi. Center for US/Mexican Studies, University of California, San Diego, 1991, p. 64.

the design of inclusionary constitutions for inclusionary states; (2) tentative answers for the resolution of the human rights dilemma on a national and global scale; and (3) the development of political channels that accomodate new demands from the realignment of social classes and their differing (often conflicting) perspectives. I shall discuss each of these elements in turn.

Designing a New Constitution for Inclusionary States

Insofar as democratic consolidation is essentially a process of "crafting,"—an exercise of conscious leadership and strategy—it is, like the task of state-building itself, a work of art. One of the first elements, which also constitutes a requirement for a well-ordered system and the promise of the democratic ideal, is the design of a new constitution and electoral system. This is vital, for a constitution sets the parameters, structures, and incentives for democratic practice (Diamond, Linz and Lipset, 1995, p. 54).

As far as designing a constitution for inclusionary states is concerned, the key problems are: (1) defining what the limits of state power and action should be, and (2) building a consensus among citizens about where those limits should be set. As already mentioned, a failure to accomplish these two tasks results in a "coordination problem." In the context of development, in the praxis of the Third World, the challenge of designing a new constitution is even more complex. For in post-colonial states there are inherited vestiges of power and privilege bound up with the laws and constitutional structure of colonialism itself. Institutional mechanisms were put in place that allowed for the constant creation and re-creation of patterns of domination and authority which were inherently un-democratic, even anti-democratic. Therefore, to simply remove the practice of formal colonialism and declare that formal independence now makes possible the realization of an institutionalized and fully consolidated democracy is nonsense.

To begin with, the crisis of the post-colonial state was the product of two forces: first, the betrayal of the revolution by the neo-colonial ruling class, and second, the failure of revolutionary movements to transform the economy and the state. How do we formulate a design for a constitution that is capable of building an IS, instead of merely duplicating the practices of the old colonial state by preserving exclusionary norms, practices and procedures? It has been suggested that "an adequate development theory . . . must focus on the way the legal order shaped institutions that fostered the emergence of new domestic economic ruling classes. Understanding that they must take the power of foreign capital as a condition, Third World country law-makers must investigate the way existing state institutions, propped up by the inherited legal order, facilitated the emergence of a bureaucratic bourgeoisie, and, all too soon, permitted the forces of national and world capitalism to strangle national-popular struggles for social change" (Seidman and Seidman, 1994, p. 111). I have already discussed this historical process earlier in this chapter with reference to the interplay between international capital accumulation processes and the practice of polyarchy throughout the Third World. It is an issue that returns to our discussion of constitutional designs for inclusionary states because an IS must effectively constrain the influence of foreign capital if it is to regain control over the integrity of its own economy. It also has implications for the degree to which the political apparatus of the state is associated with the ideals of democracy or falls into the liberal capitalist trap of subordinating popular movements and invoking exclusionary practices and policies upon its own citizens.

We must look at constitutinal designs for the IS from both an economic perspective and a political perspective. Once having outlined the dimensions of these two realms, we are better equipped to identify the areas where they overlap and either produce inclusionary or exclusionary results. We shall discuss each in turn.

First, it may be argued that politically open societies, subscribing to the rule of law, private property, and the allocation of resources through the market, grow at three times the rate—and are two and one-half times as efficient economically—in transforming inputs into national output as societies in which these rights are largely proscribed (Scully, 1992, p. 12). What this finding suggests is that exclusionary practices, although politically enforced and legally protected, are counter-productive to economic efficiency, growth, and development. Gerald Scully has argued that the material advancement of states is affected as much by the choice of economic, legal, and political institutions under which people live and work as by the resource endowments of states and their degree of technological progress. In this respect, he concludes that "each 'constitution' has an inherent level of economic efficiency. Efficiency is at its lowest in a society without freedom" (*Id.*, p. 185). This economic conclusion, however, begs the political question: What is freedom and how does a constitution either advance human freedom or inhibit it?

Second, it may be argued that legal authority is itself a form of claimed moral authority. Joseph Raz has observed that "the point is sometimes lost to sight, for legal structures transmit the authority to make law from one body to another" (Raz, 1998, p. 159). Certainly, law is a structure of authority, but there are moral reasons that can be used to justify a claim to legal authority. Because of the infrequency of such appeals to moral reasons, "this gives discourse about legal authority an appearance of being autonomous, technical legal discourse," but the fact remains that "none of this denies the fact that the law claims to be morally binding" (*Id.*, p. 159). The consequences that follow from this line of reasoning are that it is morally legitimate. This view falls apart, however, when we introduce the fact that many Latin American regimes have been regimes of "exception"—that is, they suspend the rule of law if the elites of the state declare a national emergency and invoke "martial law." Further, this view falls apart when land reform, whether in India or Latin America, is opposed for reasons of state, or merely to protect the power and position of the landed oligarchy. These are examples of exclusion that produce exclusionary results. These results have both political and economic overlap.

When viewed in combination, it is possible to argue that a unified approach to a well-ordered society that reflects the democratic ideal necessitates the balancing of the establishment of limited government with the ideals of democracy and with the rule of law. The logic of this approach is twofold. First, the views, attitudes, and beliefs of citizens about what constitutes the appropriate limits of the state are critical for comprehending the ability to maintain these limits. Second, the maintenance of boundaries on the state creates a massive social coordination problem. Because of the diversity of views, experience, and interests, individuals are unlikely to shape a consensus about the rights of citizens and the proper role of the state. Thus, the result is what some have called "coordination failure," a situation wherein "citizens are unlikely to achieve coordination without some form of organization, leadership, or other method of constructing a focal solution to their problem" (Weingast, 1997, pp. 38–39).

The "coordination problem" has two implications for maintenance of limits on the state. The first is that once citizens agree about the appropriate limits to be placed on the state, there is the possibility of the withdrawal of citizen support. Yet, the benefit of this threat is that political actors are forced to abide by those limits, thereby strengthening a consolidated democracy. The second implication is that the construction of a "coordination device" is necessary, such as a constitution, that specifies the unambiguous limits on state power (Weingast, 1997, p. 39). If these two aspects of the "coordination problem" are not addressed, it is easy to see how the praxis of democracy in Third World states degenerates into exclusionary practices, the mere struggle for power among elites, the search for unstable coalitions in the absence of consensus, and rising levels of political instability and social conflict. Recognizing these results is to recognize the costs and consequences of maintaining the ES and what is implies for democracy and inclusion in the praxis of Third World states.

Specifically, there is a need for courts and the force of an independent judiciary, constitutionally protected and mandated, if economic and social progress is to become a reality for many millions of people throughout the Third World. One of the essential tasks of development, in general, is to come to terms with this basic recognition. Legal history, from Alexander Bickel to Edmund Burke, has recognized the need for courts to affirm certain principles. Some judicial activism is needed because it leads to social and institutional change. Insofar as I am arguing for a constitutional design that is capable of producing the IS, it logically follows that courts have a role to play in determining macroeconomic policy and political stability. The courts must be independent from the pressures of concentrated wealth which, more often than not, seek to preserve privilege, perpetuate exclusion, and limit democratic rights and their exercise. What this implies is that "in order for laws and institutions to have the desired economic consequences, there must be a third party, the government, that is impartial, immune from violent or pecuniary pressures, and capable of enforcing the law and ensuring it meets with compliance" (Jarquin and Carrillo, 1998, p. 51). Unfortunately, such a government is not to be found anywhere in Latin America.

The ES in Latin America has created a situation where laws often cannot be enforced because the army does not allow it. In other countries, the lives and the property of citizens cannot be adequately protected because the government has ceded large territories to guerilla forces that impose their own rules. Other countries suffer from the tyranny of bureaucratic and political elites who place themselves above the law—they rule by law, instead of invoking the rule of law. This distinction is critical. For when rule by law creates a capitalist hegemony over people, the political result is that dominant classes forge an exclusionary socioeconomic project which eviscerates democratic activity, democratic inclusion, and democratic institution-building. In the alternative, the rule of law means more than the formal institution of democratic practices. It also means the constitutionally guaranteed provision of inclusionary practices that give substance and meaning to the democratic project, in all of its varied dimensions. This process is what creates a well-ordered society that can sustain the practice of inclusionary goverance and the legitimacy of the IS as the protector of these practices, policies and norms.

The stable democracy, or for that matter the well-ordered society, requires the maintenance and consolidation of democracy through more than just a reliance on the formal institutions of democracy such as elections and legislatures. Stability also requires a set of citizen attitudes, throughout the civil society and the market, which shows that citizens value not only the outcomes of democratic decision making but also the institutions of democracy (Weingast, 1997, p. 41). In this regard, citizens need to be willing to defend the institutions against all persons and threats to the integrity of those institutions. This is what returns us to the emphasis upon the need to establish the rule of law. The rule of law compliments the civil society, for the rule of law is an actual component of the civil society. It is an important component for it allows for freedom of association without the need for the state to intervene or use its powers to sanction (*Id.*, p. 43).

In many ways, one could conclude that the "attitudes and reactions of citizens make institutional restriction self-enforcing on political actors" (*Id.*, p. 44). This is a central aspect to the achievement of the democratic ideal in practice. Therefore, it follows that where such attitudes and reactions are absent among the citizens of Third World nations, the practice of democracy allows political actors to seek their own limited advantages at the expense of the national interest and the expense of a majority of citizens. Such a situation is a prescription for marginalization and exclusion. It is also a prescription for rising levels of political instability and social conflict.

Closely associated with the Rawlsian analysis of a well-ordered society and its democratic outlines is the related issue of "rights." In the new age of globalization there is an increasing convergence of values which is promising for the values of democracy. This is true to a lesser extent with respect to the realization of human rights. Yet as far as the tasks of the IS are concerned, the promise and the protection of human rights remains a vital issue and an ever-present task for governing and evaluating the quality of governance.

Resolving the Human Rights Dilemma

It may be argued that democracy has been easier to achieve than the protection of human rights. One explanation that may be offered for this result is that the implementation of democracy is technically more easily accomplished, as in the case of bringing a popularly elected government into existence. At the same time, there might be tremendous disagreement over which rights are basic rights and how these basic rights are to be protected. For example, some Asian nations disagree with the West on the need for comprehensive human rights protections (Graybrow, 1996, pp. 68–70). This example serves to highlight the difference between Westernization, on the one hand, and modernization, on the other.

In the praxis of Third World nations, values such as human rights may not be as readily transferable as democratic practices and procedures. Hence, what the West may consider the substance of democracy, such as certain values and principles, may not be the substance of democracy as practiced in Third World nations. Yet, this assertion is subject to debate. As Amartya Sen has noted: "Even the language used in recommending to Asia what is called 'Western democracy' imposes a geographical mode of divisiveness that springs not only from Asian intransigence but also from a Western 'priority complex'" (Sen, 1999, p. 98). Any genuine attempt to resolve what I am calling "the human rights dilemma" must confront the perceived cultural divides that inhibit constructive and meaningful dialogue and action on human rights.

To begin with, the geographical mode of divisiveness may be illusory. That is becase the much touted "Asian concept of human rights" masks not only important differences among Asians, but also ignores important commonalities between Asian and Western countries. In other words, the areas of agreement and commonality may be greater than the areas of difference and distinction. It may be merely a issue of emphasis. The human rights dilemma begins to become increasingly complicated by the way in which economic variables are juxtaposed with the criteria of human rights. For example, the conventional economic analysis emphasizes a cost-benefit-analysis. This type of evaluation is strictly *instrumental* in nature. Alternatively, human rights raises claims that have *intrinsic value*, making human rights valued for their own sake, and not merely as a means to some other end. This is a Kantian distinction, but it remains an important one with respect to this issue. For it exposes the moral bankruptcy of economic policies that attempt to divorce normative discourse from policy making which impact on the non-economic aspects of human lives and cultures.

The distinction between an instrumental criteria versus the criteria of intrinsic value needs to be recognized if the ideal of democracy is to have any relevance. For the normative claims of democracy and inclusion are not separate and distinct from human rights. Rather, democracy and inclusion are the living embodiments, practices, and procedures which emanate from the practice of human rights as normative claims upon the economy and the body politic. When viewed in this light, *the case for human rights is inclusionary because it incorporates the dimensions of political and civil rights.* There are three elements which may be enlisted to support this claim. First, human rights have intrinsic importance. Second, human rights play a consequential role in providing political incentives for economic security. Third, human rights play a constructive role in the genesis of both values and priorities (Sen, 1999, p. 99).

In terms of how this perspective may be better appreciated in the context of development and the demands of development, we are returned to the old contention that the systematic infringement of internationally recognized human rights is necessary in order to achieve rapid economic development. Is this contention an accurate one? Probably not. Further study of this contention reveals that no obvious relationship exists among economic growth, the level of economic development, and the overall protection of human rights (S. Jones, 1998, p. 125).

There are two rights/development trade-offs that are frequently invoked. One is the liberty trade-off, the other is the equity trade-off (Donnelly, 1999, p. 72). We are obliged to examine the dimensions of the liberty trade-off and the equity trade-off. Following the logic of either trade-off leads to the preservation of the ES. It also explains the praxis of democracy in the Third World, trapped between poverty and polyarchy.

The liberty trade-off is based on a perception that political rights introduce too many inefficiencies into the way in which governments proceed with respect to developmental decision-making. In other words, rapid economic development requires the non-recognition of some human rights (such as the right to organize unions) or, if unions exist, requires that laws be put in place that disallow labor strikes because the exercise of the right to strike will impede economic development. Part of what this argument overlooks is that it impedes any kind of democratic development within the political culture of the nation. Further, the argument is an apologetic argument for the ES and the practices of exclusion which subordinate classes, individuals and norms that do not easily fit within the preexisting framework of economic privilege and exploitation.

The other rights/development trade-off is the equity trade-off. Its purpose is to legitimate economic and social sacrifices, not civil and political rights. The argument is that the "immediate satisfaction of basic needs for all or the achievement of a relatively egalitarian income distribution excessively retards the progress of development" (*Id.*, p. 72). Again, this produces an argument for the preservation of the ES because it relegates the meeting of basic human needs to an undisclosed future time. If meeting basic human needs is postponed, ostensibly because efforts to realize them in the present will retard development, what kind of development are we really talking about? Is it not merely the "development of underdevelopment" for the majority who suffer under exclusionary states?

I argue that, whether democratic or authoritarian in name, these states are exclusionary states because they actively block the promotion of inclusionary growth and development by maintaining ineqitable distributional patterns and coalitions. Again, this is not merely a denial of human rights in the name of development, it is also an attempt to foreclose upon the building of a culture of peace and an inclusionary democracy. The logic of this argument and the interests behind it are not difficult to delineate. As Kothari has observed, "the State in the Third World, despite some valiant efforts by dedicated leaders in a few countries, has degenerated into a technocratic machine serving a narrow power group that is kept in power by hordes of security men at the top and a regime of repression and terror at the bottom, kept going by millions of hard-working people who must go on producing goods and services for the 'system' for if they did not, everything would collapse" (Kothari, 1989(a), p. 60).

In the aftermath of the "Asian flu" of 1998–1999, the fear of an end to the continuing production-consumption cycle is what influenced the IMF and World Bank to impose austerity measures on any Asian governments seeking relief. The pattern of power that the IMF sought to maintain would still have to be premised on compliant states willing to indulge in even more drastic exclusionary policies. Therefore, the ES is the central governing instrument, at the nation-state level, that works to effectuate exclusionary social and economic policies for the sake of continuing profit maximization while, at the same time, actively imposing exclusionary policies in the political, social, and cultural realms of life. Hence, the human rights dilemma is actually caught between poverty and polyarchy. The human rights dilemma will remain a global dilemma as long as these exclusionary policies, states, and lending institutions persist on their historical course of maintaining the ES.

This disparity between the promise of democracy in form and in substance has created ideological and practical cleavages between Western conceptions and Third World practices. This insight helps to explain why the practice of democracy in the Third World is often so far removed from the democratic ideal. It also helps to explain why in both First and Third World contexts the ideal of democracy is often far from realized in either of them. In fact, the liberty trade-off has been a mainstay of developmental dictatorships of all stripes. The equity trade-off remains a staple of many capitalist development strategies. It represents the orthodoxy of the IMF and associated Western financial institutions (Donnelly, 1999, pp. 72–73).

The major problem with the IMF orthodoxy is that the empirical basis for the trade-off arguments is weak. The equity trade-off arguments are also problematic and inconclusive in the Asian context. For example, Japan, Taiwan, and South Korea have achieved rapid economic growth with considerable equity. Actually, under the auspices of states acting more like an IS we find that aggressive state efforts to support equitable terms of trade and to develop human capital have brought economic growth and development without creating the ugly by-product of unequal income distribution. This was accomplished as basic human needs were met, not ignored. In this regard, it is possible to have a "rights-protective government" or IS that can meet basic human needs and promote economic growth and development at the same time.

This leads us back to the question of the costs of an ES. *What are the costs that stem from a denial of civil and political rights?* If a democracy that respects or promotes human rights is either too weak to be effective, or absent, officials who need not justify the effects of their policies to the electorate usually become corrupt and uncaring. The cleptocracy of the Philippines under Marcos, as well as the special-interest states of Indonesia and Mexico, for the better half of the 20th century, provide clear and convincing evidence of what the answer will probably be. If the costs that stem from a denial of civil and political rights are so high, then what constitutes a viable answer to the human rights dilemma? According to Kothari, "the movement for 'human rights' has to be conceived in the broadest possible sense and taken out of the politics of detente and other Machiavellian uses to which it has so often been put . . . Above all, the struggle of the poor and the unorganized millions around the world for economic survival, for the right to work, and for security and job tenure must be included in the movement for human rights if it is to have any meaning as a whole" (Kothari, 1989(b), p. 141). If the movement towards human rights fails, the status quo will be preserved, deepened, and widened, for "there is a growing integration in the world economy of the First, the Second and the Third Worlds: as the whole development process is transnationalized, petro-dollars are recycled" (Kothari, 1989(a), p. 66).

Returning to the issue of human rights as a substantive value in the practice of democracy, we can readily observe how elected governments need not necessarily protect human rights. This is especially the case in nascent democracies which may be crippled by problems of illiteracy, corruption, authoritarian traditions, ethnic or religious cleavages and conflicts, and winner-take-all political systems. In the case of African democracies, their fragility may be traced to the fact that voter allegiance to tribe, language, and region is stronger than to policy throughout Africa because many of these countries were the artificial creation of European powers. Insofar as democracy was imposed from without, democratic elections gave the winners everything and the losers nothing (Matloff, 1996, p. 10; French, 1996, section 4, at 4; Karathnycky, 1996).

It is assumed that the value of democratic governments is that their actions will reflect the desires of a majority of the people rather than the wishes of a select few. Given this assumption, we can argue that the ideal of democracy promotes inclusionary practices. However, there are numerous examples to the contrary. As examples of democracies at risk, Freedom House listed countries with inter-ethnic or inter-sectarian conflict (e.g., Bosnia, India, Turkey, Mali, Niger); countries in transition from communist rule (e.g., Albania, Romania, Russia); countries recovering from extended periods of guerrilla insurgencies, terrorism, and civil war (e.g., El Salvador, Nicaragua, Mozambique); and countries where the political process and judicial system are tainted by corruption (e.g., Brazil, Colombia, the Dominican Republic, Guatemala, Honduras, Paraguay, Venezuela).

In all of the aforementioned examples, we find that the praxis of democracy is not sufficient, by itself, to effectively reduce SPI, advance the cause of human rights, or promote inclusionary governance. Neither is the praxis of democracy, *as currently conceived*, capable of inducing and promoting the kind of state-building and institutional structuring that is necessary for the formulation of governmental policies that can work in conjunction with a market economy in promoting and advancing a healthy and vigorous civil society. So democracy must be reconceived. The reconception of democracy must be associated with a resolution of the human rights dilemma. Because Asia, Africa, and Latin America are becoming more sensitive to the pluralities and minorities that inhabit them, the movement of these peoples from the periphery into the centers of their societies means that governments and economic structures must respond. The response can be a more repressive ES or the building of an IS.

True, the more unified and homogenous societies of the West had less difficulty, in some ways, with the issues associated with inclusion and human rights but, as noted in Chapter 1, the pressures of "democratic exclusion" are a part of the historical evolution of the West as well. What is required, in part, to overcome the exclusionary impulse is the building of an IS. This will demand the building of mediating institutions and social structures, an end to the absolute domination of Western financial institutions over governments and nation-states in both the First and Third Worlds, and a genuine democratization of politics which follows the "Five-C's" of inclusionary governance, as discussed in Chapter 6.

If democracy, as a procedural set of practices, were capable of spreading the wealth of a society in an equitable fashion, development would proceed in conjunction with the evolution of a more harmonious civil society. Inclusionary governance, in the alternative, with democracy as its proper subset, does not neglect the interplay between an expanding market economy and an expanding and more cooperative civil society. The democratic ideal is more closely approximated when the culture and the market work together to promote democratic practices. It should be the task of the state to ensure the proper balance between the two. Yet because "the dynamic of market-oriented reforms is still poorly understood," it may be argued "that several trade-offs—notably between stabilization and growth, between social expenditures and growth, between social expenditures and the sustainability of reforms, and between political participation and the sustainability of reforms—are misconceived within the model that underlies the currently fashionable policy prescriptions" (Przeworski, 1995, pp. 15–16).

Huntington and Nelson raised this concern in the 1970s, noting: "If one's goal is to promote political participation, should one be more favorably disposed towards political elites that give higher priority to socio-economic development and economic growth, or toward elites that put greater emphasis on the achievement of social and economic equality?" (Huntington and Nelson, 1976, p. 42). Part of their answer to this question identified the problems associated with the practice of democracy itself in the praxis of Third World nations. They found that in many countries, but especially those in Latin America, "parties have appealed to the economic interests of the upper, middle, and lower-middle classes" but, at the same time, "no party has appealed to the lower classes other than in a desultory and proforma way" (*Id.*, p. 64).

By observing this quality of democratic practice in Third World nations, the alternative to failures in realizing the ideal of democracy may be implemented in the form of the principles and practices which define inclusionary governance (as outlined in the Introduction). Inclusionary states blend a commitment to economic development with a more equitable distribution of income, and participation in decision making at the state/regime level with elites. The building of an IS is the starting point for the resolution of the human rights dilemma. This is because inclusionary practices and policies stress equity. Equity as the dominant norm allows for an end to making artificial trade-offs, whether they be liberty trade-offs or equity trade-offs. Therefore, framed in this manner, the centralization of the value of equity, as a political, economic, social, and cultural norm, begins resolution of the human rights dilemma. For it serves to equate development, in its broadest sense, with inclusionary human rights practices, policies, and protections. How does this translate into everyday practice? Simply put, states that engage in the practice of institutional inclusivity have political institutions in place that allow for mediation, arbitration, discourse, and negotiation. It is in these institutional contexts that key social groups are institutionally empowered to participate in, and influence, decision making by state elites.

The value of inclusive institutions is found in their ability to guarantee membership to a broad spectrum of social groups. Also, structurally disadvantaged groups are placed closer to the levers of national decision making. Along with institutional inclusivity, another component of "inclusionary governance" is that of "groupness." It has been suggested that "groupness" may be measured by the degree of social segmentation that exists in a society and its institutions. While individuals always have multiple identities and group affiliations, the degree of segmentation in a society depends on the extent to which individuals rely on distinct identity groups, as opposed to participating in a number of overlapping and crosscutting identity groups. If there is a high degree of groupness, then there is an increase in the prospects for states to exploit conflict by the formation of conflict groups. More inclusive institutions, however, place constraints on state exploitation (Kahl, 1998, p. 91).

The Third World's experience does not give great hope to the expectation that the middle-class will come to demand democracy or inclusion for the disenfranchised. In fact in the early 1990s, both Indonesia and Malaysia developed into increasingly one-party states. More surprising, the middle-class seemed to generally support the consolidation of authoritarian rule. In the case of Singapore, the pro-democracy opposition groups derived most of their support from the lower classes. Alternatively, the burgeoning middle-class of Malaysia supported an increasingly authoritarian and interventionist state. The same could be noted of Indonesia where a prospering middle-class stood firmly on the side of the status quo (Bell, 1998, p. 23). As Daniel A. Bell has noted: "Even a 'good despotism' which manages the collective interests of the people cannot counter the tendency toward selfishness since it cannot provide the opportunity for people to cooperate and to discover common interests that may otherwise have gone unnoticed" (Bell, 1998, p. 25).

Therefore, the IS can work to effectuate the kind of social consensus needed for building opportunities for people to cooperate and to discover their common interests. Common interests can be articulated through the adoption of human rights norms. For human rights point toward that which is intrinsic in all of us as human beings. It transcends the limitations of an instrumental economic calculus that is in the service of a capitalist technocracy. Beyond the narrow confines of a consciousness preoccupied with profit maximization and the bottom line is the solution to the human rights dilemma.

Accommodating New Demands and Social Classes

Building a developmental program for inclusionary societies that are also well-ordered societies demands that we address the issues of social classes, class exclusion/inclusion, and class exploitation. While a detailed analysis of this subject is clearly beyond the scope of this book, it is essential to touch on the three aforementioned aspects of class. Why? Because the concept of class involves more than simply market-based exchanges. The concept of class is more accurately understood in the context of exploitation as a social phenonmenon and cannot be theoretically or practically confined to economic equations premised upon the independent and dependent variables which may affect the operation of market mechanisms.

According to Erick Olin Wright, there are three main reasons why we might want to ground the concept of class explicitly in exploitation rather than simply market-based life chances. First, the "exploitation-centered class concept affirms the fact that production and exchange are intrinsically linked, not merely contingently related." Second, he argues that "theorizing the interests linked to classes as grounded in inherently antagonistic and interdependent practices facilitates the analysis of social conflict." Third, and finally, he concludes that "the exploitation-centered class analysis implies that classes can exist in nonmarket societies" (Wright, 1997, p. 35).

These three points serve to act as a connecting thread to aid in understanding the dynamics of the ES, as anti-democratic state and supportive of an historically conditioned process of profit maximization that has relied on the preservation and enforcement of particular power constellations—patron/client, center/periphery, repressive bureaucratic-authoritarian models and numerous other variations—versus movements reflecting the inclusionary impulse, ranging from variations of social democratic experiments to corporatist and liberal-democratic models.

In this regard, *exploitation-centered class analysis* also serves as an interdisciplinary set of connections which serves to demonstrate that "both the development of democratic institutions and the effective role of the many in collective decision-making depend on power constellations" (Ruesschemeyer, et al., 1998, p. 75). In juxtaposition to Wright's three-pronged description of an exploitation-centered class analysis, Ruesschemeyer argues that there are three clusters of power-constellations which interact in complex ways: (1) the balance of class power; (2) the power and autonomy of the state apparatus and its articulation with civil society; and (3) the transnational structures of power (*Id.*, p. 75).

These three clusters are important for they transcend the work of earlier comparative studies which focused primarily on the public contestation of political issues and the institutions of mutual toleration of the major features of democracy while giving only secondary importance to the issue of inclusive political participation (*Id.*, p. 77). Insofar as inclusive political participation is of primary importance in my discussion of building a developmental program for inclusionary societies and an IS, it follows that an exploitation-centered class analysis, combined with an examination of power constellations, can expose the obstacles that have stood in the way of actualizing an IS. The obstacles to building an (IS), from the perspective of Wright's *exploitation-centered class analysis*, can be defined by three principal criteria:

(1) The material welfare of one group of people causally depends on the material deprivations of another.
(2) The causal relation in (1) involves the asymmetrical exclusion of the exploited from access to certain productive resources. Typically this exclusion is backed by force in the form of property rights, but in special cases it may not be.
(3) The causal mechanism which translates exclusion (2) into differential welfare (1) involves the appropriation of the fruits of labor of the exploited by those who control the relevant productive resources (Wright, 1997, p. 10).

Wright's analysis of power relationships, through his exploitation-centered class analysis, serves to outline many dimensions of a long period of historical transition to class-structured societies. Sometimes, the state seemed to stand above, or at least apart from, the society as a whole. This was despite the fact that the state was engaged in actively imposing its particular forms of class regulation on social relations. Throughout the Third World's history,

> **TABLE 7.2 The State's Primary Function in Class-Formation**
>
> 1. Ensuring the protection of the forms of property that the ruling class represents.
> 2. Ensuring that the oppressed classes are held down and do not achieve any reversal in the relations of dominant-dominated.
> 3. Regulating relations between members of the ruling class, and, through this mediation, engendering as much unity as possible in order to protect the fundamental interests of the class.
> 4. Regulating relations between all the propertied classes, including those that are not the ruling class, in order to harmonize the common interests of private property.
> 5. Raising and dispensing of resources within the society.
> 6. Intervening in the process of economic development in order to ensure patterns of accumulation consistent with the class structure of society.
> 7. Creating a bureaucracy to put into effect the laws and regulations that it introduces.
> 8. Training and educating members of the community so as to ensure the reproduction of the labor force and its citizens.
> 9. Intervening in the cultural and ideological arenas in order to ensure developments harmonious with the class structure of society.
> 10. Protecting the sovereignty of the territory over which it exercises power.
> 11. Creating the specialized instruments, institutions, and training required to command an effective coercive force without which there can be no guarantee that its other functions will be performed.
>
> SOURCE: Clive Y. Thomas, *The Rise of the Authoritarian State in Peripheral Societies*, Monthly Review Press, 1984, pp. 5–6.

as the basis of social regulation became less dependent upon social/communal ownership and increasingly more reliant on the material interests of the dominant class, the state itself became more alienated from the civil society, while still being an organic part of it. The state's primary function was to ensure that new class forms of social regulation emerged. This meant that the state had to embrace a number of functions. These functions are presented in Table 7.2.

The supplantation of indigenous models of authority by Western colonialism in the 19th and 20th centuries caused the realignment of social classes throughout the Third World and gave rise to new political and cultural elites. These new elites were educated in Europe and adopted the cultural perspectives of the European center. Returning to their homelands, they advocated and pursued policies that reflected the interests of their own class and those of their newly obtained foreign partners. In the process, they intentionally rejected many the nationalistic aspirations of their countrymen. New styles of exclusionary governance were quickly inaugurated. Unlike many authoritarian states, newly formed democratic states had to undertake a number of difficult tasks. Primarily, they had to reconcile a number of social and economic cleavages within their societies which often cut across each other in a complex fashion (Ponting, 1998, p. 393).

The task of reconciling deep social and economic cleavages was difficult enough in the praxis of First World nation-states, as the Weimar Republic clearly demonstrated. These cleavages included class and sectional interests stemming from the structure of the economic system, religious differences, and geographical differences between the center and periphery of capitalist regions, as well as ethnic and language divisions (*Id.*, p. 393). These problems are so overwhelming that, in practice, no modern state, even a core-capitalist state, that had to solve them could become fully democratic and participatory. It seems that the best that could be hoped for were governments that undertook actions which were somewhat consistent with the aspirations of large portions of the populations over relatively long periods of time (*Id.*, p. 393). The depth and breadth of this problem has been recently referred to as "durable inequality" (Tilly, 1998).

The class and sectional interests within nations create categorical distinctions. According to Tilly, "durable inequality among categories arises because people who control access to value-producing resources solve pressing organizational problems by means of categorical distinctions. Inadvertently or otherwise, those people set up systems of social closure, exclusion, and control" (*Id.*, p. 8). What this means is that multiple parties, not all of them powerful, and sometimes even victims of these exclusionary practices, acquire stakes in the solutions that are arrived at. So, while inequality has durability, there is variation in the forms that it takes. The various forms that inequality takes will be determined by a combination of factors and their interplay, depending upon the nature of the resources involved, previous sites or locations of the categories, the character of organizational problems, and the configurations of interested parties (*Id.*, pp. 8–9). From this starting point, Tilly maintains that durable inequality depends heavily on the institutionalization of categorical pairs. So what evolves is an organizational view of inequality-producing mechanisms, two of which are "exploitation" and "opportunity hoarding." These are the two causal mechanisms by wich people have established systems of "categorical inequality."

Tilly defines exploitation as a system "which operates when powerful connected people command resources from which they draw significantly increased returns by coordinating the effort of outsiders whom they exclude from the full value added by that effort" (*Id.*, p. 10). A recent example of this process from the Europe of the 1980s and 1990s is the treatment of immigrant labor in the new European Union (EU). Tilly defines opportunity hoarding as a system "which operates when members of a categorically bounded network acquire access to a resource that is valuable, renewable, subject to monopoly, supportive of network activities, and enhanced by the network's modus operandi" (*Id.*, p. 10). These two mechanisms parallel each other. But those groups who lack the power to exploit are allowed to pursue the second only if they are either ignored or tolerated by the powerful. In this sense, "often the two parties gain complementary, if unequal benefits from jointly excluding others" (Id., pp. 10–11). The end product of this process creates what I have called the ES.

The ES, then, can be seen as the product of Tilly's notion of "durable inequality," Wright's notion of "exploitation-centered class analysis," and Thomas's notion of the orgaizational functions of states to ensure new class forms of social regulation. Conceived in these ways, the ES exists to ensure that oppressed and exploited classes are held down (or permanently ascribed a place in a particular category) so that they are never empowered to achieve any reversal in the relations of domination.

Commenting on the position in which "the lower strata" find themselves, Barrington Moore, Jr., in examining the principles of social inequality, identifies three factors that promote various forms of exploitation and oppression. These three factors are: (1) the lower strata's fear of the rulers; (2) the ruler's ability to mount overwhelming force at any time; and (3) the fragmentation of the lower strata (Moore, 1998, p. 141). Because "in all sorts of states members of dominant categories ordinarily mobilize more effectively and enjoy more direct access to agents or instruments of state power than do members of subordinate categories, states usually act to reinforce—or at least to sustain—existing categorical inequalities" (Tilly, 1998, p. 203). The logic of the ES creates a "durable inequality."

What affect do democratic arrangements or conditions have on the potential elimination or amelioration of these categorical inequalities? It may be argued that democratic arrangements serve to attenuate the effects of inequality across categorical boundaries "by pitting the normally greater number of the less privileged against the superior resources of the elite," thereby producing new coalitions and alliances that often result in "a modest redistribution of resources toward less favored citizens" (Tilly, 1998, p. 203). But, except under the extreme circumstances of war, state-threatening social movements, or defeats in war (such as the Argentine generals after the Falklands War of the 1980s), we have very few examples of state-led attacks on the unequal categories themselves. It is little wonder that the ES has been so successful in both the First and Third World contexts.

Given the contours of this history of durable inequality, what are the prospects for developing the IS as a viable alternative to the accumulated thrust of the exclusionary impulse, as embodied in the state structures, economic practices, and social constellations of power in the ES? Tilly has sketched four different future scenarios. They are as follows: (1) more of the same; (2) balkanization; (3) material equalization; and (4) new categories. In the first scenario, exploitation, opportunity hoarding, emulation, and adaptation follow their current course across the globe. In the second scenario, balkanization creates small, segregated camps of hoarders. In the third scenario, for which Tilly indicates his strong personal preference, material equalization is realized through the authoritative intervention of a democratically sanctioned effort which inhibits the operations of old categories of exploitation, redistributes the surplus to guarantee all individuals a socially acceptable package of income and services, and ensures that "sorting institutions" (such as schools) attenuate the inherited practices of the past and generally weaken the links among exploitation, opportunity hoarding, and widely prevalent categorical pairs. Fourth and finally, new categories may emergence (totally new or preexisting) that gain salience through incremental action and/or political mobilization (such as situations in which revolutionary coalitions seize control of the state, or in which prophets gather followings that can be translated into a political organization and force) (Tilly, 1998, pp. 242–243). These are four different possibilities for a future in which the ES is either strengthened, diminished, or totally removed as a viable entity.

The historical movement away from the dominant status quo of the ES requires the construction of a viable alternative to exploitation, opportunity hoarding, emulation, and adaptation. Kothari's view is that the people themselves must, of necessity, intervene in the political process. This is a necessity because the removal of poverty can be a function of the pursuit of "distributive justice." As such, the removal of concentrations of wealth and the means of production in a few hand "entails much more than the mere distribution of largesse by the government and other institutions of the state" (Kothari, 1993, p. 59). He attributes these limitations to the fact that the state can achieve very little in the absence of "a revolutionary transformation of civil society" and the very centralization of state power has moved its institutions further away from the people so that it cannot function as a liberating force, but rather reflects the ills of "a centralized and increasingly corrupt state apparatus" (*Id.*, p. 59). This critique even applies to democratic states. Therefore, the much heralded "end of history" and the "spread of democracy" around the world is an empty triumphalism when it is recognized that "widespread categorical inequality threatens democratic institutions twice: by giving members of powerful categories incentives and means to *exclude* others from full benefits, and by providing visible markers for *inclusion and exclusion*" (Tilly, 1998, p. 245). These trends have led many to the conclusion that what is happening in most capitalist economies and countries throughout the world is comparable to the processes that took place in the mid-19th century—large-scale growth of capital accompanied by a rise in unemployment and/or low-paying jobs, poverty, crime, and overall human suffering (Petras and Polychronious, 1998, p. 199).

Countering these trends will require a countervailing set of norms, institutions, values and objectives that encompass and inspire the actions of new waves of labor solidarity and demand an end to bureaucratic centralization in political institutions and corporations. Calls for maximizing the redistribution of resources within civil society must also reclaim the state from those classes which profit from categorical inequality. This means the state must be reclaimed by the people themselves and viewed as both a lever and a resource for change. Such an approach is necessary at the nation-state and international levels. In this task, it will be necessary to reconcile the promotion of economic growth with concerns about equity, and especially with the protection of those who are most economically disadvantaged and vulnerable—the excluded. And so the IS offers a new paradigm for development—*inclusionary development*. Inclusionary development involves the promotion of the policies, practices and goals of the IS, as outlined in Table 7.3.

TABLE 7.3 The Policies, Practices, and Goals of the IS

(I) Policies:
A. Advance the "rule of law" and condemn the practice of "rule by law";
B. Engage in the protection and extension of human rights in all realms;
C. Promote tolerance, mutuality and cooperation between all social classes by removing the roots of categorical inequality and the connections that preserve and reinforce it;
D. Encourage the members of the civil society to increase popular participation in social movements that place claims upon the state to promote an agenda which reflects the claims of distributive justice and democratic inclusion;
E. Maintain state integrity in decision making by removing practices that advance exploitation and opportunity hoarding;
F. Advance an inclusionary agenda for inclusionary development that emphasizes material equalization by weakening the links and connections among the categories of exploitation and opportunity hoarding; and
G. Construct mediating institutions between the state and civil society which allow for greater reliance upon a variety of forms for negotiation, mediation, and the arbitration of conflicting policy choices, so as to expand the range of opportunities and resources for previously excluded individuals, groups, and classes.

(II) Practices:
A. Create, establish, and maintain an independent and impartial judiciary;
B. Establish constitutionally protected human rights categories and channels for redress of grievances;
C. Build state-society linkages which promote negotiation, mediation and arbitration in accord with the principles of an IS and inclusionary development;
D. Make economic decisions in accord with the claims of distributive justice and advanced practices of equitable distribution, so that growth is not left isolated from distributional considerations;
E. Remove categories that protect and preserve exploitation and opportunity hoarding;
F. Bring the state back in to selectively regulate market mechanisms and remedy market failures that negatively affect the poor and excluded under the rubric of an IS and the criteria of an inclusionary developmental agenda; and
G. Incorporate the poor and excluded into a participatory framework of institution-building through mediating institutions that give voice, political empowerment, and legal force to their inclusionary and equitable claims.

TABLE 7.3 *(continued)*

(III) Goals:
A. Remove the threat of the exercise of arbitrary state power from old categories that reflect the values and priorities associated with class exploitation and opportunity hoarding;
B. Enforce and expand human rights protections through domestic and international bills of rights;
C. Strengthen state and civil society linkages and bonds for accommodating the articulation of new claims which advance inclusionary development and an IS;
D. Maintain a policy orientation and state practice which is directed toward the realization of the values, norms, and priorities that are embodied in the concept and practice of distributive justice;
E. Preserve the legitimacy of the IS through maintaining the integrity of its decision making and policy making practices;
F. Eliminate absolute poverty by ensuring the meeting of basic human needs while, at the same time, working to expand the social, economic, and political space that is required for participatory inclusion and to eliminate the growth/equity trade-off and the liberty trade-off; and
G. Realize and institutionalize the newly gained rights of previously excluded groups.

E. DEMOCRACY IN THEORY AND PRACTICE

In the Third World context, elites may invoke the rhetoric of democracy to inspire social conformity, while undertaking the task of "modernization." However, the employment of democratic rhetoric does not mean that these elites pursue policies that are "democratic" in practice. Rather, expedience and convenience may just as easily be served by reference to the democratic ideal as the actual striving for the realization of conditions to which the ideal points.

Indeed, the democratic ideal may easily be turned into a false panacea. It is necessary to recognize that the democratic ideal must be made to be flexible for insertion into different cultural and normative contexts. The fact that at the periphery democracy was notable mainly by its absence in the 20th century points to the inflexible forms into which it was placed. Nowhere was this more evident than in the democracies of the semi-periphery, such as Latin America, southern Europe, and the Balkans. Unlike democratic states in the core regions, these states had weak foundations. They were subject to tremendous economic strains and often were confronted with the threat of overthrow by authoritarian regimes (Ponting, 1998, p. 405). The danger of collective violence is not limited to countries that face challenges to their sovereignty or territorial integrity. Rather, the danger of collective violence is also present in nations where social inequalities exist that "exclude large segments of the population from the effective exercise of the rights and obligations of citizenship" (Przeworski, 1995, p. 111). The factors that produce exclusion are the same factors which are major obstacles to the realization of the ideal of democracy and its actual practice in less than perfect form or in less than perfect situations.

Establishing the *meaning* of democracy is inherently difficult and necessarily complex. This reflects the fact that the term *democracy* means different things to different people. The continuing debate about democracy has most recently taken place between the proponents of procedural and substantive democracy. Put simply, this can be characterized as a debate between "rule-centered" and "outcome-centered" conceptions of democracy (Shapiro, 1997, p. 212). The great difficulty with arguments for substantive democracy is that "they assume that there is some way, independent of what democratic procedures generate, to determine what outcomes are genuinely democratic" (*Id.*, p. 213). Like it or not, the social world into which democracy is placed is a world of power relations and hierarchies. As noted above, in our review of Tilly's discussion on "durable inequality," we find that exploitation and various forms of social exclusion "are the arbitrary products of chance and the historical evolution of power relations" (*Id.*, p. 213). Any democratic theory that fails to respond to this reality is, in the final analysis, not worthy of the name.

If we recognize, however, that the historical evolution of power relations is at the core of how democracy operates in different settings, then we may be able to accommodate our understanding and appreciation to different cultures and different historical conditions. We know, at least from the standpoint of definition, what democracy is supposed to be. Democracy includes the familiar qualities of fair and equal representation, of active citizen participation, of representation in the decision-making processes of the society, of the right to vote and the right of freedom of expression, the idea of the sovereign power of the people, and, finally, the Western-liberal notion, existent since Locke, of checks and balances.

Yet at the end of the day one dominant point remains to be appreciated with respect to democracy: "Even if democracy is the regime where all subjects become citizens, only an effective state can generate the conditions that ensure the realization of citizenship" (Przeworkski, 1998, p. 111). With this in mind, I now turn to an examination of the historical experiences of Latin America and Africa. The effectiveness of their respective states, relative to the degree of their inclusionary or exclusionary policies, practices and goals, has been critical to the nature of democratic outcomes in these regions.

1. Low-Intensity Democracy and Latin America's Plight

Since 1945, democracy has not been realized in large measure throughout most of the Third World. The emergence from colonialism did not automatically grant democracy or democratic practice an immediate calling card into the lived experience of Third World states. Rather, precisely the opposite occurred in most Third World countries (Falk, 1981).

The praxological inappropriateness of "low-intensity democracy" in the Third World arises from the fact that the necessary preconditions for the effective establishment of a viable civic bond are absent. Citizenship requires: (a) an educated population (the majority of population in LDCs (lesser developed countries) remains uneducated and illiterate); (b) access to work (unemployment rates in LDCs are usually very high); and (c) a sense of being able to participate in the decision-making process of economic and political life (the majorities are usually repressed and coerced by state imposed sanctions against labor unions and other political organizations, so that a collective will cannot be shaped to articulate a political mandate for the interests of the lower classes). Hence, non-representative government is built into the system and an associational set of patron-client relationships emerges in place of democracy. These governments represent the triumph of the ES throughout Latin America.

This trend has plagued Latin American states. In particular, shifting coalitions and alternating regime structures, from military rule to civilian rule and back again, have crippled prospects for any kind of viable long-term stability in the economic as well as the political domain.

Exclusionary governance is typified by features which adhere to right-wing regimes. The most obvious features of right-wing regimes are: (1) the exclusion from power, or repression, of working class groups, or groups favoring greater equality; (2) preference for the private sector; (3) a willingness to pursue policies which lead to greater social inequality; (4) discouragement of popular participation in politics; (5) pro-Western foreign policies (especially during the Cold War); (6) anti-socialist and anti-communist rhetoric to legitimate authority; (7) appeals to "traditional values" extolling such institutions as the family, church, or past national glory; (8) claims to legitimacy based on the need for "order" without any reference to the social causes of disorder; (9) close links with civilian landed and capitalist elites; (10) the involvement of soldiers in business activity; and (11) a free market economic policy. (Pinkney, 1990, p. 14).

These features of right-wing regimes, in juxtaposition to left-wing regimes, serve to demarcate differences between Third World styles of governance in the Cold War and post-Cold War eras. In the Cold War period, despite its public commitment to democracy and reform, various US administrations frequently demonstrated their preference for anti-left and anti-communist authoritarians over left-leaning leaders who respected constitutional processes (Rabe, 1999, p. 56). Working from this perspective, military leaders falsely assumed that there could be apolitical solutions to problems of political and economic development. They also repressed the progressive organizations of civil society, such as labor unions and peasant groups, that called for more comprehensive social reforms (Rabe, 1999, p. 144). These policies and trends not only reinforced authoritarian regimes but also exacerbated exclusionary styles of governance, which in turn gave rise to the seemingly terminal problems of social violence and political conflict that have raged throughout all of Latin America (Petras, 1981; Petras, 1986; Schoultz, 1998; Schoultz, 1987; Dunkerley, 1988; LeoGrande, 1998; Castaneda, 1993; Smith, 1996).

Historian Edwin Lieuwen discovered some common themes under the rubric of "counter-revolutionary militarism," which underscored nine military takeovers between 1962 and 1967 in Latin America. In every case, he found that the military overthrow of civilian governments resulted in the adoption of a conservative or right-wing position on issues of social reform. Further, right-wing military leaders indiscriminately equated populist policies, such as land reform, with communism. His observation of the exclusionary styles of governance which right-wing military leaders embraced, enabled Lieuwen to conclude: "Without the restraining effect of the military, populist governments would probably be in power in most Latin American countries today (1967)" (Rabe, 1999, p. 144). Right-wing military regimes throughout Latin America developed bureaucratic, authoritarian regimes.

By the early 1980s, a majority of historians and political scientists concurred with the assessment of Lars Schoultz, who observed that "the great advantage of the bureaucratic-authoritarian regimes that replace popular governments is that they are able to eliminate some of the political pressures surrounding the formulation of economic policy. Because these regimes destroy the ability of popular groups to exert pressure on policy makers, they are able to implement economic policies that emphasize accumulation over distribution, growth over consumption, and . . . a free market over government intervention in the production and distribution of goods" (Schoultz, 1981, p. 11).

Similarly, Jaguaribe had already argued, in the early 1970s, that there is, as a consequence of political and economic exclusion, "a vicious circular causality between the marginality of the majority (often as much as 80 percent) of the population and the general stagnation of the system" (Jaguaribe, 1973, p. 287). In other words, the practice of "exclusionary governance" through right-wing military regimes was antithetical to equitable developmental policies as well as to political stability. The marginality of the majority created social injustice, economic deprivation, and the extermination of even the remnants of democratic practices and procedures.

In the case of Latin America, we find that income inequality was a feature of that region long before the advent of neoliberal restructuring. This is largely the case because Latin America has much more cumulative inequality than other regions of the world. Inequality has taken many forms: class, race, gender, region and religious differences. Taken together, these inequalities tend to overlap, thereby engendering rigid social structures. For example, class and economic domination coincide in Brazil and Guatemala.

Further, contrary to the neoliberal idea that "market-friendly" economic growth by itself leads to increased social homogeneity, we find that countries as diverse as Mexico, the Dominican Republic, and Nicaragua have similar levels of inequality. An explanation for this phenomenon has been set forth by Arthur Schlesinger, Jr., who has acknowledged that while capitalism has proven itself to be the supreme engine of innovation, production, and distribution, its "method, as it careens ahead, heedless of little beyond its own profits, is what Joseph Schumpeter called 'creative destruction.' In its economic theory, capitalism rests on the concept of equilibrium. In practice, its very virtues drive it toward disequilibrium" (Schlesinger, 1997, p. 8).

The various ways in which this disequilibrium manifests itself are found in features of surviving African democracies which resemble the imperfect regimes which dominate the political landscape of much of Latin America and parts of Asia. This is especially true where multi-party electoral regimes co-exist with persistent authoritarian leadership tendencies, thereby allowing for the persistence of a shallow democratic political culture (Bratton and van de Walle, 1997, p. 234).

Shallow democratic political cultures create a number of problems. First, they reinforce the experience of low-intensity democracy, which means that there is never a complete consolidation of democracy in these countries. Second, because the consolidation of a democratic political culture is an essential component of consoilidation, the absence of democratic political culture implies, by definition, that a democratic consolidation will never materialize for these countries. Put simply, democracy is not possible without democrats (*Id.*, p. 235). Third, socioeconomic inequality will persist where low-intensity democracy thrives, for the accountability of the state and the state apparatus remains virtually immune from inclusionary demands. Insofar as the ES of a low-intensity democracy allows for the preservation and maintenance of pre-existing patron-client relationships and limited electoral coalitions and alliances to guarantee victory in the next election, the time between elections is time devoted to the reinforcement of the developmental priorities of the ES and its supportive network.

There is little doubt that cumulative social inequalities represent a poor foundation for democracy. This view is born of the historical experience of Latin America, which has experienced so much social unrest and deadly conflict. The Dominican Republic, Peru, and most of Central America have suffered from high levels of political instability and violence as a consequence of these inequalities. This is historically the case with respect to the issue of land reform throughout Latin America. Most of Latin America's landed oligarchy has maintained its privileged and exclusionary rule through the mediation of brutal military regimes.

In contrast, the historical absence of hacienda agriculture and large land holdings in Costa Rica, as well as the shortage of agricultural labor that kept rural wages high, all contributed to an egalitarian social culture, which has been termed "interdependence among classes" (Booth, 1995, pp. 389–391). Costa Rica's experience has led to a fostering of its democratic prospects and low levels of social and political instability. This is because Costa Rica's culture has produced a consolidated democracy that also promotes inclusionary policies, practices, and goals. It is no accident that its leader, President Oscar Arias, was to become the winner of a Nobel Peace Prize for his efforts to bring peace to Central America, at a time when the Reagan administration was supporting violence through the contra network and the CIA (Paupp, 1987).

In order to advance economic growth and development as well as lay the foundation for the practice of democracy, the role of the state, the development of effective political parties, and viable forms of citizenship are crucial (a more detailed analysis of these relationships will be undertaken in Part H of this chapter). They are crucial elements in terms of their interlocking capacity for building a national interest/welfare agenda that incorporates and includes those groups, classes and interests that have been historically victimized by historical inequality and exclusionary politics. Therefore, strong state/society linkages are essential to overcoming social fragmentation and the dangers associated with social unrest, political violence, and deadly conflict.

2. An Overview of Africa's Experience

In the case of Africa, for example, political protest was sufficient, in the 1990s, to engender greater political participation and getting transitions started. The problem, which became evident, however, was that the protest movements that emerged as a reaction to an entrenched regime more often than not failed to have an alternative institution-building program in mind. Because of little experience with competitive politics and few precedents on which to build, the protesters' demands for political rights often failed to become actualized.

Africa, in the 1990s, experienced mass political demands throughout the continent that may have been sufficient to tip the balance in favor of multiparty elections, but protest-led reform did not necessarily lay a firm foundation for the subsequent institutionalization of democratic regimes. Lacking a sufficient heritage of political competition, democracy in Africa continues to be fragile, potentially transitory, and always threatened by reversal. Table 7.4 specifically identifies the transition outcomes for Sub-Saharan Africa (1990–94), and shows that blocked or incomplete transitions or flawed electoral transitions characterized most of the continent.

It may be argued that blocked or incomplete transitions on the African continent were a failure of democracy because the attempt to institutionalize democracy was not only burdened by Africa's colonial legacy but also by a general lack of economic development. The colonial legacy did not provide the economic or political basis for a thriving practice of democracy. In fact, political freedoms throughout the African continent were restrained by tribalism, authoritarian dictatorships (Uganda), and predatory states (Zaire, Rwanda). Without sufficient economic development, the democratic rights and freedoms demanded by protest movements could hardly be consolidated in most African states. Between independence and 1980, 106 presidential and 185 direct parliamentary elections were held in the 47 countries of sub-Saharan Africa (Table 7.5). Within this praxis, there is significant evidence to suggest that, in terms of political competition, the elections were little more than rituals. In fact, in many countries of the region, rulers could not afford to give any real electoral challenge a chance and, therefore, used elections in a self-serving manner in order to present the illusion of stability and the legitimacy of the current regime's rule.

The nature of political authority and its political institutions differ in the African praxis in several important respects from other world regions that have undergone fundamental changes in the 1980s and 1990s. The institutional nature of politics in the ancient regimes of post-colonial Africa was neopatrimonialism. The term is derived from the concept of patrimonial authority. It has been used by sociologists to designate the principles of authority in the smallest and most traditional polities. In patrimonial systems, an individual rules by reason of personal prestige and power. The great majority of the people are seen as mere extensions of the rulers household, with no rights or privileges other than those granted by the ruler. In light of this arrangement, authority is entirely personalized and decisions are made and shaped by the ruler's preferences rather than any codified system of laws.

Looking at the African continent as a whole, it is possible to discern extremes in and among Africa's neopatrimonial regimes. At one extreme, opposition parties were allowed to form and even gain entry into the legislature in a small number of countries. At the other extreme, certain governments actually banned any questioning and scrutiny of the policies formulated by an inner group of politicians. In the middle, small islands of contest were allowed and tolerated, either formally under the authority of the ruling party or independently of the state. In looking across this vast spectrum, it is easy to see the flaws in these democracies. In large measure, the stability of democratic rule was facilitated by the presence of a dominant party that was never seriously challenged. This accounts for electoral results in which the majority party in Botswana, the Gambia, and Senegal won an average of 85.8 percent, 81.7 percent, and 86.8 percent, respectively, of seats contested in multiparty elections (Bratton, 1997, p. 69). Other flaws in the African democracies reveal a pattern in which the opposition was harassed and electoral abuse was common.

Also, vacillation between democratic and authoritarian rule has been abundantly evident throughout Africa. While some countries experienced brief interludes of democratic rule, there were longer periods of authoritarianism. With the exceptions of Botswana, the Gambia, Mauritius, Senegal and Zimbabwe, scholars found 19 elections in 12 countries since 1970 in which an opposition party won at least one seat. The common characteristic of these particular elections is that they always occurred in countries where political instability (SPI) was the rule and predominant reality. These were situations where a succession of both military and civilian leaders had failed to overcome ethnoregional divisions that, in turn, served to undermine the legitimacy of the regime. The elections themselves produced charges of fraud, and their deficiencies contributed to the delegitimation of the democratic order (Bratton, 1997, p. 69).

Competition was also limited by some of Africa's single-party regimes that institutionalized limited but real competition within the ruling party. To be sure, such competition was always controlled. The function of emerging electoral institutions was to allow neopatrimonial rulers to assert presidential prerogatives over the single party, as well as to discipline the political class. One great benefit of intraparty competition was to facilitate the circulation of elites. In this way, while new players came into the system, they never threatened the actual legitimacy of the regime or the ruler himself.

Having outlined how competition has been controlled in and through Africa's emerging electoral institutions, we can better appreciate the nature of

TABLE 7.4 Indicators of Regime Transition, Sub-Saharan Africa, 1990–1994

Country	a. Frequency of Political Protest	b. Extent of Liberalization	c. Extent of Democratization	d. Level of Democracy	e. Transition Outcome
Angola	0	1	0	7	1
Benin	17	4	5	2	3
Botswana	–	1	–1	2	–
Burkina Faso	2	1	2	5	2
Burundi	7	1	1	6	1
Cameroon	19	1	0	6	2
Cape Verde Islands	3	4	4	1	3
Central African Republic	9	1	3	3	3
Chad	12	1	0	6	1
Comoros	13	4	2	4	2
Congo	6	3	3	4	3
Cote d'Ivoire	20	2	0	6	2
Djibouti	2	0	0	6	2
Equatorial Guinea	3	1	0	7	2
Ethiopia	2	3	1	6	1
Gabon	16	2	1	5	2
Gambia	–	1	–4	7	–
Ghana	6	1	1	5	2
Guinea	10	1	1	6	1
Guinea-Bissau	2	2	3	3	3
Kenya	16	1	0	6	2
Lesotho	6	2	2	4	3
Liberia	4	–1	–1	7	0
Madagascar	19	1	3	2	3
Malawi	5	0	4	2	3
Mali	14	3	4	2	3
Mauritania	11	0	0	7	2
Mauritius	–	0	1	1	–
Mozambique	1	3	4	3	3
Namibia	5	1	2	2	3
Niger	26	2	4	3	3

Between Poverty and Polyarchy 395

TABLE 7.4 *(continued)*

Country	a. Frequency of Political Protest	b. Extent of Liberalization	c. Extent of Democratization	d. Level of Democracy	e. Transition Outcome
Nigeria	26	0	−2	7	1
Rwanda	0	1	−1	7	1
Sao Tome	2	2	5	1	3
Senegal	-	1	−1	4	−
Seychelles	0	2	3	3	3
Sierra Leone	4	−1	−2	7	1
Somalia	4	0	0	7	1
South Africa	16	2	3	2	3
Sudan	8	−2	−3	7	0
Swaziland	7	1	−1	6	2
Tanzania	2	1	0	6	1
Togo	20	1	0	6	2
Uganda	1	−1	0	5	1
Zaire	22	2	−1	7	1
Zambia	12	2	3	3	3
Zimbabwe	−	2	−1	5	−
Summary					
Mean	—	1.28	1.00	4.66	—
Standard Deviation	—	1.30	2.13	2.02	—
Missing data	5	—	—	—	5
Frequency	0: 3	+37 (33f)	+24 (23f)	1–2: 10	0: 2
	1–3: 10	−10 (9f)	−23 (19f)	3–5: 15	1: 12
	4–10: 13		6–7: 22	2: 12	
	11+: 16			3: 16	

Key:
a. Total number of popular protests aimed at political goals, 1985–1994, as reported in *Africa South of the Sahara* (1986–1995).
b. Change in civil liberties score, 1988–1992, *Comparative Survey of Freedom* (1989 and 1993).
c. Change in political rights score, 1988–1994, *Comparative Survey of Freedom* (1989 and 1995).
d. Political rights score, 1994, *Comparative Survey of Freedom*, 1995.
e. 0 = precluded transition, 1 = blocked or incomplete transition, 2 = flawed electoral transition, 3 = democratic transition (all data as of December 31, 1994).
f. n = 42; figures exclude countries with multi-party regimes before 1990.

SOURCE: Bratton, *Democratic Experiments In Africa*, 1997, pp. 226–287.

political participation in the praxis of Africa between independence and the end of 1989. In this period, there were 106 presidential and 185 direct parliamentary elections in the 47 countries of the sub-Sahara, for an average of 2.30 and 4.02 elections respectively (Bratton, 1997, p. 73). Table 7.5 is an empirical presentation of these facts. When one examines these averages, scholars have found that they mask significant differences. What is revealed is that 16 countries never held a single presidential election, but 12 held four or more. In contrast to this disparity, parliamentary elections were more evenly distributed: 13 countries held two elections or fewer, and 20 held five or more.

The general conclusion that can be deduced from Table 7.5 is that the very decision not to hold direct elections was an effective way to limit participation in some countries. Hence, from our standpoint, this serves to demonstrate the shallowness or lack of "embeddedness" of the state in the society. What this means is that, in the presidential elections, the winning candidate on average received 92 percent of the vote. In 64 of those elections, the winner received above 95 percent of the vote. While more competition was tolerated in parliamentary elections, we still find that the winning party won about 83 percent of the vote and 88 percent of the seats. In fact, in 29 countries, opposition parties were disallowed from winning a single seat over the span of 150 separate elections.

F. STATE POWER IN THE THIRD WORLD AND THE EXTREMELY POOR

In the transition from a traditional social organization to the new political system no time has been allowed, for all practical purposes, for the newly emerging political state and economy to integrate democratic ideals into the objective patterns of behavior. What took Europeans centuries to create, with respect to their democratic traditions, is now expected of Third World states in terms of decades or even less. As a consequence, given the impossibility of such a rapid integration of values and such radical departures in behavior patterns and the entire normative value framework of these societies, elites easily fall prey to the kinds of "authoritarian solutions" that have characterized the pre- and post-Cold War periods (Haggard and Kaufman, 1995; Mainwaring and Scully, 1995).

Liberal democracy, which has been the purported goal of Latin American, Asian, and African elites, can be thought of as the political regime of citizenship. Such a regime is made up of some very basic and interrelated components, including the following: (1) individual autonomy, which involves personal freedom vis-a-vis all other individuals as well as individual freedom and rights vis-a-vis state power and power holders; (2) equality of rights and obligations of all individuals in a particular polity; (3) efficacy, or the ability (real or perceived) to reach desired outcomes through direct or indirect efforts; (4) accountability, or the assumption of responsibility for one's

TABLE 7:5 Elections in Sub-Saharan Africa, Independence to 1989

Country	Presidential Elections	Winner's share (mean % votes)	Legislative Elections	Winner's share (mean % seats)
Angola	0	–	0	–
Benin	3	84.2	5	100.0
Botswana	0	–	5	85.8
Burkina Faso	2	77.3	3	57.0
Burundi	1	99.6	2	81.8
Cameroon	6	97.6	8	90.9
Cape Verde Islands	0	–	2	100.0
Central African Republic	3	80.5	3	95.3
Chad	2	96.2	2	100.0
Comoros	2	99.7	3	73.7
Congo	2	100.0	5	100.0
Cote d'Ivoire	6	99.7	6	100.0
Djibouti	2	87.3	2	100.0
Equitorial Guinea	2	97.9	2	100.0
Ethiopia	0	–	6	100.0
Gabon	5	99.6	7	95.1
Gambia	2	65.7	5	81.7
Ghana	2	75.5	4	76.1
Guinea	5	99.7	4	100.0
Guinea-Bissau	0	—	0	—
Kenya	0	—	6	99.1
Lesotho	0	—	1	38.3
Liberia	6	82.6	6	89.8
Madagascar	5	86.8	7	74.2
Malawi	0	—	4	100.0
Mali	2	99.9	5	100.0
Mauritania	4	97.7	4	100.0
Mauritius	0	—	4	57.3
Mozambique	0	—	0	—
Namibia	0	—	1	—
Niger	3	99.8	3	100.0
Nigeria	2	40.6	3	56.5
Rwanda	5	97.3	5	100.0
Sao Tome	0	—	0	—
Senegal	6	87.7	7	93.4
Seychelles	3	95.6	3	100.0
Sierra Leone	2	97.6	6	62.5
Somalia	1	99.9	4	78.7
South Africa	0	—	8	71.8
Sudan	3	98.2	8	70.6
Swaziland	0	—	1	87.5
Tanzania	6	94.9	5	100.0
Togo	5	98.3	4	100.0
Uganda	0	—	4	68.4
Zaire	3	99.1	5	92.8
Zambia	5	83.4	6	89.9
Zimbabwe	0	—	1	80.0
Total/Average	106	92.0	185	88.0

SOURCE: Bratton, *Democratic Experiments In Africa*, 1997, p. 70.

needs and their consequences upon others (which is conceptually and practically inclusive, for it applies to public officials and to private individuals); (5) empathy, or the ability to place oneself in a situation or setting beyond one's own circumstances; and (6) a sense of shared belonging.

Using these definitions of citizenship as foundational to the practice of democracy in any Third World context, it becomes necessary to understand that these aspects of citizenship are mediated through political, social, and economic actors, as well as organizations and institutions that inhabit the national arena. Two central questions immediately emerge: (1) Is there a political constituency for political reform? (2) If there is such a constituency, can it prevail over domestic political forces of opposition and reaction?

To begin with, I recognize that political regimes constitute a set of rules that place limitations (constitutional restrictions) on the use of power and prescribe a given distribution of power between citizens and the state. This understanding of political regimes reveals two points that are critical. First, state power in any nation is delimited or prescribed by the "rules of the game" (usually in the form of a constitution and the balance of power between classes and the state). Second, the nature of the state/society linkages will be either strong or weak, depending on the nature and power arrangements made by the political regime in question. In the vortex of these two arenas, state power on the one hand and state/society linkages on the other, the true nature of a political regime can be discerned. Therefore, if there is a change of regime, it follows there will be a change in the "rules of the game." If there is a fundamental realignment of these rules, all the coalitions, interests and parties to the political process will change as well as the very processes of public decision making. This realignment or reconfiguration of a political regime has tremendous implications for domestic *stakeholders* who, in the final analysis, have a great deal to gain or lose from transition outcomes. This is what the struggle over state power involves.

In meeting (realizing) the desire of elites to establish quickly an appropriate investment climate, political, and social stability are prerequisites. This being the case, we find that the ideological commitment of the political elite to egalitarianism, if there ever was one, is not primarily attentive to the niceties and dictates of democratic practice but rather to meeting the needs of the immediate situation at hand. Hence, expediency governs in place of principles. If we are to accept and argue in favor of the principles and conceptions of "rights" and "rules" as ideals that are articulated for some future attainment, it is empirically quite clear that elites give only lip service to ideals as abstract goals for the society to aim at. In practice, the actual policies pursued reflect primarily the immediate class interests and political alliances that are in control of the state. In other words, it is the immediacy of the "crisis" and the problems which need to be resolved within a short span of time that places a chronological constraint on democracy. This crisis also demands a comprehensive sociopolitical performance out of democracy that democracy is too often incapable of providing. In 1985, the World Bank calculated the number of the "extremely poor" by region. Its findings are summarized, in Table 7.6.

Given the primacy of time in meeting the demands of social and political national life as well as economic choices, the Third World elites do not

TABLE 7:6 The Extremely Poor in 1985

Region	Number (millions)	Headcount Index (percent)	Poverty gap (percent)
Sub-Saharan Africa	120	30	4.0
East Asia	120	9	0.4
China	80	8	1.0
South Asia	300	29	3.0
India	250	33	4.0
Eastern Europe	3	4	0.2
Middle East and North Africa	40	21	1.0
Latin America and the Caribbean	50	12	1.0
All developing countries	633	18	1.0

Note: The poverty line in 1985 purchasing power dollars is $275 per capita per year for the extremely poor.

SOURCE: Adapted from World Bank, *World Development Report 1990*, p. 29.

practice the Western liberal ideal of democracy in the policy decision making process. Rather, they reserve the rhetoric of democracy for public speeches and, in general, domestic consumption, in order to generate a sense of legitimacy and the illusion of fairness in the public sector. Their immediate concern, after all, is political and social stability. In this respect, stability itself is essentially measured by the degree to which the region in question can adapt to quickly changing circumstances. If it cannot adjust, then the emerging situations of crises may well throw into question the regime's own life expectancy (Linz and Stepan, 1978).

In this context, it can be argued that unsolved structural problems undermine both the efficacy and the legitimacy of the regime. Nevertheless, these problems rarely constitute the cause of regime breakdown. It is only when they become acute and demand immediate response that the regime is incapable of providing that breakdowns occur. This can be brought about by rapid and massive changes in economic conditions, such as deep recessions, rampant inflation, defeat or stalemate in war, or when social dissatisfaction is expressed in more than anomic violence—generally under the leadership of a disloyal opposition—and accompanied by mass mobilization. Indeed, past and more recent history provides us with ample evidence for each and every case mentioned. The most serious crises are those in which the maintenance of public order becomes impossible within a democratic framework: when the regime needs to be reassured of the loyalty of the forces of repression; when to use such forces against one or another group becomes impossible without endangering the regime—and fragmenting coalitions, as when the disloyal opposition is perceived as capable of mobilizing large parts of the population, or strategically located sectors of it, unless the problem is solved (Linz and Stepan, 1978).

Whenever this is the case, the bureaucracy usually takes seriously the anticipated demands or aspirations of the masses, since these aspirations and demands begin to impinge upon its effectiveness and the efficient running of the state apparatus (Andrain and Apter, 1995; Huntington, 1991). Efforts at accommodations will be made by political elites, in many cases, in order to facilitate a lessening of tensions. This will involve the development of new class alliances.

Whether democracy, in practice, is a politically adaptive medium for this task is questionable. For with the emphasis on compromise, negotiations and dependence upon parties willing to bargain, as a political model, democracy is often seen as an insufficient process for Third World states. Lesser developed countries (LDCs) demand immediate solutions to immediate problems and yet do not have either an educated citizenry to act as an informed constituency, or the established representative channels that could ensure that all interest groups are fairly, or at least adequately, represented. Hence, the authoritarian drift of global governance, as seen in the ES, is at least partly rooted in the fact that given the need for immediate response, democratic practices often prove inadequate to effective policy making (Mainwaring, O'Donnell and Valenzuela, 1992; Shain and Linz, 1995). This critique brings us to the dilemma that political democracy and development theory face at the close of the 20th century.

G. STATISM, PRESIDENTIALISM, POLITICAL PARTIES, AND THE DILEMMAS OF DEVELOPMENT

The dilemma that development theory faces is found in the realization that while it is a theory designed to explicate and promote social changes, these changes are feared. As a consequence, various mechanisms have been devised to contain the effects of these changes. Some developmental theorists, while claiming to promote democratic transition, worry that democracy will bring forth a high degree of uncontrollable mass participation and social unrest (a thesis underscored by Crozier, Huntington, and Watanuki in *The Crisis of Democracy*, 1975). At the end of the day, control, discipline, containment, and institutionalization come to override all other concerns. This perspective places development theory in the service of advancing the hegemonic project of the ES. It is both an anti-democratic project and an anti-inclusionary project.

The irony is that the aim of empowering people leads to a perception of those people as a threat to democracy. This has prompted some observers to complain that it must take a special sort of ideological naiveté to persist in the belief that strengthening the state in a developing system will lead, in general, to increasing political freedom. Yet, this perspective resides at the heart of statism. *State autonomy is the hallmark of statism.* Defined in its most basic terms, an autonomous state is an organizational entity that can act and make policies that do not reflect the demands or interests of specific groups. It is, essentially, an ES. It employs the rhetoric of development and promises growth, but fails to articulate policies that would produce equitable growth. The failure to combine the project of economic growth with the issue of the equitable distribution of that growth underscores the real project of the ES. Yet, inclusionary government demands the inclusion and articulation of the demands and interests of all major classes and groups in the processes of policy formation and implementation.

Part of the problem with statism and various forms of exclusionary governance is that they view social development from the vantage point of the state and the policy makers to the exclusion of virtually everyone else. Statism has, as a result, largely given up on the democratic goal and is single-mindedly focused upon economic efficiency. Despite its limited focus, it is not hard to understand why statism has emerged in the literature of political development, since the 1980s, as a viable explanatory vehicle. As long as dictatorial leaders in the Third World find statism more helpful than democracy in legitimating their rule, authoritarianism, whether or not in the form of statism, will have its faithful followers. That is because these states have to engage in the realignment of new classes. As a result, there is the persistent pressure to build new and convenient alliances between the state and these emerging social forces. The strength of the state needs to be continuously replenished by renewing alliances, deterring societal challenges, and overcoming economic crises. This process accounts for the preservation and persistence of the ES throughout the world. Even in supposedly democratic states, guided by presidentialism and institutionalized parties, there is the danger of democratic exclusion and the preservation of an ES. The preservation of the ES is predicated upon the zero-sum character of the political game.

In those Third World states where the traditional societies have offered little in the way of what the West calls "progress," it is hard to move beyond shallow embodiments of democracy. This lack of progress (or institutionalization and consolidation) is especially pronounced in deeply divided societies where ethnicity appears to be permanent, all-encompassing, and predetermining of who will be included and excluded from both power and resources. In this context, "democratic elections take on the character of a census and produce a zero-sum game: one ethnic group or coalition or party wins by its sheer demographic weight, and others, in losing, see themselves as becoming excluded, not only from the government but also from the larger political community" (Diamond, Linz, and Lipset, 1995, p. 42). *Unfortunately, this fear of permanent exclusion is not unreasonable.*

The fear of permanent exclusion may also be found in the zero-sum character of the political game that transpires in presidential regimes. In this situation, the political game is reinforced by the fact that winners and losers are defined for the period of the presidential mandate. During this period of time, there is little hope for shifts in alliances, for broadening the base of support by national unity or by emergency grand coalitions, or even crisis situations that might lead to new elections. Rather, the losers are relegated to a waiting game of four to five years without access to executive power. In short, they remain deprived of the chance to share in the formation of cabinets and lack access to patronage. In this zero-sum game, the stakes in presidential elections for both winners and losers are so high that there is an inevitable increase in political tensions and the dangers of political and social polarization (Linz, 1994, p. 19).

The problems posed by presidentialism, under these conditions, constitute a tremendous challenge to building political parties that promote an inclusionary agenda and seek to displace an ES through the electoral process. Take, for example, the metaconstitutional powers of the president of Mexico. These metaconstitutional powers "have been mistakenly attributed to *presidencialista* tendencies in Mexican society. There is an assumption that an authoritarian political culture in Mexico leads to greater centralization of powers, which in turn leads to a very strong president" (Weldon, 1997, pp. 254–255). Rather, the actual situation is one where "the metaconstitutional powers of the president are also in part due to institutional mechanisms as well as a consensus among the elite members of the party that delegation to a central authority is in their best interest" (*Id.*, p. 255). Hence, it is the exclusionary impulse (my term) of class interests that corrupts the more inclusive potential inherent in presidentialism, thereby preserving the preexisting ES for the furtherance of limited agenda. So, while the formal process of democratic elections goes forward, behind the scenes of electoral competition elites operate to enforce a constricted agenda upon the office of the president and the society at large. In this respect, these exclusionary elites are anti-democratic.

There are two major consequences which stem from this variety of presidentialism. Because presidents can employ their "strength" to influence legislation, two categories of presidential power are determinative: constitutional and partisan. First, constitutional powers allow presidents to shape the policy output of the system. Presidents can employ these powers in the form of decree-laws or the exercise of their veto power over bills. Second, partisan powers give presidents the ability to either shape or dominate the lawmaking process. This power stems from the president's standing vis-a-vis the party system (Shugart and Mainwaring, 1997, p. 13).

The role of the party system is important. Institutionalized party systems function in various ways. They can promote compromise and moderation or, alternatively, they can exacerbate extremism and zero-sum politics. Some are more attuned to building democratic institutions than others. Thus, "an institutionalized party system, per se, does not automatically deliver or even facilitate most outcomes that one hopes a democracy will produce" (Mainwaring and Scully, 1995, p. 21). The dangers of democratic exclusion persist. They persist because of the erratic nature of democratic politics and the difficulty attached to the process of establishing legitimacy under these conditions. Governing is further complicated by the persistent pressure of powerful economic elites who retain privileged access to policy makers (*Id.*, p. 22).

1. Political and Social Stability as the Primary Pre-Condition for Economic Development

Unlike the IS, the model of the ES, as it indulges in the formation of new patterns of exclusionary governance (whether or not the regime is labeled "democratic" or "authoritarian"), will so constrain the political boundaries of decision making that large segments of the population will remain excluded. If this depiction of an ES is correct, it follows that democratic procedures, in and of themselves, are incapable of overcoming class cleavages.

As a consequence, this process results in the misuse of state power, insofar as the state's power will be used to protect the privileges of the status quo and fail to use its power in a more inclusionary manner in the service of all of the citizens of the state. What this means is that the social compact between the state and its citizens is virtually destroyed (as discussed in Chapter 2). It is the "social compact" that will have to be redesigned and reformulated, at some future time, if an IS is to develop and inclusionary development (with corresponding social policies) is to be effectuated and implemented. Without an inclusionary social compact, we find that distributional equity is cast aside. In its place, social and political instability come to increasingly define the life of the society and the quality of its governance. There is a narrowing of the dimensions of state power and the range of choices available to the state under an ES. The result is shown in Table 7.7.

The experience of the Peru of the 1980s provides a case study of the above-referenced dimensions of an ES. Peru experienced a deepening of poverty from the late 1980s and into the early 1990s. The crisis was largely the product of structural adjustment policies coupled with the failure of Peru's state to develop social policies which could have ameliorated the crisis for the poor. What the crisis proved was that "a fall in investment today increases poverty tomorrow, in both relative and absolute terms . . . Hence, as a consequence of a distributive crisis, the economy may get trapped in a vicious circle, characterized by declining investment and rising poverty" (Figueroa, 1995, p. 392). What caused Peru to fall into a crisis of distribution? The hypothesis is that macroeconomc policies which were intended to control the initial debt crisis were the basic cause. The hypothesis is based on the view that the government's choice of macroeconomic stabilization and adjustment policies—the so-called "Washington Consensus"—fell disproportionately on the poor, labor, and the excluded of Peru's social classes. As a result, the social contract between the state and the people was broken. The response of the people was rising levels of political violence. While some argued that the political violence itself was a cause of Peru's economic woes, others argued that social violence is not a cause but a consequence of Peru's distributive crisis (*Id.*, pp. 392–393).

Taking the view that Peru's social violence could be attributed to a broken social compact, it follows that if legislators fail to produce the terms of a new social contract the crisis will continue (*Id.*, p. 395). Assuming that the need for a new social contract is recognized, both within and outside of the establishment, what should the content of the new social contract be? As I

TABLE 7.7 The Dimensions of Exclusionary Governance
1. Weak States
2. Fragmented Civil Society
3. Shifting Political Coalitions
4. Short-Term Policies
5. Elite-Led Pacts
6. "Rule by Law" in place of "Rule of Law"

argued in Chapter 5, Hobbes's vision for a viable Commonwealth involved the production of and adherence to a social contract which can be viewed as an implicit agreement among the members of a society to tolerate inequality, but only up to a certain limit. Such a definition is consistent with John Rawls' proposition that "justice [as fairness] is the first virtue of institutions" (Rawls, 1971, p. 3).

Applied to the situation in Peru, when income distribution becomes unfair, the social contract breaks down. Understood in these terms, the social contract embodies both legal principles and social principles. An ES abides by neither set of principles. For an ES practices "rule by law," not the "rule of law." Further, an ES ignores inclusionary social principles by its reliance on elite-led pacts. Reliance on elite-led pacts creates a fragmented civil society, focuses on short-term policies, and encourages shifting alliances and coalitions governed by self-interest, as opposed to the national interest.

Jean Dreze and Amartya Sen have stated that social policy is intended to promote and protect the living standards of the poor (Dreze and Sen, 1991). An ES ignores social policy as a primary instrument in governance. Yet, as Figueroa has observed, "social policy is needed when economic growth alone cannot improve equity" (Figueroa, 1995, p. 396). As I argued earlier in this chapter, growth alone is insufficient and inadequate to increase the income of the poor and to meet basic human needs. Therefore, social policies are needed in order to "help establish an economic platform or floor in society, so that competition and rivalry can govern the market system and, in turn, social policies set limits on poverty . . . minimizing the risk of crossing the threshold of inequality that leads to social instability" (*Id.*, p. 396).

The responsibility of the excluded classes for political violence and economic problems may now be exposed as a tragic misrepresentation of the facts. Political violence actually results when an ES breaks the preexisting social contract and becomes recalcitrant in producing a new one that incorporates and includes social policies which establish targets for both income security (employment programs) and access to basic social services (health and education). Why is this important? It is important because when a society is in a distributive trap, income redistribution is necessary for the resumption of growth (*Id.*, p. 398). It is also a guarantee of basic needs and

Between Poverty and Polyarchy 405

rights provided by citizenship itself. If citizenship has any meaning at all, it is recognized in all of its dimensions—ethical, economic, political, and social. For, in the final analysis, a distributive crisis is the result of failures in both the market and the state. Liberalization policies will never be sufficient in themselves to correct the crisis (Ramos, 1986). That is why the policies of the ES ultimately fail. Nowhere is the failure of an ES more glaring than in the realm of a disempowered citizenship that is devoid of an equitable and viable social contract.

The achievement of citizenship—a civic fellowship—remains predicated on what is, at present, nonexistent in most Third World states; that is, a preexistent measure of cohesiveness and solidarity. Without these elements conflicts will split the civic bond, generating higher levels of political instability. As political stability is foreclosed upon, so too is the adequacy of democratic solutions. *Change is a "given" within the human condition but "order" is a human achievement.* Change and order create the dialectic for development in the Third World. The nature and direction of that change will be determined, in large measure, by the degree to which either the inclusionary or exclusionary impulse is dominant. The institutions of the state (public sphere) and those of civil society (autonomous sphere of private action) will, in larger measure, reflect the policies, practices and goals of either an ES or an IS. That determination will be crucial for the fate of democracy, human rights, and political inclusion in the praxis of the Third World.

H. BUILDING THE PRAXIS OF THE FUTURE BY POLITICAL INCLUSION

The institutional setting of a large number of Third World nations is already artificially weighted so as to disallow the realization and the articulation of the claims of some classes and/or groups. Clearly, under these circumstances, democracy is disserved. For democracy requires the realization of opportunities through social and political channels to formulate and signify preferences, as well as have those preferences weighted equally in the conduct of government. This is not possible in settings where the state and the functioning of the state are dedicated to forms of political and economic exclusion. This, in turn, creates a process of "depoliticization" of the masses, as opposed to an opening up of the possibilities for democratization. Significantly, depoliticization is a characteristic of the ES because it mirrors a technocratic consciousness and technocratic rationality. The implantation of such a state disallows the inculcation of democratic practices and inclusionary institution-building in Third World nations. This has been, in large measure, Latin America's experience.

In Africa, the experience has been different. The failure to realize democracy was not so much the imposition of a technocratic consciousness as the failure of the various African states to adopt parliamentary forms that would be capable of reflecting their own heritage of tribal societies and other governing experiences. In short, African states usually succumbed to exclusionary styles of governance (as with the "predatory state").

The challenge to building inclusionary or quasi-democratic forms of government in Africa consisted largely in overcoming the vacillations between repression and anarchy. To a large extent, this endless vacillating could be attributed to the absence of political community. In this regard, the power and influence of traditional caste divisions, tribal loyalties, religious differences, as well as racial and regional differences cannot be overemphasized. When it comes to forging an identity, these factors become important considerations, not only for the objective task of nation-building, but also for the formation of a people's consciousness and what they believe they either can or cannot undertake as people.

The European experience with democracy reflects a process of continuous negotiation and compromise, often articulated along intellectual lines associated with the abstract criterion of equality. As long as the discussion about equality persisted in the political, economic, and social realms, the extension of the principle of citizenship was also made possible and this usually resulted in more integrated societies. In short, inclusionary measures, within the democratic tradition of the Western European states, often allowed for behaviors involving compromise, cooperation, and negotiation to emerge. That path was often taken with an eye to maintaining the delicate balance of maintaining the privilege of property ownership on the one hand, and controlled access to the decision-making apparatus of the state by the lower classes on the other. Change and order found their balance in this equation and the realignment of classes that accompanied it. The balances that were ultimately struck either preserved preexisting categroies of exclusion and inequality or, in the alternative, modified categories of class to become more inclusive and less unequal. This particular path is what allowed for the formation of the multiparty systems of Europe.

In a path-breaking history of the state, entitled *Birth of the Leviathan: Building States and Regimes in Medieval and Early Modern Europe*, Thomas Ertman has argued for a combination of three factors which explain the differences in the paths of development followed by the various European polities. First, the kind of political regime which any given state came to possess by the 18th century was largely determined by the ability of national representative assemblies to resist royal pressures for absolutism. This was, in effect, a function of the nature of local government. Thus, in England, Scotland, Hungary, Poland, and Scandinavia, the result of this trend was cooperative interaction across status groups at both the local and national level. Second, the kind of state apparatus that emerged in any given polity largely reflected the impact of geomilitary competition and was the consequence of the conditions under which such apparatuses were first constructed. These conditions were fundamentally altered in the period between 1100 and the 1700s. Third, and finally, the independent influence of representative assemblies on administrative and financial infrastructures were determinative. Where such assemblies were either weak or non-existent, this influence was not sufficient to alter the ultimate character of a given state's apparatus (Ertman, 1997, pp. 317–320).

In summary, states are often unable, as a result of their history, to respond quickly or efficiently to changes in their environment. In this respect, states are forced to operate within constraints imposed by sometimes dysfunctional institutional frameworks (North, 1990, pp. 51–53). However, to the degree to which a state's apparatus is dysfunctional, in the sense that it is not "embedded" in the civil society and receptive to the various groups, classes, and interests within it, there will be a lack of governmental legitimacy and effectiveness. Such an outcome is inherent in the legacy of the ES. This dysfunction serves to explain the high levels of political instability and numerous deadly conflicts that are generated within the praxis of so many Third World states.

By extension, the recognition of dysfunctional and exclusionary institutions also serves to explain some aspects of market failures and distortions. For when cooperative interaction is diminished between status groups, at both the national and international levels, then the market reflects the most dominant economic interests of the civil society. What is jeopardized is not only the relationship between classes and the possibility of equitable distribution through market mechanisms, but also the legitimacy of the state. Social cohesion as well as multiparty and group inclusion must remain the predominant political value and goal—that is, if the state is to maintain its legitimacy. Social cohesion is also intrinsically valuable in its own right if the members of the civil society are to engage in enterprises and efforts reflective of mutual cooperation. Lastly, social cohesion is reflective of an outcome that benefits a market society—that is, if the market is to maintain the integrity of competition as opposed to surrendering to the dangers of monopoly (which often translates into political monopoly).

While the idea of "progress" served European society well as an ideology of social cohesion, thus enabling economic growth, its impact on the Third World (overall) seems to have been a disservice to growth. This, in turn, allows us to question the validity of the unilinear directionality of the concept of progress. For progress, as experienced under the auspices of late 20th century globalization, puts increasing numbers of people at the edges of social, political, and economic marginality. The uneven rate of economic growth within and between Third World states, not to mention First World states, points to the preservation of preexisting disparities in the global order—at the national and international levels (Elkins, 1995; Sassen, 1998; Baker, Epstein, and Pollin, 1998; Kitschelt, Lange, Marks, and Stephens, 1999; Held, McGrew, Goldblatt, and Perraton, 1999). The continuous incorporation and integration of Third World states into the capitalist world economy has led to the creation of what Fertado has called "centrifugal forces." In response to these forces there has been the emergence of new forms and expressions of political consciousness. It has either been placed in the service of the ES or an IS to augment the modernization process. This is, in part, why the process of modernization in the Third World has experienced such a high degree of sociopolitical instability.

The emphasis upon modernization has been overly preoccupied with form over substance. The emphasis upon growth to the exclusion of issues of social quality and equitable distribution has intensified a growing sense of unfairness and injustice at the local, regional, and nation-state levels. At the international level there has been an increasing awareness by the United Nations and NGOs that NGOs need to further develop the quality of their networks to become innovative sources of democracy as well as legitimate and effective sources of universal human rights and international justice (Tuijl, 1999, pp. 493–512).

By failing to identify the role of the state as central to development, there has been a corresponding failure to identify the characteristics of successful states. By emphasizing formal distinctions, as between democratic and authoritarian states, the substantive characteristics of styles of governance—exclusionary versus inclusionary—have been left largely unexamined. This omission has created the crisis of exclusion in the praxis of Third World nations. It is time to correct this grievous omission.

BIBLIOGRAPHY

Muthiah Alagappa, editor, *Political Legitimacy in Southeast Asia: The Quest for Moral Authority*, Stanford University Press, 1995.

Larry Alexander, editor, *Constitutionalism: Philosophical Foundations*, Cambridge University Press, 1998.

Robert R. Alford and Roger Friedland, *Powers of Theory: Capitalism, the State, and Democracy*, Cambridge University Press, 1985.

T.D. Allman, *Unmanifest Destiny: Mayhem and Illusion in American Foreign Policy—From the Monroe Doctrine to Reagan's War in El Salvador*, Doubleday & Company, 1984.

Matina Arbetman and Jacek Kugler, editors, *Political Capacity and Economic Behavior*, Westview Press, 1997.

David Apter, "Political Violence in Analytical Perspective," *The Legitimation of Violence*, edited by David E. Apter, New York University Press, 1997.

Dean Baker, Gerald Epstein and Robert Pollin, editors, *Globalization and Progressive Economic Policy*, Cambridge University Press, 1998.

Daniel A. Bell, David Brown, Kanishka Jayasuriya, and David M. Jones, editors, *Towards Illiberal Democracy in Pacific Asia*, St. Martin's Press, 1995.

Daniel A. Bell, "After the Tsunami: Will Economic Crisis Bring Democracy to Asia?," *The New Republic*, March 9, 1998.

Jagdish Bhagwati, "Poverty and Reforms: Friends or Foes?," *Journal of International Affairs*, Vol. 52, No. 1, Fall 1998.

Morris J. Blachman, William M. LeoGrande, Kenneth E. Sharpe, editors, *Confronting Revolution: Security Through Diplomacy in Central America*, Pantheon Books, New York, 1986.

Thomas Bodenheimer and Robert Gould, *Rollback: Right-Wing Power in US Foreign Policy*, South End Press, 1989.

John Booth, "Costa Rica: The Roots of Democratic Stability," *Democracy in Developing Countries: Latin America*, edited by Diamond, Linz and Lipset, Lynne Rienner Publishers, 1988 and 1989.

Michael Bratton and Nicolas Van De Walle, *Democratic Experiments in Africa: Regime Transitions in Comparative Perspective*, Cambridge University Press, 1997.

David Brown, "Democratization and the Renegotiation of Ethnicity," *Towards Illiberal Democracy in Pacific Asia*, edited by Daniel A. Bell, David Brown, Kanishka Jayasuriya and David M. Jones, St. Martin's Press, 1995.

Armando Caceres and Carlos E. Paredes, "The Management of Economic Policy, 1985–1989," *Peru's Path to Recovery: A Plan for Economic Stabilization and Growth*, Carlos E. Paredes and Jeffrey D. Sachs, editors, The Brookings Institution, Washington, D.C., 1991.

Carnegie Commission, *Final Report, Preventing Deadly Conflict*, Carnegie Corporation of New York, 1997.

Thomas Carothers, *In the Name of Democracy: US Policy Toward Latin America in the Reagan Years*, University of California. 1991.

Jorge G. Castaneda, *Utopia Unarmed: The Latin American Left After the Cold War*, Alfred A. Knopf, 1993.

Michael Chossudovsky, *The Globalisation of Poverty: Impacts of IMF and World Bank Reforms*, Zed Books, Ltd., 1997.

Christopher Clague, editor, *Institutions and Economic Development: Growth and Governance in Less-Developed and Post-Socialist Countries*, The Johns Hopkins University Press, 1997.

Michel J. Crozier, Samuel P. Huntington, and Joji Watanuki, *The Crisis of Democracy: Report on the Governability of Democracies to the Trilateral Commission*, New York University Press, 1975.

Giuseppe Di Palma, "Why Democracy Can Work in Eastern Europe," *The Global Resurgence of Democracy*, edited by Larry Diamond and Marc F. Plattner, The Johns Hopkins University Press, 1993.

Larry Diamond, Juan J. Linz, and Seymour Martin Lipset, "Introduction: What Makes for Democracy?," *Politics in Developing Countries: Comparing Experiences With Democracy*, Second Edition, edited by Larry Diamond, Juan J. Linz, Seymour Martin Lipset, Lynne Rienner Publishers, 1995.

Jack Donnelly, "Human Rights and Asian Values: A Defense of 'Western' Universalism," *The East Asian Challenge for Human Rights*, edited by Joanne R. Bauer and Daniel A. Bell, Cambridge University Press, 1999.

Denise Dresser, "Bringing the Poor Back In: National Solidarity as a Strategy of Regime Legitimation," *Transforming State-Society Strategy*, edited by Wayne A. Cornelius, Ann L. Craig, and Jonathan Fox, Center for US/Mexican Studies, University of California Press, San Diego, 1994(a).

Denis Dresser, "Embellishment, Empowerment, or Euthanasia of the PRI?— Neoliberalism and Party Reform in Mexico," *The Politics of Economic Restructuring: State-Society Relations and Regime Change in Mexico*, edited by Maria L. Cook, Kevin J. Middlebrook, and Juan M. Horcasitas, Center for US/Mexican Studies, University of California Press, San Diego, 1994(b).

Jean Dreze and Amartya Sen, "Public Actions for Social Security: Foundations and Strategy," *Social Security in Developing Countries*, edited by Ahmand Etishan, et al., Oxford University Press, 1991.

James Dunkerley, *Power in the Isthmus: A Political History of Modern Central America*, Verso, 1988.

David J. Elkins, *Beyond Sovereignty: Territory and Political Economy in the Twenty-First Century*, University of Toronto Press, 1995.

Thomas Ertman, *Birth of the Leviathan: Building States and Regimes in Medieval and Early Modern Europe*, Cambridge University Press, 1997.

Richard Falk, *Human Rights and State Sovereignty*, Holmes & Meier Publishers, Inc., 1981.

Richard Falk, *Explorations at the Edge of Time: The Prospects for World Order*, Temple University Press, 1992.

Richard Falk, "Democratic Disguise: Post-Cold War Authoritarianism," *Altered States: A Reader in the New World Order*, edited by Phyllis Bennis and Michel Moushabeck, Olive Branch Press, New York, 1993.

Richard Falk, *On Humane Governance: Toward a New Global Politics*, The Pennsylvania State University Press, 1995.

Richard Falk, "World Orders, Old and New," *Current History: A Journal of Contemporary World Affairs*, Vol. 98, No. 624, January 1999.
Richard Falk, "The Pursuit of International Justice: Present Dilemmas and An Imagined Future," *Journal of International Affairs*, Volume 52, No. 2, Spring 1999.
Howard W. French, "Can African Democracy Survive Ethnic Voting?" *The New York Times*, March 17, 1996.
Celso Fertado, *Accumulation and Development: The Logic of Industrial Civilization*, St. Martin's Press, 1983.
Adolfo Figueroa, "Peru: Social Policies and Economic Adjustment in the 1980s," *Coping with Austerity: Poverty and Inequality in Latin America*, Nora Lustig, editor, The Brookings Institution Press, Washington, D.C., 1995.
Raghav Gaiha and Vani Kulkarni, "Is Growth Central to Poverty Alleviation in India?," *Journal of International Affairs*, Volume 52, No. 1, Fall 1998.
Raymond D. Gastil, "The Past, Present and Future of Democracy," *Journal of International Affairs*, Winter 1985, Vol. 38, No. 2.
Carol Graham, *Safety Nets, Politics, and the Poor: Transitions to Market Economies*, The Brookings Institution Press, Washington, D.C., 1994.
Charles Graybrow, "South and East Asia: A Raw Deal for the Masses," in *Freedom in the World: The Annual Survey of Political Rights and Civil Liberties, 1995–1996*, Roger Kaplan, editor, at 3–4–5, 1996.
Duncan Green, *Silent Revolution: The Rise of Market Economics in Latin America*, Cassell, published in association with LAB, 1995.
Ted Robert Gurr, *Minorities at Risk: A Global View of Ethnopolitical Conflicts*, United States Institute of Peace Press, Washington, D.C., 1993.
Jurgen Habermas, *The Inclusion of the Other: Studies in Political Theory*, The MIT Press, Cambridge, Massachusetts, 1998.
David Held, Anthony McGrew, David Glodblatt, and Jonathan Perraton, *Global Transformations: Politics, Economics and Culture*, Stanford University Press, 1999.
Irving L. Horowitz, *Beyond Empire and Revolution: Militarization and Consolidation in the Third World*, Oxford University Press, 1982.
John Iliffe, *The African Poor: A History*, Cambridge University Press, 1987.
Inter-American Development Bank, *Facing Up to Inequality in Latin America: Economic and Social Progress in Latin America, 1998–1999 Report*, The Inter-American Development Bank, 1998.
Helio Jaguaribe, *Political Development: A General Theory and a Latin American Case Study*, Harper & Row, Publishers, 1973.
Edmundo Jarquin and Fernando Carrillo, editors, *Justice Delayed: Judicial Reform in Latin America*, Published by the Inter-American Development Bank, Distributed by The Johns Hopkins University Press, Washington, D.C., 1998.
Elizabeth Jelin and Eric Hershberg, editors, *Constructing Democracy: Human Rights, Citizenship, and Society in Latin America*, Westview Press, 1996.
Jacqueline Jones, *The Dispossessed: America's Underclasses from the Civil War to the Present*, Basic Books, 1992.
Sidney Jones, "The Impact of Asian Economic Growth on Human Rights,"

Fires Across the Water: Transnational Problems in Asia, edited by James Shinn, A Council On Foreign Relations Book, 1998.
Tony Judt, "The Social Question Redivivus," *Foreign Affairs*, September/October 1997, p. 98.
Colin H. Kahl, "Population Growth, Environmental Degradation, and State-Sponsored Violence: The Case of Kenya, 1991–1993," *International Security*, Fall 1998, Vol. 23, No. 2, Belfer Center for Science and International Affairs, Harvard University.
Adrian Karatnycky, "Democracy and Despotism: Bipolarism Renewed?," in *Freedom in the World: The Annual Survey of Political Rights and Civil Liberties*, 1995–1996, Roger Kaplan, editor, 1996.
Mickey Kaus, *The End of Equality*, Basic Books, 1992.
Herbert Kitschelt, Peter Lange, Gary Marks, John D. Stephens, editors, *Continuity and Change in Contemporary Capitalism*, Cambridge University Press, 1999.
Gabriel Kolko, *Confronting the Third World: United States Foreign Policy, 1945–1980*, Pantheon Books, New York, 1988.
Joyce Kolko, *Restructuring the World Economy*, Pantheon Books, New York, 1988.
Rajni Kothari, *Rethinking Development: In Search of Humane Alternatives*, New Horizons Press, New York, 1989.
Rajni Kothari, *State Against Democracy: In Search of Humane Governance*, New Horizons Press, New York, 1989(a).
Rajni Kothari, *Transformation and Survival: In Search of Humane World Order*, New Horizons Press, New York, 1989(b).
Rajni Kothari, *Poverty: Human Consciousness and the Amnesia of Development*, Zed Books Ltd., 1993.
Sanford Lakoff, *Democracy: History, Theory, Practice*, Westview Press, 1996.
Deepak Lal and M. Myint, *The Political Economy of Poverty, Equity and Growth: A Comparative Study*, Clarendon Press, Oxford, 1996.
Anatol Lieven, *Chechnya: Tombstone of Russian Power*, Yale University Press, 1998.
William M. LeoGrande, *Our Own Backyard: The United States in Central America, 1977–1992*, The University of North Carolina Press, 1998.
Juan J. Linz, "Presidential or Parliamentary Democracy: Does It Make a Difference?," *The Failure of Presidential Democracy*, edited by Juan J. Linz and Arturo Valenzuela, The Johns Hopkins University Press, 1994.
Abraham F. Lowenthal, *Partners In Conflict: The United States and Latin America*, The Johns Hopkins University Press, 1987.
Norma Lustig, editor, *Coping with Austerity: Poverty and Inequality in Latin America*, The Brookings Institution Press, Washington, D.C., 1995.
Edward Luttwak, *Turbo Capitalism: Winners and Losers in the Global Economy*, Harper Collins Publishers, 1999.
Peter McDonough, *Power and Ideology in Brazil*, Princeton University Press, 1981.
Scott Mainwaring and Timothy R. Scully, "Introduction: Party Systems in Latin America," *Building Democratic Institutions: Party Systems in Latin*

America, edited by Scott Mainwaring and Timothy R. Scully, Stanford University Press, 1995.
Jerry Mander and Edward Goldsmith, editors, *The Case Against the Global Economy—And for a Turn Toward the Local*, Sierra Club Books, 1996.
Judith Matloff, "Democracy, of a Sort, Sweeps Africa," *Christian Science Monitor*, August 7, 1996.
Jose Maria Maravall, *Regimes, Politics, and Markets: Democratization and Economic Change in Southern and Eastern Europe*, Oxford University Press, 1997.
Phil Mizen, "'Work-Welfare' and the Regulation of the Poor: The Pessimism of Post-Structuralism," *Capital & Class*, No. 65, Summer 1998.
Barrington Moore, Jr., *Moral Aspects of Economic Growth, and Other Essays*, Cornell University Press, 1998.
Ronaldo Munck, *Politics and Dependency in the Third World: The Case of Latin America*, Zed Books Ltd., 1984.
B.K. Nehru, "Western Democracy and the Third World," *Third World Quarterly*, Vol. 1, No. 2, April 1979.
Douglas C. North, *Institutions, Institutional Change and Economic Performance*, Cambridge University Press, 1990.
Terrence E. Paupp, "Between the Arrows and the Olive Branch: The Tortured Path of the War Powers Resolution in the Reagan Years," *The Journal of Contemporary Legal Issues*, Vol. 1, No. 1, 1987.
Terrence E. Paupp, "Building the Third Reconstruction Society: A Proposed United Charter for Socioeconomic Rights," *The Urban League Review*, Vol. 16, No. 1, 1993.
James F. Petras, et al., *Capitalist and Socialist Crises in the Late Twentieth Century*, Rowman & Allanheld, 1984.
James F. Petras, *Latin America: Bankers, Generals, and the Struggle for Social Justice*, Rowman & Littlefield, 1986.
James F. Petras, *Class, State, and Power in the Third World—With Case Studies on Class Conflict in Latin America*, Allanheld, Osmun/Zed Press, 1981.
James Petras and Chronis Polychroniou, "Rethinking Globalization: From The Future to the Past," *Socialism and Democracy*, Volume 12, Nos. 1–2, 1998.
Robert Pinkney, *Right-Wing Military Government*, Twayne Publishers, 1990.
Clive Ponting, *The Twentieth Century: A World History*, Henry Holt and Company, New York, 1998.
Adam Przeworski, *Sustainable Democracy*, Cambridge University Press, 1995.
Stephen G. Rabe, *Eisenhower and Latin America: The Foreign Policy of Anticommunism*, The University of North Carolina Press, 1988.
Stepen G. Rabe, *The Most Dangerous Area in the World: John F. Kennedy Confronts Communist Revolution in Latin America*, The University of North Carolina Press, 1999.
Joseph Ramos, *Neoconservative Economics in the Southern Cone of Latin America, 1973–1983*, The Johns Hopkins University Press, 1986.
John Rawls, *A Theory of Justice*, Harvard University Press, 1971.
John Rawls, *Political Liberalism*, Columbia University Press, 1993.

Joseph Raz, "On the Authority and Interpretation of Constitutions: Some Preliminaries," *Constitutionalism: Philosophical Foundations*, edited by Larry Alexander, Cambridge University Press, 1998.

William I. Robinson, *Promoting Polyarchy: Globalization, US Intervention, and Hegemony*, Cambridge University Press, 1996.

Dietrich Rueschemeyer, Evelyne Huber Stephens, and John D. Stephen, *Capitalist Development and Democracy*, The University of Chicago Press, 1992.

William Ryan, *Equality*, Pantheon Books, 1991.

David Sahn, editor, *Economic Reform and the Poor in Africa*, Clarendon Press, Oxford, 1996.

Saskia Sassen, *Globalization and Its Discontents: Essays on the New Mobility of People and Money*, The New Press, 1998.

Arthur Schlesinger, Jr., "Has Democracy a Future?," *Foreign Affairs*, September/October 1997.

David F. Schmitz, *Thank God They're on Our Side: The United States and Right-Wing Dictatorships, 1921–1965*, The University of North Carolina Press, 1999.

Lars Schoultz, *Human Rights and United States Policy Toward Latin America*, Princeton University Press, 1981.

Lars Schoultz, *National Security and United States Policy Toward Latin America*, Princeton University Press, 1987.

Lars Schoultz, *Beneath the United States: A History of US Policy Toward Latin America*, Harvard University Press, 1998.

Joseph Schwartz, *The Permanence of the Political: A Democratic Critique of the Radical Impulse to Transcend Politics*, Princeton University Press, 1995.

Gerald W. Scully, *Constitutional Environments and Economic Growth*, Princeton University Press, 1992.

Ann Seidman and Robert Seidman, *State and Law in the Development Process: Problem Solving and Institutional Change in the Third World*, St. Martin's Press, 1994.

Alex Y. Seita, "Globalization and the Convergence of Values," 30 *Cornell International Law Journal*, 1997.

Amartya Sen, "Human Rights and Economic Achievements," *The East Asian Challenge for Human Rights*, edited by Joanne R. Bauer and Daniel A. Bell, Cambridge University Press, 1999.

Ian Shapiro, "Components of the Democratic Ideal," *Understanding Democracy: Economic and Political Perspectives*, edited by Albert Breton, Gianluigi Galeotti, Pierre Salmon, and Ronald Wintrobe, Cambridge University Press, 1997.

John Sheahan and Enrique V. Iglesias, "Kinds and Causes of Inequality in Latin America," *Beyond Tradeoffs: Market Reform and Equitable Growth In Latin America*, Nancy Birdsall, Carol Graham, and Richard Sabot, editors, Inter-American Development Bank and Brookings Institutions Press, 1998.

Matthew Soberg Shugart and Scott Mainwaring, "Presidentialism and Democracy in Latin America: Rethinking the Terms of the Debate,"

Presidentialism and Democracy in Latin America, edited by Scott Mainwaring and Matthew Soberg Shugart, Cambridge University Press, 1997.

Paul E. Sigmund and Reinhold Niebuhr, *The Democratic Experience: Past and Prospects*, Praeger, 1969.

Peter H. Smith, *Talons of the Eagle: Dynamics of US /Latin American Relations*, Oxford University Press, 1996.

James Gustave Speth, "Poverty: A Denial of Human Rights," *Journal of International Affairs*, Volume 52, No. 1, Fall 1998.

James Gustave Speth, "The Plight of the Poor: The United States Must Increase Development Aid," *Foreign Affairs*, May/June 1999.

Carlos Tello, "Combating Poverty In Mexico," *Social Responses to Mexico's Economic Crisis of the 1980s*, edited by Mercedes Gonzalez de la Rocha and Agustin Escobar Latapi, Center for US/Mexican Studies, University of California, San Diego, 1991.

Goran Therborn, *What Does the Ruling Class Do When It Rules?: State Apparatuses and State Power Under Feudalism, Capitalism and Socialism*, Verso, 1980.

Clive Y. Thomas, *The Rise of the Authoritarian State in Peripheral Societies*, Monthly Review Press, 1984.

Rosemary Thorp, *Progress, Poverty and Exclusion: An Economic History of Latin America in the 20th Century*, The Inter-American Bank and the European Union, 1998.

Charles Tilly, *Durable Inequality*, University of California Press, 1998.

Chris Tilly and Charles Tilly, *Work Under Capitalism*, Westview Press, 1998.

Enrique de la Garza Toledo, "The Restructuring of State-Labor Relations in Mexico," *The Politics of Economic Restructuring: State-Society Relations and Regime Change in Mexico*, edited by Maria L. Cook, Kevin J. Middlebrook and Juan M. Horcasitas, Center for US-Mexican Studies, University of California Press, San Diego, 1994.

Peter van Tuijl, "NGOs and Human Rights: Sources of Justice and Democracy," *Journal of International Affairs*, Volume 52, No. 2, Spring 1999.

Roberto Mangabeira Unger, *Democracy Realized: The Progressive Alternative*, Verso, 1998.

Carlos M. Vilas, *Between Earthquakes and Volcanoes: Market, State, and the Revolutions in Central America*, Monthly Review Press, 1995.

Barry R. Weingast, "Democratic Stability as a Self-Enforcing Equilibrium," *Understanding Democracy: Economic and Political Perspectives*, edited by Albert Breton, Gianluigi Galeotti, Pierre Salmon, and Ronald Wintrobe, Cambridge University Press, 1997.

Jeffrey Weldon, "The Political Sources of Presidencialismo in Mexico," *Presidentialism and Democracy In Latin America*, edited by Scott Mainwaring and Matthew Soberg Shugart, Cambridge University Press, 1997.

Kurt Weyland, *Democracy Without Equity: Failures of Reform in Brazil*, University of Pittsburgh Press, 1996.

Erik Olin Wright, *Class Counts: Comparative Studies in Class Analysis*, Cambridge University Press, 1997.

Muhammad Yunus, "Poverty Alleviation: Is Economics Any Help?: Lessons from the Grameen Bank Experience," *Journal of International Affairs*, Volume 52, No. 1, Fall 1998.

Fareed Zakaria, "The Rise of Illiberal Democracy," *Foreign Affairs*, November/December 1997.

Part IV

CONCLUSION

CHAPTER 8

ESTABLISHING PERSPECTIVES ON INCLUSIONARY GOVERNANCE, INCLUSIONARY DEVELOPMENT, AND INTERNATIONAL LAW

> The understanding of a legal order . . . must be expanded to include an awareness of the prospects for upholding a fairly stable set of expectations about what is permissible and what is impermissible conduct, an awareness that shifts inquiry from the rules to the social and institutional means available for their effective implementation.
>
> Richard Falk,
> "New Approaches to the Study of International Law,"
> *The American Journal of International Law*,
> Volume 61, 1967, p. 479

> Presently, the process of transition is dominated by those who believe that the privilege of the few in the face of the misery of the many is either inevitable or actually beneficial, providing a necessary foundation for human excellence and accomplishment. The central feature of the normative challenge that I would propose as a counter rests upon an acceptance of human solidarity and all its implications, especially a shared responsibility to seek equity and dignity for every person on the planet without regard to matters of national identity, territorial boundary, or ideological affiliation.
>
> Richard Falk,
> *Revitalizing International Law*,
> 1989, p. 8

If power is to be held accountable wherever it is located—in the state, the economy, or cultural sphere—then a common structure of political action needs to be entrenched and enforced through a democratic public law. Such a notion, I believe, can coherently link the ideas of democracy and of the modern state. The key to this is the notion of a democratic legal order—an order which is bound by a democratic public law in all its affairs. A democratic

> legal order—a democratic Rechtstaat—is an order circumscribed by, and accounted for in relation to, democratic public law. The idea of such an order, however, can no longer be simply defended as an idea suitable to a particular closed political community or nation state."
>
> David Held,
> "The Transformation of Political Community: Rethinking Democracy in the Context of Globalization," *Democracy's Edges*, eds. Shapiro and Hacker-Cordon, 1999, pp. 105–106

A. THE CHALLENGE OF INCLUSION AND THE RIGHT TO DEVELOPMENT

The disciplines of international relations and international law are in a constant state of evolution, development, and reinterpretation. This book is a testament to that dynamic and an appreciation of its potentiality for writing a fundamentally different script for the 21st century than the history the 20th century has produced with respect to the concepts and practice of human rights, humane development, humane governance, cosmopolitan democracy, and inclusionary governance. To merely articulate legal rights and duties is not sufficient to remake the international world order, much less to understand it. To comprehend the international order through the lens of international law requires a shift from rule-orientation and a purely lawmaking focus toward an examination of the social and institutional means available for its ultimate realization and effective implementation. To date, exclusionary forms of governance and law making have served to effectively preclude many millions of peoples from meaningful participation in decision-making processes which directly impact their individual lives and collective destinies. Democracies as well as dictatorships have been co-equally culpable in creating and maintaining the resulting forms of exclusion which continue to deprive humanity of humane forms of governance by virtue of the exclusionary paths defended by elite privilege and indifference to human suffering and human needs.

This book has been largely dedicated to explicating the dynamics and ramifications of inclusionary forms of governance that are capable of effectively addressing and eliminating global poverty, and the denial of human rights, and of identifying exclusionary institutions, policies, and values in their various manifestations. The growing responsibility of international law and international relations theory is to make Third World nations, as subjects of international law, more qualified participants in the making of international law. To effectuate these results, the concepts and the directions for new forms of legal practice and political institutionalization, and the articulation of inclusionary values, have been set forth throughout the preceding chapters and form the basis for the discussion in this conclusion.

The right to development, at the international level, provides the larger background for discussing inclusionary governance. In 1977 and again in 1979, the United Nations Commission on Human Rights declared that there exists an internationally recognized right to development (Resolutions 4 (XXXIII) and 5(XXXV) (1979)). In this regard, the Commission set forth an endorsement of the view that there exists an equality of opportunity for development which is as much a prerogative of nations as of individuals within nations. Yet for many Third World nations on the periphery of world capitalism's centers and trade, their juridical status as formal sovereign states is contradicated by the reality of their semi-sovereign state status ("quasi-states"), even after formal decolonization. The reality of their status has resulted in their effective exclusion from broadly conceived and broadly practiced forms of inclusionary development. The political, economic, and ostensibly legal aspects of their excluded status exist in radical contradiction to the moral and ethical arguments which support the existence of a right to development at the international level. In fact, these rights are outlined in the report of the United Nations Secretary-General on the internatonal dimensions of the right to development (E/CN.4/1334 (1979)).

Despite the United Nation's position on a right to development at the Commission's 1979 meeting, one Western state delegation argued that is was not yet convinced that the right existed as a legal right recognized by international law, or that it created specific rights and corresponding obligations (E/CN.4/SR.1504, para. 32 (Australia)). The reasons for this skepticism were set forth in a subsequent report of the delegation. Among the reasons cited were that the right to development was seen as being in the category of a "third generation" of human rights, which meant that the right to peace and other allegedly "nebulous concepts" could be identified as human rights as well. The argument concluded with the assertion that "there will have to be a much better definition of the nature of the obligations which the rights create and of the manner in which humans themselves can exercise such rights" (Report of the Australian delegation to the United Nations Commission on Human Rights, Thirty-fifth Session, Geneva, 5 February–16 March 1979).

In response to the aforementioned objections, the theme of inclusionary governance represents an answer to how a right to development can be implemented and does so by virtue of the obligations that are conjoined in the exercise of legal power and political power. Such a perspective was orginally conceived of between 1968 and 1971 in the writings of Richard Falk who, in contrast to Myres McDougal, urged "the development of a systematic orientation for the study of international legal order." The purpose of such an orientation was to develop a "body of thought on the character of global interests that is as well worked out as is reflection upon the character of national interests." In a world where nation-states retained possession of predominant power in world affairs, he argued that "it is also desirable to develop sub-systemic orientations toward world order of a national, bloc, and regional variety" and that these orientations would help "to sustain the awareness that the growth of legal authority must be conjoined with the locus of political power" (Falk, 1971, p. 189). Only by adopting this particular path could international law be liberated "from a sense of its own futility" (*Id.*, p. 189).

Similarly, Louis Henkin proceeded with the proposition that international law remains condemned "constantly [to] defend its existence" and "[e]ven more earnestly . . . its relevance to world events" (Henkin, 1979, p. ix). Henkin sought to convince Realists that "law is a major force in world affairs," while presuading international lawyers to "think beyond the substantive rules of law to the function of law, the nature of its influence, the opportunities it offers, the limitations it imposes" (*Id.*, pp. 4–5). He argued that "law provides the 'submerged' rules of international relations, the definition of a state and the provision of the instruments of its interaction and communication with other states" (*Id.*, p. 21). It also serves to establish "common standards where they seem desirable (*Id.*, p. 29). Viewed in this perspective, customary law and international agreements "avoid the need for negotiating anew in every new instance" (*Id.*, p. 21). In fact, both have the capacity to "create justified expectations . . . [,] warrant confidence as to how others will behave" and, in so doing, facilitate cooperation in the pursuit of common interests (*Id.*, p. 20).

The capacity of international law to transcend the need to negotiate anew in every new instance is complemented by a phenomenological perspective, that is, "from a perspective that emphasizes the concrete phenomena of legal experience and finds support in the philosophical tradition associated with phenomenology" (Falk, 1967, p. 495). Reconciling and conjoining the roles of international law with those of international relations theory serves to explicate the historical antecedents of inclusionary governance and its promise for realizing inclusionary development, governance, and peace at the national and international levels. Inclusionary governance presents such a linkage. Inclusionary governance conjoins normative political claims with corresponding legal mandates to effectuate them. All that is lacking for the realization of inclusionary governance are mediating institutions and the political will and vision to make the quantum leap. That is because "the phenomenological approach is a technique useful for combining concrete analysis of legal problems that are intrinsically interesting with the formulation of more general ideas about the relationship between international law and international behavior" (*Id.*, p. 495).

An example of this technique may be found in the *Shimoda* case, where the legality of the use or threat of use of nuclear weapons was under consideration. The *Shimoda* case prefigured the eventual 1996 Advisory Opinion of the I.C.J. regarding the illegality of the use or threatened use of nuclear weapons (as discussed in Chapter 2). The political ramifications this ruling extend to signing a Comprehensive Test Ban Treaty (CTBT) as well as nation-states assigning one another a timetable for undertaking negotiations leading to disarmament. Some scholars have suggested that this perspective is necessary and essential in order to depict the nature and direction of the transitional shift already underway. The nature of this transitional shift brings with it an array of possibilities and plausible options, as well as "criteria for choice among the options, and an action plan by which to to maximize the possibilities through which the *preferred* option could become the *probable* option" (Falk, 1989, p. 21, italics in the orginal).

The idea that preferences count more than probabilities is an idea which resides at the heart of the model of inclusionary governance. In part,

Establishing Perspectives 423

this is because the model of inclusionary governance acknowledges that "both Machiavellian geopolitics and utopian legalism are nonviable world-order options because they fail to perceive the dominant integrationist thrust of contemporary issues" (*Id.*, p. 25). There are two central points to be derived from this assertion. First, that the "integrationist thrust" of contemporary issues constitutes what I have called the "inclusionary impulse"—the global desire of various cultures and civilizations to end disparities of wealth and power by embarking upon more inclusionary agendas at the national and international levels. Second, that the role ideas play in international law and international relations theory has gained greater normative integrity through the work of international relations theorists who consider themselves "constructivists." Constructivist approaches emphasize the impact of ideas, whereas realism and liberalism tend to focus on material factors such as power or trade (Walt, 1998, p. 40). In sum, the combination of ideas which exemplify a normative framework for world order values and their inclusionary implications with the integrationist thrust associated with contemporary issues gives greater relevance, intellectual integrity, and political legitimacy to the values, policies, and goals associated with the model of inclusionary governance. It is to this combination that we now turn.

B. EMERGING PREFERENCES AND PROBABILITIES FOR THE REALIZATION OF INCLUSIONARY GOVERNANCE

Ever since the 1977 and 1979 declaration by the United Nations Commission on Human Rights that there exists an internationally recognized human right to development, there has been increasing reliance upon the idea that there exists considerable overlap between the ethical and legal foundations of the right in international law. The report of the Secretary-General attached considerable significance to the ethical aspects of the right to development. The report cited six separate propositions of an ethical nature to support the existence of the right:

1. The promotion of development is a fundamental concern of every human endeavor.
2. In international relations there exists a duty of solidarity which is solemnly recognized in the Charter.
3. The increasing interdependence of all peoples underlines the necessity of sharing responsibility for the promotion of development.
4. It is in the economic best interests of all States to promote universal realization of the right to development.
5. Existing economic and other disparities are inconsistent with the maintenance of world peace and stability.
6. The industrialized countries, former colonial powers and some others have a moral duty of reparation to make up for past exploitation. (E/CN.4/1334, paras. 39–54).

While this accounting of the ethical foundations of the right immediately precedes consideration of the relevant legal norms, the report fails to conjoin these two themes together in a systematic manner. However, it may be argued that this link is one of major importance and warrants further examination. This is especially the case with respect to establishing the linkage between the functioning of international law and its international political context. International law has largely maintained a conceptual apparatus inherited from 1648 when the Treaty of Westphalia recognized nation-states as the only participants in international life of any legal consequence. Yet, in the late 20th century, "the emergence of regional and global actors, as well as the diminished scope of a purely private sector of domestic life, has altered greatly the stuff of international life out of which the legal order must take its shape" (Falk, 1971, p. 201).

A similar viewpoint has emerged among international relations theorists, as exemplified by Stephen M. Walt's article, "International Relations: One World, Many Theories" (Walt, 1998, pp. 29–46). International life has been transformed since the time when realist thought responded to the dynamics of the Cold War and bipolarity. The varieties of liberalism exhibited intellectual dexterity as some its strands argued that economic interdependence would discourage states from using force against one another because warfare would threaten each side's prosperity. Alternatively, another strand of liberalism contended that the spread of democratic states would initiate world peace, based on the claim that democratic states were more peaceful than authoritarian ones. Still another strand of liberalism argued that internatonal institutions, such as the IMF, could overcome selfish state beahvior by encouraging states to forego immediate gains in reliance on the promise of benefits resulting from enduring forms of cooperation. More recently, constructivist theories have emerged, no longer taking the state for granted, and regarding the interests and identities of states as "a highly malleable product of specific historical processes" thereby making constructivism especially attentive to the sources of change (*Id.*, pp. 40–41).

The constructivist position does not offer a unified set of predictions on many issues. Still, with its focus on norms, arguing that international law and other normative principles have eroded earlier notions of sovereignty and altered the legitimate purposes for which state power may be employed, constructivism has opened the door to consideration of emerging probabilities and preferences for the realization of inclusionary governance. In fact, the constructivist viewpoint is prefigured in the 1955 work of Quincy Wright, who was in search of an adequate conception of international law, writing that "a system of law must look to the past and the values of continuity, predictability, and stability, but it must also look to the future and the values of justice, progress, and peace demanded by the public opinion of the community. A valid legal discipline must reconcile vested interests with public policies and in a progressive society, whose visions of the future and interpretations of the past are continually changing, it must include means of continuous self-correction" (Wright, 1955, p. 233).

In this spirit, the notion of "justice" at the international level demands recognition of a right to development and, by extrapolation, a right to inclusionary governance. Inclusion provides the objective means and normative framework through which a right to development becomes attainable and remains sustainable. This theme is implicit in the concepts of interdependence, reparation, and solidarity—all elements of propositions set forth by the Secretary-General of the United Nations, articulating his support of the ethical nature of a right to development. Still, in many respects, the ethical claims of justice are just as to established legal foundations as they are relevant to ethical ones. In his dissenting opinion in the *South West Africa* cases (1966), Judge Padilla Nervo indicated that, in his opinion, the International Court of Justice is free to interpret the prescriptions of Article 38 of its Statute "in accordance with the constant evolution of the concepts of justice, principles of law and teachings of publicists" (I.C.J. Reports, 1966, p. 464). Similarly, in a separate opinion in the Namibia (South West Africa) case of 1971, Judge Ammoun noted: "The Court could not remain an unmoved witness in the face of the evolution of modern international law which is taking place in the United Nations through the implementation and the extension to the whole world of the principles of equality, liberty and peace in justice which are embodied in the Charter and in the Universal Declaration of Human Rights" (I.C.J. Reports, 1971, p. 72).

The emerging preferences and probabilities for the realization of inclusionary governance may be understood as the consequence of a dynamic interplay between nation-states (as forums of political power) and the degree to which international law "penetrates areas that heretofore have been the exclusive domain of national legal orders" insofar as with penetration "its tendency toward obligating or authorizing individuals directly increases" (Kelsen, 1971, p. 123). Obligations upon individuals may be derivative from sanctions imposed by international law. Alternatively, international law may leave the determination and execution of sanctions to a national legal order. In either case, the penetration of international legal norms, whether by sanctions or by international treaty, have served to create a new perspective on how to reconstitute world order and, in so doing, undertake the revitalization of international law itself.

In this regard, international courts and tribunals are late 20th century expressions of the growing jurisdiction of international law into the affairs of nations and the individuals who inhabit them. In this sense, absolute and collective liability is replaced by individual liability, and liability is based on fault. Fault can take many forms and incarnations, from inducing man-made famines to outright genocide. Whatever its particular incarnation, however, international law has so expanded the jurisdiction of human rights norms and claims that there is no escape from an evolving framework of value-preferences which centralize the value and dignity of the individual to the point where the previous claims of elite privilege are increasingly challenged with subordination to higher ordering principles. In this context, predatory globalization presents a contradictory situation. On the one hand, "the prospects for world order are enhanced on the basis of a greater worldwide unity of interests, and therefore consensus among elites, and on the diminished threat that social conflict poses." On the other hand, "the prospects for world order are threatened by the maturation under globalization of contradictions internal to capitalism" (Robinson, 1996, p. 374). The advancement of human dignity, under the auspices of inclusionary governance, is diametrically opposed to and at odds with exclusionary forms of political, financial, economic, and social exploitation legitimated by predatory globalization and its support network. Hence, a consciousness of what constitutes injustice, within and among nations, is reflective of a consciousness which asserts that injustice consists of inequalities that are not to the benefit of all (Rawls, 1971, pp. 61–62).

This emerging consciousness also represents a perspective on world order which places a premium upon a kind of global cultural convergence, one that is "partly derived from the conviction that a shared pool of values constitutes consensus" (Mazrui, 1976, p. 65). In other words, national legal orders are progressively becoming more accountable to the standards of the international legal order as the reformation of the world is taken in the direction of recognizing claims for greater social justice, enhanced economic welfare, and diminishing prospects for violence. Yet, this more humane direction remains predicated upon the requirement of "human consensus behind some core values." What this means, in practice, is that "the world of tomorrow can either be tamed through outright force or through shared values. And shared values are what constitutes cultural convergence" (*Id.*, p. 65). Viewed from this perspective, the preferences associated with the values of inclusionary governance, when widely shared, provide the foundation for a cultural convergence that has planetary dimensions.

As preferences for the values, policies, and goals of inclusionary governance evolve in accordance with the constant evolution of the concepts of justice, as has been the case with international relations since the Second World War, there is also an increasing awareness of fundamental global economic interdependence which, in contrast to predatory globalization, brings with it the acknowledgement of the responsibility of all states to contribute to world development—First, Second, and Third Worlds—in recognition of the justice-derived principle of entitlement according to need (Schacter, 1976, p. 1). The principle of entitlement according to need is unique to inclusionary governance. It is not a part of the normative structure or political ideology of the "Third Way." Neither is it an expression of the "generosity" of the G-7 nations contemplating limited forms of debt-relief for Third World peoples. Rather, the principle of entitlement according to need represents a fundamental reordering of world order, based upon inclusionary norms and claims which are, in large measure, derivative of the claims found in post-1945 international law. It is to the inclusionary principle of entitlement according to need that we now turn.

C. THE EMERGING INCLUSIONARY PRINCIPLE OF ENTITLEMENT ACCORDING TO NEED

With the world's resources controlled by a few hundred global corporations, it would seem that the fate of humanity is in the hands of transnational capital. After all, both political and financial power have become so intimately intertwined under the rubric of "globalization" that the goals, objectives, policies, and practices of governments seem virtually indistinguishable from the mandates of transnational capital. Concentrations of economic power at the international level translate into concentrations of political power at the global level. Examples abound with reference to the power wielded by the Trilateral Commission (Gill, 1990; Sklar, 1980), the Multilateral Treaty On Investment (Barlow and Clarke, 1998), the NAFTA treaty (Nader, et al., 1993), the International Monetary Fund (IMF) and the World Bank (Bello, 1994; Arrighi and Silver, 1999), and the World Trade Organization (WTO) (Wolfe, 1999, pp. 208–223; Wallach and Sforza, 1999; Conroy and West, 2000, pp. 41–55; Das, 1998; Faux, 1999, pp. 35–39; Phillips, 1999; Luttwak, 1999; Moberg, 1999; Mead, 1999; Borosage, 1999, pp. 20–21; Curtis, 1998). These constellations of power have in many ways rendered any discussion of "democracy" under such conditions virtually meaningless. From this perspective, it may seem equally meaningless to consider the idea of an emerging inclusionary principle of entitlement according to need.

Yet consideration of this principle is not incongruous when the decision-making processes affecting humanity's resources are not decided on the basis of humanity's needs, but on the basis of the drive for profit by transnational corporations and compliant governments which have made themselves clients to the demands of transnational capital. The very merger of exclusionary states with the dynamics of inherently exclusionary transnational corporations and their respective agendas has served to create the basis for a confrontation on the means of democratizing global society. The question itself reveals the interconnectedness between global democratic claims (cosmopolitan in scope), and the emerging inclusionary principle of entitlement according to need, as well as the other associated claims and prescriptions of inclusionary governance (Held, 1989).

In answer to the question of how to democratize global society, we must begin with explicating the democratic idea of the principle of entitlement as it may be applied on a global scale. Insofar as the principle of entitlement according to need is unique to inclusionary governance, this very fact exposes the inherently exclusionary nature of the current system and the rules and laws which govern it. The very language of the ideologues of globalization is inundated with a kind of anthropomorphism that obscures its essential nature. For example, the notion that "the market demands" certain directions, investments, or policies is nonsense. That is not what markets do or undertake. It is only specific people organized in classes (such as corporate executives) and their institutions (directors of the IMF, WTO, World Bank, Trilateral Commission) who make demands, in the name of the market, that constitute actual "demands" as such. Demands, made in the name of the market, are reflections of the exclusionary impulse, as the demands for protecting private wealth, privilege, and monopoly power bend legal rules and conventions to justify mergers (at the national level) and form alliances (at the international level), so as to advance economic policies which are favorable to their "their" interests. In this respect, "the 'market' is a symbol or code word for capitalists and the 'world market' for capitalists linked to multinational corporations and banks" (Petras and Polychroniou, 1999, p. 193). After all is said and done, the central and most basic questions related to the behavior of markets are essentially political questions that are ultimately resolved by state policy.

Because of the centrality of the state, even in an era of globalization, the importance of making states inclusionary and accountable to inclusionary values, policies, and goals is of primary importance for the achievement of global democratization. Understood in this context, the state can be seen as the institutional means to advance the emerging preferences and probabilities for the realization of inclusionary governance, as well as the articulation of the inclusionary principle of entitlement according to need. Indeed, there is a growing literature which emphasizes the idea "that globalization, regionalization, and market-boosting reform are not truly undercutting government authority as many observers claim. Rather, depending on the world-area and country, the trends are rebalancing the weight of government from an agenda of more or less inclusionary social policies and inward-oriented accumulation, to one of more regressive or mass-marginalizing and exclusionary social policies along with transnationalized accumulation" (Tardanico, 2000, p. 276; see also Dicken, 1998; Hollingsworth and Boyer, 1997; Sassen, 1996; Stallings, 1995).

In the advent of mass-marginalizing and exclusionary social policies, how can one seriously speak of democratizing global society? Further, how can one seriously undertake the articulation of an inclusionary principle of entitlement according to need? To consider the range and scope of these two questions, we must must address the economic, sociopolitical, international law, and democratic aspects of the principle of entitlement according to need. We shall address each in turn.

1. The Entitlement in Its Economic Aspects

Recognizing the true nature of globalization as inherently predatory by virtue of the primacy given to capital accumulation as an end itself serves to expose the exclusionary nature of the markets and states which comply with the demands of capital accumulation regardless of the human cost. In the past, critics of the right to development have asserted that few studies undertaken, to date, have conclusively established the existence of a right to development (Alston, 1987, p. 817). The criticism is largely justified, in no small measure, because the concept has been largely relegated to concerns with the terms "equity" and "ethics" while neglecting both its legal and institutional aspects. The model of inclusionary governance attempts to rectify this neglect by explicitly juxtaposing ethical and equitable claims with inclusionary models and preferences which can be legally mandated and institutionally enforced. Institutions such as the WTO and the IMF, for example, should be mandated to revise their charters to make them inclusionary of, and accountable to, the claims, rights, and preferences of Third World states.

At present, the conditionality of IMF loans still violates the domestic jurisdiction of sovereign Third World states by forcing states to impose labor

Establishing Perspectives 429

and environmental restrictions on peoples who are seeking to democratize their nation's political institutions and embark upon a more equitable distribution of wealth to meet basic human needs as well as developmental goals. This political reality places the agenda of the IMF in stark contrast to the aspirations of millions of people who are actively seeking participation and recognition of their claims in accordance with the emerging inclusionary principle of entitlement according to need. The institutional blockage of these claims characterizes the charter and practice of the IMF. The practice is also endemic to the policies and practices of the WTO. For example, in the aftermath of the GATT Uruguay Round of the early 1980s, the international coalition which had favored trade liberalization was fragmenting after more than three decades. A transnational coalition in support of a new GATT round emerged, one of whose principal goals would be to strengthen and streamline the GATT's existing dispute resolution mechanism. United States officials in the Reagan, Bush, and Clinton administrations began to regard dispute resolution reform as a major means to advance US economic interests in a manner consistent with GATT-based multilateralism.

The formation of a new dispute resolution mechanism was the centerpiece of a broader project seeking the completion of the long-delayed formal architecture of the GATT as an international organization. Under the new mechanism, timetables for hearings and panel rulings on disputes were to be accelerated. Further, panel findings are considered for adoption by a new Dispute Settlement Body (DSB), which consists of all WTO members. The central difference between the old and new dispute resolution system is that once a decision is adopted by the WTO, it is considered binding upon the country affected (Pigman, 1999, p. 197). Under this framework, a WTO decision binds a member state under the terms of the state's signature of the treaty establishing the WTO, in a manner similar to that of any other treaty commitment wherein the commitment is considered binding under international law (Congressional Research Service, (hereinafter "CRS"), 1994, p. 7). Still, an affected state must act to implement a WTO decision under the terms of its own domestic law. In this respect, WTO decisions do not possess superceding authority over domestic laws or courts of member states. In short, they do not possess the force of domestic laws themselves (Cloud, 1994, p. 2005, see also CRS, pp. 19–20).

Preceding these developments, one of the main objectives of the developed countries in inaugurating the new round of multilateral trade negotiations in GATT (the Uruguay Round) was to extract concessions and commitments from the developing countries. As the history of the DSB and the WTO reveal, the developed countries did succeed. And yet "the demand on the developing countries for further concessions has not stopped. Hardly a year had passsed after the coming into force of these negotiations, when major developed countries started putting pressure for negotiations in new areas, with the obvious objective of getting further new commitments from developing countries" (Das, The WTO Agreements, 1998, p. 7). In this context, former Director of International Trade Programmes in UNCTAD, and also former Ambassador of India to the GATT, Bhagirath Lal Das, maintains that "it becomes relevant for developing countries to examine the deficiencies and imbalances in the current agreements and propose their own agenda for the negotiations in the near future, with the objective of removing these deficiencies and imbalances and improving the operation of the agreements" (*Id.*, p. 8).

To that end, Das has made three points which are central to changing the approach and strategy of the developing countries. First, "they cannot individually face the developed countries in any serious economic negotiation" (*Id.*, p. 101). The problem arises on issues where the interests of developing and developed countries differ. Second, "they cannot expect any special favors from developed countries without indicating to them the gains which the developed countries will themselves have in extending the concessions" (*Id.*, p. 101). Third, in developed countries, it is "industry and finance, rather than the governments, which are the real operators in the economic sector." In spite of this fact, "the governments may be cooperative" and it should be recognized that "there cannot be any useful economic cooperation without the active motivation and support of the firms in industry, services and finance sectors" (*Id.*, p. 102). When viewed in combination, Das has set forth an ambitious approach to dealing with the linkages between the Third World's ethical and moral stance on the one hand and the institutional framework through which to realize those ethical and moral claims which impact directly upon the success or failure of the emerging inclusionary principle of entitlement according to need.

To make an intellectual differentiation, relative to the principle of entitlement, between moral and ethical claims on the one hand and the realization of those claims through an institutional framework on the other is to make human freedom the focus of development. By focusing the developmental task on expanding and widening the realm of human freedom is to shift traditional conceptions regarding development from a narrow concentration upon economic growth per se to inclusionary democracy. What difference does this make in the real world? What difference can a focal concentration on freedom make? In response, Amartya Sen has noted that "the differences arise for two rather distinct reasons, related respectively to the 'process aspect' and the 'opportunity aspect' of freedom" (Sen, 1999, p. 291).

First, insofar as freedom is concerned with "*processes of decision making* as well as *opportunities to achieve valued outcomes*, the domain of our interest cannot be confined only to the outcomes in the form of the promotion of high output or income . . . Such processes as participation in political decisions and social choice cannot be seen as being . . . among the *means* to development . . . but have to be understood as constitutive parts of the *ends* of development in themselves" (*Id.*, p. 291, italics in the original). The emphasis which Sen places upon "processes" as juxtaposed to "opportunities" serves to highlight Falk's criteria for choice among options when he identified a plan of action by which possibilities can be maximized through the *preferred* option which could ultimately become the *probable* option (Falk, 1989, p. 21, italics in the original). The processes of established decision making lend themselves to certain preferences. Therefore, as processes and preferences converge, as through a democratically constituted political regime, inclusionary values such as participation in decision making are centralized in practice, thereby creating opportunities for more democratic outcomes. In this way, the "process aspect" of development expands the realm of freedom, as an ideal, to be realized in practice. It is also the political and economic paradigm through which an emerging inclusionary principle of entitlement according to need is empowered and may be actualized in conformity with the claims of inclusionary governance.

Second, according to Sen, the reason for the "difference between 'development as freedom' and the more conventional perspectives on development relates to contrasts with the *opportunity aspect* itself, rather than being related to the process aspect. In pursuing the view of development as freedom, we have to examine—in addition to the freedoms involved in political, social, and economic processes—the extent to which people have the opportunity to achieve outcomes that they value and have reason to value" (Sen, 1999, p. 291, italics in the original). The "opportunity aspect" of freedom and development, as depicted in Sen's analysis, allows for the evolving convergence of moral, ethical, and cultural values with their expression in practical outcomes.

Still, at the national level, there are obstacles to realizing this evolving convergence as a result of the internationalization of many dimensions of social interaction (i.e., economic, cultural, and political), which have effectively circumscribed the nation-state's policy autonomy in many ways, the most significant of which, as already noted, involves rebalancing the force of government from an agenda of inclusionary social policies and inward-oriented accumulation to one of regressive or mass-marginalizing and exclusionary social policies in the service of transnationalized accumulation (Tardanico, 2000, p. 276). In this new international environment, many national governments increasingly play the role of "decision-takers" as they react to the actions of transnational players and more powerful foreign governments.

Global financial markets, multinational corporations, banking institutions are increasingly acting in unilateral ways with decisive effects for national policies and strategies. The ramifications of the policies and strategies of these power centers contribute to exacerbating violence and conflict around the globe. The dismantling of the former Yugoslavia and the recolonizing of Bosnia-Herzegovina under IMF auspices is a case in point. According to Michael Chossudovsky, "one cannot sidestep a fundamental question: is the Bosnian Constitution formally agreed upon between heads of state at Dayton really a constitution? A sombre and dangerous precedent had been set in the history of international relations: Western creditors had embedded their interests in a constitution hastily written on their behalf; executive positions within the Bosnian state system were held by non-citizens who were appointees of Western financial institutions. No constitutional assembly, no consultations with citizens' organizations in Bosnia and Herzegovina, no 'constitutional amendments'" (Chossudovsky, 1997, p. 257). In the context of this "hidden" history, one finds that since the onset of war in 1991, the central role of macro-economic reform has been conveniently overlooked by the global media. The glory of the "free market" has been presented as the basis and foundation for rebuilding a war-shattered economy. From this limited perspective, it has been easy for Western financial interests, governments, and the media to highlight cultural, ethnic and religious divisions as the sole cause of the crisis when, in reality, they were manifestations of a deeper process of economic and political fracturing (*Id.*, p. 259).

The true sources of Bosnia-Herzegovina's crisis were purposely distorted to hide the reality that "the ruin of an economic system, including the takeover of productive assets, the extension of markets and 'the scramble for territory' in the Balkans constitute the real cause of conflict" (*Id.*, p. 259). The global effects of the policies and dogmas of global financial markets, multinational corporations, and banking institutions made the former Yugoslavia into a mirror-image of similar economic restructuring programs that have affected millions throughout the Third World and also in the United States, Canada and Western Europe (*Id.*, p. 259). When pushed to the extreme, the "reforms" constitute the implementation of a destructive economic model premised on the articles of faith embraced by the neoliberal agenda. Its imposition upon national societies throughout the world constitutes a new age of exclusion, conflict, violence and oppression (Chomsky, 1999).

In this context, the challenge and task of legal analysis "is to find a middle ground, conjoining law to politics without collapsing the one into the other and attaining a realism that neither expects law to guarantee a peaceful world nor concludes that law is irrelevant to international peace" (Falk, 1971, p. 192). The task of political decision makers is to acknowledge that changes in the development of international law "have placed individuals, governments and non- governmental organizations under new systems of legal regulation. International law recognizes powers and constraints, and rights and duties, which have qualified the principle of state sovereignty in a number of important respects; sovereignty per se is no longer a straightforward guarantee of international legitimacy. Entrenched in certain legal instruments is the view that a legitimate state must be a democratic state that upholds certain common values" (Held, 1999, pp. 100–101). Yet, when the democratic content of the state is emptied of its autonomy and is placed on the sacrificial altar of market-driven monopoly capitalism, the force of entrenched legal instruments that support the inclusionary impulse of democracy are rendered impotent. In the case of Latin America, for example, the markets which are emerging throughout the region are characterized by little regulation, a minimal state presence, and an accentuation of liberal individualism—which vitiates more collective, communitarian, and inclusionary visions of society (Walzer, 1991; Taylor, 1990).

The pro-business rationale of these emerging markets support what Falk has termed "predatory globalization." Others have referred to these processes as "predatory capitalism." What is not in dispute, however, is that "it is a capitalism that preys on those without economic resources," such as the popular sectors and noncompetitive industries, by depriving the state of resources through its policy prescriptions (Oxhorn and Ducatenzeiler, 1998, p. 232). In the Latin American context, "governmental accountability and broad citizen participation are not only lacking . . . there is little evidence that policy makers are concerned by this lack . . . If democracy remains minimalist, it will be very difficult for it to become consolidated; the excluded cannot remain excluded forever" (*Id.*, p. 239). Exclusionary governance and the exclusionary state (ES) will ultimately collapse under the pressures generated by the inherent contradications of exclusionary policies, as well as increasing demands for political efficiency—which requires the creation and maintenance of inclusionary institutions capable of incorporating processes for both the representation and aggregation of interests. Further, variations of the inclusionary state (IS) will have to be created for the mediation of economic power's influence with the ability to re-process it in a more inclusionary direction.

It is empirically defensible to assert that variations of the IS can and should be created for the purpose of mediating the influence of economic power in a more inclusionary direction. The empirical and normative basis for this assertion finds its support in the fact that "the implied claim that there is a 'tradeoff' between material improvement and democratic quality is subject to challenge, given data from developing countries indicating that democracy is not only compatible with growth and poverty reduction but may in fact be indispensable to both" (Friedman, 1999, pp. 15–16; see also, Rodrik, 1999). There are many reasons that may be cited in support of this assertion. To consolidate democracy, elected leaders must tackle multiple tasks. These tasks include building and reforming institutions, as well as dismantling others (such as a military intelligence apparatus that spies on its own citizens). Elected leaders are responsible for managing the economy and must effectively seek solutions to the major problems their society confronts, even if progress is incremental and selective. Procedurally, democratic leaders must govern in accordance with the laws and be accountable to the constitutional arrangements they are sworn to uphold and promote. In short, while economic performance is important, the experience of "third-wave" democracies suggests that it may be less important, in the long run, than establishing inclusionary frameworks for both economic growth and governmental effectiveness, efficiency, and accountability (Diamond, Linz, and Lipset, 1995, p. 55).

2. The Entitlement in Its Sociopolitical Aspects

The pressures for inclusionary governance are building in First and Third world contexts. The overcrowding of the global village combined with growing economic, political, and social disparities and inequalities continue to encourage exclusion and separation. The problem is manifested in Western democracies where a new class of marginalized people is emerging—migrants, political and economic refugees, ethnics, inner city dwellers, and others. In this new world, "these new marginal classes are often seen as the carriers of cultural stigmata that invite exclusion on the one side and, in reaction, a new politics of group entitlements on the other. These developments may manifest themselves in Western and non-Western democracies with . . . different intensities. But at issue is always citizenship, identity, and the state" (Di Palma, 1997, p. 315).

Citizenship and democracy carry demands for certain preferences. In turn, these preferences can be mobilized into political claims for the legal recognition of particular rights and entitlements. As social movements and civil society generate more of these demands, public pressure builds to critical mass, especially in a democracy, because "there must exist multiple avenues for 'the people' to express their interests and preferences, to influence policy, and to scrutinize and check the exercise of state power continuously, in between elections as well as during them" (Diamond, 1999, p. 219). Commonly shared democratic values may act as counterweight to the hegemonic influence of unilateral corporate decision making. Recognition of the importance of shared democratic values is reflected in the concept of social policy in the emerging European Union, especially as economic and democratic values are harmonized or placed into contest. For example, "the more unequal the primary distribution is, the more relevant the corrective role of redistribution becomes. Therefore, primary distribution is also a major concern of social policy" (da Costa, 1997, p. 100). This is especially the case with respect to market economies. The claims of inclusionary governance have an enlarged significance with regard to the institutional dimension insofar as "it seems clear that social policy has been closely related to government action, an aspect that is currently under debate, both for philosophical reasons (neo-liberalism) as well as because of problems related to public expenditure and public deficit. This has to do with the assimilation of the notion of welfare to the the idea of a welfare state, which hinders the global mobilization of all the resources, public and private . . . to achieve social goals, which should be defined and implemented with the participation of all the relevant social actors" (*Id.*, p. 100).

The inclusion and incorporation of all the relevant social actors represents the inclusionary claim of an IS, in recognition of the political reality that "'regimes' may survive from the neo-liberal era, but state capitalism is not the most fertile ground for their formation" (Cox, 1997, p. 64). The inherited regimes of state capitalism sought to propose "a means of reconciling the accumulation and legitimation functions brought into conflict by the economic and fiscal crises of the 1970s and by hyper-liberal politics" (*Id.*, p. 65). Yet the prescription of state capitalism is not necessarily transferable from one country to another because "different countries are more or less well-equipped by their historical experience for the adoption of the state-capitalist developmental path with or without socialist coloration" (*Id.*, p. 65). In this situation, "hyper-liberalism is the ideology of globalization in its most extreme form," which accounts for the fact that "state capitalism is an adaptation to globalization that responds . . . to society's reaction to the negative effects of globalization" (*Id.*, p. 66). According to some scholars, this situation gives rise to the need to ask ourselves "whether there are longer-term prospects that might come to fruition following a medium-term experiment with state capitalism" (*Id.*, p. 66).

One implication to be drawn from this analysis is that national governments need to move from a place of being "decision-takers" to a place of being "decision-makers"—not in the service of exclusionary forms of transnational capital accumulation, but in the service of inclusionary principles which adhere to the emerging inclusionary principle of entitlement according to need. This approach is essential in the task of adopting and asserting inclusionary claims when national governments are faced with the objective reality of a GATT framework which elevates the priority to be accorded unencumbered trade. The IS alternative, under these circumstances, becomes more appealing and more attainable. For "if the state-capitalist solution were to be but an interim stage, the prospect of turning around the segmenting, socially disintegrating, and polarizing effects of globalization rests upon the possibility of the emergence of an alternative political culture that would give greater scope to collective action and place a greater value on collective goods" (*Id.*, p. 66). This is what inclusionary governance and a democratic public order promise and embody—an alternative political culture which centralizes the importance of collective goods so as not to abandon the poor, marginalized, unemployed, members of a declining middle class, and the dispossessed. Yet, under the current arrangements of state capitalism and particular international organizational arrangements, such as the GATT, the recognition of the power imbalances which currently exist expose the reality that the GATT framework operates at the regional level to make "an electoral choice of social democracy almost impossible to implement in practice" (Falk, 1999, p. 74).

Acting effectively as counterbalances—not a zero-sum rivalry—to the GATT framework are transnational democratic goals which are "designed to reconcile global market operations with the well-being of peoples and with the carrying capacity of the earth" (Falk, 1999, p. 136). Undertaking this kind of reconciliation between global market forces and the inclusionary principle of entitlement represents a recognition of the fact that "these powerful elements of the existing global setting provide many beneficial opportunities for improving the material, social, and cultural experience of peoples throughout the world" (Falk, 1999, pp. 168–169). An alternative to the state-capitalist solution, to become a reality, implies that "whole segments of societies would have to become attached, through active participation and developed loyalties, to social institutions engaged in collective activities. They would have to be prepared to defend these institutions in time of adversity. The condition for a restructuring of society and polity in this sense would be to build a new coalition of social forces capable of becoming an alternative basis of polity. Europe's social history has known such movements" (Cox, 1997, pp. 66–67).

While these movements influenced European societies, they never completely fulfilled their aims. That is because no single society or nation could do it alone without international cooperation and support from other communities and polities. Therefore, "movements of this kind would have to grow simultaneously in several countries" (*Id.*, p. 67). Yet to embark upon this path will require the evolution of an international legal regime which is supportive of such a socioeconomic and sociopolitical outcome. To do this will require the creation of an international legal regime which complements a new international political order which embodies the preferences for and probabilities of an emerging democratic public order. Such a democratic legal order has been defined as "a democratic *Rechtstaat* . . . an order which is circumscribed by, and accounted for in relation to, democratic public law" (Held, 1999, p. 106).

The practical framework for such an order would have to possess the capacity to engage deliberative and decision-making centers beyond national territories. Such a framework would have to be inclusive of cross-border and transnational groupings. An arrangement of this kind would be necessary "when 'lower' levels of decision making cannot manage and discharge satisfactorily transnational or international policy questions, and when the principle of democratic legitimacy can only be properly redeemed in a transnational context" (*Id.*, p. 106). In the context of contemporary forms of globalization, what this framework implies is that "for democratic law to be effective it must be internationalized" (*Id.*, p. 106). This concept is not foreign to international law.

3. The Entitlement in Its International Law Aspects

The concept of international *jus cogens* presupposes the emergence of a body of fundamental legal principles that are binding upon all members of the international community in all circumstances (Danilenko, 1993, pp. 211–252). The idea of a "higher law" of overriding importance has been gaining acceptance both in state practice and in legal doctrine. For example, such an approach was first embodied in the 1969 Vienna Convention on the Law of Treaties (1155 UNTS 331) and it was subsequently confirmed by the 1986 Vienna Convention on the Law of Treaties (UN Doc. A/Conf. 129/15 (1986)).

From a law-making perspective, the importance of the principle of *jus cogens* in international law is found in the fact that states have increasingly developed a practice of relying on the concept of *jus cogens* in their efforts to achieve profound changes in the existing law. For those nations seeking rapid legal reforms, the concept is regarded as a powerful tool for the renovation and revitalization of existing legal norms and political structures, practices, and institutions. In fact, the proponents of reform have discovered that by working to create a few preemptory principles they may be able to bring about radical changes in the entire system of existing legal relationships. Examples of this reform process can be found in Article 64 of the Vienna Convention on the Law of Treaties which states: "If a new preemptory norm of general international law emerges, any existing treaty which is in conflict with that norm becomes void and terminates." Also, in the Draft Articles on State Responsibility, there is the assertion in Article 18(2) that "an act of the state which, at the time when it was performed, was not in conformity with what was required of it by an international obligation in force for that state, ceases to be considered an internationally wrongful act if, subsequently, such an act has become compulsory by virtue of a preemptory norm of general international law" (2 YILC 74 (1976 II)).

In various areas of international law, efforts have been made to introduce new preemptory rules of general international law. Examples include the negotiating process at UNCLOS III, the Declaration of Principles Governing the Sea-Bed and the Ocean Floor (UN Doc. A/Res. 2749 (1970)), the United Nations Convention on the Law of the Sea (UN Doc. A/Conf. 62/122 (1982)), the Charter of Economic Rights and Duties of States (UN Doc. A/Res. 3281

Establishing Perspectives

(1974)), and the possibility of relying on *jus cogens* as discussed in the ILC meetings on the Draft Code of Offenses Against the Peace and Security of Mankind (UN Doc. A/CN. 4/404 (1987)). Taken in combination, these examples provide a significant counter-argument to the allegation that the international community has not agreed in any specific legal instrument that the right to development does not exist. What this criticism does reflect is "an unduly restrictive view of the processes by which norms of international law may emerge," especially when one considers that "many of the elements which are essential components of the right to development are already recognized in a variety of legal instruments which are of significance in determining what constitute norms of internatonal law" (Alston, 1987, p. 818). As elaborated in the discussion of the principle of *jus cogens*, it may be argued that such norms are the product of an evolving process of international law making. Therefore, it is far from dispositive to assert that a right to development or an emerging principle of entitlement according to need does not yet exist or is not referred to in specific terms in existing instruments.

Existing human rights instruments are a primary source for asserting that both the right to development, as well as the inclusionary principle of entitlement according to need, are in fact internationally recognized and accepted as being a normative component of international law. On this point, of all the international declarations of rights, the European Convention for the Protection of Human Rights and Fundamental Freedoms (1950) remains noteworthy. As its preamble indicates, the declaration seeks "to take the first steps for the collective enforcement of certain rights stated in the Universal Declaration." In this regard, "the European initiative was and remains a most radical legal innovation: an innovation which, against the stream of state history, allows individual citizens to initiate proceedings against their own governments" (Held, 1999, p. 101). Further, with United Nations support and encouragement, human rights regimes in other regions of the world have worked to promote the entrenchment of rights at regional levels. The promotion of "positive regionalism" has dramatically altered the landscape of international law and its connection to both world order values and those of inclusionary governance.

Regionalism has achieved "positive results in relation to specified world order values in several substanative sectors and various geographic settings, most significantly in Europe, but also in the Asia/Pacific region region, Latin America, Africa, and the Middle East" (Hettne, 1994). The promotion of inclusionary values and forms of governance can be traced to the fact that "from a world order perspective, regionalism's role is to create a new political equilibrium in politics that balances the protection of the vulnerable and the interests of humanity as a whole (including future generations) against the integrative, technological dynamic associated with globalism" (Falk, 1995, p. 87). Yet, the open question is whether regionalism can be democratically conditioned. The dangers associated with negative globalism remain as dangerous and antithetical forces to inclusionary governance, human rights, and democratization. In this context, regionalism has emerged as an important site of struggle and "as an exemplification of opposed forces" (*Id.*, p. 88).

The limits of regionalism are exposed as we contemplate the furtherance of inclusionary democracy in a transnational setting, incorporating

Central and Eastern Europe. Because democracy is a process which must be learned, the learning curve has been conditioned, in large measure, by both geography and history. As Simai has observed, "democracy is . . . a process which must be learned on the basis of national political experiences. It also has a strong international 'demonstration effect,' but this can play a limited role since it cannot influence the interests and determine the attitudes of the masses. The shaping of democratic political culture in its different concrete manifestations has been the result of long processes of learning in the West. One of the important dimensions of backwardness in Central and Eastern Europe has been the limited, underdeveloped nature of its political culture" (Simai, 1997, p. 218). On a more hopeful note, Przeworski observes that "as the history of Socialist parties in Western Europe demonstrates, all political forces face the alternatives of joining or vanishing, and, except for the Anarchists, who persevered in resisting 'the siren song of elections,' they all joined" (Przeworski, 1991, p. 74).

4. The Entitlement in Its Democratic Aspects

As far as democracy is concerned, there are many models to choose from. The United States model of federalism, for instance, views the "demos-constraining" aspect of federalism as essentially beneficial because it has the capacity to protect individual rights from being infringed upon by the central government's potential for producing populist majorities. But "when examined from the point of view of equality and efficacy, both of which are as important to the consolidation of democracy as is liberty, the picture becomes more complicated" (Stepan, 1999, p. 23). There is an important distinction between that which is *"demos-constraining"* and that which is *"demos-enabling."* For example, "in multinational polities . . . some groups may be able to participate fully as individual citizens only if they acquire, as a group, the right to have schooling, mass media, and religious or even legal structures that correspond to their language and culture" (*Id.*, p. 31).

Given these historical and cultural variations, the liberal tradition's emphasis upon individualism as the ultimate guarantor of rights and right-claims remains open to question. In fact, an objective assessment of liberalism's claims about its universalism and its corresponding emphasis upon individualism may be more supportive of exclusionary forms of governance and democracy, thereby creating a "democratic deficit" (see Chapter 4). As Stepan has observed, "while individual rights are universal, it is simply bad history to argue that in actual democracies all rights have been universal" (*Id.*, p. 32). After all, the struggle to reconcile "the imperatives of political integration with the legitimate imperatives of cultural difference has led countries to award certain minorities group-specific rights, such as those given to French-speaking Quebec in Canada, to cultural councils in Belgium, and to Muslim family courts in India" (*Id.*, p. 32). Regardless of these differences in the democratic experience, the primary point is that the democratic state is obligated to ensure that no group-specific right violates individual or universal rights. Hence, the danger of exclusionary versions of democracy must be counter-balanced by inclusionary governance and inclusionary democratic claims which are respectful and protective of the delicate balance between political integration on the one hand and the imperatives of group-specific rights on the other.

In his review of patterns of democratic forms of government in thirty-six countries, Arend Lijphart concluded his study with two major findings. First, that the great variety of formal and informal rules and institutions which are found in democracies can be reduced to a clear two-dimensional pattern on the basis of "the contrasts between majoritarian and consensus government." Second, as to the policy performance of democratic governments, "majoritarian democracies do not outperform the consensus democracies on macroeconomic management . . . but the consensus democracies do clearly outperform the majoritarian democracies with respect to the quality of democracy and democratic representation" (Lijphart, 1999, p. 301). This finding demonstates Lijphart's view that consensus democracies perform better in what he calls "the kindness and gentleness of their public policy orientation" (*Id.*, p. 301). In this regard, we may jatapose what Stepan called "demos-enabling" with Lijphart's "consensus democracies," and what Stepan called "demos-constraining" with Lijphart's "majoritarian democracies." Fundamentally, the differentiation constitutes, at least as far as public policy orientation is concerned, the differences which exist between the IS and the ES, whether the institutions of government are labeled democratic or not.

In the final analysis, these differentiations and distinctions are, in combination, vital considerations to be taken into account when assessing the obstacles and opportunities for an emerging inclusionary principle of entitlement according to need. As such, each of the aforementioned concepts is part of a cluster of issues to be addressed when undertaking the examination of inclusionary governance and its various democratic incarnations. For example, in capitalist democracy, the separation between civic status and class position moves in two different directions. On the one hand, socioeconomic position does not determine the right to citizenship. This fact is what is *democratic* in capitalist democracy. On the other hand, the power which resides in the capitalist to appropriate the surplus labor of workers is not dependent on a privileged juridical or civic status. Rather, capitalist democracy reveals that civic equality does not directly affect or significantly modify class inequality. That is, at the end of the day, what limits democracy in capitalism. Even with juridical equality and universal suffrage, class relations between capital and labor survive. In that sense, "political inequality in capitalist democracy not only coexists with socioeconomic inequality but leaves it fundamentally intact" (Wood, 1995, p. 213). It is this proclivity to maintain socioeconomic inequality which accounts for the survival and extension of the ES, exclusionary practices, and results even within societies which are constituted along formally "democratic" lines.

The survival of socioeconomic inequality within capitalist democracies and its exclusionary nature, as exemplified in growing wage-disparities and widening circles of poverty, constitutes the political, social, and juridical challenge to the claims of inclusionary governance. Inclusionary governance and inclusionary democracy stress the point that the right to development and the principle of entitlement according to need are more than just a synthesis of existing rights. It would be a fundamental mistake to view the right to development solely in terms of its international legal significance, for to do so would be to undermine and to underestimate its potentially major psychological significance within the international community. Additionally, "it serves to highlight the need to create a new international order, in social and cultural as much as in economic terms, to accompany the achievement of a new national order through improved respect for human rights" (Alston, 1987, p. 819). Alston has suggested that what is needed is a "bringing together of a variety of existing rights" and then, by emphasizing the need for international cooperation to achieve development, use it to make the "right to development" highlight "a dimension of specific rights which is sometimes overlooked" (Id., p. 819). Among these rights to development would be the right to food and the right to be free from hunger. Both of these rights are articulated in Article 11 of the International Covenant on Economic, Social and Cultural Rights. When viewed in light of the right to development, these rights stand for the proposition that "the amount and type of food required must be adequate not only for that purpose but also to facilitate the endeavors of the individual to realize his potential" (Id., p. 819).

At the most basic level, international law claims, as through the International Covenant on Economic, Social and Cultural Rights, identify the convergence of the normative force of law with its role in addressing the problems associated with poverty, human rights, and state sovereignty. The human right to subsistence (which is an element of the principle of entitlement according to need), stands for the proposition that there is a certain minimal level of well-being below which no individual should be allowed to fall. In this context, "malnutrition, lack of shelter, and the absence of protection from disease leave persons incapable of engaging in . . . autonomous activity" and it is precisely the protection of such activity "which is often thought to justify concern for civil and political rights in the first place" (Jones, 1999, p. 60). So, if the right to subsistence exists, "the indirect argument for susbsistence rights shows that there is a link between these 'socioeconomic' rights and the more traditional civil and political rights" (Id., p. 61). Human potential, under this analysis, can only be realistically advanced by the linkage of socioeconomic rights with civil and political rights, thereby rendering the case for the the practice and enactment of the principle of entitlement according to need a part of the inclusionary democratic project, as well as its underlying mandate. Explicating the dimensions of this mandate constitutes the topic to which we now turn.

D. THE LINKAGE OF SOCIOECONOMIC RIGHTS WITH POLITICAL/CIVIL RIGHTS IS THE TASK OF AN INCLUSIONARY DEMOCRATIC PROJECT

The mandate of the inclusionary democratic project is to undertake all necessary steps to bring about the practice and enactment of the principle of entitlement according to need. The dimensions of this mandate extend to

Establishing Perspectives

considerations of: (1) the right to self-determination as complementary to and potentially integrated with the right to development; (2) the linkage of self-determination with the development and enjoyment of human rights; (3) the right to participation and inclusion in governmental decision making, so as to unite the political community with the individual, insofar as civil, political, and economic rights, taken as a whole, describe and guarantee the rights of human existence; (4) the achievement of self-determination to uphold other human rights and other international norms; (5) inclusionary political associations and institutions that can accommodate the constant flux of circumstances, which also implies the evolution of a reconstructed notion of sovereignty, of which self-determination is an integral part; and (6) the redefinition of self-determination and "development" insofar as development is as much a prerogative of nations as of individuals within nations. We shall discuss each of these dimensions of the inclusionary democratic project in turn.

(1) *The right to self-determination is complementary to and integrated with the right to development.* The right to development has been broadly conceived and redefined in the second half of the 20th century by both First and Third World states. The right to development has implications for both the juridical notions of sovereignty and self-determination because an internationally constructed and recognized human rights regime has increasingly been forced to confront the objective problems associated with hunger, poverty, and global deprivation. Revised notions of utilitarianism have come to possess radical implications for global social policy. One such implication is the demand for a significant redistribution of wealth and resources from rich countries to poor. The demand also carries with it support for institutional changes "designed to ensure that the basic interests of everyone are protected, regardless of the citizenship of the individuals concerned" (Jones, 1999, p. 49).

By releasing the right to development from the bondage of a narrowly construed definition of sovereignty, the direction of international law has taken a turn toward a more utilitarian mandate. People, regardless of their national citizenship, should not be starving and trapped in poverty. In fact, it has been asserted that "redistributive taxation is an ethically acceptable way of dealing with large-scale impoverishment" for "if each human being has a right to be exempt from the hardships to which poverty gives rise, it is unacceptable to contain redistribution within nation-state boundaries for such a limitation threatens to leave many individuals in poverty" (*Id.*, p. 223).

Appreciation of this argument is prefigured in Rawls' "law of peoples." Rawls argues, in radical terms, that there is a fundamental "distinction between the law of peoples and the law of nations, or international law. The latter is an existing or positive legal order, however incomplete it may be in some ways, lacking, for example, an effective scheme of sanctions such as normally characterizes domestic law. The law of peoples, by contrast, is a family of political concepts with principles of right, justice, and the common good, that specify the content of a liberal conception of justice worked up to extend to and apply to international law. It provides the concepts and principles by which law is to be judged" (Rawls, 1999, p. 536).

Insofar as "peoples" have the right to self-determination, it is rather axiomatic that the right to development is contingent upon the viability of self-determiantion as an ordering principle of national and international life. Insofar as the right to development is an all-encompassing one, it is the rubric underneath which the linkage of socioeconomic rights with political/civil rights is to be concretely effectuated. The realization and enforcement of this linkage cannot remain abstract; therefore it falls to peoples and states to undertake the task of an inclusionary democratic project which brings national and international law into compliance with the claims associated with the articulated rights of self-determination and development. Insofar as there is little if any empirical evidence which offers support to the view that the creation of conditions which enable a state to realize its right to development will automatically lead to the creation of similarly favorable conditions for the realization of the right to development by individuals within the state, the Commission on Human Rights has reiterated that "development is as much a prerogative of nations as of individuals within nations" (Resolution 5 (XXXV) (1979), para.1).

Following this interpretative thrust, one scholar has recently asserted that "self-determination is a collective right. As such, it is related to the role the community plays vis-a-vis the individual. For the collective right to be carried out, however, certain preconditions must be met. Primary among these is the ability of those within the community to determine the goals and direction of the community—that is, to participate in the self-determining process" (Mills, 1998, p. 82). Participation as an objective political option represents the inclusionary democratic project at work in the task of effectuating the linkage between socioeconomic claims, as a matter of right, with the simultaneous articulation of political and civil rights in the processes of decision making and policy choice. Thus conceived, participation becomes an expression of the Rawlsian "law of peoples" by virtue of its assertion of a family of political concepts which centralize the political concepts of right, justice, and the common good. In this context, the right to self-determination is complementary to and integrated with the right to development.

(2) *The linkage of self-determination with the development and enjoyment of human rights also implies that human rights are a pre-condition for communal self-determination.* Communal self-determination cannot be divorced from human rights (Mills, 1998, p. 83). In this critical sense, "self-determination is a human right along with civil, political, and economic rights which, taken as a whole, describe and guarantee the rights of human existence" (*Id.*, p. 83). The argument is buttressed by the assertion that "the indirect argument for subsistence rights shows that there is a link beteen these 'socioeconomic' rights and the more traditional civil and political rights" (Jones, 1999, p. 61). The linkage is further established under the auspices of an inclusionary democratic project that focuses upon "piecing together fresh counter-hegemonic strategies . . . to ensure that democratic structures at all levels address the concerns of the great mass of citizens and not merely those of political elites" (Luckham, 1998, p. 315).

This interpretation applies especially to a highly diverse group of states which have emerged from Marxist and neo-Marxist theoretical traditions. While historical experience may have "alterted them to the traps of liberal democracy and market capitalism . . . as in Allende's Chile, Sandinista Nicaragua, or present-day South Africa," they have gained "a new appreciation of liberal rights and freedoms" and have tended to be "critical of the commandist proclivities of revolutionary movement and democratic centralism in socialist states" (*Id.*, pp. 315–316). The net result of this political gestalt is the argument that both socialism and democracy need to be reconstituted from the bottom up. This means a greater affirmation of gender and minority rights (*Id.*, p. 316). Having come to this historical juncture, there are distinct implications to be derived for the form and practice of democratic governance that is undertaken. These implications include, significantly, "a commitment to broader conceptions of citizenship than assured by liberal democracy on its own" as well as an "insistence on social and economic as well as political rights" (*Id.*, p. 316). Viewed in combination, recognizable right-claims are in the process of emerging which have an individualistic orientation, but are part of an indivisible whole with those rights which retain an essentially collectivist orientation.

The result is an inclusionary human rights regime which establishes the legal, social, cultural, political, and economic aspects of an inclusionary democratic project. It has been suggested that "only if this indivisibility is maintained will the danger of excessive emphasis on one aspect or the other be avoided" (Alston, 1987, p. 819). In a number of critical areas this insight is especially relevant. Specifically, it is relevant if one maintains that human rights are universal moral entitlements, i.e., that they are held equally by all human beings. The blending of welfare rights with civil and political rights suggests that "human rights, if not recognized within a given local jurisdiction, should generate international protest and action designed to protect the victims of such injustice" (Jones, 1999, p. 72). Pursuant to this interpretation, in order to achieve self-determination while at the same time upholding other human rights and international norms, "a variety of forms of political association outside of the sovereignty discourse need to be recognized which keep communities together in one kind of association, while permitting them to pursue their 'common lives' in others" (Mills, 1998, p. 94).

(3) *The right to participation and inclusion in governmental decision making unites the political community with the individual, insofar as civil, political, and economic rights, taken as a whole, describe and guarantee the rights of human existence.* In the post-Cold War world, with the collapse of bipolarity and the globalization of trade and finance, as well as corresponding concerns with the international plight of labor and the global environment, there is a growing philosophical, political, and legal recognition that a discursively grounded "system of rights" cannot be confined to the inherent limitations of one particular constitutional state because these concerns implicate the need for the globalization of rights. The political community, in the broadest sense, is now a cosmopolitan society which requires an inclusionary democratic project capable of uniting socioeconomic rights with political and civil rights.

As Habermas has argued, "the discrepancy between, on the one hand, the human-rights content of classical liberties and, on the other, their forms as positive law, which initially limits them to a nation-state, is just what makes one aware that the discursively grounded 'system of rights' points beyond the constitutional state in the singular toward the globalization of rights. As Kant realized, basic rights require, by virtue of their semantic content, an international, legally administered 'cosmopolitan society'" (Habermas, 1996, p. 456). The reasons for this assertion are not limited to pure discourse. The reasons to be given are also reflective of the situation in contemporary Western societies governed by the rule of law and the recognition that "politics has lost its orientation and self-confidence before a terrifying background: before the conspicuous challenges posed by ecological limits on economic growth and by increasing disparities in the living conditions in the Northern and Southern Hemispheres . . . in the face of the risks of renewed ethnic, national, and religious wars, nuclear blackmail, and international conflicts over the distribution of global resources" (*Id.*, p. xlii). Given these trends, it may be asserted that "only a democratic citizenship that does not close itself off in a particularistic fashion can pave the way for a *world citizenship* which is already taking shape today in worldwide political communications" (*Id.*, p. 514, italics in the original).

As to the role of international law, however, the principal conclusion is that "challenges set for law by the evolving needs of international life must be taken into account, but not at the expense of sacrificing the autonomy of the legal order" (Falk, 1971, p. 200). Even as drastic modifications and alterations in international affairs and relations come about, and as efforts are made to move from exclusionary forms of governance to more inclusionary modes, "as a matter of policy it seems essential in a world divided by tension and conflict to keep alive some respect for law as a transcendent social order, that is, to maintain some respect for law as a normative order that posits the way states ought to act as well as explains in legal language the way states do act" (*Id.*, p. 200). By retaining the transcendent power of law as a normative order, "even in highly political settings it remains useful to invoke rules of law as criteria of judgment, if for no other reason to mobilize domestic and international public opinion on some basis other than a mere appeal to expediency" (*Id.*, p. 200). This perspective on international law is rightly critical of jurisprudential deference to geopolitics, "which often functions as an unconscious determinant of juridical analysis" and serves to erode "the role of international law in promoting a preferred world order in the form of humane governance for the planet" (Falk, 1998, p. 200).

In short, it is necessary for the future of international law that it overcome its historical and jurisprudential deference to geopolitical concerns and the ideological orientation of those Western powers which endorsed the "Washington Consensus" of the 1980s and early 1990s. That is, it is necessary if inclusionary preferences are to be effectively translated into probabilities. Otherwise, the experience of recent decades, which has endorsed an economic policy shaped by a neoliberal criteria dedicated to the primacy of capital efficiency in the allocation of resources, will effectively subvert the principle of entitlement according to need, as well as evolving definitions of self-determination and human rights claims of a cosmopolitan variety. The geopolitics of the old order, which has traditionally defended privatization, liberalization, and neoliberal prescriptions for Eastern Europe, Russia, and Third World states, will continue to act as a hegemonic jurisprudence for capital accumulaton, regardless of the human cost.

The pursuit of international justice will require, among other things, the task of reconciling the promotion of economic growth with concerns about equity, and especially with the protection of those who are most economically vulnerable or disadvantaged (Falk, 1999, p. 430). This is particularly important in a situation where mainstream economists continue to stress the efficient allocation of society's scarce resources while, at the same time, "harsh social realities call into question the consequences of this means of allocation . . . Resources are not used 'efficiently' when there remain large amounts of unused industrial capacity and millions of unemployed workers. Modern capitalism appears totally incapable of mobilizing these untapped human and material resources" (Chossudovsky, 1998, p. 305). This situation has created a global crisis. A solution to this crisis has not been forthcoming as far as dealing with the exclusionary dimensions and results of the crisis are concerned. In part, solutions have not been set forth because "the internatonal order has inadequately addressed humanity's drastic problems, which has led many to call for a reexamination of the relationship between the individual and the state" (Felice, 1996, p. 63). While the crisis has worsened over the course of the last fifty years of the 20th century, there are international precedents for addressing the crisis in its current forms. The precedents include advances in international law, but significantly transcend these advances. There is, in other words, a separation between international law, per se, and the law of peoples, which needs to be bridged if the current global crisis is to move toward a humane resolution. The degree to which it is humane will, in large measure, be determined by the degree to which it is inclusive of both the civil and political rights of individuals as well as their socioeconomic claims.

From an international law perspective, it would be helpful to return to the innovative approach taken in the Algiers Declaration of the Rights of Peoples, adopted on July 4, 1976. Its preamble serves as a vivid reminder that dominant capitalist tactics and structures are at the root of a great deal of global human misery, "including a basic explanation of the general failure to realize those minimal rights associated with the basic needs of the peoples of the world" (Falk, 1981, p. 192). The Algiers Declaration also serves notice on governments, multinational corporations, and international banks and financial institutions, that their activities are subject to worldwide scrutiny and from a vantage point that is higher than that of national governments (*Id.*, p. 193). Now, the force and integrity of the declarations' claims are themselves subject to question, such as: "How shall we regard the Algiers Declaration?" "Does it purport to be law?" "On behalf of what community does it speak?" "Who appointed the authors of this declaration to speak on behalf of 'the peoples' of the world?" (*Id.*, p. 199). While governments failed to directly or indirectly participate in shaping the declaration, the fundamental claim of the Algiers Declaration is that "the peoples of the world possess the ultimate law-making authority, and that the validity of of governmental law-making capacity rests on a prior delegation of competence by the people" (*Id.*, p. 199).

The view contained in the Algiers Declaration reflects Rawls' definition of how the "law of peoples" is distinct from the traditional formulations of international law and that "this distinction between the law of peoples and the law of nations should be straightforward" (Rawls, 1999, p. 536). States rely on narrow definitions of "sovereignty" to bolster their claims to jurisprudential legitimacy and geopolitical "realities" while, in the alternative, the "law of peoples" rests on expanded definitions of self-determination and human rights. The "law of peoples" transcends the liberal idea that persons are first citizens and "as such free and equal members of society who hold those basic rights as the rights of citizens. It requires only that persons be responsible and cooperating members of society who can recognize and act in accordance with their moral duties and obligations" (Rawls, 1999, p. 552). In the case of the Algiers Declaration, membership in "society" means the global society.

Rawls' perspective is more widely incorporated within human rights discourse and jurisprudence because empirical investigations of international law and state practice, in addition to normative and theoretical interrogations of the social purpose of the state, have come to suggest that "the state cannot claim to be the sole arbiter of proper conduct within a particular territorial expanse. Rather, it is subject to a wide array of restrictions on its conduct, particularly with regard to the treatment of individuals and groups" (Mills, 1998, p. 126). Increasingly, the state is viewed as "an amalgamation of individuals and groups, all of which have certain rights and obligations with respect to each other, the juridical entity—the state—of which they are a part, and the wider international community" (*Id.*, p. 127).

If there is a rejection of this trend toward interdependence, the result may be the destruction of the bridge between individual rights—which are the foundation of modern human rights theory—and the need to complement the individual's rights with collective human rights. This complementarity between individual and collective rights must take into account: (1) the fact that individual rights can often only be satisfied in a collective context; (2) the collectivist traditions which dominate the cultural and political institutions of many developing countries; and (3) the political reality of the sovereign state as the dominant negotiating unit at the international level (Alston, 1987, p. 820). Rawls' concept of the law of peoples supplies a recent legitimation of collectivist human rights claims and their inclusionary capacity to establish the normative linkage of socioeconomic rights with political/civil rights in the tasks associated with an inclusionary democratic project. Still, Rawls' concept of the law of peoples does not stand alone. It is augmented by some established principles of international law. For example, to create a norm of customary international law, assuming that a state practice exists, means that the practice must be accompanied by an intention to state a legal principle. In other words, there must be a conception on the part of the state actors that the practice is required by international law. Thus, mere conduct is not sufficient to raise a practice to the level of principle. The conduct must be motivated by a conviction of obligation—*opinio juris* (Bergman, 1987, p. 239).

In this context, international law constitutes more than international morality. When states act in conformity with the precepts of international law, whether through diplomats and statesmen, or through national actions consistent with the principles and precepts of international law, the practice engaged in gives legitimation to the norms in question, whether the norms are based on treaty or custom (*Id.*, p. 232). Further, Third World nations have increasingly looked to the UN General Assembly as an international source for law making and the creation of a new normative structure which will enable them to be placed on a more equal playing field with the West. The consequence of this growing reliance has blurred the distinction between political and legal obligation insofar as UN resolutions have come to be considered the applicable rule of law. In this context, the Rawlsian concept of the law of peoples has found its institutional expression through the resolutions of the General Assembly and also discovered its legal significance enhanced vis-a-vis these same resolutions. Political and legal obligations may eventually be imposed on the conduct of Western-based financial institutions which have historically ignored the normative and practical implications of General Assembly resolutions.

Take, for example, the role of IMF conditionality requirements in the loan adustment process and its impact upon basic needs, socioeconomic claims, and the exercise of civil and political rights in recipient countries. To begin with, "conditionality" is not a legal term because it is not mentioned in the Articles of Agreement. However, the conditionality of IMF credits refers to the economic policies which the IMF expects a member to follow in order to be able to make use of the Fund's general resources (Gester, 1987, p. 535). As Third World governments sign off on these agreements, they are exposed to the unequal and hierarchical nature of the national and international income distribution and power structure. As such, the stabilization programs are manifestations of the reluctance of the dominant and hegemonic project of international finance to avoid serious discussions on distributional questions. The IMF becomes a tacit ally to global forces which seek to prevent a reduction or mitigation of the existing inequalities. In turn, the maintenance of inequalities creates new forms of political, economic, legal, social, and cultural exclusion for many millions of people. The inescapable conclusion is that in the absence of a clear policy to promote greater equality and reduce the existing inequalities, the eradication of poverty becomes a utopian fantasy.

The unification of socioeconomic rights claims with civil/political rights claims would have the effect of imposing a basic needs approach to conditionality. Further, it would also have an anti-exclusionary emphasis which would force governments throughout the Third World to transform their current political structures to become more inclusionary. Why? Because with the establishment of a basic needs oriented performance criteria, both IMF officials and the heads of Third World governments would have to end a practice which has allowed elites to shift the burden of adjustment to the weaker segments of society.

We may ask why this has not been done before. Why have exclusionary states continued exploitative practices with such drastic outcomes and growing rates of poverty? In part, the answer is that governments have conveniently been allowed to blame the IMF for the hardships of the stabilization programs in spite of the fact that they carry a large measure of responsibility for the result. In this regard, "it is part of the services of the IMF not to refuse the blame in public in order to discharge the governments of an often unpleasant domestic political situation. So, the IMF, looking after the interests of the foreign creditors and governments mainly pursuing the interests of a small elite, may become allies at the cost of the politically voiceless poor" (Gester, 1987, p. 542). The ES is a product of the dialectic which exists between international processes of capital accumulation and the political defense of elite interests, which maintain their power and profit at the expense of the poor and marginalized. The ES continues to exist as the antithesis of the IS and an international human rights regime. The continued lack of accountability which the ES and the IMF enjoy serves to underscore the observation that "it seems that while human rights has won the battle with sovereignty, it does not know what to do with the victory" (Mills, 1998, p. 194).

The challenge of working to unify socioeconomic rights (universal and inclusionary in scope) with political/civil rights constitutes a tentative answer. The scope of this challenge is well-articulated by Felice who notes that "a stark global reality of misery informs the discussion of the right to development at the United Nations. Economic globalization—a single, integrated world economy—has had a profound effect on human existence, structurally limiting equality of opportunity. One-fourth of our world is rich, while the vast majority is poor. The most vicious ethnic strife is among the poor. Migration is not permitted. Redistribution of income is not considered" (Felice, 1996, p. 78). The task of the inclusionary democratic project is to embark upon the unification of socioeconomic rights with political/civil rights so that such a redistribution of income is the result. In this way, the historical promise of the right to development and the fulfillment of the principle of entitlement according to need can be achieved and universally recognized. Such a result would heal the current gap between the claims of international law and the law of peoples. Inclusionary governance, under this rubric, would be able to bring integrity to both by fulfilling the promises which are inherent in each.

(4) *The achievement of self-determination upholds other human rights and other international norms which are conducive to realizing the goals, values, policies, and norms of inclusionary governance and the mandate of the inclusionary democratic project, which is to bring about the practice and enactment of the principle of entitlement according to need.* The reality of an interdependent world creates a transformed environment in which the principle of self-determination takes on new dimensions and added significance. The principle's enhanced significance and transformatory capacity in both international law and international relations is derived from the dialectical forces associated with new modalities of collaborative or combative operations on the one hand, and of shared subjectivities on the other.

The implications for inclusionary governance, in its democratic forms, of the practice and enactment of the principle of entitlement according to need, as well as the right to development, arise out of the realization that "any systematic suppression of human rights by any government produces deprivatory effects not only upon its own people, but also upon peoples beyond the border" (Chowdhury, 1987, p. 98). As McDougal and Reisman

Establishing Perspectives

expressed it, "when such acts precipitate major inclusive deprivations, jurisdiction is internationalized and inclusive concern and measures become permissible" (McDougal and Reisman, 1968). Exclusionary forms of governance have arisen as a consequence of the interaction between states and the evolving multilateral regime associated with international capital and globalization. Inclusive deprivations are expressions of this interaction, especially in the context of globalization's capacity to undermine the normative achievements of the old multilateralism, "especially through its tendency to impose the discipline of global and regional capital upon states" (Falk, 1999, p. 106). The gulf between inclusive deprivations on the one hand, and the claims of inclusionary governance and humane governance on the other exposes the hypocrisy of the neoliberal ideology.

Neoliberal ideology is incompatible with the project of inclusionary and humane governance because it confines the role of the new multilateralism to the civil and political domain, thereby avoiding accountability to socioeconomic claims related to human rights, equity, and justice concerns. This rather pessimistic assessment arises out of the duality of the relationship between neoliberalism and the transnational mobility of capital. It is a situation which exposes the vulnerability of workers in high wage countries, "reinforcing their hostility to immmigrant labor and a special resistance to most categories of transnatonal economic migration" (Falk, 1999, p. 102; see also Pena, 1997, pp. 317–324). In an integrated world, therefore, it is "hypocritical to concede, on the one hand, interdependence and cooperation among nations and peoples in social, economic, political and cultural activities which directly affect behavior toward human rights while, on the other hand, denying common international responsibility to breaches of those rights arising from the same social intercourse. In other words, international law has erected artificial territorial nationalism and personalism in the area of social responsibility to otherwise transnational causes and effects" (Gutto, 1987, p. 289).

In few areas of international life is this hypocrisy more evident than in the IMF's structural adjustment programs—that are "conducive to a form of 'economic genocide' which is carried out through the conscious and deliberate manipulation of market forces" (Chossudovsky, 1997, p. 37)—which affect the lives of more than four billion people. In this international environment, income disparities between nations are superimposed on wide income disparities between social-income groups within nations. This means that in many Third World nations, "at least 60 percent of national income is concentrated in the upper 20 percent of the population" while in many low and middle-income developing countries, 70 percent of rural households have a per capita income which is between 10 and 20 percent of the national average" (*Id.*, p. 41; see also Falk, 1975, pp. 17–22).

These disparities are largely the consequence of two interrelated factors: the structure of commodity trade and the unequal division of labor. These disparities extend from Third World countries to the countries of the former Soviet bloc, placing them in a subordinate status in the global economic system. Recognition of this emerging situation has great implications for the Wesphalian model of world order, which assumed that states are, to a greater or lesser degree, the exclusive agents of instrumentalization. However, in a globalized world economy, "states are themselves increasingly instrumentalized by concealed external forces, such as markets and profit margins, and their instrumentalization is expressed by way of the weakening of commitment to such foreign policy goals as human rights and environmental protection, and to the rerouting of these tasks to the United Nations" (Falk, 1995, p. 76). This trend provides support for "an argument in favor of 'resituating the state,' that is, strengthening its capacity to mediate between market drives and populist social forces" (Id., p. 76). Yet to strengthen the capacity of the state as a mediator between market drives and populist forces exposes the reality that such a "resituation" of the state will remain in an arena of global reform that is "likely to remain contested and unresolved" (Falk, 1999, p. 51).

There are a number of factors as to why the state remains an important and vitally contested arena of power. First, governance involves more than merely good public administration and managerial skill. While economic reforms, political liberalization, and globalization have altered the function and potentially the nature of the state, the state remains the source of patronage and retains its status as the prize for social contenders for whom power rather than control of production remains the key asset (Sayigh, 1999, pp. 228–230). Second, while social cleavages have always existed, the point is that they play a new role within the framework of structural alignments in the domestic and international economies. At the regional level, the state has proven adept at retaining the means of political leverage and control while, at the same time, reclaiming its central role as mediator. So, in both political and managerial terms, the state is uniquely equipped to act as not only the central mediator of disputes but can also be an effective guarantor of a free market economy, civil society, and, potentially, inclusionary forms of democracy (Id., p. 230). However, the potential for building inclusionary forms of democracy has been blocked throughout many parts of the Third World because the presumed impact of democracy as a global value has been largely contained "by such mechanisms as periodic elections to assemblies with severely constrained powers or appointment to consultative councils" (Id., p. 228). Given these limitations, the mere freedom to form political parties has "not compensated for the loss of protection previously offered to lower income groups by corporatism in the welfare state" (Id., p. 228). Hence, the growth of exclusionary governance has actually coincided with the spread of democracy as it has been institutionalized under these constrained conditions and practices.

The expansion of exclusionary forms of governance, operating under the rubric of political democracy, exposes the fact that political/civil rights must be ultimately conjoined with socioeconomic rights and the principle of entitlement according to need in order that inclusionary states may be created in order to meet the needs of lower income groups and actualize the right to development. However, continuing forms of exclusion and the general state of economic underdevelopment, which exists in almost all the countries of Asia, Africa, and Latin America, exposes the reality that "human rights progress, while definitely subversive of statist pretensions . . . still remained generally compatible with the maintenance of existing geopolitical structures of authority and wealth in the world and, as such, exerted only a marginal influence" (Falk, 1999, p. 98). Given this history, it is not altogether inaccurate to conclude that, "at the global level, as at that of the nation-state, the free market does not promote stability or democracy. Global democratic capitalism is as unrealizable a condition as world-wide communism" (Gray, 1998, p. 21).

Both authoritarian and exclusionary practices, as well as some critical arenas of democratic capitalism, have been rendered effectively immune from external human rights pressures, whether these pressures emanate from individual states, the UN, or transnational forces. Such a result should be of no surprise, in spite of the promise of GATT reform or the processes associated with trade liberalization. The reason for skepticism is that "institutional reform is practically useless, when the basic concept remains unchecked. Experience with previous reforms of GATT shows clearly the fallacy of such an approach in attempting to resolve basic conceptual conflicts. Efforts should thus be concentrated on overcoming the dominance of the major trading countries in GATT in order to achieve an equal balance of interests between developed and LDCs by adapting the GATT concept to the divergent trade needs and problems of both groups" (Ibrahim, 1987, p. 430). Together, the World Bank, the IMF, and the WTO provide a level of global economic management that has led to the wholesale reorganization of economies and societies in the South (Redclift and Sage, 1999, p. 137). Also, institutional reform is practically useless because of the growing "incongruence between the increasing market orientation of international law and the inability of international governance institutions or of many sovereign states to cope with the problems of inequality that markets alone do not resolve" (Kingsbury, 1999, p. 67; see also Jones, 1999, p. 228). There is still an impasse on the issue of social standards around the globe, which exemplifies the complexity of the contending interests converging to shape a post-Cold War global social policy (Deacon, 1999, p. 236).

At the close of the 20th century, the inescapable conclusion is that the commitment to the universal formal equality of states in the context of the sovereignty model has not resolved the most critical underlying problems of the global order. In terms of state capacity to manage issues of national economic and social policy, their ability to represent and regulate, and their guarantees of property rights and civil rights, many putative states have exhibited only the trappings of the effective functions of states, not their substance. Hence, the traditional sovereignty-based system has proven itself to be a tragedy and travesty for the excluded, marginalized and dispossessed, "in which priorities of good governance and human welfare have been subordinated to a very formal commitment to ineffective structures" (*Id.*, p. 84). The ineffectiveness of these structures is not limited to issues of mere efficiency, but extends in an egregious manner into systems of exclusionary governance and the reinforcement of a network of exclusionary states around the globe. If international law is to reclaim its role in advancing global society toward workable and visionary solutions, it must be reconstituted to accommodate the concerns of the excluded, and provide effective enforcement mechanisms for their inclusion into the frameworks of national and international decision making.

In this task, the role and purpose of international law can and must be "reconstituted," along with the role of a "resituated" state, capable of acting as a mediator between market drives and populist pressures. After all, both the state and international law deal with boundary issues. With respect to law, "in a most primitive sense international law posits boundaries upon conflict. These boundaries function as limits upon the means available to states in contention with one another" (Falk, 1971, p. 193). Obviously, law's role in this context has been applied to states in a period of warfare. Yet, in an age of globalization, with "economic warfare" and "competitiveness" replacing traditional boundary considerations, there are new boundaries to be identified. These are the boundaries of poverty and wealth, opportunity and disadvantage, disparities of power and wealth versus an equitable balance of each. The right to development, the achievement of broadly shared patterns of self-determination, the realization of the principle of entitlement according to need—all constitute the conceptual universe of inclusionary governance and its political, normative, and legal claims upon nation-states and the institutions which affect global governance in all of its forms and manifestations.

The question arises: How do we create and apply international law standards that are capable of advancing inclusionary rights and principles of democratic governance on a global basis? While the expression "source of law" is figurative and highly ambiguous, "it is used not only to designate the different methods of creating law but also to characterize the reason for the validity of law, and especially the ultimate reason. The constitution of a state determines the organs and the procedure of legislation. General international law or the community constituted by international law also has its 'constitution.' The constitution of the international community is the set of rules of international law which regulate its creation, or, in other terms, which determine the 'sources' of international law" (Kelsen, 1966, p. 437). However, it may be argued that, in the context of international law, any notion of a "constitution" is misplaced "because it may create a misleading impression that the international legal order possesses the same qualities, including a constitutional machinery for law-making, as domestic legal orders" (Danilenko, 1993, p. 15).

The reality is that the international community lacks even a superficial semblance of the constitutionally institutionalized machinery of law making which is typical to a developed domestic legal order. As the UN Secretary-General Javier Perez de Cuellar observed: "We do not always think of the world community as possessing a coherent law making mechanism" (60 ILA 78, 79 (1982)). In spite of this observation, there are certain fundamental rules governing law-making. If these fundamental rules were absent, there would be no modern system of international law at all. Treaties, custom, general principles of international law, the concept of *jus cogens*, all constitute avenues through which nations pressing for rapid legal reforms can seek the renovation of their respective domestic societies as well as incorporate international legal norms respective of human rights through bills of rights.

It has also been suggested that "new community-based types of lawmaking may become a reality . . . when global interdependence reaches such a high degree that it becomes a force compelling states to abandon the idea of sovereignty in favor of the overriding interests of the community as a whole" (Danilenko, 1993, p. 304). To establish these overriding interests, it has been suggested that the international community undertake those tasks associated with the realization of global constitutionalism. In the most broadly conceived terms, however, a concern with global constitutionalism "implies a conception of justice and order . . . inspired by an acceptance of world order values, which are themselves always in the process of gestation and evolution, expressive of democratizing concerns but also protective of limits on political options" (Falk, 1993, p. 15).

Part of the difficulty with realizing global constitutionalism is that there is no single set of cross-civilization values which rise to the level of world order values, as exemplified by differing conceptions of what is constitutive of "human rights" (Donnelly, 1994, pp. 97–117). Further, world order values are still emerging in the unfinished context of a struggle between sovereignty on the one hand and self-determination on the other. While sovereignty is far from dead, its unquestionable status as a norm has rightly been devalued by the events which shaped the history of the 20th century. Compliance with international human rights standards has been far from complete since 1945. The crises of genocide in Rwanda (Prunier, 1995), as well as the tragedy of Kurdistan (Randall, 1997), are testimony to sovereign non-compliance with human rights standards. In addition, new forms of slavery have arisen in the context of the new global economy, creating a whole new group of excluded persons considered as economically "disposable" (Bales, 1999). Along with these trends, modern plagues have come to be increasingly associated with the linkage between infections and inequalities (Farmer, 1999). And, where the practice of sovereignty has been used as an excuse of elites to embark upon civil wars and the terrorizing of their own people, the proliferation of refugee crises have come to be a symbol of the practice of exclusionary governance and the entrenched dominance of the ES as an unfettered vehicle for exacerbating state violence and forcing massive migrations of peoples (Loescher, 1993; Zolberg, Suhrke, and Aguayo, 1989; Korn, 1999; UNHCR, 1993; UNHCR, 1995).

A devaluation of old conceptions of sovereignty is necessary because sovereignty not only impedes rule-making; it may also obstruct compliance control. Case studies which exemplify this process involve the war in Chechnya (Lapidus, 2000), the conflict over Nagorno-Karabakh (Maresca, 2000), the tragedy of Somalia (Menkhaus and Ortmayer, 2000), the failure to act in the case of Rwanda (Suhrke and Jones, 2000), and a coup and collapse in the Congo (Zartman and Vogeli, 2000). While violence could have been prevented, in too many cases it has not been prevented. The leadership of the nations involved often made choices, in the name of sovereignty, to undertake actions leading to deadly conflict that were neither legally nor morally justified. Still, sovereignty is not merely negative, for it may play a positive role in effectuating greater state responsibility. This is particularly the case with regard to explicating the purposive sources of ethnic conflict and the responsibility of national leaders for such conflicts. The Carnegie Commission issued a study on preventive diplomacy, for example, which concluded that "while all these conflicts have deep historical roots, the driving and dominant dynamic was more purposive than primordialist, much more the consequence of a volitional calculus than historical determinism. . . . To be sure, history has its legacies. . . . But there was nothing inevitable about deadly conflicts in any one of these cases. . . . They were fed, shaped, manipulated, directed, and turned toward the purposes of leaders and others whose interests were served by playing the ethnic card" (Jentleson, 2000, p. 322).

Global interdependence has at least served to reveal that there are many arenas of common concern which promote international consensus. This emerging consensus is partially responsible for trends to reshape and reconfigure international law and its applications. One consequence of this trend is the Realists' incorporation into their legal analysis of the materials and perspectives native to the traditional practitioners of statecraft. This has led to the allegation that they have obliterated the distinction between law and politics—that they have substituted Machiavelli for Grotius (Farer, 1998, p. 331). The union of law and politics has opened up space for greater emphasis upon the normative features of international life, thereby allowing international law to attain greater practical expression in statecraft. Whatever the merits of the allegation, there is a growing consensus that "some normative framework is necessary even if one agrees that conflict prevention, mitigation, and termination will usually be approached most effectively in a flexible, mediatory posture rather than a rigorous, hierarchicial, rule-directed one" (Id., p. 346). Ideally, politics involve the practice of mediation leading to conflict prevention, while law, too often, has been conceived in its more traditional and limited function as a rule-directed exercise, open to varying interpretations. Yet, the reality is that "political decision-making need not require the exclusion of international law" (Falk, 1967, p. 481). However, if political decision making does exclude international law from its calculus, then "such an exclusion of law from the procedures of political decision-making does suggest a willingness to conceive of national interest as exclusively defined by national will and by the realtive capabilities of interested parties to assert control over the event in question" (Id., p. 481).

With the expansion of a more normative legal framework, the evolution of new overriding interests, expressive of the entire international community, requires the unification and inclusion of normative concerns which transcend the traditional focus of international law with its preconceptions about the hallowed nature of geopolitics as currently structured. This means that the international legal community, if it is responsive to the need to incorporate political practices of humane governance with established norms, has the choice of remaking the world by acknowledging that there has been no disappearance of the North-South divide. Indeed, the real challenge is that the international legal community, regional communities, and individual nation-states merely make changes in the way that the North-South divide is being managed (Acharya, 1999, p. 97). In other words, the choice is between the defense of established practices of exclusionary governance or, in the

Establishing Perspectives

alternative, a movement toward more inclusionary forms of governance that reconcile the normative claims of inclusion with the practice and exercise of raw political power.

With the expansion of a more normative legal framework, the overriding interests of the international community are beginning to find new normative and legal expression in the context of the rights of indigenous peoples (Falk, 1989, pp. 199–220), the growing acceptance of governmental accountability vis-a-vis the Nuremberg principle (*Id.*, pp. 221–227), a growing concern with the protection of the environment in light of the dangers associated with the long-term effects of nuclear war (*Id.*, pp. 167–195), growing international law restraints placed upon biological weaponry (*Id.*, pp. 127–154), and the evolution of a legal regime for the control of nuclear weapons (*Id.*, pp. 105–126). To this impressive list, we have the capacity to make some additions. Insofar as the achievement and recognition of the right of self-determination upholds other human rights and international norms which are conducive to realizing the goals, values, policies and norms of inclusionary governance, we may assert that the right of self-determination also gives rise to supplying the legal foundation for a global democratic project which is inclusionary in scope, by virtue of its capacity to effectuate the practice and enactment of the principle of entitlement according to need.

(5) *Political associations and institutions must become inclusionary, or be created to be inclusionary, in order to accommodate the constant flux of circumstances, which also implies the evolution of a reconstructed norm of sovereignty, of which self-determination is an integral part. A reconstructed norm of sovereignty must encompass: (a) an acknowledgment of the evolving correspondence between the principles of justice in domestic law and international law, (b) an acknowledgment that the principle of equity is not a concept limited to judicial decision making, and (c) an acknowledgment that the operation of large modern states as law-oriented bureaucracies assures the automatic application of international law in many areas of transnational activity.* The historical application of the legal doctrine of sovereignty has been diminished in the last half of the 20th century. While there are many explanations offered for it, two need to be emhasized here. First, sovereignty is not an absolute good insofar as the state that claims sovereignty deserves respect only as long as it protects the basic rights of its citizens and subjects. Second, there are circumstances in which the moral good of sovereignty must yield to superior values and imperatives, such as those of "global humanity" and "humane governance," which allow for the protection of human beings from evils such as the violation of basic human rights to life and security, in all of its dimensions (Hoffmann, 1998, p. 159; see also Chomsky, 1994). In this regard, the project of inclusionary democratic governance has three major implications for a reconstructed norm of sovereignty.

First, a reconstructed norm of sovereignty is an acknowledgment of the evolving correspondence between the principles of justice in domestic law and in international law. The late 20th century's global politics has created a new normative context for the correspondence between domestic and international law applications of the principles of justice. This correspondence has been accelerated by the growing interdependence of domestic economies and societies, as well as their interactions with the international realm. In large measure, for example, great legal advances have been made against racial discrimination (Lauren, 1988; Banton, 1996). For this reason, "whatever principles of justice we are prepared to acknowledge in the domestic case, we should be prepared to acknowledge in the international case as well" (Beitz, 1979, 1999, p. 200).

While the establishment of an extensive global trading network may not rise to the level of justifying such an analogy, the Rawlsian conception of justice as fairness and the law of peoples may justify such an analogy. Its justification, under this rubric, would allow the concept of "justice as reciprocity" to come into play with all of its normative and practical implications. Further, the Rawlsian argument conceives of society as more than a system of simple exchange. Whether at the domestic or international level, then, mere exchange is not enough to constitute activation of the principles of justice and reciprocity, except insofar as unequal exchange exposes the injustices and lack of reciprocity between the Northern and Southern hemispheres. Acknowledgment of this non-reciprocity opens the possibilities for a kind of corrective equity to enter into an assessment of trading agreements because "the basic law of the trading system is that of supply and demand within a free trade regime. While the system recognizes the paramount importance of this law to the efficient operation of the global marketplace, it has also come to accommodate principles of equity to remedy its harsher effects on the weakest parties" (Franck, 1995, p. 58). Hence, the Rawlsian notion of reciprocity has legal and economic ramifications which also point to the need to create a more inclusionary trading regime, supported by international law standards reflective of the principles of justice, equity, and reciprocity.

Politically, the inclusionary thrust of these changes would have objective ramifications for the legislative arrangements produced by nation-states and serve to accelerate greater compliance on their part with the demands and principles embodied in international law. In a new afterword to his classic book *Political Theory and International Relations*, Beitz notes that "the growth and structure of the world economy . . . and the elaboration of global finance and regulatory regimes only strengthen the impression of an evolving global basic structure with consequences for individual life prospects whose scale and character are analogous to those of the institutional structure of domestic society. Indeed, it seems increasingly difficult to distinguish the one from the other; the structures of the world political economy so interpenetrate those of domestic society that one is often at a loss to assign the causal responsibility for structural inequalities to one or the other level" (Beitz, 1979, 1999, p. 202). Beitz is not alone in coming to terms with this dilemma. The implications obviously reach into previously held conceptions of sovereignty and explain, in part, why the legal concept of sovereignty needs to be reconstructed so as to accommodate the new global sociopolitical and socioeconomic environment.

Arrighi and Silver have observed that "unlike the global financial expansion, the proliferation in the number and variety of transnational business organizations and communities is a novel and probably irreversible feature of the present hegemonic crisis. It has been a major factor in the disintegration of the US hegemonic order and can be expected to continue to shape ongoing systemic changes through a general, though by no means universal, disempowerment of states" (Arrighi and Silver, 1999, p. 278). The disempowerment of states implies a disempowerment of the concept of sovereignty, as previously conceived. Therefore, the reconstruction is an inevitable development for the dawn of the 21st century. All that remains unresolved is the nature, scope, and depth of its reconstruction and whether its reconstruction will move in the direction of the value preferences of exclusionary or inclusionary forms of governance.

Second, a reconstructed norm of sovereignty is an acknowledgment that the principle of equity is not a concept limited to judicial decision making. Rather, "it may also be the basis for mitigating the legal parameters established by a treaty system; or it may be the basis for an altogether new legal institutional regime. Some instances of both the former and the latter are found in the laws established to create a global market for commodities" (Franck, 1995, p. 58). Yet the focus of international law is not limited to the efficient operation of the global marketplace. The focus of international law extends into those realms of human concern which are touched by considerations of the principles of equity so as "to remedy its harsher effects on the weakest parties" (Id., p. 58). The enlargement of the parameters of legal, ethical, normative, economic, social, and political concerns with regard to the weakest parties creates a practical opening for addressing the problems of exclusion, in all of the aforementioned arenas, and the possibilities for building a more inclusionary framework for governance in each of these arenas. After all, "in the developed states, the gap between rich and poor is addressed through extensive, if still inadequate remedial programs which are widely accepted by all classes as a necessary part of the social compact" (Id., p. 414).

Further, in the developed nations, there are more elaborate systems of wealth transfer, which include programs such as Head Start for poor children who have been marginalized by deprivation or broken families, educational scholarships, and the provision of a variety of programs to resocialize human aspirations and functionality. Yet "the international community provides very little of these rudiments of economic and social fairness for its most deprived" (Id., p. 414). Because of this disparity, the 1960s witnessed the growth the Non-Aligned Nations Movement (NAM), while the 1970s brought a campaign for a New International Economic Order. Countering these trends, the 1980s and 1990s brought about the dismantling of the welfare state, in First and Third World contexts, and the rise of neoliberal orthodoxy with its emphasis upon structural adjustment programs, privatization, economic liberalization, and the Reagan/Thatcher-doctrine which stressed the "rolling back of the state" in order to disaggregate the realm of state responsibility from the provision of welfare rights, which were previously viewed as inherent in a viable social contract/compact.

The legacy of the 1980s and 1990s for millions of people in both the First and Third Worlds is a legacy of state-sanctioned marginalization and exclusion (Grieder, 1997). In order to gloss over the crises rendered by the decline of the welfare-state and the rise of exclusionary forms of governance at all levels, elites sought "to reconcile the obvious contradiction between a free market ideology and a technological nationalism" by allowing US officials to indulge "the pretense that defense and commerical life were wholly separate realms" (Kuttner, 1991, p. 193). They are not separate realms. The ramifications of their mutual interdependence constitute a strong argument for not only a reconstructed legal conception of sovereignty, but also an acknowledgment of the evolving correspondence between the principles of justice in domestic law as well as international law. Only in the discovery of this correspondence can the promise of humane governance and the inclusionary democratic project find an expression of global unity, prefigured in social movements seeking self-determination and, ultimately, realized within the legal framework at both domestic and international levels.

Third, and finally, the operation of large modern states as law-oriented bureaucracies assures the automatic application of international law in many areas of transnational activity (Falk, 1971, p. 196). Both legal advisors to governments and the domestic courts of large states assume the general applicability of international law. In most cases, a government is interested in "satisfying the expectations of the parties in controversy about the requirements of law, and does not have any inclination to assert any governmental policy at variance with international law—even in the event of such variance" (Id., p. 196). Having made this general observation, a more detailed discussion is in order regarding the "contradictions" of capitalist democracies.

There are left-wing theories and conservative theories about these contradictions. It is necessary to mention them at this point in reference to the full scope of the problems confronted by large-scale capitalist democracies in modern states, reacting to the international forces of globalization and the pressures of populist democratic constituencies. On the left, theories of "late capitalism" have predicted an imminent "legitimacy crisis" of the state. In response to this crisis, the state "was compelled to instrumentalize its democratically based power in order to fulfill the ever more demanding functional requisites of the capitalist economy" while, at the same time, respecting those capital interests which could not, on their own account, be "normatively justified under the criterion of 'governability'" (Scharpf, 1999, p. 33; see also Offe, 1972, 1984; Habermas, 1973, 1976). On the conservative side, by contrast, "theories of 'overloaded' government predicated an inflation of political demands in competitive mass democracies which would force governments to intensify taxation and economic regulation to an extent that would eventually destroy the viability of capitalist economies" (Scharpf, 1999, p. 33). From either of these perspectives, the inescapable conclusion was that the precarious symbiosis of a democratic state and a capitalist economy could not long endure.

The precarious symbiosis of the democratic state and a capitalist economy has reached new dimensions in the case of the regional efforts being undertaken to build the EU. Some critics have argued that it is a thoughtless and inadequately prepared attempt to impose a certain type of unfamiliar bureaucratic style of governance on new member countries. The implication

Establishing Perspectives 459

is that, at the very heart of the EU organization, there resides "an ignorance of, or ignoring of, the deepest civic traditions and habits, the cultural psychology of the various states" (Conquest, 2000, p. 261). The gulf that lies between the democratic state and the capitalist economy is even more evident when it is possible to point to certain advantages under the EU, though none under Maastrict or the Euro, which have accrued in precisely those areas of governance that have nothing to do with political assimilation. And, it has been asserted, "even economically, they do not balance out the disadvantages incurred from other parts of the bargain" (*Id.*, p. 263). This result is, to a large extent, the consequence of the fact that the EU is a forced creation "and it has proved inadequate to finding a joint foreign policy with the rest of the democratic world, or even as yet within its own councils" (*Id.*, p. 265). Despite these particular shortcomings, however, the EU can be considered to be a power of international significance in the international system through the capabilities of both the Union and its Member States. Furthermore, "its economic strength and the network of relationships that it has created in the international political economy encompass an area that is undergoing substantive change as a consequence of the relative decline of the United States" (Whitman, 1998, p. 148).

This First World undertaking is mirrored in developing countries which "have begun restructuring the nature of their intervention in the domestic economy, liberalizing their domestic trade and investment regimes, privatizing state-owned enterprises, and pursuing a variety of economic reforms" (Biersteker, 1995, p. 174). This undertaking is in direct conflict with the meaning of "development" as defined by the Brandt Commission Report, published in 1980, which argued that "we must not surrender to the idea that the whole world should copy the models of highly industrialized countries," but rather "development strategies which used to aim at increasing production as a whole will have to be modified and supplemented in order to achieve a fairer distribution of incomes taking into account the essential needs of the poorest strata and the urgency of providing employment for them" (Brandt Commission, 1980, pp. 23–24). The issue of governmental accountability to address the problems of the poorest strata return us to the implications that this accountability demands of governments and the inclusionary claims of international social movements, as well as international law.

To begin with, the dynamics of globalization and state responses to it have transformed the basic discourse of development. With the removal of the fundamental opposition between the capitalist West and the socialist East, the boundaries of development discourse have been extended beyond old conceptual and ideological boundaries. In the new Post-Cold War world, Luttwak has defined the hidden effects of free market capitalism as "turbo-capitalism," which accounts for a paradigm shift from "power politics" to "geo-economics" (Luttwak, 1999, pp. 133–151). The old traditional power politics invoked the means of military strength, diplomacy, propaganda, and weapons development to effectuate the goals of territorial security, expansion, influence over other states, and the achievement of prestige. The shift that has occured, however, toward "geo-economics" has created two new categories of "means." The first set of means propels state-assisted and directed private entities toward high-risk research and development and market-penetration investments. The second set of means, solely in the domain of the state, involves tariffs, quotas, regulatory and covert impediments to imports, and reliance on economic and technical intelligence. In combination, these "means" are designed to reach certain designated goals, including the conquest or defense of roles in strategic industries (i.e., telecommunications, information technology, biotechnology, aerospace). The implications of this shift from "power politics" toward "geo-economics" have both political and economic components. On the economic side, there are implications for severe comparative disadvantage for firms in targeted industries if unprotected or poorly protected by ineffective or uncooperative state bureaucracies and governments. Additionally, there is the danger of chronic overcapacity in sectors in which state-assisted firms compete for market shares beyond profitability limits. These trends may also result in the waste of resources by overinvestment. On the political side, "geo-economics" is power-enhancing for governing elites, who cannot control plain business. In this context, "geo-economic" struggles may replace "power politics" in stimulating national cohesion while, at the same time, eroding residual power politics alliances (*Id.*, p. 134).

The implications for international law arising from Luttwak's analysis are vital to appreciate the differences which are even more stark between forms of exclusionary governance versus those of inclusionary governance. Further, the implications for development discourse have also been fundamentally altered as a consequence of this paradigm shift. Therefore, I suggest that it will be necessary to work toward a convergence of international legal analysis with an analysis of the inclusionary potential and possibilities for development discourse. From an international law perspective, Thomas Franck has posited that with respect to economic fairness, the 1970s campaign for a New International Economic Order (NIEO) had already shifted attention to the international system "both as the cause and perpetrator of injustice and as the locus of appropriate remedial measures. This shift has occurred at a time when the globalization of so much that affects the quality of life has begun to impinge on the consciousness of even the most fortunate of citizenries" (Franck, 1995, p. 415).

This transformation of consciousness is already evident in the context of the aforementioned contradictions between the democratic state and the imperatives of the capitalist economy, within the context of the EU (Tridimas, 1999; Winter, Curtain, Kellermann, Witte, 1996; Cumper and Wheatley, 1999; Sorensen, 1996; Miles and Thranhardt, 1995; Ucarer and Puchala, 1997; Hooghe and Marks, 1999; Moravcsik, 1998; Rosa, 1999; Hettne, 1997). Still, what holds even greater global meanings and implications are the ramifications for moving toward inclusionary governance at all levels (governmental, business, legal, economic, social, and cultural) which are implicated in "the convergence of these historic tendencies" which have "laid the foundation for a widening communitarian consensus that in the world, as in the state, the happenstance of affluence carries a responsibility to alleviate the condition of the less fortunate: a responsibility which transcends the historic accident of national boundaries" (*Id.*, p. 415).

Establishing Perspectives 461

To speak of our current ability and potential to transcend the accident of national boundaries is to speak of both a reconstruction of the legal notion of "sovereignty" and, at the same time, unlock the dynamics of self-determination (Chen, 1976, pp. 198–261). These are the dynamics which accompany a redefined concept of "development," for "development" is as much a prerogative of nations as of individuals within nations. The implication is that in both First and Third World states, those practices, institutions, and policies which have historically promoted exclusionary governance (in all of its forms) can be held accountable to an international consensus which demands inclusionary governance, as a matter of law as well as of right. At that point in time, the normative potential of inclusionary governance may be conjoined with the objective and practical requirements of inclusionary governance. It is to the potential union between the normative potential of inclusionary governance with the practical requirements of inclusionary governance that we now turn.

(6) *Self-determination redefines "development" and "development" redefines self-determination insofar as the right to development and to inclusionary democratic governance is as much a prerogative of nations as individuals within nations. The maximum application of the "principle of fairness" also requires a close scrutiny of the international system's rules, with a view to challenging exclusionary forms of governance while, at the same time, enhancing the claims of inclusionary governance, such as the "principle of entitlement according to need."* Just as the developed countries have established intricate entitlement programs in order to enhance the opportunities of their poorer citizens and to extend the range of social inclusion, so too the international community in the decades since the 1960s has worked to create a number of entitlement programs designed to reduce the gap between the economic power of developed countries and developing countries. The stated goals of these programs has been to promote self-sufficiency and competitiveness. This has been largely effectuated through the transfer of funds and technology from developed to developing nations (Franck, 1995, p. 416). Yet this effort has left the problems of social, political, economic, and cultural exclusion still largely unaddressed. This result reflects the fact that the effort which has been undertaken has been also aimed at realizing and mandating principles of distributive justice, thereby creating tensions between the developed and developing worlds. In this context, both donors and recipients have been disappointed. The remaining challenge for the international community and for international law is to more closely approximate the ideals of the principle of distributive justice, as well as inclusionary governance, "if entitlements are to become a significant tool for promoting equality and prosperity in the international system" (*Id.*, p. 416).

The obstacles which present themselves to the principle of entitlement according to need, distributive justice, principles of fairness and equity, and the claims of inclusionary governance, are the challenge that all governments must face in the early 21st century: "to figure out ways to reduce their intervention in some areas, and to retool and refocus their intervention in others, while preserving the public trust" (Yergin, 1998, p. 373). A new role for government is essential, for there is no market without government to define the rules and context. The role of government, in this context, extends far beyond the economics of the marketplace, for it will also determine the civic space that is allowed or disallowed to citizens to practice democracy to be included in the processes of decision making or excluded from it. In this respect, "democracy is consolidated when it becomes self-enforcing, that is, when all the relevant political forces find it best to continue to submit their interests and values to the uncertain interplay of the institutions" (Przeworski, 1991, p. 26).

Yet the fact is also that governments cannot spend all of their time consulting and negotiating—they must have the power to govern (Przeworski, 1995, p. 83). Effective governance, in this context, should and must be inclusionary if it is to be both efficient and effective. Therefore, as market-oriented reforms are undertaken, these reforms must link concerns with growth together with practical strategies for protecting the material welfare of citizens against the transitional costs of reforms and "for making full use of democratic institutions in the formulation and implementation of reform policies" (*Id.*, p. 89). Assessing the costs of reform at the national, regional, and international levels is vital, for "industrial policies, social policies, and political compromises cost money, and trade-offs are inevitable" but the "trade-offs must be determined by the democratic process" for, to be successful, "reforms must explicitly aim at growth, income security, and democracy" (*Id.*, p. 90).

As far as the impact of inclusionary governance is concerned, it is also necessary to acknowledge that "within a reenergized democratic vision, egalitarianism has an important but subsidiary place. The range and quality of the lives a society makes possible are what matter most . . . Everyone should inherit from society . . . a set of basic rights and resources needed to set upon a course of life, and to sustain it against the extremes of misfortune and insecurity. Everyone should therefore have at hand the tools necessary to effective economic and civic action" (Unger, 1998, p. 167). In practical terms, however, this analysis implies that "political and social linkages are widely regarded as indispensable for the stability of political regimes" and that, in their absence, new social movements are the only remaining avenue which potentially offer people new kinds of linkage (Aarts, 1995, p. 227). From this perspective, "the growth of critical citizens is really a challenge. Democracies need to adapt to present-day politics and the new style of participatory politics. The challenge to democracies is whether they can continue to evolve, to guarantee political rights, and increase the ability of citizens to control their lives" (Dalton, 1999, pp. 76–77).

E.   MOVING TOWARD INCLUSION

The challenge to democracies is one that is intimately tied to the protection of and respect for human rights. As this conclusion has stressed, human rights are not just political and civil, but also embody socioeconomic dimensions and claims. The enduring question remains, however, which is: Where to begin? It is easy for international lawyers to overlook the revolutionary nature of the demands for international economic justice (Kahn,

1995, pp. 249–262). In large measure, this is because of the excessive concentration on the formulation of a legal agenda of tasks awaiting them. The scope of the legal agenda is daunting, for it involves everything from treaty-making as a function of modern associative diplomacy to an analysis of the theoretical premises of treaty taxonomy (Johnston, 1997).

The articles and subarticles of the Charter of Economic Rights and Duties of States still require the investment of time and talent in order to delineate, explicate, and articulate the dimensions and interconnectedness of issues involving sovereignty over resources, foreign investment, the proper international role and boundaries of transnational corporations, the lawful nationalization of foreign property, international trade, the transfer of technology, the nature and scope of the charters which guide international financial institutions such as the IMF and World Bank, as well as trading regimes such as the GATT and WTO (Benedek, 1995, pp. 274–288), and the exploitation of the international seabed. After all is said and done, the central problem of this international economic arena is "a matter of international justice rather than of international law, of norms *de lege ferenda* rather than *de lege lata*, of desired rather than actual law" (Stone, 1984, p. 111, italics in the original). We are, in short, returned to the distinction mentioned earlier, between preferences and probabilities. Our challenge in realizing the claims of inclusionary governance around the globe depends, in large measure, upon healing the gulf between preferences and probabilites.

In the context of the UN Charter, the content of the charter and other provisions regarding the NIEO have been a mixed bag of both established legal norms and emerging norms. Mere exhortations have made efforts to give the NIEO any singular legal status an exercise in futility. This sense of futility arises out of the incongruous nature of the doctrine of each state's permanent sovereignty over its own resources on the one hand, and demands for transfers of resources from developed to underdeveloped countries based on interdependence and reciprocity on the other. The crux of the problem is evident when challenging the absolutism of each developed state's claim to sovereignty over its own resources. Those seeking to transcend this absolutism must face the difficult challenge of bringing clarity to the blurred distinction between existing legal entitlements on the one hand, and demands that changes in those entitlements be negotiated in varied and subtle forms on the other. In this undertaking, UNCTAD and the G-7 have rarely agreed. Eventually, however, the movement toward inclusionary forms of governance will force an agreement which addresses the equitable distribution of wealth and income within and between nations. As Gabriel Kolko has noted, "the strongest argument for the equitable distribution of wealth and income is not that it maximizes economic incentives and growth, which it probably does not in the strictly short-term manner that dominant economic thought calculates, but rather that it stabilizes economies and societies in ways that are much more likely to prevent the emergence of atavistic, reactionary, and ultimately materially highly destructive political forces. It is social stability within states that remains the precondition for peace between them, and the loss of mythical capitalist efficiencies to attain these goals is a positive achievement. For the central issue of economics today is civilization's survival, which requires doing whatever increases the chances for peace as opposed to militarism and war" (Kolko, 1994, p. 481).

Yet in the battle for the contested terrain of power, states, and markets seeking the "commanding heights" both need to preserve something of the classical demand for formal law. This is because a genuinely democratic society, as well as a democratic world order, requires a high degree of legal regularity and predictability to achieve autonomous and uncoerced political deliberation and action. The classical liberal call for forms of calculable and norm-based state action remains a key element for any and all deliberations. This is especially difficult to attain given the legal history of the 20th century, where a process of legal deformalization has provided many innovative interpretations. Yet the lesson to be gleaned from this history is that "if contemporary law is undergoing a gradual deformalization, this is much because formal law conflicts with powerful social and political interests" (Scheuerman, 1994, p. 3). In light of this trend, "formal law today is threatened at least partly because it contains critical elements that challenge capitalist-based social inequalities and a number of deeply undemocratic trends in contemporary political systems" (Id., p. 3).

Exclusionary states and exclusionary forms of governance are characteristic of deeply undemocratic political systems. As such, the legal systems associated with these exclusionary states and international regimes means that "the legal order, too, often drags behind new demands placed on political actors" (Id., p. 198). Therefore, it will be necessary, if inclusionary governance is to succeed, that we also recognize that a naive faith in the legal status quo can even endanger democracy itself because of its inherently conservative nature and the fact that "every legal order obviously embodies the political achievements of past struggles and previous generations. Even though a democratic system best minimizes the consequences of this natural conservatism, we can never be sure that they have been altogether vanquished, and every genuinely democratic view of politics would do well to recognize this" (Id., p. 198). A genuinely democratic view of politics recognizes, as did Kant, that law differs from morality in the formal properties of legality, but "the correct response to the danger of an unmediated moralization of power politics is 'not the demoralization of politics, but rather the democratic transformation of morality into a system of positive laws with legal procedures for their application and implementation.' Human rights fundamentalism is avoided not by renouncing the politics of human rights, but only through a cosmopolitan transformation of the state of nature among states into a legal order" (Habermas, 1998, p. 201). Inclusionary governance represents and sets forth a strategy for the cosmopolitan transformation of the state of nature among states into a legal order.

The ability of citizens to control their own lives, by virtue of their rights as human beings, is the most critical and fundamental human concern at the dawn of the 21st century. The inclusionary nature of our planetary interdependence and our personal interdependence is real. Its claim lays claim to us all. With it, duties and obligations come attached to the rights inherent in the claim. Those duties and obligations involve meeting our responsibilities toward the excluded, neglected, poor, and dispossessed of the world. In this regard, "one step toward the development of an adequate conception of international law consists in describing its various modes of impinging upon state behavior" (Falk, 1971, p. 192). This book has sought to outline the various modes of how inclusionary governance, as a strategy of governance and as a set of normative values, policies and goals, may be empowered to impinge upon state behavior in First and Third World nation-states, as well as throughout the interdependent linkages which constitute our global village.

BIBLIOGRAPHY

Kees Aarts, "Intermediate Organizations and Interest Representation," *Citizens and the State*, edited by Hans-Dieter Klingemann and Dieter Fuchs, Oxford University Press, 1995.

Amitav Acharya, "Developing Countries and the Emerging World Order: Security and Institutions," *The Third World Beyond the Cold War: Continuity and Change*, edited by Louise Fawcett and Yezid Sayigh, Oxford University Press, 1999.

Philip Alston, "The Right to Development at the International Level," *Third World Attitudes Toward International Law: An Introduction*, edited by Frederick E. Snyder and Surakiart Sathirathai, Martinus Nijhoff Publishers, 1987.

Giovanni Arrighi and Beverly J. Silver, et al., *Chaos and Governance in the Modern World System*, University of Minnesota Press, 1999.

Kevin Bales, *Disposable People: New Slavery in the Global Economy*, University of California Press, 1999.

Michael Banton, *International Action Against Racial Discrimination*, Clarendon Press, Oxford, 1996.

Maude Barlow and Tony Clarke, *MAI—The Multilateral Agreement on Investment and the Threat to American Freedom*, Stoddart, 1998.

Charles R. Beitz, *Political Theory and International Relations*, With a New Afterword by the Author, Princeton University Press, 1999.

Walden Bello, et al., *Dark Victory: The United States, Structural Adjustment, and Global Poverty*, Pluto Press with Food First and Transnational Institute (TNI), 1994.

Wolfgang Benedek, "Implications of the Principle of Sustainable Development, Human Rights and Good Governance for the GATT/WTO," *Sustainable Development and Good Governance*, edited by Konrad Ginther, Erik Denters, and Paul de Waart, Martinus Nijhoff Publishers, 1995.

Mark S. Bergman, "The Norm-Creating Effect of a General Assembly Resolution on Transnational Corporations," *Third World Attitudes Toward International Law: An Introduction*, edited by Frederick E. Snyder and Surakiart Sathirathai, Martinus Nijhoff Publishers, 1987.

Thomas J. Biersteker, "The 'Triumph' of Liberal Economic Ideas in the Developing World," *Global Change, Regional Response: The New International Context of Development*, edited by Barbara Stallings, Cambridge University Press, 1995.

Robert L. Borosage, "The Battle in Seattle," *The Nation*, December 6, 1999.

The Brandt Commission, *North-South: A Programme for Survival*, Pan Books, 1980.

Lung-Chu Chen, "Self-Determination as a Human Right," *Toward World Order and Human Dignity: Essays in Honor of Myres S. McDougal*, edited by W. Michael Reisman and Burns H. Weston, The Free Press, 1976.

Noam Chomsky, *World Orders Old and New*, Columbia University Press, 1994.

Noam Chomsky, *The New Military Humanism: Lessons from Kosovo*, Common Courage Press, 1999.
Michel Chossudoveky, *The Globalisation of Poverty: Impacts of IMF and World Bank Reforms*, Zed Books, Ltd. and Third World Network, 1997.
Michel Chossudovsky, "Global Poverty in the Late 20th Century," *Journal of International Affairs*, Vol. 52, No. 1, Fall 1998.
S. Chowdhury, "The Status and Norms of Self-Determination in Contemporary International Law," *Third World Attitudes Toward International Law: An Introduction*, edited by Frederick E. Snyder and Surakiart Sathirathai, Martinus Nijhoff Publishers, 1987.
David S. Cloud, "Critics Fear GATT May Declare Open Season on US Laws," *Congressional Quarterly*, July 23, 1994.
Congressional Research Service Report for Congress, "World Trade Organization: Institutional Issues and Dispute Settlement," August 3, 1994.
Robert Conquest, *Reflections on a Ravaged Century*, W.W. Norton & Company, 2000.
Michael E. Conroy and Sarah E. West, "The Impact of NAFTA and the WTO on Chiapas and Southern Mexico: Hypotheses and Preliminary Evidence," *Poverty or Development: Global Restructuring and Regional Transformations in the US South and the Mexican South*, edited by Richard Tardanico and Mark B. Rosenberg, Routledge, 2000.
Robert Cox, "Structural Issues of Global Governance: Implications for Europe," *A New Europe in the Changing Global System*, edited by Richard Falk and Tamas Szentes, United Nations University Press, 1997.
Peter Cumper and Steven Wheatley, editors, *Minority Rights in the "New" Europe*, Martinus Nijhoff Publishers, 1999.
Mark Curtis, *The Great Depression: Anglo-American Power and World Order*, Pluto Press, 1998.
Alfredo Bruto da Costa, "Social Policy and Competitiveness," *The Social Quality of Europe*, edited by Wolfgang Beck, Laurent van der Maesen, and Alan Walker, Kluwer Law International, 1997.
Russell J. Dalton, "Political Support in Advanced Industrial Democracies," *Critical Citizens: Global Support for Democratic Government*, edited by Pippa Norris, Oxford University Press, 1999.
G.M. Danilenko, *Law-Making in the International Community*, Martinus Nijhoff Publishers, 1993.
Bhagirath Lal Das, *The WTO Agreements: Deficiencies, Imbalances and Required Changes*, Zed Books, Ltd. and Third World Network, 1998.
Bob Deacon, "Social Policy in a Global Context," *Inequality, Globalization, and World Politics*, edited by Andrew Hurrell and Ngaire Woods, Oxford University Press, 1999.
Giuseppe Di Palma, "Market, State, and Citizenship in New Democracies," *Inequality, Democracy, and Economic Development*, edited by Manus I. Midlarsky, Cambridge University Press, 1997.
Larry Diamond, Juan Linz, and Seymour Martin Lipset, "Introduction: What Makes for Democracy?," *Politics in Developing Countries: Comparing Experiences with Democracy*, Second Edition, Lynne Rienner Publishers, 1995.

Larry Diamond, *Developing Democracy: Toward Consolidation*, The Johns Hopkins University Press, 1999.
Peter Dicken, *Global Shift*, 3d ed. rev., The Guilford Press, 1998.
Jack Donnelly, "Post-Cold War Reflections on the Study of International Human Rights," *Ethics & International Affairs*, Volume 8, 1994.
Richard Falk, "New Approaches to the Study of International Law," *The American Journal of International Law*, Volume 61, 1967.
Richard Falk, "The Relevance of Political Context to the Nature and Functioning of International Law: An Intermediate View," *The Relevance of International Law*, edited by Karl Deutsch and Stanley Hoffman, Anchor Books, Doubleday & Company, Inc., 1971.
Richard Falk, *A Study of Future Worlds*, The Free Press, 1975.
Richard Falk, *Human Rights and State Sovereignty*, Holmes & Meier Publishers, Inc., 1981.
Richard Falk, *Revitalizing International Law*, Iowa State University Press, 1989.
Richard Falk, "The Pathways of Global Constitutionalism," *The Constitutional Foundations of World Peace*, edited by Richard Falk, Robert Johansen, and Samuel Kim, State University of New York Press, 1993.
Richard Falk, "Regionalism and World Order After the Cold War," *Saint Louis-Warsaw Transatlantic Law Journal*, Volume 1995.
Richard Falk, *Law in an Emerging Global Village: A Post-Westphalian Perspective*, Transnational Publishers, Inc., 1998.
Richard Falk, *Predatory Globalization: A Critique*, Polity Press, 1999.
Richard Falk, "The Pursuit of International Justice: Present Dilemmas and An Imagined Future," *Journal of International Affairs*, Volume 52, No. 2, 1999.
Tom Farer, "Conclusion: What Do International Lawyers Do When They Talk About Ethnic Violence and Why Does It Matter?," *International Law and Ethnic Conflict*, edited by David Wippman, Cornell University Press, 1998.
Paul Farmer, *Infections and Inequalities: The Modern Plagues*, University of California Press, 1999.
Jeff Faux, "Slouching Toward Seattle: Will Trade Overwhelm Democracy—Or Stimulate a New Global Politics?," *The American Prospect*, Volume 11, No. 2, December 6, 1999.
William F. Felice, *Taking Suffering Seriously: The Importance of Collective Human Rights*, State University of New York Press, 1996.
Thiomas M. Franck, *Fairness in International Law and Institutions*, Clarendon Press, Oxford, 1995.
Steven Friedman, "South Africa: Entering the Post-Mandela Era," *Journal of Democracy*, Volume 10, Number 4, October 1999.
Richard Gerster, "The IMF and Basic Needs Conditionality," *Third World Attitudes Toward International Law: An Introduction*, edited by Frederick E. Snyder and Surakiart Sathirathai, Martinus Nijhoff Publishers, 1987.
Stephen Gill, *American Hegemony and the Trilateral Commission*, Cambridge University Press, 1990.
John Gray, *False Dawn: The Delusions of Global Capitalism*, The New Press, 1998.

William Grieder, *One World, Ready or Not: The Manic Logic of Global Capitalism*, Simon & Schuster, 1997.
S.B.O. Gutto, "Violation of Human Rights in the Third World: Responsibility of States and TNCs," *Third World Attitudes Toward International Law: An Introduction*, edited by Frederick E. Snyder and Surakiart Sathirathai, Martinus Nijhoff Publishers, 1987.
Jurgen Habermas, *Legitimationsprobleme im Spatkapitalismust*, Suhrkamp, 1973.
Jurgen Habermas, *Legitimation Crisis*, Heinemann, 1976.
Jurgen Habermas, *Between Facts and Norms: Contributions to a Discourse Theory of Law and Democracy*, translated by William Rehg, The MIT Press, 1996.
Jurgen Habermas, *The Inclusion of the Other: Studies in Political Theory*, edited by Ciaran Cronin and Pablo De Greiff, The MIT Press, 1998.
David Held, *Political Theory and the Modern State: Essays on State, Power, and Democracy*, Stanford University Press, 1989.
David Held, "The Transformation of Political Community: Rethinking Democracy in the Context of Globalization," *Democracy's Edges*, edited by Ian Shapiro and Casiano Hacker-Cordon, Cambridge University Press, 1999.
Louis Henkin, *How Nations Behave: Law and Foreign Policy*, 2d Edition, 1979.
Bjorn Hettne, *The New Regionalism: Implications for Development and Peace*, WIDER/UNC, 1994.
Bjorn Hettne, "Europe in a World of Regions," *A New Europe in the Changing Global System*, edited by Richard Falk and Tamas Szentes, United Nations University Press, 1997.
Stanley Hoffmann, *World Disorders: Troubled Peace in the Post-Cold War Era*, Rowman & Littlefield Publishers, Inc., 1998.
J. Rogers Hollingsworth and Robert Boyer, editors, *Contemporary Capitalism: The Embeddedness of Institutions*, Cambridge University Press, 1997.
Liesbet Hooghe and Gary Marks, "The Making of a Polity: The Struggle Over European Integration," *Continuity and Change in Contemporary Capitalism*, edited by Herbert Kitschelt, Peter Lange, Gary Marks, and John D. Stephens, Cambridge University Press, 1999.
Tigani E. Ibrahim, "Developing Countries and the Tokyo Round," *Third World Attitudes Toward International Law: An Introduction*, edited by Freerick E. Snyder and Surakiart Sathirathai, Martinus Nijhoff Publishers, 1987.
Bruce J. Jeetleson, "Preventive Diplomacy: Analytical Conclusions and Policy Lessons," *Opportunities Missed, Opportunities Seized: Preventive Diplomacy in the Post-Cold War World*, edited by Bruce W. Jentleson, Carnegie Commission On Preventing Deadly Conflict, Rowman & Littlefield Publishers, Inc., 2000.
Douglas M. Johnston, *Consent and Commitment in the World Community: The Classification and Analysis of International Instruments*, Vol. 22, Procedural Aspects of International Law Book Series, Transnational Publishers, Inc., 1997.
Charles Jones, *Global Justice: Defending Cosmopolitanism*, Oxford University Press, 1999.

Rahmatullah Kahn, "The Thickening Web of International Law," *Issues in Global Governance: Papers Written for the Commission on Global Governance*, Kluwer Law International, 1995.

Benedict Kingsbury, "Sovereignty and Inequality," *Inequality, Globalization, and World Politics*, edited by Andrew Hurrell and Ngaire Woods, Oxford University Press, 1999.

Hans Kelsen, *Principles of International Law*, Second Edition, revised and edited by Robert W. Tucker, Holt, Rinehart and Winston, Inc., 1966.

Hans Kelsen, "The Essence of International Law," *The Relevance of International Law*, edited by Karl Deutsch and Stanley Hoffman, Anchor Books, Doubleday & Company, Inc., 1971.

Gabriel Kolko, *Century of War: Politics, Conflict, and Society Since 1914*, The New Press, 1994.

David A. Korn, *Exodus Within Borders: An Introduction to the Crisis of Internal Displacement*, Brookings Institution Press, 1999.

Robert Kuttner, *The End of Laissez-Faire: National Purpose and the Global Economy After the Cold War*, Alfred A, Knopf, 1991.

Gail E. Lapidus, "The War in Chechnya: Opportunities Missed, Lessons to Be Learned," *Opportunities Missed, Opportunities Seized: Preventive Diplomacy in the Post-Cold War World*, edited by Bruce W. Jentleson, Carnegie Commission On Preventing Deadly Conflict, Rowman & Littlefield Publishers, Inc., 2000.

Paul G. Lauren, *Power and Prejudice: The Politics and Diplomacy of Racial Discrimination*, Westview Press, 1988.

Arend Lijphart, *Patterns of Democracy: Government Forms and Performance in Thirty-Six Countries*, Yale University Press, 1999.

Gil Loescher, *Beyond Charity: International Cooperation and the Global Refugee Crisis*, Oxford University Press, 1993.

Robin Luckham, "Are There Alternatives to Liberal Democracy?," *The Democratic Developmental State: Politics and Institutional Design*, edited by Mark Robinson and Gordon White, Oxford University Press, 1998.

Edward Luttwak, *Turbo-Capitalism: Winners and Losers in the Global Economy*, Harper Collins Publishers, 1999.

Edward N. Luttwak, "Globalizers are the Bolsheviks of Their Day," *The Los Angeles Times*, December 10, 1999.

Myres S. McDougal and W.M. Reisman, "Rhodesia and the United Nations: The Lawfulness of International Concern," *The American Journal of International Law*, Volume 62, 1968.

John Maresca, "The International Community and the Conflict over Nagorno-Karabakh," *Opportunities Missed, Opportunities Seized: Preventive Diplomacy in the Post-Cold War World*, edited by Bruce W. Jentleson, Carnegie Commission On Preventing Deadly Conflict, Rowman & Littlefield Publishers, Inc., 2000.

Ali A. Mazrui, *A World Federation of Cultures: An African Perspective*, The Free Press, 1976.

Walter Russell Mead, "Skewered in Seattle: In the Suites and on the Streets, Few Agreed," *Los Angeles Times*, December 5, 1999.

Kenneth Menkhaus and Louis Ortmayer, "Somalia: Misread Crises and Missed Opportunities," *Opportunities Missed, Opportunities Seized: Preventive Diplomacy in the Post-Cold War World*, edited by Bruce W. Jentleson, Carnegie Commission On Preventing Deadly Conflict, Rowman & Littlefield Publishers, Inc., 2000.

Robert Miles and Dietrich Thranhardt, *Migration and European Integration: The Dynamics of Inclusion and Exclusion*, Pinter Publishers, 1995.

Kurt Mills, *Human Rights in the Emerging Global Order: A New Sovereignty?*, St. Martin's Press, Inc., 1998.

David Moberg, "Seattle Showdown: Citizens Stand Up to the WTO," *In These Times*, November 28, 1999.

Andrew Moravcsik, *The Choice for Europe: Social Purpose and State Power from Messina to Maastricht*, Cornell University Press, 1998.

Ralph Nader, et al., *The Case Against Free Trade: GATT, NAFTA, and the Globalization of Corporate Power*, Earth Island Press and North Atlantic Books, 1993.

Claus Offe, *Strukturprobleme des kapitaliistischen*, Suhrkamp, 1972.

Claus Offe, *Contradictions of the Welfare State*, Hutchinson, 1984.

Philip Oxhorn and Graciela Ducatenzeiler, "Conclusions: What Kind of Democracy?" *What Kind of Market?, What Kind of Democracy What Kind of Market?: Latin America in the Age of Neoliberalism*, edited by Philip D. Oxhorn and Graciela Ducatenzeiler, The Pennsylvania State University Press, 1998.

Devon G. Pena, *The Terror of the Machine: Technology, Work, Gender, and Ecology on the US-Mexico Border*, CMAS Books, The Center for Mexican American Studies, The University of Texas at Austin, 1997.

James Petras and Chronis Polychroniou, "Rethinking Globalization: From the Future to the Past," *Socialism And Democracy*, Vol. 12, Nos. 1–2, 1998.

Kevin Phillips, "The Stealth Coup: The WTO and the Fed Have Essentially Become Two New Branches of Government, in Many Ways More Powerful Than Congress and the President—Who Elected Them Anyway?," *The Los Angeles Times*, November 21, 1999.

Geoffrey Allen Pigman, "States, Sovereignty and Trade," *Trade Politics: International, Domestic and Regional Perspectives*, edited by Brian Hocking and Steven McGuire, Routledge, 1999.

Gerard Prunier, *The Rwanda Crisis: History of a Genocide*, Columbia University Press, 1995.

Adam Przeworski, *Democracy and the Market: Political and Economic Reforms in Eastern Europe and Latin America*, Cambridge University Press, 1991.

Adam Prezeworkski, et al., *Sustainable Democracy*, Cambridge University Press, 1995.

Jonathan C. Randal, *After Such Knowledge, What Forgiveness? My Encounters with Kurdistan*, Farrar, Straus and Giroux, 1997.

John Rawls, *A Theory of Justice*, Harvard University Press, 1971.

John Rawls, "The Law of Peoples," *John Rawls: Collected Papers*, edited by Samuel Freeman, Harvard University Press, 1999.

Michael Redclift and Colin Sage, "Resources, Environmental Degradation, and Inequality," *Inequality, Globalization, and World Politics*, edited by Andrew Hurrell and Ngaire Woods, Oxford University Press, 1999.

William I. Robinson, *Promoting Polyarchy: Globalization, US Intervention, and Hegemony*, Cambridge University Press, 1996.

Dani Rodrik, *The New Global Economy and Developing Countries*, Overseas Development Council, 1999.

Jean-Jacques Rosa, *Euro-Error*, translated from French under the direction of Andrea Lyn Secara, Algora Publishing, 1998.

Saskia Sassen, *Loss of Control? Sovereignty in an Age of Globalization*, Columbia University Press, 1996.

Yezid Sayigh, "Globalization Manqué: Regional Fragmentation and Authoritarian-Liberalism in the Middle East," *The Third World Beyond the Cold War: Continuity and Change*, by Louise Fawcett and Yezid Sayigh, Oxford University Press, 1999.

Oscar Schacter, "The Evolving International Law of Development," *Columbia Journal of Transnational Law*, Volume 15, 1976.

Fritz W. Scharpf, *Governing in Europe: Effective and Democratic?*, Oxford University Press, 1999.

William E. Scheurman, *Between the Norm and the Exception: The Frankfurt School and the Rule of Law*, The MIT Press, 1994.

Amartya Sen, *Development As Freedom*, Alfred A. Knopf, 1999.

Mihaly Simai, "The Agenda of European Politics in the 1990s," *A New Europe in the Changing Global System*, edited by Richard Falk and Tamas Szentes, United Nations University Press, 1997.

Holly Sklar, editor, *Trilateralism: The Trilateral Commission and Elite Planning for World Management*, South End Press, 1980.

Jens Magleby Sorensen, *The Exclusive European Citizenship: The Case for Refugees and Immigrants in the European Union*, Avebury, 1996.

Barbara Stallings, editor, *Global Change, Regional Response: The New International Context of Development*, Cambridge University Press, 1995.

Alfred Stepan, "Federalism and Democracy: Beyond the US Model," *Journal of Democracy*, Volume 10, No. 4, October 1999.

Julius Stone, *Visions of World Order: Between State Power and Human Justice*, The Johns Hopkins University Press, 1984.

Astri Suhrke and Bruce Jones, "Preventive Diplomacy in Rwanda: Failure to Act or Failure of Actions?," *Opportunities Missed, Opportunities Seized: Preventive Diplomacy in the Post-Cold War World*, edited by Bruce W. Jentleson, Carnegie Commission on Preventing Deadly Conflict, Rowman & Littlefield Publishers, Inc., 2000.

Richard Tardanico, "Poverty or Development?," *Poverty or Development: Global Restructuring and Regional Transformations in the US South and the Mexican South*, edited by Richard Tardanico and Mark B. Rosenberg, Routledge, 2000.

C. Taylor, *Invoking Civil Society*, Working Papers and Proceedings of the Center for Psychosocial Studies, No. 31, 1990.

Takis Tridimas, *The General Principles of EC Law*, Oxford University Press, 1999.

Emek M. Ucarer and Donald J. Puchala, editors, *Immigration into Western Societies: Problems and Policies*, Pinter Publishers, 1997.

Roberto Mangabeira Unger, *Democracy Realized: The Progressive Alternative*, Verso, 1998.

United Nations High Commissioner for Refugees (UNHCR), *The State of the World's Refugees: The Challenge of Protection*, Penguin Books, 1993.

United Nations High Commissioner for Refugees (UNHCR), *The State of the World's Refugees, 1995—In Search of Solutions*, Oxford University Press, 1995.

Lori Wallach and Michelle Sforza, *Whose Trade Organization? Corporate Globalization and the Erosion of Democracy—An Assessment of the World Trade Organization*, Public Citizen, 1999.

Stephen M. Walt, "International Relations: One World, Many Theories," *Foreign Policy*, No. 110, Spring 1998.

M. Walzer, "A Better Vision: The Idea of Civil Society. A Path to Social Reconstruction," *Dissent*, Spring 1991.

Richard G. Whitman, *From Civilian Power to Superpower? The International Identity of the European Union*, St. Martin's Press, Inc., 1998.

Jan A. Winter, Deirdre M. Curtin, Alfred E. Kellermann, Bruno de Witte, editors, *Reforming the Treaty on European Union: The Legal Debate*, Kluwer Law International, 1996.

Robert Wolfe, "The World Trade Organization," *Trade Politics: International, Domestic and Regional Perspectives*, edited by Brian Hocking and Steven McGuire, Routledge, 1999.

Ellen M. Wood, *Democracy Against Capitalism: Renewing Historical Materialism*, Cambridge University Press, 1995.

Daniel Yergin and Joseph Stanislaw, *The Commanding Heights: The Battle Between Government and the Marketplace That Is Remaking the Modern World*, Simon & Schuster, 1998.

I. William Zartman and Katharina R. Vogeli, "Prevention Gained and Prevention Lost: Collapse, Competition, and Coup in Congo," *Opportunities Missed, Opportunities Seized: Preventive Diplomacy in the Post-Cold War World*, edited by Bruce W. Jentleson, Carnegie Commission On Preventing Deadly Conflict, Rowman & Littlefield Publishers, Inc., 2000.

Aristide R. Zolberg, Astri Suhrke, and Sergio Aguayo, *Escape from Violence: Conflict and the Refugee Crisis in the Developing World*, Oxford University Press, 1989.

INDEX

AFRICA, 167, 312, 330–331, 405–406
  Elections in Sub-Saharan Africa, 397
  Political situation in, 392–396
ALGIERS DECLARATION, xxv, xxvii, 445
ANARCHY
  Hobbes and, 258–259, 274
APARTHEID, 177–178
  Global apartheid, 15, 16
ARBITRATION, 192–197
ARGENTINA
  Union Civica Radica (UCR), 62–64
ARISTOCRACY, 225
ARMS RACE, 79
ASYLUM, xlv

BIBLIOGRAPHY
  Hobbes, Thomas, 276–283
  Inclusion, exclusion, and the reconstitution of power, lvii–lx
  Inclusionary governance and international law, 466–473
  Inclusionary versus exclusionary governance, 342–348
  Media, 142–147
  Moving toward exclusion, 198–207
  Nuclear disarmament and militarization, 105–112
  Poverty and polyarchy, 409–416
  Preface to inclusionary governance, 45–50
BLAIR, TONY, 261–262
BOSNIA, 211, 215
BOSNIA-HERZEGOVINA, 432
BRAZIL, 185–187, 191
  Brazil and South Africa
    Comparative view, 168–172
BRUNDTLAND COMMISSION, lv

CAPITALISM, 173–174
  Demands of, 353
  Globalization under capitalism and democracy, 222–223
  Marxists and, 220
  Predatory globalization, 432
  Turbo-capitalism, 361
CHILE, 183
CHINA, 367
CIVIL SOCIETY
  Task of in the Commonwealth, 265–267
CLASS, 172–175
COLD WAR, 14, 21, 71, 81, 96, 138, 389, 443
COMMUNIST PARTY, 248
COMPREHENSIVE TEST BAN TREATY (CTBT), 76, 77, 84, 85, 86, 92
CORPORATISM, 323–324
COSTA RICA, 391
COUNTER-REVOLUTIONARY MILITARISM, 390

DECLARATION ON THE GRANTING OF INDEPENDENCE TO COLONIAL COUNTRIES AND PEOPLES, xxv
DELHI DECLARATION, 85–86
DEMOCRACY
  Capitalism and, 7–10
  Competing conceptions of, 245 et seq.
  Consequences of democratic types, 247
  Entitlements and, 438–440
  European social democracy, 322–323
  Exclusionary states
    Dynamics of structural change, 364–366
    Failure of liberal capitalist revolutions, 362–364
    Illiberal democracy in, 362–367
    Responsibility of state toward the poor, 366–367
  Globalization under capitalism and, 222–223
  Hobbes and, 225
  Poverty and, 358–362

DEMOCRACY *(continued)*
  Representative democracy, 319
  Theories of
    Press clause interpretation, 121
  Theory and practice of, 386–396
    Africa, 392–396
    Latin America and, 387–392
DEMOCRATIC EXCLUSION, 151–197
  Arbitration, mediation, negotiation, 192–193, 259
  Brazil and South Africa, 168–172
  Brazil in the late 70s, 185–187
  Class, race, and ethnicity, 155, 172–175
  Decision making
    Tolerance, equitable distribution and continuity in, 187–189
  Dictatorship and democracy, 191–192
  Dynamics of, 159–179
  Exclusionary states as anti-developmental states, 177–179
  First and Third world states, 153
    Democratic exclusion in, 167–168
    The ideal and practice of democracy, 179182
  Globalization and the promotion of common values, 175–177
    Democratic exclusion in, 167–168
  Integration or separation, 163–164
  Introduction, 151–159
    Current situation, 153–157
    What is inclusion, 157–159
  Neoliberal model, 153 et seq.
  Political exclusion, 151 et seq.
  South Africa and the U.S., 164–167
  State powerlessness
    Repression and exclusionary governance, 183–184
  State/society relationship, 189–191
    Uniting the agendas of state and civil society, 156, 193–197
DEVELOPMENT, RIGHT TO, 420–426
  See also as subhead to other topics
DISARMAMENT
  Joint Statement of Agreed Principles for Disarmament Negotiations, 79
DISPUTE SETTLEMENT BODY (DSB), 429

ECO-IMPERIALISM, 17
EGOISTIC MAN, 238–240
EMBEDDED AUTONOMY, 324–326
EQUITABLE DISTRIBUTION, 187–189
ETHNIC UNITY, 160
ETHNICITY, 172–175
EUROPEAN CONVENTION ON THE PROTECTION OF HUMAN RIGHTS AND FUNDAMENTAL FREEDOMS, 36–37, 437
EUROPEAN SOCIAL CHARTER, 27–30
EUROPEAN UNION, xxix, xxx, xxxi, xxxv, 176
  Inclusion vs exclusion, xxxvi–xlvii
EXCLUSIONARY GOVERNANCE
  See also INCLUSIONARY GOVERNANCE
  Billionaires, xxxiv
  Definition, xix
  Dimensions of, 404
  Exclusionary impulse, 305
  Global dimension of exclusion, 299–301
  Outmoded, 42
  Richest and poorest countries, 20
  Trends toward, xxviii
  Widening scope of, xlvii–l
EXCLUSIONARY STATE (ES)
  See also EXCLUSIONARY GOVERNANCE
  Africa, 167
  Anti-development states, 177–179
  Definition, xx, 5
  Inhumane governance, 18
  Latin America, 167
  Repression and, 183
  Status quo and, 191
  United States and, xxxiii
EXPLOITATION-CENTERED CLASS ANALYSIS, 381–384

FALK, RICHARD, xxiv, 20
FRANCK, THOMAS, xlviii, xlix

GENERAL AGREEMENT ON TARIFFS AND TRADE (GATT), xxix, xxxv, 264, 429, 435, 451, 463
GLOBALIZATION, 260, 426–433
  Promotion of common values and, 175–177

Three-tiered social structure,
  262–263
GOVERNANCE
  See also EXCLUSIONARY
    GOVERNANCE, INCLUSIONARY
    GOVERNANCE
  Patterns of, 19
GROTIUS, HUGO, xxiii

HABERMAS, JURGEN, 249–251, 355,
  443
HELSINKI DECLARATION, 218
HOBBES, THOMAS, xxii
  Absolute sovereign
    Fragile nature of, 257
    Hobbes' meaning by term, 228 et
      seq.
    Nature of sovereignty, 241
  Exegesis on, 209–283
  Founding of the Hobbesian state,
    240–256
  General will, 259 et seq.
  Global commonwealth and culture
    of peace, 256–257
  Good government and, 226
  Guaranteed economic minimum,
    254–256
  Inclusionary governance and, 252 et
    seq.
  Introduction, 210–11
  Leviathan
    Application to modern times, 212
      et seq.
  Limited government and, 229–231,
    257
  Monarchy, democracy, and aristocracy, 225–229
  Moral minimum, 252–254
  Overcoming the Hobbesian
    dilemma, 215–216, 223–231
  Political unity and, 268
  Political violence, 253
  Rich sharing with poor, 252
  Rule of law and, 232–240
  Social contract and, 244–252,
    259–265, 274
    Negotiation and, 244–252
  Views on law, 232–240
HUMAN DEVELOPMENT REPORT, 16
HUMAN RIGHTS, 374–380, 437,
  442–443

INCLUSIONARY GOVERNANCE
  See also as subhead to other topics
  Accommodating new demands and
    social classes, 380
  Civil society in the Commonwealth,
    265–275
  Coherence, 338–339
  Cohesiveness, 337–338
  Conclusion, 41–44
  Congruence, 336–337
  Consensus, 330–333
  Consistency, 333–336
  Constitution for, 370–374
  Continuing struggle for, 296–299
  Covenant for a new democratic
    order, 34–35
    Legal framework for, 35–41
  Definition, xix, 4, 157
  Demand for, 15–18
  Democratic norms and, 21–24
  Development success and, 367–385
  Dynamics of democratic exclusion,
    151–197
    See also DEMOCRATIC EXCLUSION
  Equity enhancing reform, 321
  Exclusionary globalization and, 10–21
    Developing a new security agenda,
      13–15
  Exclusionary governance
    Inclusionary governance versus,
      287–348, 327–329
    Introduction, 288–294
  Global Social Charter, 27–30
  Global dimensions of exclusion,
    299–301
  Hobbes and, 224, 228
  Human rights and, 374–380
  Inclusion/exclusion dilemma,
    321–322
  Inclusionary principles, 310
  International democratic policy, 22–24
  International law and, 419–465
  Introduction, 3–7
  Major obstacles to, 294–301
  Media
    See MEDIA
  Neo-liberalism and
    See NEO-LIBERALISM
  Obstacles to, 294–310
  Political inclusion
    Necessity for, 405–408, 455

INCLUSIONARY GOVERNANCE
    (continued)
  Polyarchy and neoliberalism and, 304–305
  Poverty and violence, 309–310
  Privilege vs. promotion of inclusion, 303
  Promoting effectiveness and efficiency in governance, 339–341
  Seek a newer world, 7–10
  Social bargains, need for, 319–322
  Sociopolitical aspects, 433–436
  Solutions for achieving, 310–341
  State and society, 10
  Underlying causes of internal conflict, 311–329
    Cultural and perceptual factors, 317–319
    Economic and social factors, 316–317
    Political factors, 314–316
    Structural factors, 312–314
    Well-ordered society and, 369–385
INCLUSIONARY STATE (IS), 156, 157
  Continuity in decision-making process, 188
  Control, implications of, xxiii
  Definition, xx
  Distribution of income, 188
  Ideal civil society, xxi
    See also CIVIL SOCIETY
  IS and ES
    Differences, 187–189
  Model of governance, xxi
  Moving towards inclusion, 462–465
  Policies, practices, and goals of, 388–389
  Principles of, 340–341
  Purpose of, xxi
  Socioeconomic rights and, 440–462
  Tolerance, 187–189
INTEGRATION
  Integration or separation, 163–164
INTER-AMERICAN DEVELOPMENT BANK (IDB), 292
INTERNATIONAL COURT OF JUSTICE (ICJ)
  Nuclear weapons, 76, 92, 93
INTERNATIONAL COVENANT ON ECONOMIC, SOCIAL AND CULTURAL RIGHTS, 440

INTERNATIONAL FINANCIAL INSTITUTIONS (IFI), 27, 28
INTERNATIONAL HUMAN RIGHTS COURT, xlii
INTERNATIONAL LABOR ORGANIZATION (ILO), xl
INTERNATIONAL LAW
  Emerging global context of, xxxi–xxxv
  Entitlement and, 436–438
  Inclusionary governance and, 419–473
  Right to development, 421 et seq.
  Role in IS, xxi
INTERNATIONAL MONETARY FUND (IMF), 289, 300, 301, 302, 307, 376, 377, 427–429. 447, 448, 449, 463
INTERNATIONAL ORGANIZATION FOR MIGRATION (IOM), xliv

JUS SANGUINIS, xlii
JUS SOLI, xlii

KANT, IMMANUEL, xxii, xxiii, xxiv, 11
  Perpetual Peace, xxvi, xxvii
KENNEDY, JOHN F.
  Nuclear policy, 79–80
KOSOVO, 210, 211, 215

LATIN AMERICA, 25–26, 167, 184, 263, 288, 294, 295
  Low-intensity democracy and, 387–392
LESSER DEVELOPED COUNTRIES (LDC), li, 65, 321, 334, 387
LEVIATHAN
  See HOBBES, THOMAS
LOCKE, JOHN, 229, 257

MAASTRICT TREATY, xxix, xxx
MACHIAVELLI, 272, 423, 454
MEDIA
  Balkan tragedy, 140
    Independent opinion and, 140–141
  Compassion fatigue, 139
  Concentration of ownership, 136
  Conservative think tanks, 118
  Corporate profits, 120
  Electronic republic and the manufacture of consent, 136–142
    Exclusionary governance and, 137
    Spin, use of, 138

Index 479

  Exclusionary governance and,
    120–121
  Double-speak, use of, 129
  Exploitation by mass media, 124
    Third Reich and, 124
  For profit vs non profit, 118
  Free press, 123, 126
  Globalization of, 113–147
  Information technologies, 114
  Introduction, 114–127
  Measuring media change, 122
  Media giants, 114
  Moral, free and civil space, 129
  Obstacles to change, 140
  Rich media, poor democracy, 117,
    127–130
    Poverty rate and, 119
  Rise of network society, 130–136
  Transnational corporate influence, 124
  Undemocratic nature of, 119
  Voice and accountability, 123
MEDIATION, 192–197
MEXICO, 190, 193, 291, 294,
    359–360, 368, 370
  Bailout of, 299–300
MILITARIZATION
  See also NUCLEAR DISARMAMENT
  Antidemocratic nature of, 56
  Armament culture, 55
  Building "security communities' for
    sustainable peace, 62–64
  Deterrence and balance of power,
    107–108
  Globalization of, 51–112
  Inclusionary measures for advancing
    peace, 78–84
  Introduction, 52–57
  Military state capitalism, 73
  Non-military incentives, 102–104
  Post-1945 world, 64–66
  Profit motive, 81–82
  Rogue state hypothesis, 82
MILITARY-INDUSTRIAL COMPLEX
    (MIC), 115
MILLS, C. WRIGHT, 115
MONARCHY, 225
MORAL MINIMUM, 252–254

NATIONALISM
  Hypotheses on nationalism and war,
    217–218

  Role of, 214–222
NATO, xxx, 58
NEGOTIATION, 192–197
  Negotiation of the agents
    Hobbes and, 244–252
NEO-LIBERALISM, 259–265
  Contesting the neo-liberal dogma,
    306–309
  Free markets and, 294
  Main elements of, 289–290
NEW REPUBLIC, 131, 133
NEWLY INDUSTRIALIZED COUNTRY
    (NIC), 59, 60
NON-ALIGNED NATIONS MOVE-
    MENT (NAM), 58, 59, 60, 457
NON-GOVERNMENTAL ORGANIZA-
    TION (NGO), 352, 408
NORTH AMERICAN FREE TRADE
    ASSOCIATION (NAFTA), xxix,
    xxxv, 264, 427
NUCLEAR DISARMAMENT, 51–112
  See also MILITARIZATION
  Antarctic Treaty, 91
  Atomic diplomacy, 57 et seq.
  Building exclusionary monopolies,
    57–61
  Hiroshima and Nagasaki, 57
  Inclusionary governance and, 87 et
    seq.
  Introduction, 52–57
  Legality of nuclear weapons, 66–77
  Limited nuclear war, 74
  Nuclear Non-Proliferation Treaty
    (NPT), 75–76
  Nuclear winter, 83
  Summary of proposals to ban threat
    of mass destruction, 69–70
  Sustaining norms of nuclear restraint,
    84–104
    Cost factor, 86, 88
    Seven factors, 86–104
  Technology and, 52 et seq.
NUREMBERG PRINCIPLES, xxv, 39, 68,
    72, 73–74, 76

ORGANIZATION FOR ECONOMIC
    COOPERATION AND DEVELOP-
    MENT, (OECD), 256, 307
ORGANIZATION FOR SECURITY AND
    COOPERATION IN EUROPE
    (OSCE), xliv

PACTA SUNT SERVANDA, 36
PEACE
  Hobbes and, 256–265
  Inclusionary measures for advancing peace, 79–84
PERU, 403, 404
PLATO, 233
POLITICAL PARTIES
  Development and, 400–405
POLITICIZED DECISION-MAKING, xlvi
POLYARCHY, 304–305
  See also POVERTY
  Between poverty and polyarchy, 349–416
  Definition, 350
  Third World and, 350 et seq.
POVERTY
  Between poverty and polyarchy, 349–416
  Extremely poor in 1985, 399
  Meeting needs of poor, 306–309
  Social policy and, 305–306
  Socialization of, 358–362
    Democratic crises in First and Third World states, 360–362
    Violence, of, 309–310
PREDATORY STATE, 181–182
PRESIDENTIALISM
  Development and, 400–405
PRIVILEGE
  Inclusion and, 303–304
PROPERTY RIGHTS, 258
PROTECTIVE SECURITY, 42

QUASI-STATES, 296–299

RACE, 172–175
RATNER, STEVEN, xxx
  Description and prescription, xxii
RAWLS, JOHN, 302, 369, 441, 445–446, 456
REAGAN, RONALD, xxxiii, 261
REFUGEES, xlv
REGIONALISM
  Limitations of, 437–438
RESOLUTION ON PERMANENT SOVEREIGNTY OVER NATURAL RESOURCES, xxv
ROSTOW, W.W., 300
ROTH, BRAD, 31–32
RULE OF LAW, 326–327
  Hobbes and, 232–240
  Rule by law and, 232–240
RUSSIA, 180, 248, 248, 338
RWANDA TRIBUNAL, 39, 139, 156, 181, 182

SEGREGATION, 165
SELF-DETERMINATION, 24–27, 34, 218, 448–462, 461–462
  Human rights and, 442–443
  Right to, 441–443
  Test for determining, 30 et seq.
SEN, AMARTYA, 123
SERBIA, 156
SHIMODA CASE, 422
SOCIAL COMPACT
  Hobbes and, 224–229, 244 et seq.
SOCIAL EXCLUSION, xxxviii
SOCIAL POLICY, 305–306
SOCIAL QUALITY
  Definition, xxxvii
SOCIAL SCIENCES, 247
SOCIAL SECURITY SYSTEM, 117
SOCIOECONOMIC RIGHTS, 440–462
SOCIOPOLITICAL INSTABILITY (SPI), 261, 271, 303, 330
SOUTH AFRICA, 181, 243, 334
  Brazil and South Africa
    Comparative view, 168–172
  Inequality and exclusion, 164–167
SOUTH KOREA, 301
SOUTH WEST AFRICA CASES, 425
SOVEREIGNTY
  Democratic peace thesis and, 219–220
  Doctrine of, 216–219
  Reevaluation of, 453, 457
STATISM
  Development and, 400–405
STRATEGIC ARMS LIMITATION TALKS (SALT), 80
STRATEGIC ARMS REDUCTION TALKS (START), 80, 81
STRATEGIC DEFENSE INITIATIVE (SDI), 81
STRUCTURAL ADJUSTMENT PROGRAMS (SAP), 154, 294
SUSTAINABLE DEVELOPMENT, 18
  Achieving peace through, 19–21

TECHNOCRATIC DECISION-MAKING, xlvi

Index

THIRD WAVE, 7, 290
  Critique of neoliberal view, 7
THIRD WAY, xlix, 261 et seq., 302–303
THIRD WORLD, xxv, 6, 60, 296, 335
  See also POVERTY
  Bottom-up pressures and top-down initiatives, 323–324
  Capitalist experiments in, 364–365
  Democracy and, 179–182, 220–222, 349–416
  Democratic exclusion in, 167–168
  Exclusionary governance and, 268
  Media and, 128
  Nuclear weapons and, 89
  Quasi-states, 221, 297
  State power and the poor, 396–400
TIME WARNER, 115–116, 124–125, 131
TOLERANCE, 187
TRANSNATIONAL CAPITALIST CLASS (TCC), 260
TRANSNATIONAL CORPORATIONS (TNC), 115, 132
TREATY OF PARIS, 75
TRILATERAL COMMISSION, 427

UNCTAD, 429
UNESCO
  Declaration on the Mass Media, 132–135
UNITED NATIONS COMMISSION ON HUMAN RIGHTS, 421, 423
UNITED NATIONS CONFERENCE ON SCIENCE AND TECHNOLOGY FOR DEVELOPMENT (UNCSTD), 65–66
UNITED NATIONS DEVELOPMENT PROGRAM (UNDP), 16
UNITED NATIONS HIGH COMMISSIONER FOR REFUGEES (UNHCR), xliv
UNITED STATES
  Affirmative action, 162
  Constitution of, 158–159
  Discrimination, 161
  Disparities of wealth, 159
  Double standards, 162–163
  Drugs, war on, 162
  Federalism, 438
  Globalization-from-below, xxxii
  Imperial democracy, 141
  Inclusionary governance and, 157–159
  inequality and exclusion, 164–167
  Military state capitalism, 73
  New globalism after WWII, 53
  Over preparation for regional conflicts, 83
  Poverty rate, 119
  Racial discrimination, 162
  Second-class citizens and, 126–127
  Slavery and, 160–161
  Support of dictatorships, 354
  Treaties U.S. is not a party to, xxxii
UNIVERSAL DECLARATION OF HUMAN RIGHTS, xxv, 43
UNIVERSAL DECLARATION ON THE RIGHTS OF PEOPLES, xxvi

VIENNA CONVENTION ON THE LAW OF TREATIES, 436
VIOLENCE
  Political violence, 363

WAR
  Debt and, 308–310
  Hypotheses on nationalism and war, 217–218
  Role of, 214–222
WASHINGTON CONSENSUS, xxxiii, xxxv, 9, 25, 260, 261, 403, 444
WESTPHALIAN MODEL, 23 et seq., 31 et seq., 59, 216
WORLD BANK, xxxvi, 28, 153, 289, 302, 307, 309, 427, 451
  Policies no help to poor, 9
WORLD TRADE ORGANIZATION (WTO), xxxvi, 429, 463
  Exclusionary politics of, xx, xxix

YUGOSLAVIA, 219
YUGOSLAVIA TRIBUNAL, 39

ZAIRE, 156, 181, 182